Learn to Read in Japanese

A Glossary

9,700 Japanese Terms Used in
Learn to Read in Japanese,
Volumes I, II, III & IV

Including Definitions,
Word Derivations,
Mnemonics and Synonyms

by
Roger Lake and Noriko Ura

Copyright © 2022 by Roger Lake
All rights reserved

Learn to Read in Japanese

A Glossary

Contents

Introduction	vii
Glossary	1
Proper Nouns	402
Counting and Time Words	410
The Differences Between Wa and Ga	413
Books in the *Learn to Read in Japanese* Series	416

This page intentionally left blank.

Introduction

This glossary lists more than 9,700 Japanese terms that students will encounter in the four volumes of our *Learn to Read in Japanese* series. They include nearly every Japanese word used in those books, as well as a number of Japanese phrases. Our purpose in compiling this volume has been to make it easier for students to learn vocabulary as they read, by providing prompt access to definitions, memory aids and synonyms.

We supply two kinds of memory aids for the words in the Glossary section of this book. For many terms, these consist of explanations that describe how certain words are derived from other known Japanese words. When such explanations aren't feasible, we provide mnemonics which are intended to help students to remember the terms' definitions and pronunciations. We also include synonyms, or at least "related terms," for a large number of the words, and these are marked by the symbol "cf." which stands for the Latin word *confer*, meaning "compare."

Near the end of this volume, we provide a list of almost all of the Proper Nouns (the names of people and places) that are used in our books, totaling more than 300 names. In addition, you will find eight lists of Counting and Time words: Counting Numbers (objects), Counting Numbers (people), Days of the Month, Days of the Week, Months, Number of Months, Ordinary Numbers, and Time of Day.

Finally, we provide an appendix, "The Differences Between Wa and Ga," which lists 15 guidelines that may be helpful when students are considering which of those two particles to use in Japanese sentences.

Please visit us at JapaneseAudioLessons.com for more information, including guides to Japanese grammar.

This page intentionally left blank.

Glossary of Vocabulary Terms from the *Learn to Read in Japanese* Books

Aachisuto アーチスト = an artist; cf. related terms listed at geijutsuka

Abaremawaru 暴れまわる = to rampage, run riot; from abareru = to become violent + mawaru = to turn

Abareru 暴れる = to become violent; *she abandoned her red rooster after it became violent*

Abiru 浴びる = to bathe, to receive (praise or attention) abundantly; *after I bathe, I drink a biiru (beer)*; cf. nyuuyoku suru = to take a bath

Abunai 危ない = dangerous, risky, doubtful, life-threatening; *in Abu Dhabi the nights can be dangerous*; cf. related terms listed at ayashii and at kiken na

Abura 油 = oil; *they poured sacred oil on a Buddha statue*

Abura 脂 = fat; *that Abu Dhabi ram has a lot of fat on its bones*; cf. shibou = fat

Aburagiru 脂ぎる = to become greasy or oily; *the abura (fat) got into the gears, and now they are greasy*

Aburakkoi 脂っこい = greasy, fatty; *the abura (fat) on the coin made it greasy*; cf. aburappoi = greasy, fatty, oily

Aburami 脂身 = fatty meat; *the abura (fat) in this meat makes it fatty meat*

Aburappoi 脂っぽい = greasy, fatty, oily; *the abura (fat) on the table points to the conclusion that some greasy food was eaten here*; cf. aburakkoi = greasy, fatty

Acchi あっち – see achira

Achira あちら = that person, place or way over there; *a cheerful rabbit is over there*

Aen 亜鉛 = zinc; *the artist entertained us by using zinc to create fire*; cf. related terms listed at tanso

Aete ieba あえて言えば = if I had to say; from aete = venturing + ieba = if I say

Aete あえて = daring to do something, venturing; this can also be spelled 敢えて; *the attitude of entertainers on that television show is one of venturing into risky territory*

Agameru 崇める = to worship or adore; *again my meditation session was ruined because you were loudly worshipping your idol*; cf. related terms listed at ai suru

Agaru 上がる = to become shy or nervous; *when I become nervous, my heart rate agaru (goes up)*

Agaru 上がる = to climb, to go up, to rise (prices), to increase, to enter a house; *if you are against the rules, please climb onto this platform*; cf. noboru = to rise; cf. takamaru = to rise; cf. other related terms listed at hairu and at noboru = to climb

Agaru 上がる = to finish, used after an intransitive verb stem; *Agatha Christie went to her room, and the novel was finished*; cf. -ageru = to finish, used after a transitive verb stem; cf. other related terms listed at owaru

Agaru 揚がる = to be deep fried; the intransitive form of ageru = to fry

Ageku 挙句 = a negative outcome, e.g., ageku ni, or ageku no hate ni, both of which = even worse, in the end; *the argumentative guest drank Kool-Aid with my niece and, even worse, they got into the vodka, leading to a negative outcome, in the end*

Agemono 揚げ物 = deep-fried food; from ageru = to deep fry + mono = thing; cf. related terms listed at tabemono

Ageru 上げる = to finish (used after a

transitive verb stem); *if you <u>ageru</u> (raise) your voice, I will <u>finish</u> our conversation*; cf. -agaru = to finish, used after an intransitive verb stem; cf. other related terms listed at owaraseru

Ageru 上げる = to give, to raise or lift, to fly (a kite), to hold (a ceremony), to turn up (volume); *I will give you the art the guest <u>ruined</u> if you can <u>lift</u> it*; cf. mochiageru = to elevate, raise up, flatter; cf. okosu = to raise, to cause, to wake someone; cf. oshiageru = to boost or push up; cf. takameru = to raise; cf. other related terms listed at ataeru

Ageru 揚げる = to hoist, to fry in deep fat; *after I <u>fry</u> food <u>in deep fat</u>, I <u>ageru</u> (lift) it with tongs and put it on a plate*

Ago 顎 = a chin or jaw, usually written あご; *I hurt my <u>chin</u>, and I'm in <u>agony</u>*; cf. gaku = a chin or jaw, used as a word component

Ahiru アヒル = a duck; *the <u>African heat</u> ruined the nest where the <u>ducks</u> were living*; cf. related terms listed at tori

Ai 愛 = love; *we feel <u>love</u> for <u>ice</u> cream*; cf. related terms listed at aijou

Ai 藍 = indigo; *her <u>eyes</u> are dark blue, almost <u>indigo</u>*; cf. related terms listed at ao

Ai suru 愛する = to love; from ai = love + suru = to do; cf. agameru = to worship or adore; cf. aikou suru = to love; cf. itsukushimu = to love or be affectionate, to cherish, to pity; cf. natsuku = to become emotionally attached

Aibou 相棒 = a buddy or partner; *<u>Ike</u> is boring, but he's my <u>buddy</u>*; cf. related terms listed at nakama

Aibu 愛撫 = a caress; *I put <u>ice</u> in her <u>booze</u>, and she gave me a <u>caress</u>*

Aida 間 = interval, time, distance, gap, between, among, relationship; *<u>Ida</u> waited for a long <u>time</u>*; cf. related terms listed at jikan

Aida ni 間に = during, between, while; from aida = interval, time, distance + -ni = a suffix that forms an adverb; cf. saichuu = in the midst of, during

Aidoru アイドル = idol, young star, TV personality

Aijou 愛情 = love, affection; *in <u>Iceland</u>, <u>J</u>oan of Arc fell in <u>love</u>*; cf. ai = love; cf. aikou = love, adoration; cf. jou = emotion, affection; cf. koi = love; cf. konomi = liking, taste; cf. renai = romantic love; cf. shitsuren = unrequited love, lost love; cf. suuhai = adoration, worship

Aikawarazu 相変わらず = as usual; *<u>as usual</u>, there was <u>ice</u> at the <u>car wash</u>, and there were <u>rats</u> at the <u>zoo</u>*

Aikou 愛好 = love, adoration; *we feel <u>love</u> for <u>ice cold milk</u>*; cf. related terms listed at aijou

Aikou suru 愛好する = to love; from aikou = love; cf. related terms listed at ai suru

Aikousha 愛好者 = fan, enthusiast; from aikou = adoration + sha = person

Aimai na 曖昧な = ambiguous, vague, unsure; *<u>I might</u> go to the party, but I'm <u>unsure</u>*; cf. related terms listed at fumei

Ainori 相乗り = riding together; from aite = partner + noru = to board a vehicle

Airon wo kakeru アイロンをかける = to iron; from airon = iron + kakeru = to expend

Aisatsu あいさつ = greetings, salutation, a polite set phrase used when meeting or parting from someone; this is sometimes spelled 挨拶; *when <u>E</u>isenhower met his <u>satisfied supervisor</u>, he used a <u>polite set phrase of meeting</u> ("good morning") to express <u>greetings</u>*; cf. eshaku = a bow, salute, greeting, nod

Aishou 愛称 = a pet name; *at the <u>ice show</u>, some of the skaters had <u>pet names</u>*; cf.

related terms listed at namae

Aishou 相性 = affinity, compatibility; *she has an affinity for ice shows*

Aiso 愛想 = amiability, friendliness, cheerfulness (this can also be pronounced aisou); *when Ike was sober, his amiability increased*

Aiso ga ii 愛想がいい = sociable; from aiso = amiability + ii = good; cf. shakouteki = social, sociable

Aite = 相手 opponent or partner; *I drink iced tea and play tennis with my partner*; cf. kataki = enemy, rival; cf. teki = an enemy or opponent

Aitou 哀悼 = condolences; *I put ice on his toe as I offered condolences for his injury*; cf. related terms listed at okuyami

Aitou no i 哀悼の意 = condolences; from aitou = condolences + iken = an opinion; cf. related terms listed at okuyami

Aitsu あいつ = that damn person; *that damn person put ice in my tsuitcase (suitcase)*; cf. boushi = a certain man; cf. chikushou = a beast or brute, a repulsive person or thing; damn it! (interjection); cf. kare = he, him, boyfriend; cf. nanigashi = so-and-so, one, that person; cf. yarou = a guy or rascal; cf. yatsu = he, a guy, a thing or object (derogatory); cf. yarou = a guy or rascal; cf. yatsura = they

Aiyou 愛用 = favorite thing, habitual use; from aijou = love + riyou suru = to use; cf. koubutsu = favorite food; cf. okiniiri = a favorite thing or person

Aizou 愛憎 = simultaneous love and hate; *when I visited the ice cream zone, I felt simultaneous love and hate, since I love ice cream but hate to gain weight*

Aizu 合図 = a sign or signal; *when Ike visited the zoo, he was sending a signal about his concern for animals*; cf. kizashi = a sign or omen; cf. shirushi = a sign or symbol

Aji あじ = horse mackerel; *the aristocratic genius prefers horse mackerel*

Aji 味 = taste; *the agile deer like the taste of grass*; cf. amami = sweetness; cf. bimi = good flavor; cf. fuumi = taste or flavor; cf. karami = salty taste; cf. kuchiatari = taste; cf. umami = a 5th taste category recognized in Japan; cf. other related terms listed at fuumi

Ajisai あじさい = hydrangea; *the agile scientists studied hydrangeas*

Ajitsuke 味付け = seasoning, flavor; from aji = taste + tsukeru = to attach; cf. related terms listed at fuumi

Ajiwau 味わう = to taste, savor, relish; *as she savored the cake, she said, "this aji (taste) is wow!"*; cf. kuchi ni suru = to taste, eat, speak of

Aka 垢 = dirt; *our academy has dirt floors*; cf. dojou = soil, breeding ground; cf. doro = mud; cf. nendo = clay; cf. tsuchi = soil, earth; cf. yogore = dirt or a stain

Aka 赤 = red; the noun form of akai = red

Akachan 赤ちゃん = a baby or infant; from akai = red + chan = a suffix used to express affection and intimacy; cf. related terms listed at kodomo

Akai 赤い = red; *the academic eats red peppers*; cf. makka = bright red

Akaji 赤地 = a red background; from akai = red + ji = chi = ground; cf. cf. related terms listed at haikei

Akame 赤目 = a red eye; from akai = red + me = eye; cf. related terms listed at me

Akanbou 赤ん坊 = a baby; *the baby got into a candy bowl*; cf. related terms listed at kodomo

Akari 明かり = light; *the academy that Ringo attended was full of light*; cf. related terms listed at hikari

Akarui 明るい = bright, colorful, cheerful; *the academy gave Louis a colorful diploma*; cf. azayaka = colorful, bright,

- vivid, impressive, beautiful; cf. kagayakashii = brilliant, bright, splendid; senmei = bright, clear, vivid
- Akashi 証 = proof, certificate; *here is the certificate I received from the Academy of Sheep Farming*; cf. shouko = evidence, proof, testimony; cf. shoumei = proof, identification
- Akashingou 赤信号 = a red light (traffic); from akai = red + shingou = a traffic signal; cf. aoshingou = a green light
- Akasu 飽かす = to bore or tire; this is the transitive form of akiru = to get tired of
- Akatsuki 暁 = daybreak, beginning, ending; *at the Academy of Tsuki (moon) Studies, classes end at daybreak*; cf. related terms listed at hajime ni and at yoake
- Akegata 明け方 = daybreak; from akeru = to end or expire + yuugata = evening; cf. related terms listed at yoake
- Akeppanashi 開けっ放し = leaving open; from akeru = to open + -ppanashi = to leave something unfinished
- Akeru 明ける = to start, end or expire; *if you akeru (open) my diary, our relationship will end, and a new one may start*; cf. related terms listed at hajimaru
- Akeru 開ける = to open or unwrap, transitive; *when I had my art show, an artistic Kennedy ruined it by opening a competing show*; cf. related terms listed at hiraku
- Aki 秋 = fall (season), autumn; *Achilles visited us in the autumn*; cf. similar terms listed at kisetsu
- Akibin 空き瓶 = an empty bottle; from aku = to become vacant + bin = a bottle; cf. related terms listed at tsubo
- Akichi 空地 = vacant land, a vacant lot; from aku = to become empty or vacant + chi = ground or place; cf. similar terms listed at basho
- Akikan 空き缶 = an empty can; from aku = to become vacant + kan = a can; cf. related terms listed at kan
- Akinai 商い = trade, business; from akinau = to trade in; cf. boueki = international trade; eigyou = business; cf. jigyou = business or enterprise; cf. kagyou = trade, business, occupation; cf. kagyou = a family business; cf. kigyou = enterprise or company; cf. kougyou = industry; cf. koumu = public business; cf. shoubai = business; cf. shouyou = business; cf. other related terms listed at kaisha and at kougyou
- Akinau 商う = to trade in or sell; *Achilles is now trading in military equipment*; cf. related terms listed at uru
- Akiraka na 明らかな = obvious, clear; this can sometimes be spelled 顕らかな; *it's obvious that a key to the locker is needed*; cf. kiyoi = clear, pure; cf. meiryou na = obvious, clear; cf. rekizen = evident, clear, distinct; cf. senmei = bright, clear, vivid; cf. sukitootta = transparent, clear
- Akirameru 諦める = to give up or abandon hope; *Achilles' ramen was ruined because he gave up on it*
- Akireru 呆れる = to be disgusted or astonished; *Achilles ate the red roosters, and I was astounded*; cf. related terms listed at akiru and at odoroku
- Akiru 飽きる = to get tired of; *Achilles ruined his toys after he got tired of them*; cf. akireru = to get disgusted or astonished; cf. hekieki suru = to get tired of; cf. iradatsu = to get irritated, to fret; cf. koriru = to learn a lesson or get sick of; cf. unzari suru = to get disgusted, to be fed up with
- Akita 秋田 = the name of a prefecture and also a type of dog; from aki = autumn + ta = rice paddy, e.g., tanbou = rice paddy
- Akka suru 悪化する = to go from bad to worse; *the academy went from bad to worse*

Akke 呆気 = dumbfounded, taken aback; *the ad for Kennedy's campaign dumbfounded me*

Akogareru 憧れる = to admire, to long for; *the acorns in the garden attracted the red rooster which admired them*; cf. shitau = to adore or yearn for; cf. other related terms listed at kanshin suru

Aku 悪 = evil; *her acute poisoning was caused by an evil rival*; cf. related terms listed at warui

Aku 空く = to become vacant; *the acupuncture clinic became vacant*

Aku 開く = to open or start (intransitive), to come to an end; *they accused me of negligence after the window opened and it started to rain*; cf. kurihirogeru = to unfold, to open

Akuheki 悪癖 = bad habit; from aku = evil + heki = habit

Aku'i (Akui) 悪意 = malice, ill will; from aku = evil + imi = meaning; cf. keno = hatred, disgust; cf. onnen = a grudge, malice, hatred; cf. urami = a grudge, animosity

Akuma 悪魔 = a devil or evil spirit; *the accumulation of magic events suggests that we are dealing with a devil or evil spirit*; cf. oni = a devil, or a cruel person

Akumu 悪夢 = a nightmare; from aku = evil + mu = a dream, e.g. muchuu = a daze; cf. related terms listed at yume

Akusho 悪書 = a harmful book; from aku = evil + sho = a document; cf. related terms listed at hon

Akushu 握手 = a handshake; *I received acupuncture for my shooting arm, and it improved my handshake*

Akushuu 悪習 = a bad habit, evil practice; from aku = evil + shuukan = custom; cf. related terms listed at shuukan

Akushuu 悪臭 = a bad smell; *the acupuncturist's shoes had a bad smell*; cf. related terms listed at kaori

Akutenkou 悪天候 = bad weather; from aku = evil + tenkou = weather; cf. related terms listed at tenki

Ama 尼 = a nun; *I met a nun while visiting the Amazon*; cf. nisou = a nun or priestess

Ama 天 = the sky, used as a word component; *the sky is big in the Amazon*

Ama no gawa 天の川 = the Milky Way; from ama = sky + gawa = kawa = river

Amadoi 雨樋 = a rain gutter; from ama = ame = rain + doi = gutter; *my doily was flushed down the gutter*

Amagasa 雨笠 = a rain hat; from ama = ame = rain + gasa = kasa = hat; cf. related terms listed at boushi

Amai 甘い = sweet; *the amateur's ice cream is too sweet*;

Amami 甘味 = sweetness; from amai = sweet + mi = taste, eg., shumi = hobby or taste; cf. amasa = sweetness; cf. other related terms listed at aji

Amari ni mo あまりにも = excessively; from amari = very much + ni = a suffix that forms an adverb + mo = even

Amari 余り = surplus, remainder, more than, very much, not very (with negative constructions); from amaru = to be be left over; cf. anmari = unusually, extremely, very much, not very (with negative constructions), irrational, cruel; cf. sahodo = not so, not particularly, not very, not that much; cf. other related terms listed at yoyuu and at ooi ni

Amaru 余る = to be left over, to remain, to be in excess; *Amanda ruined the food that was left over*; cf. nokoru = to stay behind, to remain

Amasa 甘さ = sweetness; from amai = sweet + sa = a suffix that creates a noun; cf. amami = sweetness

Amatsubu 雨粒 = raindrop; from ama = ame = rain + tsubu = drop; cf. related terms listed at tsubu

Amayakasu 甘やかす = to indulge or spoil (a person); *in the Amazon, the Yankee casually spoiled his monkey*; cf. dekiai suru = to dote on or indulge

Ame 雨 = rain, rainfall; *sometimes we get rain in America*; cf. doshaburi = pouring rain; cf. ooame = a heavy rain; cf. yuudachi = an evening rain shower

Ameagari 雨上がり = after the rain; from ame = rain + agaru = to finish; *the balloon will agaru (rise) after we finish adding helium*

Amerikaka アメリカ化 = Americanization; from amerika = the U.S. + ka = a nominalizing suffix, adding the meaning "ization"

Ami 網 = a net, a spider's web; *my amigo (friend, in Spanish) gave me a butterfly net*

Amikake 網掛け = shaded font; from ami = a net + kakeru = to hang

Amu 編む = to knit; *she knitted an amulet (a piece of jewelry hung around the neck)*

An 案 = idea, plan, proposal; *Queen Anne had a lot of plans*; cf. related terms listed at kikaku, at omoi, and at teian

An 暗 = dark, used as a word component; *ants can work in the dark*

Ana 穴 = hole; *the anatomy class studied the seven holes in a dog's head*; cf. hariana = a pinhole, the eye of a needle; cf. sukima = hole, gap

Anadoru 侮る = to look down on, despise or make light of; *he uses analogies to donkeys and rudeness against those he looks down on*; cf. ibaru = to look down on, to brag; cf. sagesumu = to look down on, to scorn or despise

Anata あなた = you; *I saw you at the anatomy talk*; cf. anatagata = you (plural); cf. kimi = you (used mostly by men and boys); cf. omae = you (informal men's speech); cf. omaera = you (plural)

Anatagata あなた方 = you (plural); from anata = you + gata = kata = honorable person; cf. related terms listed at anata

Ane 姉 = older sister; *my older sister tells a lot of anecdotes*; cf. similar terms listed at kyoudai

An'i (Ani) 安易 = easygoing, lightly, easily; *Little Orphan Annie was an easygoing girl*; cf. karugaru = lightly, easily, carelessly

Ani 兄 = older brother; *my older brother eats like an animal*; cf. similar terms listed at kyoudai

Ankeeto アンケート = questionnaire; from the French enquete; *she made an anklet out of the questionnaire*

Anmari あんまり = unusually, extremely, very much, not very (with negative constructions), irrational, cruel; cf. related terms listed at amari

Anna あんな = that kind over there, that sort over there, such; *the anatomy teacher is that kind of person over there*; cf. related terms listed at konna

Annai 案内 = information, guidance, showing around; *he likes showing people around at night*; cf. sendou = guidance, leadership; cf. shidou = guidance; cf. other related terms listed at jouhou

Ano あの = that over there, those over there; *that over there is an artistic Norwegian*

Ano あの = well, say, errr…; *well, let's keep this anonymous*

Anou あのう – see ano = well

Anpi 安否 = safety or welfare; *that anvil on the piano is a safety hazard*; cf. fukushi = welfare; cf. other related terms listed at chian

Anpontan あんぽんたん = a simpleton or fool; *that simpleton put an anvil on a pony before leading it into a tanning booth*; cf. related terms listed at baka

Ansatsu 暗殺 = assassination; from an = dark + satsujin = murder; cf. related terms listed at satsujin

Anshin 安心 = peace of mind, relief; *my aunt bought new shingles for her peace of mind*; cf. anshinkan = a sense of security; cf. hitoanshin = a feeling of relief; cf. kanwa = relief, alleviation, relaxation

Anshin suru 安心する = to feel relief or peace of mind; from anshin = peace of mind, relief; cf. related terms listed at yasuragu

Anshinkan 安心感 = a sense of security; from anshin = peace of mind, relief + kanjiru = to feel; cf. related terms listed at anshin

Anshou 暗証 = a code or password; *you need a password to watch the animal show*; cf. anshou bangou = code number

Anshou bangou 暗証番号 = code number; from anshou = a code or password + bangou = number

Antai 安泰 = peace, security; *my aunt went to Thailand to work for peace and security*; cf. related terms listed at heiwa

Antei 安定 = stability; *my aunt's kitchen table was a symbol of stability*

Anteika 安定化 = stabilization; from antei = stability + ka = a nominalizing suffix

Anzan 暗算 = mental calculation; *when Queen Anne visited Zanzibar, she did a mental calculation of the number of Queen Anne chairs there*; cf. related terms listed at keisan

Anzen 安全 = safety, security; *my aunt turned to Zen for safety and security*; cf. related terms listed at chian

Anzensei 安全性 = safety, security; from anzen = safety, security + sei = nature; cf. related terms listed at chian

Ao 青 = blue (or green); the noun form of aoi = blue (or green); cf. ai = indigo; cf. aoao = fresh and green; cf. kon (no) = dark or navy blue; cf. kon'iro = navy blue; cf. noukon = dark blue

Aoao 青々 = fresh and green; from aoi = blue (or green); cf. related terms listed at ao

Aogu 仰ぐ = to look up, look up to, ask for advice, depend on; *the owl and the goose looked up at the sky*; cf. related terms listed at miru

Aoi 青い = blue (or green), unripe, inexperienced; *the Arctic ocean extended east under a blue sky*; cf. related terms listed at ao

Aori あおり = a gust of wind; *the owl that was perched on a reed was knocked over by a gust of wind*; cf. related terms listed at kaze

Aoritateru あおり立てる = to flap strongly or stir up fiercely; *the owl on the reed tateru (stands) and flaps his wings strongly*; cf. habataku = to flap (wings)

Aoshingou 青信号 = a green light (traffic); from aoi = blue (or green) + shingou = a traffic signal; cf. akashingou = a red light

Apiiru アピール = appeal, in the sense of being attractive to people; cf. miryoku = attractiveness, charm

Appu suru アップする = to upload

Apuri アプリ = app (application)

Arai 粗い = coarse, rugged; *the artist's rhymes were rather coarse*; cf. arai = violent, rough, rude; cf. related terms listed at somatsu

Arai 荒い = violent, rough, rude; *when violent, rough and rude people assemble, a riot can break out*; cf. arai = coarse, rugged; cf. oozappa = rough, broad, sketchy; cf. other related terms listed at ranbou and at shikkei

Arainagasu 洗い流す = to wash away or rinse off; from arau = to wash + nagasu = to flush; cf. related terms listed at arau

Arashi 嵐 = storm; *an Arab who is a Shiite was caught in a storm*; cf. taifuu = a typhoon

Arasoi 争い = fighting, conflict; from arasou = to fight; cf. related terms listed at issen

Arasou 争う = to fight, dispute or compete; *the Arab soldiers will fight*; cf. iiarasou = to quarrel or dispute; cf. kenka suru = to quarrel or fight; cf. kisou = to compete with; cf. shiai suru = to compete; cf. taikou suru = to oppose or fight; cf. tatakau = to fight, make war

Arasu 荒らす = to lay waste, damage, devastate, break into, invade; *Arafat sued his enemies for damaging his car*; cf. related terms listed at kizutsukeru

Arata 新た = fresh, new; *the Arabesque tapestry was fresh and new*; cf. related terms listed at atarashii

Aratamaru 改まる = to be renewed; the intransitive form of aratameru = to change

Aratameru 改める = to change, renovate, correct; *we are going to renovate a cage for our Arabian tame rooster*; cf. related terms listed at kaeru

Aratamete 改めて = again, anew, another time, formally; *the Arabian tame terriers came again, anew and another time*; cf. futatabi = again; cf. mata = again, also, and, as well as; cf. saisan = many times, again and again; cf. sara ni = again, furthermore

Arau 洗う = to wash; *I asked Raul Castro to wash the dishes*; cf. arainagasu = to wash away or rinse off; cf. sentaku suru = to wash laundry

Arawareru 現れる = to appear or show up; *the Arab warrior owned some red roosters, and he always showed up to feed them*; cf. shutsugen suru = to appear; cf. waku = to gush out, well up, appear; cf. yatte kuru = to turn up, come along

Arawasu 著わす = to write or publish; *Yasser Arafat washed his suit and then sat down to write a book*; cf. related terms listed at kaku and at keisai suru

Arawasu 表す = to signify, represent or express; to reveal or show; this can also be written 現わす; *Arafat watched Superman, who seemed to represent some hope that the problem could be solved*; cf. related terms listed at iiarawasu and miseru

Arayuru あらゆる = all, every possible; *Arafat said the youths were rude after they called him every possible name*; cf. ari to arayuru = every single; cf. other related terms listed at kanou

Are あれ = hey! *hey! there's an American restaurant*

Are あれ = that over there; *that over there is an African restaurant*

Arehateru 荒れ果てる = to fall into ruin; *while arguing at a restaurant, I learned that the Harvard tennis courts were rumored to be falling into ruin*; cf. areru = to be stormy or rough, to fall into ruin

Arera あれら = those over there; from are = that over there + ra = a suffix that makes the preceding pronoun plural

Areru 荒れる = to be stormy or rough, to fall into ruin; *the American red rooster noticed that the weather was stormy and rough as it crossed the road*; cf. arehateru = to fall into ruin

Ari to arayuru ありとあらゆる = every single; from aru = to exist + to = if + arayuru = every possible; cf. arayuru = all, every possible

Arieru 有りえる = is possible; (this can also be pronounced ariuru); *that an aristocrat could be erudite is possible*; cf. related terms listed at kanou

Arigatai 有難い = grateful, welcome; the

noun form of arigatou = thank you

Arigatami 有り難み = worth or value; *the aristocratic gallant tall mediator showed his value during the negotiations*; cf. related terms listed at kachi

Arigatou 有難う = thank you; *the aristocratic gallant Tolstoy always said thank you*; cf. doumo = thank you, somehow or somewhat, probably; cf. sumimasen = I'm sorry, excuse me, thank you

Arikata 在り方 = the way things are; from arimasu = to exist + kata = direction; cf. related terms listed at keisei

Aritai ありたい = I want (something) to exist. For example, heiwa de aritai = I want peace to exist. Utsukushiku aritai = I want to be beautiful. Kirei de arita = I want to be pretty. Iru, meaning "to exist," is not used in the same way, i.e., one cannot say ~~iritai~~. cf. tai = want to do

Ariuru 有りうる – see arieru

Aru ある = a, a certain, some, used as an adjective prior to a noun; from aru = to exist

Aru ある = to exist (used for inanimate objects), to happen, to experience; *Aruba exists in the Caribbean*; cf. de wa aru = to exist (in contrast to something that doesn't exist); cf. dearu = to exist (animate or inanimate); cf. degozaimasu = to exist humbly (animate or inanimate); cf. irassharu = to come, go or exist (animate) honorably; cf. iru = to exist (animate); cf. orareru = to exist honorably (animate); cf. oru = to exist humbly (animate); cf. sonzai suru = to exist (animate or inanimate)

Arubaito アルバイト = part-time job; *I got a part-time job in Aruba at Easter towing tour boats*; cf. related terms listed at shigoto

Arukaseru 歩かせる = to make someone walk; the causative form of aruku = to walk

Arukimawaru 歩き回る = to walk around; from aruku = to walk + mawaru = to turn; cf. related terms listed at aruku

Aruku 歩く = to walk; *after I arrive in Aruba and drink some Kool-Aid, I plan to walk*; cf. arukimawaru = to walk around; cf. sanpo suru = to walk

Asa 朝 = morning; *the assault was scheduled in the morning*; cf. gozen = morning, a.m.; cf. kesa = this morning; cf. souchou = early morning

Asa 麻 = hemp, linen; *he assaulted me with a hemp and linen rope*

Asa ito 麻糸 = linen thread; from asa = linen + ito = thread; cf. ito = thread, string

Asagao 朝顔 = Japanese morning glory; from asa = morning + gao = kao = face; cf. related terms listed at hana

Asagohan 朝ご飯 = breakfast; from asa = morning + gohan = a meal; cf. similar terms listed at shokuji

Asahi 朝日 = morning sun, rising sun; from asa = morning + hi = sun

Asai 浅い = shallow, superficial, frivolous, wretched, shameful; *the assault in Ireland was shameful, and it was done for shallow and frivolous reasons*; cf. related terms listed at mittomonai

Asaichi 朝一 = first thing in the morning; from asa = morning + ichi = number one

Asatte あさって = the day after tomorrow; this can also be spelled 明後日, in which case it can also be pronounced myougonichi; *there's a plot to assault Ted Kennedy the day after tomorrow*

Ase 汗 = sweat; *asses sweat when they work*

Ase wo kaku 汗をかく = to sweat; from ase = sweat + kaku = to draw and other meanings

Aseru 焦る = to be in a hurry or impatient, to

be flustered; *when the <u>asses</u> see the <u>rooster</u>, they get <u>flustered</u>*; cf. hayaru = to be impatient or hotblooded; cf. awateru = to become confused, to panic, to be in a hurry or a frenzy; cf. muzumuzu = to feel itchy, to be impatient or eager to do something

Ashi 足 = foot or leg; *his <u>feet</u> and <u>legs</u> look <u>ashy</u> due to a low oxygen level*; cf. related terms listed at ude

Ashi no kou 足の甲 = top of the foot; from ashi = foot + the possessive no + koura = shell

Ashi wo arau 足を洗う = to cut ties with; literally "to wash the feet," similar to "washing one's hands" of something in English; cf. related terms listed at kiru

Ashiato 足跡 = footprints; from ashi = foot + ato = trace or track

Ashikubi 足首 = an ankle; from ashi = foot + kubi = neck

Ashioto 足音 = footsteps; from ashi = foot + oto = sound

Ashita 明日 = tomorrow; *<u>tomorrow</u> let's take that <u>ashy</u> tapestry to the dump*; cf. asu = tomorrow; cf. myounichi = tomorrow

Asobi 遊び = play, diversion, game, having a good time; from asobu = to play; cf. goraku = diversion, recreation, entertainment

Asobu 遊ぶ = to play; *the <u>associate</u> <u>bootmaker</u> let his children <u>play</u>*; cf. tawamureru = to play, to be amused (with something)

Asoko あそこ = over there; *the <u>associate's</u> <u>cola</u> is <u>over</u> <u>there</u>*

Asu 明日 = tomorrow; *I <u>assume</u> he will come <u>tomorrow</u>*; cf. related terms listed at ashita

Ataeru 与える = to give, award, cause; *if I attain erudition, I will <u>give</u> my goods to the poor*; cf. ageru = to give, to raise or lift, to fly (a kite), to hold (a ceremony), to turn up (volume); cf. hodokosu = to donate, perform, give time; cf. juyo suru = to confer or award; cf. kifu suru = to donate; cf. kudasaru = to give to someone in the speaker's in-group, by someone outside the group who has equal or greater age or status; cf. kureru = to give to a member of the speaker's in-group, by someone in the group or by someone outside the group who has equal or inferior status; cf. megumu = to bless, show mercy, give money, bestow a favor, etc.; cf. okuru = to give a present; cf. sashiageru = to give humbly; cf. sazukeru = to give or grant; cf. yaru = to give to someone of equal or lower status or to a member of the speaker's in-group, to do, to get along; cf. zoutei suru = to donate or present a gift; cf. other related terms listed at hikiokosu

Atai 値 = value, price; this can also be spelled 価; *<u>a Thai</u> guy is checking the <u>price</u>*; cf. related terms listed at kachi and at nedan

Atai suru 値する = to be worth it, to deserve it; from atai = value; this can also be spelled 価する; *<u>a Thai</u> vacation is <u>worth</u> the money*

Atama 頭 = head, brain; *I <u>attached a machine</u> to my <u>head</u>*; cf. nou = a brain; cf. tou = head, counter for large animals; cf. toubu = head, cranium; cf. zunou = brains, head

Atarashii 新しい = fresh or new; *I use my <u>new</u> catapult to <u>attack</u> rats with flying <u>shingles</u>*; cf. arata = fresh, new; cf. shin = new, used as a word component; cf. shinsen = fresh

Atari 当たり = a hit or success; from ataru = to hit

Atari 当たり = per, apiece, when used as a suffix; *my brother and I had one <u>Atari</u> game <u>apiece</u>*; cf. ni tsuki = per, apiece, because of, regarding

Atari 辺り = neighborhood, area; *the <u>Atari</u> headquarters is in this <u>neighborhood</u>*; cf. related terms listed at fukin

Atarimae 当たり前 = natural, reasonable,

ordinary, the norm; *for the Atari company to build an office mae (in front of) the station seems reasonable*; cf. related terms listed at tekitou

Ataru 当たる = to hit, to win; *a tall rooster fell from its perch and hit me*; cf. related terms listed at utsu = to hit

Atatakai 暖かい = warm (atmosphere); *Ataturk talked about kayaking on that warm day*; cf. related terms listed at atatakai = warm (objects)

Atatakai 温かい = warm (objects); *Ataturk talked about kayaking as he waved his warm paddle*; cf. atatakai = warm (atmosphere); cf. attakai = warm, mild, genial

Atatakasa 暖かさ = warmth; from atatakai = warm (atmosphere) + sa = a suffix that makes a noun from an adjective; cf. related terms listed at atsusa

Atatamaru 温まる = to get warm, intransitive; *after we attacked the tax collectors, we were marooned, and we built a fire to get warm*

Atatameru 温める = to heat or warm up, transitive; the transitive form of atatamaru = to get warm

Atchi あっち – see achira

Ate 宛 = addressed to, used as a suffix; from ateru = to address

Atehamaru 当てはまる = to apply (a rule or law), to be applicable; from ateru = to hit + hamaru = to fall into

Ateru 宛てる = to address (mail); *I addressed my letter to "A Terribly Rude Person"*

Ateru 当てる = to touch (by hand), hit, win, guess correctly, to call on, to allot; *a terribly rude person touched me on the subway*; cf. related terms listed at katsu, at fureru and at utsu

Atesaki 宛先 = an address or destination; *I mailed a tennis ball and some salty quiche to that destination*; cf. juusho = an address

Atetsuke 当て付け = insinuation, spiteful remark; *when you told the architect that his tennis racket should have stayed in his tsuitcase (suitcase), that was a spiteful remark*

Ato 後 = after, another (with a number); *I will buy another atomic clock after lunch*; cf. related terms listed at hoka and at kongo

Ato 後 = the rear, the rest; *my atomic clock is in the rear of my house*; cf. related terms listed at ushiro

Ato 跡 = trace, track, mark, ruin; *the atomic bomb project left traces of radiation*; cf. ato = a mark or footprint, used as a word component; cf. atokata = trace, vestige; cf. konseki = traces, vestiges; cf. nagori = traces, remnants; cf. nokori = remainder, balance

Ato 痕 = a mark or footprint, used as a word component; *the atomic bomb left a mark when it was dragged across the floor*; cf. related terms listed at ato = trace

Atokata 跡形 = trace, vestige; from ato = trace or track; + kata = shape; cf. related terms listed at ato = trace

Atsude no 厚手の = thick (paper, fabric, etc.); from atsui = thick + de = te = hand

Atsui 厚い = thick; *at the Swedish house, they had thick curtains*; cf. related terms listed at koi

Atsui 暑い = hot (atmosphere); *at the Swedish house, the weather was hot*; cf. atsui = hot (objects); hokahoka = steaming hot, very warm; cf. mushiatsui = hot and humid; cf. mushimushi = hot and humid

Atsui 熱い = hot (objects); *at the Swedish house, the walls were hot*; cf. related terms listed at atsui = hot (atmosphere)

Atsukamashii 厚かましい = impudent, shameless; *at Superman's party, Karl Marx and his Shiite friends were impudent*;

cf. related terms listed at shikkei

Atsukai 扱い = treatment, service; from atsukau = to take care of

Atsukau 扱う = to deal with or deal in, to take care of; *I <u>dealt with</u> a wolf after it <u>attacked</u> my <u>superior cows</u>*; cf. related terms listed at shori suru

Atsumaru 集まる = to meet or assemble; the intransitive form of atsumeru = to collect; cf. related terms listed at shuugou suru

Atsumeru 集める = to collect, gather, attract, summon; *<u>at the supermarket</u> I received a <u>meeru</u> (email) asking me to <u>gather</u> some fruit for dinner*; cf. hakiatsumeru = to sweep up together; cf. hirou = to pick up, to find, to gather; cf. karu = to hunt (animals), to gather (flowers, mushrooms, fruit); cf. yoseru = to send, gather or bring closer; cf. other related terms listed at kaishuu suru

Atsuryoku 圧力 = pressure; from atsu = pressure, e.g., ketsuatsu = blood pressure; + ryoku = force; cf. ketsuatsu = blood pressure; cf. kiatsu = atmospheric pressure; cf. suiatsu = water pressure

Atsusa 暑さ = heat; from atsui = hot + sa = a suffix that makes a noun from an adjective; cf. atatakasa = warmth; cf. mousho = fierce heat, heat wave; cf. netsu = heat, fever; cf. nukumori = warmth

Attakai 暖かい = warm, mild, genial; a variant of atatakai = warm; cf. related terms listed at atatakai = warm (objects)

Atto iu mani あっという間に = in the blink of an eye; *a <u>tow</u> truck driver can take <u>your money in the blink of an eye</u>*; cf. matataku ma ni = in an instant

Attou suru 圧倒する = to overwhelm, overpower; *<u>American tornadoes overwhelm</u> residents*

Attouteki 圧倒的 = overwhelming; from attou suru = to overwhelm + teki = related to

Au 会う = to meet; *we will <u>meet</u> in <u>Austria</u>*; cf. related terms listed at deau

Au 合う = to match or agree with, to come together; *we <u>came together</u> in <u>Austria</u>, and our outfits <u>matched</u>*

Au 遭う = to be involved (in an accident, etc.), to get caught in, encounter, meet; *the <u>owl</u> was <u>involved in</u> an <u>accident</u>*; cf. related terms listed at deau and at kakawaru

Awa 泡 = bubbles, foam; *I was <u>awakened</u> by <u>bubbles</u> flowing into my house*; cf. kihou = an air bubble

Awa Odori 阿波踊り = a dance festival held during Obon in Tokushima City; *I was <u>awakened</u> by the <u>odori</u> (dance) <u>festival</u>*

Awai 淡い = thin, faint, pale, fleeting; *I was <u>awakened</u> by an <u>eagle</u> making a <u>faint fleeting</u> sound*; cf. related terms listed at kasuka

Aware 哀れ = pity, misery; *are you <u>aware</u> of the <u>misery</u> you caused me?* cf. related terms listed at doujou

Aware na 哀れな = pitiable, miserable; from aware = misery

Awaseru 合わせる = to join together, to harmonize or adjust, to match speed, etc; *while the doctors <u>await serum</u>, they will <u>join together</u> to prepare the patient*

Awaseru 会わせる = to introduce people to each other; this is the causative form of au = to meet

Awatadashii あわただしい = hasty; *your decision to <u>awaken</u> me was <u>tadashii</u> (correct) since circumstances made you <u>hasty</u>*; cf. keisotsu = thoughtless, careless, hasty

Awateru 慌てる = to become confused, to panic, to be in a hurry or a frenzy; *<u>awakened</u> by a <u>terrorist</u>, I was in a <u>frenzy</u>*; cf. aseru = to be in a hurry or impatient, to be flustered

Ayamachi 過ち = fault, mistake; *the Ayatollah got mad when the chief made a mistake*; cf. related terms listed at ketten

Ayamari 誤り = a mistake; from ayamaru = to make a mistake; cf. related terms listed at ketten

Ayamari 謝り = an excuse or apology; from ayamaru = to apologize

Ayamaru 誤る = to make a mistake; *the Ayatollah was marooned because a sailor made a mistake*; cf. related terms listed at machigaeru

Ayamaru 謝る = to apologize; *after a shipwreck, the Ayatollah was marooned on a desert island, and later the ship's owners apologized*

Ayashii 怪しい = suspicious, doubtful; *the Ayatollah thought that some of the Shiites were of doubtful loyalty*; cf. abunai = dangerous, risky, doubtful, life-threatening; cf. ayaui = dangerous, uncertain, insecure; cf. etai no shirenai = questionable, untrustworthy, enigmatic, suspicious; cf. utagawashii = doubtful

Ayatsuru 操る = to control, manipulate, handle; *the Ayatollah's tsuitcase (suitcase) was ruined when the airline handled it roughly*; cf. related terms listed at shori suru

Ayaui 危うい = dangerous, uncertain, insecure; *the Ayatollah said that whiskey is dangerous*; cf. related terms listed at ayashi and kiken na

Ayauku 危うく = barely, almost; from ayaui = dangerous, insecure; cf. hobo = almost, about; cf. hotondo = mostly, just about, almost; cf. ni chikai = almost; cf. other related terms listed at yatto

Aza あざ = a bruise, birthmark, black eye; *I asked Zach for money, and he gave me this bruise*; cf. related terms listed at dabokushou

Azakeru 嘲る = to ridicule, mock or scoff; *my friend scoffed at me for keeping azaleas in Kennedy's room*

Azamuku 欺く = to deceive or trick; *they deceived me into thinking that I could send azaleas to the moon from Kuwait*; cf. related terms listed at uragiru

Azayaka 鮮やか = colorful, bright, vivid, impressive, beautiful; *the art that I saw in Zach's yacht and car was vivid and beautiful*; cf. other related terms listed at akarui, at inshouteki and at utsukushii

Azukaru 預かる = to keep, be in charge of, take care of; *I am in charge of that azul (blue, in Spanish) car*; cf. ban wo suru = to watch or take care of; cf. hokan suru = to keep a close watch over, to take good care of; cf. iji suru = to maintain; cf. tamotsu = to keep or maintain; cf. tasu = to take care of business, to add numbers, to add something; cf. teire wo suru = to take care of; cf. tsukisou = to accompany or take care of

Ba 馬 = a horse, used as a suffix; *there are a lot of horses in Barcelona*; cf. similar terms listed at uma

Baai 場合 = case or situation; *in case the bar runs out of ice, we will find ourselves in a difficult situation*; cf. related terms listed at keisei

Bachiatari na (or no) 罰当たりな = spiteful, sinful, cursed; *the bad cheese that they serve at the Atari company is cursed*

Bai 倍 = double, times, -fold, often used as a suffix; *let's buy two times or double the quantity*; cf. related terms listed at -do

Bai 杯 – see hai

Baibai 売買 = buying and selling; *since you're busy buying and selling, I'll say bye bye*; cf. related terms listed at uriage

Baigaku 倍額 = double the amount; *he will buy us a gallon of Kool-Aid, but he wants to be repaid double the amount*; cf. baizou = double; cf. nijuu = double

Baikai 媒介 = a carrier, medium or agent, mediation; *I'm looking for an agent to buy kites for me*; cf. baitai = a medium; cf. chuukai = mediation

Baikaku 倍角 = double-sized font; *when I filled out the order to buy Karl some Kool-Aid, I used double-sized font*

Baikyaku 売却 = selling, or a sale; *since I want to buy a kayak, I'm looking for a sale*; cf. related terms listed at uriage

Baishaku 媒酌 = matchmaking; *I'm going to buy a shack for my matchmaking office*

Baishin 陪審 = a jury; *the jury weighed the teachings of the Bible vs. those of Shinto*

Baishou 賠償 = compensation, reparation; *we received compensation for the damage caused to our neighborhood by the bike show*; cf. hoshou = compensation

Baitai 媒体 = a medium (e.g., air is a medium for sound); from baikai = a carrier or medium + tai = a body, e.g., buttai = a body (physics); cf. related terms listed at baikai

Baiten 売店 = stall, booth, kiosk; from hanbai = sales + ten = store, e.g., tenin = store clerk; cf. related terms listed at mise

Baito バイト = part-time work, an abbreviation of arubaito = part-time work; cf. related terms listed at shigoto

Baiu 梅雨 = rainy season (June and early July); this is the less common pronunciation, compared to tsuyu; *during the rainy season, the bayou was flooded*; cf. related terms listed at kisetsu

Baiuzensen 梅雨前線 = seasonal rain front; from baiu = rainy season; + zen = before, e.g., gozen = before noon; + sen = line

Baiyou 培養 = cultivation, nurture, culture; *I'm buying yogurt so that I can start a culture and make my own in the future*; cf. related terms listed at kousaku

Baizou 倍増 = double; *when I buy Zooey's quiche, I order a double quantity*; cf. baigaku = double the amount; cf. nijuu = double

Bajou 馬上 = horseback, horse riding; *the barber joked that he was going to take up horse riding*

Baka バカ = a stupid person; *he may be a stupid person, but he has a baccalaureate degree*; cf. anpontan = a simpleton or fool; cf. boke = a fool

Bakari ばかり = approximately, just (finished, etc.) a while ago, only, nothing but, always or constantly; *the bakery is approximately a block away, and I just discovered it, but they are only open in the mornings*

Bakari ni ばかりに = just because, on account of; from bakari = only + ni = by

Bakkari ばっかり — see bakari

Bakkin 罰金 = a penalty or fine; *if you back in to the parking spot, you pay a fine*; cf. batsu = discipline, penalty; cf. choukai = reprimand, discipline; cf. seisai = a punishment or sanction

Bakuchi 博打 = gambling; *the barmaid thinks it's cool to cheat when she's gambling*; cf. kakegoto = gambling; cf. tobaku = gambling

Bakuchiku 爆竹 = firecracker; from bakudan = bomb + chiku = bamboo; cf. hanabi = fireworks

Bakudai ばくだい = enormous, vast; *the barber in Kuwait died and was given an enormous funeral*; cf. related terms listed at ookii

Bakudan 爆弾 = bomb; *in the back of the Uber car, the dancer concealed a bomb*; cf. genbaku = atomic bomb; cf. genshi-bakudan = an atomic bomb

Bakufu 幕府 = the shogunate administration; *at a bar in Kuwait, I foolishly raged against the shogunate administration*

Bakuga 麦芽 = malt (a grain such as barley which is softened in water and allowed to germinate, used in brewing and distilling); *after drinking* malt *liquor, the* bartender *poured* Kool*-Aid on the* gambler

Bakuhatsu 爆発 = an explosion or eruption; from bakudan = bomb + hatsu = discharge, departure; cf. funka = a volcanic eruption; cf. haretsu = an explosion or rupture

Bakuro 暴露 = exposure or revelation; *I* badgered Kooky Roy *Rogers, hoping for a* revelation

Bakuzen 漠然 = obscure, vague; *my* barber *in* Kuwait *practices* Zen*, but I find his beliefs* obscure; cf. related terms listed at fumei and at kasuka

Bakuzen to shita 漠然とした = ambiguous, uncertain, vague; from bakuzen = obscure or vague + to suru = to regard as; cf. fumei = unknown, uncertain

Bamen 場面 = a scene; *the* barber's mentor *admired the* scene; cf. genba = actual spot, scene, site, location; cf. koukei = a scene or sight; cf. nagame = a view or scene

Bamu ばむ = a suffix creating a verb that indicates that something is in the state of the preceding noun; *I'm watching a* bad movie, like the preceding one

Ban 晩 = evening, night; *we eat* bananas in the evening; cf. yoru = night; cf. yuube = evening, yesterday evening; cf. yuugata = evening, dusk; cf. yoi = evening, the early hours of the night

Ban 番 = a watch (guard) or turn, a number in a series; *please* watch *the baby during the* banquet; cf. junban = one's turn, order; cf. other related terms listed at keibi

Ban wo suru 番をする = to watch, take care of; from ban = a watch; cf. related terms listed at azukaru

Banare ばなれ = a suffix meaning quitting, stopping, or a loss of interest; e.g., chichibanare = weaning a baby, kurumabanare = a loss of interest in cars; from banareru = hanareru = to separate from or leave

Bangohan 晩ご飯 = the evening meal; from ban = even + gohan = a meal; cf. similar terms listed at shokuji

Bangou 番号 = number; *they* banned *golfers from hitting more than a fixed* number *of balls*; cf. guusuu = an even number; cf. kazu = a number; cf. kisuu = an odd number; cf. hansuu = half the number; cf. kahansuu = a majority; cf. nengou = name of an era, a year number; cf. ninzuu = number of people; cf. sosuu = a prime number; cf. soutousuu = a considerable number; cf. suu = a number; cf. suuji = a numeral or figure; cf. tasuu = a large number, a majority

Bangumi 番組 = TV or radio program; *I saw a* TV program *about a* band *that eats* gummy *snacks*

Banji 万事 = everything, all; *if you* ban jeans, all *of the ranchers will complain*; cf. bantan = everything, all; cf. issai = everything (with positive verbs); cf. nanigoto = everything (with positive verbs); cf. nanimokamo = everything; cf. subete = everything, all, the whole, entirely; cf. zenbu = all, everything; cf. zentai = whole

Banken 番犬 = a watchdog; *the* bank *where* Ken *keeps his money has a* watchdog; cf. related terms listed at inu

Bannen 晩年 = one's last years; from ban = evening + nen = year

Banpaku 万博 = a world fair; *the* banker *and the* padre *drank* Kool*-Aid at the* world fair

Bansou 伴奏 = musical accompaniment; *the* band *provided the* soldiers *with* musical accompaniment *as they marched*

Bantan 万端 = all, everything; *if you* ban tanning, then all *of the people will leave the beach*; cf. related terms listed at banji

Banzai 万歳 = 10,000 years, used as a cheer

meaning "long live!"; from ban = man = 10,000 + zai = sai = age or years; cf. related terms listed at nen

Bara バラ = rose; *after he was freed, Barabbas gave Pilate a rose*; cf. related terms listed at hana

Baribari バリバリ = energetically, actively; *bareebooru (volleyball) games on Bali are played energetically*

Basabasa バサバサ = rustling, fluttering, flapping; *on Barcelona's sandy beaches, many birds make a fluttering sound*; cf. habataki = fluttering of wings

Basho 場所 = a place; *sometimes badgers show up at this place*; cf. akichi = vacant land, a vacant lot; cf. chi = ground, earth, place; cf. chikei = terrain; cf. funinchi = place of new post or appointment; cf. genba = actual spot, scene, site location; cf. genchi = location, the place, local; cf. gotouchi = here, where one comes from; cf. hekichi = a remote place; cf. ichi = position, location; cf. ichizuke = placement, location; cf. jimen = ground; cf. juutakuchi = a residential district; cf. kaijou = venue, site of an event; cf. kankouchi = tourist sites; cf. kasho = a point or place; cf. kyokuchi = a locality or limited area; cf. kyoten = location, base; cf. meisho = a famous place; cf. meishou = a place of scenic beauty; cf. numachi = swampland; cf. riku = land; cf. shikichi = a location or site; cf. tochi = land, place; cf. tokoro = a place or part; cf. touchi = this place, here

Bassai 伐採 = logging; *the bad scientist was logging the forest*; cf. batsuboku = logging

Bassui 抜粋 = an excerpt or extract; *here's an excerpt from the book "Bass Fishing in Sweden"*; cf. shouhon = an excerpt, abstract or abbreviated transcript

Bassui suru 抜粋する = to extract, excerpt or select; from bassui = an excerpt or extract

Bassuru 罰する = to punish or penalize; *after the banker's suit was ruined, the dry cleaner was penalized*

Basutei バス停 = bus stop; from basu = bus + tei = stop; *the tailor works near the bus stop*

Batan バタン = a thud, bang, slam, crash; *in Baghdad the tank arrived with a bang*; cf. gashan = a crash, bang, breaking sound

Batou 罵倒 = abuse, disparagement; *I receive abuse when I serve bad tofu*; cf. related terms listed at hihan

Batou suru 罵倒する = to abuse or yell at; from batou = abuse, disparagement; cf. related terms listed at ijimeru

Batsu 罰 = discipline, penalty; *if you wear that bat suit to work, you will encur a penalty*; cf. related terms listed at bakkin

Batsuboku 伐木 = logging; *they were doing some logging to make bats for the bony Kool-Aid salesman*; cf. bassai = logging

Batsugun 抜群 = outstanding, fabulous; *a bat suit plus a toy gun add up to a fabulous Halloween outfit*; cf. related terms listed at joutou

Battari ばったり = with a thud, unexpectedly, suddenly; *the battery failed suddenly and unexpectedly*; cf. related terms listed at igai and at kyuu ni

Batteki suru 抜擢する = to select; *some batty techies selected the entertainment for tonight*; cf. related terms listed at erabu

Beisaku 米作 = rice growing, rice crop; *the baby dropped a sack of cookies into the rice crop*; cf. 米作 komezukuri = rice cultivation; cf. other related terms listed at inasaku and at sakumotsu

Beki べき = must, should (social responsibility); this follows a plain speech verb and is itself followed by da or desu; *Becky must do a lot of things*; cf. related terms listed at seneba

Bekkyo 別居 = separation of family members; *since I've taken up begging in*

Kyoto, I've become *separated from* my *family*; cf. syonyms listed at wakare

Ben 弁 = a dialect, used as a word component, e.g., nagoyaben = the Nagoya dialect; *my knowledge of the local dialect benefited me*

Bengi 便宜 = convenience, assistance; *for your convenience, you may use this bench to support your guitar*; cf. related terms listed at enjo

Bengi wo hakaru 便宜を図る = to accommodate or suit the convenience of; from bengi = convenience + hakaru = to attempt

Bengoshi 弁護士 = lawyer; *we hired a lawyer for the benefit of our goats and sheep*

Benkai 弁解 = excuse, justification; *I made up an excuse for the benefit of the Kaiser*; cf. kikkake = excuse, catalyst, motive, impetus; cf. koujitsu = an excuse or pretext; cf. moushiwake = apology, excuse; cf. riyuu = reason, excuse

Benki 便器 = toilet bowl, urinal, bedpan; from benri = convenient + ki = container; *I keep quiche in a container*

Benkyou 勉強 = study; *when Benjamin Franklin was in Kyouto, he was immersed in study*; cf. gaku = study or learning; cf. gakushuu = study or learning; cf. kenkyuu = research, study; cf. moubenkyou = studying extra hard; cf. ryuugaku = study abroad

Benkyou suru 勉強する = to study or learn; from benkyou = study; cf. manabu = to study or learn; cf. mi ni tsukeru = to take on, to learn or acquire knowledge, to wear clothes, etc.; cf. narau = to learn or study

Benkyouka 勉強家 = a diligent student; from benkyou = study + ka = a person

Benri 便利 = convenient, handy; *the bench that Ringo bought was convenient*; cf. tegoro = handy, affordable

Bentou 弁当 = a boxed lunch; *I asked Benjamin Franklin to put some tofu in my box lunch*; cf. ekiben = a boxed lunch sold at train stations

Benza 便座 = toilet seat; from benki = toilet bowl + za = to sit, e.g., zabuton = floor cushion; cf. related terms listed at seki

Benzetsu 弁舌 = eloquence, persuasiveness; *Benjamin Franklin wore a Zen tsuit (suit) and was praised for his eloquence*

Bessou 別荘 = a summer house, villa or cottage; *we have a better sofa at our summer house*; cf. related terms listed at ie

Bessouchi 別荘地 = an area of villas or holiday homes; from bessou = a summer house or villa + chi = ground; cf. related terms listed at chitai

Betsu 別 = separate, different, extra, other, another; *I bet Superman comes from a different planet*; cf. related terms listed at hoka

Betsu ni 別に = particularly; from betsu = different + -ni = a suffix that forms an adverb; cf. related terms listed at toku ni

Betsu no 別の = another (defined object, person or place); *I bet Superman has another girlfriend*; cf. related terms listed at hoka

Betsu to shite 別として = other than, except for; from betsu = separate + to shite = as; cf. yori hoka = other than

Betsumune 別棟 = separate building, outbuilding; *I bet Superman and the moon experts are in that outbuilding*; cf. related terms listed at tatemono

Bi 美 = beauty; *I can see beauty at the beach*; cf. biyou = beauty of figure or form

Biiru ビール = beer

Bijin 美人 = a beautiful woman; *many beach jin (people) are beautiful women*; cf. related terms listed at onna

Bijutsu 美術 = visual art; *Being juts out into the world through the visual arts*; cf.

related terms listed at geijutsu

Bijutsukan 美術館 = an art museum or gallery; from bijutsu = visual arts + kan = large building; cf. geijutsukan = an art museum; cf. hakubutsukan = a museum (other than art)

Biki 引き = -off (price reduction); from biku = hiku = to pull

Bikkuri びっくり = being surprised or shocked; *I was surprised that the beef curry was so good*

Bikou 備考 = notes or remarks; *the beef was cold, and I made some remarks about it to the waitress*; cf. chuu = notes

Bikouran 備考欄 = a remarks column; from bikou = remarks + ran = column; cf. ran = a column (newspaper)

Bimi 美味 = good flavor; *the beef meal contained some good flavors*; cf. related terms listed at aji

Bimyou 微妙 = subtle, delicate; *the beast meowed when it smelled the delicate fragrance*; cf. related terms listed at binkan

Bin 便 = a service or convenience; also = a flight, e.g., chokkoubin = a nonstop flight; *having beans delivered is a convenience; we played bingo on the flight*

Bin 瓶 = a bottle, jar or decanter (this can also be pronounced kame = an earthenware jar); *I keep beans in that jar*; cf. related terms listed at tsubo

Binbou 貧乏 = poverty, poor person; *the beans that Bo Peep picks are given to poor people*; cf. fujiyuu = disability, discomfort, poverty; cf. hihei = exhaustion, impoverishment, ruin; cf. hinkon = poverty; cf. hinkonsha = poor people; cf. konkyuu = poverty

Binetsu 微熱 = a slight fever; from bi = delicate, minute; *that beak is minute*; + netsu = fever

Biniiru ビニール = vinyl

Biniiru bukuro ビニール袋 = a plastic bag; from biniiru = vinyl + bukuro = fukuro = a bag

Binkan na 敏感な = sensitive, delicate; *that bean can is sensitive and delicate, so don't squeeze it*; cf. bimyou = subtle, delicate; cf. sensai = fragile, sensitive, delicate

Binsen 便箋 = writing paper, stationery; *you can get writing paper at the bingo center*; cf. related terms listed at kami

Biru ビル = a building; cf. related terms listed at tatemono

Bitoku 美徳 = virtue; *at the beach, I saw a totally cool lifeguard rescue a swimmer, and I admired her virtue*; cf. related terms listed at yosa

Biyou 美容 = beauty of figure or form; *I poured beer into the yogurt and admired the beauty of the shapes it made*; cf. bi = beauty

Biyoushi 美容師 = a beautician; from biyou = beauty + shi = expert, e.g., ishi = a physician

Bocchan 坊っちゃん = another person's son, a boy (often spelled 坊ちゃん); *the boring chants are coming from that boy*; cf. related terms listed at otoko

Bochi 墓地 = cemetery, graveyard, churchyard; *the bones of the chief were buried in a cemetery*; cf. bohi = a gravestone or tombstone; cf. haka = a gravestone, cemetery or tomb; cf. hakaba = a cemetery; cf. kofun = an ancient tomb or burial mound

Bohi 墓碑 = a gravestone or tombstone; *here is the tombstone of our bold hero*; cf. related terms listed at bochi

Boin (Bo'in) 母音 = a vowel; *the boring intern kept mixing up her vowels*; cf. shiin = a consonant

Bojou 慕情 = longing, yearning; *Bo Peep and Joan of Arc had a longing for peace*

Boke ボケ = a fool; *riding in a boat while drinking from a keg makes you look like a fool*; cf. related terms listed at baka

Boki 簿記 = bookkeeping; *the boring king focused exclusively on bookkeeping*

Bokin 募金 = fundraising; *Bo Peep went to the kindergarten to do some fundraising*

Bokoku 母国 = one's native country; from bo = mother, e.g., sobo = grandmother; + koku = country; cf. related terms listed at sokoku

Bokokugo 母国語 = one's native language; from bokoku = one's native country + go = words, e.g., eigo = English; cf. related terms listed at gengo

Boku 僕 = I or me, used by men and boys; *I am a bony Kool-Aid salesman*; cf. related terms listed at watashi

Bokujou 牧場 = a stock farm, ranch, or pasture; *the bony Kool-Aid salesman joked about buying a stock farm, ranch or pasture*; cf. related terms listed at noujou

Bokujuu 墨汁 = India (black) ink; *a bony Kuwaiti jeweler signed his name in India ink*; cf. sumi = ink stick, black ink; cf. shuniku = red ink used for seals

Bokushi 牧師 = a pastor or minister; *the bony Kool-Aid salesman gave a sheepdog to his pastor*

Bon 盆 = a tray; also, a summer festival usually known as obon; *I received my bonus on a tray*; cf. ozen = a four-legged tray for festive food

Bon 本 – see hon

Bonjin 凡人 = an ordinary person; from bon = mediocre, e.g., heibon = ordinary; + jin = person; cf. ippanjin = ordinary people

Bonnou 煩悩 = worldly desire; *the bold nobles were consumed by worldly desire*; cf. related terms listed at shomou

Bonodori 盆踊り = a dance performed at Obon; from Bon = summer festival + odori = dance

Bonsai 盆栽 = a miniature potted plant; cf. related terms listed at shokubutsu

Bon'yari (Bonyari) ぼんやり = dim, vague, hazy, absent-minded, inattentive; *as a bonus, I received a yakuza ring, but I am absent-minded and only have a dim memory of that*; cf. related terms listed at ussura

Bon'you na (Bonyou na) 凡庸な = mediocre, commonplace; *that bony yodeler is mediocre*; cf. related terms listed at taitei

Bookaru ボーカル = vocals; cf. related terms listed at kashou

Boppatsu 勃発 = an outbreak or sudden occurrence; *after Bo Peep patted her supervisor on the back, she experienced an outbreak of regret*; cf. hassei = an outbreak or occurrence

Boshuu 募集 = recruitment; *we are in charge of recruitment of a ship crew, and we are looking for people with boat shoes*

Boshuu suru 募集する = to recruit; from boshuu = recruitment; cf. tsunoru = to advertise, recruit, intensify

Bosotto ぼさっと = absent-mindedly, vacantly, idly; *the bored soldiers cut their toenails and stared absent-mindedly*

Bossuru 没する = to sink, go down, to set, to pass away, to die, to disappear; *the boat carrying Superman and his rooster sank and disappeared*; cf. botsu = to drown, sink, disappear, or die; cf. chinbotsu suru = to sink; cf. kakureru = to conceal oneself or disappear; cf. kieru = to disappear or extinguish (intransitive); cf. kieuseru = to disappear or die; cf. nakunaru = to run out or disappear; cf. nigesaru = to take flight or disappear; cf. shizumu = to set (sun or moon), to sink (intransitive), to feel depressed; cf. useru = to disappear or vanish; cf. other related terms listed at shinu

Botamochi ぼたもち = azuki bean mochi; from bota = azuki beans; *that boy has a talent for preparing azuki beans*; + mochi = rice cake; cf. related terms listed at ryouri

Botchan 坊ちゃん – see bocchan

Botsu 没 = to drown, sink, disappear, or die; *I stay away from boats because they may sink, and I may drown and die*; cf. oboreru = to drown, or to indulge in; cf. other related terms listed at bossuru and at shinu

Botsugo 没後 = after death; from botsu = to die + go = after

Bottou 没頭 = immersing (oneself); *after my boat was hit by a torpedo, I jumped out and immersed myself in the water*

Bou 棒 = a stick; *I made a boat out of sticks*

Bou 某 = so-and-so, one, used as a word component; *so-and-so is a bore*

Boudai na ぼうだいな = huge, enormous, gigantic; *they boasted of a dike that was enormous*; cf. related terms listed at ookii

Boudou 暴動 = rebellion, revolt, riot; *a bold dophin led a rebellion at the aquarium*; cf. related terms listed at hangyaku

Bouei 防衛 = defense; *Tarzan boasts about the apes that provide defense at his jungle hideout*

Boueki 貿易 = international trade or commerce; *we conduct international trade, selling bows and arrows at the eki (station) to foreigners*; cf. related terms listed at akinai

Bouenkyou 望遠鏡 = a telescope; *when I'm bored with the entertainment in Kyouto, I use my telescope to view the stars*; cf. kenbikyou = a microscope; cf. mushimegane = a magnifying glass

Bougai 妨害 = an interference, disturbance, intrusion or obstacle; *the boring guide was an obstacle to our enjoyment of the museum*; cf. kanshou = interference, intervention; cf. other related terms at shougai

Bougai suru 妨害する = to interfere, intrude or disturb; from bougai = an interference, disturbance, intrusion or obstacle

Boujitsu 某日 = a certain day; from bou = so-and-so + jitsu = a day, e.g., heijitsu = a weekday

Bouka 防火 = fire prevention, fireproofing; from bouei = defense + kaji = fire

Boukan suru 傍観する = to be an onlooker; *I was an onlooker when Bo Peep toured Canada*

Bouken 冒険 = adventure, risk; *the boyish Kennedy liked adventure*; cf. kiken = danger; cf. kiki = crisis, danger

Bouryoku 暴力 = violence, brutality; *after the bowlers drank Leo's Kool-Aid, they drifted into violence*

Bouseki 紡績 = spinning (textiles); *she boasted that the selfish king admired her spinning (of cloth)*

Boushi 帽子 = a hat; *Bo Peep and her sheep wear hats*; cf. amagasa = a rain hat; cf. ichimegasa = a straw hat worn by women; cf. kasa = a straw hat or lamp shade;

Boushi 某氏 = a certain man; from bou = so-and-so + shi = mister; cf. related terms listed at aitsu

Boushi 防止 = prevention; *we sell boldly colored sheets for the prevention of boredom in bed*; cf. yobou = prevention

Boushitsu 房室 = room, bedroom of a married couple, atrium or ventricle (heart); *the boldly colored sheets are in the bedroom of that married couple*; cf. related terms listed at -shitsu

Bousui 防水 = waterproofing; *my boat from Sweden has good waterproofing*

Boyaku ぼやく = to grumble or complain;

Bono took my *yak* to *Kuwait, and I complained*; cf. kujou wo iu = to complain; cf. uttaeru = to sue, appeal or complain of

Bu 部 = a part or section, used as a word component, e.g., buchou = a section manager, a counter for copies of a newspaper or magazine; *we divided the booze into three parts*; cf. related terms listed at ichibu

Buatsui 分厚い = bulky, heavy; *I tried to read a book at the Swedish house, but it was too bulky*; cf. omoi = heavy

Bubun 部分 = a part of something; *this boot that belonged to Daniel Boone is a part of history*; cf. related terms listed at ichibu

Buchou 部長 = a division manager; from bubun = a part of something + chou = a leader or chief; cf. synonynms listed at shunou

Budou ぶどう = grapes; *the boot by the door is full of grapes*; cf. related terms listed at kudamono

Budou 武道 = the way of the samurai, martial arts; from buki = weapon + dou = way, e.g., douro = road

Bugyou 奉行 = a Samurai magistrate; *that Sumurai magistrate is drinking booze and eating gyoza*

Buji ni 無事に = safely, quietly, without problems; *I loaded the booze into the Jeep with my niece without problems*

Bujoku 侮辱 = insult, contempt, disrespect; *your Buddhist jokes are an insult to my faith*

Buka 部下 = a subordinate person; from bubun = a part of something + ka = below

Bukatsu 部活 = club activities; from bu = section; + katsudou = activity

Buki 武器 = weapon, arms; *the bookkeeper carried a weapon*; cf. heiki = a weapon or arms; cf. kakuheiki = nuclear weapon; cf. kyouki = a lethal weapon

Bukiyou 不器用 = clumsy; *I'm clumsy, and when I was booking the yoga class, I dropped the phone twice*; cf. related terms listed at heta

Bukka 物価 = prices (in general); *the prices of booze in California are rising*; cf. related terms listed at nedan

Bukkaku 仏閣 = a Buddhist temple; *the Buddha appeared to Karl the Kool-Aid vendor when he was visiting a Buddhist temple*; cf. related terms listed at tera

Bukkyou 仏教 = Buddhism; *I read a book kyou (today) about Buddhism*

Bukuro 袋 – see fukuro

Bumon 部門 = category, class, section; *the booze that the monks make is in a class by itself*; cf. kaikyuu = class, rank, caste; cf. kyuu = class, level, grade; cf. sou = a layer, stratum, social class, story (of a building)

Bun 分 – see -fun

Bun 分 = a share or quantity; *Daniel Boone ate his share of the food*; cf. related terms listed at wakemae

Bun 文 = a sentence or composition; *Daniel Boone's composition was written in complete sentences*; cf. related terms listed at sakuhin

Bungaku 文学 = literature; from bun = a composition + gaku = study; cf. related terms listed at hon

Bunka 文化 = culture; *Daniel Boone's cabin reflected frontier culture*; cf. shokubunka = food culture

Bunkai 分解 = disassembly, decomposing; *Daniel Boone's kite was in a state of disassembly*

Bunkazai 文化財 = cultural assets; from bunka = culture + zaisan = assets; cf. related terms listed at tomi

Bunkiten 分岐点 = a crossroads, juncture, watershed; *at the crossroads, students are bunking ten to a room*

Bunmyaku 文脈 = context; *Daniel Boone liked to drink Miami Kool-Aid in the context of kids' parties*

Bunpitsu 分泌 = secretion; *Daniel Boone met two Petes when he encountered St. Peter and Peter Pan, and his endorphin secretions increased*

Bunpou 文法 = grammar; *Daniel Boone was a poet who knew his grammar*

Bunretsu 分裂 = division, separation; *after his separation from his wife, Daniel Boone started wearing retro suits*; cf. related terms listed at wakare

Bunseki 分析 = analysis; *Daniel Boone gave the selfish king an analysis of the problem*; cf. chousa = investigation, survey, analysis;

Bunshou 文章 = sentence, composition, writing; *Daniel Boone showed us his composition*; cf. related terms listed at sakuhin

Buntan 分担 = one's share or assignment; *Daniel Boone took a tank of gasoline which was his share*; cf. related terms listed at wakemae

Buntan suru 分担する = to share; from buntan = one's share; cf. shikiru = to divide or partition; cf. wakeru = to divide or share; cf. waru = to break glass or wood, to divide or cut

Buppin 物品 = article, things, goods; from butsu = thing + pin = hin = goods, e.g., seihin = manufactured goods; cf. related terms listed at sanbutsu

Burabura ぶらぶら = strolling, roaming; *while strolling, Daniel Boone rambled on about booze and rabbits*

Buranko ブランコ = swing; *the swing was painted blanco (white, in Spanish)*

Bureiku ブレイク = a break, in the sense of sudden popularity

Buri ぶり = a suffix meaning "it's like," e.g., ninkiburi = so popular; *a burrito is like a sandwich*; from buru = to assume the air of, to behave like; cf. furi = pretense or appearance

Buri ni ぶりに = after an interval, e.g., ichinen buri ni = after one year's interval; *I gave a burrito to my niece, after an interval when she hadn't eaten one*; cf. buri = "it's like"; cf. related terms listed at hisashiburi ni

Buronzu ブロンズ = bronze; cf. similar terms listed at dou = copper

Buru ぶる = to assume the air of, to behave like; *those Buddhists rule their monastery and behave like kings*

Buruburu ぶるぶる = to shiver with cold or fear; *my boots were ruined, and soon I was shivering*

Bushi 武士 = a warrior or samurai; from budou = the way of the samurai + shi = a man, e.g., heishi = a soldier; cf. samurai = a Japanese warrior

Busoku 不足 – see fusoku

Busshitsu 物質 = material, substance; *the Buddha's sheets were made from a previously unknown substance*; cf. monogoto = a matter or thing

Buta 豚 = a pig or a despicable person; *Daniel Boone tackled a pig*

Butai 舞台 = stage, setting; *Daniel Boone showed off his tiger on stage*; cf. dan = stage

Butai 部隊 = force, unit, corps; *when the Buddha was tired, a rescue unit came to pick him up*; cf. related terms listed at guntai

Butsu ぶつ = to hit (a person); *my father hit me after I ruined his boots*; cf. related terms listed at utsu = to hit

Butsu 物 = a thing or object, matter; *boots are important things to have*

Butsubutsu ぶつぶつ = grunt, grumble, complaint; from butsu = thing; *the lumberjacks complained about their boots and other people's boots*; cf. related terms at kujou

Butsudan 仏壇 = Buddhist altar found in Japanese homes; *the boots that I dance in are stored next to our Buddhist altar*

Butsukeru ぶつける = to hit; a variation of butsu = to hit

Butsuzou 仏像 = image or statue of Buddha; from butsu = Buddha + zou = image; *I saw an image representing the signs of the Zodiak*

Buttai 物体 = object or body (in physics); from butsu = thing + tai = body, e.g., taijuu = body weight; cf. related terms listed at shugo

Buyou 舞踊 = dancing or dance; *after drinking some booze, the yogi started dancing*; cf. odori = dance

Buzoku 部族 = a tribe or clan; from bubun = a part of something; + zoku = a family or tribe, e.g., kazoku = a family; cf. han = clan (feudal period); cf. jinshu = a race of people; cf. minzoku = an ethnic group; cf. uji = a clan

Byou 秒 = a second (1/60 minute), used as a word component; *the bee owner sees a bee fly by every second*

Byoudou 平等 = equal; *the beer that I ordered was by the door, but I had an equal amount in the refrigerator*; cf. hitoshii = same, equal

Byouin 病院 = a hospital; from byouki = illness + -in = an institution

Byoujou 病状 = condition related to health; from byouki = sick + joutai = condition; cf. related terms listed at keisei

Byouki 病気 = illness, sickness, disease; *the beerhall owner ate so much quiche that he developed an illness*; cf. densen = an infection; cf. densen byou = an infectious disease; cf. ekibyou = a plague or epidemic; cf. gan = cancer; cf. haien = pneumonia; cf. hakike = nausea; cf. hifuen = dermatitis; cf. haigan = lung cancer; cf. ikaiyou = a stomach ulcer; cf. kafunshou = hay fever; cf. kaiyou = an ulcer; cf. kansen = infection, contagion; cf. kansenbyou = a contagious disease; cf. kansenshou = an infectious disease; cf. kebyou = a feigned illness; cf. kekkaku = tuberculosis; cf. ketsumakuen = conjunctivitis; cf. naizou shikkan = an internal disease; cf. noushuyou = a brain tumor; cf. nousocchuu = a stroke; cf. nyuugan = breast cancer; cf. shikkan = a disease; cf. tennentou = smallpox; cf. uirususei shikkan = a viral disease

Byounin 病人 = a sick person; from byouki = sickness + nin = a person

Byousha suru 描写する = to describe; *he described the B.O. (body odor) coming from the shack*; cf. related terms listed at iiarawasu

Byoushin 秒針 = the second hand on a clock; from byou = a second + shin = a needle

Byoutou 病棟 = hospital ward; *the B.O. (bacterial overgrowth) in my toe was treated in a hospital ward*

Byuffe ビュッフェ = buffet

Cha 茶 = tea; *Prince Charles drinks tea*; cf. ocha = green tea; cf. koucha = black tea; cf. maccha = powdered green tea for ceremonies; cf. ryokucha = green tea; cf. sencha = green tea

Chaimu チャイム = a chime or doorbell; cf. related terms listed at suzu

Cha'iro (Chairo) 茶色 = light brown; from cha = tea + iro = color; cf. chakasshoku = dark reddish brown; cf. kasshoku = dark brown; cf. tan kasshoku = light brown

Chakasshoku 茶褐色 = dark reddish brown; from cha'iro = light brown + kasshoku = dark brown; cf. related terms listed at chairo

Chaku 着 = arrival, order of arrival (in a race); *at the end of the race, the athletes receive either champagne or Kool-Aid, depending on their order of arrival*; cf. related terms listed at touchaku

Chakuchi 着地 = landing; from chaku = arrival, e.g., touchaku = arrival + chi = ground

Chakunan 嫡男 = an heir or oldest son; *my eldest son bought a nice chandelier in Kuwait for our nanny*; cf. related terms listed at musuko

Chakuriku suru 着陸する = to land; from chaku = arrival + riku = land; cf. jouriku suru = to land; cf. maioriru = to swoop down on, to alight; cf. ririku suru = to take off (flight)

Chakusui 着水 = landing on the water; from chaku = arrival, e.g., touchaku suru = to arrive; + sui = water, e.g., suiei = swimming

Chakuyou 着用 = wearing or having on; *Prince Charles bought a kooky suit with yogurt stains on it, and he is wearing it*

Chakuyou suru 着用する = to wear or put on clothes; from chakuyou = wearing or having on; cf. haku = to put on or wear lower body clothing or shoes; cf. kaburu = to wear something on the head; cf. kiru = to put on or wear clothes; cf. mi ni tsukeru = to take on, to learn or acquire knowledge, to wear clothes, etc.; cf. tsukeru = to wear (clothing or accessories)

Chan ちゃん = a suffix used after a person's name to express affection and intimacy; *I chant with my intimate friends*

Chanbara チャンバラ = sword fighting, referring to a genre of samurai movies; *the channel in the bar at the ranch was tuned to a sword-fighting movie*

Chanoyu 茶の湯 = the tea ceremony; from cha = tea + the possessive no + yu = hot water

Chanson シャンソン = song (a French word); cf. related terms listed at uta

Chanto ちゃんと = properly, exactly, without fail; *we chant old hymns exactly, without fail*; cf. kanarazu = without fail, for certain; cf. kicchiri = without fail, precisely, tightly; cf. kichinto = properly, tidily; cf kitto = for sure, without fail; cf. other related terms listed at choudo

Chi 地 = ground, earth, place; *I know a cheap place to eat*; cf. related terms listed at basho

Chi 血 = blood; *my cholesterol is so high that my blood is like cheese*; cf. related terms listed at ketsueki

Chi ga sawagu 血が騒ぐ = to get excited; from chi = blood + sawagu = to make a fuss; cf. moriagaru = to swell, rise, get excited

Chian 治安 = safety, public order; *the police chief expressed anxiety about public order in the city*; cf. anpi = safety or welfare; cf. anzen = safety, security; cf. anzensei = safety, security

Chibi ちび = small child, runt, dwarf; *the dwarf likes cheap beer*; cf. related terms listed at kodomo

Chichi 乳 = milk, mother's milk; *we buy milk and make cheap cheese*

Chichi 父 = my father, used in the third person; *my father likes cheap cheese*; cf. otousan = father

Chichioya 父親 = a father; from chichi = father + oya = a parent; cf. related terms listed at otousan

Chichishibori 乳搾り = milking or a milker; from chichi = milk + shiboru = to squeeze

Chie 知恵 = wisdom, intelligence; *if you eat cheese and eggs, you may develop wisdom*; cf. chinou = intelligence, intellect; cf. joushiki = common sense

Chigaeru 違える = to change, to make a

mistake; the potential form of chigau = to differ; cf. related terms listed at kaeru = to change

Chigau 違う = to differ (verb), different or wrong (adjective); *the chiggers in Australia differ from the ones in New Zealand*; cf. kotonaru = to differ

Chigiru 契る = to vow or pledge; *he pledged to keep the cheap geese off the roof*

Chihou 地方 = region, district; *the cheese we hope to eat will differ in each region*; cf. related terms listed at chitai

Chi'i (Chii) 地位 = rank, status, position; from chi = ground + i = rank or place; cf. related terms listed at kurai

Chi'iki (Chiiki) 地域 = region or area; *in this region, we produce cheese for an Eastern king*; cf. related terms listed at chitai

Chi'iki shakai (Chiiki shakai) 地域社会 = a regional community; from chi'iki = a region + shakai = society

Chiisai 小さい = small, young, trivial, low (sound); *the cheap scientist left a small tip*; cf. gokuchiisai = very small; cf. kogata = small size; cf. komakai = small, detailed; cf. sasayaka na = small, modest; cf. semai = narrow, small; cf. shoukibo = small-scale

Chijimu 縮む (spelled chidimu in electronic dictionaries) = to shrink or become short, to cringe; *cheap jeans suit my mood, but they shrink in the wash*

Chijin 知人 = an acquaintance or friend; from chi = to know, e.g., chishiki = knowledge; + jin = person; cf. related terms listed at tomodachi

Chijou 地上 = above ground; *the chief joked that he wanted to be buried above ground*

Chika 地下 = a basement, underground; from chi = ground + ka = below

Chikagai 地下街 = underground shopping mall; *in Chicago, our guide took us to an underground shopping mall*; cf. hankagai = a business or shopping district

Chikagoro 近頃 = recently, lately, nowadays; from chikai = close + goro = approximate time; cf. related terms listed at saikin = recently

Chikai 近い = close, near, almost, soon; *a cheap kite landed close to me*; cf. chikaku ni = close to, near, almost, before long; cf. majika = proximity, soon, nearby; cf. mijika ni = close at hand, closely related; cf. soba ni = close to, beside; cf. sugusoba = very near; cf. temoto = at hand, nearby

Chikaku 近く = neighborhood or vicinity, nearly; the adverbial form of chikai = close, used as a noun or as an adverb; cf. related terms listed at fukin

Chikaku ni 近くに = close to, near, almost, before long; from chikaku = vicinity + ni = to; cf. related terms listed at chikai

Chikan 痴漢 = a sexual pervert; *that sexual pervert lures children with cheap candy*; cf. hentai = a pervert or perversion, metamorphosis (insect)

Chikara 力 = force, power, energy, ability; *we have the power to import cheese in caravans*; cf. hakuryoku = dynamism, power; cf. ikioi = force, power, energy, spirit; cf. kakki = liveliness, energy; cf. katsuryoku = energy, vitality; cf. ryoku = power, used as a suffix; cf. seiryoku = energy, vigor, vitality

Chikarazoe 力添え = assistance, support; from chikara = force + zoeru = soeru = to support; cf. related terms listed at enjo

Chikashitsu 地下室 = a basement; from chika = underground + shitsu = room; cf. related terms listed at -shitsu

Chikatetsu 地下鉄 = a subway; from chi = ground + ka = below; *there's a car below my window*; + tetsu = iron

Chikau 誓う = to vow, pledge or swear; *I vow to buy you a cheap cow*

Chikazukeru 近づける = to draw something near, to introduce a person to another (this is spelled chikadukeru in electronic dictionaries); from chikai = close + tsukeru = to attach; cf. related terms listed at hikitsukeru

Chikazuku 近づく = to approach (this is spelled chikaduku in electronic dictionaries); the intransitive form of chikazukeru; cf. omomuku = to go or tend toward; cf. sashikakaru = to come near or approach

Chikei 地形 = terrain; *he grows cheap cane on that terrain*; cf. related terms listed at basho

Chiku 竹 = bamboo, used as a suffix; *I drink cheap Kool-Aid from a bamboo cup*; cf. take = bamboo

Chikoku 遅刻 = lateness, late coming; *he stopped to buy cheese and Coke, and that caused his lateness*

Chikuji 逐次 = one by one, sequentially, successively; *the cheap Kool-Aid packets were loaded into the Jeep one by one*; cf. related terms listed at tsugitsugi ni

Chikurin 竹林 = a bamboo grove; *I drank cheap Kool-Aid with Ringo in the bamboo grove*; cf. related terms listed at mori

Chikushou 畜生 = a beast or brute, a repulsive person or thing; damn it! (interjection); *when we were drinking cheap Kool-Aid at the shore, we were attacked by beasts*; cf. related terms listed at aitsu

Chikyuu 地球 = the Earth, the globe; *the cheese in Cuba is the best on the Earth*; cf. related terms listed at sekai

Chimei 地名 = a place name; also, chimei no (or na) = famous; from chi = ground + mei = name; cf. chomei = famous; cf. nadakai = famous; cf. yuumei = famous; cf. related terms listed at namae

Chimeido 知名度 = fame; *the cheerful mailman's doughnut recipe earned him fame*; cf. koumei = fame; cf. na = name or fame; cf. yuisho = history, pedigree, lineage, fame

Chimeishou 致命傷 = a fatal mistake or injury; *his fatal mistake was to serve cheap mayonnaise to the Shougun*; cf. related terms listed at ketten and at kizu

Chin 賃 = wage, pay, rent, fare; *I'm saving my wages to buy a chin strap*; cf. chinage = a wage increase; cf. chingin = a wage; cf. gekkyuu = monthly salary; cf. houkyuu = a salary; cf. kyuuryou = salary or wages; cf. nenpou = an annual salary; cf. nikkyuu = a daily wage; cf. shuunyuu = income; cf. taiguu = treatment (of customer), salary and benefits

Chinage (Chin'age) 賃上げ = a wage increase; from chin = wages, fee + ageru = to raise; cf. related terms listed at chin

Chinami ni ちなみに = in passing, incidentally; *in the China meeting, my niece mentioned in passing that she is getting married*; cf. tokoro de = by the way

Chinamu ちなむ = to derive from or be related to; *the chief's nasty moods were related to his headaches*; cf. kan suru = to be related to, concerning

Chinbotsu suru 沈没する = to sink; *the Chinese boats sank*; cf. related terms listed at bossuru

Chingin 賃金 = wage; *Mr. Chin had gingko trees and paid wages to their caretakers*; cf. related terms listed at chin

Chinjutsu 陳述 = a statement, an oral report; *he made a statement saying that, since the patient's chin juts out, he will need surgery*; cf. related terms listed at sengen

Chinka suru 鎮火する = to put out a fire; *I hurt my chin in the cathedral while putting out a fire there*

Chinmoku 沈黙 = silence; *after I hit him on the chin on mokuyoubi (Thursday), I've heard nothing but silence from him*; cf.

related terms listed at seijaku

Chinou 知能 = intelligence, intellect; *he has the intelligence to avoid putting cheese in his nose*; cf. related terms listed at chie

Chinretsu 陳列 = an exhibition or display; *Mr. Chin's retro suits are in this display*; cf. related terms listed at tenji

Chinseki 珍石 = unusual stones; *hold up your chin for a sentimental kiss, and I will give you an unusual stone*

Chintsuuzai 鎮痛剤 = a pain medicine; *after my chin collided with a tsuitcase (suitcase) in Zaire (former name of the Congo), I had to take pain medicine*; cf. related terms listed at kusuri

Chippu チップ = a tip or gratuity, or a piece of advice

Chirakaru 散らかる = to be in a mess; the intransitive form of chirakasu

Chirakasu 散らかす = to scatter around, to mess up; *the cheerful rabbi carried the soup, but he spilled it and messed up the floor*

Chiru 散る = to fall, scatter, disperse; *the cheap rubies fell and scattered on the ground*

Chiryou 治療 = medical treatment; *these Cheerios are effective as a medical treatment*; cf. iryou = medical treatment; cf. teate = medical treatment

Chiryouhou 治療法 = remedy, cure; from chiryou = medical treatment + houhou = method; cf. related terms listed at kusuri

Chisetsu 稚拙 = unskilled, childish, crude; *after the children set soup on the table, the place settings looked childish*; cf. related terms listed at heta

Chishiki 知識 = knowledge, learning; *to make cheese from sheep's milk in Kiev takes knowledge*; cf. gaku = study or learning; cf. gakushuu = study or learning; cf. hakubutsu = wide learning, natural history; cf. kyouyou = education, learning; cf. miyoumimane = learning by imitation; cf. ninshiki = awareness, recognition, knowledge; cf. zoukei = knowledge, mastery; cf. zoukeifukai = scholarship, learning

Chisso 窒素 = nitrogen; *the chief soprano liked nitrogen in his coffee*; cf. related terms listed at tanso

Chissoku 窒息 = suffocation, choking; *when I ate the cheese soaked in vinegar, it caused choking*

Chissoku suru 窒息する = to choke or suffocate; from chissoku = suffocation, choking

Chitai 地帯 = zone, area, district; *cheap tires can be found in that district*; cf. bessouchi = an area of villas or holiday homes; cf. chihou = region, district; cf. chiiki = region or area; cf. gun = county or district; cf. gunbu = rural districts; cf. ittai = region or zone; cf. ryoudo = territory; cf. sangakuchi = mountain lands

Chitsujo 秩序 = order, discipline, method; *since we want to keep good order, anyone who cheats Empress Josephine will be arrested*; cf. seiton = orderliness

Chittomo ちっとも = not at all; *a chief told Monet to stop painting, but he listened not at all*; cf. related terms listed at zenzen

Chizu 地図 = a map; *you smeared cheese on this map*

Chochiku 貯蓄 = savings; *I chose cheap Kool-Aid to maximize my savings*; cf. chokin = savings

Chokin 貯金 = savings; *too much household savings is choking the Japanese economy*; cf. chochiku = savings

Chokka 直下 = directly under; *I choked on cabbage when I was directly under her window*; cf. shita = below, inferior

Chokkaku 直角 = a right angle; *we chose Karl the Kool-Aid vendor to draw a right*

angle; cf. kakudo = an angle

Chokkei 直径 = diameter; _I choked on a piece of cake because its diameter was too large_; cf. enshuu = a circumference; cf. hankei = a radius

Chokkoubin 直行便 = nonstop flight; _I chose corn and beans to eat on the nonstop flight_

Chokugo ni 直後に = immediately after or behind; from chokusetsu = directly + go = after; cf. related terms listed at saki ni

Chokumen suru 直面する = to face or be involved with, to confront with; _if you choke those Ku Klux Klan men, they will confront you_; cf. tai suru = to face toward, to confront; cf. taiketsu suru = to confront; cf. other related terms listed at kakawaru

Chokusen 直線 = a straight line; from socchoku = straightforward + sen = a line; cf. related terms listed at gyou

Chokusetsu 直接 = directly; _when he chokes you, it sets you back, but at least he acts directly_; cf. massugu ni = directly or straight

Chokuzen 直前 = just before; _he choked the Zen monk just before the funeral_; cf. sunzen = just before; cf. other related terms listed at saki ni

Chomei 著名 = famous; _Margaret Cho's maid became famous_; cf. chimei = famous; cf. nadakai = famous; cf. yuumei = famous

Chonmage ちょんまげ = topknot (hair style for samurai or sumo wrestler); _after I chose negativity, Ma (mother) and her guest tied a topknot in my hair_

Chosha 著者 = a writer; _he chose a lady with a shawl to be the writer of his biography_; cf. hissha = writer; cf. sakka = writer

Chotto ちょっと = a little, just a moment; _Margaret Cho's toe hurt a little, for just a moment_; cf. related terms listed at ittan and at sukoshi

Chottoshita ちょっとした = somewhat, quite; from chotto = a little + shita = did; cf. ikuraka = somewhat, a little; cf. nandaka = a little, somewhat

Chou 町 = a town or district, used as a word component; _I chose to live in this town_

Chou 腸 = intestines, bowel; _I choked when I ate beef intestines_; cf. related terms listed at naizou

Chou 超 = super, ultra; _Margaret Cho is a super comedian_

Chou 長 = a chief or leader, used as a suffix; or = long, used as a prefix; _we chose her to be our leader_; _she chose a long skirt_

Choubo 帳簿 = an account book; _Margaret Cho is bored by account books_

Choubou 眺望 = a view; _I chose a boat with a big window so that I could enjoy the view_; cf. related terms listed at nagame

Chouda 長蛇 = a long snake, a long line (of people, etc.); _the long snake chose a dark hole for its lair_; cf. hebi = a snake

Choudai ちょうだい = please, used to address children; _please don't choke the diver_; cf. related terms listed at kudasai

Choudo ちょうど = exactly; _we chose this door because it was exactly what we needed_; cf. chanto = properly, exactly, without fail; cf. masa ni = exactly, naturally, certainly, on the verge; cf. pittari = tightly, exactly, ideally

Chouin 調印 = signature, sealing; _Margaret Cho used red ink for her signature_; cf. shomei = a signature

Chouji 弔辞 = a message of condolence or a memorial address; _Margaret Cho sent a Jeep with a message of condolence_; cf. related terms listed at okuyami

Choujikan 長時間 = a long time; from chou = long; _she chose a long skirt_; + jikan = time; cf. choukikan = a long time; cf. nagai aida = a long time

Choujinteki 超人的 = superhuman; from chou = super; *Margaret Cho did a super job during her performance*; + jin = person + teki = related to

Choujo 長女 = an eldest daughter; from chou = a chief or leader + josei = a girl; cf. related terms listed at musume

Choujou 超常 = paranormality, anomalous phenomena; *Margaret Cho told jokes about paranormal phenomena*

Choujou 頂上 = summit; *Margaret Cho told a joke at the summit*; cf. chouten = the top or climax; cf. itadaki = summit; cf. mine = mountain peak; cf. teppen = top, summit; cf. touge = a mountain pass or peak, a crucial point

Choukai 懲戒 = reprimand, discipline; *the boy received a reprimand for choking the Kaiser*; cf. related terms listed at bakkin

Choukai 朝会 = morning meeting or assembly; from choushoku = breakfast + kaigi = meeting; cf. related terms listed at kaigi

Choukai 聴解 = listening comprehension; *after glaucoma choked my eyes, I had to work on my listening comprehension*

Choukairyoku 聴解力 = listening comprehension; from choukai = listening comprehension + ryoku = force, power

Choukan 朝刊 = morning newspaper; *I choked on candy while reading the morning newspaper*; cf. related terms listed at shinbun

Chouki 長期 = long-term; from chou = long, e.g., choukyori = a long distance; + ki = season, e.g., jiki = season; cf. tanki = short-term

Choukikan 長期間 = a long time; *when I was choking on candy, it took a long time for my friends to respond*; cf. choujikan = a long time; cf. nagai aida = a long time

Choukoku 彫刻 = a sculpture or carving; *the sculpture was crafted from chocolate and drenched in Coke*

Choukou 兆候 = a symptom or sign; *Margaret Cho had a cold, judging from her symptoms*; cf. shoujou = symptoms, condition of a patient

Choukyori 長距離 = long distance; from chou = long; *she chose a long skirt*; + kyori = distance cf. enkyori = long distance; cf. enpou = a long way, a distant place

Choume 丁目 = city block, district of a town; *he chose some men to work in his district*

Choumiryou 調味料 = flavoring, seasoning; *I choked during a meal with Pope Leo because the seasoning was too spicy*; cf. related terms listed at fuumi

Chounan 長男 = oldest son; *the oldest son choked the nanny*; cf. related terms listed at musuko

Chouonpa 超音波 = ultrasound; from chou = super or ultra + onpa = a sound wave

Chouri 調理 = cooking; *Margaret Cho retired so that she could concentrate on cooking*; cf. jisui = cooking for oneself; cf. ryouri = cooking, cuisine; cf. other related terms listed at ryouri

Chourishi 調理師 = a chef; from chouri = cooking + shi = expert or teacher; *the sheep herder is an expert in his field*; cf. ryourinin = a chef or cook

Chousa 調査 = investigation, survey, analysis; *we chose Samsung to conduct the investigation*; cf. bunseki = analysis; cf. kansoku = observation, survey; cf. other related terms listed at kensa

Chousei 調整 = adjustment; *before I could start my chores at Safeway, I had to make an adjustment to my uniform*

Chousen suru 挑戦する = to challenge or attempt; *the party chose a senator to challenge the president*; cf. related terms listed at tamesu

Choushi 調子 = condition, way, manner, style; *the <u>chores</u> I do for my <u>sheep</u> improve their living <u>condition</u>*; cf. related terms listed at keisei

Chousho 長所 = merit, a strong point; *he was <u>chosen</u> by the <u>Shogun</u> for his <u>merit</u>*; cf. tokui = pride, strong point

Choushoku 朝食 = breakfast; from chou = morning; *I do my <u>chores</u> in the <u>morning</u>*; + shokuji = a meal; cf. similar terms listed at shokuji

Choushou 嘲笑 = ridicule; *Margaret <u>Cho</u>'s <u>show</u> contained a good deal of <u>ridicule</u>*; cf. karakau = to ridicule or jeer

Choushuu 聴衆 = audience; *Margaret <u>Cho</u> threw her <u>shoes</u> at the <u>audience</u>*; cf. kaishuu = an audience or congregation; cf. kankyaku = audience, spectator; cf. kansensha = spectator

Chouten 頂点 = the top or climax; from choujou = a summit + ten = a point; cf. related terms listed at choujou

Chouwa 調和 = harmony or balance; *he <u>chose</u> to <u>walk</u> in order to enhance <u>harmony</u> in the world and tip the <u>balance</u> away from machines*; cf. wa = harmony, total; cf. yuuwa = harmony

Chuu 中 = in the middle of, in the process of, during, among; *I <u>chew</u> gum while I'm <u>in the process of</u> driving*; cf. related terms listed at nagara

Chuu 宙 = space or sky; *it's hard to <u>chew</u> food in <u>space</u>*; cf. related terms listed at sora

Chuu 注 = notes; *I <u>choose</u> to take <u>notes</u> during the lectures*; cf. bikou = notes or remarks

Chuu ni uku 宙に浮く = to float in air; from chuu = space + uku = to float

Chuubi 中火 = a medium fire; from chuuou = middle + bi = hi = fire

Chuubu 中部 = center (e.g., the center of a town), middle, heart; from chuu = middle + bu = section or part; cf. chuuou = center, middle; cf. chuushin = center, core, focus; cf. chuushinchi = a center or metropolis; cf. chuusuu = center, the most important person or thing; cf. kakushin = a core, center, central issue, kernel; cf. mannaka = center, middle; cf. naka = inside or middle; cf. nakaba = middle, half-way, in-between; cf. nakagoro = about the middle; cf. ou =center or middle, used as a word component; cf. uchi = inside, middle, center; cf. other related terms listed at ichibu

Chuudan 中断 = interruption; *if he <u>chews</u> on the <u>dancer</u>, it will cause an <u>interruption</u> in the show*; cf. related terms listed at chuushi

Chuudoku 中毒 = addiction, poisoning; *his <u>addiction</u> made him <u>chew</u> on <u>documents</u>, and this led to his <u>poisoning</u>*

Chuudokusha 中毒者 = an addict; from chuudoku = addiction + sha = a person; cf. joushuusha = an addict

Chuugaeri 宙返り = somersault; from chuu = space + gaeru = kaeru = to return

Chuugakkou 中学校 = a junior high school or middle school; from chuushin = center or core + gakkou = school; cf. related terms listed at gakkou

Chuugen 中元 = a midsummer gift, usually expressed as ochuugen; *I <u>choose</u> <u>Genghis</u> to select the <u>midsummer</u> <u>gift</u>*; cf. related terms listed at okurimono

Chuui 中尉 = a first lieutenant; *the <u>first lieutenant</u> was <u>chewing gum</u>*; cf. related terms listed at shikan

Chuui 注意 = caution, warning; *he exercises <u>caution</u> when he's <u>chewing fish</u>, to avoid <u>bones</u>*; cf. related terms listed at keikoku

Chuuibukai 注意深い = attentive, cautious, careful; from chuui = caution + bukai = fukai = deep; cf. shinchou = careful, prudent

Chuuihou 注意報 = a weather warning; from chuui = a warning + yohou = a forecast; cf. related terms listed at keikoku

Chuuijikou 注意事項 = important points, precautions; from chuui = caution + jikou = item

Chuujun 中旬 = around the middle of a month; from chuu = middle + jun = season; cf. shojun = the first ten days of a month; cf. kouhan = the latter half

Chuuka ryouri 中華料理 = Chinese cuisine; from chuuka = Chinese food; *I choose to take a car to get Chinese food*; + ryouri = cuisine

Chuukai 仲介 = mediation; *I will choose the Kaiser to do the mediation*; cf. related terms listed at baikai

Chuukaisha 仲介者 = mediator; from chuukai = mediation + sha = a person

Chuuken 中堅 = mainstay, nucleus, main body, middle standing, center field (baseball); *we choose Kennedy to act as the mainstay of our cause in the Senate*; cf. shutai = core, nucleus, protagonist, subject (as opposed to object)

Chuuken 忠犬 = a faithful dog; from chuusei = loyalty + ken = dog; *Ken and Barbie have a dog*; cf. related terms listed at inu

Chuuko 中古 = used, second hand; *he sits in his used car and chews coconuts*; cf. chuukosha = a used car; cf. furugi = used clothes

Chuukoku 忠告 = advice or admonition; *his advice was to choose Coke*; cf. kankoku = recommendation, advice; cf. soudan = consultation, advice

Chuukosha 中古車 = used car; from chuuko = used; + sha = car; cf. related terms listed at chuuko and at kuruma

Chuumoku 注目 = attention; *if you chew moku (wood), you will get attention*

Chuumon suru 注文する = to order or request; *if you are going to request a painting for me, I choose the Monet*; cf. toriyoseru = to order or send away for; cf.

other related terms listed at tanomu

Chuuou 中央 = center, middle; from chuu = middle + ou = middle; cf. related terms listed at chuubu

Chuuou 中欧 = central Europe; from chuu = middle + oushuu = Europe; cf. related terms listed at oushuu

Chuusei 中世 = the Middle Ages; from chuu = middle + seiki = centuries

Chuusei 忠誠 = loyalty, allegiance; *when shopping, I choose Safeway because I feel loyalty to it*; cf. chuuseishin = loyalty, faithfulness

Chuuseishin 忠誠心 = loyalty, faithfulness; from chuusei = loyalty + shin = heart; cf. chuusei = loyalty, allegiance

Chuusen 抽選 = a lottery or raffle; *they used a lottery to choose the next senator*; cf. related terms listed at takarakuji

Chuusha 注射 = injection; *during the injection, I chewed shark cartilage*

Chuusha 駐車 = parking (e.g., a car); *I chew shark cartilage while parking my car*

Chuushajou 駐車場 = a parking lot or parking spot; from chuusha = parking + jou = a place

Chuushi 中止 = suspension, stoppage, interruption; *if the dog chews the sheets, there will be a suspension of dog food deliveries*; cf. chuudan = an interruption; cf. chuuzetsu = interruption, suspension, abortion; cf. kousoku = a stoppage, tightness or block, an infarction; cf. teisha = stopping (a vehicle); cf. teishi = stoppage or suspension

Chuushin 中心 = center, core, focus; from chuu = middle + shin = heart, mind; cf. shouten = focus or central issue; cf. other related terms listed at chuubu

Chuushinchi 中心地 = a center or metropolis; from chuushin = a center + chi = ground; cf. related terms listed at chuubu

Chuushinteki 中心的 = central; from chuushin = central, core or focus + teki = related to; cf. related terms listed at shouten

Chuushoku 昼食 = lunch; from chuu = in the middle of + shokuji = a meal; cf. similar terms listed at shokuji

Chuushou 抽象 = an abstraction; *I choose to show my modern paintings because I like abstraction*

Chuushouteki na 抽象的な = abstract or vague; from chuushou = an abstraction + teki = related to; cf. related terms listed at kasuka

Chuusuu 中枢 = center, the most important person or thing; *I choose Superman as the most important person and the center of our society*; cf. related terms listed at chuubu

Chuuto 中途 = in the middle, half-way; *as I was chewing my toast, he burst into the middle of my breakfast*; cf. related terms listed at tochuu de

Chuuton 駐屯 = stationing (troops), occupancy; *if we choose Tony Blair for Prime Minister, he may favor stationing troops overseas*

Chuuton suru 駐屯する = to station (troops); from chuuton = stationing

Chuutou 中東 = the Middle East; from chuu = middle + tou = east

Chuuzetsu 中絶 = interruption, suspension, abortion; *if you chew my Zen tsuit (suit), I will order a suspension of your dog food*; cf. related terms listed at chuushi

Chuuzou 鋳造 = casting or minting; *we will choose Zooey to be in charge of the casting*

Chuuzuri 宙づり = suspended in midair; from chuu = space or sky + tsurusu = to hang up

Da だ – see desu

Daasu ダース = a dozen

Dabodabo ダボダボ = loose clothing, plenty of (when pouring a liquid); from double double; cf. related terms listed at fuku

Daboku 打撲 = a bruise; an abbreviation of dabokushou = a bruise; cf. related terms listed at dabokushou

Dabokushou 打撲傷 = a bruise; *if you throw darts at the bony Kool-Aid salesman, he will show you his fighting skills, and you will end up with a bruise*; cf. aza = a bruise, birthmark, black eye; cf. daboku = a bruise

Dachou ダチョウ = an ostrich; *one of the dancer's chores was to feed the ostriches*

Daeki 唾液 = saliva; *Darwin visited the eki (station) and slipped on some saliva*; cf. related terms listed at yodare

Dai だい = desu ka = is it? used with "wh" questions (where, who, what), e.g., doushitan dai = what's up? cf. kai = desu ka, used with yes-no questions

Dai 代 = a certain age, a generation, a lifetime; *when I reached a certain age, I went on a diet*; cf. related terms listed at jidai

Dai 代 = cost, price, used as a suffix; *the price was a dime*

Dai 台 = a stand, base or platform; a counter for machines; *he keeps a jar of dimes on a stand, one for each of his machines*; cf. hoomu = a platform; cf. kyoudan = a podium or platform

Dai 大 = big, serious, very; used as a prefix, e.g., daimondai = a big problem; *that's a big dike*; cf. related terms listed at ookii

Dai 第 = an ordinal number indicator, used as a prefix, e.g., dai ichi = first; *I was the first to dive into the pool*

Daibu 大分 = considerably, a lot; *the diet that the Buddha followed helped him considerably*; cf. related terms listed at kanari (no)

Daibubun 大部分 = the major part, the majority; from dai = large + bubun = a part of something; cf. related terms listed at mottomo

Daibutsu 大仏 = a large statue of Buddha; from dai = large + butsu = Buddha

Daichou 大腸 = the large intestine; from dai = large + chou = intestine; cf. related terms listed at naizou

Daidai 代々 = for generations, hereditary; from dai = a generation, a certain age

Daidokoro 台所 = a kitchen; from dai = a stand + dokoro = tokoro = a place

Daieiteikoku 大英帝国 = the British Empire; from dai = large + eikoku = Great Britain + teikoku = an empire

Daigaku 大学 = a college or university; from dai = large + gaku = study or learning; cf. ritsudai = a private university; cf. shuuritsudai = a state university; cf. other related terms listed at gakkou

Daigakusei 大学生 = a college student; from daigaku = a college + sei = a person; cf. related terms listed at gakusei

Daihyou suru 代表する = to represent; *a diet of healing yogurt represents a different approach to weight loss*

Daihyoutorishimariyaku 代表取締役 = a representative director (a director chosen by a board to represent it); from daihyou = representative + torishimariyaku = a company director

Daiichi 第一 = number one, i.e., the most, the best or the first; from dai = ordinal number indicator + ichi = one; cf. ichiban = number one; cf. other related terms listed at hajime ni, at mottomo and at saikou

Daiichiji 第一次 = the first; from dai = number, e.g., daisan = number three; + ichi = one + ji = next or following, e.g., jikai = next time; cf. related terms listed at hatsu

Daiichiji sekai taisen 第一次世界大戦 = World War I; from daiichiji = the first + sekai = world + tai = big + sensou = war; cf. dainiji sekai taisen = World War II

Daiichininsha 第一人者 = leading person; from dai ichi = number one, i.e., the most, the best, or the first; + nin = person + sha = person

Daiji 大事 = important, precious; *my dyed jeans are important to me*; cf. related terms listed at juuyou

Daijin 大臣 = a Cabinet minister; *that cabinet minister dyed his jeans*; cf. related terms listed at souri

Daijoubu 大丈夫 = all right; *the diet that Job recommended was all right*; cf. junchou = no problem, doing well; cf. ryoukou = favorable, satisfactory; cf. yuuri = advantageous, favorable

Daikakusei 大覚醒 = the Great Awakening, a religious revival in the English colonies in America during the 18th century; from dai = big + kakusei = waking up

Daikibo 大規模 = large-scale; from dai = large + kibo = scale or scope; *the scale of the king's bowling alley was impressive*; cf. related terms listed at kibo and at ookii

Daikon 大根 = a large white winter radish; from dai = big + kon = a root, e.g., konkyo = a basis or foundation; cf. related terms listed at yasai

Daikyuu 代休 = compensatory time off; *the diver went to Cuba during her compensatory time off*; cf. related terms listed at yasumi

Daimyou 大名 = a samurai lord; *the samurai lord said that before he died, he wanted to meet a yogi*; cf. related terms listed at shujin

Dainashi 台無し = messy, spoiled; *when you diet and gnash your teeth, my appetite is spoiled*

Dainashi ni suru 台無しにする = to mar or ruin; from dainashi = messy, spoiled; cf. related terms listed at horobosu

Dainiji 第二次 = the second; from dai = number, e.g., daisan = number three; + ni = two + ji = next or following, e.g., jikai = next time; cf. otsu = the second, the latter

Dainiji sekai taisen 第二次世界大戦 = World War II; from dainiji = the second + sekai = world + tai = big + sensou = war

Dairi 代理 = representation, agent, proxy; *I keep a diary about my representation by my agent*

Dairiten 代理店 = an agency or agent; from dairi = representation + ten = store

Daishinsai 大震災 = a great earthquake; from dai = big + shinsai = a great earthquake; cf. related terms listed at jishin

Daishou 大小 = large and small; from dai = large + sho = small; *I saw large and small people at the diet show*

Daisongai 大損害 = great damage; from dai = tai = big + songai = loss or harm; cf. related terms listed at sawari

Daisuki 大好き = a great liking; from dai = big + suki = a liking

Daitai 大体 = approximately, mostly, about, general; *in general, I dye my ties about once a year*; cf. related terms listed at taitei and at yaku = about

Daitan 大胆 = bold or brave; *you must be brave to dive into that tank*

Daitasuu 大多数 = a majority; from dai = big + tasuu = a large number; cf. related terms listed at mottomo

Daiteitaku 大邸宅 = a mansion; from dai = big + teitaku = a mansion; cf. teitaku = a mansion or residence; cf. yashiki = an estate, mansion or residence

Daitoshi 大都市 = a large city; from dai = big + toshi = a city; cf. related terms listed at shi

Daitouryou 大統領 = president (of a country); *the diver told Pope Leo that he was searching for the president*

Daizu 大豆 = soybean; *if an elephant eats too many soybeans, he may die at the zoo*

Dakara だから = because, therefore; from da = it is + kara = since; cf. desu kara = because, therefore; cf. shitagatte = accordingly or therefore; cf. to iu koto desu (or to iu koto da, or tte iu koto desu) = therefore, or something is reported to be true; cf. to iu wake desu (or to iu wake da) = therefore or as a result; cf. wake desu (or wake da) = therefore

Dake だけ = only, simply; *Darwin's kettle was the only one they had*; cf. nomi = only, nothing but; cf. shika = except for only; cf. tada = only, simply, merely; cf. tanni = merely, only; cf. tatta = only, simply, merely (often used with numbers); cf. yuuitsu = only, sole, unique

Dake atte だけあって = because, as might be expected from; *Dad wears Keds at the tennis club, as might be expected*; cf. related terms listed at node

Dake de naku だけでなく = not only but also, e.g., jousha ken dake de naku = not only a boarding ticket but also; from dake = only + de = from + naku = not existing

Dake demo だけでも – see dake wa

Dake ni だけに – see dake atte

Dake wa だけは (or dake demo) = at least, as much as one can (when used after a plain verb); from dake = only + wa = as for; cf. dake demo = at least, as much as one can; cf. demo = however, but, any, even, at least, or something, as well; cf. semete = at least

Dakeatte だけあって – see dake atte

Dakedo だけど = although, but; from da = it is + kedo = but; cf. related terms listed at demo

Dakiageru 抱き上げる = to hold up in one's arms; from daku = to hug + ageru = to raise; cf. related terms listed at daku

Dakishimeru 抱きしめる = to hug someone tightly; from daku = to hug + shimeru = to close; cf. related terms listed at daku

Daku 抱く = to embrace, hold or hug; *Dad drank some Kool-Aid and embraced me*; cf. dakiageru = to hold up in one's arms; cf. dakishimeru = to hug someone tightly; cf. houyou suru = to embrace or hug; cf. idaku = to embrace or hold, to entertain (an idea); cf. kakaeru = to embrace or hold; to employ (a person)

Dakuryuu 濁流 = a muddy stream; *the builders of the dam in Kuwait reused old construction debris and piled it across a muddy stream*; cf. related terms listed at kawa

Dakyou 妥協 = a compromise; *my daughter took a job in Kyouto as a compromise*; cf. jouho = a concession or compromise

Dama 玉 – see tama

Damaru 黙る = to keep silent; *when my dad was marooned, he kept silent for a year*; cf. shizumaru = to become calm or quiet

Damasu だます = to trick, cheat or deceive; *in Damascus, Superman tricked his foes*; cf. madowasu = to delude or seduce; cf. uragiru = to betray or deceive

Dame だめ = bad or wrong; *Darwin's memory was bad*; cf. related terms listed at warui

Dan 壇 = a stage; *a dancer needs a stage*; cf. butai = a stage

Dan'atsu (Danatsu) suru 弾圧する = to oppress or suppress; *the dancer I met at Superman's house said that the government had oppressed her*; cf. shiitageru = to persecute or oppress; cf. other related terms listed at houmuru

Danbou 暖房 = heating, heater; *the dancer boasted about her space heater*

Dandan だんだん = gradually; *the dancing dandelion gradually lost its petals*; cf. related terms listed at shidai ni

Dangai 断崖 = precipice, cliff; *the dancing guy fell off a cliff*; cf. gake = cliff; cf. zeppeki = a precipice

Dangan 弾丸 = a bullet; *the dancer and Gandalf were struck by bullets*; cf. tama = a bullet

Dan'in (Danin) 団員 = a group member; from dantai = a group of people + in = a member of a group, e.g., kaishain = a company employee; cf. ichiin = a member; cf. in = a group member (used as a suffix)

Danjiri だんじり = a float or portable shrine used in festivals; *the dancing genius released a pigeon from the top of the float*

Danjo 男女 = men and women; from dansei = man + josei = woman

Dankai 段階 = stage of development or step; *the dancer worked for the Kaiser at a certain stage of her development*; cf. gendankai = present stage, current phase

Danketsu suru 団結する = to unite or consolidate; *I put dandelions and ketchup in my soup in order to unite yellow and red colors*; cf. ketsugou suru = to unite

Danko 断固 = resolute; *the dancer who went to Colombia was resolute about winning the dance contest*; cf. ganko = stubborn

Danna 旦那 = husband, master; *my husband was a dancing Nazi*; cf. related terms listed at shujin

Dannasan 旦那さん = male customer, master; from danna = master + san = an honorific suffix; cf. related terms listed at shujin

Danpen 断片 = piece; *the dancer's pen fell and broke into pieces*; cf. hahen = a fragment; cf. hashikure = a scrap or piece, an unimportant person; cf. hitokake = one piece

Danro 暖炉 = a fireplace or stove; *the <u>dancer</u> <u>roasted</u> chestnuts in the <u>fireplace</u>*; cf. ro = a fireplace or furnace

Dansa 段差 = a difference in level; from dan = a step, e.g., kaidan = stairs; + sa = a gap, e.g., jisa = a time difference

Dansei 男性 = male, a man; *the <u>dancing</u> <u>sailor</u> is a <u>male</u>*; cf. related terms listed at otoko

Danshi 男子 = boy, male; from dansei = male + shi = child; *that <u>boy</u> <u>dances</u> with <u>sheep</u>*; cf. related terms listed at otoko

Dansou 断層 = fault, discrepancy, gap; *the <u>dancer</u> and the <u>soldier</u> <u>found</u> <u>fault</u> with each other*; cf. suki = gap, opening, carelessness, inattentiveness; cf. sukima = gap, hole; cf. other related terms listed at ketten

Dantai 団体 = group of people, an organization; *a <u>group</u> of <u>dancing</u> <u>tigers</u>*; cf. gekidan = a theatrical company; cf. gunshuu = a group of living things (including people), a crowd or community; cf. ha = group, sect, school; cf. habatsu = a faction; cf. han = a group; cf. ichidan = a group; cf. kensetsuhan = a construction group; cf. kumi (or gumi) = group, team, school class; cf. mure = herd, crowd, group; cf. oozei = many, a crowd of people; cf. renchuu = a group of people, a crowd; cf. shuudan = a group; cf. soshiki = an organization; zattou = a crowd, congestion

Danyuu 男優 = an actor; *that <u>dancing</u> <u>youth</u> is an <u>actor</u>*; cf. related terms listed at haiyuu

Darake だらけ = full of, covered with; *Charles <u>Darwin</u> would <u>rake</u> the lawn when it was <u>covered with</u> leaves*; cf. related terms listed at juuman

Darashinai だらしない = sloppy, untidy, careless; *when the city of <u>Dallas</u> <u>shinai</u> (doesn't do) trash pickup, the streets get untidy*

Dare 誰 = who; *<u>who</u> is wearing the <u>dark</u> <u>red</u> shirt?* cf. donata = who, used in more polite situations

Dare datte 誰だって = anyone, everyone; from dare = who + da = it is + tte = reportedly; cf. related terms listed at daredemo

Daredemo 誰でも = anyone; from dare = who + demo = as well; cf. dare datte = anyone, everyone; cf. daremo = everyone or anyone (with positive constructions), no one (with negative constructions)

Dareka 誰か = someone; from dare = who + ka = a question marker

Daremo 誰も = everyone or anyone (with positive constructions), no one (with negative constructions); from dare = who + mo = even; cf. related terms listed at daredemo

Darou だろう – see deshou

Darui だるい = lethargic, sluggish, dull; *the <u>dancer</u> <u>ruined</u> the show with her <u>sluggish</u> performance*

Dasha 打者 = a batter (baseball); *the <u>batter</u> wore a <u>damp</u> <u>shawl</u>*; + sha = a person

Dasshutsu 脱出 = flight or escape; *after the <u>dancer</u> <u>shoots</u> <u>you</u>, she will attempt an <u>escape</u>*; cf. toubou = escape, flight; cf. tousou = escape, flight

Dasu 出す = to take out, put out; *I will <u>take</u> <u>out</u> your <u>dark</u> <u>suit</u>*; cf. morasu = to let out, to omit; cf. hipparidasu = to take out, drag out

Date 建て = story (of a building), e.g., kono ie wa ikkai date desu = this is a one-story house; from dateru = tateru = to build or put upright

Datou na 妥当な = right, appropriate, reasonable; *after my <u>daughter</u> stubbed her <u>toe</u>, it was <u>appropriate</u> for her to take a break*; cf. related terms listed at tekitou na

Datsugoku 脱獄 = a jailbreak; *after his jailbreak, he drove a Datsun to a cafe and ordered gold Kool-Aid*

Datsumou 脱毛 = hair loss; *after my Datsun collided with a lawn mower, I began to experience hair loss*; cf. datsumoushou = baldness (as a disorder)

Datsumoushou 脱毛症 = baldness (as a disorder); from datsumou = hair loss + shoujou = symptom; cf. datsumou = hair loss

Dattara だったら = if it's the case; the conditional form of da = desu = it is; this can sometimes replace nara = if or in case; cf. related terms listed at moshi

Datte だって = because, something is reportedly true, well; from da = it is + tte = reportedly; cf. desutte = reportedly, used by women; cf. other related terms listed at node

De で = at, in (space), on, in (time), by (means of), from, of, because of, and; cf. ni = at, by, for, from, in, on, to, per; cf. other related terms listed at node

De 出 = origin, birth, stock; from deru = to leave

De gozaimasu でございます = (it) is humbly; from de = from + gozaimasu = to exist humbly; cf. desu = (it) is

De sae でさえ – see sae

De wa aru ではある = to exist (in contrast to something that doesn't exist); from dearu = to exist + wa, indicating contrast; cf. related terms listed at aru

Deaeru 出会える = to be able to meet; the potential tense of deau = to meet; from deru = to go out + au = to meet

Deai 出会い = an encounter; from deau = to meet; cf. related terms listed at kaigi

Deaikei 出会い系 = an online dating website; from deai = an encounter + keitou = system

Dearu である = to exist (animate or inanimate); from de = from + aru = to exist; cf. related terms listed at aru

Deau 出会う = to meet (by chance), to encounter; from deru = to go out + au = to meet; cf. au = to meet; cf. au = to be involved, to get caught in, to encounter or meet; cf. me ni kakaru = to meet humbly; cf. mukaeru = to meet/welcome; cf. sessuru = to border on, adjoin or encounter; cf. saikai suru = to meet again; cf. shiriau = to meet; cf. souguu suru = to encounter

Debabouchou 出刃包丁 = a knife or cutting tool; *the debacle started when Bo Peep chose to bring a knife to a party*; cf. hamono = a knife or cutting tool; cf. houchou = a kitchen knife

Deeta mou データ網 = a data network; from deeta = data + mou = network

Degozaimasu でございます = to exist humbly (animate or inanimate); from de = from + gozaimasu = to exist humbly; cf. related terms listed at aru

Deguchi 出口 = an exit; from deru = to go out + guchi = kuchi = mouth

Dehajimeru 出始める = to begin to appear; from deru = to go out + hajimeru = to begin

Deisui 泥水 = muddy water, red-light district; *my date was sweet, but he took me to the red-light district*; cf. related terms listed at mizu

Dekai でかい = huge; *the deck on the Kaiser's yacht is huge*; cf. related terms listed at ookii

Dekakeru 出かける = to go out, leave; *the dentist called Kennedy in his room before he went out*; cf. related terms listed at deru

Dekiagaru 出来上がる = to be completed or ready; from dekiru = to be able + agaru = to finish (when used as a suffix)

Dekiai suru 溺愛する = to dote on or indulge; *a deaf king in Ireland doted on his only son*; cf. amayakasu = to indulge or spoil (a person)

Dekigoto 出来事 = occurrence, event; from dekiru = to be able + goto = koto = thing; cf. genshou = a phenomenon; cf. jiken = an event, incident or case

Dekiru 出来る = to be able to do, to be ready, to be built or produced; *I am able to install decking below the roof*

Dekiru dake できるだけ = as much as possible; from dekiru = to be able to do + dake = only; cf. related terms listed at narubeku

Dekiru dake hayaku できるだけ早く = as soon as possible; from dekiru dake = as much as possible + hayaku = the adverbial form of hayai = early

Demae 出前 = a (food) delivery or catering service; *the deaf maestro started a catering service*; cf. takuhaibin = a home delivery service

Demo でも – see temo

Demo でも = however, but, any, even, even though, at least, or something, as well; *we can't even go to the party, but at least we can watch the demolition*; cf. dakedo = although, but; cf. dake wa = at least, as much as one can (when used after a plain verb); cf. ga = but; cf. kedo = but, however; cf. keredo(mo) = although, but, nevertheless; cf. shikashi = however, but

Denai でない = is not, am not, are not; the negative form of dearu = to exist

Denchi 電池 = a battery; *the dentist's cheap drill runs on batteries*

Denchuu 電柱 = telephone pole or electricity pole; *the dentist will choose to install telephone poles outside her office*; cf. hashira = a pillar, post or column

Dengen 電源 = electric power source; from denki = electricity + gen = source, e.g., kigen = origin; cf. related terms listed at kigen

Dengon 伝言 = a message; *the dentist sent Gonzalez a message*; cf. kotozuke = a message

Denki 電気 = electricity, an electric light; *the dentist in Kiev paid for electricity*

Denkigama 電気釜 = an electric rice cooker; from denki = electricity + gama = kama = a pot in which rice is cooked

Denpyou 伝票 = a receipt, bill or slip; *the dentist in Pyonyang sent me a bill*; cf. kanjou = bill, check, calculation; cf. ryoushuusho = a receipt; cf. suitou = receipts and disbursements

Denryoku 電力 = electric power; from denki = electricity + ryoku = power

Denryokumou 電力網 = electrical power grid; from denryoku = electric power + mou = network, e.g., deeta mou = a data network

Denryuu 電流 = electric current; *when the dentist reused an old drill, he felt some electric current flowing into his hand*

Densen 伝染 = an infection; *the dentist sensed an infection*; cf. related terms listed at byouki

Densen 電線 = an electric or telephone wire; from denki = electricity + sen = line

Densen byou 伝染病 = infectious disease; from densen = infection + byouki = illness; cf. related terms listed at byouki

Densetsu 伝説 = a legend; *there is a legend about a dentist who set Superman's implants*; cf. related terms listed at hanashi

Densha 電車 = a train; from denki = electric + sha = a vehicle; cf. futsuu = ordinary, usual, general, average; this can also = local train; cf. kaisoku densha = an express train; cf. kisha = a train with a steam locomotive (or an ordinary train); cf.

kyuukou = an express train; cf. ressha = a train; cf. shinkansen = a bullet train; cf. tokkyuu = limited express (train)

Densha chin 電車賃 = train fare; from densha = train + chin = fare; *I hold my fare under my chin while boarding*; cf. unchin = fare

Denshi 電子 = electron, electronic; *the dentist solved the Shiite's problem with an electronic drill*

Denshi renji 電子レンジ = a microwave oven; from denshi = electronic + renji = a range or over

Dentou 伝統 = tradition, heritage; *the dentist toasted his heritage*; cf. isan = inheritance, legacy, heritage

Dentou 電灯 = electric light; *the dentist's toe collided with the electric light*; cf. keikoutou = a fluorescent light

Dentouteki 伝統的 = traditional; from dentou = tradition + teki = related to; cf. kotenteki = classical, old-fashioned

Denwa 電話 = a telephone; from denki = electricity + kaiwa = a conversation

Deru 出る = to come out, go out, leave, attend or participate; *when the dentist entered the room, I left*; cf. dekakeru = to go out, leave; cf. hanareru = to separate from or leave; cf. saru = to leave; cf. shuppatsu suru = to depart or start out; cf. tachinoku = to evacuate, vacate; cf. other related terms listed at shusseki suru

Desae でさえ = even, but, however; from de = of + sae = even; cf. related terms listed at sae

Deshou でしょう = it probably is; *it probably is a dental show*

Desu です = (it) is; *it is a dessert from Uruguay*; cf. de gozaimasu = (it) is humbly

Desu kara ですから – see dakara

Desutte ですって = reportedly, used by women; from desu = (it) is + tte = reportedly; cf. datte だって = because, something is reportedly true, well

Detarame でたらめ = nonsense; *the dentist talked about ramen, but it was all nonsense*

Dewa では = well, then; *well, I dented the wall*

Do 度 = times (frequency), degree (temperature, etc.), counter for occurrences, used as a suffix; *the dophin came two times*; cf. -bai = double, times, -fold; cf. -kai = times (frequency), counter for occurrences; cf. reido = zero degrees

Doa ドア = a door; to = a door; cf. tobira = a front door, a title page

Dobu 溝 = a ditch, used as a word component; *the dozing bookkeeper was snoring in a ditch*

Dobumizu 溝水 = ditch water; from dobu = a ditch + mizu = water; cf. related terms listed at mizu

Docchi どっち – see dochira

Dochira どちら = which, who, where

Dochiraka to iu to どちらかと言うと = if I had to say; from dochiraka = either + to = quote + iu = to say + to = if

Dochiraka どちらか = either, one of the two; from dochira = which + ka = a question marker; cf. kaku = each, every, either

Dochiramo どちらも = both, either; from dochira = which + mo = even

Dochiratomo どちらとも = both; from dochira = which, who, where + tomo ni = together

Dohyou 土俵 = a ring used for sumo wrestling, surrounded by rice bales; *a dozing healer from Oregon sat near the sumo ring*

Dojou 土壌 = soil, breeding ground; *the dorm where Joan of Arc lived was a breeding ground* for rebellion, and it was situated on good *soil*; cf. related terms listed at aka

Dokidoki ドキドキ = thump-thump, pitter-patter, to palpitate; from the sound a heart makes when it beats

Dokitto ドキッと = feeling a shock, startling; *the dozing king hurt his toe when he was feeling a shock from an earthquake*

Dokka どっか = an abbreviation of dokoka = somewhere

Dokkai 読解 = reading comprehension; *the dopes who work for the Kaiser have poor reading comprehension*

Doko どこ = where; *where is the dolphin's coach?*

Dokodemo どこでも = anywhere; from doko = where + demo = as well; cf. dokoka = somewhere, anywhere

Dokoka どこか = somewhere, anywhere; from doko = where + ka = a question marker; cf. dokodemo = anywhere

Dokomo どこも = everywhere, wherever, nowhere or nothing (in negative constructions); from doko = where + mo = even; cf. itaru tokoro = everywhere

Dokoroka どころか = on the contrary or conversely; *when Bob Dole bought a Corolla car, people said, "On the contrary, you should have gotten a Ford"*; cf. gyaku = contrary, opposite, antithetical; cf. kaette = conversely, rather, all the more; cf. soredokoroka = on the contrary; cf. taishouteki ni = diametrically opposite

Doku 毒 = poison; *that document is contaminated with poison*; cf. dokubutsu = poison; cf. shokuchuudoku = food poisoning

Dokubutsu 毒物 = poison; from doku = poison + butsu = thing; cf. related terms listed at doku

Dokuha suru 読破する = to finish reading a book; *the documentary was about a Harvard man who had just finished reading a book*

Dokuji 独自 = original, unique; *the documentarian's Jeep was unique*; cf. dokutoku = unique, original, characteristic; cf. koseiteki = unique, individualistic; cf. myou = odd, unique, strange; cf. tokushu na = unique, peculiar, special; cf. yuiitsu = only, sole, unique

Dokuritsu 独立 = independence; *the document contained written suggestions about how to achieve independence*

Dokuritsu shite iru 独立している = is independent; from dokuritsu = independence; cf. shutaiteki = independent, responsible

Dokusai 独裁 = a dictatorship; *I saw a documentary about the psychological tactics employed by the dictatorship*

Dokusaisha 独裁者 = a dictator; from dokusai = a dictatorship + sha = person

Dokusen 独占 = a monopoly; *they have a monopoly on copying documents for senators*

Dokusha 読者 = a person who reads; from dokusho = reading + sha = person

Dokushin 独身 = single, unmarried; *as he dove into the harbor in Kuwait, the Shinto priest asked himself why he was still unmarried*; cf. mikon = unmarried

Dokusho 読書 = reading; *this document shows signs of extensive reading*

Dokushou 独唱 = solo singing; from dokushin = single, unmarried; + shou = to sing energetically, e.g., gasshou = chorus; cf. related terms listed at kashou

Dokusousei 独創性 = originality, creativity; *the documentary about soldiers and sailors demonstrated their creativity in solving problems*

Dokutoku 独特 = unique, original,

characteristic; from dokusousei = originality + toku = special; cf. dokuji = original, unique; cf. koseiteki = unique, individualistic; cf. myou = odd, unique, strange; cf. yuiitsu = only, sole, unique

Dokyou 度胸 = courage or audacity; *the doe in Kyouto Station must have had a lot of courage to venture so far*; cf. related terms listed at yuuki

Donaru 怒鳴る = to shout or yell; *Donald Duck came into the room and started yelling*; cf. himei wo ageru = to scream; cf. sakebu = to shout, yell or scream; cf. wameku = to yell or shriek

Donata どなた = who, used in more polite situations; *who was the one that Donald tagged?* cf. dare = who

Donburi 丼 = a porcelain bowl (for noodles, rice, etc.), or a meal served in such a bowl; *the donkey was buried with a porcelain bowl*; cf. related terms listed at tsubo

Donichi 土日 = Saturday and Sunday; from doyoubi = Saturday + nichiyoubi = Sunday

Donkan 鈍感 = insensitive; *the donkey that Queen Anne bought seemed insensitive to pain*

Donkusai 鈍くさい = slow, stupid, irritating; from donkan = insensitive + kusai = smelly; cf. nibui = dull, dim-witted, slow

Donna どんな = what kind of, what; *what kind of person is Madonna?*

Don'yoku na (Donyoku na) 貪欲な = avaricious, greedy; *the donkey ate all of the yogurt and cookies in a greedy way*

Donzoko どん底 = the depths; *when the donkey saw Zooey's cobra, it jumped off the boat and sank to the depths*; cf. related terms listed at soko

Doori 通り = a street or way (used as a suffix), in accordance with; from dooru = tooru = to passs through; cf. related terms listed at michi

Dore どれ = which or what; *which door is red?*

Doredake どれだけ = how much, to what extent; from dore = which + dake = only; cf. related terms listed at ikura

Doredemo どれでも = any one; from dore = which + demo = any

Dorehodo どれほど = how much, how long, how far; from dore = which + hodo = extent; cf. related terms listed at ikura

Dorei 奴隷 = a slave; *that dome was raised by slaves*

Dorei seido 奴隷制度 = slavery; from dorei = a slave + seido = a system

Doreka どれか = any of, one of, which one; from dore = which + ka = a question marker

Doremo どれも = both, either, any, all, every; neither or none (in negative constructions); from dore = which + mo = also

Doro 泥 = mud; *the dopy robot got stuck in the mud*; cf. related terms listed at aka

Dorobou 泥棒 = thief; *Dorothy's boyfriend is a thief*; cf. related terms listed at hannin

Doronuma 泥沼 = a marsh, bog or swamp; from doro = mud + numa = swamp; cf. numa = a swamp; cf. numachi = swampland

Doryoku 努力 = effort; *the dorm stocks yogurt and cookies in an effort to please*; cf. funtou = hard struggle, strenuous effort; cf. katsudou = action, activity; cf. katsuyaku = activity, great efforts, conspicuous service; cf. torikumi = initiative, effort, dealing with

Dosha 土砂 = earth and sand; *the doughnuts they gave to the Shah were full of earth and sand*; cf. suna = sand

Doshaburi どしゃ降り = pouring rain; from dosha = earth and sand; + buru = furu = to precipitate; cf. related terms listed at ame

Dotchi どっち – see dochira

Dou どう = how, what, would you like; *how was the doughnut? would you like another one?* cf. dou yattara = by what means, how (can); cf. ikaga = how, would you like (more polite)

Dou 同 = the same, used as a prefix; *we like the same doughnuts*; cf. related terms listed at onaji

Dou 堂 = a hall or public chamber, used as a suffix; *they have a nice hall in the Dominican Republic*

Dou 銅 = copper; *the doorknob is made of copper*; cf. buronzu = bronze; cf. oudou = brass; cf. seidou = bronze; cf. related terms listed at tanso

Dou itashimashite どういたしまして = you're welcome, it's nothing; from dou = how + the te form of itasu = to do humbly, so literally this means "how doing humbly," which might imply that what I did was insignificant

Dou iu どう言う = what sort of; from dou = how + iu = to say

Dou ni demo nare どうにでもなる = let come what will; literally "to how, even though, become" (this is the imperative tense; to form the imperative tense of a "u" verb, add "e" to the verb root, i.e., the pre-u form)

Dou yattara どうやったら = by what means, how (can); from dou = how + yattara = if to do (from yaru = to do); cf. related terms listed at dou

Doubutsu 動物 = an animal; from dousa = movement + butsu = thing; cf. ikimono = a living creature; cf. kachiku = domestic animals, livestock, cattle; cf. kemono = an animal; cf. seibutsu = a living creature; cf. yajuu = a wild animal

Doubutsuen 動物園 = a zoo; from doubutsu = an animal + en = a park, e.g., kouen = a public park

Douchuu 道中 = along the way; from douro = a road + chuu = in the middle of; cf. related terms listed at tochuu de

Douga 動画 = movie, video, animation; *I saw a video about a doughnut shop in a garage*; cf. related terms listed at eiga

Dougu 道具 = a tool, appliance, utensil; *I have a tool for cleaning my dopy goose*; cf. related terms listed at souchi

Douhan 同伴 = companionship; *the Doberman and Hansel enjoyed their companionship*

Douhan suru 同伴する = to go together, to accompany; from douhan = companionship; cf. tsukisou = to accompany, chaperone, take care of

Doui 同意 = the same opinion, agreement; *we are in agreement that this bread is too doughy*; cf. related terms listed at shouchi

Douji ni 同時に = at the same time; from dou = the same; *the doughnuts are the same at both shops*; + jikan = time + -ni = a suffix that forms an adverb; cf. ippen ni = all at once, at the same time; cf. issei ni = all at once, at the same time, all together; cf. issho = together, identical, at the same time; cf. nagara = while, at the same time; cf. todouji ni = at the same time, as well

Doujou 同情 = sympathy, pity; *when the door hit Joan of Arc, everyone felt sympathy*; cf. aware = pity, misery; cf. jihi = mercy; cf. kyoukan = sympathy

Douka どうか = please, somehow or other; from dou = how + ka = a question marker; cf. related terms listed at nantonaku

Douka shita no どうかしたの = is something up, is something wrong? from douka = somehow or other + shita = did

Doukan suru 同感する = to have the same opinion or feeling; *the dopes in Canada have the same opinions as the dopes in the*

U.S.

Douketsu 洞穴 = a cave; this is an alternative pronunciation of hora'ana = a cave; *sitting in his cave, the dope pours ketchup into his soup*; cf. related terms listed at horaana

Doukutsu 洞窟 = a cave or grotto; *the doe cut Superman when it ran out of the cave*; cf. related terms listed at horaana

Doukyonin 同居人 = roommate; *I met a dopy Kyoto ninja who became my roommate*

Doukyuusei 同級生 = a classmate; *my classmate eats doughnuts with Cuban sailors*; cf. kyuuyuu = a classmate

Doumei 同盟 = an alliance, league or union; *in the Dominican Republic, some mayors formed an alliance*; cf. related terms listed at rengou

Doumeigun 同盟軍 = an allied army, coalition forces; from doumei = an alliance + guntai = an army; cf. related terms listed at guntai

Doumo どうも = thank you, somehow or somewhat, probably; *somehow I bought a doughnut at the motel which was probably old, but I ate it and said thank you*; cf. nazeka = somehow; cf. other related terms listed at arigatou and at osoraku

Doumyaku 動脈 = artery; *the doorman drank so much Miami Kool-Aid that his arteries hardened*; cf. joumyaku = a vein; cf. kekkan = blood vessel; cf. myaku = pulse or vein

Dounen 同年 = that year, the same year, the same age; from dou = the same + nen = year; cf. related terms listed at nen

Dounyuu 導入 = introduction, leading in; *our doorman in Nyuuyooku (New York) gave us an introduction to our neighbors*; cf. shoukai = introduction

Douran 動乱 = disturbance, commotion; *during the disturbance, the crowd opened the door and ransacked the store*; cf.

hendou = change, commotion, uproar

Douri 道理 = truth, reason; *I have a reason for buying a dory, since I will use it to cross the river and seek the truth*; cf. related terms listed at hontou

Douri de 道理で = no wonder; from douri = reason

Douri ni 道理に = rightly, or in accordance with, e.g., jikan douri ni = on time; from douri = truth, reason + -ni = a suffix that forms an adverb; cf. ni sotte = in accordance with, along

Douro 道路 = a road; *Dorothy and the scarecrow walked along a road*; cf. related terms listed at michi

Douryou 同僚 = a pal, colleague or coworker; *the doughnuts that Leo is eating were brought in by a coworker*; cf. related terms listed at nakama

Dousa 動作 = movement; *the dozing salaryman made a movement*; cf. undou = exercise, sport, action, movement

Dousatsu 洞察 = insight, discernment; *the doorman read satisfying Superman novels to enhance his insight into the criminal mind*

Douse どうせ = anyhow, after all; *the dozing settlers don't do any work after all*; cf. related terms listed at kekkyoku and at tonikaku

Dousha 同社 = the same company; from dou = the same, e.g., douji = at the same time; + kaisha = company; cf. related terms listed at kaisha

Doushi 動詞 = a verb; *"to downshift" is a verb*; cf. doushi = a peer; cf. related terms listed at shugo

Doushi 同士 = fellow, mutual, companion; *the dozing sheepdog belongs to my companion*; cf. related terms listed at nakama and at tagai

Doushite どうして = why or how; *why did*

you hang the <u>doorman</u>'s <u>sheet</u> over the <u>television</u>? cf. related terms listed at naze

Doushite mo どうしても = by any means, no matter what, after all, at any rate, surely; from doushite = how + mo = even

Dousoukai 同窓会 = an alumni meeting; *the <u>door</u>men were <u>sober</u> and <u>kind</u> at the <u>alumni</u> <u>meeting</u>*

Doutai 胴体 = body, torso; *having a <u>doughnut</u> <u>time</u> every day makes your <u>torso</u> expand*; cf. related terms listed at karada

Doutoku 道徳 = morality, moral, ethics; *he consumes only <u>doughnut</u>s, <u>tofu</u> and <u>Kool</u>-Aid, since he questions the <u>morality</u> of <u>eating meat</u>*; cf. kachikan = sense of values, value system; cf. rinri = ethics; cf. rinrigaku = ethics (a branch of philosophy)

Doutokujou 道徳上 = morally, from a moral point of view; from doutoku = morality + jou = above, e.g., jouzu = skillful

Douwa 童話 = a fairy tale; *<u>doughnut</u> <u>wars</u> only occur in <u>fairy</u> <u>tales</u>*; cf. related terms listed at hanashi

Douyara どうやら = somehow or other; *if you leave a <u>doughnut</u> in the <u>yard</u> with an <u>apple</u>, <u>somehow</u> <u>or</u> <u>other</u> they will be gone by the next day*; cf. related terms listed at nantonaku

Douyou 動揺 = uneasiness, agitation; *the <u>door</u>man ate the <u>yogurt</u> with <u>uneasiness</u>*; cf. related terms listed at kinchou

Douyou 同様 = similar, same; *the <u>door</u>man ate the <u>yogurt</u>, which was the <u>same</u> as always, in a <u>similar</u> way*; cf. related terms listed at onaji

Douyou ni 同様に = similarly; from douyou = similar, same + -ni = a suffix that forms an adverb

Douzo どうぞ = go ahead (or come this way); *the <u>dozing</u> <u>owner</u> opened his eyes and told me to <u>go</u> <u>ahead</u>*

Douzou 銅像 = a bronze statue; from seidou = bronze + zou = a statue

E へ = to, for, toward; cf. ni = at, by, for, from, in, on, to, per

E 柄 = a handle; *this <u>handle</u> is for my <u>egg</u> cooker*; this can also be pronounced gara = a pattern, a body build

E 絵 = a picture, painting or drawing; *this is a <u>painting</u> of an <u>egg</u>*; cf. ema = a drawing or painting of a horse; cf. emakimono = a scroll that tells a story with pictures; cf. fuukeiga = a landscape painting; cf. hekiga = a mural painting; cf. kaibou zu = anatomical drawings; cf. kaiga = a painting; cf. makimono = a scroll painting; cf. nihonga = a Japanese painting; cf. penkie = a picture painted with oil paint, especially a mural in a public bath; cf. sashie = an illustration; cf. suisaiga = a watercolor painting; cf. zu = a drawing, illustration or picture; cf. zushi = an illustration

Ebi エビ = shrimp or prawn; *I drank excellent <u>beer</u> with the <u>shrimp</u> meal*

Eda 枝 = a branch; *my eccentric <u>dad</u> was hanging from a <u>branch</u>*

Edamame 枝豆 = boiled or steamed soybeans, literally "branch beans" since historically often sold while still attached to the branch; from eda = branch + mame = bean

Egakidasu 描き出す = to delineate, express or imagine; from egaku = to depict, draw or describe + dasu = to put out; cf. related terms listed at iiarawasu

Egaku 描く (also pronounced kaku) = to draw, paint, depict, describe; *I learned to <u>paint</u> <u>egg</u> <u>art</u> in <u>Kuwait</u>*; cf. nuru = to paint, plaster, spread, smear

Egao 笑顔 = a smiling face; *when she is throwing <u>eggs</u> at <u>owls</u>, she has a <u>smiling</u> <u>face</u>*; cf. related terms listed at kao

Ehon 絵本 = a picture book; from e = picture + hon = book

Eibun 英文 = English text; from eigo =

English + bunshou = sentence

Eibun dokkai 英文読解 = English reading comprehension; from eibun = English text + dokkai = reading comprehension

Eien 永遠 = eternity; *when I fly on ANA (All Nippon Airways), it seems to take an eternity to get to Japan*; cf. eikyuu = eternity, forever

Eiga 映画 = a movie or film; *I saw an aging Gandalf in that movie*; cf. douga = movie, video, animation; cf. gazou = picture (film, TV)

Eigagan 映画館 = a move theater; from eiga = movie + kan = a large building; cf. gekijou = a theater

Eigo 英語 = the English language; *the aging golfer spoke the English language*

Eigoryoku 英語力 = English ability; from eigo = English + ryoku = power

Eigyou 営業 = business; *our business is selling aging gyoza*; cf. related terms listed at akinai

Eiji 英字 = English text, English alphabet; from eigo = the English language + ji = character

Eikaiwa 英会話 = English conversation; from eigo = English + kaiwa = conversation; cf. related terms listed at kaiwa

Eikou 栄光 = glory, eminence; *adherence to their ancient code led them to glory*; cf. related terms listed at kouei

Eikyou 影響 = influence, effect; *the ancient temples in Kyouto have an influence on the entire country*; cf. eikyouryoku = influence, clout; cf. kekka = an effect or result; cf. kouka = an effect; cf. kouryoku = an effect

Eikyouryoku 影響力 = influence, clout; from eikyou = influence + ryoku = force; cf. related terms listed at eikyou

Eikyuu 永久 = eternity, forever; *aging Cubans seem to live for an eternity*; cf. eien = eternity

Eimin 永眠 = death; *the aging mink was approaching its death*; cf. karoushi = death from overwork; cf. seikyo = death; cf. shi = death; cf. shikyo = death; cf. toushi = freezing to death; cf. uejini = death from starvation

Eimin suru 永眠する = to die; from eimin = death; cf. related terms listed at shinu

Eisakubun 英作文 = English composition; from eigo = English + sakubun = composition; cf. related terms listed at sakuhin

Eisei 衛星 = satellite; *eight sailors watched the satellite*

Eisei 衛生 = hygiene, sanitation; *honest Abe went to Safeway for his hygiene products*; cf. hoken = health preservation, hygiene

Eiseiteki 衛生的 = sanitary, hygienic; from eisei = sanitation + teki = related to

Eiwa jiten 英和辞典 = English-Japanese dictionary; from eigo = English + wa = Japanese, e.g., washoku = Japanese food; + jiten = dictionary; cf. similar terms listed at jiten = an encyclopedia

Eiyaku 英訳 = an English translation; from eigo = English + honyaku = a translation; cf. related terms listed at honyaku

Eiyou 栄養 = nutrition; *honest Abe ate yogurt for good nutrition*; cf. jiyou = nourishment, nutrition; cf. youbun = nourishment

Eiyuu 英雄 = a hero; *the aviator who flew to the Yukon was a hero*; cf. gouketsu = a hero or great man; cf. shujinkou = hero, heroine, protagonist, lead; cf. yuusha = a brave man or hero

Eizou 映像 = images, pictures (screen), film; *I watched a film about some ancient Zodiac signs*; cf. related terms listed at zou

Ejiki 餌食 = prey or victim; *the edgy king was the victim of a coup*; cf. related terms listed at hisaisha

Eki 駅 = a railway station; *Edward the King left the station*

Ekiben 駅弁 = boxed lunch sold at train station; from eki = station + bentou = a boxed lunch

Ekibenyasan 駅弁屋さん = a store at a station that sells boxed lunches; from ekiben = boxed lunch sold at station + ya = store + san = honorific suffix

Ekibyou 疫病 = plague, epidemic; from eki = epidemic; *an excellent king healed people during the epidemic*; + byouki = illness; cf. related terms listed at byouki

Ekisentorikku エキセントリック = eccentric

Ekisha 易者 = a fortune teller; *Edward the King visited a shack to consult a fortune teller*

Ekitai 液体 = liquid; *when Edward the King was tired, he drank a stimulating liquid from a flask*

Ema 絵馬 = a drawing or painting of a horse; *the emancipated people made drawings of horses*; cf. related terms listed at e

Emakimono 絵巻物 = a scroll that tells a story with pictures; from e = a picture + makimono = a scroll painting; cf. related terms listed at e

Emoji 絵文字 = an ideograph; from e = picture + ji = character; cf. related terms listed at ji

Emon 衣紋 = clothes or dress; *the energetic monks made their own clothes*; cf. related terms listed at fuku

Emonkake 衣紋掛け = a kimono stand; from emon = clothes + kakeru = to hang

Emono 獲物 = game (hunting) or catch (fishing); *when Eskimos get mono (things) from hunting or fishing, we call them game or catch*

En 円 = yen, a Japanese currency unit, a circle; *I encourage you to spend some yen*

En 縁 = relation, bond, kinship, fate; *entertainers have a bond with their audience*; cf. related terms listed at kanrensei

En 煙 = smoke, used as a word component; *a train's engine produces smoke*

Enban 円盤 = a disk or platter; *the engineer mashes bananas on this disk*

Endaka 円高 = appreciation of the yen, a strong yen; from en = yen + dakai = takai = high

Endoyuuzaa エンドユーザー = end user

Engi 演技 = a performance (stage); from enjiru = to perform + gijutsu = skill; cf. related terms listed at shutsuen

Engi 縁起 = omen, sign of luck, origin, causation; *those energetic geese are a sign of luck and a good omen*; cf. related terms listed at zenchou = premonition

Enja 演者 = a performer or actor; *the energy that Jack Nicholson brought to the studio made him a great actor*; cf. related terms listed at haiyuu

Enjiru 演じる = to perform or act; *an engineer and his rooster will perform*; cf. konasu= to digest, to be able to use, to manage, to do completely, to perform or be good at; cf. okonau = to conduct or perform, to do, to carry out

Enjo 援助 = assistance, support; *I enjoy the support of my family*; cf. bengi = convenience, assistance; cf. chikarazoe = assistance, support; cf. fuyou = support, raising (of children); cf. hojo = assistance, support; cf. ouen = support; cf. sasae = support; cf. sewa = looking after, assistance, usually expressed as osewa; cf. seien = support, cheering; cf. shien = support; cf. shiji = support

Enjou suru 炎上する = to blaze up, burn; *the French king encouraged Joan of Arc to fight against the English, but in the end she* got *burned*; cf. related terms listed at moeru

Enkai 宴会 = party or banquet; *the entertainer brought some kites to the banquet*; cf. paati = a party

Enkaku 沿革 = history, development; *I encouraged Karl the Kool-Aid vendor to describe the history and development of the Kool-Aid industry*; cf. other related terms listed at hattatsu and at rekishi

Enkatsu 円滑 = smooth, harmonious; *my energetic cats engage in smooth and harmonious play*; cf. related terms listed at nameraka

Enkei 円形 = circular; from en = a circle + keitai = a form

Enkei 遠景 = background, distant view; *some engineers were eating cake in the background*; cf. haikei = background

Enki 延期 = postponement; *if you encourage kicking, there will be a postponement of the match*; cf. yuuyo = a postponement or reprieve

Enki suru 延期する = to postpone; from enki = postponement; cf. miawaseru = to exchange glances, to postpone, to refrain from doing something; cf. miokuru = to see off (e.g., to an airport), to let pass or postpone, to wait and see

Enkyori 遠距離 = long distance; *the engineer went to Kyoto to realize his dreams, and he had to travel a long distance*; cf. choukyori = long distance; cf. enpou = a long way, a distant place

Enmoku 演目 = a program (e.g., theatrical); *the entertainer drank more Kool-Aid after he saw the program that he was expected to perform*

Enogu 絵具 = artist's paint; from e = a painting + no (understood but not written) + gu = a tool; cf. penki = paint

Enpitsu 鉛筆 = pencil; *after he got a new pencil, the engineer peeled the paint off*

and dropped it into his *tsoup* (soup)

Enpou 遠方 = a long way, a distant place; *the enthusiastic policeman traveled a long way to arrest the suspect* cf. enkyori = long distance; cf. choukyori = long distance

Enryo 遠慮 = hesitation, reserve, restraint, modesty; *we have to encourage Pope Leo because he shows too much hesitation*; cf. jishuku = self-restraint, self-discipline; cf. kigane = hesitation or reserve; cf. related terms listed at kenkyo

Enryo suru 遠慮する = to hesitate or hold back; from enryo = hesitation; cf. kigane wo suru = to hesitate; cf. mayou = to lose direction, to get lost, to hesitate; cf. shiburu = to hesitate or be reluctant

Ensei 遠征 = an expedition; *we enjoyed sailing during our expedition*; cf. related terms listed at tanken

Enseitai 遠征隊 = an expeditionary group; from ensei = an expedition + butai = a unit

Enshou 炎症 = inflammation; from en = inflammation, e.g., haien = pneumonia; + shoujou = symptoms

Enshuu 円周 = circumference; *the engineer designed shoes that could be used to walk the circumference of the earth*; cf. related terms listed at chokkei

Ensou 演奏 = musical performance; *her performance begins at the end of the drum solo*; cf. related terms listed at shutsuen

Ensoukai 演奏会 = concert or recital; from ensou = performance + kaigi = meeting; cf. related terms listed at shutsuen

Entotsu 煙突 = a chimney; *when he saw the chimney, the engineer said that it was totally superfluous*

Entou 円筒 = a cylinder; *the energy of a tornado creates a cylinder of air*

Enzetsu 演説 = a speech; *I made a speech about an enzyme, but etiquette required me to share credit with Sue*; cf. kouen = a speech or lecture; cf. kougi = a lecture; cf. other related terms listed at jugyou = a lesson

Enzetsu suru 演説する = to make a speech; from enzetsu = a speech

Erabu 選ぶ = to choose or select; *during the era of Bush, we had to choose a senator*; cf. batteki suru = to select; cf. sentaku suru = to choose; cf. yoru = to choose or select

Erai 偉い = great, excellent, eminent, distinguished; *it was an error to throw ice at that distinguished woman*; cf. related terms listed at idai and at joutou

Eri 襟 = a collar or lapel; *Eric Clapton had lipstick on his collar*

Eru 得る = to get, earn, understand, receive something undesirable (like a punishment); *if you are erudite, you can get, earn and understand things*; cf. related terms listed at shutoku suru and at wakaru

Esa 餌 = animal food or bait; *the Eskimos use sardines as animal food*; cf. related terms listed at tabemono

Eshaku 会釈 = a bow, salute, greeting, nod; *the man at the entrance to the shack acknowledged me with a bow*; cf. aisatsu = greetings, salutation, a polite set phrase used when meeting or parting from someone; cf. mukae = greeting, welcome; cf. ojigi = a bow

Esute エステ = aesthetic

Etai 得体 = nature or character; *the expert tile setter has a unique character*; cf. seishitsu = character or nature; cf. shizen = nature; cf. shizenkai = nature, the natural world

Etai no shirenai 得体の知れない = questionable, untrustworthy, enigmatic, suspicious; from etai = nature or character + the possessive no + shirenai = cannot know; cf. related terms listed at ayashii

Etsu 悦 = ecstasy, joy, rapture; *the etchings that Superman bought gave him joy*; cf. related terms listed at shiawase

Etsu ni iru 悦に入る = to be gratified or happy; from etsu = joy + iru = to go in; cf. hitori etsu ni iru = to be pleased with oneself; cf. ki ni iru = to like or favor; cf. yorokobu = to be happy or delighted

Etsuran 閲覧 = inspection, reading, browsing (e.g., the web); *we keep etchings of Superman at the ranch, where they are available for browsing or inspection*; cf. related terms listed at tenken

Fu 不 = negation, used as a word component, e.g., fuan = insecurity; *the foolish President focused on negation*; cf. related terms listed at mu

Fu 府 = urban prefecture, e.g., Kyoutoufu = Kyoto Prefecture; *they serve good food in that urban prefecture*; cf. similar terms listed at ken

Fuan 不安 = insecurity, anxiety, uneasiness; from fu = negation + anzen = safety, security; cf. fuantei = instability, insecurity; cf. other related terms listed at kinchou

Fuankan 不安感 = an uneasy feeling, sense of anxiety; from fuan = anxiety, uneasiness + kanjiru = to feel; cf. related terms listed at kinchou

Fuantei 不安定 = instability, insecurity; from fu = negation + antei = stability; cf. fuan = insecurity, anxiety, uneasiness

Fuben 不便 = inconvenient; from fu = negation + benri = convenient

Fubo 父母 = parents; *the parents were foolish bores*; cf. related terms listed at oya

Fuchaku 付着 = adhesion, cohesion; *I spilled food, champagne and Kool-Aid, and they caused adhesion of my shoes to the floor*; cf. related terms listed at yuchaku

Fuchuui 不注意 = carelessness, inattention; from fu = negation + chuui = caution; cf. suki = gap, opening, carelessness, inattentiveness

Fudan 普段 = usual, casual, everyday; *the foolish dancer was casual in her everyday workouts*; cf. related terms listed at taitei

Fuda 札 = label, tag, sign, game card; *my foolish daughter wears a sign on her clothes*; cf. hyoushiki = a written sign; cf. nefuda = price tag; cf. nifuda = tag, label, sign

Fude 筆 = writing brush; *the foolish debutante brushed her teeth with a writing brush*; cf. mouhitsu = a writing or painting brush; cf. tawashi = a scrubbing brush

Fudousan 不動産 = real estate; *if you get into real estate sales, your food will be mostly doughnuts and sandwiches*

Fudousanya 不動産屋 = a real estate office or realtor; from fudousan = real estate + ya = a shop or store

Fudoutoku 不道徳 = immoral; from fu = negation + doutoku = morality; cf. related terms listed at warui

Fue 笛 = a flute or whistle; *the food expert carries a whistle to summon waiters*; cf. kiteki = a steam whistle

Fueru 増える = to increase (intransitive); *in Fukuoka, erudite people's numbers increase every year*; cf. zouka suru = to increase

Fufuku 不服 = dissatisfaction, complaint; *the foolish guy from Fukuoka was full of complaints*; cf. fuman = dissatisfaction; cf. other related terms listed at kujou

Fugou 富豪 = a person of great wealth; *he claimed to be a person of great wealth, but all he had was fool's gold*; cf. kanemochi = a rich person

Fugu フグ = a blowfish or puffer fish; *a food that Goofy liked was puffer fish*; cf. related terms listed at sakana

Fuhai 腐敗 = decomposition, decay, corruption; *the food that we hide outside the refrigerator might be prone to decay*

Fuhai suru 腐敗する = to decay or rot; from fuhai = decomposition, decay, corruption; cf. kuchiru = to rot or decay

Fuhen no 普遍の = constant, unchanging, eternal; *the food the hens eat is unchanging*; cf. ittei no = fixed, settled, constant, uniform; cf. taemanai = constant, incessant; cf. other related terms listed at mugen

Fuhou 不法 = illegal; from fu = negation + houritsu = law; cf. ihou = illegal

Fuhou 訃報 = an obituary, news of a person's death; *I read the obituary of a person who checked into a Fukuoka hotel and never checked out*

Fuhyou 不評 = bad reputation or review, unpopularity; from fu = negation + hyouban = reputation; cf. related terms listed at hyouban

Fui 不意 = sudden, abrupt; *the foolish eagle's attack was abrupt*; cf. related terms listed at ikinari

Fui wo tsuku 不意をつく = to take by surprise; from fui = sudden + tsuku = to arrive

Fu'inki (Fuinki) 雰囲気 (fun'iki is a less common pronunciation) = atmosphere, ambience, mood, air; *those fools are winking at me, and it's affecting the ambience of the party*; cf. igokochi = comfort in a particular ambience

Fuji 藤 = wisteria, usually spelled ふじ; *the foolish genius cut down the wisteria vine*; cf. related terms listed at hana

Fujin 婦人 = woman; *on Mt. Fuji's north slope, a woman lives*; cf. related terms listed at onna

Fujiyuu 不自由 = disability, discomfort, poverty; from fu = negation + jiyuu = freedom; cf. binbou = poverty, poor person; cf. hinkon = poverty

Fukai 深い = deep; *the foolish Kaiser jumped*

into the <u>deep</u> end

Fukaketsu 不可欠 = indispensable; *he spills <u>food</u> in the <u>car</u> and puts <u>ketchup</u> in his <u>soup</u>, but he is <u>indispensable</u> to our project*; cf. related terms listed at hitsuyou

Fukameru 深める = to deepen or elaborate; *when the <u>foolish cabbie</u> met <u>Rudolph</u>, he <u>elaborated</u> on his scheme to develop a flying taxi with a red nose*

Fukanou 不可能 = impossible; from fu = negation + kanou = possible; cf. related terms listed at muri

Fukeiki 不景気 = an economic recession; from fu = negation + keiki = a business condition; cf. fukyou = an economic recession

Fukeru 老ける = to age or lose one's youthful appearance; *the <u>foolish Kennedy</u> ruined his health and began <u>to age</u>*; cf. oiru = to grow old

Fukikakeru 吹きかける = to blow or breathe on; *the foolish king called Kennedy's room and told him to blow on his eyeglasses*; cf. fuku 吹く = to blow, breathe, whistle, play a wind instrument; cf. iki wo suru = to breathe

Fukin 付近 = neighborhood; *I serve <u>food</u> at the <u>kindergarten</u> in our <u>neighborhood</u>*; cf. atari = neighborhood, area; cf. chikaku = neighborhood or vicinity; cf. hen = environs, vicinity; cf. kinjo = neighborhood; cf. kinrin = neighborhood, vicinity; cf. ryouiki = an area, domain or field; cf. soba = neighborhood, vicinity; cf. shuuhen = neighborhood, vicinity; cf. yoko = side or width

Fukinaosu 葺きなおす = to repair a roof; from fuku = to thatch a roof + naosu = to repair

Fukinshin na 不謹慎な = indiscreet; from fu = negation + kinshin = self-restraint

Fukitsu 不吉 = ill omen, unlucky, ominous; *these <u>foolish kittens</u> from <u>Sudan</u> are <u>unlucky</u>*; cf. related terms listed at zenchou = premonition

Fukkatsu 復活 = revival, restoration; from fuku = to repeat, e.g., fukushuu = review; + katsu = life, e.g., seikatsu = life, livelihood; cf. fukkyuu = restoration, resumption of service; cf. henkan = a return or restoration

Fukkyuu 復旧 = restoration, resumption of service; *the <u>foolish Cuban</u> visited the phone company to demand a <u>resumption of service</u>*; cf. fukkatsu = revival, restoration

Fuku 吹く = to blow, breathe, whistle, play a wind instrument; *the wind <u>blows</u> in <u>Fukuoka</u>, and we can <u>breathe</u> easily*; cf. related terms listed at fukikakeru

Fuku 拭く = to wipe or mop; *I <u>mopped</u> the floor in <u>Fukuoka</u>*; cf. nuguu = to wipe

Fuku 服 = clothing; *they wear nice <u>clothes</u> in <u>Fukuoka</u>*; cf. dabodabo = loose clothing, plenty of (when pouring a liquid); cf. emon = clothes or dress; cf. fukusou = outfit, dress style, attire; cf. furugi = used clothes; cf. ifuku = clothing; cf. irui = clothing; cf. ishou = clothing, costume; cf. kimono = a kimono; cf. nishiki = brocade, fine dress; cf. sebiro = a business suit; cf. wafuku = Japanese clothing, kimono; cf. youfuku = Western-style clothing; cf. yukata = an informal summer kimono

Fuku 福 = good luck, fortune; *I had the <u>good luck</u> to visit <u>Fukuoka</u>*; cf. related terms listed at kouun

Fuku ふく = to thatch a roof; *I'll give you some <u>food</u> and <u>Kool</u>-Aid if you <u>thatch</u> my roof*

Fukubu 腹部 = abdomen, stomach; *in <u>Fukuoka</u>, I spilled <u>booze</u> on my <u>abdomen</u>*; cf. related terms listed at onaka

Fukujiteki 副次的 = secondary; *in <u>Fukuoka</u>, jeans are worn by <u>techies</u> who think that fashion is of <u>secondary</u> importance*; cf. tsumaranai = dull, uninspiring, unimportant, tedious, worthless

Fukujuu 服従 = obedience, submission; *the*

submission and obedience of the Fukuoka jury in the presence of the judge was remarkable

Fukujuu suru 服従する = to obey or submit; from fukujuu = obedience, submission; cf. shitagau = to obey or follow

Fukujuushoku 副住職 = vice-priest; in Fukuoka a jury shocked the community by finding a vice-priest guilty; cf. related terms listed at juushoku

Fukumen 覆面 = mask; the Fukuoka men were wearing masks; cf. related terms listed at men

Fukumeru 含める = to include, the transitive form of fukumu = to contain

Fukumu 含む = to contain; in Fukuoka I saw a movie that contained violent content; cf. kuwaeru = to add or include

Fukuro 袋 = a bag, sack, or pack; people carry bags along Fukuoka roads; cf. hyou = a bag or bale; cf. ippyou = one bag; cf. komedawara = a bag of rice; cf. tawara = a straw bag

Fukusanbutsu 副産物 = a byproduct; in Fukuoka sandals and boots can be made from byproducts of the leather industry; cf. related terms listed at sanbutsu

Fukusayou 副作用 = a side-effect; in Fukuoka, I ate some salty yogurt and suffered some side-effects

Fukusei 複製 = reproduction, copy; the Fukuoka sailor made a copy of his will; cf. utsushi = a copy

Fukushi 福祉 = welfare; in Fukuoka, clean sheets are provided by the welfare department; cf. anpi = safety or welfare

Fukushuu 復習 = a review (e.g., of lessons); the Fukuoka shoe store manager did a review of her business policies

Fukusou 服装 = outfit, dress style, attire; from fuku = clothes + souchi = equipment;

cf. related terms listed at fuku

Fukutsuu 腹痛 = stomachache; from fukubu = stomach + tsuu = pain, e.g., zutsuu = headache

Fukuyasan 服屋さん = a clothing store; from fuku = clothing + ya = store + san = an honorific suffix; cf. related terms listed at mise

Fukuyou suru 服用する = to take medicine; eating Fukuoka yogurt is like taking medicine

Fukuzatsu 複雑 = complicated, difficult; at the Fukuoka airport, they zapped my tsuitcase (suitcase) with radiation for some complicated reason; cf. wazurawashii = complicated, troublesome; cf. other related terms listed at muzukashii

Fukyou 不況 = an economic recession; in both Fukuoka and Kyoto, there is an economic recession; cf. fukeiki = an economic recession

Fukyuu no 不朽の = eternal, immortal; the foolish Cuban bought a potion to make himself immortal; cf. related terms listed at mugen

Fukyuu suru 普及する = to become popular or widespread; food fads in Cuba have become widespread; cf. hayaru = to become popular or successful; cf. hiromaru = to pervade or become widespread

Fuman 不満 = dissatisfaction; from fu = negation + manzoku = satisfaction; cf. fufuku = dissatisfaction, complaint

Fumei 不明 = unknown, uncertain; from fu = negation + mei = bright, obvious, e.g., setsumei = explanation; cf. aimai na = ambiguous, vague, unsure; cf. bakuzen = obscure or vague; cf. bakuzen to shita = ambiguous, uncertain, vague; cf. mumei = anonymous, unknown

Fumetsu no 不滅の = immortal, eternal; from fu = negation + metsubou = destruction; cf. related terms listed at mugen

Fuminshou 不眠症 = insomnia; from fu = negation + suimin = sleep + shoujou = symptoms

Fumoto 麓 = foot of a mountain, base; usually spelled ふもと; *the foolish motorcyclists raced up the foot of a mountain*; cf. sanroku = the base of a mountain; cf. yamasuso = the foot or base of a mountain; cf. other related terms listed at kichi

Fumu 踏む = to step on; *the foolish mover stepped on our cat*

Fun 分 = minute (60 seconds); this can also be pronounced -pun or -bun, depending on the number preceding it; *we had fun for a minute*

Funabin 船便 = ship mail; from funa = fune = boat + bin = service, e.g., yuubin = mail

Fune 船 = a ship or boat; this can also be spelled 舟; *a boat took us to the funeral*; cf. gyosen = a fishing boat; cf. kamotsusen = a cargo ship; cf. kisen = a steam ship; cf. kobune = a small boat; cf. watashibune = a ferry

Fungai suru 憤慨する = to be indignant, to resent; *the funny guy was indignant that no one laughed at his jokes*; cf. ikidooru = to resent or get indignant

Fun'iki (Funiki) 雰囲気 – see fuinki

Funin 赴任 = one's post or place of appointment; *the foolish ninja went to his post on the wrong date*

Funinchi 赴任地 = the place of a (new) post or appointment; a combination of funin = one's post or appointment + ninchi = a post or appointment; cf. related terms listed at basho

Funka 噴火 = a volcanic eruption; *the funny car was trapped in a volcanic eruption*; cf. related terms listed at bakuhatsu

Funshitsu suru 紛失する = to lose (something); *I had some funny sheets, but I lost them*; cf. related terms listed at okiwasureru

Funsou 紛争 = a dispute or fight; *I got into a dispute with a funny soldier*; cf. related terms listed at issen

Funsui 噴水 = water fountain; *a funnel carried the Swedish water into the water fountain*

Funtou 奮闘 = hard struggle, strenuous effort; *the funny toad made a strenuous effort to catch the fly*; cf. related terms listed at doryoku

Furareru 振られる = to be given the cold shoulder or rejected; the passive form of furu = to wave, shake or jilt someone

Furatsuku ふらつく = to wander aimlessly, to stagger, to waver; *after I got to furansu (France) with a tsuitcase (suitcase) full of Kool-Aid, I wandered aimlessly*; cf. hourou suru = to wander

Fureru 触れる = to touch, to make contact with something, often unintentionally, to experience things like air, Nature & electric current; *the foolish red rooster touched the electric fence*; cf. ateru = to touch or hit; cf. sawaru = to touch or feel, usually intentional

Furi ふり = pretense or appearance; *the wolf in a furry costume has the appearance or pretense of being a sheep*; cf. buri = "it's like"; cf. other related terms listed at mitame

Furidasu 降り出す = to begin to rain or snow; from furu = to precipitate + dasu = to put out; cf. related terms listed at furu

Furikaeru 振り替える = to change a bill, to transfer money, to switch or move over; from furu = to wave or shake + kaeru = to replace or exchange

Furikaeru 振り返る = to turn the head, look back, think back; *Lot's wife was furious and wanted to kaeru (return), and she looked back at Sodom*; cf. furimuku =

to turn around; cf. kaerimiru = to look back on

Furikake ふりかけ = a dry Japanese seasoning sprinkled on rice; etc.; from furikakeru = to sprinkle

Furikakeru ふりかける = to sprinkle; from furu = to shake or wave + kakeru = to pour; cf. maku = to sow, sprinkle, scatter

Furikomu 振り込む = to transfer; *the furious Communist transferred the Party's money to his own account*; cf. norikaeru = to transfer (trains)

Furimawasu 振り回す = to swing, to wave about; from furu = to shake or wave + mawasu = to turn; cf. related terms listed at furu = to wave

Furimidasu 振り乱す = to dishevel (hair); from furu = to wave or shake + midasu = to disarrange, the transitive form of midareru = to become windblown (hair)

Furimuku 振り向く = to turn around; *I was furious when I had to move the Kool-Aid packages in the display and turned around to talk to the manager*; cf. related terms listed at furikaeru

Furin 不倫 = adultery, immorality; from fu = negation + rinri = ethics

Furiotosu 振り落とす = to throw or shake off; from furu = to wave or shake + otosu = to drop

Furisosogu 降り注ぐ = to rain incessantly, to pour down (this can also be used for sunlight); from furu = to precipitate + sosogu = to pour

Furo 風呂 = a Japanese bath or bathtub; *in Fukuoka I rose from the bath*; cf. onyoku = a warm bath; cf. sentou = a public bath; cf. yokujou = a bath, bathtub, bathhouse, bathroom; cf. yokusou = a bathtub

Furoba 風呂場 = a bathroom (for bathing); from furo = a Japanese bath + basho = place; cf. related terms listed at senmenjo

Furu 振る = to wave, shake or swing, to jilt or dump someone, and many other meanings; *he waved at the foolish rooster*; cf. furimawasu = to swing, to wave about; cf. te wo furu = to wave or shake the hand

Furu 降る = to precipitate rain or snow (but not frost, dew or mist); *the foolish rooster hid whenever it precipitated*; cf. furidasu = to begin to rain or snow; cf. oriru = to precipitate frost, dew or mist

Furueru 震える = to tremble; *his food ruined, the erudite man trembled as the winter approached*; cf. yureru = to sway, shake or rock

Furugi 古着 = used clothes; from furui = old + shitagi = underwear; cf. related terms listed at chuuko and at fuku

Furuhon 古本 = second-hand book; from furui = old + hon = book; cf. related terms listed at hon

Furui 古い = old, ancient (not used to refer to living things); *I was furious when they ruined the old tomb*

Furumai 振る舞い = behavior; *the food was ruined by Michael Jackson's behavior*; cf. fuuzoku = manners or customs; cf. gyougi = conduct, behavior, manners; cf. koudou = behavior, actions; cf. koui = deed, action; cf. okonai = act, behavior; cf. taisaku = measures (actions), strategy

Furumau 振る舞う = to behave, to treat to food or drink; the verb form of furumai = behavior; cf. mau = to dance; cf. okonau = to conduct or perform, to do, to carry out

Furusato 故郷 = hometown, homeland (this can also be pronounce kokyou, with the same meaning); *it was foolish to ruin the satellite tower in my hometown*; cf. hasshouchi = a birthplace or place of origin; cf. inaka = rural area, hometown; cf. jimoto = local, hometown; cf. kokyou = hometown; cf. kyouri = hometown; cf. sato = hometown; cf. shusshin = birthplace, hometown

Furyou 不良 = delinquent, poor condition; *foolish Pope Leo was in poor condition*; cf. related terms listed at keisei and at somatsu

Fusa 房 = a bunch, cluster, tassel; *food is satisfying when it comes in bunches*; cf. related terms listed at taba

Fusagu 塞ぐ = block, to stop up, close; *they fuss and argue and block our way*; cf. related terms listed at shimeru

Fusai 負債 = debt; *it was foolish to stay silent as you piled up debt*; cf. saimu = debt; cf. shakkin = debt

Fusaku 不作 = poor harvest; from fu = negation + sakuhin = creation; cf. related terms listed at sakumotsu

Fuse 布施 = an offering; *the food that we sent was an offering*

Fusegu 防ぐ = to prevent or defend; *I filled the fuse with metallic goo to prevent another blackout*

Fusei 不正 = wrongdoing, unlawfulness, dishonesty; from fu = negation + seikaku = truthful; cf. related terms listed at tsumi

Fusei torihiki 不正取引 = dishonest dealings; from fusei = dishonesty + torihiki = business deal

Fuseijitsu 不誠実 = insincere, dishonest; from fu = negation + seijitsu = sincere; cf. hanpa = insincere, incomplete, insufficient

Fuseiritsu 不成立 = a failure; from fu = negation + seiritsu = coming into existence; cf. related terms listed at shippai

Fuseru 伏せる = to lay an object upside down or face down, to lie down, to cast one's eyes down; *the foolish seller made it a rule to lay his merchandise face down*; cf. related terms listed at yoko ni naru

Fushi 節 = knot (wood), joint (body), melody; *the food the sheep were eating caused their joints to swell*; cf. related terms listed at kansetsu and at uta

Fushigi 不思議 = mysterious, strange, magical; *the food that I put out for the sheep and the geese disappeared, which was strange*; cf. shinpiteki = mysterious; cf. other related terms listed at kimyou

Fushinsha 不信者 = a person who doesn't believe, an unbeliever; from fu = negation + shinjiru = to believe + sha = a person; cf. kyouto = an adherent (of a religion)

Fushou 負傷 = injury, wound; *that foolish guy shows everyone his wound*; cf. kega = an injury; cf. kizu = a scar, injury or wound

Fushouji 不祥事 = scandal; *when the foolish short guy stole a Jeep, he caused a scandal*; cf. shuubun = a scandal

Fusoku 不足 = lack or shortage; *the food is soaked with sauce, but there's a lack of flavor*; cf. ketsujo = a deficiency or lack; cf. other related terms listed at naki

Futa 蓋 = a cover, bottle cap or lid; *when I have a full tank of water, I put a cover on it*; cf. sen = a bottle cap, cork or stopper

Futago 双子 = twins; from futatsu = two + go = ko = a child

Futamata 二股 = a parting of the way, two-timing; from futatsu = two + mata = a thigh

Futamata kakeru 二股かける = to two-time or have two lovers at once, to sit on the fence; from futamata = two-timing + kakeru = to expend

Futan 負担 = responsibility, burden, charge; *the foolish tanning center owner had to take responsibility for causing skin cancer, and he carried that burden*; cf. jama = burden, disturbance; cf. omoni = a burden; cf. other related terms listed at tsutome

Futatabi 再び = again; *again, he put food on the tatami mat for the beast*; cf. related terms listed at aratamete

Futo ふと = accidentally, suddenly, casually; *the foolish Tory accidentally fell down*; cf.

related terms listed at kyuu ni

Futoi 太い = thick, boldface (letters), deep (voice), brazen or rude; *the foolish toy maker made his dolls too thick*; cf. related terms listed at koi

Futokoro 懐 = bosom, heart; *I sleep on a futon in my Corolla, and that's where my heart is*; cf. related terms listed at kokoro

Futokoro ga hiroi 懐が広い = is kind-hearted; from futokoro = heart + hiroi = spacious; cf. related terms listed at yasashii = kind

Futon 布団 = floor cushion, or Japanese bedding; *foolish Tony Blair spilled coffee onto his Japanese bedding*

Futorisugi 太りすぎ = overweight; from futoru = to gain weight + sugiru = to exceed

Futoru 太る = to gain weight; *since I gained weight, I have to sleep on the futon in that room*; cf. koeru = to put on weight, to become fertile

Futosa 太さ = thickness; from futoi = thick + sa, a suffix that makes a noun from an adjective

Futou 不当 = unjust or unfair; from fu = negation + touzen = justly, natural; cf. related terms listed at rifujin

Futsukayoi 二日酔い = a hangover; from futsuka = two days (or the second day, in this case) + you = to get drunk

Futsuu 普通 = ordinary, usual, general, average; this can also = local train; *in the usual or general case, the foot that the supervisor uses for kicking is the right one*; cf. heikin = average, mean; cf. soujite = in general, on the whole; cf. other related terms listed at densha and at taitei

Futtou suru 沸騰する = to boil; from futtou = boiling; cf. related terms listed at nieru

Futtou 沸騰 = boiling, seething; *the foolish toad stayed in the water until it was boiling*

Fuu 風 = appearance, condition, style; *the appearance of buildings in Fukuoka reveals a certain style*; cf. related terms listed at keisei

Fuubutsu 風物 = natural features, characteristic things like scenery, customs, etc.; from fuu = style + butsu = thing

Fuubutsushi 風物詩 = a thing that reminds us of a particular season; from fuubutsu = characteristic things + shi = poetry

Fuufu 夫婦 = married couple; *that married couple may be foolish, but they make good food*

Fuukei 風景 = a view, scenery or landscape; *the foolish caterer wasted time looking at the scenery*; cf. related terms listed at nagame

Fuukeiga 風景画 = a landscape painting; from fuukei = landscape + ga = drawing, e.g., manga = comics; cf. related terms listed at e

Fuumi 風味 = taste or flavor; *the food in that meal had a delicious flavor*; cf. aji = taste; cf. ajitsuke = seasoning, flavor; cf. choumiryou = flavoring, seasoning; cf. kami = seasoning or flavor; cf. other related terms listed at aji

Fuun 不運 = bad luck; from fu = negation + un = luck; cf. related terms listed at kouun

Fuurin 風鈴 = wind chime; *foolish Ringo hung wind chimes inside his house*; cf. related terms listed at suzu

Fuuryuu 風流 = refined; *sometimes food can be reused and refined into something better*; cf. related terms listed at jouhin

Fuusa 封鎖 = a blockade; *foolish Saruman tried to set up a blockade of Gandalf's castle*

Fuusai 風采 = personal appearance or presence; *the foolish scientist neglected her personal appearance*

Fuutou 封筒 = an envelope; *he was furious*

about the <u>tomato</u> sauce staining the <u>envelope</u>

Fuuzoku 風俗 = manners or customs; *our <u>custom</u> is to eat <u>food</u> with <u>Zooey</u>'s <u>Kool</u>-Aid*; cf. related terms listed at furumai

Fuwa 不和 = discord, disagreement; a discordant or hostile relationship; from fu = negation + wa = harmony; cf. related terms listed at kankei

Fuwafuwa ふわふわ = fluffy, floating, frivolously, spongy, soft; from fluffy

Fuwari ふあり = softly, gently, lightly; *the <u>food</u> that the <u>warrior</u> ate was prepared <u>gently</u>*; cf. related terms listed at karugaru and at sotto

Fuyasu 増やす = to increase (transitive); the transitive form of fueru = to increase

Fuyou 扶養 = support, raising (of children); *the <u>foolish</u> <u>yogi</u> failed to pay child <u>support</u>*; cf. related terms listed at enjo

Fuyu 冬 = winter; *the dancer said "I <u>fooled</u> <u>you</u>" after escaping during the <u>winter</u>*; cf. related terms listed at kisetsu

Fuyukai 不愉快 = unpleasant; from fu = negation + yukai = pleasant; cf. iya = unpleasant, disgusting

Fuzai 不在 = absence; from fu = negation + zai = to exist or stay, e.g., taizai suru = to stay (at a hotel, etc.); cf. kesseki = absence; cf. nasa = absence, nonexistence; cf. rusu = absence, being away from home

Ga が = but; *he's <u>gabby</u>, <u>but</u> he has a good heart*; cf. related terms listed at demo

Gachi がち = a tendency to do something, used after a verb stem; e.g., yasumigachi = a tendency to rest or be absent; *I have a <u>tendency</u> <u>to</u> look for <u>gas</u> that's <u>cheap</u>*; cf. keikou = tendency, inclination, trend; cf. muki = direction, suitability, tendency

Gai 外 = outside, used as a word component, e.g., gaibu = the outside world; this can also be pronounced soto = outside; cf. related terms listed at soto

Gai 害 = harm; *that <u>guy</u> caused me <u>harm</u>*; cf. related terms listed at sawari

Gaiaku 害悪 = evil, a bad influence; from gai = harm + aku = evil; cf. related terms listed at warui

Gaibu 外部 = the outside world, exterior; *this is a <u>guidebook</u> to the <u>outside world</u>*; cf. gai = outside, used as a word component; cf. related terms listed at ichibu and at soto

Gaijin 外人 – see gaikokujin

Gaikan 外観 = surface, exterior; *that <u>guy</u> uses <u>candles</u> to light the <u>exterior</u> of his house*; cf. gaiken = appearance; cf. hyoumen = surface, exterior; cf. men = mask, face, surface or aspect; cf. omote = surface, front

Gaiken 外見 = appearance; from gai = outside, e.g., gaijin = foreigner; + ken = to look, e.g., haiken suru = to look humbly; cf. related terms listed at mitame

Gaikoku 外国 = a foreign country; from gaibu = the outside world + koku = country; cf. related terms listed at kuni

Gaikokujin 外国人 = a foreigner; from gaikoku = a foreign country + jin = a person

Gaikotsu 骸骨 = a skeleton; *the <u>guide</u> took two <u>coats</u> and wrapped the <u>skeleton</u> that he found on the mountain*; cf. related terms listed at hone

Gaikou 外交 = diplomacy; from gaikoku = a foreign country + koushou = negotiation

Gainen 概念 = a concept or general idea; *a spiritual <u>guide</u> taught my <u>negative</u> <u>nephew</u> some <u>concepts</u> about enlightenment*; cf. kousou = a plan or concept

Gairai 外来 = foreign, outpatient (as opposed to inpatient); from gai = outside, e.g., gaijin = a foreigner; + rai = to come, e.g., rainen = next year; cf. kaigai = overseas, foreign

Gairai no 外来の = from outside, foreign, outpatient (as opposed to inpatient); from gai = outside, e.g., gaijin = foreigner; + rai = to come, e.g., rainen = next year

Gairaishu 外来種 = non-native species; from gairai = foreign + shurui = variety or type

Gaisan 概算 = a rough estimate; from gainen = a general idea + sansuu = arithmetic; cf. oyoso = an estimate or outline, approximately

Gaishite 概して = generally, for the most part; from gainen = a general idea + suru = to do; cf. related terms listed at taitei

Gaishutsu 外出 = going out; from gaibu = the outside world + shutsu = emerging or exiting

Gaitou 街灯 = a street light; *the guide hit his toe on a street light*

Gaitou 該当 = application, correspondence; *the guide used his toe to show the correspondence between the map on the ground and the trail we were following*; cf. related terms listed at moushikomi

Gaitou suru 該当する = to correspond, apply or fall under; from gaitou = application, correspondence

Gaiyou 概要 = an outline or summary; from gainen = a concept or general idea + youkou = an outline or main point

Gajou 賀状 = a New Year's card; *the gambler and Joan of Arc always send each other New Year's cards*; cf. nengajou = a New Year's card

Gaka 画家 = an artist or painter; *the painter put gas in his car*; cf. related terms listed at geijutsuka

Gakai 瓦解 = a collapse or downfall; *Gandalf's kite business underwent a collapse*

Gake 崖 = a precipice or cliff; *gallant Ken leaped from the cliff to rescue Barbie*; cf. related terms listed at dangai

Gakka 学科 = a subject of study; from gaku = study or learning + ka = a course

Gakkari がっかり = disappointment; *the amount of gas that I can carry in my car is a disappointment*; cf. genmetsu = disillusionment; cf. hikan fee = pessimism, disappointment; cf. kakusei = waking up, disillusionment; cf. rakutan = disappointment, dejection, discouragement

Gakki 学期 = a semester; *the gawky king only attended for one semester*

Gakki 楽器 = a musical instrument; *the gawky musicians all had musical instruments*; cf. gengakki = a stringed instrument; cf. wagakki = a traditional Japanese musical instrument

Gakkou 学校 = a school; *I took a gardening course in school*; cf. chuugakkou = a junior high school or middle school; cf. daigaku = a college or university; cf. juku = cram school, private school; cf. koukou = a high school; cf. shijuku = a private school (in a house); cf. shougakkou = an elementary school; cf. shougaku = elementary school

Gaku 学 = study or learning; *his study is of gardens in Kuwait*; cf. related terms listed at benkyou and at chishiki

Gaku 額 = a sum of money; *I paid a sum of money for a gallon of Kool-Aid*; cf. related terms listed at kikin

Gaku 顎 = a jaw or chin, used as a word component; *I injured my jaw in a garden in Kuwait*; cf. ago = a jaw or chin

Gakubu 学部 = a department of a university, an undergraduate; from gaku = study + bu = section

Gakudan 楽団 = orchestra or band; from ongaku = music; + dantai = group

Gakufu 楽譜 = sheet music; *I spilled a gallon of Kool-Aid and some food on your sheet music*

Gakui 学位 = a degree (academic); from gaku = study + i = rank or place; cf. gakushigou = a bachelor's degree

Gakukansetsu 顎関節 = the jaw (temporomandibular) joint; from gaku = a jaw + kansetsu = a joint

Gakureki 学歴 = academic background; from gaku = learning, e.g., gakusei = a student; + rekishi = history

Gakusei 学生 = a student; from gaku = study or learning + sei = a person; cf. daigakusei = a college student; cf. joshikousei = a female high school student; cf. jukusei = a cram school student; cf. seito = a student; cf. shuusai = an outstanding student or an able person

Gakusha 学者 = a scholar; from gaku = learning + sha = a person

Gakushi 学士 = a university gradute; from gaku = study + shi = a man, e.g., heishi = a soldier; cf. sotsugyousei = a graduate

Gakushigou 学士号 = a bachelor's degree; from gakushi = a university graduate + gou = a number, e.g., bangou = a number; cf. gakui = a degree

Gakushuu 学習 = study, learning; from gaku = learning, + shuu = learning by repeating, e.g., renshuu = practice; cf. related terms listed at benkyou and at chishiki

Gakuzen 愕然 = shock, astonishment, terror; *when I drank a gallon of Kool-Aid, the Zen monk expressed shock*; cf. related terms listed at osore

Gaman 我慢 = patience, endurance; *the garbage man has patience and endurance*; cf. related terms listed at nintai

Gamanzuyosa 我慢強さ = patience, perseverance (this is spelled gamanduyosa in electronic dictionaries); from gaman = patience + zuyoi = tsuyoi = strong + sa, a suffix that makes a noun from an adjective; cf. related terms listed at nintai

Gamen 画面 = an (electronic) screen, a picture or photo; *Gandalf mended the TV screen*; cf. related terms listed at men

Gamigami がみがみ = nagging, griping; *the gambler will serve as a mediator to try to stop the griping*; cf. related terms listed at kujou

Gan 癌 = cancer, usually written がん; *Gandalf can cure cancer*; cf. related terms listed at byouki

Gan chiryou がん治療 = cancer treatment; from gan = cancer + chiryou = medical treatment

Ganban 岩盤 = bedrock; *Gandalf dug a bank vault into bedrock*; cf. related terms listed at ishi = a pebble

Ganbaru 頑張る = to persevere, to do one's best; *when Gandalf is at a bar with his roommates, he does his best to control his drinking*; cf. related terms listed at tsuzukeru and at zensho suru

Gangan ガンガン = splitting or pounding (headache), intense, a lot, e.g., gangan suru = to have a splitting or pounding (headache); gangan taberu = to eat a lot; *Gandalf and his gang split the enemy and then had a lot to eat*

Ganjitsu 元日 = New Year's Day; *Gandalf met the jittery superstar on New Year's Day*; cf. related terms listed at shougatsu

Ganjou 頑丈 = sturdy, strong; *Gandalf and Joan of Arc are sturdy and strong*; cf. related terms listed at tsuyoi

Ganka 眼科 = ophthalmology; *Gandalf calculates that he can make money from ophthalmology*; cf. related terms listed at gankagaku

Gankagaku 眼科学 = the study of ophthalmology; from ganka = ophthalmology + gaku = study; cf. ganka = ophthalmology; cf. hi'nyoukika = a urology department; cf. i = a doctor, or the field of medicine; cf. jibiinkouka =

otorhinolaryngology; cf. jibika = ear, nose & throat specialty; cf. naika = internal medicine; cf. shika = dentistry, dental clinic; cf. shounika = pediatrics

Ganko 頑固 = stubborn; *Gandalf has a cold, but he is too stubborn to take medicine*; cf. danko = resolute

Gankyou 眼鏡 = eyeglasses (this can also be read "megane," with the same meaning); *Gandalf went to Kyouto to get some eyeglasses*; cf. megane = eyeglasses

Ganseki 岩石 = rock; *Gandalf buried the selfish king in rock*; cf. related terms listed at ishi = a pebble

Ganshou 岩礁 = reef; *Gandalf hurt his shoulder on the reef*

Gan'yuu (Ganyuu) 含有 = content; *that gang of youths posted hateful content on the internet*; cf. naiyou = content, substance; cf. nakami = contents

Gappei 合併 = a merger, combination or union; *the merger reduced the gap in pay between the two companies*; cf. related terms listed at rengou

Gara 柄 = a pattern, a body build; this can also be pronounced e = a handle; *I keep patterns in my garage*

Garasu bari ガラス張り = glass-sided; from garasu = glass; + baru = haru = to stretch or spread; *Hawaiian roosters spread their wings*

Garou 画廊 = an art gallery; from gaka = an artist + rouka = a hallway

Garu がる = appears to (have certain feelings), used as a suffix after i adjective stems (to make an i adjective stem, remove the final "i"), or after na adjectives; e.g., hoshii = desiring, hoshigaru = appears to desire; also, tabetagaru = appearing to want to eat, derived from tabetai = to want to eat + garu; also, iyagaru = appears to dislike; *Gandalf's room appears to be enchanted*; cf. -gachi = a tendency to do something

Gashan ガシャン = a crash, bang, breaking sound; *Gandalf broke into the shanty with a crash*; cf. batan = a thud, bang, slam, crash

Gashi 餓死 = starvation; *the garden was full of sheep suffering from starvation*; cf. ue = hunger, starvation

Gashi suru 餓死する = to die of starvation; from gashi = starvation; cf. ueru = to starve, to be thirsty or hungry

Gassaku 合作 = collaboration, joint work; *I went out to the garden with a sack of seeds, to start a collaboration with my neighbor*

Gasshou 合唱 = a chorus; *it was a ghastly show, but I sang in the chorus*

Gasshoudan 合唱団 = chorus goup, choir; from gasshou = chorus + dantai = group

Gasshuukoku 合衆国 = a federal state; *the gambler took off his shoes and drank a Coke when he arrived in the federal state*

Gata 形 – see kata

Gatsu 月 – see getsu

Gawa 側 = side, used as a suffix, e.g., madogawa = the window side; *there was a gas war on that side of town*; cf. related terms listed at hou = direction or side

Gazou 画像 = picture (film, TV); from gamen = an electronic picture + zou = an image; cf. related terms listed at eiga

Geemu ki ゲーム機 = game machine; from geemu + kikai = machine; cf. related terms listed at kikai

Gehin 下品 = vulgar, coarse, indecent; *the guest hinted that our behavior was vulgar*; cf. related terms listed at mittomonai

Gei 芸 = art or craft, animal trick; *arts, crafts and tricks were all a game to him*; cf. related terms listed at geijutsu

Geijutsu 芸術 = art; *she gazes at the bay window that juts out from the house and* declares it a kind of *art*; cf. bijutsu = visual art; cf. gei = art or craft, animal trick; cf. tougei = ceramic art

Geijutsuka 芸術家 = an artist; from geijutsu = art + ka = person; cf. aachisuto = an artist; cf. gaka = a painter or artist

Geijutsukan 芸術館 = art museum; from geijutsu = art + kan = large building; cf. bijutsukan = an art museum or gallery; cf. hakubutsukan = a museum (other than art)

Geiko 芸子 = geisha; *the gay coder was infatuated with a geisha*; cf. related terms listed at geisha

Geimaiko 芸舞妓 = geisha and maiko; from geisha + maiko; cf. related terms listed at geisha

Geinin 芸人 = actor, performer; from gei = art or craft + nin = person; cf. related terms listed at haiyuu

Geinou 芸能 = entertainment, performance; *the gay Norwegians put on a performance*; cf. related terms listed at shutsuen

Geisha 芸者 = a geisha; from gei = art + sha = person; cf. geiko = a geisha; cf. geimaiko = geisha and maiko; cf. hangyoku = an apprentice or child geisha; cf. maiko = an apprentice geisha

Geka 外科 = surgery; *Genghis Khan underwent surgery*; cf. shujutsu = surgery

Geki 劇 = a play; *I saw the guests kissing during the play*; cf. gikyoku = a drama or play; cf. kageki = an opera

Geki 激 = violent, intense, passionate, used as a word component; *the guest who took our keys was intense*

Gekidan 劇団 = a theatrical company; from geki = a play + dantai = a group of people; cf. related terms listed at dantai

Gekido 激怒 = fury, outrage; *he felt fury when he saw the guest key in the door*; cf. related terms listed at uppun

Gekigen 激減 = sharp decrease; from geki = intense + genshou = a decrease; cf. related terms listed at genshou

Gekijou 劇場 = a theater; from geki = play + jou = place; cf. eigagan = a move theater

Gekirei 激励 = encouragement; *when I saw the guest eating quiche in the rain, I offered her some encouragement that the weather would improve*; cf. seien = support, cheering, encouragement; cf. shourei = encouragement or promotion

Gekisen 激戦 = fierce competition or battle; from geki = intense + sensou = war; cf. related terms listed at issen = battle

Gekiteki 劇的 = dramatic, exciting; from geki = a play + teki = related to

Gekitsuu 激痛 = intense, sharp pain; from geki = intense + tsuu = pain, e.g., zutsuu = headache; cf. related terms listed at itami

Gekkanshi 月刊誌 = monthly magazine; from getsu = month + kankou suru = to publish + shi = magazine, e.g., zasshi = magazine; cf. related terms listed at zasshi

Gekkyuu 月給 = monthly salary; from getsu = month + kyuuryou = salary; cf. related terms listed at chin

Gen 弦 = a bow or string (for a musical instrument); *Genghis always kept an extra guitar string handy*; cf. related terms listed at himo

Gen'an (Genan) 原案 = the original proposal or plan; from gen'in = source + teian = proposal; cf. related terms listed at teian

Genba 現場 = actual spot, scene, site, location; *Genghis was shot in this bar, so this is the scene of the crime*; cf. related terms listed at bamen and at basho

Genbaku 原爆 = atomic bomb; an abbreviation of genshibakudan; from genshi = atom + bakudan = bomb; cf. related terms listed at bakudan

Genchi 現地 = location, the place, local; from genjitsu = reality + chi = ground or place; cf. related terms listed at basho

Gendai 現代 = modern times, nowadays; *Genghis would be put on a diet if he lived nowadays*; cf. related terms listed at ima

Gendankai 現段階 = present stage, current phase; from gendai = modern times + dankai = a stage of development; cf. dankai = a stage of development or step

Gengakki 弦楽器 = a stringed instrument; from gen = a string + gakki = a musical instrument; cf. related terms listed at gakki

Gengo 言語 = language; *Genghis had a goal to learn new languages*; cf. bokugo = one's native language; cf. hougen = a dialect; cf. keigo = honorific language; cf. kotoba = language, word

Gengogaku 言語学 = linguistics; from gengo = language + gaku = learning, e.g., gakusei = student

Gen'in (Genin) 原因 = cause, origin, source; *Genghis had international ambitions, and they were the cause of his endless wars*; cf. related terms listed at kigen

Genjitsu 現実 = reality, fact; *Genghis Khan was a jittery superstar, and that's a fact*; cf. related terms listed at hontou

Genjou 現状 = present condition; *Genghis jokes about our present condition*; cf. related terms listed at keisei

Genkai 限界 = limit; *Genghis flew kites along his borders to mark the limit of his domain*; cf. gentei = restriction, limit; cf. hodo = extent, degree, limits, moderation, approximate time, about so much; cf. kagiri = limit, degree, as far as possible, the end; cf. kiri = an end or limit; cf. seigen = limit, restriction; cf. sokubaku = a restraint, restriction, or confinement; cf. waku = a frame, framework, limit

Genkaku 厳格 = stern, strict; *Genghis called the Kool-Aid ban excessively strict*; cf. kibishii = stern, strict

Genkaku 幻覚 = hallucination; *Genghis drank the cactus juice and had hallucinations*; cf. gensou = fantasy, illusion; cf. maboroshi = illusion, vision; cf. sakkaku = an illusion or misunderstanding

Genkan 玄関 = entranceway; *Genghis Khan's palace had a grand entranceway*

Genki 元気 = healthy, fine, energetic; *Genghis learned that his kidneys were healthy*; cf. gouken = vigor, health, sturdiness; cf. joubu = healthy, hearty, strong; cf. mubyou = in perfect health; cf. sukoyaka = vigorous, healthy, sound

Genkin 現金 = cash; *Genghis was a king who always paid in cash*

Genko 拳固 = a fist, usually spelled げんこ; *when Genghis wanted corn, he would slam his fist on the table*; cf. kobushi = a fist

Genkou 原稿 = a draft or manuscript; *Genghis told the court to suppress the manuscript*; cf. related terms listed at sengen

Genkouhan 現行犯 = in the act, red-handed; *since Genghis had cold hands, he dropped the crowbar, and they caught him in the act*

Genkyuu suru 言及する = to mention or refer to; *the report mentioned the fact that Genghis had gone to Cuba*

Genmai 玄米 = brown or unpolished rice; *Genghis had mice that ate brown rice*; cf. related terms listed at gohan

Genmetsu 幻滅 = disillusionment; *when Genghis met Superman, he felt disillusionment*; cf. related terms listed at gakkari

Genpatsu 原発 = nuclear power; *Genghis patted the supervisor on the back after he developed nuclear power*

Genri 原理 = a principle; *Genghis realized that he should adhere to his principles*; cf. related terms listed at rinen

Genryou 原料 = raw materials; *Genghis Khan and Pope Leo started a company to harvest raw materials*; cf. related terms listed at zairyou

Gensan 原産 = place of origin, habitat; from gen'in = cause + san = to produce, e.g., sangyou = industry; cf. related terms listed at kigen

Genshi 原子 = atom; *Genghis said that his sheets were made of atoms*

Genshibakudan 原子爆弾 = an atomic bomb, often abbreviated to genbaku; from genshi = atom + bakudan = a bomb; cf. related terms listed at bakudan

Genshiro 原子炉 = a nuclear reactor; from genshi = an atom + ro = a furnace

Genshou 現象 = phenomenon; *Genghis said that the shore was a natural phenomenon*; cf. related terms listed at dekigoto

Genshou 減少 = a decrease; *Genghis showed how a tax decrease could help the people*; cf. gekigen = a sharp decrease; cf. kaishou = reduction, cancellation, resolution; cf. ochikomi = a decline; cf. sakugen = a curtailment or reduction; cf. shukushou = a reduction or cutback

Genshou suru 減少する = to decrease; from genshou = a decrease; cf. hangen suru = to reduce by half; cf. heru = to reduce, to dwindle, to lose (weight), to get hungry (hara ga heru); cf. kagen suru = to moderate, downgrade; cf. keigen suru = to reduce or alleviate; cf. otoroeru = to become infirm, to decline; cf. otosu = to drop (transitive), to lose, to decrease; cf. sageru = to hang (transitive), lower, reduce, remove; cf. shizumeru = to alleviate or suppress, to calm; cf. sutareru = to become obsolete, to decline; cf. teika suru = to decrease; cf. tenraku suru = to fall or decline

Genshu suru 厳守する = to observe strictly (regulations, etc.); *Genghis had shoes that had to be polished every day, and his instructions for doing so were observed strictly*; cf. related terms listed at mamoru

Genshuku na 厳粛な = solemn or serious; *Genghis wore shoes from Kuwait for solemn occasions*; cf. related terms listed at maji

Genso 元素 = an element (chemical); *Genghis sold elements like silver to earn money*

Gensoku 原則 = a general rule; *as a general rule, Genghis soaks in the tub every night*; cf. related terms listed at kisoku

Gensou 幻想 = fantasy, illusion; *Genghis and his soldiers were fooled by an illusion*; cf. genkaku = hallucination; cf. maboroshi = illusion, vision; cf. mousou = a fantasy or delusion

Gensouteki 幻想的 = fantastic, magical; from gensou = fantasy, illusion + teki = related to; cf. mahou no = magical

Gentei 限定 = restriction, limit; *Genghis taped the restrictions on a wall*; cf. related terms listed at genkai

Genzai 現在 = nowadays, present time; *Genghis said that the zeitgeist (spirit of the age) at the present time was decadent*; cf. related terms listed at ima

Genzei 減税 = tax reduction; from genshou = a decrease + zeikin = tax; cf. related terms listed at zeikin

Geppu 月賦 = a monthly installment or payment; *the guest was poor, but she kept up with her monthly payments*; cf. related terms listed at hensai

Geri 下痢 = diarrhea; *I had diarrhea after visiting the Getty Museum*

Geru ゲル = a ger = a yurt, a traditional portable home common in central Asia

Gesui 下水 = sewage; *the guest's Swedish*

meatballs fell into the sewage; cf. related terms listed at mizu

Gesuikan 下水管 = a sewer pipe; from gesui = sewage + kan = a pipe or tube; cf. related terms listed at kuda

Geta 下駄 = Japanese clogs; *when I went to get apples, I wore my Japanese clogs*; cf. related terms listed at kutsu

Getsu 月 = month, used as a word component, e.g., sengetsu = last month; *he will get super rich in a month*

Getsugaku 月額 = a monthly sum; from getsu = month + kingaku = a sum of money; cf. related terms listed at kikin

Getsugakusei 月額制 = a monthly payment system; from getsugaku = a monthly sum + seido = system; cf. similar terms listed at seido

Getsumatsu 月末 = the end of a month; from getsu = month + matsu = end, e.g., shuumatsu = a weekend; cf. similar terms listed at shuumatsu

Gichou 議長 = a chairperson; from kaigi = a meeting + chou = a chief

Giin 議員 = a member of a legislature; from gikai = a national assembly, Congress or Diet; + in = a group member; cf. related terms listed at in

Gijutsu 技術 = technology, technique, skill; *this guitar juts out in various places, demonstrating the technique of its maker*; cf. gikou = technique, skill; cf. nouryoku = skill, ability, competence; cf. tegiwa = skill, performance, tact; cf. waza = skill, technique

Gikai 議会 = a national assembly, Congress or Diet; *the geeky Kaiser spoke to the national assembly*; cf. related terms listed at kokkai

Gikou 技巧 = technique, skill; *the geeky coder was known for his skill and his innovative techniques*; cf. related terms listed at gijutsu

Gikyoku 戯曲 = a drama or play; *I saw a drama about geese at the Kyoto Kool-Aid Club*; cf. related terms listed at geki

Gimon 疑問 = a question or doubt; *the guitar-playing monkey was consumed by doubt*; cf. related terms listed at utagai

Gimu 義務 = unlimited duty to the emperor, ancestors and descendants; *the geese on the moor must perform their unlimited duty to their offspring*; cf. giri = moral debt, limited duty to the outside world; cf. kinmu = service, duty, work; cf. ninmu = duty, mission; on = indebtedness, obligation, gratitude

Gin 銀 = silver; *I paid silver for this gin*; cf. related terms listed at tanso

Ginga 銀河 = Milky Way, galaxy; from gin = silver + ga = river, e.g., unga = canal

Ginkou 銀行 = a bank; *there's a ginkgo tree outside that bank*

Ginkou furikomi 銀行振り込み = bank transfer; from ginkou = bank + furikomu = to transfer

Ginmi suru 吟味する = to check in detail, to examine; *we will examine whether gin was served at the meeting*; cf. related terms listed at sousaku suru

Giri 義理 = moral debt, limited duty to the outside world; *the captain felt giddy during the storm, but he had to do his limited duty*; cf. gimu = unlimited duty to the emperor, ancestors and descendants; cf. kinmu = service, duty, work; cf. ninmu = duty, mission

Girigiri ギリギリ = at the last moment, just barely; *the gears rewound and the geese were released at the last moment*

Giron 議論 = discussion, controversy, argument; *the geese that Ronald Reagan kept in his yard caused some controversy*; cf. related terms listed at rikutsu

Gisei 犠牲 = a victim, a sacrifice; *the geese*

were *saved for the sacrifice*; cf. related terms listed at hisaisha

Gisei ni suru 犠牲にする = to sacrifice; from gisei = sacrifice + ni suru = to make A into B

Gisei wo harau 犠牲を払う = to make sacrifices for, to pay dearly for; from gisei = a sacrifice + harau = to pay

Giseisha 犠牲者 = a victim; from gisei = a victim + sha = a person; cf. related terms listed at hisaisha

Gishi 技師 = engineer; *the engineer keeps his gear wrapped in a sheet of plastic*

Gishiki 儀式 = ritual, ceremony, formality; *during the ceremony, geese were presented to the Shiite king*; cf. shiki = a ceremony or rite

Giwaku 疑惑 = a suspicion or doubt; *some geese were recruited for the war against the Kool-Aid industry, but they had doubts about their mission*; cf. related terms listed at utagai

Go ご = an honorific or humble prefix; *this is an honorable goat*; cf. o = an honorific or humble prefix

Go 後 = after, used as a suffix; *I will go after you*; cf. related terms listed at kongo

Go 碁 = a Japanese board game; *my goal when playing a Japanese board game is to win*

Go 語 = language, word; *my goal is to learn new words in a foreign language*

Goannai ご案内 – see annai

Gobu 五分 = half, 50%, tie; from go = five + bu = part (**Note:** this can also be read as gofun = five minutes); cf. related terms listed at han

Gobusata ご無沙汰 = a long silence, not contacting for a while; from go = a humble prefix + bu = mu = negation + sata = communication; cf. related terms listed at seijaku

Gochisou ご馳走 = a delicacy; *the goat cheese sold out, since it was a delicacy*; cf. related terms listed at tabemono

Gofuku 呉服 = cloth (for Japanese clothes), textile; *if you go to Fukuoka, you should buy some textiles*; cf. related terms listed at nuno

Gofukuya 呉服屋 = a dry goods store, a kimono store; from gofuku = cloth (for Japanese clothes) + ya = a shop or store; cf. related terms listed at mise

Gogo 午後 = afternoon, p.m.; *let's go golfing in the afternoon*; cf. related terms listed at hiru

Gohan ご飯 = cooked rice, a meal; *the ghost offered Hansel some cooked rice*; cf. genmai = brown or unpolished rice; cf. hakumai = white rice; cf. kome = uncooked white rice; cf. mochigome = glutinous rice; cf. raisu = rice; cf. shari = rice prepared for sushi; cf. related terms listed at ryouri and at tabemono

Goi 語彙 = vocabulary; *the goalie spend his evenings learning new vocabulary*; cf. goui = agreement; cf. related terms listed at kotoba

Gokai 誤解 = a misunderstanding; *due to a misunderstanding, the gold to pay the Kaiser didn't arrive*; cf. kanchigai = a misunderstanding, wrong guess

Gokoku 五穀 = the five grains (wheat, rice, beans, awa and kibi; awa and kibi are kinds of millet); from go = five + kokumotsu = grain; cf. related terms listed at mugi

Gokoku houjou 五穀豊穣 = a bumper crop; from gokoku = the five grains + houjou = good harvest; cf. related terms listed at sakumotsu

Goku ごく = quite, extremely, very (this can also be spelled 極 or 極く); *the gold Kool-Aid is extremely good*; cf. related terms listed at ooi ni

Gokuchiisai 極小さい = very small; from goku = extremely + chiisai = small; cf. related terms listed at chiisai

Gomen (nasai) ごめん(なさい) = I'm sorry, excuse me; *I'm sorry that those goat men and some nasty scientists made me late*; cf. related terms listed at sumimasen

Gomi ゴミ = trash, garbage; *the goat was meaning to pick through the trash*

Gomibako ゴミ箱 = a wastebasket or garbage can; from gomi = garbage + hako = bako = a box; cf. related terms listed at hako

Gomu ゴム = gum, rubber, an eraser

Gongen 権現 = an incarnation of Buddha, an avatar; *Gonzalez thinks Genghis Khan was an incarnation of Buddha*

Goraku 娯楽 = diversion, recreation, entertainment; *golf and racketball are recreations*; cf. asobi = play, diversion, game, having a good time

Goran ご覧 = honorably seeing or looking; *were you honorably seeing gophers on that ranch?*

Goran ni naru ご覧になる = to see, look or watch honorably; from goran = honorably seeing or looking; cf. related terms listed at miru

Gorenraku ご連絡 = honorable contact or communication; from go = an honorific prefix + renraku = contact or communication; cf. tsuushin = communication

Goro 頃 – see -koro

Gorogoro ゴロゴロ = purring, grumbling, thundering, rumbling; *the goat rode in a cart that rumbled down the road*

Gosenzosama ご先祖様 = very honorable ancestor; from go = honorific prefix + senzo = ancestor + sama = honorific suffix; cf. related terms listed at senzo

Goshigoshi ゴシゴシ = scrubbing, rubbing vigorously; *when we bathe the goats and the sheep, we subject them to vigorous scrubbing*

Goshounou kudasai ご笑納ください = please accept; from go = honorific prefix + shounou = acceptance

Goto ni ごとに = each, every; *the golfers told my niece to find each ball*; cf. kaku = each, every, either; kakuji = each, every, either; cf. kakuji no = each, one's own; cf. meimei = each, individual; cf. sorezore = each, respectively, severally

Gotoshi 如し = like, as if, the same as; *the golden tomatoes that he feeds his sheep are like the red ones that we feed ours*; cf. related terms listed at onaji

Gotouchi ご当地 = here, where one comes from; from the honorific go + touchi = this place or this town; cf. related terms listed at basho

Gou 号 = a suffix denoting a number or a name (e.g., of a train, rocket, ship, etc.); for example, ichigou = number one; nozomigou = the Nozomi train (a Shinkansen super express train); *our goats all have numbers and names*

Goui 合意 = consent or agreement; *we made an agreement to go east*; cf. goi = vocabulary; cf. related terms listed at shouchi

Gouka 豪華 = wonderful, gorgeous; *your gold car is gorgeous*; cf. related terms listed at idai and at utsukushii

Goukaku suru 合格する = to pass an exam or be accepted to a school; *if she can go to cactus country and interview, she will be accepted to the University of Arizona*

Goukei 合計 = sum, total; *this is the total number of goats living in the cave*; cf. sougaku = total amount

Gouken 剛健 = vigor, health, sturdiness; *the goats in Kenya are know for their vigor*; cf.

related terms listed at genki

Gouketsu 豪傑 = a hero or great man; *the great man hid his gold in a kettle of soup*; cf. related terms listed at eiyuu

Goukin 合金 = an alloy; from yuugou = fusion + kinzoku = metal

Goukon 合コン = group blind dates; *I met a golfer and a conehead at the group blind date*

Goukyuu suru 号泣する = to cry aloud, lament; *when the goat saw the smashed cucumber, it cried aloud*; cf. related terms listed at nageku

Gouman na 傲慢な = insolent, arrogant; *she lives in a golden mansion and is arrogant*; cf. ouhei = arrogant

Goumon 拷問 = torture; *he underwent torture until he revealed the location of the gold and the money*

Gourei 号令 = a command or order; *the ghost raced around issuing commands*; cf. meirei = a command or order; cf. sashizu = direction, command, order

Gouryuu 合流 = confluence (of rivers), merge (of traffic); *the goats drank reused water at the confluence of the rivers*

Gousetsu 豪雪 = a tremendous snowfall; from gouka = wonderful + setsu = snow; cf. related terms listed at yuki

Goutou 強盗 = a burglar, robber; *the burglar stole a gold toaster*; cf. related terms listed at hannin

Gozaimasu ございます = to exist humbly (the plain speech form, gozaru = to exist, is archaic), often used in the form de gozaimasu = (it) is; *if you go to Zaire with master, be sure to remind him that you humbly exist*

Gozen 午前 = morning, a.m.; *I golfed with the Zen monk in the morning*; cf. related terms listed at asa

Gozonji desu ご存知です = honorably knows; from the honorific "go" + zonjiru = to know honorably; cf. related terms listed at shiru

Guai 具合 = a condition; *since the goose fell through the ice, it isn't in good condition*; cf. related terms listed at keisei

Guchi 愚痴 = a complaint; *I have a complaint about my Gucci handbag*; cf. related terms listed at kujou

Gumi 組 – see kumi

Gun 軍 = an abbreviation of gunbu = a military force

Gun 郡 = county or district; *they employ goons in that county*; cf. related terms listed at chitai

Gunbu 軍部 = a military force; from gunjin = a soldier + bubun = a part of something; cf. gun = a military force

Gunbu 郡部 = rural districts; from gun = county + bu = part or section; cf. related terms listed at chitai

Gundan 軍団 = an army corps; from gunjin = soldier + dantai = group; cf. related terms listed at guntai

Gunjin 軍人 = a soldier; *the soldier keeps a gun in the pocket of his jeans*; cf. related terms listed at heishi

Gunkan 軍艦 = a warship, battleship; *guns from Canada were deployed on a battleship*

Gunshuu 群衆 = a group of people, a crowd or mob; *I keep a gun in my shoe in case a crowd of people attacks me*; cf. related terms listed at dantai

Gunshuu 群集 = a group of living things (including people), a crowd or community; *I keep a gun in my shoe in case a group of living things attacks me*; cf. related terms listed at dantai

Gunsou 軍曹 = a sergeant; *the sergeant distributed guns to the soldiers*; cf. related terms listed at shikan

Guntai 軍隊 = an army; *the <u>army</u> will need <u>guns</u> to fight the <u>Thai</u> soldiers*; cf. butai = a force, unit, or corps; cf. doumeigun = an allied army, coalition forces; cf. gundan = an army corps; cf. rikugun = an army; cf. wagagun = our army

Gurai ぐらい – see -kurai

Gurai nara ぐらいなら = gurai nara = kurai nara = approximately case, used to express the idea that one choice is the lesser of two evils, often followed by hou ga ii, or hou ga mashi da; for example, sensou ni itte shinu gurai nara, nigeru hou ga mashi da = to go to war and die approximately case, it would be better to run away (i.e., it would be better to run away than to die in war); from gurai = approximately or something like + nara = in case

Guramarasu グラマラス = glamorous

Guruguru ぐるぐる = turning round and round, going around in circles; *I keep going from <u>guru</u> to <u>guru</u> and feel like I'm <u>going</u> <u>around</u> <u>in</u> <u>circles</u>*; cf. gurutto = turning in a circle, going around, encircling

Gurume グルメ = gourmet, referring to gourmet (delicious) food

Gurutto ぐるっと = turning in a circle, going around, encircling; *the <u>guru</u> <u>told</u> <u>me</u> to keep <u>going</u> <u>in</u> <u>a</u> <u>circle</u>*; cf. guruguru = turning round and round, going around in circles

Gussuri ぐっすり = sound asleep; *after the <u>goofy</u> <u>supervisor</u> <u>retired</u>, he spent his days <u>sound</u> <u>asleep</u>*

Gutai 具体 = concrete, tangible, material; *the <u>goon</u> went to <u>Thailand</u> and demanded <u>tangible</u> rewards*; cf. yuukei (no) = material, physical

Gutaiteki 具体的 = specific, concrete, tangible; from gutai = concrete, tangible, material + teki = related to

Gutsugutsu ぐつぐつ = simmering or boiling gently; *the <u>goofy</u> <u>tsupervisor</u> (supervisor) brought a <u>goose</u> in his <u>tsuitcase</u> (suitcase), and now it's <u>simmering</u> on the stove*

Gutsugutsu nieru ぐつぐつ煮える = to simmer; from gutsugutsu = simmering or boiling gently + nieru = to be cooked or boiled; cf. related terms listed at nieru

Guusuu 偶数 = an even number; *the <u>goofy</u> <u>supervisor</u> thinks that <u>even</u> <u>numbers</u> are <u>lucky</u>*; cf. related terms listed at bangou

Guuzen 偶然 = coincidence, e.g., guuzen no icchi = a coincidence; *a <u>goose</u> showed up at the <u>Zen</u> center by <u>coincidence</u>*; cf. icchi = agreement, coincidence, conformity, cooperation

Guuzen ni 偶然に = coincidentally; from guuzen = coincidence + ni = by

Gyaku 逆 = contrary, opposite, antithetical; *the <u>geeky</u> <u>yakuza</u> (gangster) has a <u>contrary</u> <u>temperament</u>*; cf. related terms listed at dokoroka

Gyakusetsu 逆説 = paradox; *the <u>geeky</u> <u>yakuza</u> (gangster) <u>settled</u> on a <u>soup</u> with a bittersweet flavor, which sounds like a <u>paradox</u> (i.e., bitter and sweet)*

Gyakuten 逆転 = reversal, sudden change; *the <u>geeky</u> <u>yakuza</u> playing <u>tennis</u> made a <u>sudden</u> <u>change</u> in his strategy*; cf. related terms listed at henka

Gyogyou 漁業 = fishing business; *our <u>fishing</u> <u>business</u> sells fish <u>gyoza</u> to <u>gyoza</u> lovers*

Gyojou 漁場 = fishing ground; *I'm going to the <u>fishing</u> <u>ground</u> to catch a fish in order to make <u>gyoza</u> for <u>Joan</u>*

Gyoku 玉 = a gem or jewel; this can also be read as tama = ball, bead, jewel or bullet; *I'll give you some <u>gyoza</u> and <u>Kool</u>-Aid for that <u>jewel</u>*

Gyosen 漁船 = fishing boat; *before making fish <u>gyoza</u>, the <u>senator</u> catches fish in his <u>fishing</u> <u>boat</u>*; cf. related terms listed at fune

Gyoson 漁村 = fishing village; *the fish gyoza my son bought came from a fishing village*

Gyotto ぎょっと = being startled; *I was startled when the gyoza fell onto my toe*

Gyou 行 = a line; *this gyoza has lines on it*; cf. chokusen = a straight line; cf. gyouretsu = a line or queue; cf. retsu = a row or line; cf. sen = a line or track; cf. suji = streak (line), fiber, muscle, tendon, story line, logic, lineage

Gyougi 行儀 = conduct, behavior, manners; *I admired his behavior in feeding his gyoza to the geese*; cf. related terms listed at furumai

Gyouji 行事 = event, function; *we ate gyoza in the Jeep during the event*; cf. moyooshi = an event or meeting

Gyoumu 業務 = business, affairs; *as I ate gyoza during the movie, I thought about business affairs*; cf. shomu = general affairs

Gyoumuka 業務課 = general affairs section of a company; from gyoumu = affairs + ka = section; cf. shomuka = the general affairs section of a company

Gyouretsu 行列 = a line or queue; *I spilled gyoza on my retro suit while standing in line*; cf. related terms listed at gyou

Gyousei 行政 = government administration; *our government administration checks to see whether gyoza is safe to eat*; cf. related terms listed at kanri

Gyouseki 業績 = accomplishments, results, performance (business); *we make gyoza and sell it to the king's household, and the performance of our business is good*; cf. related terms listed at seiseki

Gyousha 業者 = a trader or merchant; *that merchant sold gyoza to the Shah*; cf. shounin = a merchant or shopkeeper; cf. urinushi = a seller or vendor

Gyousho 行書 = semi-cursive script; from gyou = a line + sho = a document; cf. related terms listed at kaisho

Gyoushou 行商 = peddling; *the gyoza that we bought before the show came from a peddling business*; cf. related terms listed at uriage

Gyoushuku 凝縮 = condensation; *the condensation from the melting gyoza got onto my shoes from Kuwait*

Gyoushukusui 凝縮水 = condensed water; from gyoushuku = condensation + sui = water, e.g., suiei = swimming

Gyouten suru 仰天する = to be astounded or amazed; *the gyoza was so tender that I was amazed*; cf. related terms listed at odoroku

Gyoza ギョーザ = pan-fried dumplings stuffed with minced pork and vegetables, pot stickers; *the geek yodeled while Zach made pot stickers*

Gyuuniku 牛肉 = beef; *when the geeky youth was near Kuwait, he ate some beef*; cf. matsuzaka gyuu = a type of Wagyu beef; cf. murasawa gyuu = another type of Wagyu beef; cf. wagyuu = Wagyu beef

Gyuunyuu 牛乳 = cow's milk; *the geeky youth went to Nyuuyoku (New York) to get cow's milk*

Ha 刃 = a blade; *this blade has a handle attached to it*; cf. related terms listed at hamono

Ha 歯 = a tooth; *Prince Harry lost a tooth*; cf. related terms listed at mushiba

Ha 派 = group, sect, school; *each group wears distinctive hats*; cf. related terms listed at dantai

Ha 葉 = a leaf; *at harvest time, leaves turn colors*; cf. happa = a leaf; cf. kareha = dry or withered leaves; cf. konoha = foliage, leaves of trees; cf. ochiba = fallen leaves; cf. shinryoku = new green leaves

Haa はあ = well, what? *what? you're going*

to Hawaii?

Ha'aku suru (Haaku suru) 把握する = to comprehend or understand; *the Harvard-trained acupuncturist understands my problem*; cf. related terms listed at wakaru

Haba 幅 = width; *the Hawaiian barber is concerned about her width*; cf. yoko = side or width

Habahiroi 幅広い = extensive, broad; from haba = wide + hiroi = spacious; cf. kouhan'i = extensive; cf. zenmenteki = all-out, general, extensive, full-scale, over-all, complete

Habamu 阻む = to block or stop; *in Habana, Cuba, that movie is being blocked from theaters*; cf. related terms listed at shimeru

Habataki 羽ばたき = fluttering of wings; *on Halloween, the barber looked tacky in spite of the fluttering of his wings*; cf. basabasa = rustling, fluttering, flapping

Habataku 羽ばたく = to flap (wings); *the Hawaiian bat will attack you, flapping its wings*; cf. aoritateru = to flap strongly or stir up fiercely

Habatsu 派閥 = a faction; *that faction wears Hawaiian bat suits*; cf. related terms listed at dantai

Habukeru 省ける = to be able to omit or to cut down (cost); the potential form of habuku = to be able to omit or to cut down (cost)

Habuku 省く = to omit or to cut down (cost); *I will cut down on my expenses for Hawaiian booze and Kool-Aid*; cf. morasu = to let out, to omit

Hacchuu 発注 = placing an order; *the harbormaster will choose when to place the order*

Hachi ハチ, or 蜂, = bee; *the bees were hatching in their hive*

Hachi 鉢 = a bowl or flower pot; *an egg is hatching in that bowl*; cf. related terms listed at tsubo

Hachimitsu 蜂蜜 = honey; from hachi = bee + mitsu = honey; *when I meet Superman I will give him some honey*

Hachiue 鉢植え = a potted plant; from hachi = bowl + ueru = to plant; cf. related terms listed at shokubutsu

Hada 肌 = skin, personality; *my Hawaiian daughter has good skin and a nice personality*; cf. hifu = skin; cf. kawa = skin, peel; cf. kawa = leather, skin, hide

Hadagi 肌着 = underwear; from hada = skin + giru = kiru = to wear; cf. shitagi = underwear

Hadaka 裸 = nudity; *a Hawaiian dancer used a camera to document nudity in show business*

Hade 派手 = showy, gaudy, colorful; *the Hawaiian debutante wore a showy costume*; cf. jimi = subdued, inconspicuous; cf. related terms listed at utsukushii

Hae ハエ = housefly; *the hall entrance is full of houseflies*; cf. related terms listed at mushi

Haenai iro 生えない色 = a dull color; from haenai = dull; *when Hansel entered night school, he wore dull colors*; + iro = color

Haeru 映える = to shine or look attractive; *Hansel is erudite and looks attractive*; cf. related terms listed at teru

Haeru 生える = to grow or sprout; *Hansel is an erudite farmer who knows how to make things grow*; cf. hatsuiku suru = to develop or grow; cf. mebaeru = to bud or sprout; cf. moeru = to sprout or bud; cf. oishigeru = to grow thickly; cf. shigeru = to grow luxuriantly or thickly; cf. seichou suru = to grow; cf. sodatsu = to grow up or be brought up

Hagaki はがき = a postcard; from ha = leaf + kaku = to write

Hagasu 剥がす = to strip (the skin) from something, to reveal, usually written はがす, sometimes expressed as and written 剥ぐ hagu; the <u>Hawaiian</u> <u>gambler</u> <u>sued</u> after I <u>revealed</u> his secrets

Hagemasu 励ます = to cheer or encourage (there is no plain speech equivalent); when we go to the market, I <u>encourage</u> my boss by saying, "<u>Haggle Master</u>"; cf. related terms listed at seien suru

Hagemu 励む = to be diligent or make an effort (there is no "masu" form); after our <u>Hawaiian</u> <u>guest</u> <u>moved out</u>, she <u>made an effort</u> to live on her own and <u>was diligent</u> in her job search; cf. related terms listed at zensho suru

Hageru 剥げる = to come off or peel off, usually written はげる; the <u>Hawaiian</u> <u>guest</u> <u>rued</u> the day when the paint <u>peeled off</u> her car; cf. nukeru = to come out or come off, to fall out, to escape, to be missing

Hageshii 激しい = fierce, tempestuous, crowded (traffic), frequent (change); our <u>Hawaiian</u> <u>guest</u> was a <u>Shiite</u> with a <u>fierce</u> demeanor; cf. mouretsu = fierce, fervent

Hagu 剥ぐ = to strip (the skin) from something, to reveal, usually written はぐ, sometimes expressed as 剥がす hagasu; the <u>happy goose stripped</u> the kernels from the cob; cf. related terms listed at miseru

Haguki 歯茎 = the gums (mouth); from ha = a tooth + guki = kuki = a stalk or stem

Hagukumu 育む = to nourish or nurture; a bird <u>hatched</u> a <u>goose</u> in a <u>coop</u> under a <u>moon</u> and <u>nurtured</u> it; cf. related terms listed at yashinau

Hagureru はぐれる = to lose sight of one's companions, to miss a chance; in the <u>hall</u>, the <u>goose</u> and the <u>red rooster lost sight of each other</u>

Haha 母 = my mother, used to talk about her in the third person; <u>my mother</u> says <u>haha</u> when I make mistakes; cf. hahaoya = mother; cf. okaasan = mother

Hahaoya 母親 = mother; from haha = mother + oya = parent; cf. related terms listed at haha

Hahen 破片 = fragment; the <u>hacker's</u> <u>henchmen</u> broke my monitor into <u>fragments</u>; cf. related terms listed at danpen

Hai 杯 = a counter for cups, bowls, etc; ippai = 1 cup, nihai = 2 cups, sanbai = 3 cups; <u>Heidi</u> always keeps track of <u>how many cups</u> of sake she drinks

Hai 灰 = ashes; I <u>hide</u> <u>ashes</u> under a layer of dirt

Hai 肺 = a lung; the <u>hikers</u> felt tightness in their <u>lungs</u>

Haiboku 敗北 = a defeat; when <u>Heidi</u> challenged the <u>bony</u> <u>Kool</u>-Aid seller, she suffered a <u>defeat</u>

Haiden 配電 = distribution of electricity; from haifu = distribution; + denki = electricity; cf. related terms listed a haifu

Haieki 廃駅 = abandoned station; they decided to <u>hide</u> from <u>Edward</u> the <u>King</u> in an <u>abandoned station</u>

Haien 肺炎 = pneumonia; the x-rays showed <u>pneumonia</u> at the <u>high end</u> of the lungs; cf. related terms listed at byouki

Haifu 配布 = distribution; he <u>hides food</u> after the monthly <u>distribution</u>; cf. haiden = distribution of electricity; cf. haitatsu = delivery or distribution; cf. hanpu = distribution; cf. ryuutsuu = distribution

Haigan 肺がん = lung cancer; from hai = lung + gan = cancer; cf. related terms listed at byouki

Haiiro 灰色 = grey; from hai = ashes + iro = color

Haikan 配管 = plumbing or piping; *Hiawatha went to Canada to study plumbing*

Haikankei 配管系 = a pipe system; *Hiawatha visited a Canadian cave to study its pipe system*

Haikankou 配管工 = a plumber; *Hiawatha asked a Canadian corporation to train him as a plumber*

Haikei 背景 = background; *there were hikers and cavers in the background*; cf. akaji = a red background; cf. enkei = background, distant view; cf. murasakiji = a purple background; cf. shiroji = a white background

Haiken suru 拝見する = to see or read humbly; *when Heidi and Ken humbly see a new book, they want to read it humbly*; cf. yomu = to read; cf. other related terms listed at miru

Haiki 廃棄 = disposal, abandonment; *we arranged for the disposal of our hiking equipment*

Haiki 排気 = exhaust, ventilation; from haisui = drainage + kuuki = air

Haiku 俳句 = a style of Japanese poetry, or a poem written in this style; *I wrote a poem about hiding cookies*; cf. related terms listed at shi

Hainyou 排尿 = urination; from haisui = drainage + nyou = urine; cf. related terms listed at hi'nyou

Hairetsu 配列 = arrangement, disposition; *Heidi's retro suits were hung up in a particular arrangement*

Hairikomu 入り込む = to come into or go into; from hairu = to enter + komu = to get crowded; cf. related terms listed at hairu

Hairu 入る = to enter, to contain; *Heidi's rooster entered the barn*; cf. agaru = to climb, go up, rise (prices), enter a house; cf. hairikomu = to come into or go into; cf. haitte kuru = to come in; cf. tachiiru = to enter, meddle or be nosy; cf. totsunyuu suru = to enter or rush into

Hairyo 配慮 = consideration, concern; *I will hide Pope Leo out of concern for his safety*; cf. kentou = examination, investigation, consideration, cf. kizukai = consideration, concern; cf. kokorozukai = thoughtfulness, care, consideration, cf. kouryo = consideration; cf. shikou = thought, consideration

Haiseki 排斥 = exclusion, boycott, shut-out; *he was hired by the selfish king to enforce a boycott*

Haiseki suru 排斥する = to expel, boycott or shut out; from haiseki = exclusion, boycott; cf. houridasu = to expel, abandon, neglect

Haisha 歯医者 = a dentist; from ha = tooth + isha = a physician

Haisha 配車 = dispatching cars; from haifu = distribution + sha = a car

Haishi suru 廃止する = to abolish, repeal; *we want to abolish the custom of hiding sheep from the tax collector*

Haishutsu 輩出 = turning out in great numbers; *that hiker shoots some of the birds that are turning out in great numbers*

Haisou 配送 = delivery; *Heidi's sonar equipment came in that delivery*; cf. haitatsu = delivery or distribution

Haisui 排水 = drainage; *we hired some Swedes to dig a drainage ditch*

Haisui no jin 背水の陣 = back to the wall, last stand; *we hiked to the Swiss Alps, took some notes, drank some gin, and made our last stand*

Haisuikou 排水溝 = drainage, gutter, ditch; *Heidi's sweet corn was grown in a ditch*; cf. related terms listed at unga

Haitatsu 配達 = delivery or distribution;

Heidi puts on a tattered suit before starting her deliveries; cf. haisou = delivery; cf. haifu = distribution; cf. ryuutsuu = distribution

Haitte kuru 入ってくる = to come in; from hairu = to enter + kuru = to come; cf. related terms listed at hairu

Haiyuu 俳優 = an actor or actress; *the actress was hiding in the Yukon*; cf. danyuu = an actor; cf. enja = a performer or actor; cf. geinin = an actor or performer; cf. joyuu = an actress; cf. yakusha = an actor or actress

Haizara 灰皿 = an ashtray; from hai = ashes + zara = sara = a dish

Haizoku 配属 = assignment or attachment (of a person or animal); *Heidi started drinking Zooey's Kool-Aid after her assignment to Zooey's office*; cf. shitei = designation, assignment

Haji 恥 = shame, dishonor; *I feel shame that I forgot my hat in the Jeep*; cf. hazukashime = a shame or disgrace

Haji wo kaku 恥をかく = to be embarrassed, to lose face; from haji = shame + kaku = to perspire

Hajikeru はじける = to burst open; *Hansel jeered when Ken ruined the watermelon by dropping it, causing it to burst open*

Hajiketobu はじけ飛ぶ = to pop out, fly off, burst open; from hajikeru = to burst open + tobu = to fly

Hajimaru 始まる = to begin; the intransitive form of hajimeru; cf. akeru = to start, end or expire; cf. tsuku = to start, set out, obtain a position

Hajime はじめ – see wo hajime

Hajime 始め = a beginning; *Happy Jimmy met his wife at the beginning of 1945*; cf. kaien = the start of a performance; cf. kaishi = a start or commencement; cf. saisho = first, beginning; cf. shuushi = beginning and ending, from beginning to end

Hajime ni 初めに = at first; from hajimeru = to start something + -ni = a suffix that forms an adverb; cf. akatsuki = daybreak, beginning, ending; cf. dai ichi = number one, i.e., the most, the best or the first; cf. hatsu no = the first or beginning; cf. saisho = first, beginning; cf. sentou = vanguard, first; cf. shoki = a beginning or initial stage; cf. shuushi = beginning and ending, from beginning to end; cf. tousho = at first, beginning

Hajimemashite はじめまして = I'm glad to meet you; the polite te form of hajimeru = to start something

Hajimeru 始める = to start something (transitive); *he put his hat in the Jeep and checked his meeru (email) before he started his work*; cf. kaishi suru = to start or initiate; cf. -kakaru = to start doing something (when used as a suffix); cf. kakeru = to begin or be about to begin (when used as a suffix); cf. tachiageru = to start something, to start up; cf. torikakaru = to begin or set out, to launch or start; cf. yaridasu = to begin (transitive)

Hajimete 初めて = the first time; *Happy Jimmy met Ted Kennedy for the first time*

Hajimete de nai 初めてでない = not the first time; a contraction of hajimete de wa nai

Hajiru 恥じる = to feel shame; *the Harvard genius ruined his dorm room and then felt shame*; cf. hazukashigaru = to feel ashamed, embarrassed or shy

Haka 墓 = a gravestone, cemetery, or tomb, usually expressed as ohaka; *after participating in a hackathon, he ended up in the cemetery*; cf. tsukaana = a grave; cf. other related terms listed at bochi

Hakaba 墓場 = cemetery; from haka = graveyard + basho = place; cf. related terms listed at bochi

Hakai 破壊 = destruction; *the hardhearted Kaiser caused the destruction of his country*; cf. hametsu = devastation, ruin

Hakai suru 破壊する = to destroy; from hakai = destruction; cf. related terms listed at kowasu

Hakari 量り = a scale; from hakaru = to weigh

Hakaru 計る = to measure, gauge or time something; this can also be spelled 測る; *the hackathon room was measured in advance*; cf. keiryou suru = to measure or compute; cf. sokutei suru = to measure

Hakaru 測る = to measure, gauge or time something; this can also be spelled 計る; *the hackathon room was measured in advance*; cf. keiryou suru = to measure or compute; cf. sokutei suru = to measure

Hakaru 謀る = to plot or attempt; this can also be spelled 図る; *at the hackathon some rude men plotted against me*; cf. related terms listed at tamesu

Hakaru 図る = to plot or attempt; this can also be spelled 謀る; *at the hackathon some rude men plotted against me*; cf. related terms listed at tamesu

Hakaru 量る = to weigh; *at the hackathon there were rumors that they would weigh us*

Hakase 博士 = a doctoral degree holder; *it was hard to hear the cassette on which the doctoral degree holder had recorded his lecture*

Haken 覇権 = hegemony, supremacy; *the happy Kennedys had hegemony in their home district*

Haken suru 派遣する = to send (a person), to dispatch; *during the harvest, Ken would send Barbie to watch the workers*; cf. tsukawasu = to dispatch

Haki suru 破棄する = to abolish or cancel; *they canceled the hockey game*

Hakiatsumeru 掃き集める = to sweep up together; from haku = to sweep + atsumeru = to gather; cf. related terms listed at atsumeru

Hakikakeru 吐きかける = to spit; from haku = to spit + kakeru = to hang

Hakike 吐き気 = nausea; from haku = to vomit + ke = ki = feeling; cf. other similar terms listed at byouki

Hakkan 発汗 = perspiration; *the hacker ate candy all day and sat in his perspiration*

Hakken 発見 = a discovery; *the harbor where the Kennedys kept their boats was the site of a discovery*; cf. hakkutsu = excavation, discovery; cf. hatsumei = an invention

Hakken suru 発見する = to discover; from hakken = discovery; cf. related terms listed at mitsukeru

Hakki 発揮 = exhibition, display, manifestation; *the hockey game was a display of skill*; cf. related terms listed at tenji

Hakkiri はっきり = clearly, distinctly; *the Hawaiian kitty was clearly unhappy*; cf. kukkiri = clearly

Hakkou suru 発行する = to issue (a publication) or publish; *the Harvard Corporation publishes a magazine*; cf. related terms listed at keisai suru

Hakkou suru 発酵する = to ferment; *we harvest corn and ferment it*

Hakkutsu 発掘 = excavation, discovery; *my Hawaiian kutsu (shoes) got muddy during the excavation*; cf. hakken = discovery

Hako 箱 = a box or case; *I keep a hat and coat in that box*; cf. gomibako = a garbage can; cf. masu = a small square measuring box, sometimes used for sake

Hakobu 運ぶ = to convey, transport, carry; *she carried my hat, coat and boots*; cf. hansou suru = to convey or carry; cf. katsugu = to carry on one's shoulder; cf.

keitai suru = to carry; cf. mochidasu = to bring up, to carry out, to run away with, to mention something; cf. ninau = to carry or bear; cf. seou = to carry on one's back, to shoulder a burden; cf. tazusaeru = to carry with; cf. tewatasu = to hand to or submit; cf. watasu = to carry across, pass or hand over

Haku 吐く = to vomit, spit, exhale, puff; *the hackers' Kool-Aid made me vomit*

Haku 履く = to put on or wear lower body clothing or shoes; *I put on my shoes near the harbor in Kuwait*; cf. related terms listed at chakuyou suru

Haku 掃く = to sweep; *the hackers sweep up after the hackathon*; cf. hakiatsumeru = to sweep up together

Haku 泊 = an overnight stay; ippaku = a one-night stay; sanpaku = a three-night stay; *we scheduled an overnight stay at the harbor in Kuwait*

Haku 迫 = force, urge, imminent; used as a word component; *these Hawaiian cookies reduce my tendency to use force to solve problems*

Hakubutsu 博物 = wide learning, natural history; *the hacker studied cool boots, and he had acquired wide learning about them*; cf. related terms listed at chishiki

Hakubutsukan 博物館 = a museum (other than art); from hakubutsu = wide learning + kan = a large building; cf. bijutsukan = an art museum or gallery; cf. geijutsukan = an art museum

Hakuchou 白鳥 = a swan; *the hackers chose a swan as their logo*; cf. related terms listed at tori

Hakuchuu 伯仲 = fierce competition, well-matched; *for their online games, the hackers choose teams that are well-matched*; cf. related terms listed at issen

Hakudatsu suru 剥奪する = to deprive of; *the hackers took his Datsun and deprived him of transportation*

Hakugai 迫害 = persecution; *they harmed the Kuwaiti guy when they subjected him to persecution*

Hakuhatsu 白髪 = grey or white hair; *he wears hackers' hats to hide his grey hair*; cf. related terms listed at ke

Hakui 白衣 = a white uniform; from haku = white, e.g., hakuhatsu = white hair; + ifuku = clothing; cf. seifuku = a uniform

Hakujou suru 白状する = to confess or admit; *the hacker went to Joan of Arc to confess his crimes*; cf. jihaku suru = to confess; cf. kokuhaku suru = to confess

Hakumai 白米 = white rice; *the hacker had mice that ate white rice*; cf. related terms listed at gohan

Hakurai no 舶来の = imported; *the harbor in Kuwait brings in rice that is imported*; cf. yu'nyuu = imported

Hakuraihin 舶来品 = imported goods; from hakurai no = imported + hin = goods; cf. hakuraimono = imported things

Hakuraimono 舶来物 = imported things; from hakurai no = imported + mono = a tangible thing; cf. hakuraihin = imported goods

Hakuryoku 迫力 = dynamism, power; from haku = force + ryoku = power; cf. related terms listed at chikara

Hakushu 拍手 = applause; *at the harbor in Kuwait, the shooting star was met with applause*; cf. kassai = applause

Hamabe 浜辺 = beach; *the Hawaiian mansion is best because it's near a beach*; cf. related terms listed at kaihin

Hamaru はまる = to fall into or be caught, to fit in or into (intransitive); *the Hawaiian marine climbed onto the roof and fell into a trap*; cf. mitsukaru = to be caught or found; cf. tsukamaru = to be caught

Hameru はめる = to put on, to fit or mold (transitive); *I hammered Ruth's ring into* shape before I <u>put</u> <u>it</u> <u>on</u> her finger; cf. related terms listed at oku

Hametsu 破滅 = devastation, ruin; *the <u>Har</u>vard delegation <u>met</u> <u>Superman</u> to see if he could prevent the <u>devastation</u> of their campus*; cf. hakai = destruction

Hamigaki 歯磨き = toothpaste; from ha = a tooth + migaku = to brush

Hamono 刃物 = a knife or cutting tool; *the <u>ham</u>mock in the <u>no</u>rth wing was cut with a <u>knife</u>*; cf. debabouchou = a knife or cutting tool; cf. ha = a blade; cf. houchou = a kitchen knife

Han 半 = half; *<u>Hans</u>el ate <u>half</u> of Gretel's cookie*; cf. gobu = half, 50%, tie; cf. hanbun = half; cf. kouhan = the latter half; cf. kouki = second half (of a period)

Han 反 = anti-; *<u>Hans</u>el is <u>anti</u>-witch*

Han 斑 = a group; *<u>Hans</u>el joined a <u>group</u> of witch-fighters*; cf. related terms listed at dantai

Han 藩 = a clan (feudal period); *the men in that <u>clan</u> are <u>hands</u>ome*; cf. related terms listed at buzoku

Han suru 反する = to oppose, to be inconsistent with; from han = anti + suru = to do; cf. related terms listed at sakarau

Hana wo tsuku 鼻をつく = to be smelly or stink; from hana = nose + tsuku = to adhere; cf. kusai = smelly, stinking, suspicious

Hana 花 = a flower; *I gave the <u>Ha</u>waiian <u>nanny</u> a <u>flower</u>*; cf. asagao = Japanese morning glory; cf. bara = a rose; cf. fuji = wisteria; cf. hanabira = a (flower) petal; cf. hanataba = a bouquet; cf. hasu = lotus; cf. kaika = flowers blooming; cf. kiku = chrysanthemum; cf. kusabana = flowering plants, flower; cf. ran = an orchid; cf. touka = a peach blossom

Hana 鼻 = nose; *the <u>Ha</u>waiian <u>nanny</u> has a tiny <u>nose</u>*

Hanabi 花火 = fireworks; from hana = flower + bi = hi = fire; cf. bakuchiku = a firecracker

Hanabira 花弁 = a (flower) petal; *<u>Hann</u>ah's <u>bees</u> <u>ran</u> past the <u>petals</u>, heading for the <u>nectar</u>*; cf. related terms listed at hana

Hanaji 鼻血 = nosebleed; from hana = nose + ji = chi = blood; cf. related terms listed at hanajiru

Hanajiru 鼻汁 = nasal discharge; from hana = nose + jiru = shiru = soup, or liquid; cf. hanaji = a nose bleed; cf. hanamizu = nasal mucous

Hanamaru はなまる = flower circle = an award given to school children when they do good work, similar to a gold star; from hana = flower + maru = circle

Hanami 花見 = a cherry blossom viewing party; from hana = flower + miru = to watch

Hanamizu 鼻水 = nasal mucous; from hana = nose + mizu = water; cf. related terms listed at hanjiru

Hanamuko 花婿 = a bridegroom; *<u>Hann</u>ah met a <u>moody</u> <u>corpora</u>l who became her <u>bridegroom</u>*; cf. related terms listed at hanayome

Hanarabi 歯並び = a row or set of teeth; from ha = a tooth + narabu = to line up; cf. related terms listed at mushiba

Hanarebanare 離れ離れ = scattered, apart; from hanareru = to separate from or leave

Hanareru 離れる = to separate from or leave; *<u>Hann</u>ah owned a <u>red</u> <u>rooster</u>, but she had <u>to separate from</u> it*; cf. wakareru = to separate or be divided; cf. other related terms listed at deru

Hanaru 放る = to be released or get free; *<u>Hann</u>ah's <u>rooster</u> was <u>released from</u> its <u>pen</u>*; this can also be pronounced houru = to throw away

Hanashi 話し = talk, story; from hanasu = to

talk, speak or tell; cf. densetsu = a legend; cf. douwa = a fairy tale; cf. itsuwa = an anecdote; cf. jitsuwa = a true story; cf. kiji = an article or news story; cf. kijutsu = a written description; cf. mono-gatari = a story; cf. mukashibanashi = legends, reminiscences, old stories; cf. tanpen = a short story; cf. uwasa = rumor, gossip

Hanashiau 話し合う = to discuss; from hanasu = to talk + au = to come together; cf. related terms listed at hanasu

Hanashikakeru 話しかける = to address or talk to someone; from hanashi = talk + kakeru = to spend (time, money, etc.), among many other meanings; cf. related terms listed at hanasu

Hanasu 放す = to release, loosen; *Hannah helped Superman to release the hostages*; cf. yurumeru = to abate or loosen (transitive); cf. other related terms listed at tokihanatsu

Hanasu 話す = to talk, speak or tell; *Hannah and Superman like to talk*; cf. hanashiau = to discuss; cf. hanashikakeru = to address or talk to someone; cf. happyou suru = to announce, publish or reveal; cf. hyouji suru = to indicate or express; cf. iikaesu = to talk or answer back, to say repeatedly; cf. iu = to say, tell, speak; cf. katariau = to talk together; cf. kataru = to talk; cf. kuchi wo kiku = to speak; cf. ossharu = to say or tell honorably; cf. monogataru = to tell or indicate; cf. mousu = to say, speak or tell; cf. moushiageru = to say, speak or tell humbly; cf. noberu = to tell or state; cf. ronjiru = to discuss or argue; cf. shaberu = to talk or chat

Hanasu 離す = to separate; the transitive form of hanareru = to separate from; cf. related terms listed at hikihanasu

Hanataba 花束 = a bouquet; from hana = flower + taba = a bundle; cf. related terms listed at hana

Hanatsu 放つ = to fire, to release, emit; a variation of hanasu = to release; cf. utsu = to fire a gun

Hana'uta (Hanauta) 鼻歌 = humming; from hana = nose + uta = song

Hanaya 花屋 = a flower shop; from hana = flower + ya = store

Hanayaka 華やか = dazzling, gorgeous; *Hannah's yak art is gorgeous*; cf. mabushii = dazzling, blinding; cf. other related terms listed at utsukushii

Hanayome 花嫁 = a bride; from hana = flowers + yome = a bride; cf. hanamuko = a bridegroom; cf. musumemuko = a son-in-law; cf. shinpu = a bride; cf. shinrou = a bridegroom; cf. yome = a bride

Hanbai 花火 = sales, marketing; *Hansel buys his cars from the sales department*; cf. related terms listed at uriage

Hanbaibu 販売部 = a sales department; from hanbai = sales + bubun = a part of something

Hanbun 半分 = half; from han = half + bun = a share or quantity; cf. related terms listed at han

Hanchou 班長 = a squad or group leader; *Hansel was chosen as group leader*; cf. related terms listed at shunou

Handan 判断 = judgment, decision; *to hand the dancer a victory was the judge's judgment and decision*; cf. hanketsu = a judgment (court); cf. hantei = a judgment or decision; cf. hyouketsu = a decision or verdict; cf. kesshin = a decision or determination; cf. ketsui = a decision or determination; cf. kettei = a decision; cf. saiban = a trial or judgment; cf. senkoku = a sentence or judgment

Hane 羽 = feather, wing; *I saw a bird with feathers at Haneda Airport*; cf. tsubasa = wing; cf. umou = down, feathers

Han'ei (Hanei) 繁栄 = prosperity; *we achieved prosperity by selling handy aprons*; cf. hatten = development, prosperity; cf. kouryuu = a rise, prosperity; cf. seikyou = success, prosperity

Han'ei (Hanei) suru 繁栄する = to prosper; from han'ei = prosperity; cf. related terms listed at sakaeru

Haneru 跳ねる = to jump or hop, to splash; *Hansel is an erudite guy who likes to jump*; cf. related terms listed at tobu = to jump

Hanga 版画 = woodblock print; *he keeps his woodblock print in an airplane hanger*

Hangaku 半額 = a 50% discount; from han = half + gaku = a sum of money; cf. waribiki = a discount

Hangeki 反撃 = a counterattack; from hantai = opposition + totsugeki = attack; cf. related terms listed at shuugeki

Hangen suru 半減する = to reduce by half; from hanbun = half + genshou = decrease; cf. related terms listed at genshou suru

Hangyaku 反逆 = rebellion, treason, betrayal; *the hanged yakuza was guilty of treason*; cf. boudou = rebellion, revolt, riot; cf. hankou = rebellion, defiance, resistance; cf. hanran = an uprising or revolt; cf. muhon = a mutiny or rebellion

Hangyakusha 反逆者 = a traitor; from hangyaku = rebellion + sha = a person

Hangyoku 半玉 = apprentice or child geisha; from han = half + gyoku = a jewel; cf. related terms listed at geisha

Han'i (Hani) 範囲 = extent, area, range; *Hansel's eagle patrols a large area*; cf. hodo = extent, degree, limits, moderation, approximate time, about so much, compared to, not as much as (with negative constructions)

Hanji 判事 = a judge; *the judge impounded Hansel's Jeep*; cf. related terms listed at saibankan

Hankagai 繁華街 = business or shopping district; *the handsome captain will guide us on a tour of the shopping district*; cf. chikagai = underground shopping mall

Hankei 半径 = radius; from han = half + chokkei = diameter; cf. related terms listed at chokkei

Hanketsu 判決 = judgment (court); *Hansel put ketchup in his soup as he pondered the judgment of the court*; cf. related terms listed at handan

Hankou 反抗 = rebellion, defiance, resistance; *Hansel stands against the corporations in defiance*; cf. related terms listed at hangyaku

Hanma ハンマー = a hammer

Hanmei suru 判明する = to prove to be, to become clear; *the handmaid proved to be a thief*; cf. related terms listed at sumu

Hanmen 反面 = the other or opposite side, on the other hand; *Hansel's mentor lives on the other side of the alley*; cf. related terms listed at hou = direction or side

Hannin 犯人 = criminal, culprit; *they hang nin (people) who are criminals*; cf. dorobou = a thief; cf. goutou = a burglar, robber; cf. hanzaisha = a criminal; cf. sagishi = a swindler; cf. touzoku = a robber or burglar

Hannou 反応 = reaction, response; *Hansel went to Norway in order to get a reaction from Gretel*

Hannya 般若 = prajna, wisdom, insight into the nature of reality (Buddhism); *the handsome yak driver had achieved prajna*

Hanpa 半端 = insufficient, incomplete, insincere; *Hansel's Pa was insincere and gave an incomplete explanation about the witch*; cf. fuseijitsu = insincere, dishonest; cf. other related terms listed at tarinai

Hanpu 頒布 = distribution; after *Hansel jumped into the pool, a wide distribution of water drops appeared on the sidewalk*; cf. related terms listed at haifu

Hanran 反乱 = an uprising or revolt; from hantai = opposition + ranbou = violent; cf. related terms listed at hangyaku

Hanron 反論 = an objection or rebuttal; *since Hansel thought that I was wrong, he raised on objection*; cf. hitei = a rejection or denial; cf. igi = an objection

Hanryo 伴侶 = a spouse or companion; *handsome Leo was a presentable companion*; cf. related terms listed at nakama

Hansei 反省 = scrutiny, self-scrutiny, regret; *Hansel sagely recognized that the birds were eating the crumbs and did self-scrutiny*; cf. shingi = discussion, scrutiny; cf. other related terms listed at koukai = regret

Hansha 反射 = reflection; *the reflection showed Hansel holding a sharp sword*

Hansha suru 反射する = to reflect; from hansha = reflection; utsusu = to project (onto a screen), to reflect

Hanshatekini 反射的に = reflexively; from hansha = reflection + teki = related to

Hanshi 半紙 = common Japanese writing paper; literally, "half a paper"; *Hansel gave the Shiite some writing paper*; cf. related terms listed at kami

Hanshi 藩士 = a feudal retainer or warrior; from han = clan + bushi = a warrior or samurai

Hanshoku 繁殖 = proliferation, breeding, propaganda; *Hansel is shocked by nuclear proliferation*; cf. seishoku = reproduction, procreation

Hansode 半袖 = short sleeves; from han = half + sode = a sleeve; cf. related terms listed at sode

Hansoku 販促 = a sales promotion; *after standing all day for a sales promotion, Hansel soaked his feet*; cf. shusai = sponsorship, promotion, hosting; cf. sokushin = propagation, promotion

Hansou 帆走 = sailing; *Hansel had a sophisticated knowledge of sailing*; cf. related terms listed at koukai

Hansou 搬送 = transportation, conveyance, delivery; *Hannibal and his soldiers needed transportation to travel to Rome*; cf. related terms listed at ourai

Hansou suru 搬送する = to convey or carry; from hansou = conveyance; cf. related terms listed at hakobu

Hansuu 半数 = half the number; from han = half + suuji = numeral; cf. related terms listed at bangou

Hantai 反対 = opposition, the reverse; *due to the opposition we face, our hands are tied*; cf. teikou = resistance, opposition; cf. teikouryoku = power of resistance

Hantai hyou 反対票 = an opposing vote or voice; from hantai = opposition + hyou = a vote; cf. related terms listed at hyou

Hantei 判定 = judgment, decision; *the handsome tailor listened to the court's judgment*; cf. related terms listed at handan

Hantou 半島 = a peninsula; from han = half + tou = island

Hanzai 犯罪 = a crime; *Hansel went to Zaire (former name of the Congo), to investigate a crime*; cf. related terms listed at tsumi

Hanzaisha 犯罪者 = a criminal; from hanzai = crime + sha = person; cf. related terms listed at hannin

Haori 羽織 = short jacket worn over kimono; *she keeps Hawaiian Oreos in the pockets of her short jacket*

Happa 葉っぱ = leaf; *the Hawaiian padre studied leaves*; cf. related terms listed at ha = a leaf

Happoushu 発泡酒 = sparkling wine, low-malt beer; *I'm happy the old shoemaker gave us some sparkling wine and low-malt beer*; cf. related terms listed at sake

Happyou 発表 = an announcement or publication, a statement; *I'm happy that you are making the announcement*; cf.

related terms listed at sengen

Happyou suru 発表する = to announce, publish or reveal; from happyou = an announcement or publication, a statement; cf. related terms listed at shiraseru

Hara 原 = a field or meadow; *he harasses me in the field*; cf. hatake = a field for cultivation or field of expertise; cf. nohara = a field; cf. ryouiki = an area, domain or field; cf. ta = a rice field; cf. tahata = field (crops); cf. tanbo = a rice field

Hara 腹 = stomach, abdomen; *a Hawaiian rascal stabbed me in the stomach*; cf. related terms listed at onaka

Hara ga heru 腹が減る = to become hungry; from hara = stomach, abdomen + heru = to reduce, lose (weight), to get hungry; cf. related terms listed at onaka ga suku

Hara ga suku 腹がすく = to be hungry; from hara = stomach + suku = to become empty; cf. related terms listed at onaka ga suku

Hara ga tatsu 腹が立つ = to become angry; from hara = stomach + tatsu = to stand; cf. related terms listed at okoru = to get angry

Harau 払う = to brush away, to pay (money or attention); *the hackers and Raul Castro brushed away all complaints and paid for anti-virus software*; cf. shiharau = to pay

Hare 腫れ = swelling, boil; from hareru = to swell up

Hareru 晴れる = to be sunny, to clear up; *Hansel's red rooster comes out when it's sunny*

Hareru 腫れる = to swell up; *the happy red rooster swelled up with pride*; cf. moriagaru = to swell, rise, get excited

Haretsu 破裂 = an explosion or rupture; *Hansel was wearing his retro suit when there was a rupture of the gas line, followed by an explosion*; cf. related terms listed at bakuhatsu

Hari 張り = tension, tone, willpower, pride; *the hairy archer increased the tension in the bow*; cf. other related terms listed at hokori and ishi

Hari 針 = a needle; *Prince Harry is good with needles*; cf. shin = a needle

Hariageru 張り上げる = to raise (one's voice); from haru = to stretch + ageru = to raise

Hariana 針穴 = a pinhole, the eye of a needle; from hari = a needle + ana = a hole; cf. related terms listed at ana

Harikiru 張り切る = to be in high spirits, enthusiastic, eager; *Prince Harry keeps his room clean because he is enthusiastic about cleanliness*; cf. necchuu suru = to be absorbed in, to be enthusiastic about

Harishigoto 針仕事 = sewing, needlework; from hari = needle + shigoto = work; cf. saihou = sewing

Haritsuke 貼り付け = pasting; from haru = to paste + tsukeru = to attach

Haritsuku 張り付く = to cling to; *Prince Harry tsuku (adheres), in fact clings, to his values*; cf. related terms listed at kuttsuku

Haru 張る = to stretch, to spread, to put up (e.g., a tent), to fill (transitive), to paste, to become tense, to be expensive; *the Hawaiian ruler stretched a rope across his throne room and filled his bathtub with wine*; cf. related terms listed at kakageru and at shiku

Haru 春 = spring (season); *it was spring when King Harold's rule began*; cf. similar terms listed at kisetsu

Haru 貼る = to paste, stick or attach; this can also be spelled 張る; *the Hawaiian ruler pasted signs on the walls*; cf. soeru = to attach to, to garnish a dish, to help or support; cf. tsukeru = to attach, install, and many other meanings

Harukaze 春風 = a spring breeze; this can

also be pronounced shunpu, with the same meaning; from haru = spring + kaze = wind

Hasamaru 挟まる = to get between, to get caught in; *the <u>handsome</u> <u>salaryman</u> <u>ruined</u> his shoe when it <u>got</u> <u>caught</u> between two stones*; cf. related terms listed at mitsukaru

Hasami はさみ = scissors; *I use <u>scissors</u> to cut <u>Hawaiian</u> <u>salty</u> <u>meat</u>*

Hasamu 挟む = to hold or place between, to pinch; *the <u>handsome</u> <u>salaryman</u> <u>moved</u> his chopsticks in such a way that they <u>pinched</u> his food*; cf. tsumamu = to pick up or eat with fingers, to pinch

Hasan 破産 = bankruptcy; *<u>Hansel</u> had to shovel <u>sand</u> after his <u>bankruptcy</u>*; cf. hatan = failure, bankruptcy; cf. tainou = deliquency (failure to pay)

Hasei 派生 = derivation; *<u>harpists</u> <u>say</u> that their instrument is a <u>derivation</u> of hunting bows*; cf. hassei suru = to break out

Hashi 橋 = a bridge; *we were <u>hashing</u> out our problems on the <u>bridge</u>*

Hashi 端 = end, edge, border; *I marked the <u>edge</u> of the court with <u>hashi</u> (chopsticks)*

Hashi 箸 = chopsticks; *I eat <u>hash</u> made from <u>eels</u>, using <u>chopsticks</u>*

Hashika はしか = measles; *while we were <u>hashing</u> out our problems in the <u>car</u>, I noticed a spot of <u>measles</u> on my arm*

Hashikure 端くれ = a scrap or piece, an unimportant person; *an <u>unimportant</u> <u>person</u> is smoking <u>hashish</u> and drinking <u>Kool-Aid</u>*; cf. related terms listed at danpen

Hashira 柱 = pillar, post, column; *he smokes <u>hashish</u> with his <u>radical</u> friends behind that <u>column</u>*; cf. denchuu = telephone pole or electricity pole

Hashirimawaru 走り回る = to run around; from hashiru = to run + mawaru = to turn; cf. related terms listed at hashiru

Hashirinuku 走りぬく = to run through, to outrun; from hashiru = to run + nuku = to extract, omit, outrun or surpass; cf. related terms listed at hashiru

Hashirisaru 走り去る = to run away; from hashiru = to run + saru = to leave; cf. related terms listed at nigeru

Hashiru 走る = to run or rush; *the <u>hashish</u> <u>ruined</u> his chances, but he <u>ran</u> the race anyway*; cf. hashirimawaru = to run around; cf. hashirinuku = to run through, to outrun; cf. kakeagaru = to run up; cf. kakemeguru = to run about; cf. kakeoriru = to run down (e.g., a flight of stairs); cf. kakeru = to run

Hassei 発生 = an outbreak or occurrence; *<u>Hawaii</u> was <u>saved from</u> an <u>outbreak</u> of <u>disease</u>*; cf. boppatsu = an outbreak or sudden occurrence

Hassei suru 発生する = to break out, generate, breed, occur; from hassei = an outbreak; cf. okiru = to occur, to get up, to wake up; cf. okoru = to happen, to originate, to break out; cf. shoujiru = to arise, occur, bring about

Hasshin 発信 = dispatch, transmission; *the <u>happy</u> <u>Shinto</u> priest sends <u>dispatches</u> to his followers*

Hasshou 発祥 = origin; *the <u>harbor</u> and <u>show</u> business are among the <u>origins</u> of the wealth in New York*; cf. related terms listed at kigen

Hasshouchi 発祥地 = a birthplace or place of origin; from hasshou = origin + chi = place; cf. related terms listed at furusato

Hasu 蓮 = lotus; *I wrapped my <u>Hawaiian</u> <u>souvenirs</u> in <u>lotus</u> leaves*; cf. related terms listed at hana

Hata はた = a loom; *that <u>Hawaiian</u> guy has a <u>talent</u> for weaving on a <u>loom</u>*

Hata 旗 = banner, flag; *the <u>Hawaiian</u> <u>tavern</u> was flying a <u>flag</u>*; cf. kokki = a national flag

Hatachi 二十歳 = 20 years old; this can also

be pronounced nijuusai; *when I was 20 years old, I visited a Hawaiian tavern and ordered cheese*

Hatajirushi 旗印 = an emblem, slogan or insignia on a flag; from hata = flag + jirushi = shirushi = a sign or symbol; cf. related terms listed at kizashi

Hatake 畑 = field for cultivation or field of expertise; *in Hawaii, a tall Kennedy farms a field*; cf. related terms listed at hara

Hataku はたく = to strike, knock, dust, beat; *the hacker paid his taxes in Kuwait, but they still used to knock him around*; cf. related terms listed at utsu

Hatan 破綻 = failure, bankruptcy; *the Hawaiian tank factory was a failure*; cf. related terms listed at hasan

Hatarakimono 働き者 = a hard-working person; from hataraku = to labor + mono = person; cf. related terms listed at hito

Hataraku 働く = to labor; *I labor making hats for Arabs in Kuwait*; cf. related terms listed at shigoto suru

Hatashite はたして = really, ever; from hatasu = to accomplish or realize

Hatasu 果たす = to accomplish or realize; *when Prince Harry talked to Superman, he realized his dream*; cf. jikkou suru = to implement; jisshi suru = to carry out or effect; cf. jitsugen suru = to realize or effect; cf. nashitogeru = to accomplish or complete; cf. shikkou suru = to carry out or execute; cf. tassei suru = to accomplish; cf. togeru = to accomplish; cf. tsuranuku = to penetrate, to accomplish, to carry out; cf. yaritogeru = to accomplish

Hato 鳩 = pigeon, dove; *the pigeons eat ham and toast*

Hatoba 波止場 = a pier or wharf; *in Hawaii people eat toast at bars near the piers*; cf. sanbashi = a wharf, bridge, jetty or pier

Hatsu 発 = counter for gunshots or explosions; the pronunciation varies according to the number preceding it, e.g, ippatsu, nihatsu, sanpatsu, or manpatsu (1, 2, 3, or 10,000 explosions); this also = departure, e.g., toukyou hatsu = departing from Tokyo; *some gunshots passed through their hats prior to their departure*

Hatsu (no) 初(の) = the first or beginning; *it was the first time we had worn our hats*; cf. related terms listed at hajime ni

Hatsubai suru 発売する = to sell, put on the market; from hatsu = departure + bai = to sell, e.g., hanbai = sales; cf. related terms listed at uru

Hatsudensho 発電所 = a power plant; from hatsu = departure + denki = electricity + sho = a place

Hatsuga 発芽 = germination, budding, sprouting; *I have some old hats in the garage that I filled with dirt and use for sprouting new seeds*; cf. mebae = budding

Hatsugen 発言 = a statement or remark; *the hats that Genghis wore caused some critical remarks*; cf. related terms listed at sengen

Hatsu'iku (Hatsuiku) 発育 = development or growth (physical); *the children's hats were infested with ear cooties, which stunted their growth*; cf. seichou = growth

Hatsu'iku (Hatsuiku) suru 発育する = to develop or grow; from hatsu'iku = development or growth (physical); cf. related terms listed at haeru

Hatsumei 発明 = an invention; *the hats that we wore in May were made possible by an invention that occurred in April*; cf. hakken = a discovery

Hatsumoude 初詣 = first shrine visit of the year; from hatsu = the first; *we are wearing our hats for the first time this season*; + moude = shrine visit; cf. similar terms listed at houmon

Hatsuon 発音 = pronunciation; *somehow their pronunciation is better when their hats are on*

Hatsurainichi 初来日 = the first visit to Japan; from hatsu = the first + rainichi = a visit to Japan; cf. similar terms listed at houmon

Hatsuseri 初競り = opening of an auction; our *hats* are a *serious* concern when we dress up for the *opening of an auction*

Hattatsu 発達 = progress, development; the *hacker* is wearing a *tattered suit*, but he's making *progress*; cf. enkaku = history, development; cf. hatten = development; cf. kaihatsu = development, exploitation; cf. kaikon = cultivating new land; cf. shinka = progress; cf. tenkai = develop-ment; cf. zenshin = an advance, progress

Hatten 発展 = development, prosperity; *as a result of development* in our town, we're seeing more people wearing *hats* and playing *tennis*; cf. related terms listed at hanei and at hattatsu

Hayai 早い = early, fast, (too) soon, simple, quick; *the Hawaiian yacht arrived at Easter, which was a bit early*; cf. related terms listed at hayai = speedy

Hayai 速い = speedy, fast; *the Hawaiian yacht is easy to steer and fast*; cf. hayai = early, fast, (too) soon, simple, quick; cf. hayame = early, fast; cf. jinsoku na = fast, prompt; cf. kibin na = nimble, quick; cf. saisoku = fastest; cf. subayai = nimble, speedy

Hayakuchi 早口 = speaking fast; from hayai = fast + kuchi = mouth

Hayame 早め = early, fast; *the happy yak met his partner early and fast*; cf. related terms listed at hayai

Hayaoki 早起き = early rising; from hayai = early + okiru = to get up

Hayaru はやる = to be impatient or hotblooded; *Hansel's yak room held some hotblooded and impatient animals*; cf. aseru = to be in a hurry or impatient, to be flustered; cf. muzumuzu = to feel itchy, to be impatient or eager to do something

Hayaru はやる = to become popular or successful; *the happy yakuza makes it a rule to give to charity, and he has become popular*; cf. related terms listed at fukyuu suru

Hayashi 林 = a grove; *when we visited the grove after the fire, the hay on the ground was ashy*; cf. related terms listed at mori

Hazakura 葉桜 = a cherry tree in leaf; from ha = a leaf + zakura = sakura = cherry

Hazu はず = should, ought, surely, an expectation that something will exist or occur, usually used as a suffix; *they should be wearing hats at the zoo*; cf. related terms listed at seneba

Hazukashigaru 恥ずかしがる = to feel ashamed, embarrassed or shy; from hazukashii = ashamed, embarrassed, shy; + garu = appears to be; cf. hajiru = to feel shame

Hazukashii 恥ずかしい = ashamed, embarrassed, shy; *at Prince Harry's zoo, they are cashing in by selling body parts, and they should be ashamed*

Hazukashime 辱め = a shame or disgrace; from hazukashimeru = to dishonor; cf. haji = shame, dishonor

Hazukashimeru 辱める = to humiliate, dishonor or rape; *Prince Harry's zoo is cashing in via meeru (email), and that is humiliating the royal family*

Hazumu 弾む = to become lively, to accelerate; *at the Hawaiian zoo, the movies accelerate when the animals are watching*; cf. kasoku suru = to accelerate

Hazureru 外れる = to fail, lose or miss, to come off, to be dislocated, to stray; *at the Hawaiian zoo, a red rooster tried to catch a fly, but it missed*; cf. ochiru = to fail, fall or go downhill; cf. shippai suru = to fail or make a mistake; cf. suberu = to slide, slip or fail an exam; zasetsu suru = to be frustrated, to collapse or fail

Hazusu 外す = to remove or take off, to miss, to go away; *I took off my hat and my zoot suit and went away*; cf. nozoku = to remove; cf. nugu = to remove clothing; cf. torinozoku = to remove; cf. torisaru = to remove or eliminate

Hea ヘアー = hair; cf. related terms listed at ke

Hebi 蛇 = a snake; *the snake wrapped itself around a heavy beam*; cf. chouda = a long snake, a long line (of people, etc.)

Hedataru 隔たる = to be distant; *I'm trying to be distant from those heavy dancers on that tar roof*

Hedateru 隔てる = to separate (by time, distance, etc.), to isolate, to divide, to interpose; *let's separate ourselves from the heavy dancers in the television room*; cf. related terms listed at hikihanasu

Hei 塀 = a fence or wall; *she hates fences and walls*; cf. related terms listed at kakine

Heian jidai 平安時代 = the Heian era of Japanese history, lasting from 794 to 1185

Heibon 平凡 = commonplace, mediocre, ordinary; *I hate bones in fish, but they are a commonplace problem when eating seafood*; cf. related terms listed at taitei

Heien 閉園 = a closing (park, etc.); *since I hate the entertainers in that show, I don't mind its closing*; cf. heisa = closing, shutdown; cf. shimekiri = a closing or deadline

Heihou 平方 = square (e.g., square meters); *I hate homes that are square*

Hei'in (Heiin) 兵員 = military personnel; from heitai = a soldier + in = a group member; cf. related terms listed at shikan

Heijitsu 平日 = weekdays; *in Hades, the jittery superstar says that every day is like a weekday*; cf. related terms listed at yokujitsu

Heika 陛下 = the Emperor, Your Majesty; *we hail the car that carries the Emperor*; cf. related terms listed at ou

Heiki 兵器 = a weapon or arms; *the hated king amassed weapons*; cf. related terms listed at buki

Heiki 平気 = unconcerned, nonchalant, calmness; *the hated king is nonchalant*; cf. ochitsuki = composure, calmness, serenity; cf. reisei = calm, composure; cf. other related terms listed at nanigenai and at reisei

Heikin 平均 = average, mean; *that halo-wearing king is just average*; cf. futsuu = ordinary, usual, general, average

Heikou suru 閉口する = to be annoyed; *when hail strikes the corn, I get annoyed*

Heion na 平穏な = peaceful, calm; *a fear of Hades is the only thing that keeps him peaceful*; cf. related terms listed at odayaka

Heiryoku 兵力 = military force; from heitai = soldier + ryoku = force

Heisa 閉鎖 = closing, shutdown; *haze in Sapporo caused a shutdown of an airport*; cf. heien = a closing (park, etc.); shimekiri = a closing or deadline

Heisa suru 閉鎖する = to close down; from heisa = closing; cf. shimeru = to close; cf. tojiru = to close or shut

Heisha 弊社 = our company (humble expression); from hei = collapse, e.g., hihei = ruin; + kaisha = a company; cf. related terms listed at kaisha

Heishi 兵士 = soldier; *he hated sheep farming, so he became a soldier*; cf. gunjin = soldier; cf. heitai = soldier; cf. other related terms listed at shikan

Heitai 兵隊 = soldier; *when he first became a soldier, he was hazed and tied to a chair*; cf. related terms listed at heishi

Heiten 閉店 = closed store, closing up a store (for the day), going out of business; *I hate it when my tendonitis forces me to close the store*; cf. related terms listed at mise

Heiwa 平和 = peace, tranquility; *after the hatred of war, it's wonderful to have peace*; cf. antai = peace; cf. yasuragi = peace of mind, tranquility

Heiyou suru 併用する = to use simultaneously; *I hate yogurt, but I use it simultaneously with a fiber supplement*

Heizan 閉山 = closing a mine or a mountain (to climbers); *due to the haze, Queen Anne closed the mountain*

Heki 癖 = a habit or mannerism, e.g., akuheki = a bad habit; *he has a habit of losing helicopter keys*; cf. related terms listed at shuukan

Hekichi へき地 = a remote place; *the healthy king was cheered by his vacation in a remote place*; cf. related terms listed at basho

Hekieki suru 辟易する = to feel overwhelmed, to get tired of, to get irritated by; *I lost my helicopter keys at the eki (station), and I feel overwhelmed*; cf. related terms listed at akiru

Hekiga 壁画 = mural painting; *the heavy king sat in the garden and watched as the mural was painted*; cf. related terms listed at e

Hen 変 = funny, strange, clumsy; *that hen looks strange and acts in funny ways*; cf. related terms listed at heta and at kimyou

Hen 辺 = environs, vicinity; *the hen is somewhere in this vicinity*; cf. related terms listed at fukin

Henbou 変貌 = a transformation or change of appearance; *since this hen was born, there has been a transformation of our farm*; cf. related terms listed at henka

Hendou 変動 = change, commotion, uproar; *as the hen dozed, change was taking place on the farm*; cf. douran = disturbance, commotion; cf. other related terms listed at henka

Henji 返事 = a reply; *her reply caused King Henry to jeer*; cf. related terms listed at kotae

Henka 変化 = change, variety; *Henry VIII called for change and variety*; cf. gyakuten = a reversal or sudden change; cf. henbou = a transformation or change of appearance; cf. hendou = a change or commotion; henkaku = change, transformation; cf. henkou = a change or alteration; cf. henshin = a transformation

Henkaku 変革 = change, transformation; *Henry VIII wanted Karl the Kool-Aid vendor to effect a transformation of the Kool-Aid industry*; cf. related terms listed at henka

Henkan 返還 = a return or restoration; *Henry VIII worked by candle light as he planned for the restoration of his royal prerogatives*; cf. related terms listed at fukkatsu

Henken 偏見 = prejudice or bigotry; *hens in Kenya are the victims of prejudice*

Henkou 変更 = a change or alteration; *if the hens are cold, we have to make an alteration to their coop*; cf. related terms listed at henka

Henkyaku suru 返却する = to return something borrowed; *Henry VIII was a kayaker who always returned the paddles that he borrowed*; cf. kaesu = to return something, to repeat, to overturn, to retaliate

Henpin 返品 = returned goods; *since the new hen pinched me, I'm sending it back as returned goods*; cf. related terms listed at sanbutsu

Hensai 返済 = repayment, reimbursement; *Henry VIII was silent about repayment of the money he borrowed*; cf. geppu = a monthly installment or payment; cf. shiharai = a payment

Henshin 変身 = transformation; *King Henry's shingles underwent a transformation after the heavy rains*; cf. related terms listed at henka

Henshuu 編集 = editing; *Henry VIII would shoot people if he didn't like their editing*

Henshuusha 編集者 = editor; from henshuu = editing + sha = person

Hensou 変装 = a disguise; from hen = strange + fukusou = attire

Hentai 変体 = pervert or perversion, metamorphosis (insect); *the hens are tired of those perverts*; cf. chikan = a sexual pervert; cf. tousaku = perversion

Heru 減る = to reduce, to dwindle, to lose (weight), to get hungry (hara ga heru); *the herald ruined his health when he lost weight*; cf. related terms listed at genshou suru

Heru 経る = to pass (time), to go through or by way of; *as I passed time in the canyon, the helicopter ruined the view of the scenery as it went through*

Herumetto ヘルメット = helmet

Heta 下手 = unskillful; *I want to help Tarzan, but I'm unskillful*; cf. bukiyou = clumsy; cf. chisetsu = unskilled, childish, crude; cf. hen = funny, strange, clumsy; cf. tsutanai = clumsy, unskillful

Hevimetaru ヘヴィーメタル = heavy metal

Heya 部屋 = a room; *Helen keeps her yak in that room*; cf. related terms listed at -shitsu

Hi 日 = sun, sunlight, day; *during the day, the hero lies in the sun*; cf. related terms listed at taiyou and at yokujitsu

Hi 火 = fire; *fire produces heat*; cf. related terms listed at kaji

Hi 費 = cost or expense, used as a suffix; from hiyou = cost; cf. related terms listed at nedan

Hibachi 火鉢 = a brazier or pan for holding lighted coals; from hi = fire + bachi = hachi = a bowl

Hibi ひび = crack, fissure; *some Himalayan bees are living in that crack*; cf. wareme = a crack, fissure or chasm

Hibi 日々 = daily, every day, days; from hi = day + bi = hi = day; cf. hinichi = date, number of days; cf. higoto ni = day after day

Hibiki 響 = echo, repercussion, sound; from hibiku = to resound; cf. related terms listed at oto

Hibiku 響く = to resound, to be heard far away; *I got the heebie jeebies in Kuwait when I heard mortar fire resound*

Hibon 非凡 = unusual, outstanding; *in the healing professions, bonuses are unusual and are only awarded for outstanding work*; cf. related terms listed at kawatta

Hidari 左 = the left-hand side; *there is a hideous aristocrat on the left side*; cf. migi = the right-hand side

Hideri 日照り = dry weather, drought; *the Himalayan dairy farm was stricken by drought*; cf. related terms listed at tenki

Hidoi ひどい = inhuman, cruel, painful, violent, terrible; *the hideous oily monster was cruel and terrible*; cf. hiretsu na = mean, contemptible, vicious; cf. iyashii = despicable, mean; cf. sanzan na = devastating, terrible; cf. zangyaku na = cruel, inhuman; cf. other related terms listed at ranbou

Hieiri 非営利 = nonprofit; *I hear that eighty nonprofit organizations are operating in this town*

Hieru 冷える = to get cold or chilly, intransitive; the intransitive form of hiyasu = to cool or chill; cf. sameru = to become cool

Hifu 皮膚 = skin; *the hero foolishly tattooed his skin*; cf. related terms listed at hada

Hifuen 皮膚炎 = dermatitis; from hifu = skin + enshou = inflammation; cf. related terms listed at byouki

Higai 被害 = damage or loss; *the hideous guide caused damage to my tent*; cf. related terms listed at sawari and at sonshitsu

Higaimousou no 被害妄想の = paranoid; from higai = damage + mousou = a delusion

Higaisha 被害者 = a victim; from higai = damage + sha = a person; cf. related terms listed at hisaisha

Higashi 東 = east; *when building the fence, the hero left a gap for the sheep on the east side*; cf. similar terms listed at minami

Higata 干潟 = a tidal flat; *I found a hideous gander covered with tar on the tidal flat*

Hige ひげ = a beard; *the Himalayan guest had a beard*; cf. kuchihige = a moustache

Higeki 悲劇 = a tragedy; *when the heel found the guest key, it led to a tragedy*

Higenjitsuteki 非現実的 = unrealistic; from hi = negative, e.g., hinan = criticism; + genjitsu = reality + teki = related to

Higoro 日頃 = usual, everyday; *the hero herds goats on the road every day which is usual for him*; cf. related terms listed at taitei

Higoto ni 日ごとに = day after day; from hi = day + goto ni = each; cf. hibi = daily

Higure 日暮れ = nightfall, dusk; *sometimes I hear the goose outside the restaurant at dusk*; cf. kure = year-end, nightfall

Hihan 批判 = criticism; *the hero was handsome, but he received a lot of criticism*; cf. batou = abuse, disparagement; cf. hihyou = review, criticism; cf. hinan = criticism, accusation, blame; cf. hyouron = review, criticism; cf. kougeki = attack, criticism; cf. shisseki = a reprimand or rebuke; cf. warukuchi = slander, abuse

Hihan suru 批判する = to criticize; from hihan = criticism; cf. hihyou suru = to criticize; cf. hinan suru = to criticize, accuse, blame; cf. kougeki suru = to attack or criticize; cf. shikaru = to scold

Hihei 疲弊 = exhaustion, impoverishment, ruin; *some of the healers in Haiti suffer from exhaustion and impoverishment*; cf. related terms listed at binbou

Hihyou 批評 = review, remark, criticism; *the hero said "Hi-yo Silver," and this remark was mentioned in the reviews and criticisms that he received*; cf. related terms listed at hihan

Hihyou suru 批評する = to criticize; from hihyou = review, remark, criticism; cf. related terms listed at hihan suru

Hihyouka 批評家 = a critic; from hihyou = criticism + ka = person

Hiideru 秀でる = to excel or surpass; *the heat at Easter in the debutante's room surpassed previous records, but she excelled in her studies*; cf. sugureru = to excel; cf. other related terms listed at oikosu

Hiji 肘 = an elbow, often written ひじ; *if you hear a Jeep coming, pull in your elbows*; cf. hiza = knee, lap

Hijou 非常 = an emergency (see alternate meaning below); *the healers joked during the emergency, and the patient died*; cf. kinkyuu = an emergency; cf. masaka = something expected, an emergency, by no means, never; cf. rinji = temporary, extraordinary, emergency

Hijou na 非常な = extreme, great (see alternate meaning above); *the healers joked that the patient had a great personality;* cf. related terms listed at idai

Hijou ni 非常に = extremely; from hijou = extreme + -ni = a suffix that forms an adverb; cf. related terms listed at ooi ni

Hijun 批准 = ratification; *we expect ratification of the treaty to protect the Himalayan jungle*

Hikaeru 控える = to refrain from, to take notes, to be imminent (an event), to be in waiting; *the <u>hick</u> will <u>kaeru</u> (return) after <u>taking</u> <u>notes</u>, <u>refraining from</u> criticism, and <u>being</u> <u>in</u> <u>waiting</u>*; cf. related terms listed at tsutsushimu

Hikaku 比較 = a comparison; *I <u>hear</u> that <u>Karl</u> the <u>Kool</u>-Aid vendor makes <u>comparisons</u> between his product and other beverages*; cf. shougou = comparison, collation

Hikakuteki 比較的 = comparatively; from hikaku = a comparison + teki = related to; cf. wari to = relatively, comparatively

Hikan 悲観 = pessimism, disappointment; *his <u>heel</u> <u>cancer</u> reinforced his <u>pessimism</u>*; cf. related terms listed at gakkari

Hikan suru 悲観する = to be pessimistic, to feel hopeless; from hikan = pessimism

Hikari 光 = light, ray, brilliance; from hikaru = to shine, glitter or stand out; cf. akari = light; cf. shizenkou = natural light;

Hikaru 光る = to shine, glitter or stand out; *the <u>hideous</u> <u>candle</u> on the <u>roof</u> is shining*; cf. related terms listed at teru

Hiki 匹 = a counter for small animals or bolts of cloth; *that <u>small</u> <u>animal</u> gave me a <u>hicky</u>*

Hikidashi 引き出し = a drawer; from hiku = to pull + dasu = to take out

Hikihanasu 引き離す = to separate, surpass or outrun; from hiku = to pull + hanasu = to separate (the transitive form of hanareru = to separate from); cf. hanasu = to separate; cf. hedateru = to separate (by time, distance, etc.), to isolate, to divide, to interpose; cf. hikisaku = to tear off or separate; cf. other related terms listed at oikosu

Hikiiru 率いる = to lead; *since I wanted <u>to</u> <u>lead</u> my dorm, I bought some <u>heated</u> <u>quiche</u> and <u>eels</u> for my <u>roommates</u>*; cf. michibiku = to guide, direct, lead

Hikikae ni 引き換えに = in exchange; from hikikaeru = to exchange + -ni = a suffix that forms an adverb

Hikikaeru 引き換える = to exchange or convert; from hiku = to pull + kaeru = to replace or exchange; cf. related terms listed at koukan suru

Hikikaesu 引き返す = to repeat, to retrace one's steps, to return; from hiku = to pull + kaesu = to repeat

Hikimodosu 引き戻す = to bring back or restore; from hiku = to pull + modosu = to return or put back

Hikinobasu 引き延ばす = to delay; *the <u>Himalayan</u> <u>king</u> had <u>no</u> <u>basu</u> (bus), so he <u>delayed</u> his trip*

Hikiokosu 引き起こす = to cause or trigger; from hiku = to pull + okosu = to cause, or to wake someone up; cf. ataeru = to give, award, cause; cf. kamoshidasu = to engender, to bring about, to cause, to give rise to; cf. kamosu = to brew, to bring about; cf. okosu = to raise, to cause, to wake someone

Hikiotoshi 引き落とし = a debit or withdrawal; from hikiotosu = to debit a bank account

Hikiotosu 引き落とす = to pull down, to debit a bank account; from hiku = to pull + otosu = to decrease

Hikisaku 引き裂く = to tear off or separate; from hiku = to pull + saku = to rip; cf. related terms listed at hikihanasu and at saku

Hikishio 引き潮 = low tide; from hiku = to pull + shio = tide; cf. related terms listed at shio

Hikitomeru 引き止める = to restrain; from hiku = to pull + tomeru = to stop

Hikitoru 引き取る = to take back, take over, claim, take charge of, to leave; from hiku = to pull + toru = to take; cf.

Hikiukeru = to take charge of, to undertake; cf. tantou suru = to be responsible or in charge

Hikitsugu 引き継ぐ = to succeed to, take over; from hiku = to pull + tsugu = to inherit; cf. related terms listed at tsugu

Hikitsukeau 引き付けあう = to pull together; from hikitsukeru = to pull + au = to fit or match; cf. related terms listed at hikitsukeru

Hikitsukeru 引き付ける = to attract, draw, pull; from hiku = to pull + tsukeru = to attach; cf. chikazukeru = to draw something near, to introduce a person to another; cf. hikitsukeau = to pull together; cf. hiku = to pull, to attract, to look up, to subtract, to draw a line, to install utilities; cf. hipparu = to pull toward oneself

Hikiukeru 引き受ける = to take charge of, to undertake; from hiku = to pull + ukeru = to receive; cf. uketamawaru = to hear, to be told, to undertake, to take (a message or reservation), to comply; cf. hikitoru = to take back, take over, claim, take charge of; cf. tantou suru = to be responsible or in charge

Hikkaku 引っかく = to scratch or claw; *that hideous cactus plant scratched me*

Hikkomeru 引っ込める = to retract claws; from hiku = to pull + komeru = to go into, to get crowded

Hikkoshi 引っ越し = moving, changing residence; from hikkosu = to move

Hikkosu 引っ越す = to move (one's dwelling); *the hero and his cobra viewed Sudan as a good place to move to*; cf. kosu = to exceed, pass, cross, move (residence); cf. utsurisumu = to change one's residence; cf. utsuru = to move (one's lodging), to change or be infected with, to change target of interest

Hikkurikaesu ひっくり返す = to turn over, to knock over; from hiku = to pull + kurikaesu = to repeat; cf. related terms listed at kutsugaesu

Hikoku 被告 = the defendant or accused; *the accused is said to have heated Coke and poured it on the victim's head*

Hikou 飛行 = aviation, flight; *I hear that your corporation is expanding into aviation*; cf. koukuu = aviation, flying

Hikouki 飛行機 = an airplane; from hikou = aviation + kikai = a machine

Hiku 引く = to pull, to attract, to look up, to subtract, to subside, to draw a line, to install utilities (e.g., gas); *when I pull this curtain aside, I can see the heating and cooling controls*; cf. sanshou suru = to refer to or consult (dictionary); cf. other related terms listed at hikitsukeru

Hiku 弾く = to play a piano or guitar; *to play a guitar is to hiku (pull) strings*; cf. kanaderu = to play a stringed instrument

Hikui 低い = low, small (sound), short (person); *the short guy had the hiccups during the Easter service*; cf. mijikai = short

Hikutsu na 卑屈な = servile, subservient; *a barber who is subservient was asked to give Superman a haircut, and he cut Superman because he was told to do so*

Hikutsuku ひくつく = to twitch; *sometimes heated Kool-Aid tsuku (adheres) to my nose and makes it twitch*

Hima 暇 = free time; *while my wounds were healing on Mars, I had a lot of free time*

Himan 肥満 = overweight, obesity; *the hero was eating only mangos because he was overweight*

Himan ritsu 肥満率 = the obesity rate; from himan = obesity + ritsu = percentage

Himantai 肥満体 = an overweight body; from himan = overweight + tai = body; *my body is tired*; cf. related terms listed at karada

Himatsubushi 暇潰し = killing time; this

can also be written 暇つぶし; from hima = free time + tsubusu = to waste (time)

Hime 姫 = a princess; *the princess was attracted to he-men*; cf. oujo = a princess

Himei wo ageru 悲鳴をあげる = to scream; from himei = scream + ageru = to raise up; cf. donaru = to shout or yell; cf. sakebu = to shout, yell or scream

Himei 悲鳴 = scream, shriek, cry of distress; *he majored in psychology, but I hear his screams every night*; cf. related terms listed at kakegoe

Himen 罷免 = dismissal, discharge; *the Himalayan men faced dismissal*; cf. related terms listed at kaiko

Himen suru 罷免する = to dismiss (from a job); from himen = dismissal, discharge; cf. kaiko suru = to dismiss (from employment)

Himitsu 秘密 = a secret; *it's a secret that he meets you*; cf. naisho = secret

Himo ひも = rope, string; *we tied the hemodialysis machine together with string*; cf. gen = a bow or string (for a musical instrument); cf. ito = thread, string;

Hin 品 = refinement, elegance, goods, article; *the Hindu was known for his refinement and the goods he produced*

Hina ひな = a chick or a doll; *the hero saved the nanny's doll*; cf. ningyou = a doll

Hinadan ひな壇 = a doll stand; from hina = a doll + dan = a stage

Hinamatsuri ひな祭り = Dolls' Festival, or Girls' Festival, held on March 3; from hina = a doll; *I hear Nancy got a doll*; + matsuri = a festival

Hinan 避難 = a refuge or shelter; *the Himalayan nanny found refuge in Europe*; cf. hinanjo = a shelter place

Hinan 非難 = criticism, accusation, blame; *when I gave a hearing aide to our nanny, I received criticism, since her hearing is fine*; cf related terms listed at hihan

Hinan suru 非難する = to criticize, accuse, blame; from hinan = criticism, accusation, blame; cf. related terms listed at hihan suru

Hinanjo 避難所 = a shelter place; from hinan = a shelter + jo = place

Hinata 日向 = sunny place, in the sun; *the excessive heat at the national talent show was due to the fact that they held it in the sun*

Hinata bokko 日向ぼっこ = basking in the sun; from hinata = in the sun + bokko = basking; *I was basking in the sun with some bowlers from Korea*

Hindo 頻度 = frequency of occurrence; from hinpan = frequent + do = time, e.g., kondo = this time; cf. kaisuu = frequency; cf. shindousuu = frequency

Hinichi 日日 = a date, the number of days; this can also be spelled 日にち; from hi = day + nichi = day, date; cf. hizuke = date; cf. nichiji = a date; cf. other related terms listed at hibi

Hinichijou 非日常 = the unusual or unexpected; from hijou = extreme + nichijou = usual; cf. nichijou = ordinary, usual; cf. related terms listed at igai

Hinichijouteki 非日常的 = extraordinary, unusual; from hinichijou = the unusual or unexpected; + teki = related to; cf. hibon = unusual, outstanding; cf. rinji = temporary, extraordinary, emergency; cf. kawatta = different, unusual, strange

Hiniku 皮肉 = sarcasm, cynicism, irony; *when I hear you say that the niku (meat) I cooked was great, I detect a hint of sarcasm*

Hinkon 貧困 = poverty; *if we hinder the Congo from exporting gold, we will increase its poverty*; cf. binbou = poverty, poor person; cf. fujiyuu = disability, discomfort, poverty

Hinkonsha 貧困者 = poor people; from hinkon = poverty + sha = a person; cf. related terms listed at binbou

Hinpan na 頻繁な = frequent, incessant; *in India, Hindu pans are a frequent sight*

Hinshi 品詞 = part of speech; *a Hindu asked a Shiite to list the parts of speech*; cf. related terms listed at shugo

Hinshitsu 品質 = product quality; *these Hindu sheets are of high quality*; cf. kouhinshitsu = high product quality; cf. koukyuu = high class or quality; cf. ryoushitsu = fine quality; cf. -shitsu = quality

Hinyari ひんやり = cool, chilly; *the Hindu's yard was really chilly*; cf. suzushii = cool

Hi'nyou (Hinyou) 泌尿 = urination; *I can hear the neo-Nazi's urination activity next door*; cf. hainyou = urination; cf. oshikko = urination

Hi'nyouki (Hinyouki) 泌尿器 = the urinary organs; from hi'nyou = urination; + ki = container, e.g., benki = toilet bowl

Hi'nyoukika (Hinyoukika) 泌尿器科 = urology; from hi'nyou = the urinary organs + kagaku = science; cf. related terms listed at gankagaku

Hippariau 引っ張り合う = to pull from both ends, to play tug of war; from hipparu = to pull + au = to match or come together

Hipparidasu 引っ張り出す = to take out, drag out; from hipparu = to pull + dasu = to take out; cf. dasu = to take out, put out

Hipparu 引っ張る = to pull toward oneself; *the hippie parent was on the roof, pulling wires toward himself*; cf. related terms listed at hikitsukeru

Hira 平 = even, flat, peace; an abbreviation of hiratai = flat, simple; cf. related terms listed at taira

Hirakikakeru 開きかける = to start to open, to be about to open; from hiraku = to open + kakeru = to start to do something; *the car that Kennedy ruined was starting to show its age*

Hiraku 開く = to open or unfold, to hold (e.g., a meeting), transitive or intransitive; *when I open my shoe store I will display high heels on racks*; cf. akeru = to open or unwrap

Hiratai 平たい = flat, simple; *I hear that the rascal's tires are flat*; cf. related terms listed at kantan and at taira

Hirataku suru 平たくする = to make flat; from hiratai = flat, simple

Hiraya 平屋 = one-story house; *I keep my Himalayan rams and yaks in a one-story house*; cf. related terms listed at ie

Hiretsu na 卑劣な = mean, contemptible, vicious; *the heel who is wearing that retro suit is vicious*; cf. related terms listed at hidoi

Hiroba 広場 = plaza, town square; *the hero battled criminals in the plaza*

Hirogaru 広がる = to spread out, to extend (intransitive); *the hero's garden was ruined when the neighboring rabbit colony spread out*; cf. nobiru = to lengthen or stretch, to be postponed or prolonged (intransitive)

Hirogeru 広げる = to spread or expand, to unfold (transitive); *the hero and his guest ruined the carpet by unfolding it in the ocean*; cf. related terms listed at shiku

Hiroi 広い = wide, spacious; *the hero found it easy to fit his stuff into the spacious apartment*; cf. related terms listed at ookii

Hiroihiroi 広い広い = very big; from hiroi = large or spacious; cf. related terms listed at ookii

Hiromaru 広まる = to pervade or become widespread; from hiroi = spacious + maru

= round, whole; cf. related terms listed at fukyuu suru

Hiromeru 広める = to publicize, propagate, spread; from hiroi = spacious; cf. sokushin suru = to promote or propagate

Hirosa 広さ = width, expanse, area; from hiroi = wide, spacious + sa = a suffix that makes a noun from another word; cf. related terms listed at menseki

Hirou 披露 = announcement, demonstration; *there was an announcement that the hero would give a demonstration of his special powers*; cf. related terms listed at sengen

Hirou 拾う = to pick up, to find, to gather; *the hero picked up the car that had fallen onto the child*; cf. toriageru = to take up or feature, to adopt, to take away, to pick up; cf. toru = to get, take, pick up, to take off a hat or watch, etc.; cf. tsumamu = to pick up or eat with fingers, to pinch; cf. other related terms listed at atsumeru

Hirou 疲労 = fatigue, weariness; *the hero's performance was affected by fatigue*; cf. tsukare = fatigue

Hirouen 披露宴 = wedding reception; *the hero entertained us at his wedding reception*

Hiru 昼 = noon, afternoon, daytime; *the heat ruined our picnic at noon*; cf. gogo = afternoon, p.m.; cf. hiruma = daytime; cf. nicchuu = daytime, during the day

Hirugohan 昼ご飯 = lunch; from hiru = noon + gohan = a meal; cf. similar terms listed at shokuji

Hiruma 昼間 = daytime; from hiru = daytime + ma = duration of time, e.g., mamonaku = before long; cf. related terms listed at hiru

Hirune 昼寝 = a nap; from hiru = noon + neru = to sleep; cf. inemuri = a catnap

Hiruyasumi 昼休み = a lunch break; from hiru = noon + yasumi = a break

Hisai 被災 = being a victim, suffering from; *the heroic scientist was a victim of bad luck*

Hisaisha 被災者 = a victim; from hisai = being a victim + sha = person; cf. ejiki = prey or victim; cf. gisei = a victim, a sacrifice; cf. giseisha = a victim; cf. higaisha = a victim

Hisan na 悲惨な = woeful, pitiable, miserable; *those hideous sandals are pitiable*; cf. related terms lised at ki no doku

Hisashiburi ni 久しぶりに = after a long interval; from hisashi = long time or old; *his sash is buried for a long time*; + buri ni = after an interval; cf. buri ni = after an interval; cf. shibaraku = a short time [this can also mean "it's been a long time (since I've seen you, etc.),", when followed by desu]

Hishigeru 拉げる = to be crushed; the intransitive form of hishigu = to crush

Hishigu 拉ぐ = to crush; *the Himalayan sheep fell on the goose and crushed it*

Hisho 秘書 = a secretary; *the secretary goes to Hispanic shows*

Hisoka ni 密かに = secretly, behind the scenes; *the hero sold his car secretly*

Hisomeru ひそめる = to knit (the eyebrows); *while he sold medicine to Ruth, he knitted his eyebrows*

Hissha 筆者 = writer; *the writer lived in a hideous shack*; cf. chosha = writer; cf. sakka = writer

Hisshi 必死 = frantic, desperate, inevitable death; from hitsuyou = necessary + shinu = to die

Hissu no 必須の = essential, imperative, necessary; *this Himalayan suit is necessary if you want to attend the wedding*; cf. kanjin na (or no) = essential, most important, crucial; cf. other related terms listed at hitsuyou

Hitai 額 = forehead; *he tied a bandana around his forehead*

Hitasu 浸す = to soak, dip, drench or dunk; *the hero sitting in a tavern was Superman, and he soaked his bread in olive oil*; cf. tsukeru = to soak or marinade

Hitasura ひたすら = nothing but; *the Himalayan tanner's supervisor ran out of the room, and nothing but an apology could make him come back*

Hitei 否定 = a rejection or denial; *if he hears the tape, he will issue a denial*; cf. kyohi = rejection, refusal; cf. massatsu = erasure, denial, ignoring (an opinion); cf. other related terms listed at hanron

Hito 人 = a person; *Emperor Hirohito was a person*; cf. hatarakimono = a hard-working person; cf. honnin = the person in question; cf. hitobito = people; cf. hitotachi = people; cf. jinbutsu = a person; cf. jinrui = the human race; cf. jinzai = a talented or capable person, human resources; cf. kata = an honorable person; cf. mono = a humble person; cf. murabito = a village person; cf. nihonjin = a Japanese person; cf. ningen = a human being; cf. shinjin = a newcomer; cf. shomin = common people, the masses; cf. other related terms listed at sha

Hitoanshin 一安心 = a feeling of relief; from hitotsu = one + anshin = relief; cf. related terms listed at anshin

Hitoban 一晩 = one night; from hitotsu = one + ban = night

Hitobito 人々 = people; from hito = person + bito = hito = person; cf. related terms listed at hito

Hitochigai 火と違い = a case of mistaken identity; from hito = person + chigau = to differ

Hitogara 人柄 = personality or character; *when I learned that the hero stored torpedoes in his garage, I understood more about his personality*; cf. related terms listed at jinkaku

Hitogiki 人聞き = reputation, respectability; from hito = person + giku = kiku = to hear; cf. related terms listed at hyouban

Hitogiki warui 人聞き悪い = disgraceful, disreputable; from hitogiki = reputation + warui = bad; cf. related terms listed at mittomonai = shameful, disgraceful

Hitokake ひとかけ = one piece; from hitotsu = one + kakeru = to be chipped; cf. related terms listed at danpen

Hitokoto 一言 = a single word, a brief comment; from hitotsu = one + kotoba = word; cf. related terms listed at kotoba

Hitokuchi 一口 = a mouthful, one word; from hitotsu = one + kuchi = mouth; cf. related terms listed at kotoba

Hitokui 人喰い = cannibalism, man-eating; from hito = person + kuu = to eat

Hitome 一目 = a glance or glimpse; from hitotsu = one + me = eyes

Hitome 人目 = public gaze; from hito = a person + me = eyes

Hitomebore 一目ぼれ = to fall in love at first sight; from hitome = a glimpse + boreru = horeru = to fall in love

Hitomi 瞳 = a pupil (eye); *he told me that my pupils looked dilated*

Hito'oyogi (Hitooyogi) ひと泳ぎ = a swim; from hitotsu = one + oyogu = to swim

Hitori de 一人で = by or for oneself; from hitori = one person; cf. related terms listed at jibun de

Hitori etsu ni iru 一人悦に入る = to be pleased with oneself; from hitori = one person + etsu ni iru = to be happy

Hitoribocchi 一人ぼっち = solitude, loneliness; from hitori = one person + bocchi = loneliness; *he played bocce ball to escape his loneliness*; cf. related terms listed at kodoku

Hitorigurashi 一人暮らし = living alone; from hitori = one person and gurashi = kurashi = life

Hitosashiyubi 人差し指 = an index finger; from hito = person + sasu = to hold up + yubi = a finger

Hitoshii 等しい = same, equal; *the number of hito (people) who own sheep is equal to the number who own cattle*; cf. byoudou = equal

Hitotabi ひとたび = once, for a moment; from hitotsu = one + tabi = occasion; cf. related terms listed at ittan

Hitotachi 人達 = people; from hito = person + tachi = a suffix making the previous noun plural; cf. related terms listed at hito

Hitotoki 一時 = for a moment, for a while; this can also be read as ichiji = one o'clock, or ichiji = for awhile; from hitotsu = one + toki = time; cf. related terms listed at ittan

Hitotsu hitotsu 一つ一つ = one by one, carefully; from hitotsu = one object; cf. tsugitsugi ni = one after the other; cf. zokushutsu = appearing one after the other; cf. zutsu = each or by (as in "one by one")

Hitoyaku 一役 = a role, a contribution to a situation; from hitotsu = one + yaku = a role or service, e.g., yaku ni tatsu = to make use of; cf. yaku = a role or service

Hitoyaku kau 一役買う = to take on a role, to take part; from hitoyaku = a role + kau = to buy or appreciate

Hitoyama 一山 = a pile of something, one mountain; from hitotsu = one + yama = a mountain

Hitozato 人里 = human habitation; from hito = people + zato = sato = village; *there is a satellite tower in the village*; cf. seisoku = habitation

Hitozukiai 人付き合い = social disposition, socializing; from hito = people + tsukiau = to associate with

Hitsudan 筆談 = communicating in writing; *she communicated in writing about the heat in Sudan*

Hitsuji 羊 = sheep; *this sheep often hits you and your genius friend*

Hitsujikai 羊飼い = shepherd; from hitsuji = sheep + kainushi = pet owner; cf. kainushi = a shepherd or pet owner

Hitsujuhin 必需品 = a necessary or essential item; *the heat in Sudan in June will hinder your work unless you bring necessary items like air conditioners*

Hitsuyou 必要 = necessary, necessity; *if he hits you, the yogi should be punished, since it's necessary that everyone obey the rules*; cf. fukaketsu = indispensable; cf. hissu no = essential, imperative, necessary; cf. hitsuzen = inevitable, necessary; cf. hitsuzenteki = inevitable, necessary; cf. yamu wo enai = unavoidable, inevitable

Hitsuyou wa arimasen 必要はありません = it isn't necessary; from hitsuyou = necessity + nai = doesn't exist; cf. related terms listed at koto wa nai

Hitsuyousei 必要性 = necessity; from hitsuyou = necessry + sei = nature; cf. hitsuzensei = inevitability, necessity

Hitsuzen 必然 = inevitable, necessary; *when it heats up, the Zen monks will turn on the air-conditioning, since it's necessary for their concentration*; cf. hitsuyou = necessary; cf. hitsuzenteki = inevitable, necessary

Hitsuzensei 必然性 = inevitability, necessity; from hitsuzen = inevitable, necessary + sei = nature; cf. hitsuyousei = necessity

Hitsuzenteki 必然的 = inevitable, necessary; from hitsuzen = inevitable, necessary + teki = related to; cf. hitsuyou = necessary; cf. hitsuzen = inevitable, necessary

Hiyakedome 日焼け止め = sunscreen; from hi = sun + yaku = to grill or toast + domeru = tomeru = to stop

Hiyaku 飛躍 = leaping, making great strides; from hi = to fly, e.g., hikouki = airplane; + yaku = a leap

Hiyakuteki ni 飛躍的に = rapidly; from hiyaku = leaping + teki = related to + -ni = a suffix that forms an adverb; cf. related terms listed at kyuusoku

Hiyasu 冷やす = to cool or chill, transitive; the *hero* liked *yak soup*, and he would *chill* it by adding *ice*; cf. samasu = to cool, transitive

Hiyou 費用 = cost; *healing yogurt has a high cost*; cf. related terms listed at nedan

Hiyu 比喩 = a simile or metaphor; *the hero used a simile*

Hiza 膝 = knee, lap; *he's a little drunk and has fallen onto his knees*; cf. hiji = elbow

Hiza wo tsuku 膝をつく = to fall to one's knees; from hiza = a knee + tsuku = to stick

Hizuke 日付 = a date; from hi = day + tsukeru = to attach; cf. related terms listed at hinichi

Ho 帆 = a sail; *she used a sail to get home*

Hobo ほぼ = almost, about; *the hobo had traveled almost all the way home*; cf. related terms listed at ayauku

Hodo ほど = extent, degree, limits, moderation, approximate time, about so much, compared to, not as much as (with negative constructions); *the host doles out the drinks only to the extent necessary*; cf. han'i = extent, area, range; cf. other related terms listed at genkai and at yaku

Hodokosu 施す = to donate, perform, give time; *I will hold the door while my co-supervisor donates food*; cf. related terms listed at ataeru

Hodou 歩道 = sidewalk; *the homeless doorman slept on the sidewalk*; cf. houdou = public news or report; cf. hosou = pavement

Hoedasu 吠え出す = to bark; from hoeru = to bark + dasu = to put out; cf. related terms listed at naku = to chirp

Hoeru 吠える = to bark, howl, roar, cry; *that hostess is erudite, but her dog barks too much*; cf. related terms listed at naku = to chirp

Hogaraka na ほがらかな = bright, sunny, cheerful; *that person has a home with a garage and a car, and she is always cheerful*

Hogei 捕鯨 = whaling; *I hope Bill Gates joins the fight against whaling*

Hogo 保護 = protection, care; *Homer's goal was the protection of the environment*; cf. kokorozukai = thoughtfulness, care, consideration; cf. teire = care; cf. yougo = protection

Hogosha 保護者 = parent or guardian; from hogo = protection, care + sha = person; cf. related terms listed at oya

Hogureru ほぐれる = to unravel, untie, undo, solve; *we hope that the goose and the red rooster can solve their differences after we untie them*; cf. kaiketsu suru = to solve, settle or resolve; cf. toku = to untie

Hoho 頬 = cheek; *Santa says Ho Ho when you pinch his cheek*; cf. hoo = cheek

Hohoemu 微笑む = to smile; *Santa said ho ho after the excellent movie and he smiled*; cf. related terms listed at warau

Hojo 補助 = assistance, support; *when he was at home, Jonah gave assistance to his family*; cf. related terms listed at enjo

Hoka 他 = other, another; this can also be spelled 外; *Homer's car was parked on another street*; cf. ato = after, another (with a number); cf. betsu = separate, different, extra, other, another; cf. betsu no = another (defined object, person or place); cf. hoka ni = another, as well, besides; cf. hoka no = another (undefined object, person or place), other; cf. mou = already, before long, another, more

Hoka naranai 他ならない = nothing but; this can also be spelled 外ならない; from hoka = another + naranai = does not become

Hoka ni 他に = another, as well, besides; this can also be spelled 外に; from hoka = another + -ni = a suffix that forms an adverb; cf. related terms listed at hoka

Hoka no 他の = another (undefined object, person or place), other; this can also be spelled 外の; from hoka = another; cf. related terms listed at hoka

Hokahoka ホカホカ = steaming hot, very warm; *we hope the candle under the pot makes it steaming hot*; cf. related terms listed at atsui

Hokan suru 保管する = to keep a close watch over, to take good care of; *our hosts in Canada took good care of us*; cf. related terms listed at azukaru

Hokekyou 法華経 = the Lotus Sutra; *we hope that Kennedy will go to Kyouto and study the Lotus Sutra*

Hoken 保健 = health preservation, hygiene; *my horse in Kentucky benefits from good hygiene, since we are dedicated to its health preservation*; cf. eisei = hygiene, sanitation; cf. hozon = preservation

Hoken 保険 = insurance; *the home that Ken and Barbie live in is covered by insurance*

Hokenjo 保健所 = a health care center; from hoken = health preservation + jo = place

Hokkyokusei 北極星 = North Star; *at the hotel, we drank Kyoto Kool-Aid, and then we set sail using the North Star as a reference*; cf. hoshi = a star

Hokori ほこり = dust; *my home in Korea is full of dust*

Hokori 誇り = pride; from hokoru = to take pride in; cf. hari = tension, tone, willpower, pride; cf. jiman = pride, boast; cf. jishin = self-confidence; cf. manshin = pride, self-conceit; cf. tokui = pride, strong point; torie = merit or good point

Hokorobi 綻び = a tear or a seam that has come apart; from hokorobiru = to tear apart

Hokorobiru 綻びる = to be torn or tear apart, to begin to bloom (flower); *Homer had a coronary (heart attack) when his biru (building) was torn apart*

Hokoru 誇る = to take pride in, to boast of; *after playing hockey in Korea, Rudolph boasted of his "nose for the net"*

Hokou 歩行 = walking; *the hobo from Colombia is walking down the road*; cf. related terms listed at sanpo

Hokubu 北部 = northern parts; *my home and my cool boots are in the northern part of the country*; cf. related terms listed at ichibu

Hokui 北緯 = northern latitude; from hoku = north, e.g., hokubu = northern parts; + ido = latitude; cf. related terms listed at ido

Hokuou 北欧 = northern Europe; from hokubu = northern parts + oushuu = Europe; cf. related terms listed at oushuu

Hokyuu suru 補給する = to supply or supplement; *we hope that Cuba will supplement our relief efforts in the Caribbean*; cf. houkyuu = a salary; cf. oginau = to supplement or compensate; cf. other related terms listed at kyoukyuu suru

Homare 誉れ = honor or distinction; *Homer married a rebel, who said that it was an honor to be his wife*; cf. related terms listed at kouei

Homeru 褒める = to praise, admire or speak well of; this can also be spelled 誉める;

we all *praise* Homer; cf. shousan suru = to praise, admire, commend; cf. zessan suru = to praise highly

Hon 本 = a book; *I read a book about Honduras*; cf. akusho = a harmful book; cf. bungaku = literature; cf. furuhon = a second-hand book; cf. ikkan = one volume (book); cf. jijoden = an autobiography; cf. kyoukasho = a textbook; cf. sasshi = a booklet or pamphlet; cf. shouseki = a book; cf. shousetsu = a novel; cf. tankoubon = a special book, separate volume; cf. techou = a pocket notebook; cf. zousho = a book collection or library

Hon 本 = a counter for long objects, used as a suffix; this can also be pronounced bon or ppon, depending on the number preceding it; *I drank from a lot of long objects (i.e., bottles) in Honduras*

Honba 本場 = home, habitat, center, authentic; from hontou = true + basho = place; cf. related terms listed at uchi

Hondo 本土 = mainland; *Honda keeps its dough (money) on the mainland*; cf. related terms listed at tairiku

Hondou 本堂 = a main temple building; from honba = a center + dou = a hall; cf. related terms listed at tatemono

Hone 骨 = a bone; *I research bone diseases with the help of my home network*; cf. gaikotsu = a skeleton; cf. kotsu = skeleton, bone; cf. sekitsui = the spine; cf. sekitsuikotsu = a vertebra; cf. zugaikotsu = a skull

Honjitsu 本日 = today, this day, the designated day; *Honduras will welcome the jittery superstar today*; cf. kyou = today

Honkaku 本格 = serious, genuine, original method or procedure; *when he was buying a Honda, Karl the Kool-Aid vendor was serious and genuine*; cf. junsui na (or no) = pure, pure-blooded, genuine; cf. other related terms listed at maji

Honki 本気 = seriousness, earnestness; *I noticed his seriousness as he was honking his horn*

Honkyochi 本拠地 = a headquarters or base; *Hong Kong vs. Kyoto: the chief is wondering where to locate his headquarters*; cf. honsha = head or main office; cf. other related terms listed at kichi

Honmono 本物 = the real or genuine article; from hontou = truth + mono = tangible thing; cf. jitsubutsu = the real thing

Honne 本音 = real intention, what one really thinks; *he has a home in the Netherlands, and his real intention is to return to it*

Honnin 本人 = the person in question; from hontou = true or real + nin = person; cf. related terms listed at hito

Honoka ほのか = faint, dim, slight; *she holds her nose when a candle is lit, but she still smells a faint odor*; cf. related terms listed at kasuka

Honoo 炎 = blaze, flame; *there was a flame burning at my home in northern Oregon*; cf. related terms listed at kaji

Honpou na 奔放な = unrestrained, free, wild; *the Honduran police are unrestrained*; cf. jiyuu na = unfettered, free; cf. jiyuu honpou = freewheeling, behaving with abandon; cf. yasei = wild (referring to plants or animals)

Honrou suru 翻弄する = to play with or trifle with, to toss about (a ship); *I played with a dog on a Honduran road*

Honsekichi 本籍地 = permanent address; *my permanent address is in Honduras, where I sell quiche cheaply*

Honsha 本社 = head or main office; from hontou = reality + kaisha = company; cf. honkyochi = a headquarters or base; cf. other related terms listed at kyoku

Honten 本店 = a main store or head office; from honba = a home or center + ten = a store; cf. related terms listed at mise

Hontou 本当 = truth, reality, real, true, genuine; in *Honduras, tornadoes cause real damage*; cf. douri = truth, reason; cf. genjitsu = reality, fact; cf. jijitsu = fact or truth; cf. jitsu = reality, truth; cf. jissai = reality, fact; cf. makoto = sincerity, truth; cf. shinsou = truth, real situation; cf. shinjitsu = truth, reality; cf. shin (no) = true, genuine, real

Hontou ni 本当に = really, truly; from hontou = truth + ni = a suffix that forms an adverb; cf. jitsu ni = really, indeed, truly

Hontou no 本当の = real, true, genuine; from hontou = truth + the possessive no; cf. related terms listed at shin no

Honya 本屋 = a bookstore; from hon = book + ya = a store; cf. related terms listed at mise

Honyaku 翻訳 = translation; *in Honduras, a yak herder earns money by doing translations*; cf. eiyaku = an English translation; cf. yaku = a translation

Ho'nyuu (Honyuu) 哺乳 = lactation, suckling; *the lactation occurred in a home in Nyuuyooku (New York)*

Ho'nyuu doubutsu (Honyuu doubutsu) 哺乳動物 = a mammal; from ho'nyuu = lactation + doubutsu = an animal

Honzuki 本好き = a book lover; from hon = book + zuki = suki = liking; cf. inuzuki = a dog lover; cf. sakezuki = a drinker, someone who likes sake

Hoo 頬 = cheek; *a hornet stung my cheek*; cf. hoho = cheek

Hoobaru 頬張る = to stuff one's cheeks or fill one's mouth with food; *the hobo came into the barroom and stuffed his cheeks with food*

Hoomu ホーム = a platform; *when I show home movies, I put my projector on a platform*; cf. related terms listed at dai = a stand

Hoppou 北方 = northward; *I hope that the police look northward during their search*

Hora ほら = look! *look! there's a hole in the ramp*

Horaana 洞穴 = cave, den; this can also be pronounced douketsu; from hora = cave; *the cave is home to rats*; + ana = hole; cf. doukutsu = a cave or grotto; cf. su = nest, animal habitat, cobweb, honeycomb, den

Hori 堀 = a canal, moat or ditch; *the holy temple was surrounded by a moat*; cf. related terms listed at unga

Horiateru 掘り当てる = to find or strike (gold, etc.); from horu = to dig + ateru = to hit; cf. related terms listed at mitsukeru

Horobiru 滅びる = to perish, to be ruined, to be destroyed; *my horoscope says that our biru (building) will be destroyed*; cf. related terms listed at shinu

Horobosu 滅ぼす = to ruin or destroy; *my horoscope suggests that I buy a boat soon, since a flood is coming which will destroy our town*; cf. dainashi ni suru = to mar or ruin; cf. kowasu = to break or destroy; cf. kuzusu = to dismantle, pull down, destroy, throw off balance; cf. utsu = to shoot at, attack, defeat, destroy

Horu 彫る = to engrave, carve or chisel; *Homer ruined the door when he carved his initials on it*; cf. related terms listed at kiru

Horu 掘る = to dig; *the hostess was rude when I asked her to dig a hole*

Horyo 捕虜 = prisoner of war, captive; *Homer and Pope Leo were taken prisoner*; cf. shuujin = a prisoner; cf. toriko = captive, prisoner

Hosa 補佐 = aid, help; *the hobo stood in the sand and waited for help*; cf. related terms listed at kyuujo

Hoshi 星 = a star; *horses and sheep admire stars*; cf. hokkyokusei = North Star

Hoshii 欲しい = desiring; *this is the kind of*

home the *Shii*tes are *desiring*; cf. synonyms listed at shomou

Hoshou 保証 = guarantee, assurance; *I will give you a guarantee that you will love the horror show*

Hoshou 補償 = compensation; *we received compensation after the horrow show*; cf. baishou = compenstion, reparation

Hoshou suru 保証する = to guarantee; from hoshou = guarantee; cf. kakuho suru = to guarantee or maintain

Hoshu 保守 = maintenance, conservation; *he has a hole in his shoe, but he will repair it because he believes in conservation*; cf. iji = maintenance

Hoshuteki 保守的 = conservative; from hoshu = conservation + teki = related to

Hosoi 細い = narrow, thin, fine; *Homer arranged the soy beans in narrow lines*; cf. related terms listed at semai

Hosonagai 細長い = long and narrow; from hosoi = narrow + nagai = long; cf. related terms listed at nagai and at semai

Hosou 舗装 = pavement; *when Homer got sober he found himself on the pavement*; cf. hodou = a sidewalk

Hossa 発作 = fit, attack, seizure; *when the horse saw the snake, it had a fit*

Hosu 干す = to dry or to air; *I hope this suit will dry before the wedding*

Hosuteru ホステル = a hostel

Hotaru 蛍 = a firefly, often written ホタル; *Santa went home to talk to Rudolph about incorporating fireflies into his sleigh lighting*; cf. related terms listed at mushi

Hotoke 仏 = Buddha; *the Buddha enjoyed hottokeeki (pancakes)*

Hotondo ほとんど = mostly, just about, almost; *the hot water ondo (temperature) was almost scalding*; cf. related terms listed at ayauku

Hotteoku ほっておく = to leave alone or neglect; *Homer tested the old Kool-Aid and decided to leave it alone*

Hotto suru ホッとする = to feel relief, to relax; *when I put a hot towel on my face, I feel relief and relax*; cf. related terms listed at kutsurogu and at yasuragu

Hou 方 = direction or side, than, compared to, alternative; *my home is in that direction*; cf. -gawa = side (used as a suffix); cf. hanmen = the other or opposite side; cf. hyouri = two sides, inside and out; cf. mukou = the other side; cf. ryouhou = both, both sides; cf. ryoumen = both sides; cf. temae = before, this side; cf. uchigawa = inside or interior; cf. uramen = the back side; cf. yoko = side or width; cf. other related terms listed at houkou

Hou 法 = method, law; *Homer obeys the law*; cf. related terms listed at houhou

Hou 邦 = home country or Japan, used as a word component; *my home is in my home country*

Hou ga ii 方がいい = it would be better to do, e.g., yasunda hou ga ii = it would be better to rest (usually this employs the past form of the verb); this construction can also be used with other adjectives, e.g., iki no hou ga hidoi = going is more awful; from hou = direction or side + ii = good

Houan 法案 = legislation; *we hope that Queen Anne will support this legislation*

Houbi 褒美 = a reward or prize; *the hostess found some beer and earned a reward*; cf. houshuu = a reward or remuneration; cf. kenshou = an award or prize; cf. shou = a prize; cf. shouyo = a reward or bonus; cf. taishou = a grand prize

Houchiki 報知機 = alarm; *our host had a cheeky son who kept setting off the fire alarm*

Houchou 包丁 = a kitchen knife; *my home chores involve using a kitchen knife*; cf. debabouchou = a knife or cutting tool; cf.

hamono = a knife or cutting tool

Houdai 放題 = a suffix meaning without restriction, e.g., tabehoudai = all you can eat; *I hope to diet, but now I eat without restriction*

Houdou 報道 = report, information or news; *there was a report that the hotel's doors were left unlocked*; cf. hodou = sidewalk; cf. related terms listed at houkokusho and at jouhou

Houfu na 豊富な = abundant, full of; *Whole Foods stocks abundant groceries*; cf. yutaka = rich, abundant

Hougaku 邦楽 = traditional Japanese music; from hou = home country + ongaku = music

Hougen 方言 = a dialect; *in the home where Genghis was raised, they spoke a Mongolian dialect*; cf. related terms listed at gengo

Houhou 方法 = method; *Santa's method for deflecting questions is to reply "Ho Ho"*; cf. hou = method, law; cf. ikikata = a way of life; cf. shiji = instructions, directions; cf. shikata = way (of doing), method; cf. shiyou = means, method; cf. shudan = a means or way; cf. teguchi = a method or trick; cf. yarikata = a way of doing something

Hou 邦 = home country, Japan, used as a word component; *my home is in my home country*

Houjou 豊穣 = good harvest, fertile; *Homer joked that he was still fertile and might have been responsible for the good harvest*; cf. related terms listed at sakumotsu

Houka 砲火 = gunfire; *homes in California sometimes get damaged by gunfire*

Houka suru 放火する = to commit arson; *someone committed arson on my home in California*

Houken 封建 = feudalistic; *the hotel where Kennedy stayed looked feudalistic*

Houken jidai 封建時代 = the feudal period; from houken = feudalistic + jidai = era

Houki ホウキ = a broom; *they use a broom to sweep the ice before the hockey games*

Houkoku 報告 = a report, information; *we have a report that Homer's Coke is contaminated*; cf. related terms listed at houkokusho and at jouhou

Houkokusho 報告書 = a written report; from houkoku = a report + sho = a document; cf. houdou = public news or report; cf. houkoku = a report, information

Houkou 方向 = direction, way; *the horse and the colt are going in that direction*; cf. hou = direction or side; cf. kazamuki = wind direction; cf. kurashimuki = life direction

Houkou 芳香 = perfume or fragrance; *the horse and its colt were doused with perfume*; cf. related terms listed at kaori

Houkyuu 俸給 = a salary; *he sells homes in Cuba for a good salary*; cf. hokyuu suru = to supply or supplement; cf. other related terms listed at chin

Houmen 放免 = a release (from custody), discharge, setting free; *the police released the holy men after their arrest for begging*; cf. shakuhou = release, liberation, or acquittal

Houmen suru 放免する = to acquit, release or let loose; from houmen = a release; cf. related terms listed at tokihanatsu

Houmon 訪問 = a visit or call; *I paid a visit to the doctor to get some hormones*; cf. hatsumoude = first shrine visit of the year; cf. hatsurainichi = the first visit to Japan; cf. moude = a temple or shrine visit; cf. ohakamairi = a visit to a grave; cf. omairi = a humble visit to a shrine, grave, etc; cf. omiyamairi = a shrine visit; cf. otozure = a visit or arrival; cf. rainichi = a visit to Japan

Houmon suru 訪問する = to visit; from

houmon = a visit or call; cf. otozureru = to visit or arrive; cf. tazuneru = to visit; cf. ukagau = to visit or ask

Houmuru 葬る = to bury or suppress; *Homer's mood was ruined when he had to bury his dog*; cf. danatsu suru = to oppress or suppress; cf. umeru = to bury, to fill up (e.g., a hall, a seat or a vacant position), to plug gaps, to make amends, to cover

Hounin 放任 = noninterference, giving someone a free hand; *Homer treated the ninjas in accordance with his policy of noninterference*

Hounin suru 放任する = to give free rein, to leave a person to himself or herself; from hounin = noninterference

Houridasu 放り出す = to expel, abandon, neglect; from houru = to throw away or neglect + dasu = to put out; cf. haiseki suru = to expel, boycott or shut out; cf. other related terms listed at suteru

Hourikomu 放り込む = to throw into; from houru = to throw away + komu = to get crowded; cf. related terms listed at nageru

Houritsu 法律 = a law; *Homer's written suggestions were incorporated into the law*; cf. related terms listed at kisoku

Hourou suru 放浪する = to wander; *the hobo on the road is wandering*; cf. furatsuku = to wander aimlessly, to stagger, to waver

Houru 放る = to throw away or neglect; *I threw away the hotel's rulebook*; this can can also be pronounced hanaru = to be released or get free; cf. related terms listed at suteru

Housaku 豊作 = a good harvest, bumper crop; *please hold the sack while I fill it with fruit from our bumper crop*; cf. related terms listed at sakumotsu

Houseki 宝石 = a jewel or precious stone; *in the home of the selfish king, I saw jewels*

Houshanou 放射能 = radioactivity; *my home is a shack in Norway, and it's contaminated by radioactivity*

Houshi 奉仕 = service, ministry; *the hotel provides sheets as part of its service*; cf. related terms listed at kinmu

Houshi 胞子 = a spore; *the holes in my sheets let spores get into my bed*

Houshin 方針 = policy, principle, direction; *the hotel's shingles were fireproof, as per policy*; cf. seisaku = policy; cf. shugi = doctrine, rule, principle

Houshuu 報酬 = a reward or remuneration; *these homely shoes were my reward*; cf. related terms listed at houbi

Housou 放送 = a broadcast; *we hope that the soldiers will be able to hear the broadcast*; cf. saihousou = a re-broadcast

Houtei 法廷 = a court of law; *the homely tailor sued his customer in the court of law*; cf. saibansho = a court of law

Houteki 法的 = legal; from hou = law + teki = related to

Houwa 飽和 = saturation; *the hose poured water onto the ground until saturation was reached*; cf. houwa joutai = saturation

Houwa joutai 飽和状態 = saturation; from houwa = saturation + joutai = condition

Houyou 包容 = magnanimity, tolerance; *when the hornet stung the yogi, he showed tolerance*; cf. related terms listed at kanyou

Houyou 法要 = a Buddhist memorial service; *I brought home-made yogurt to the Buddhist memorial service*

Houyou suru 抱擁する = to embrace or hug; *the homely yogi embraced us*; cf. related terms listed at daku

Houyouryoku 包容力 = tolerance, broad-mindedness; from houyou = tolerance + ryoku = force; cf. related terms listed at kanyou

Hoyuu 保有 = possession, ownership; *one of my possessions is a home in the Yukon*; cf. shoyuu = ownership

Hoyuu suru 保有する = to own; from hoyuu = possession; cf. motsu = to have or own; cf. yuu suru = to own or be endowed with

Hozon 保存 = preservation; *when Homer zones out in front of he TV, he neglects the preservation of his food*; cf. hoken = health preservation

Hyakka 百科 = many objects (for study); from hyaku = one hundred + ka = section or category, e.g., kagaku = science

Hyakkajiten 百科事典 = an encyclopedia; from hyakka = many objects + jiten = an encylopedia; cf. similar terms listed at jiten = an encyclopedia

Hyakushou 百姓 = a farmer; *Himalayan yaks were featured in a cool show put on by farmers*; cf. noufu = a farmer; cf. nouka = a farmer or farmhouse

Hyotto ひょっと = possibly; *the Lone Ranger said "Hi-yo" when his toe encountered an object, which he thought was possibly a snake*; cf. related terms listed at kamoshiremasen

Hyotto suru to ひょっとすると = possibly, maybe; from hyotto = possibly; cf. related terms listed at kamoshiremasen

Hyou 俵 = a bag or bale, or a counter for bags; *a healer from Oregon gave me a bag*; cf. fukuro = bag, sack, pack

Hyou 氷 = ice, used as a word component; *the Lone Ranger said "Hi-yo" when he saw ice*; cf. koori = ice

Hyou 票 = a vote; *the healer from Oregon had one vote*; cf. hantai hyou = an opposing vote or voice; cf. touhyou = voting, vote

Hyou 表 = a surface, chart or diagram; *the healer from Oregon put a diagram on the surface of the table*; cf. related terms listed at men

Hyou suru 表する – see hyousu

Hyouban 評判 = reputation, popularity, rumor; *"Hi-yo Silver" was banned, and this affected the Lone Ranger's reputation and popularity*; cf. fuhyou = bad reputation or review, unpopularity; cf. hitogiki = reputation, respectability; cf. kouhyou = favorable review, good reception; cf. ninki = popularity; cf. taimen = a reputation; cf. teihyou = reputation, notoriety

Hyougen 表現 = an expression; *the Lone Ranger said "Hi-yo" when he saw Genghis, as an expression of delight*

Hyougen suru 表現する = to express or describe; from hyougen = an expression; cf. related terms listed at iiarawasu

Hyouhakuzai 漂白剤 = bleach; *when the healer from Oregon met the hacker from Kuwait in Zaire (former name of the Congo), they threw bleach at each other*

Hyouji 表示 = an indication, expression, or showing; *the healer from Oregon was a genius who used many informative expressions*; cf. related terms listed at kehai

Hyouji suru 表示する = to indicate or express; from hyouji = an indication or expression; cf. related terms listed at hanasu

Hyoujou 表情 = facial expression; *when the Lone Ranger said "Hi-yo Joe," Joe's facial expression brightened*

Hyouka 評価 = assessment, evaluation; *high yogurt prices caused a change in the evaluation of that company*

Hyouka suru 評価する = to value, to appreciate; from hyouka = evaluation; cf. kanshou suru = to appreciate (seeing, reading, listening, etc.); cf. taisetsu ni suru = to value or treasure, to take good care of; cf. other related terms listed at sonkei suru

Hyouketsu 評決 = a decision or verdict; *the*

healer from Oregon put ketchup in his soup as he waited for the verdict in his trial; cf. related terms listed at handan

Hyoukou 標高 = elevation, height above sea level; *the Lone Ranger said "Hi-yo" when he experienced the cold at a high elevation*

Hyoumei 表明 = a declaration or announcement; from hyousu = to express + seimei = a statement; cf. related terms listed at sengen

Hyoumen 表面 = surface, exterior; *the Lone Ranger said "Hi-yo" when he saw the men who were on the surface of the moon*; cf. gaikan = surface, exterior; cf. men = mask, face, surface or aspect; cf. omote = surface, front

Hyouri 表裏 = two sides, inside and out; *the Lone Ranger said "Hi-yo" at the rear of the house and again at the front, so he said it on two sides*; cf. related terms listed at hou = direction

Hyouron 評論 = criticism, review; from hyouka = assessment + kouron = argument; cf. related terms listed at hihan

Hyouryuu 漂流 = drifting; *the healer from Oregon reused a compass that he found drifting in the ocean*

Hyoushi 拍子 = musical time or rhythm; *the healer from Oregon and his sheep dance to a rhythm*

Hyoushiki 標識 = a written sign; *the Lone Ranger said "Hi-yo" when he saw that some Shiites from Kiev were building a sign*; cf. related terms listed at fuda

Hyoushou 表彰 = public acknowledgment, commendation; *I saw a healer from Oregon on a TV show, where he received a commendation*

Hyousu 表す = to express or show; this can also be expressed as hyou suru; *the healer from Oregon and Superman expressed respect for each other*; cf. related terms listed at iiarawasu and at miseru

Hyouteki 標的 = a target; *the Lone Ranger said "Hi-yo" when he saw that some techies were shooting at a target*; cf. mato = target, center of attention

Hyoutenka 氷点下 = below freezing; from hyou = ice + ten = point + ka = below

Hyouzan 氷山 = iceberg; from hyou = ice; *the Lone Ranger said "Hi-yo" when he saw ice;* + zan = san = mountain

I 位 = rank or place, used as a suffix; *she achieved first place in the east*; cf. related terms listed at kurai = rank

I 医 = a doctor, or the field of medicine; from isha = a doctor; cf. related terms listed at isha

I 胃 = stomach; *the eagle had a full stomach*; cf. related terms listed at onaka

I 意 = mind, heart; *her heart and mind were eager to help*

Ian 慰安 = consolation, comfort, recreation; *we visited the eastern Andes for recreation*; cf. related terms listed at kokochiyosa

Ian ryokou 慰安旅行 = a pleasure trip, a company recreational trip; from ian = recreation + ryokou = travel; cf. related terms listed at ryokou

Ibaru 威張る = to look down on, to brag; *the Eagles fans in the bar were rude and bragged about their team's victory*; cf. jiman suru = to brag; cf. other related terms listed at anadoru

Ibento イベント = event

Icchi 一致 = agreement, coincidence, conformity, cooperation, e.g., guuzen no icchi = a coincidence; *we are in agreement that we all feel itchy, but it may be a coincidence*; cf. guuzen = coincidence; cf. kyoudou = cooperation, sharing; cf. kyouryoku = cooperation; cf. other related terms listed at shouchi

Icchouen 一兆円 = 1 trillion yen; from ichi = one + chou = trillion; *Margaret Cho earned a trillion yen last year*; + en = yen

Ichi 位置 = position, location, situation; *we eat cheaply at that location*; cf. related terms listed at basho and at keisei

Ichi 壱 = one, usually written 一; *one leg is itchy*

Ichiba 市場 = market (as a physical place); *I got my itchy bandana at the market*; cf. 市場 shijou = market (as an abstract idea)

Ichiban 一番 = number one; from ichi = one + ban = number in a series; cf. related terms listed at daiichi

Ichibu 一部 = a part or portion; from ichi = one + bubun = a part of something; cf. bubun = a part of something; cf. chuubu = center (e.g., the center of a town), middle, heart; cf. gaibu = the outside world, exterior; cf. hokubu = northern parts; cf. kabu = the lower part; cf. naibu = inside; cf. nanbu = southern parts; cf. nanseibu = the southwestern part; cf. seibu = the western parts; cf. tokoro = a place or part

Ichidan to 一段と = better (or worse) than usual, all the more; *itchy Dan told me that the new medicine made him itch all the more*

Ichidan 一団 = group; *itchy Dan belongs to a support group*; cf. related terms listed at dantai

Ichigo イチゴ = strawberry; *I'm itching to go to the strawberry patch*

Ichiin 一員 = a member; *the itchy investigator is a member of the police department*; cf. danin = a group member; cf. in = a group member (used as a suffix)

Ichiji 一時 = for a while; from ichi = one + jikan = time (this can also be read as ichiji = one o'clock, or hitotoki = for a moment, for awhile); cf. related terms listed at ittan

Ichijirushii 著しい = remarkable, conspicuous; *at ichiji (1:00) he was rushing, which was remarkable and conspicuous*; cf. kencho na = conspicuous, remarkable; cf. odorokubeki = surprising, remarkable

Ichiman'en (Ichimanen) 壱万円 = 10,000 yen, usually written 一万円; from ichi = one + man = 10,000 + en = yen

Ichimegasa 市女笠 = a straw hat worn by women; *as the itchy men gathered sand, they wished that they had the straw hats worn by women*; cf. related terms listed at boushi

Ichimokusan 一目散 = at full speed; *when the itchy guy needed more Kool-Aid and sandwiches, he drove to the store at full speed*

Ichinenjuu 一年中 = all year round, from ichi = one + nen = year + juu = throughout

Ichinichi 一日 = one day; from ichi = one + nichi = day

Ichinichijuu 一日中 = all day long, throughout the day; from ichinichi = one day + juu = throughout

Ichininmae 一人前 = becoming adult, coming of age; *the itchy ninja and the maestro have both worked hard at becoming adults*

Ichiou 一応 = more or less, tentatively, for the time being; *I'm itching to live near the ocean for the time being*; cf. related terms listed at toriaezu

Ichiren 一連 = a series; from ichi = one + renzoku = a series

Ichiryuu no 一流 = first-rate; *those itchy reusable hats are first-rate*; cf. related terms listed at idai

Ichiwa 一把 = a bundle or bunch; from ichi = one + wa = a bundle; *the itchy warrior was a bundle of nerves*; cf. related terms listed at taba

Ichiwa 一羽 = one bird; from ichi = one + wa = a counter for birds; cf. related terms listed at tori

Ichiya 一夜 = one evening, overnight; from ichi = one + ya = night, e.g., konya = tonight; cf related terms listed at tetsuya

Ichiyaku 一躍 = suddenly, overnight; from ichi = one + yaku = leap; cf. related terms listed at kyuu ni

Ichizen 一膳 = one bowl (of cooked rice); from ichi = one + zen = a counter for bowls of cooked rice

Ichizoku 一族 = family, household, relatives; from ichi = one + kazoku = family; cf. related terms listed at kazoku

Ichizu ni 一途に = wholeheartedly, earnestly; *the itchy animals at the zoo and my niece wholeheartedly wish for a cure*

Ichizuke 位置づけ = placement, location; from ichi = position + tsukeru = to attach (**Note**: this is spelled "ichiduke" in electronic dictionaries); cf. related terms listed at basho

Ichou 胃腸 = the stomach and intestines; from i = stomach + chou = intestines; cf. related terms listed at naizou and at onaka

Idai 偉大 = great, grand; *the eagle's dive from the sky was great*; cf. erai = great, excellent; cf. gouka = wonderful, gorgeous; cf. hijou = extreme, great; cf. ichiryuu no = first-rate; cf. kyouiteki = marvelous, miraculous; cf. migoto = wonderful; cf. soudai = magnificent, imposing; cf. soukan na = spectacular, magnificent; cf. subarashii = wonderful, superb, excellent; cf. sugoi = great, wonderful, terrific, terrible; cf. suteki = great, wonderful; cf. taishita = considerable, great

Idaku 抱く = to embrace or hold, to entertain (an idea); *he entertained the idea of training eagles to dance in Kuwait*; cf. related terms listed at daku

Idenshi 遺伝子 = a gene; *we can identify sheep using their genes*

Ido 井戸 = water well; *the eastern door leads to a water well*

Ido 緯度 = latitude; *people at that latitude tend to worship idols*; cf. hokui = northern latitude; cf. keido = longitude; cf. nan'i = southern latitude

Idomu 挑む = to challenge or contend for; *the eager doorman moved across town to challenge his rivals for a job*; cf. related terms listed at tamesu

Idou suru 移動する = to move (both transitive and intransitive); *both an eagle and a doe can move around*; cf. iten suru = to move (a business, etc.); cf. nokeru = to move something; cf. ugokasu = to move something; cf. utsusu = to move or transfer something; cf. other related terms listed at ugoku

Ie いえ = no; *no, I don't have an earache*

Ie 家 = house, household, family, home; *my house is yellow*; cf. bessou = a summer house, villa or cottage; cf. hiraya = one-story house; cf. ikka = a house, a family; cf. ikken = one house; cf. ikkenya = detached house; cf. ikko = one house or household; cf. ittou = one house; cf. juukyo = dwelling; cf. juutaku = a residence or house; cf. kaoku = a house or building; cf. koya = cabin, hut; cf. machiya = a townhouse, or a tradesman's house; cf. shotai = household, family; cf. wagaya = my house; cf. zaijuu = residence cf. other related terms listed at teitaku and at uchi

Ifuku 衣服 = clothing; *at Easter in Fukuoka, I wore new clothes*; cf. related terms listed at fuku

Igai 以外 = with the exception of; *with the exception of the easy guys, I can't beat anyone at chess*

Igai 意外 = unexpected; *the eating guide contained some unexpected advice*; cf. battari = with a thud, unexpectedly, suddenly; cf. hinichijou = the unusual or unexpected; cf. masaka = something unexpected, an emergency, by no means, never; cf. omoigakenai = unexpected; cf. tamatama = unexpectedly, by chance; cf. tondemonai = unthinkable, unexpected

Igaku 医学 = medical science; from isha = physician + gaku = study

Igata 鋳型 = a mold or cast; *at Easter, Gandalf makes taffy in a mold*; cf. related terms listed at kata

Igen 威厳 = dignity; *it was easy for Genghis to behave with dignity*

Igi 異議 = an objection; *I have an objection to eating geese*; cf. related terms listed at hanron

Igo 以後 = hereafter, thereafter, since; *his ego only strengthened thereafter*; cf. related terms listed at irai and at kongo

Igokochi 居心地 = comfort in a particular ambience; from iru = to reside + gokoro = kokoro = heart + chi = ground or soil; cf. fuinki = atmosphere, ambience, mood air; cf. related terms listed at kokochiyosa

Ihai 遺灰 = ashes (of the deceased); *the eagle flew high to avoid the ashes from the cremation fire*

Ihan 違反 = offense; *eagle handling is an offense*

Ihou 違法 = illegal; *my Eastern home is illegal, and I have to tear it down*; cf. fuhou = illegal

Ii いい = good, fine, enough; *if you eat it in the evening, that will be good*; cf. kekkou = fine, good, rather; cf. yoi = good; cf. yoroshii = good

Ii ne いいね = a "like"; literally "good, huh"

Ii okureru 言い遅れる = to say something late; from iu = to speak + okureru = to be delayed

Iiarasou 言い争う = to quarrel or dispute; *on Easter, Arafat sold his share in his yacht after he quarreled with the other owners*; cf. related terms listed at arasou

Iiarawasu 言い表す = to express or narrate; from iu = to speak + arawasu = to signify or represent; cf. arawasu = to signify or represent; cf. byousha suru = to describe; cf. egakidasu = to delineate, express or imagine; cf. hyougen suru = to express or describe; cf. hyousu = to express or show

Iikaesu 言い返す = to talk or answer back, to say repeatedly; from iu = to speak + kaesu = to return something; cf. kotaeru = to answer; cf. other related terms listed at hanasu

Iikagen いい加減 = irresponsible, careless, lukewarm, half-hearted, reasonable or moderate, considerably, quite; *the eagle caught Genghis behaving in an irresponsible and careless way*

Iikagen ni shinasai いい加減にしなさい = act properly, don't be irresponsible; from iikagen = irresponsible; **Note**: in this expression, you are saying the opposite of what you mean, i.e., you are actually saying "act irresponsibly"; this may be due to the fact that the negative form of nasai, nasaruna, is no longer in active use in Japanese

Iikagen ni shiro いい加減にしろ = don't overdo it; from iikagen = irresponsible; **Note**: in this expression, you are saying the opposite of what you mean, i.e., you are actually saying "act irresponsibly"; this may be due to the fact that the negative form of nasai, nasaruna, is no longer in active use in Japanese

Iikikaseru 言い聞かせる = to tell someone to do something, to warn or persuade; from iu = to speak + kikaseru = to make hear; cf. imashimeru = to admonish, warn, prohibit, be cautious; cf. satosu = to warn or advise

Iin 委員 = a committee member; from iinkai = a committee; cf. related terms listed at in

Iinkai 委員会 = committee; *it was easy to*

see the *incompetence* of the *Kaiser's committee*

Iisugi 言い過ぎ = an exaggeration; from iisugiru = to exaggerate; cf. kagon = an exaggeration; cf. kochou = an exaggeration

Iisugiru 言い過ぎる = to exaggerate or say too much; from iu = to say + sugiru = to exceed

Iji 維持 = maintenance; *it's easy for Jeep owners to perform maintenance on their cars*; cf. hoshu = maintenance, conservation

Iji suru 維持する = to maintain; from iji = maintenance; cf. related terms listed at azukaru

Ijime いじめ = bullying, teasing; from ijimeru = to bully or abuse

Ijimeru 苛める = to bully or abuse, usually written いじめる; *it's easy to jeer at my messy room, but you don't have to abuse me*; cf. batou suru = to abuse or yell at; cf. nonoshiru = to revile, abuse or swear at; cf. ranyou suru = to abuse, misuse

Ijin 偉人 = an exceptional person; *the easygoing genius is an exceptional person*

Ijou 以上 = not less than, now that, beyond, further, more than, this is all, above-mentioned; *at Easter, Joan of Arc would eat not less than three eggs*

Ijou 異常 = abnormal, bizarre; *the eels that Joan of Arc caught were abnormal and bizarre*; cf. related terms listed at kawatta

Ijuu suru 移住する = to migrate or immigrate; *the eastern Jews migrated west*

Ijuusha 移住者 = immigrant, migrant; from ijuu suru = to immigrate + sha = person; cf. imin = an immigrant or emigrant

Ika イカ = squid; *Icarus liked to eat squid*; cf. surume = dried shredded squid

Ika 以下 = below, less than, the following, the rest; *the numbers of eagles in California are below their historic levels, as shown by the following data*; cf. shita = below, inferior; cf. other related terms listed at tsugi

Ikada いかだ = a raft; *Icarus and his dad crossed on a raft*

Ikaga 如何 = how, would you like, usually spelled いかが; *how would it be if I gave some Easter candy to Gandalf?* cf. related terms listed at dou

Ikaiyou 胃潰瘍 = a stomach ulcer; from i = stomach + kaiyou = an ulcer; cf. related terms listed at byouki

Ikan 遺憾 = regret (noun); *I feel regret after eating that candy*; cf. related terms listed at koukai

Ikan na 遺憾な = regrettable, unsatisfactory; from ikan = regret; cf. related terms listed at zannen

Ikan nagara 遺憾ながら = regrettably; from ikan = regret + nagara = while, at the same time

Ikanaru いかなる = any kind of; *when he performed any kind of flying stunts, Icarus was the subject of nasty rumors*

Ikashi 生かし = making the most of, keeping alive; from ikasu = to make the most of, to keep alive

Ikasu 生かす = to make the most of, to keep alive; *before Easter, I casually asked my wife if she was going to make the most of the opportunity to wear her new dress*; cf. katsuyou suru = to make the most of

Ike 池 = a pond; *it's easy to wash my kettle in the pond*; cf. related terms listed at mizuumi

Ikebana 生け花 = Japanese flower arrangement; from ikeru = to arrange (flowers) + bana = hana = flowers

Ikei 畏敬 = awe and respect, reverence; *I bowed to the eagle's cage out of reverence*;

cf. related terms listed at sonkei

Ikemasen いけません = bad, unacceptable, prohibited; from ikeru = to be able to go, so literally this means "it cannot go"; cf. naranai = must not, cannot help, one must

Ikemen イケメン = good-looking guy, hunk; *I eat ketchup with those men, who are all good-looking guys*

Iken 意見 = an opinion; *Easter in Kentucky is the best, in my opinion*; cf. kenkai = a viewpoint or opinion; cf. setsu = theory, opinion

Ikenai いけない – see ikemasen

Ikeru 生ける = to arrange (flowers); *in the evening I went to Kennedy's room to help him arrange flowers*

Iki wo suru 息をする = to breathe; from iki = breath; cf. related terms listed at fukikakeru

Iki 息 = breath; *your breath smells icky*; cf. kokyuu = breath, respiration

Iki 行き = going, or bound for; from iku = to go

Ikidooru 憤る = to resent or get indignant; *she resented the icky doru (dollar) bill she received as change*; cf. fungai suru = to be indignant

Ikikata 生き方 = a way of life; from ikiru = to live + kata = a method; cf. related terms listed at houhou

Ikimono 生き物 = a living creature; from ikiru = to live + mono = tangible thing; cf. related terms listed at doubutsu

Ikinari いきなり = all of a sudden, without warning; *an Eastern king showed up at Narita without warning*; cf. fui = sudden, abrupt; cf. kyuu = urgent, sudden, unexpected, steep, rapid; cf. kyuugeki = abrupt or rapid; cf. kyuusei no = acute or sudden; cf. totsuzen no = abrupt or sudden; cf. toutotsu = sudden, abrupt

Ikinobiru 生き延びる = to survive or live long; from ikiru = to live + nobiru = to extend

Ikioi 勢い = force, power, energy, spirit; *there is a lot of energy in the icky oil industry*; cf. related terms listed at chikara and at seishin

Ikiru 生きる = to live; *I live near some icky ruins*; cf. iru = to reside; cf. katsudou suru = to be active; cf. katsuyaku suru = to be active, implying successful or energetic activity; cf. kurasu = live or make a living; cf. okuru = to spend time, live one's life, send a thing, escort a person; cf. seikatsu suru = to maintain a lifestyle; cf. seisoku suru = to reside; cf. sumu = to reside; cf. tabete iku = to make a living; cf. yadoru = to lodge or dwell

Ikka 一家 = a family, a house; from ichi = one + ka = a house, e.g., kazoku = family; cf. related terms listed at ie and at kazoku

Ikkaiten 一回転 = one revolution or rotation; from ichi = one + kaiten = rotation; cf. related terms listed at kaiten

Ikkaku 一角 = corner, section, point; from ichi = one + kaku = corner, e.g., shikaku = a square or rectangle; cf. related terms listed at kado

Ikkan 一巻 = one volume (book); from ichi = one + kan = a counter for books; *I read a book about Easter candy*; cf. related terms listed at hon

Ikkan 一貫 = consistency, coherence, integration; *the consistency of their Easter candy is remarkable*; cf. related terms listed at kosa

Ikkanshite 一貫して = consistently; from ikkan = consistency + shite = doing

Ikken 一軒 = one house; from ichi = one + ken = house; *Ken and Barbie live in a house*; cf. related terms listed at ie

Ikkenya 一軒家 = detached house; from ikken = one house + ya = house; cf. related terms listed at ie

Ikki ni 一気に = in one gulp, in one breath; from ichi = one + ki = spirit or air + ni = by

Ikkin 一斤 = one loaf of bread; from ichi = one + kin = a counter for loaves of bread; *I got a loaf of bread at my kindergarten*

Ikko 一戸 = one house or household; from ichi = one + ko = a counter for houses; cf. related terms listed at ie

Ikkoku 一刻 = a moment, an instant; *the eagle spilled the Coke in an instant*;; cf. related terms listed at shunkan

Ikkou ni 一向に = completely, not at all (in negative sentences); *this Eastern cold front nearly froze my plants and was completely and not at all what I wanted*; cf. ikou = thereafter; cf. other related terms listed at zenzen

Ikoi 憩い = rest; *after we study the ecosystem of the eagles we should get some rest*; cf. related terms listed at yasumi

Ikoi no ba 憩いの場 = a place for relaxation; from ikoi = rest + basho = place

Ikoru イコール = equals

Ikou 以降 = hereafter, thereafter, since; *at Easter I had a cold, and thereafter I haven't felt well*; cf. ikkou ni = completely; cf. other related terms listed at irai and at kongo

Iku 行く = to go; *I will go to buy medicine for my ear cooties*; cf. mairu = to come or go humbly; cf. irassharu = to come, go or exist humbly

Ikubun 幾分 = somewhat, somehow, to some extent; *the ear cooties that Daniel Boone had were somewhat larger than usual*; cf. related terms listed at nandaka

Ikura いくら = how much, even if; *how much does the Italian kuura (cooler) cost?* cf. doredake = how much, to what extent; cf. dorehodo = how much, how long, how far

Ikuraka いくらか = somewhat, a little; from ikura = how much + ka = a question marker; cf. dokoka = somewhere; cf. chottoshita = somewhat, quite; cf. ikutsuka = some, several; cf. nandaka = a little, somewhat

Ikusa 戦 = battle; *I carry ear cooties in a sack when I go into battle and scatter them on my enemies*; cf. related terms listed at issen

Ikusei 育成 = training, cultivation, promotion; *I received training in the detection of ear cooties in sailors*; cf. related terms listed at kunren

Ikutsu いくつ = how many or how old; *how many ear cooties can fit in a tsuitcase (suitcase)?*

Ikutsuka いくつか = some, several; from ikutsu = how many + ka = question marker; cf. related terms listed at ikuraka

Ima 今 = now; *imagine that you are in Heaven now*; cf. gendai = nowadays, modern times; cf. genzai = nowadays, present time; cf. ima sara = now, after a long time; at this late hour; cf. imadoki = the present day; cf. imaya = now, now at last, right now; cf. kindai = modern times, present day; cf. toudai = the present age

Ima 居間 = living room; *imagine that this is your living room*; cf. related terms listed at shitsu

Ima ni mo 今にも = soon, at any time; from ima = now + ni = at + mo = even; cf. related terms listed at mamonaku

Ima sara 今更 = now, after a long time; at this late hour; from ima = now + sara ni = again, furthermore; cf. related terms listed at ima

Imada 未だ = as yet, still, not yet finished; *my imaginary daughter hasn't shown up as yet*; cf. related terms listed at mada

Imada ni 未だに = even now, still, until this very day; *my imaginary daughter and my niece still have not appeared*; cf. related terms listed at mada

Imadoki 今どき = the present day; from ima = now + doki = toki = time; cf. related terms listed at ima

Imashimeru 戒める = to admonish, warn, prohibit, be cautious; *I imagine that there are sheep in the Mexican ruins, but I warn you not to visit them*; cf. keikai suru = to be cautious or watch out; cf. kinjiru = to prohibit

Imaya 今や = now (in contrast to the past), now at last, right now; from ima = now + yatto = at last; cf. related terms listed at ima

Imi 意味 = meaning, sense, significance; *the meaning of "imitation" is "something copied from an original"*; cf. wake = reason, meaning

Imiai 意味合い = nuance, implication; from imi = meaning + au = to match; cf. shisa = an implication or suggestion

Imin 移民 = an immigrant or emigrant; from idou suru = to move + min = people, e.g., shimin = a citizen; cf. ijuusha = an immigrant or migrant

Imo 芋 = potato; *eating potatoes stimulates positive emotions*; cf. jagaimo = Irish potato; cf. yaki imo = roasted sweet potato; cf. related terms listed at yasai

Imouto 妹 = a younger sister; *my little sister has immobile toes*; cf. similar terms listed at kyoudai

In 員 = a group member, used as a suffix; *group members are insiders*; cf. danin = a group member; cf. giin = a member of a legislature; cf. ichiin = a member; cf. iin = a committee member; cf. kaiin = a group member

In 院 = an institution, used as a suffix; *that institution works to promote industry*

Ina 否 = negate or deny, used as a word component; *your inappropriate behavior caused us to deny your request*

Inai 以内 = within, inside of, less than, used as a suffix; *on Easter night, I was inside the house for less than an hour*; cf. related terms listed at miman and at naka

Inaka 田舎 = rural area, hometown; *when he was inactive, Karl Marx would go to his hometown*; cf. related terms listed at furusato

Inasaku 稲作 = rice cultivation, rice crop; *you're using inappropriate sacks to store the rice crop*; cf. beisaku = rice growing, rice crop; cf. komezukuri = rice cultivation; cf. kousaku = cultivation; cf. nougyou = agriculture; cf. rakunou = dairy farming; cf. saibai = cultivation; cf. other related terms listed at sakumotsu

Inazuma 稲妻 = lightning; *at the inaugural, I was zooming around with Ma (Mother) when we got struck by lightning*

Inbou 陰謀 = a plot or conspiracy; *they hatched the conspiracy on the inbound train*

Inbun 韻文 = verse or poetry; *when intoxicated, Daniel Boone wrote poetry*; cf. sanbun = prose; cf. other related terms listed at shi

Ine 稲 = a rice plant; *this rice plant is inexpensive*; cf. related terms listed at shokubutsu

Inemuri 居眠り = a catnap; *it's inevitable that Muriel will take a catnap during the meeting*; cf. hirune = a nap

Ingen いんげん = beans, an abbreviation of ingenmame = string beans; cf. related terms listed at mame

Ingenmame いんげん豆 = green bean, string bean; *it's ingenious the way some mame (beans) conceal their beans in pods, and we call those string beans*; cf. related terms listed at mame

Inkan 印鑑 = a stamp or seal; *the incantation was stamped with a seal*

Inkei 陰茎 = a penis; *the insolent caterer has a penis*

Inn'en (Innen) 因縁 = a pretext for an attack; *the pretext for the attack on the policeman was incompetent enforcement of the law*

Inochi 命 = life, most precious possession or person; *my innocent children are my most precious possessions*; cf. isshou = a lifetime, all through life; cf. jinsei = human life; cf. kekkon seikatsu = married life; cf. kurashi = living, life; cf. seikatsu = livelihood, life (daily existence); cf. sei = life, a living thing or person; cf. seimei = life, existence; cf. shiseikatsu = private life; cf. yo no naka = the world, society, life

Inochizuna 命綱 = lifeline; from inochi = life + zuna = tsuna = rope

Inori 祈り = prayer; from inoru = to pray; cf. related terms listed at shomou

Inoru 祈る = to pray; *the innocent roosters prayed for peace*; cf. matsuru = to pray, worship, celebrate

Inoshishi 猪 = a wild boar; *the innocent sheep and their Shiite owners were frightened by a wild boar*

Inryoku 引力 = gravitation; *there was an accident involving Leo's Kool-Aid and gravitation, in which my pants got wet*

Inryou 飲料 = a beverage; *we invited Pope Leo to drink a beverage with us*; cf. nomimono = a beverage

Insatsu 印刷 = printing; *when he saw the printing, the Indian was satisfied with the super work*

Insatsu jutsu 印刷術 = the printing art; from insatsu = printing + jutsu = art or skill, e.g., shujutsu = surgery

Insei 陰性 = negative, gloomy; *she is so negative that she is driving me insane*; cf. related terms listed at makkura

Inshoku 飲食 = drinking and eating; *she was in shock when she saw how much drinking and eating was going on*; cf. inshu = drinking alcohol

Inshou 印象 = impression; *the insects on the shore made an impression on me*; cf. kanji = impression, perception, feeling; cf. kanmei = a deep impression; cf. kansou = impressions, thoughts

Inshouteki 印象的 = impressive; from inshou = impression + teki = related to; cf. azayaka = colorful, bright, vivid, impressive, beautiful; cf. kanshin = impressive, admirable; cf. rippa = splendid, impressive; cf. sugoi = terrific

Inshu 飲酒 = drinking alcohol; from in = drinking, e.g., inshoku = eating and drinking; + shu = alcohol, e.g., nihonshu = Japanese sake; cf. inshoku = eating and drinking

Inshu'unten (Inshuunten) 飲酒運転 = drunken driving; from inshu = drinking alcohol + unten = driving

Insutabae インスタ映え = something that looks attractive on Instagram; from insutaguramu = Instagram + baeru = haeru = to look attractive

Insutorakutaa インストラクター = instructor

Inu 犬 = a dog; *the Inuits keep dogs*; cf. banken = a watchdog; cf. chuuken = a faithful dog; cf. iyashiken = healing dogs; cf. kaiinu = a pet dog; cf. keisatsuken = a police dog; cf. moudouken = a guide dog; cf. mouken = a savage dog

Inuzuki 犬好き = a dog lover; from inu = dog + zuki = suki = to like; cf. similar terms listed at honzuki

In'you (Inyou) 引用 = a quotation or citation; *the intelligent yogi recited inspiring quotations*; cf. meigen = a wise or famous saying

In'you suru (Inyou suru) 引用する = to quote or refer to; from in'you = a quotation

Iou 硫黄 = sulfur; <u>Ee</u>y<u>o</u>re's garden was fertilized with <u>sulfur</u>; cf. related terms listed at tanso

Ippai 一杯 = one cup, glass, spoon or bowl; this also means "full"; after you <u>eat</u> that <u>pie</u>, I will give you <u>one glass</u> of milk, if your stomach isn't <u>full</u>; cf. related terms listed at juuman

Ippai de 一杯で = at the end of (a year, etc.); from ippai = full

Ippan ni 一般に = commonly, generally, usually; my <u>Easter pants</u> are <u>usually</u> colorful; cf. related terms listed at taitei

Ippan ni koukai 一般に公開 = usually open to the general public; from ippan ni = generally, usually + koukai = opening to the public

Ippanjin 一般人 = ordinary people; from ippan ni = commonly + jin = person; cf. bonjin = an ordinary person

Ippanteki ni 一般的に = commonly, generally, usually; from ippan = usually + teki = related to + -ni = a suffix that forms an adverb; cf. related terms listed at taitei

Ippatsu 一発 = one blow, shot, attempt; from ichi = one + patsu = departure, e.g., shuppatsu = departure; cf. related terms listed at kokoromi

Ippen 一片 = a piece or slice; the <u>eager</u> <u>pen</u>guin ate the last <u>slice</u> of fish; cf. related terms listed at ittai

Ippen 一遍 = one time, once; the <u>eager</u> <u>pen</u>guin jumped out of the water <u>one time</u>; cf. related terms listed at ittan

Ippen de 一遍で = the first time; from ippen = once + de = of

Ippen ni 一遍に = all at once, at the same time; from ippen = one time + ni = by; cf. related terms listed at douji ni

Ippin 一品 = one item, article, dish or course; from ichi = one + pin = hin = goods; cf. similar terms listed at ittai

Ippin ryouri 一品料理 = a la carte; from ippin = one dish + ryouri = cuisine; cf. related terms listed at ryouri

Ippo 一歩 = one step, level, stage; a small degree or amount; from ichi = one + po = to walk, e.g., sanpo = walk

Ippou 一方 = one side, the other party, on the other hand, meanwhile; this can also be read as hitokata = one person; from ichi = one + pou = hou = direction or side; cf. synonyms listed at katahou

Ippunkan 一分間 = one-minute duration; from ippun = one minute + kan = interval or space

Ippyou 一俵 = one bag; from ichi = one + pyou = hyou = a bag; cf. similar terms listed at fukuro and at ittai

Iradatsu 苛立つ = to get irritated, to fret; when my <u>Ira</u>nian <u>Datsu</u>n broke down, I <u>got</u> <u>irritated</u>; cf. related terms listed at akiru

Irai 以来 = since (after a point in time); I've been <u>eating rice since</u> I was a child; cf. igo = hereafter, thereafter, since; cf. ikou = hereafter, thereafter, since; cf. kara = from, since, after, because, therefore; cf. -kiri = since (after a point in time); cf. sore kara = and then, after that

Irai 依頼 = a request or commission; we have a <u>request</u> for some <u>Easter rhymes</u>; cf. related terms listed at seikyuu

Irasshai いらっしゃい = welcome; the imperative form of irassharu; cf. related terms listed at youkoso

Irasshaimase いらっしゃいませ = welcome (used in shops); a more formal version of irasshai = welcome; cf. related terms listed at youkoso

Irassharu いらっしゃる = to come, go or exist honorably; in <u>Iran</u>, the <u>Shah's rule</u> affected everyone who <u>came</u>, <u>went</u> or <u>existed honorably</u>; cf. iku = to go; cf. kuru = to come; cf. mairu = to come or go humbly; cf. other related terms listed at aru

Irei 異例 = exceptional, unprecedented, singular; *the eagle race was exceptional*; cf. related terms listed at tokubetsu

Irekaeru 入れ替える = to replace, to shift or change places; from ireru = to insert + kaeru = to replace; cf. related terms listed at koukan suru

Ireru 入れる = to insert or let in, to make coffee or tea; *when I eat red roosters, I insert spices into the recipe*; cf. related terms listed at mochikomu

Iriguchi 入口 = entrance; from ireru = to insert or let in + guchi = kuchi = mouth

Iro 色 = color; *iron has a warm color*; cf. shikisai = color, hue

Iroiro 色々 = various, manifold; *we have various irons made of iron for sale*; cf. related terms listed at kazukazu

Ironna いろんな = an abreviation of iroiro na = various, manifold; cf. related terms listed at kazukazu

Irozuku 色ずく = to change color (esp. leaves); from iro = color + zuku = tsuku = to adhere

Iru いる = to exist (used for animate beings); *the eager rooster exists*; cf. related terms listed at aru

Iru 入る = to go in, come in, flow in, set in; *the eager rooster went in to the barn*

Iru 射る = to hit or shoot (an arrow); *it was easy to ruin the balloon by shooting it*; cf. related terms listed at utsu = to hit

Iru 煎る = to roast or toast; *it's easy to ruin breakfast by toasting the bread too much*; cf. related terms listed at niru

Iru 要る = to need or require; *the east room needs some paint*

Iru 居る = to reside; *the Italian rooster resides on a farm*; cf. related terms listed at ikiru

Irui 衣類 = clothing; *at Easter, King Louis wore new clothes*; cf. related terms listed at fuku

Iruka イルカ = dolphin; *that dolphin will easily ruin your camera if you hand it over*; cf. related terms listed at sakana

Iryou 医療 = medical treatment; from isha = doctor + chiryou = medical treatment; cf. related terms listed at chiryou

Isagiyoi 潔い = unhesitating, manly, wholehearted, sportsmanlike; *Queen Isabella served geese and yogurt at Easter for her wholehearted supporters*; cf. ririshii = manly, dignified, gallant

Isakai いさかい = a fight or quarrel; *after Esau took Jacob's kite, they had a quarrel*; cf. related terms listed at issen

Isamashii 勇ましい = courageous, invigorating; *Isaac is mashing potatoes in the army, which he joined because he was courageous and thought that military life would be invigorating*; cf. yuukan na = brave

Isan 遺産 = inheritance, legacy, heritage; *my inheritance was an eel sandwich*; cf. dentou = tradition, heritage; cf. souzoku = a succession or inheritance

Iseki 遺跡 = ruins, remains; *at Easter the selfish king attacked and left the town in ruins*; cf. nokori = remainder, balance, remnant

Isha 医者 = a physician, usually expressed as oisha; *the eager Shah summoned a physician*; cf. i = a doctor, or the field of medicine; cf. ishi = physician

Ishi 医師 = physician; *my physician eats sheep*; cf. related terms listed at isha

Ishi 意志 = will, willpower; *the eastern Shiites had a lot of willpower*; cf. hari = tension, tone, willpower, pride; cf. kiryoku = willpower, mental energy

Ishi 石 = a pebble or stone; *it's easy to make a*

shield *that will protect us from* stones; cf. ganban = bedrock; cf. ganseki = rock; cf. iwa = rock; cf. koishi = a pebble or small stone; cf. seki = a stone

Ishibei 石塀 = a stone wall; *the* Irish sheep *and the* bay *were separated by a* wall; cf. related terms listed at kakine

Ishiki 意識 = consciousness; *when I* eat sheep *from* Kiev, *I sense their* consciousness; cf. ninshiki = awareness, recognition, knowledge

Isho 遺書 = a will; *he included money for the* Easter show *in his* will; cf. yuigon = a will; cf. yuigonsho = a written will

Ishoku 衣食 = clothing and food; from ifuku = clothing + shokuji = a meal; cf. ishokujuu = clothing, food & shelter

Ishokujuu 衣食住 = clothing, food & shelter (the necessities of life); from ifuku = clothing + shokuji = meal + juusho = address; cf. ishoku = clothing and food

Ishou 衣装 = clothing, costume; *she bought a* costume *to wear to the* Easter show; cf. related terms listed at fuku

Ishuku 萎縮 = withering, atrophy, contraction; *the* Italian shoemaker *went to* Kuwait *to be treated for* withering, contraction *and* atrophy

Ishuku suru 萎縮する = to flinch, wince, cower or recoil; from ishuku = contraction

Isogashii 忙しい = busy; *as an* isolated gadfly *in the* Shiite *community, he was* busy

Isogu 急ぐ = to hurry; *the* isolated goose *had to* hurry *to escape the fox*

Isoide 急いで = hurriedly; the te form of isogu = to hurry

Issai 一切 = everything (with positives) or nothing, not at all or never (with negatives); Eastern psychology *is* everything *to me, or,* Easter psychology *is* not *helping me* at all; cf. related terms listed at banji and at zenzen

Issei ni 一斉に = all at once, at the same time, all together; *it's* easy *to* say *that you will do it if everyone else will do it* at the same time; cf. related terms listed at douji ni and at issho ni

Issen 一戦 = battle, game, bout; *it was* easy *for the* senator *to get tickets to the* game; cf. arasoi = fighting, conflict; cf. funsou = a dispute or fight; cf. gekisen = fierce competition or battle; cf. hakuchuu = fierce competition, well-matched; cf. ikusa = battle; cf. isakai = a fight or quarrel; cf. kattou = conflict, friction; cf. kenka = a quarrel or fight; cf. kouron = argument, quarrel; cf. kyougi = an athletic competition; cf. kyousou = competition; cf. senran = war, strife; cf. sensou = war; cf. shiai = a competition or game; cf. taisen = competition; cf. tokkumiai = a scuffle; cf. yosen = a preliminary contest or heat

Issen 一銭 = 0.01 yen; from ichi = one + sen = money; *the* senator *needs* money *for her campaign*

Issho 一緒 = together, identical, at the same time; *the* Easter shows *were* identical, *and they were held* at the same time; cf. related terms listed at douji ni and at issho ni

Issho ni 一緒に = together; from issho = together, identical, at the same time + -ni = a suffix that forms an adverb; cf. issei ni = all at once, at the same time, all together; cf. matomete = all together, all at once; cf. minna de = all together, all told, in sum; cf. tomo ni = together

Isshoku 一色 = one color, same tendency, everyone caught up in the same thing; *the* Italian *was* shocked *by the art that employed only* one color; cf. similar terms listed at ittai

Isshou 一升 = an old liquid measurement unit equaling 1.8 liters; *we drank* 1.8 liters *of wine before attending the* Easter show

Isshou 一生 = a lifetime, all through life; *that* Easter show *will satisfy me for* a lifetime; cf. isshougai = a lifetime, all through life;

Isshou kenmei 一生懸命 = with all one's might; *at the Easter show, Ken and May sang with all their might*; cf. related terms listed at zenryoku

Isshoubin 一升瓶 = a 1.8 liter bottle; from isshou = 1.8 liters + bin = a bottle; cf. related terms listed at tsubo

Isshougai 一生涯 = a lifetime, all through life; from ichi = one + shougai = one's lifetime; cf. related terms listed at isshou

Isshu no 一種の = a kind of, a type of; from ichi = one + shurui = type; cf. related terms listed at shurui

Isshun 一瞬 = one moment or instant; *the eagle's shunt was only plugged for one instant*; cf. related terms listed at shunkan

Isshun de 一瞬で = in an instant; from isshun = one instant + de = from or of; cf. related terms listed at kyuu ni

Isshuu 一周 = round, tour; from ichi = one + shuu = circumference; *the skaters's shoes were scattered around the circumference of the rink*

Isshuuki 一周忌 = the first anniversary of a death; from isshuu = one round or tour + ki = a death anniversary; cf. sankaiki = the second anniversary of a death; there is no ~~nishuuki~~ or ~~nikaiki~~; cf. related terms listed at shuunen

Issou 一層 = all the more, more than before; *after he lost his birthright, Esau hated Jacob all the more*; cf. kaette = conversely, rather, all the more; cf. yokei = excessive, all the more

Issui 一睡 = a wink (of sleep); *at Easter, the Swedish pastor doesn't get a wink of sleep*

Isu 椅子 = chair; *on Easter the superintendent will sit in a fancy chair*; cf. related terms listed at seki

cf. shougai = one's lifetime or career; cf. wagashougai = my lifetime; cf. other related terms listed at inochi

Ita 板 = (wooden) board or (metal) plate; *I sawed a board for my Italian friend*

Itadaki 頂き = peak, summit; *I wore an Italian dark kimono when I climbed to the summit*; cf. related terms listed at choujou

Itadaku 頂く = to receive humbly, to eat or drink humbly; *I will humbly receive Italian dark Kool-Aid*; cf. morau = to receive

Itai 痛い = painful, aching; the adverbial form of itamu = to feel pain

Itai 遺体 = a dead body; *an eagle from Thailand ate the dead body*; cf. related terms listed at karada

Itamashii 痛ましい = poignant, pitiable, tragic; *the Italian was mashing potatoes which was tragic for the potatoes*; cf. related terms listed at kanashii

Itameru 炒める = to cook or fry; *the Italian men ruined the pasta when they fried it*; cf. related terms listed at niru

Itameru 痛める = to injure or cause pain; the transitive form of itamu = to feel pain; cf. related terms listed at kizutsukeru

Itami 痛み = pain; from itamu = to feel pain; cf. gekitsuu = sharp, intense pain; cf. kirikiri = sharp pain, grinding, chafing; cf. kunou = agony, anguish, suffering; cf. kurushimi = suffering, pain, hardship; cf. kurushisa = pain, suffering; cf. kutsuu = pain, agony; cf. shikushiku = with a dull pain, upset, weeping; cf. tsurasa = pain or bitterness; cf. youtsuu = low back pain; cf. zukizuki = throbbing pain; cf. zutsuu = a headache

Itamu 痛む = to feel pain; *I felt pain during that Italian movie*; cf. uzuku = to ache or throb

Itaru 至る = to lead to, to reach, to result in; *this road leads to some Italian ruins*; cf. tsuujiru = to lead to, reach by phone, communicate, flow, be knowledgeable; cf. other related terms listed at oyobu

Itaru tokoro 至るところ = everywhere; from itaru = to lead to + tokoro = place; cf. dokomo = everywhere, wherever, nowhere or nothing (in negative constructions)

Itasu 致す = to do humbly; *he sewed Italian suits and did it humbly*; cf. related terms listed at suru

Itazura いたずら = mischief, prank, trick; *at the Italian zoo, a rabbi played a trick on me*

Iten suru 移転する = to move, used for businesses, etc.; *the Eastern tennis club will move to a new location*; cf. idou suru = to move (an object); cf. nokeru = to move something; cf. ugokasu = to move something

Ito 糸 = thread, string; *during the evening the tobacco is tied with thread*; cf. asa ito = linen thread; cf. other related terms listed at himo

Itonamu 営む = to run a business, to conduct (a ceremony); *we run a business selling instruments with eerie tonal qualities to musicians*

Itsu いつ = when; *he eats when he's hungry*

Itsu no hi ka いつの日か = one of these days, someday; from itsu = when + the possessive no + hi = day + ka = question marker; cf. itsuka = sometime, some day, in the future, once, before

Itsu no manika いつの間にか = before one realizes it; *after she eats the nomads' nearby cattle, she falls asleep before she realizes it*

Itsudemo いつでも = always, any time; from itsu = when + de = of + mo = also

Itsuka いつか = sometime, some day, in the future, once, before; in some cases, this can also mean "when?"; from itsu = when + ka = a question marker; cf. itsu no hi ka = one of these days, someday

Itsukushimu 慈しむ = to love or be affectionate, to cherish, to pity; *he eats cookies with the sheep on the moor because he loves both cookies and sheep*; cf. related terms listed at ai suru

Itsumo いつも = always, usually, every time; *when she eats moldy bread, she always complains*; cf. shikiri ni = often, frequently, eagerly; cf. tsune ni = always, continually; cf. zutto = always, all the while, all the way, very much, far more

Itsunomanika いつの間にか – see itsu no ma ni ka

Itsuwa 逸話 = an anecdote; *she tells anecdotes while she eats walnuts*; cf. related terms listed at hanashi

Itsuwaru 偽る = to lie, deceive or pretend; *he eats waffles in the room and lies about it*; cf. uso wo tsuku = to tell a lie

Ittai 一体 = one body or unit, what on earth! from ichi = one + tai = body, e.g., taionkei = body thermometer; cf. hitokake = one piece; cf. hitokoto = a single word, a brief comment; cf. hitokuchi = a mouthful, one word; cf. ikkan = one volume (book); cf. ikken = one house; cf. ikko = one house or household; cf. ippen = a piece or slice; cf. ippin = one item, article, dish or course; cf. ippyou = one bag; cf. ittou = one house; cf. isshoku = one color

Ittai 一帯 = region or zone; *in this region, people eat Thai food*; cf. related terms listed at chitai

Ittai ichi 一対一 = one on one; from ichi = one + tai suru = to face toward + ichi = one

Ittan 一旦 = for a moment, once; *once I got my Italian tan, I was happy*; cf. chotto = a little, just a moment; cf. hitotabi = once, for a moment; cf. hitotoki = for a moment, for awhile; cf. ichiji = for a while; cf. ippen = one time, once; cf. ittoki = for a moment, for awhile; cf. shoushou = a little, just a moment

Ittei no 一定の = fixed, settled, constant, uniform; *the eels' tails grow to a fixed length*; cf. fuhen no = constant, unchanging, eternal

Itteki 一滴 = one drop; from ichi = one + teki = a drop; cf. related terms listed at tsubu

Ittoki 一時 = for a moment, for a while; from ichi = one + toki = time (this could also be read as hitotoki, with the same meaning, or as ichiji = for a while, or as one o'clock); cf. related terms listed at ittan

Ittou 一棟 = one house; from ichi = one + tou = counter for large buildings, e.g., byoutou = a hospital ward; cf. related terms listed at ie; cf. other similar terms listed at ittai

Iu 言う = to say, tell or speak; *he likes to say he's European*; cf. related terms listed at hanasu

Iu made mo naku 言うまでもなく = needless to say; from iu = to say + made = as far as + mo = even + naku, the adverbial form of nai = negation; literally, this = to say so far even is not, i.e., not necessary; cf. orosoka = neglect, negligence, not to mention, needless to say

Iwa 岩 = rock; *the eastern wall is made from rock*; cf. related terms listed at ishi = a pebble

Iwai 祝い = a celebration or congratulation, or a congratulatory gift; from iwau = to celebrate or congratulate; cf. shukuga = a celebration; cf. shukugakai = a celebration

Iwaigoto 祝い事 = a celebration; from iwau = to celebrate + goto = koto = thing

Iwau 祝う = to celebrate or congratulate; *eels?, wow!, let's celebrate*; cf. matsuru = to pray, worship, celebrate

Iwayuru いわゆる = what is called, so to speak; *eagles and wasps are united in ruling over their domains in what is called the animal world*

Iya いや = no, a variation of ie = no; this can also = wow! or hey!

Iya 嫌 = unpleasant, disgusting; *that eerie yacht is disgusting*; cf. fuyukai = unpleasant

Iyaa いやあ – see iya (no, wow! or hey!)

Iyahon イヤホン = earphones

Iyashii 卑しい = despicable, mean; *to put iyahon (earphones) on sheep is despicable*; cf. related terms listed at hidoi

Iyashiken 癒し犬 = healing dogs; from iyasu = to heal + ken = dog; cf. related terms listed at inu

Iyasu 癒す = to heal, cure, quench (thirst); *the iyahon (earphones) that Superman uses can cure hearing loss*; cf. naosu = to cure or heal

Iyoiyo いよいよ = more and more, increasingly, at last; *Eeyore and Eeyore's friends started coming around more and more*; cf. masumasu = increasingly, more and more; cf. other related terms listed at tsui ni

Izakaya 居酒屋 = a pub or bar; from i = dwelling, e.g., ima = living room; + zakaya = sakaya = liquor store; cf. related terms listed at ryoutei

Izen 以前 = ago (suggesting a long time), before; *eastern Zen was popular before western Zen*; cf. related terms listed at saki ni

Izumi 泉 = a spring or fountain; *there is a spring at the Eagle Zoo in Michigan*; cf onsen = a hot spring

Izure いずれ = which, soon, someday, in the end; *the eagle zoo rescues birds which may someday be released back into the wild*; cf. related terms listed at mamonaku and at tsui ni

Jaa じゃあ = well, then; *well, the jam is good*

Jagaimo じゃが芋 = an Irish potato; *Mick Jagger's aunt had an emotional attachment to Irish potatoes*; cf. related terms listed at imo

Jaguchi 蛇口 = a water faucet; *after eating a jar of gooey cheese, I looked for a water faucet*

Jakuniku kyoushoku 弱肉強食 = survival of the fittest; literally, "the weak are meat that the strong eat"; from jaku = weak; *Jack Nicholson's tennis game is weak*; + niku = meat; + kyou = strong; *a strong man lives in Kyouto*; + shokuji = meal

Jama 邪魔 = burden, disturbance, hindrance; *when he wears pajamas to the theatre, it creates a disturbance*; cf. futan = responsibility, burden; cf. omoni = a burden; cf. other related terms listed at sawari and shougai

Janru ジャンル = genre

Jari 砂利 = gravel; *driving on gravel is jarring*; cf. saiseki = rubble, broken stone

Jarimichi 砂利道 = a gravel path; from jari = gravel + michi = a path; cf. related terms listed at michi

Ji 字 = a character or letter; *the genius writes beautiful characters*; cf. emoji = an ideograph; cf. moji = a character or letter

Ji 時 = time, o'clock, used as a suffix; *the genius kept time in her head and always knew what o'clock it was*

Ji 父 = father, used as a word component; *my father drives a Jeep*

Jibiinkouka 耳鼻咽喉科 = otorhinolaryngology, or the medical science of the ear, nose and throat; *while driving his Jeep to the beach, he became incoherent and and hit a car, due to side-effects from his otorhinolaryngology medicines*; cf. related terms listed at gankagaku

Jibika 耳鼻科 = ear, nose & throat specialty; *put on your jeans, grab some beer, get in the car, and let's go see the ear, nose & throat specialist*; cf. related terms listed at gankagaku

Jibun 自分 = self; *the jeans that Daniel Boone bought were for himself*; cf. jiko = self; cf. onore = self; cf. ware = self

Jibun de 自分で = by oneself; from jibun = self; cf. hitori de = by or for oneself; cf. jiriki = by oneself; cf. jishin = by oneself, personally; cf. jitai = oneself, itself; cf. mizukara = for one's self, personally

Jidai 時代 = era, times, days; *the genius died during that era*; cf. dai = a certain age, a generation, a lifetime; cf. jiki = time, season; cf. kigen = an era, A.D.; cf. nendai = age, generation, period; cf. yo = world, era, age

Jidou 児童 = a child; *a child opened the Jeep door*; cf. related terms listed at kodomo

Jidou 自動 = automatic; from jibun = self + dousa = movement

Jidouhanbaiki 自動販売機 = vending machine; from jidou = automatic + hanbai = sales + kikai = machine; cf. related terms listed at kikai

Jidouhikiotoshi 自動引き落とし = an automatic debit from a bank account; from jidouhikiotsu = to automatically debit a bank account

Jidouhikiotosu 自動引き落とす = to automatically debit a bank account; from jidou = automatic + hikiotosu = to debit a bank account

Jidousha 自動車 = a car; from jidou = automatic + sha = a car; cf. related terms listed at kuruma

Jidouteki 自動的 = automatic; from jidou = automatic + teki = related to

Jigoku 地獄 = hell; *the genius saw a ghost in Kuwait who came straight from hell*

Jigyou 事業 = business or enterprise; *I take Jeeps full of gyoza to restaurants as part of my business*; cf. related terms listed at akinai and at kaisha

Jihaku 自白 = a confession (to a crime); *in his confession, the genius said that he* intended to *harm* Kuwait

Jihaku suru 自白する = to confess (to a crime); from jihaku = a confession; cf. related terms listed at hakujou suru

Jiheishou 自閉症 = autism; from jibun = self + hei = to close, e.g., heiten = closed store + shoujou = symptoms

Jihi 慈悲 = mercy; *Jesus healed the leper out of mercy*; cf. related terms listed at doujou

Jihyou 辞表 = written resignation; *when his horse got hit by a Jeep, the Lone Ranger said "Hi-yo" and submitted his written resignation*; cf. taishoku = retirement from office, resignation

Jiin 寺院 = Buddhist temple; from ji = temple; *that temple has a Jeep*; + in = institution, e.g., byouin = hospital; cf. related terms listed at tera

Jijitsu 事実 = fact or truth; ji = an intangible thing, e.g., jijou = reason, facts; + jitsu = reality, fact; cf. related terms listed at hontou

Jijitsujou 事実上 = in reality, actually; from jijitsu = truth + jou = above, e.g., jouzu = skillful

Jijoden 自叙伝 = an autobiography; *Jeep jokes were often found in the dentist's autobiography*; cf. related terms listed at hon

Jijou 事情 = reason, situation, facts, circumstances; *under the circumstances, we lent the Jeep to Joan*; cf. other related terms listed at jitai, ken and riyuu

Jikai 次回 = next time; *the genie promised to bring me a kite the next time we meet*; cf. kondo = this time or next time

Jikan 時間 = time, hour, duration of time; *when the genius got cancer, she knew she didn't have much time*; cf. aida = interval, time, distance; cf. jiki = time, season; cf. jikoku = time, hour; cf. kankaku = an interim, interval, pause or space; cf. kikan = duration, period; cf. machijikan = waiting time; cf. sonzoku = duration, continuance; cf. toki = time; cf. tsukihi = time, years

Jikandoori 時間通り = on time; from jikan = time + doori = street or way

Jikannai 時間内 = on time; from jikan = time + nai = inside or within

Jikatsu 自活 = supporting one's self; from jibun = self + katsu = life, livelihood

Jikei 字形 = character style or form; from ji = character + keitai = a form

Jiken 事件 = an event, incident, case; *the Jeep from Kentucky was involved in an incident*; cf. related terms listed at dekigoto

Jiki 時期 = time, season; *I will lend you the Jeep keys at the right season*; cf. related terms listed at jidai and at jikan

Jikken 実験 = experiment; *the genius and Ken conducted an experiment*

Jikkou 実行 = implementation, execution, realization; *the gypsy coalition took care of the plan's implementation*; cf. related terms listed at jitsugen

Jikkou suru 実行する = to implement; from kikkou = implementation, execution, realization; cf. related terms listed at hatasu

Jiko 事故 = an accident; *in the accident, a Jeep ran over a cobra*

Jiko 自己 = self; *my jeans and coat are an expression of my self*; cf. related terms listed at jibun

Jikochuushinteki 自己中心的 = selfish; from jiko = self + chuushin = center + teki = related to; cf. wagamama = selfish, spoiled

Jikoku 時刻 = time, hour; *it's time to get in the Jeep and drink Coke*; cf. related terms listed at jikan

Jikou 事項 = matter, item, facts; *the Jeep is always cold, so that's an item we need to fix*; cf. related terms listed at ken

Jiku 軸 = axle, axis, center; *the Jeep from Kuwait has a broken axle*; cf. tatejiku = a vertical axis; cf. yokojiku = a horizontal axis

Jiku ni suru 軸にする = to center around; from jiku = a center + ni suru = to make A into B

Jimaku 字幕 = subtitle; *when Jimmy Carter got macular degeneration, he couldn't read subtitles*

Jiman 自慢 = pride, boast; *the G-man (government man) had pride*; cf. related terms listed at hokori

Jiman suru 自慢する = to brag; from jiman = boast; cf. ibaru = to look down on, to brag

Jimen 地面 = ground; *the G-men (government employees) lay down on the ground*; cf. related terms listed at basho

Jimi 地味 = subdued, inconspicuous; *Jimmy Carter wore an inconspicuous tie*; cf. hade = showy, gaudy

Jimintou 自民党 = the Liberal Democratic Party; from jiyuu = liberty + minshu = democracy + seitou = political party; cf. jiyuutou = the Liberal Party

Jimoto 地元 = local, hometown; from ji = ground, e.g., jishin = earthquake; + moto = base; cf. kyokuchiteki = local; cf. other related terms listed at furusato

Jimu 事務 = office work; *when the genius was in the mood, she did office work*

Jimuin 事務員 = an office worker; from jimu = office work + in = a group member

Jimusho 事務所 = an office; from jimu = office work + sho = a place

Jin 人 = a person, used as a suffix; *the genius is a good person*; cf. related terms listed at -sha = a person

Jinan 次男 = a second son; *the genius hired a nanny to care for her second son*; cf. related terms listed at musuko

Jinbutsu 人物 = a person, especially one of rank or note; from jin = a person + butsu = a tangible thing, e.g., doubutsu = an animal; cf. related terms listed at hito

Jinchi 陣地 = encampment, position; *the gin was cheap in our encampment*

Jindai 甚大 = very great, enormous, serious; *the genius designed a dike that was enormous*; cf. related terms listed at ookii

Jinguu 神宮 = high-status (imperial) Shinto shrine; *the genius hired Goofy to guard the high-status shrine*; cf. related terms listed at jinja

Jinin suru 辞任する = to resign from a position; *the genius was a ninja who had resigned his position*; cf. related terms listed at jishoku suru

Jinja 神社 = a Shinto shrine; *the genius took some jam to the Shinto shrine*; cf. jinguu = high-status (imperial) Shinto shrine; cf. miya = a palace or shrine

Jinji 人事 = personnel; *those personnel wear jeans and ride around in a Jeep*

Jinjika 人事課 = personnel department; from jinji = personnel + ka = a section

Jinkaku 人格 = personality, character; *the genius collects cactus plants, in accordance with his prickly character*; cf. hitogara = personality or character; cf. kosei = individuality, personality; cf. seikaku = personality

Jinkou 人口 = population; *there is a large population of genial Koreans*

Jinkou 人工 = man-made, artificial; from jin = person + kou = crafted object, e.g., koujou = factory; cf. jinkou = population

Jinmei 人名 = a person's name; from jin = a person + meishou = a name; cf. related terms listed at namae

Jinmen 人面 = a human face; from jin = person + men = surface; cf. related terms listed at kao

Jinmenseki 人面石 = a stone with a human face; from jinmen = a human face + seki = stone; *the selfish king sat on a stone*

Jinmon 尋問 = interrogation; *a genius named Monet was subjected to interrogation*

Jinrikisha 人力車 = a rickshaw; from jin = person + rikisha = rickshaw = a vehicle pulled by a man

Jinrui 人類 = the human race; *the genie asked King Louis to make a wish that would benefit the human race*; cf. related terms listed at hito

Jinsei 人生 = human life; *my human life is to drink gin behind the Safeway store*; cf. related terms listed at inochi

Jinshin 人身 = the human body, one's person; from jin = person + shin = body; cf. related terms listed at karada

Jinshu 人種 = a race of people; from jin = person + shurui = type; cf. related terms listed at buzoku

Jinsoku na 迅速な = fast, prompt; *when my jeans are soaked, I dry them in a fast dryer*; cf. related terms listed at hayai

Jintai 人体 = the human body; from jin = a person + nikutai = the human body; cf. related terms listed at karada

Jintoku 仁徳 = benevolence or goodness; *the jeans that you gave me are totally cool, and I really appreciate your benevolence*; this can also be pronounced nintoku; cf. yoki = goodness, good; cf. yosa = goodness

Jintsuu 陣痛 = labor pains; *the genius tsued (sued) the hospital over her labor pains*

Jinushi 地主 = a land owner; from ji = land, e.g., jishin = earthquake; + nushi = a master; cf. related terms listed at mochinushi

Jinzai 人材 = a talented or capable person, human resources; *these jeans are being eyed by some talented people*; cf. related terms listed at hito

Jinzou 腎臓 = a kidney; *the genius zoned out when the teacher discussed kidneys*; cf. related terms listed at naizou

Jiriki 自力 = by oneself; from jibun = one's self + riki = force; *Ricky exerts a lot of force*; cf. related terms listed at jibun de

Jirojiro じろじろ = staringly, scrutinizing; *the genius had a robot that looked around staringly*

Jisa 時差 = time difference; *the genius saw that the time difference was 13 hours*

Jisaboke 時差ぼけ = jet lag; *the genius saw that boring Ken was suffering from jet lag*

Jisatsu 自殺 = suicide; from jibun = self + satsujin = murder

Jisha 自社 = one's company; from jibun = self + kaisha = company; cf. related terms listed at kaisha

Jishaku 磁石 = magnet or compass; *the Jeep in that shack holds my magnet collection*; cf. rashinban = a compass

Jishin 地震 = an earthquake; *my Jeep was struck by shingles during the earthquake*; cf. daishinsai = a great earthquake; cf. shinsai = a great earthquake

Jishin 自信 = self-confidence; from jibun = self + shinjiru = to believe; cf. related terms listed at hokori = pride

Jishin 自身 = by oneself, personally; from jibun = self + shin = person; cf. related terms listed at jibun de

Jishinka 自信家 = a person with self-confidence; from jishin = self-confidence + ka = person

Jisho 辞書 = a dictionary; *the genius showed us his dictionary*; cf. similar terms listed at jiten = an encyclopedia

Jishoku suru 辞職する = to resign; *the*

genius was <u>shocked</u> when he was asked <u>to resign</u>; cf. jinin suru = to resign from a position; cf. taishoku suru = to retire; cf. yameru = to resign

Jishu 自主 = independence, autonomy; from jibun = self + shuji = master

Jishuku 自粛 = self-restraint, self-discipline; the <u>genius</u> wanted some <u>shoes</u> from <u>Ku</u>wait but exercised <u>self-restraint</u> and didn't buy them; cf. kinshin = penitence, discipline, house-arrest, self-restraint; cf. other related terms listed at enryo

Jishuteki ni 自主的に = independently, voluntarily; from jishu = independence, autonomy + teki = related to + -ni = a suffix that forms an adverb

Jisoku 時速 = speed; the <u>Jee</u>p got <u>soaked</u> due to the <u>speed</u> at which it was driven; cf. sokudo = speed

Jissai 実際 = reality, fact; the <u>genius sighed</u> when he learned the <u>facts</u>; cf. related terms listed at hontou = truth, reality

Jissai no tokoro 実際のところ = to tell the truth, as a matter of fact; from jissai = reality, fact + tokoro = moment or place; cf. jitsu wa = really, as a matter of fact

Jisseki 実績 = accomplishment, achievement; the <u>genius</u> told the <u>self</u>ish <u>k</u>ing about his <u>accomplishments</u>; cf. related terms listed at seiseki

Jissen 実践 = implementation, practice; the company promoted the <u>implementation</u> of a <u>Jeep Center</u> which would encourage the <u>practice</u> of off-roading; cf. related terms listed at jitsugen

Jisshi 実施 = enforcement, implementation; using a <u>Jeep</u>, we took the <u>sheep</u> to the pasture and carried out the <u>implementation</u> of our plan; cf. related terms listed at jitsugen

Jisshi suru 実施する = to carry out or effect; from jisshi = enforcement, implementation; cf. related terms listed at hatasu

Jisuberi = a landslide; from ji = chi = earth + suberu = to slide

Jisui 自炊 = cooking for oneself; *when the genius lived in <u>Sw</u>eden, he learned to do <u>cooking for himself</u>*; cf. related terms listed at chouri

Jitai 事態 = situation, circumstance; *the <u>Jee</u>p's <u>ti</u>re was <u>fl</u>at, so we had to deal with that <u>situation</u>*; cf. jijou = reason, situation, facts, circumstances; cf. joukyou = circumstances; cf. jousei = situation, circumstances; cf. joutai = condition, circumstances; cf. kyouguu = circumstances, environment; cf. tsugou = circumstances, convenience; cf. other related terms listed at keisei

Jitai 自体 = oneself, itself; *the <u>genius</u> was <u>tired</u> of doing everything <u>himself</u>*; cf. related terms listed at jibun de

Jitaku 自宅 = one's home; from jibun = self + taku = home; cf. related terms listed at uchi

Jiten 事典 = an encyclopedia; *the <u>genius</u> read <u>ten</u> <u>en</u>cyclopedias*; cf. eiwa jiten = an English-Japanese dictionary; cf. hyakkajiten = an encyclopedia; cf. jisho = a dictionary; cf. jiten = a dictionary

Jiten 辞典 = a dictionary; *the <u>genius</u> stopped the <u>ten</u>nis match to consult a <u>dictionary</u>*; cf. similar terms listed at jiten = an encyclopedia

Jitensha 自転車 = a bicycle; from jibun = self + unten = operation of a machine + sha = a car or wheeled vehicle

Jitsu 実 = reality, fact; *the <u>jittery</u> <u>su</u>perstar had to face the <u>facts</u>*; cf. related terms listed at hontou = truth, reality

Jitsu ni 実に = really, indeed, truly; from jitsu = reality + ni = a particle that creates an adverb; cf. hontou ni = really, truly

Jitsu no 実の = real, biological; from jitsu to reality + the possessive no; cf. related terms listed at shin no

Jitsu wa 実は = really, as a matter of fact; from jitsu = reality, fact + wa = as for; cf. cf. jitsuwa = a true story; cf. jissai no tokoro = to tell the truth, as a matter of fact

Jitsubutsu 実物 = real thing or person; from jitsu = reality + butsu = tangible thing; cf. honmono = the real article

Jitsubutsu dai 実物大 = actual size; from jitsubutsu = real thing + dai = big

Jitsugen 実現 = implementation, materialization, realization; *the jittery superstar asked Genghis to help with the implementation of his plan*; cf. jikkou = implementation, execution, realization; cf. jissen = implementation, practice; cf. jisshi = enforcement, implementation; cf. shikou = execution, enforcement

Jitsugen suru 実現する = to materialize, realize, effect; from jitsugen = realization; cf. related terms listed at hatasu

Jitsuryoku 実力 = capability, proficiency; from jitsu = reality or fact + ryoku = power

Jitsuwa 実話 = a true story; from jitsu = reality or truth + wa = to speak, e.g., kaiwa = conversation; cf. jitsu wa = as a matter of fact; cf. related terms listed at hanashi

Jitto じっと = fixedly, intently, motionlessly; *the genius toasted us with a fixed stare*

Jiyou 滋養 = nourishment, nutrition; *the the genius said that yogurt provides good nutrition*; cf. related terms listed at eiyou

Jiyuu 自由 = freedom, liberty; *the genius used his money to buy freedom*

Jiyuu honpou 自由奔放 = freewheeling, behaving with abandon; from jiyuu = freedom + honpou = unrestrained; cf. related terms listed at honpou

Jiyuu na 自由な = unfettered, free; from jiyuu = freedom; cf. honpou = unrestrained, wild, free

Jiyuuseki 自由席 = unreserved seats; from jiyuu = freedom + seki = a seat

Jiyuutou 自由党 = the Liberal Party; from jiyuu = liberty + seitou = political party; cf. jimintou = the Liberal Democratic Party

Jizen 事前 = in advance, prior; *the abbot sent the Jeep to the Zen temple in advance of his visit*; cf. related terms listed at saki ni

Jizen 慈善 = charity; *the genius visited the Zen center for a charity event*

Jo 所 = a place, used as a suffix, e.g., kenmonjo = a checkpoint

Jobun 序文 = a preface or introduction; *Empress Josephine asked Daniel Boone to write the preface to her book about Napoleon*

Jojo ni 徐々に = gradually, step by step; *Jonah and Job kneeled and gradually cleaned the floor*; cf. related terms listed at shidai ni

Jokou suru 徐行する = to slow down; *Jonah's commute slowed down after Labor Day*

Jokyo 除去 = removal; *Jonah went to Kyoto for the removal of a tooth*; cf. related terms listed at tsuihou

Joou 女王 = queen; from josei = female + ou = king; cf. kougou = an empress; cf. kougou heika = Her Majesty the Empress; cf. kouhi = a queen; cf. ouhi = a queen

Josainai 如才ない = clever, shrewd; *she is clever and jokes with scientists at night*; cf. related terms listed at kashikoi

Josei 女性 = a woman or girl, female; *Jonah saved a girl from the whale*; cf. related terms listed at onna

Josetsu suru 除雪する = to remove snow; *Jonah is our settlement's super pioneer, and he is good at removing snow*

Joshi 女子 = a woman or girl; *Jonah's sheep were shepherded by a girl*; cf. related terms listed at onna

Joshikousei 女子高生 = a female high school student; from joshi = woman or girl + koukou = high school + sei = a person; cf. related terms listed at gakusei

Joshu 助手 = an assistant; *Jonah's shoes were polished by his assistant*

Jou 城 = a castle, used as a suffix; *Joan of Arc stayed in that castle*; this can also be read as shiro = a castle; cf. related terms listed at shiro

Jou 場 = a place, used as a suffix, e.g., kaijou = the site of an event; *this place where I live is a joke*

Jou 情 = emotion, affection; *Joan of Arc had strong emotions*; cf. related terms listed at aijou and at kankaku

Jou 錠 = a counter for pills, used as a suffix; from jouzai = a tablet or pill

Jou 畳 = a counter for tatami mats; *Joan of Arc sat on a tatami mat*

Joubu 丈夫 = healthy, hearty, strong; *Joan of Arc was a boon to the French cause, since she was healthy, hearty, and strong*; cf. related terms listed at genki and at tsuyoi

Joudan 冗談 = a joke, humor; *the jokes the dancer told proved she had a sense of humor*

Jouhanshin 上半身 = the upper body; from jou = above + han = half + shin = body; cf. kahanshin = the lower body

Jouhatsu 蒸発 = evaporation; from jouki = steam + hatsu = departure

Jouhin na 上品な = elegant, graceful, refined; *Joan said that Hindu culture was refined*; cf. fuuryuu = refined; cf. koushou na = noble, high-brow, refined; cf. miyabita = gracious, elegant, refined; cf. onga = graceful, affable; cf. yuuga = elegant

Jouho 譲歩 = a concession or compromise; *Joan hoped that a compromise could be found*; cf. dakyou = a compromise

Jouhou 情報 = information, news; *we have information about Joan's hotel*; cf. annai = information, guidance, showing around; cf. houdou = public news or report; cf. houkoku = report, information; cf. kokoroatari = some information; cf. kouhou = public relations, publicity, information; cf. otosata = news, letter; cf. sata = information, communication, command, affair; cf. shirase = notification, news; cf. shousoku = whereabouts, news; cf. tayori = news, letter

Joui 上位 = high rank; from jou = above, e.g., jouzu = skillful; + i = rank; cf. related terms listed at kurai = rank

Jouin 上院 = an Upper House or Senate; from jou = above, e.g., jouzu = skillful; + in = an institution; cf. related terms listed at kokkai

Joukan 上官 = a superior officer; from jou = above, e.g., jouzu = skillful; + shikan = a military officer; cf. related terms listed at shikan

Jouken 条件 = condition, requirement; *the jokes that Ken tells are a requirement of his employment*

Jouki 蒸気 = vapor, steam; *I was only joking when I said that I saw steam coming out of your ears*; cf. suijouki = water vapor

Jouki kikan 蒸気機関 = a steam engine; from jouki = steam + kikan = an engine; cf. related terms listed at kikan

Joukuu 上空 = the sky, upper air; from jou = up or above, e.g., jouzu = skillful; + kuu = sky, e.g., kuuki = air; cf. kuuchuu = mid-air; cf. other related terms listed at sora

Joukyaku 乗客 = a passenger; *Joan and the kayaker were passengers*

Joukyou 状況 = circumstances; *we joke about Kyouto's circumstances*; cf. related terms listed at jitai

Joumae 錠前 = a lock; *Joan of Arc told her maestro to get better locks*

Joumuin 乗務員 = crew member (of a vehicle); from joumu = transport-related work; *when Joan of Arc was in the mood, she did transport-related work*; + in = member

Joumyaku 静脈 = a vein; *after Joan drank some Miami Kool-Aid, her veins started throbbing*; cf. similar terms listed at doumyaku

Jounetsu 情熱 = enthusiasm, passion; *Joan of Arc wanted network superiority for her cell phone, since talking on the phone was her passion*; cf. related terms listed at nesshin

Jourei 条例 = an ordinance; *Joan raced her car in violation of a city ordinance*; cf. related terms listed at kisoku

Jouren 常連 = a regular customer; *Joan stopped at the rental car office, where she was a regular customer*; cf. related terms listed at kyaku

Jouriku suru 上陸する = to land, to hit (typhoon); from jou = above, e.g., jouzu = skillful; + riku = land; cf. related terms listed at chakuriku suru

Jouryuu 蒸留 = distillation; *Joan of Arc reused her brother's still for her alcohol distillation business*; cf. related terms listed at jouzou

Jouryuushu 蒸留酒 = distilled liquor; from jouryuu = distillation + shu = alcohol; *I spilled alcohol on my shoes*; cf. shouchuu = a Japanese spirit distilled from sweet potatoes, rice, etc.

Jousei 情勢 = situation, circumstances; *in those circumstances, Joan of Arc felt safe*; cf. related terms listed at jitai

Jousha 乗車 = taking a train or a bus; *Joan of Arc wore a shawl when she was taking a bus*; cf. toujou = boarding (a ship or plane)

Joushi 上司 = supervisor, a superior (in a company); *Josephine the Shiite is my supervisor*; cf. senpai = a senior, elder, predecessor; cf. toshiue = a senior or older person; cf. uwayaku = someone who is superior or senior

Joushi 上肢 = an arm or upper limb; from jou = above, e.g., jouzu = skillful; + shi = a limb (arm or leg); cf. related terms listed at ude

Joushiki 常識 = common sense; *Joan bought her sheep in Kiev, which shows her common sense*; cf. related terms listed at chie

Joushoku 常食 = a staple food; *Joan of Arc shocked us when she refused her staple food*; cf. related terms listed at tabemono

Joushou 上昇 = rising, ascending, climbing; *I saw the rising of Michael Jordan's shoulders as he jumped*; cf. nobori = an ascent; cf. other related terms listed at zouka

Joushuusha 常習者 = an addict; *Joan of Arc sold her shoes and her shawl to help some drug addicts*; cf. chuudokusha = an addict

Jousuiki 浄水器 = a water purifier; *after she got a water purifier, Joan of Arc started making Swedish quiche*

Joutai 状態 = condition, circumstances, state; *under the circumstances, Joan was tired*; cf. related terms listed at jitai and keisei

Joutatsu 上達 = improvement (in skill, etc.); *Joan's tattered suit shows some improvement over the last one she sewed*; cf. related terms listed at kaizen

Joutou 上等 = excellent, very good; *Joan of Arc's tomatoes were excellent*; cf. batsugun = outstanding, fabulous; cf. erai = great, excellent; cf. mezamashii = outstanding, striking; cf. subarashii = wonderful, superb, excellent; cf. sugureta = excellent; cf. yuushuu = excellent, outstanding, prominent

Jouyaku 条約 = a treaty or pact; *Joan of Arc and the yakuza signed a peace treaty*

Jouzai 錠剤 = a tablet or pill; _Joan of Arc went to Zaire to get her sleeping pills_

Jouzou 醸造 = brewing, distilling; _Joan of Arc and Zooey are into brewing beer_; cf. jouryuu = distillation; cf. shuzou = sake brewing

Jouzu 上手 = skillful, proficient; _Joan's zucchini were the result of skillful gardening_; cf. tannou = 1) skillful, or 2) enjoyment/satisfaction; cf. takumi na = skillful; cf. umai = skillful, delicious, successful

Joyuu 女優 = an actress; _Josephine was a youth who wanted to be an actress_; cf. related terms listed at haiyuu

Juchuu 受注 = receiving an order; _the junior clerk chews gum while he receives orders_

Jugyou 授業 = a class, lesson or teaching; _we bring juice and gyoza to class_; cf. koushuukai = classes, lessons, a course; cf. kouza = an academic course or lecture; cf. kyoukun = moral, teaching, lesson; cf. nikka = daily lesson or routine; cf. other related terms listed at enzetsu

Jugyouryou 授業料 = tuition fee; from jugyou = a class + -ryou = a fee

Juken 受験 = taking an exam; _the juice that Ken brought gave him energy when he was taking an exam_

Juken suru 受験する = to take an exam; from juken = taking an exam

Jukensei 受験生 = examinee; from juken suru = to take an examination; + sei = a person; cf. jukensha = examinee

Jukensha 受験者 = examinee; from juken suru = to take an examination; + sha = person

Jukou 受講 = attending lectures; _the junior corporal spends his time attending lectures_

Jukousei 受講生 = students attending lectures; from jukou = attending lectures + sei = a person

Juku 塾 = cram school, private school; _I'm going to private school to learn how to repair jukeboxes_; cf. related terms listed at gakkou

Jukusei 塾生 = a cram school student; from juku = cram school + seito = student; cf. related terms listed at gakusei

Jukusu 熟す = to ripen or mature; _the jukebox in Sudan contained fruit which was ripening_; cf. minoru = to ripen; cf. ureru = to ripen

Jukusui suru 熟睡する = to sleep well; _when the jukebox plays sweet music, I sleep well_; cf. related terms listed at neru

Jukutatsu 熟達 = mastery; _his jukebox holds some tattered souvenirs that reflect his mastery of the music business_; cf. zoukei = knowledge, mastery

Jukyou 儒教 = Confucianism; _the juror from Kyouto believed in Confucianism_; cf. koushi = Confucius

Jumoku 樹木 = trees; _trees that give us juice are the most cool_; cf. related terms listed at ki

Jumyou 寿命 = lifespan; _the jubilant cat meowed when it learned that it would be given seven more lives, extending its lifespan_

Jun 旬 = season (for specific products); _it's the season to buy jungle gear_; cf. related terms listed a kisetsu

Junban 順番 = one's turn, order; _the junior ate a banana while he awaited his turn_; cf. ban = a watch (guard) or turn

Junbi 準備 = preparation; _I've made preparations for warding off jungle bees_; cf. related terms listed at youi

Junbi bantan 準備万端 = every preparation, suggesting that one is completely ready; from junbi = preparation + bantan = all, everything; cf. related terms listed at youi

Junchou 順調 = no problem, doing well; _the_

junior <u>chose</u> a major and is <u>doing</u> well; cf. related terms listed at daijoubu

Junjo 順序 = order, sequence; *the <u>juniors</u> followed <u>Jonah</u> in <u>sequence</u>*

Junkan 循環 = circulation, circular movement; *this <u>junk</u> from <u>Canada</u> arrived here via the <u>circulation</u> of the currents*; cf. meguri = circumference, tour, circulation

Junkin 純金 = pure gold; from junsui = pure + kin = gold; cf. related terms listed at ougon

Junn'ou (Junnou) 順応 = adaptation; *living creatures in <u>jungles</u> and <u>oceans</u> show signs of <u>adaptation</u> to climate change*; cf. tekiou = adaptation, accommodation

Junsa 巡査 = patrolman; *the <u>junior</u> <u>salaryman</u> flagged down a <u>patrolman</u>*; cf. related terms listed at keikan

Junsui na (or no) 純粋な = pure, pure-blooded, genuine; *since the <u>junior</u> was <u>sweet</u>, I assumed that she was <u>pure</u>*; cf. honkaku = serious, genuine, original method or procedure; cf. other related terms listed at seijou

Jushou suru 受賞する = to win an award or prize; *at the <u>jewelry</u> <u>show</u>, I <u>won</u> a <u>prize</u>*; cf. related terms listed at katsu

Juu 中 = throughout, used as a suffix; *we drink <u>juice</u> <u>throughout</u> the day*; cf. related terms listed at nagara

Juu 銃 = a gun; *the <u>jury</u> was guarded with <u>guns</u>*; cf. related terms listed at teppou

Juubun 十分 = enough; ; this can also be read as juppun = 10 minutes *the <u>juice</u> that Daniel <u>Boone</u> brought is <u>enough</u>*

Juuden suru 充電する = to charge (a battery); *the <u>junior</u> <u>dentist</u> <u>charged</u> her phone*

Juudenki 充電器 = a battery charger; from juuden suru = to charge + ki = a container, e.g., benki = a toilet bowl

Juudou 柔道 = judo, a sport similar to wrestling; *I consume <u>juice</u> and <u>doughnuts</u> after <u>judo</u> practice*; cf. juujutsu = a Japanese martial art

Juuji suru 従事する = to work or engage in (a profession); *I have these <u>juice-stained</u> <u>jeans</u> because I <u>work</u> in a juice shop*; cf. related terms listed at shigoto suru

Juujitsu 充実 = fullness, completion, perfection; *the <u>junior</u> executive told the <u>jittery</u> <u>superstar</u> that the superstar's art had reached a state of <u>fullness</u>, <u>completion</u> and <u>perfection</u>*; cf. kansei = completion

Juujutsu 柔術 = a Japanese martial art; this can also be pronounced juujitsu; *the <u>jukebox</u> <u>juts</u> out and blocks the entrance to the <u>Japanese</u> <u>martial</u> <u>arts</u> center*; cf. juudou = a Japanese sport

Juukyo 住居 = dwelling; *the <u>jeweler</u> lived in <u>Kyoto</u>, in a <u>dwelling</u>*; cf. related terms listed at ie

Juuman 充満 = being filled with; *that <u>junior</u> <u>manager</u> is <u>full</u> <u>of</u> hot air*; cf. darake = full of, covered with; cf. ippai = one cup, glass, spoon or bowl, or full of

Juuman suru 充満する = to be filled with; from juuman = being filled with; cf. umaru = to be buried (in), to be filled (with)

Juumin 住民 = a resident; from juutaku = a residence + kokumin = a citizen

Juunan na 柔軟な = flexible; *the <u>junior</u> <u>nanny</u>'s work schedule was <u>flexible</u>*

Juuroudou 重労働 = heavy labor; from juu = heavy, e.g., taijuu = a person's weight; + roudou = manual labor; cf. related terms listed at shigoto

Juusei 銃声 = the sound of a gunshot; from juu = a gun + onsei = a voice

Juushii ジューシー = juicy; cf. mizumizushii = juicy

Juusho 住所 = an address; *the <u>jewel</u> <u>show</u> is at this <u>address</u>*; cf. atesaki = an address or destination

Juushoku 住職 = chief priest of a Buddhist temple; *the juke box shocked the chief priest*; cf. fukujuushoku = a vice-priest; cf. sou = a monk or priest; cf. souryo = a monk or priest; cf. zensou = a Zen monk

Juusou 重曹 = baking soda; *the junior asked about the amount of sodium in baking soda*

Juutai 渋滞 = gridlock (traffic); *I always carry juice in Thailand in case of traffic gridlock*; cf. konzatsu = crowdedness, congestion

Juutaku 住宅 = residence, house; from juu = to reside, e.g., juusho = an address; + otaku = home; cf. related terms listed at ie

Juutakuchi 住宅地 = a residential district; from juutaku = a residence + chi = a place; cf. juutakugai = a residential area; cf. other related terms listed at basho

Juutakugai 住宅街 = a residential area; from juutaku = a residence + gai = a town or district, e.g., hankagai = a shopping district; cf. juutakuchi = a residential district

Juutan じゅうたん = a carpet or rug; *the jewels got tangled up in the carpet*

Juuyou 重要 = important; *juice and yogurt are important parts of our diet*; cf. juyou = a demand or request; cf. daiji = important, precious; cf. taisetsu = important, beloved; cf. taishita = considerable, great, important; cf. toutoi = sacred, important, valuable

Juuyousei 重要性 = importance; from juuyou = important + sei = nature

Juuzei 重税 = heavy taxes; *my jeweler and his zany friends pay heavy taxes*; cf. related terms listed at zeikin

Juyo suru 授与する = to confer or award; *the jubilant yogi awarded prizes*; cf. related terms listed at ataeru

Juyou 需要 = a demand or request; *they made a demand for juice and yogurt*; cf. juuyou = important; cf. other related terms listed at seikyuu

Ka か = or; *I want a cat or a canary*; cf. related terms listed at soretomo

Ka 下 = below, used as a suffix, e.g., chika = underground; *there's a car below my window*

Ka 化 = a nominalizing suffix (adds the meaning "-ization" to make a noun from another word), e.g., amerikaka = Americanization; *cart is a noun*

Ka 家 = a person, used as a suffix, e.g., seijika = a politician; *that person has a car*; cf. related terms listed at sha

Ka 科 = an academic department or course, used as a suffix; *I worked in an academic department in California*; cf. kamoku = an academic course

Ka 蚊 = a mosquito; *that mosquito flew into the car*; cf. related terms listed at mushi

Ka 課 = a chapter, lesson or section, a counter for chapters of a book; *this chapter and this lesson are about cathedrals*; cf. shou = a chapter

Ka to omottara かと思ったら – see ka to omou to

Ka to omou to かと思うと = as soon as, no sooner than, a moment ago, just recently; from ka = a question marker + to = a quote marker + omou to = if I think; literally, this means "question, if I think," suggesting that something happens at the speed of thought

Kaban カバン = bag, briefcase, suitcase; *there are cabbages and bananas in that bag*

Kabe 壁 = wall; *he threw the bottle of cabernet sauvignon against the wall*

Kabin 花瓶 = a vase; *I saw a vase in the cabin*; cf, related terms listed at tsubo

Kabin na 過敏な = overly sensitive; from kagon = exaggeration + binkan = sensitive

Kabocha かぼちゃ = pumpkin, squash; *on the cattle boat, the champion ate only pumpkins*; cf. related terms listed at yasai

Kabu 下部 = the lower part; from ka = below + bubun = a part of something; cf. related terms listed at ichibu

Kabu 株 = stock, stump, or a counter for small plants; *I sit on a stump surrounded by small plants as I check my stock in a caboose company*

Kabuka 株価 = a stock price; from kabu = stock + bukka = price

Kabuki 歌舞伎 = a form of traditional Japanese drama; *while Karl was booking the hotel, I watched traditional Japanese drama*; cf. nou = Noh, old-style Japanese theater

Kabureru かぶれる = to develop a rash or inflammation, to be influenced; *in Kabul, the red rooster developed a rash*

Kaburu 被る = to wear something on the head, to be covered with something; *the kabuki player entered the room wearing a wig*; cf. related terms listed at chakuyou suru

Kachi 価値 = value; *he's catching a lot of balls, and we recognize his value to the team*; cf. arigatami = worth or value; cf. atai = value, price; cf. kakaku = price, value

Kachikan 価値観 = sense of values, value system; from kachi = value + kan = to look over, e.g., kankou = sightseeing; cf. related terms listed at doutoku

Kachiku 家畜 = domestic animals, livestock, cattle; from katei = home + chikushou = a beast; cf. related terms listed at doubutsu

Kachime 勝ち目 = chance of success, odds; *the odds of catching Mexico in the tournament are slim*

Kachinuku 勝ち抜く = to win through; from katsu = to win + nuku = to surpass; cf. related terms listed at katsu

Kachitoru 勝ち取る = to win/take; from katsu = to win + toru = to take; cf. related terms listed at katsu = to win

Kachou 課長 = a section manager; from ka = section; *we carved the fruit into sections*; + chou = chief or leader; cf. related terms listed at shunou

Kaden 家電 = consumer electronics or electrical appliances; from katei = home or household + denki = electricity

Kado 角 = an outside corner; this can also be read as tsuno = antler or horn; *I hit my head on the corner of a car door*; cf. ikkaku = corner, section, point; cf. machikado = a street corner; cf. magarikado = a street corner or a bend in the road; cf. sumi = an inside corner; cf. sumikko = a corner, nook or recess

Kado 過度 = excess, immoderation; *she used excess force to close the car door*; cf. related terms listed at yoyuu

Kadouka かどうか = whether or not; from ka = question marker + dou = how + ka = a question marker; cf. kainaka = whether or not

Kaen 火炎 = fire; *let's call the engineers to put out the fire*; cf. related terms listed at kaji

Kaeri 帰り = returning; from kaeru = to return

Kaerimiru 顧みる = to look back on; from kaeru = to return + miru = to look; cf. related terms listed at furikaeru

Kaeru カエル = a frog; *the frog always kaeru (returns) to his home*

Kaeru 変える = to change or transform, transitive; *Karl was erudite and changed all of the clocks*; cf. aratameru = to change, renovate, correct; cf. chigaeru = to change or alter something; cf. kirikaeru = to change, convert or switch over

Kaeru 帰る = to go back or return, to go home; *Karl* was *erudite* and always *went home* to study; cf. modoru = to return

Kaeru 替える = to replace or exchange (this can also be spelled 換える); *Karl was erudite and replaced the books he lost*; cf. related terms listed at koukan suru

Kaeru 返る = to return, to restore; *Karl was erudite and returned to the library*; *Karl was erudite and restored the books he damaged*

Kaesu 返す = to return something, to repeat, to overturn, to retaliate; *let's call your eccentric supervisor and return this to her*; cf. henkyaku suru = to return something borrowed; cf. related terms listed at kutsugaesu

Kaette かえって = conversely, rather, all the more; from kaeru = to change or transform; cf. mushiro = rather; cf. other related terms listed at dokoroka and at issou

Kafun 花粉 = pollen; from ka = flower, e.g., kabin = vase; + fun = powder; *that powder on your nose looks funny*

Kafunshou 花粉症 = hay fever; from kafun = pollen + shoujou = symptoms; cf. related terms listed at byouki

Kagaku 化学 = chemistry; *if you study chemistry, you will be able to determine the number of sugar molecules in a can of Gandalf's Kool-Aid*; cf. kagaku = science

Kagaku 科学 = science; *if you study science, you will be able to calculate the number of atoms in a gallon of Kool-Aid*; cf. kagaku = chemistry

Kagaku gijutsu 科学技術 = science and technology, or scientific technique; from kagaku = science + gijutsu = technique

Kagakusha 化学者 = a chemist; from kagaku = chemistry + sha = a person

Kagakusha 科学者 = a scientist; from kagaku = science + sha = a person

Kagameru かがめる = to bend or stoop; *Karl Marx and Gandalf went to see some Mexican ruins and had to stoop to get through the doorways*; cf. kussuru = to bend or yield to

Kagami 鏡 = mirror; *when Karl Marx is gaming, he uses mirrors to see what's happening behind him*

Kagayakashii 輝かしい = brilliant, bright, splendid; from kagayaku = to shine; cf. related terms listed at akarui

Kagayaku 輝く = to shine, glitter, sparkle; *when the cat in the garden saw the yak, its eyes sparkled*; cf. related terms listed at teru

Kage 影 = shadow, silhouette; *the carving of a gecko cast a shadow on the ground*

Kage 陰 = shade, gloominess; *I called out to the guest to come into the shade*

Kageki 歌劇 = opera; from kashu = singer + geki = play

Kageki 過激 = aggressive, radical; *Karl Marx demanded the guest key in an aggressive way*; cf. seme no = aggressive, offensive

Kagemusha 影武者 = a double (an impersonator); this is also the name of a Japanese movie, whose title was translated as "Shadow Warrior"; *I called the guests to come and see the moody Shah, but he was only an impersonator*

Kagen suru 加減する = to moderate, downgrade; *the carpenter that Genghis hired downgraded his plans for the new palace*; cf. related terms listed at genshou suru

Kagi 鍵 = a key or clue; *I use a key to lock the cage holding my captive geese*

Kagiranai 限らない = it isn't limited to, or not necessarily; from kagiru = to be limited to; cf. related terms listed at kanarazu shimo

Kagiri 限り = limit, degree, as far as possible, the end; from kagiru = to be limited; cf. related terms listed at genkai

Kagiri wa 限りは = as long as, used after a plain negative verb, e.g., taifuu ga konai kagiri wa = as long as a typhoon doesn't come; from kagiri = limit + wa = as for

Kagiru 限る = to be limited to, to limit or restrict; e.g., ni kagiru = it's limited to; *she can call geese and roosters, but otherwise her skills are limited*

Kago 籠 = a basket or cage; this is usually writen かご; *we use baskets to carry cargo*; cf. ori = cage or cell; cf. torikago = a bird cage

Kagon 過言 = exaggeration; *to say that all the cars are gone is an exaggeration*; cf. related terms listed at iisugi

Kagu 嗅ぐ = to sniff or smell; *that carpenter is goofy in that he smells wood before cutting it*

Kagu 家具 = furniture; *that Canadian goose is sitting on my furniture*

Kagyou 家業 = a family business; *our family business supplies cabbage for gyoza*; cf. related terms listed at akinai

Kagyou 稼業 = trade, business, occupation; *in my restaurant business, I calculate how much gyoza we will need every week*; cf. related terms listed at akinai

Kahanshin 下半身 = the lower body; from ka = below, e.g., chikatetsu = subway; + han = half + shin = body; cf. jouhanshin = the upper body

Kahansuu 過半数 = a majority; from kajou = excess + hansuu = half the number; cf. related terms listed at bangou and at mottomo

Kahei 貨幣 = money, currency; *camels eat hay, which costs money*; cf. related terms listed at kinsen

Kai かい = desu ka = is it?, used with yes-no questions, e.g., nozoite minai kai = won't you look into it? *is it that you fly kites?* cf. dai = desu ka, used with "wh" questions (where, who, what)

Kai 回 = times (frequency), counter for occurrences, used as a suffix; *I flew my kite five times before it broke*; cf. related terms listed at -do

Kai 貝 = shellfish, a seashell; *you were kind to give me your seashell*

Kai 階 = a counter for floors of a building (for the first floor, use ikkai); *the Kaiser stayed on the top floor*

Kaibou 解剖 = anatomy, autopsy, dissection; *the Kaiser boasted about his strong anatomy*

Kaibou zu 解剖図 = anatomical drawings; from kaibou = anatomy + zu = a drawing; cf. related terms listed at e

Kaibutsu 怪物 = a monster; *the monster stole the Kaiser's boots*; cf. kaijuu = a monster

Kaichiku 改築 = reconstruction; *the Kaiser gives us cheap Kool-Aid in return for reconstruction work*; cf. related terms listed at kaisou

Kaichou 会長 = chairman of the board; from kaisha = a company + chou = leader or chief; cf. related terms listed at shunou

Kaichuu 懐中 = one's pocket; *the Kaiser chooses to keep his hands in his pockets*

Kaichuu dentou 懐中電灯 = flashlight; from kaichuu = pocket + dentou = electric light

Kaidan 会談 = a consultation, conversation or conference; from kaigi = a meeting + soudan = a consultation; cf. related terms listed at soudan

Kaidan 階段 = steps, stairs; *the Kaiser chased the dancer up the stairs*

Kaidoku 買得 = a bargain; *the Kaiser*

thought that the *documentary* was a *bargain* and bought several tickets to it

Kaidou 街道 = highway, path; *the Kaiser built doughnut shops along the highway*; cf. related terms listed at michi

Kaien 開演 = start of a performance; *the Kaiser entered just before the start of the performance*; cf. related terms listed at hajime

Kaifuku 回復 = recovery; *touching the Kaiser's fuku [clothing] hastened her recovery from her illness*; cf. kyuuyou = rest, recuperation, recreation; cf. ryouyou = recovery, recuperation

Kaifuku suru 回復する = to recover from illness, to improve; from kaifuku = recovery; cf. related terms listed at ryouyou suru

Kaiga 絵画 = a painting; *the Kaiser gallantly gave one of his paintings to a lady*; cf. related terms listed at e

Kaigai 海外 = overseas, foreign; from kaiyou = an ocean + gaibu = the outside world; cf. gairai = foreign, outpatient (as opposed to inpatient)

Kaigan 海岸 = a beach or coast; *I flew kites with Gandalf at the beach*; cf. related terms listed at kaihin

Kaigi 会議 = a meeting, conference or convention; *the meeting was held to discuss the Kaiser's geese*; cf. choukai = a morning meeting or assembly; cf. deai = an encounter; cf. kaigou = a meeting or assembly; cf. kaiken = a meeting or interview; cf. kondan = a meeting or talk; cf. mikkai = a secret meeting; cf. moyooshi = an event or meeting; cf. soukai = a general meeting; cf. taikai = convention, tournament, rally; cf. uchiawase = a preparatory meeting

Kaigou 会合 = a meeting or assembly; *the meeting was held to discuss the Kaiser's gold*; cf. related terms listed at kaigi

Kaigun 海軍 = navy; *the Kaiser buys guns for his navy*

Kaigyou 開業 = opening a business; *the Kaiser wants to sell gyoza, so that's why he's opening a business*

Kaihatsu 開発 = development, exploitation; *the Kaiser's hatsus (hats) were purchased with money he made from development and exploitation*; cf. sakushu = exploitation; cf. shuudatsu = plundering, exploitation; cf. other related terms listed at hattatsu

Kaihatsu suru 開発する = to develop; from kaihatsu = development; cf. kaitaku suru = to develop (wilderness), to open up (new markets, etc.)

Kaihi 会費 = membership fee; *the Kaiser heeded advice and paid the membership fee*

Kaihi 回避 = evasion, avoidance; *the Kaiser heeded his generals' advice and followed a strategy of avoidance*

Kaihi suru 回避する = to evade or avoid; from kaihi = evasion, avoidance; cf. manugareru = to avoid or be exempted from; cf. sakeru = to avoid

Kaihin 海浜 = seaside; *the Kaiser met some Hindus at the seaside*; cf. hamabe = beach; cf. kaigan = a beach or coast; cf. kishi = a beach; cf. kohan = a lake shore or lakeside; cf. sunahama = a sandy beach; cf. taigan = the opposite shore

Kaihou suru 解放する = to emancipate, liberate or release; *we want to liberate the Kaiser's horses*; cf. related terms listed at tokihanatsu

Kai'in 会員 (Kaiin) = a group member; from kaigi = a meeting + in = a group member; cf. related terms listed at in

Kai'inu 飼い犬 (Kaiinu) = pet dog; from kau = to keep a pet + inu = dog; cf. related terms listed at inu

Kaijou 会場 = venue, site of an event; from kaigi = meeting + jou = place; cf. related terms listed at basho

Kaijou 海上 = above the sea; from kai = ocean, e.g., kaigai = overseas; + jou = above

Kaijuu 怪獣 = a monster; *the Kaiser served juice to the monster*; cf. kaibutsu = a monster

Kaika 開花 = flowers blooming; *the kind captain invited us to visit during flowers-blooming season*; cf. related terms listed at hana

Kaikadoki 開花時 = blossoming time; from kaika = blossoming + doki = toki = time

Kaikaeru 買い替える = to buy a replacement; from kau = to buy + kaeru= to replace

Kaikaku suru 開花する = to reform; *the Kaiser ordered Karl the Kool-Aid vendor to reform the Kool-Aid industry*; cf. kaisei suru = to revise, reform, amend

Kaikei 会計 = accounting; *the accounting department keeps track of the Kaiser's cake and other food expenses*

Kaiken 会見 = a meeting or interview; *the Kaiser and Kennedy had a meeting*; cf. menkai = an interview; cf. mensetsu = an interview; cf. other related terms listed at kaigi

Kaiketsu 解決 = solution, settlement, resolution; *the Kaiser poured ketchup into his soup as he pondered a settlement, solution or resolution of his problem*

Kaiketsu suru 解決する = to solve, settle or resolve; from kaiketsu = solution, settlement, resolution; cf. related terms listed at hogureru

Kaiko 蚕 = a silkworm; *the Kaiser's corporation raises silkworms*

Kaiko 解雇 = discharge, dismissal; *the kind coach was facing dismissal*; cf. himen = dismissal, discharge; cf. kubi = dismissal, firing from a job

Kaiko suru 解雇する = to dismiss (from employment); from kaiko = discharge, dismissal; cf. himen suru = to dismiss (from a job)

Kaikon 開墾 = cultivating new land; *the Kaiser focused on the Congo as a site for cultivating new land*; cf. related terms listed at hattatsu

Kaikyou 海峡 = a channel or strait; from from kai = ocean, e.g., kaigai = overseas; + kyoukoku = a canyon

Kaikyuu 階級 = class, rank, caste; *the Kaiser and his cute queen occupy the highest rank*; cf. bumon = category, class, section; cf. kyuu = class, level, grade; cf. shaku'i = peerage, court rank; cf. sou = a layer, stratum, social class, story (of a building); cf. other related terms listed at kurai

Kaimamiru 垣間見る = to take a peep at, to catch a glimpse of; *the kind man miru (sees) me when he catches a glimpse of me*

Kaimono 買い物 = shopping; from kau = to buy + mono = a tangible thing

Ka'inaka (Kainaka) か否か = whether or not; from ka = a question marker + ina = deny; *your inappropriate behavior caused us to deny your request*; + ka = a question marker; cf. kadouka = whether or not

Kainushi 飼い主 = a shepherd or pet owner; *the Kaiser's new sheep herder is a pet owner*; cf. hitsujikai = a shepherd

Kairo 回路 = circuit, cycle, process; *the kite rose and fell in a kind of cycle*; cf. katei = process; cf. seizoukatei = manufacturing process

Kaisai suru 開催する = to hold a meeting or open an exhibition; *the kind psychologists will hold a meeting*; cf. moyoosu = to hold an event

Kaisan suru 解散する = to break up or dismiss (a meeting, etc.); *the Kaiser and Santa dismissed the meeting*

Kaisei suru 改正する = to revise, reform, amend; *following the Kaiser's sage advice,* we will <u>reform</u> the laws; cf. kaikaku suru = to reform

Kaisetsu suru 解説する = to explain, comment or interpret; *the <u>Kaiser</u> <u>sets</u> his book aside and <u>explains</u> his plans*; cf. setsumei suru = to explain or illustrate

Kaisha 会社 = a company, corporation or office; *the <u>Kaiser</u> and the <u>Shah</u> started a <u>company</u>*; cf. dousha = the same company; cf. heisha = our company (humble expression); cf. jigyou = business or enterprise; cf. jisha = one's company; cf. kigyou = an enterprise or company; cf. kisha = your company; cf. kogaisha = a subsidiary company; cf. sha = a company; cf. tousha = this company; cf. unsougaisha = a shipping company; cf. wagasha = our company; cf. zaibatsu = a financial combine or business conglomerate; cf. other related terms listed at akinai and at kyoku

Kaishain 会社員 = a company employee; from kaisha = a company + in = a group member; cf. related terms listed at seishain

Kaishaku 解釈 = an explanation or interpretation; *the <u>Kaiser</u> had the men <u>shackl</u>ed until they could produce an <u>explanation</u>*; cf. setsumei = an explanation or illustration

Kaishi 開始 = start, commencement; *the <u>Kaiser's</u> <u>sheep</u> ranch project will have its <u>start</u> next year*; cf. related terms listed at hajime

Kaishi suru 開始する = to start or initiate; from kaishi = commencement; cf. related terms listed at hajimeru

Kaisho 楷書 = block or standard style of printed typeface, square script (calligraphy); *the <u>Kaiser</u> attended a <u>show</u> of <u>square-script</u> calligraphy*; cf. gyousho = semi-cursive script; cf. sousho = cursive or "grass" script

Kaishou 解消 = reduction, cancellation, resolution; *the <u>Kaiser</u> came to the <u>shore</u> and worked out a <u>resolution</u> to the sailor's strike and a <u>reduction</u> in tension*; cf. related terms listed at genshou

Kaishuu 会衆 = an audience or congregation; *the <u>Kaiser</u> threw his <u>shoe</u> at the <u>audience</u>*; cf. related terms listed at choushuu

Kaishuu suru 回収する = to recover, recall, collect (bills or trash); *the <u>Kaiser's</u> <u>shoe</u> was <u>recovered</u> after he lost it*; cf. atsumeru = to collect, gather, attract, summon; cf. toru = to hire, adopt, collect or pick up

Kaishuu suru 改宗する = to convert (to a religion); *the <u>Kaiser</u> will <u>shoot</u> anyone who <u>convert</u>s from his religion*

Kaisoku 快速 = express, high speed, mobility; *the <u>Kaiser</u> <u>soak</u>ed in the tub on his <u>express</u> train*; cf. kousoku = high speed

Kaisoku densha 快速電車 = express train; from kaisoku = express + densha = train; cf. related terms listed at densha

Kaisou 改装 = renovation, remodeling; *the <u>Kaiser</u> ordered his <u>soldiers</u> to help with the <u>renovation</u> of his palace*; cf. kaichiku = reconstruction; cf. kaizou = remodeling; cf. okoshi = revitalization

Kaisou 海藻 = seaweed; this can also be spelled 海草; *the <u>k</u>ind <u>sold</u>ier gave us some <u>seaweed</u>*; cf. mo = algae, seaweed

Kaisui 海水 = sea water; from kai = ocean, e.g., kaigai = overseas; + sui = water, e.g., suiei = swimming; cf. related terms listed at mizu

Kaisuiyoku 海水浴 = bathing in the ocean; from kaisui = sea water + yoku = bathing, e.g., yokushitsu = a bathroom

Kaisuu 回数 = frequency; from kai = times + suuji = numeral; cf. hindo = frequency of occurrence; cf. shindousuu = frequency

Kaitaku suru 開拓する = to develop (wilderness), to open up (new markets, etc.); *the <u>Kaiser</u> paid <u>taxes</u> to <u>Ku</u>wait after he <u>developed</u> some raw land there*; cf. kaihatsu suru = to develop

Kaitakusha 開拓者 = a pioneer; from

kaitaku suru = to develop + sha = a person; cf. senkusha = originator, pioneer

Kaite 買手 = a buyer; from kau = to buy + te = hand

Kaitei 海底 = the bottom of the sea; *the Kaiser's tape recorder sank to the bottom of the sea*; cf. related terms listed at soko = the bottom

Kaiteki 快適 = pleasant, agreeable, comfortable; *the Kaiser found the techie to be pleasant, and he was comfortable with her*; cf. related terms listed at kokoroyoi

Kaiten 回転 = rotation; *that kite has a tendency to do excessive rotation*; cf. ikkaiten = one revolution or rotation; cf. senkai = rotation, turning

Kaiten suru 回転する = to revolve or rotate; from kaiten = rotation; cf. related terms listed at mawaru

Kaitori 買い取り = a purchase or sale; from kaimasu = to buy + toru = to take; cf. kounyuu = a purchase

Kaitou 回答 = a reply; *the Kaiser told her that his reply might be delayed*; cf. related terms listed at kotae

Kaiwa 会話 = a conversation; *the Kaiser liked to walk during his conversations*; cf. eikaiwa = an English conversation; cf. oshaberi = chatting

Kaiyou 海洋 = ocean; *a kayak with a yogi in it was lost in the ocean*; cf. related terms listed at umi

Kaiyou 潰瘍 = an ulcer; *the Kaiser ate yogurt for his ulcer*; cf. related terms listed at byouki

Kaizen 改善 = improvement; *the Kaiser went to the Zen temple seeking personal improvement*; cf. joutatsu = improvement (in skill, etc.); cf. koujou = improvement; cf. koushin = renewal or improvement; cf. yakushin = progress

Kaizoku 海賊 = a pirate; *pirates stopped our ship and took our kites and Zooey's Kool-Aid*

Kaizou 改造 = remodeling; *the Kaiser created a zone in which architectural remodeling was allowed*; cf. related terms listed at kaisou

Kaji 火事 = fire; *let's call the genius to put out the fire*; cf. hi = fire; cf. honoo = blaze, flame; cf. kaen = fire; cf. kasai = fire; cf. sumibi = a charcoal fire; cf. takibi = a bonfire; cf. yowabi = a low fire

Kajiru かじる = to chew or bite; *Karl Marx had his jeans ruined when a dog chewed them*; cf. kamu = to bite or chew

Kajitsu 果実 = berry, nut, fruit; *let's call the jittery superstar and give him these berries*; cf. related terms listed at kudamono

Kajou 過剰 = excess, surplus; *call Joan if you have any excess money*; cf. related terms listed at yoyuu

Kajuen 果樹園 = an orchard; from ka = fruit; *I carved some fruit*; + jumoku = trees + en = park, e.g., kouen = park

Kajuu 果汁 = fruit juice; *cantaloupe juice is one kind of fruit juice*; cf. related terms listed at shiru

Kakaeru 抱える = to embrace or hold; to employ (a person); *when she called a cab, the erudite woman was holding a phone*; cf. related terms listed at daku and at yatou

Kakageru 掲げる = to put up (e.g., a flag); *the California carpenter who was staying in the guest room put up a flag*; cf. haru = to stretch, spread or put up (eg., a tent); cf. sasu = to hold up (e.g., an umbrella), to fill or insert; cf. tateru = to build or put upright

Kakaku 価格 = price, value; *cabbage, cactus and Kool-Aid are sold for a low price*; cf. related terms listed at kachi and nedan

Kakari 係 = a person in charge, duty; this can also be spelled 係り ; *the person in charge* *can carry* his weight and discharge his *duty*

Kakarichou 係長 = an assistant section chief; from kakari = a person in charge + chou = chief; cf. related terms listed at shunou

Kakariin 係員 = a person in charge; from kakari = person in charge + in = a member, e.g., kaishain = a company employee

Kakaru かかる = to start doing something, used as a suffix; this can also = to span, to hang, to cross, to cost, to deal with, to suffer from, and many other meanings; *the card-carrying roofer started repairing the roof, but he suffered from a fear of heights*; cf. related terms listed at hajimeru, at sagaru and at wazurau

Kakaru 掛かる = to take (time), to cost (money), to hang, to depend on, to get a phone call; *the card-carrying roofer takes his time and costs us money*

Kakaru 架かる = to span; *the cab carried Rudolph over a bridge that spanned the river*; cf. related terms listed at oudan suru

Kakawarazu かかわらず = regardless, in spite of, nevertheless (usually expressed as ni kakawarazu or ni mo kakawarazu); this can also be spelled 拘わらず; *the cacao beans that Washington fed his rabbits in Zurich were not good for them; nevertheless I didn't interfere*; cf. ni mo kakawarazu = regardless, in spite of, nevertheless; cf. shikamo = moreover, nevertheless, and yet; cf. sore ni shitemo = nevertheless, at any rate

Kakawaru 関わる = to be involved in or connected with (this can also be spelled 係わる); *if you call a cab, it's warui (bad), since then you will be involved*; cf. kakawarazu = regardless; cf. au = to be involved (in an accident, etc.); cf. chokumen suru = to face or be involved with, to confront with

Kakeagaru 駆け上がる = to run up; from kakeru = to run + agaru = to rise; cf. related terms listed at hashiru

Kakegoe 掛け声 = a shout or cheer; from kakeru = to spend + goe = koe = voice; cf. himei = a scream, shriek or cry of distress; cf. kansei = a cheer or shout of joy; cf. sakebigoe = a scream; cf. zekkyou = a scream or shriek

Kakegoto 賭け事 = gambling; from kakeru = to gamble + goto = koto = thing; cf. related terms listed at bakuchi

Kakei 家系 = lineage, geneology; *Karl Marx sat in a cave, working on his geneology charts*

Kakemeguru 駆け巡る = to run about; from kakeru = to run + meguru = to go around; cf. related terms listed at hashiru

Kakeoriru 駆け降りる = to run down (stairs, etc.); from kakeru = to run + oriru = to descend; cf. related terms listed at hashiru

Kakeru 掛ける = to expend or spend (e.g., time, money, love), to extend, to hang (a picture), to make (a phone call), to multiply, to put on (glasses), to pour or sprinkle onto, to burden someone, to secure (e.g., a lock), to sit down, to begin or be about to begin (when used as a suffix, e.g., yomikakeru = to begin to read), among many other meanings; *I called Kennedy's room to see if he would spend time with me*; cf. mabusu = to cover or sprinkle with; cf. sosogu = to pour; cf. suwaru = to sit; cf. other related terms listed at hajimeru, sageru and sugosu

Kakeru 欠ける = to lack, to be chipped; *the camera that Kennedy ruined lacks a lens*; cf. kaku = to lack

Kakeru 賭ける = to bet or gamble; *I called Kennedy's room to see if he wanted to gamble*

Kakeru 駆ける = to run; *I called Kennedy's room to see if he wanted to run*; cf. related terms listed at hashiru

Kaketsu suru 可決する = to approve or

pass (legislation); *after the legislature passed the new law, Karl Marx poured ketchup into his soup*; cf. sandou suru = to approve or endorse

Kaki 夏季 = the summer season; *I wore my khaki uniform during the summer season*; cf. related terms listed at kisetsu

Kaki 柿 = a persimmon; *my cocky neighbor brags about his persimmon tree*; cf. related terms listed at kudamono

Kakiageru 書き上げる = to finish writing; from kaku = to write; + ageru = to finish, when used after a transitive verb stem, e.g., shiageru = to finish doing

Kakikata 書き方 = a way of writing; from kaku = to write + kata = a method

Kakine 垣根 = hedge, fence; *my cocky neighbor put up a fence*; cf. hei = a fence or wall; cf. ishibei = a stone wall; cf. saku = a fence; cf. tessaku = an iron fence

Kakki 活気 = liveliness, energy; *he's cocky, but he has a lot of energy*; cf. related terms listed at chikara

Kakko カッコ = parenthesis or bracket; this can also be spelled 括弧; *I calculated the co-payments and wrote them in parentheses*

Kakko ii かっこいい = good-looking; from kakko, an abbreviation of kakkou = form + ii = good; cf. kakkoyoi = good-looking, stylish; cf. ko'iki = stylish, conceited; cf. oshare = stylish

Kakkoku 各国 = each country; from kakuji = each + koku = country; cf. related terms listed at kuni

Kakkou 格好 = form, appearance, suitability; *he carved some coral into jewelry that had an attractive appearance*; cf. related terms listed at kata and at mitame

Kakkoyoi カッコ良い = good-looking, stylish; from kakkou = form, appearance + yoi = good; cf. related terms listed at kakko ii

Kako 過去 = the past; *I worked for a California corporation in the past*

Kakoku 苛酷 = severity, rigor, cruelty (nouns), or harsh (a na adjective); this can also be spelled 過酷; *in their cruelty, they banned cashews and Coke, which was harsh*; cf. kibishii = stern, rigid, strict, harsh; cf. kibishisa = strictness, severity

Kakomu 囲む = to surround or circle; *a carpentry corporation moved some stones when they built a fence to surround a well*; cf. meguru = to go or come around, to surround; cf. torikakomu = to surround; cf. torimaku = to surround

Kakou 河口 = mouth of a river; *that car turned a corner and ended up in the mouth of a river*

Kakou 火口 = a crater, a burner (e.g., on a furnace); from kazan = a volcano + kou = a mouth, e.g., 河口 kakou = the mouth of a river

Kaku – see 描く egaku

Kaku かく = to perspire, e.g., ase wo kaku = to sweat; *I perspired in the car in Kuwait*

Kaku 各 = each, every, either; *Karl the Kool-Aid vendor likes each variety of Kool-Aid*; cf. dochiraka = either, one of the two; cf. other related terms listed at goto ni

Kaku 書く = to write; *Karl the Kool-Aid vendor wrote me a letter*; cf. arawasu = to write or publish; cf. egaku = to draw, paint, depict, describe; cf. kijutsu suru = to describe in writing; cf. sakusei suru = to draw up (document), prepare, write, make, produce; cf. shirusu = to record or write

Kaku 核 = nucleus; *Karl the Kool-Aid vendor and his colleagues form the nucleus of the sales force*

Kaku 欠く = to lack; *Karl's Kool-Aid lacks sugar*; cf. kakeru = to lack, to be chipped

Kaku 閣 = a tower or palace, used as a word component; *Karl* the *Kool*-Aid vendor lives in a *tower*

Kakuchi 各地 = every place, various places; from kaku = each, every + chi = ground; cf. kakuji = each, one's own

Kakuchou 拡張 = expansion, enlargement; *Karl* the *Kool*-Aid vendor *chose* a strategy devoted to *expansion* of his sales territory; cf. related terms listed at shinshutsu

Kakudai 拡大 = magnification, enlargement; *Karl* the *Kool*-Aid vendor went on a *diet* after noticing an *enlargement* of his body; cf. related terms listed at shinshutsu

Kakudo 角度 = an angle; from kaku = a corner, e.g., shikaku = a rectangle; + do = degree; cf. chokkaku = a right angle

Kakueki 各駅 = each station; from kaku = each + eki = station

Kakugo 覚悟 = preparedness, readiness; when *Karl* the *Kool*-Aid vendor plays *golf*, his *preparedness* is evident

Kakuheiki 核兵器 = nuclear weapon; from kaku = nucleus + heiki = a weapon; cf. related terms listed at buki

Kakuho suru 確保する = to ensure or secure; *when Karl the Kool-Aid vendor came to my home, he said that I should secure the doors with locks*; cf. hoshou suru = to guarantee

Kakuji 各自 = each, every, either; from kaku = each + jibun = by oneself; cf. related terms listed at goto ni

Kakuji no 各自の = each, one's own; from kakuji = each; cf. related terms listed at goto ni

Kakujitsu 確実 = guaranteed, reliable; *Karl the Kool-Aid vendor told the jittery superstar that his Kool-Aid was guaranteed*; cf. kenjitsu = steady, reliable, solid; cf. tonomoshii = reliable, trustworthy

Kakujitsu ni 確実に = certainly; from kakujitsu = guarantee + -ni = a suffix that forms an adverb; cf. related terms listed at tashika ni

Kakumau 匿う = to shelter, shield or hide, transitive; *Karl* the *Kool*-Aid vendor went to *Maui* to *hide* the evidence from the police; cf. related terms listed at kakusu

Kakumei 革命 = revolution; *Karl Marx drank Kool-Aid with his maid while plotting the revolution*

Kakumo かくも = so (e.g., so much, so many, etc.); *Karl* the *Kool*-Aid vendor's *motorcycle is so fast*; cf. kore hodo = so much, this much

Kakunin 確認 = confirmation, check; *Karl* the *Kool*-Aid vendor asked the *ninja* for *confirmation* of his order

Kakunin suru 確認する = to confirm, validate or check; from kakunin = confirmation or check; cf. tashikameru = to ascertain or confirm; cf. tsukitomeru = to find out, locate, ascertain

Kakureru 隠れる = to conceal oneself or disappear; *Karl* the *Kool*-Aid vendor bought some *red roosters*, and then he *disappeared*; cf. komoru = to seclude oneself, to be confined in cf. shinobu = to conceal oneself; cf. other related terms listed at bossuru

Kakuryou 閣僚 = a Cabinet member; from naikaku = the Cabinet + kanryou = a government official

Kakusei 覚醒 = waking up, disillusionment; *Karl the Kool-Aid vendor posed as a sage, but his followers experienced a waking up and a disillusionment*; cf. related terms listed at gakkari

Kakushi 隠し = hidden, used as a prefix, e.g., kakushido = a hidden door; from kakusu = to hide

Kakushin 核心 = a core, center, central issue, kernel; *Karl the Kool-Aid vendor's Shinto faith is at the center of his life*; cf. related terms listed at chuubu

Kakusu 隠す = to hide or cover up (transitive); *Karl the Kool-Aid vendor's supervisor told him to hide the evidence from the police*; cf. kakumau = to shelter, shield or hide, transitive; cf. oou = to cover, conceal, wrap, disguise; cf. moguru = to dive or hide; cf. tsutsumu = to wrap up

Kakuteru カクテル = a cocktail (alcoholic drink)

Kakutoku suru 獲得する = to win or obtain; *that cactus is totally cool, and I hope to win it in a contest*; cf. related terms listed at katsu and at shutoku suru

Kama 窯 = an oven, furnace or kiln; *Karl Marx built an oven*

Kama 釜 = a pot in which rice is cooked; *Karl Marx bought a pot for cooking rice*; cf. related terms listed at tsubo

Kama 鎌 = a sickle or scythe; *I called a master arborist to fix a tree damaged by a sickle*

Kamainaku 構いなく – see okamainaku

Kamameshi 釜飯 = a rice, meat and vegetable dish served in a pot; from kama = a pot in which rice is cooked + meshi = rice or food; cf. related terms listed at ryouri

Kamau 構う = to care about, to mind; *she cares about her cabin on Maui*; cf. ki ni naru = to worry, care about, to be bothered by; cf. ki ni suru = to mind, care about or worry; cf. tonchaku suru = to care about

Kamawazu 構わず = not minding; from kamawanaide = kamawazuni = not minding (from kamau = to mind)

Kame 亀 = turtle, tortoise; *the turtle is a friend of the camel*; cf. umigame = a sea turtle

Kame 瓶 = an earthenware jar (this can also be pronounced bin = a bottle, jar or decanter); *the camel drank from an earthenware jar*; cf. related terms listed at tsubo

Kamei 加盟 = participation, joining; *the cabby and the maid discussed joining a club*; cf. related terms listed at sanka

Kami 加味 = seasoning, flavor; *the cabbage and the meat have good flavoring*; cf. related terms listed at fuumi

Kami 神 = a god; *the Catholics meet to pray to their god*; cf. megami = goddess, female deity

Kami 紙 = paper; *I called a meeting to discuss the paper shortage*; cf. binsen = writing paper, stationery; cf. hanshi = common Japanese writing paper; cf. katagami = pattern paper; cf. noshigami = gift-wrapping paper

Kami 髪 = hair; *that commie (communist) has long hair*; cf. related terms listed at ke

Kamigata 髪型 = hair style; from kami = hair + gata = kata = form

Kaminari 雷 = thunder or lightning; *the Commies from Narita heard thunder and saw lightning*; cf. raimei = thunder

Kaminoke 髪の毛 = hair; from kami = hair + the possessive no + ke = fur; cf. related terms listed at ke

Kamitsu 花蜜 = nectar; from ka = flower, e.g., kafun = pollen; + mitsu = honey, e.g., hachimitsu = honey

Kamo かも – see kamoshiremasen

Kamoku 科目 = academic course; *the academic course about camels is the most cool*; cf. ka = an academic department or course, used as a suffix

Kamoshidasu 醸しだす = to engender, to bring about, to cause, to give rise to; from kamosu = to bring about + dasu = to put out; cf. related terms listed at hikiokosu

Kamoshiremasen かもしれません = maybe, possibly, might be; *when I called Moses, he said that he shiremasen (can't* know) *if there will be a party, but* <u>possibly</u> *there* <u>might</u> <u>be</u>; cf. hyotto = possibly; cf. hyotto suru to = possibly, maybe; cf. moshikashitara = perhaps, maybe; cf. moshikashite = perhaps, maybe; cf. moshikasuruto = perhaps, maybe

Kamoshirenai かもしれない – see kamoshiremasen

Kamosu 醸す = to brew, to bring about, to cause; *watching military dramas has* <u>caused</u> *me to start wearing* <u>camouflaged</u> <u>suits</u>; cf. kamoshidasu = to engender, to bring about, to cause, to give rise to; cf. other related terms listed at hikiokosu

Kamotsu 貨物 = freight; *the amphibious* <u>car</u> *drove through the* <u>moats</u>, *loaded with* <u>freight</u>

Kamotsusen 貨物船 = a cargo ship; from kamotsu = freight + sen = a boat, e.g., kisen = a steam ship; cf. related terms listed at fune

Kamu かむ = to bite or chew; <u>Camus</u> <u>chewed</u> *his food carefully*; cf. kajiru = to chew or bite

Kan 乾 = dry, used as a word component, e.g., kandenchi = a dry cell battery; *this* <u>candy</u> *is* <u>dry</u>

Kan 感 = sensation, emotion, feeling; from kanjiru = to sense or feel; cf. related terms listed at kankaku

Kan 棺 = a coffin; *I lit some* <u>candles</u> *near her* <u>coffin</u>

Kan 管 = a pipe or tube; *I make* <u>candles</u> *by pouring wax into* <u>tubes</u>; cf. related terms listed at kuda

Kan 缶 = a tin can, jar or container; *I have a* <u>jar</u> *of* <u>candy</u>; cf. akikan = an empty can; cf. utsuwa = container or receptacle, ability

Kan 貫 = a counter for pieces of sushi; *that* <u>Canadian</u> *usually eats three* <u>pieces</u> <u>of</u> <u>sushi</u>

Kan 間 = interval or space, used as a suffix; <u>Kan</u>sas *is in the* <u>space</u> *between Nebraska and Oklahoma*

Kan 館 = a large building, used as a suffix; *they manufacture* <u>cans</u> *in that* <u>large</u> <u>building</u>

Kan shite 関して = concerning, regarding; from kan suru = concerning, to be related to; cf. related terms listed at ni tsuite

Kan suru 関する = to be related to, concerning; *I am* <u>related</u> <u>to</u> *some* <u>Canadians</u>; cf. chinamu = to derive from or be related to; cf. other related terms listed at ni tsuite

Kana かな = I wonder; <u>I</u> <u>wonder</u> *how they do it in* <u>Canada</u>

Kanaderu 奏でる = to play a stringed instrument; *a* <u>Canadian</u> <u>debutante</u> *named Ruth* <u>plays</u> *a* <u>stringed</u> <u>instrument</u>; cf. hiku = to play a piano or guitar

Kanaeru 叶える = to grant or answer a request, to meet requirements; the transitive form of kanau = to be fulfilled; cf. related terms listed at oujiru

Kanai 家内 = one's wife; <u>my</u> <u>wife's</u> <u>cat</u> <u>is</u> <u>nice</u>; cf. nyoubou = one's wife; cf. okusan = another person's wife; cf. shufu = a housewife; cf. tsuma = a wife (one's own or another person's)

Kanarazu 必ず = for certain, without fail; <u>Canadian</u> <u>rascals</u> *come to the* <u>zoo</u> *every week* <u>without</u> <u>fail</u>; cf. related terms listed at chanto

Kanarazu shimo 必ずしも = not necessarily (when used with a negative verb); <u>Canadian</u> <u>rascals</u> *at the* <u>zoo</u> *stealing* <u>Shi</u>ite <u>motorcycles</u> *will* <u>not</u> <u>necessarily</u> *get caught*; cf. kagiranai = it isn't limited to, or not necessarily; cf. wake de wa nai = not necessarily

Kanari かなり = considerably, quite; *that* <u>canary</u> *is* <u>quite</u> <u>fat</u>; cf. daibu = considerably, a lot; cf. nakanaka = not easily or readily (with negative constructions), quite or considerably (with positive constructions)

Kanashii 悲しい = sad; *Canadian Shiites are sad in the winter*; cf. itamashii = poignant, pitiable, tragic; cf. muzan na = heartless, tragic

Kanashimi 悲しみ = sadness; from kanashimu = to feel sad; cf. nageki = sorrow; cf. shuushou = grief, sorrow

Kanashimu 悲しむ = to feel sad; *after the Canadian Shiite saw the movie, he felt sad*

Kanau 叶う = to come true or be fulfilled (referring to a wish or dream); *California is now a dream come true for many immigrants*

Kanawanu 叶わぬ = an archaic way of saying kanawazu = kanawanaide = not being fulfilled

Kanawazu 叶わず = kanawanaide = not being fulfilled; from kanau = to come true or be fulfilled

Kanbai 完売 = sold out; *you can buy it until it's sold out*; cf. urikire = sold out

Kanban 看板 = a signboard; *the signboard states that candy is banned*; cf. related terms listed at kokuban

Kanbashii 芳しい = fragrant; *the can you are bashing is emitting a fragrant liquid*; cf. kaori takaku = fragrant, aromatic

Kanbatsu 干ばつ = a drought; *the Canadian bats were affected by the drought*; cf. related terms listed at tenki

Kanben 勘弁 = pardon, forgiveness; *I left the candy on the bench, and I beg your pardon*; cf. kannin = forgiveness; cf. yousha = pardon, forgiveness; cf. yurushi = forgiveness

Kanbu 幹部 = an executive; *that executive drinks only Canadian booze*; cf. related terms listed at shunou

Kanchigai 勘違い = misunderstanding, wrong guess; from kan = intuition, e.g., kanben = pardon; + chigai = difference; cf. gokai = a misunderstanding; cf. sakkaku = an illusion or misunderstanding

Kanchou 官庁 = a government office; *the Canadian did chores at a government office*; cf. related terms listed at kyoku

Kandai na 寛大な = understanding, lenient, tolerant, generous, broad-minded; *since I'm generous, I will give him a Canadian dime*; cf. related terms listed at kanyou

Kandenchi 乾電池 = a dry cell battery; from kan = dry + denchi = a battery

Kandou suru 感動する = to be moved; *I was moved by her candor*

Kane 金 = money; *I spent money on canned eggplant*; cf. related terms listed at kinsen

Kane 鐘 = a bell, gong or chimes; *a Canadian expert built the bell for the steeple*; cf. related terms listed at suzu

Kanemochi 金持ち = a rich person; from kane = money + motsu = to have or own; cf. fugou = a person of great wealth

Kaneru 兼ねる = to serve multiple purposes at the same time, to be unable to do (when used as a suffix); *the Canadian eggs in the room can serve multiple purposes, but we are unable to eat them*

Kangae 考え thinking, thought; from kangaeru = to think or consider; cf. related terms listed at omoi

Kangaeru 考える = to think or consider; *that kangaroo is erudite and thinks a lot*; cf. related terms listed at omou

Kangaetsuku 考えつく = to think of; from kangaeru = to think + tsuku = to adhere; cf. related terms listed at omoidasu

Kangei 歓迎 = a welcome; *the kangaroo at the gate gave us a warm welcome*

Kangetsukai 観月会 = a moon-viewing party; from kankou = sightseeing + getsu = moon + kaigi = meeting

Kangofu 看護婦 = female nurse; *the female*

nurse can go to the *funeral*

Kangoku 監獄 = jail, prison; *I smuggled some candy and gold Kool-Aid into the jail*; cf. keimusho = prison; cf. kouchisho = a jail or detention center

Kani カニ = a crab; this is often spelled かに; *Karl's knee was pinched by a crab*

Kanimiso カニみそ = miso-like paste found in a crab's intestinal area; from kani = crab + miso = fermented bean paste

Kanja 患者 = a patient; *that patient likes Canadian jazz*

Kanji 感じ = impression, perception, feeling; from kanjiru = to feel or sense; cf. related terms listed at inshou and at kankaku

Kanji 漢字 = Chinese characters used in Japanese writing

Kanjin na (or no) 肝心な = essential, most important, crucial; *Canadian jeans are an essential item when logging trees*; cf. hissu no = essential, imperative, necessary

Kanjiru 感じる = to feel or sense; *I feel or sense the meaning of the kanji found in the ruined castle*; cf. sacchi suru = to perceive

Kanjou 勘定 = bill, check, calculation; *in Canada, we joked about who should pick up the check*; cf. denpyou = a receipt, bill or slip; cf. other related terms listed at keisan

Kanjusei 感受性 = sensitivity; *I developed a sensitivity to that canned juice they sell at Safeway*; cf. shinkei = nerves, sensitivity

Kankaku 感覚 = a sense or feeling; *when he got to Canada, Karl the Kool-Aid vendor had a sense that he would succeed*; cf. jou = emotion, affection; cf. kan = sensation, emotion, feeling; cf. kanji = an impression, perception or feeling; cf. ki = spirit, soul, feeling, intention, inclination; cf. kibun = a feeling; cf. kigen = mood, feeling; cf. kimochi = a feeling; cf. kimochiyoi = a good feeling, feeling good; cf. kokochi = feeling, sensation, mood; cf. moe = feelings of affection directed at certain anime or manga characters; cf. nen = sense or feeling

Kankaku 間隔 = an interim, interval, pause or space; *Canada provided Karl the Kool-Aid vendor with some space to recover during that interval*; cf. related terms listed at jikan

Kankan カンカン = anger, clanging noise, used in the phrase "kankan ni okoru" = to get furious; *when I feel anger, I dance the cancan*; cf. related terms listed at uppun

Kankatsu 管轄 = jurisdiction or control; *I have jurisdiction over my Canadian cats*; cf. related terms listed at seigyo

Kankei 関係 = relationship, connection; *our relationship began in a Canadian cave*; cf. fuwa = a discordant or hostile relationship; cf. setsuzoku = connection, attachment, link, conjunction; cf. other related terms listed at kanrensei

Kanki 歓喜 = exhilaration, joy; *this canned quiche gives me joy*; cf. related terms listed at shiawase

Kanki suru 歓喜する = to exhilarate or feel joy; from kanki = joy

Kankin 監禁 = incarceration, confinement; *the kangaroo's kinky owner was sentenced to incarceration*

Kankoku 勧告 = recommendation, advice; *his recommendation was to drink a can of Coke*; cf. chuukoku = advice or admonition; cf. soudan = consultation, advice

Kankou 観光 = sightseeing; *I went sightseeing to see canned corn*; cf. kenbutsu = sightseeing, watching (e.g., sports)

Kankou 観光する suru = to sightsee; from kankou = sightseeing

Kankou suru 刊行する = to publish; *the Canadian corporation publishes a newsletter*; cf. related terms listed at keisai suru

Kankouchi 観光地 = tourist sites; from kankou = sightseeing + chi = ground; cf. related terms listed at basho

Kankoukyaku 観光客 = a tourist; from kankou = sightseeing + kyaku = customer

Kankyaku 観客 = an audience or spectator; from kan = to look over, e.g., kankou = sightseeing; + kyaku = customer; cf. related terms listed at choushuu

Kankyou 環境 = environment, surroundings; *if you drop candy wrappers on the street in Kyouto, you will mess up the environment*; cf. kyouguu = circumstances, environment; cf. mawari = surrounding; cf. shuui = surroundings

Kanman 干満 = ebb and flow; *the Canadian mansion was affected by the ebb and flow of the tides*

Kanmei 感銘 = a deep impression; *the Canadian maid's reply left a deep impression*; cf. related terms listed at inshou

Kanmuri 冠 = a crown; *can Muriel ever put on the crown?* cf. related terms listed at oui

Kannai 管内 = within the jurisdiction; *the regulations for canning at night are within our jurisdiction*

Kannai 館内 = in the building; from kan = a large building; + nai = inside

Kannin 堪忍 = forgiveness; *I received forgiveness for my fruit-canning errors*; cf. kanben = pardon, forgiveness

Kanningu カンニング = cheating, from "cunning"

Kanojo 彼女 = she, her, girlfriend; *she said her calculations were no joke*

Kanou 可能 = possible; *it's possible to cook it with Canola oil*; cf. arayuru = all, every possible; cf. arieru = is possible; cf. ariuru = is possible; cf. okoriuru = to be possible to occur

Kanousei 可能性 = a possibility; *it's a possibility to cook with Canola and save money*

Kanpa 寒波 = a cold wave (weather event); *the Canadian padre died during the cold wave*; cf. mousho = fierce heat, heat wave

Kanpai 乾杯 = cheers! *let's eat some Canadian pie, have a drink, and say cheers!*

Kanpeki na 完璧な = perfect, complete, flawless; *the candy we ate in Peking was perfect*; cf. kanzen na = perfect, entire; cf. zenmenteki = all-out, general, extensive, full-scale, over-all, complete

Kanran 観覧 = a viewing; *we visited a Canadian ranch for a viewing of the scenery*

Kanransha 観覧車 = a Ferris wheel; from kanran = a viewing + sha = a car

Kanren 関連 = related, associated; *the Canadian rental car was related to the incident*

Kanrensei 関連性 = relatedness or relationship; *the Canadian rental car was used by a sailor who had a relationship with the renter*; cf. en = relation, bond, kinship, fate; cf. kankei = relationship, connection; cf. naka = relationship; cf. tsukiai = association, relationship

Kanri 管理 = supervision, administration, management; *she's in management at a company that sells Canadian rings*; cf. gyousei = government administration; cf. keiei = management; cf. keiri = management, accounting; cf. seigyo = control, governing, checking; cf. soujuu = management, handling, operation

Kanryou 官僚 = a government official or bureaucrat; *in Canada, Pope Leo became a bureaucrat*; cf. koukan = a high-ranking official

Kanryou suru 完了する = to finish; *I finished drinking the soda in the can that*

Pope Leo gave me; cf. related terms listed at owaraseru

Kansatsu 観察 = observation; *he made the observation that a Canadian guy sat on Superman's sandwich*; cf. kansoku = observation, survey

Kansei 完成 = completion; *in Canada, a new Safeway store is reaching completion*; cf. juujitsu = fullness, completion, perfection

Kansei 歓声 = cheer, shout of joy; *when the kangaroo was saved, the people shouted cheers*; cf. related terms listed at kakegoe

Kansei na 閑静な = quiet (neighborhood); *the Canadian sailor came from a quiet town*; cf. related terms listed at odayaka

Kansei suru 完成する = to finish, accomplish, complete (transitive); from kansei = completion; cf. related terms listed at owaraseru

Kansen 感染 = contagion, infection; *the Canadian senator warned about the risk of contagion from the epidemic disease*; cf. related terms listed at byouki

Kansen 観戦 = watching a game, observing; *the Canadian senators were watching a game*

Kansenbyou 感染秒 = an infectious disease; from kansen = infection + byouki = illness; cf. related terms listed at byouki

Kansensha 観戦者 = spectator; from kansen = watching a game + sha = person; cf. related terms listed at choushuu

Kansenshou 感染症 = infectious disease; from kansen = infection + shoujou = symptoms; cf. related terms listed at byouki

Kansetsu 関節 = joint (e.g., knee); *the cancer doctor set up a super clinic for joint problems*; cf. fushi = knot (wood), joint (body), melody; cf. tsugime = a joint or seam

Kansha 感謝 = gratitude; *I feel gratitude to the kangaroo's shadow which saved me from being trampled*; cf. kyoushuku = gratitude; cf. on = indebtedness, obligation, gratitude; cf. onrei = thanks, gratitude; cf. orei = gratitude, thanks

Kanshi 監視 = monitoring, watching, inspection; *the Canadian sheepdogs were in charge of monitoring the sheep*; cf. related terms listed at tenken

Kanshin 感心 = impressive, admirable; *the candy from the Shinto temple was impressive*; cf. related terms listed at inshouteki

Kanshin 関心 = concern, interest, e.g., kanshin ga aru = to have an interest or concern; *in Canada, Shinto artifacts are regarded with interest and concern*; cf. kyoumi = interest

Kanshin suru 感心する = to admire or be impressed; from kanshin = impressive; cf. akogareru = to admire, to long for; cf. kantan suru = to admire or be astonished

Kanshou 干渉 = interference, intervention; *I felt interference when I walked into the waves on the Canadian shore*; cf. bougai = an interference, disturbance, intrusion or obstacle

Kanshou 鑑賞 = appreciation (e.g., of art), listening (to music), watching (works of art), reading (literature); *you can show your appreciation by giving me money*

Kanshou suru 鑑賞する = to appreciate (seeing, reading, listening, etc.); from kanshou = appreciation; cf. hyouka suru = to value, to appreciate

Kanshuu 慣習 = a usual custom; similar to shuukan = a custom, but with the order of characters reversed; cf. related terms listed at shuukan

Kansoku 観測 = observation, survey; *our survey will determine how often Canadians soak in their tubs, based on direct observations*; cf. kansatsu = observation; cf. chousa = investigation, survey, analysis

Kansou 乾燥 = dryness; *that <u>Canadian soap</u> causes <u>dryness</u> of my skin*

Kansou 感想 = impressions, thoughts; from kanji = impression, perception, feeling; + souzou = imagination; cf. related terms listed at inshou

Kantan 簡単 = simple and easy; *getting a <u>Canadian tan</u> is <u>easy</u> during the summer*; cf. hiratai = flat, simple; cf. tanjun = simple; cf. tegaru = easy, informal, cheap, quick; cf. yasashii = easy; cf. youi = easy, simple, plain; cf. yuttari = comfortable, easy, loose

Kantan suru 感嘆する = to admire or be astonished at; *I <u>admire Canadian tanks</u>*; cf. related terms listed at kanshin suru and at odoroku

Kantoku 監督 = a director, superintendent, or manager (e.g., of a sports team); *the <u>director</u> made a movie about <u>Canada</u> that was <u>totally cool</u>*; cf. keieisha = a business manager or owner

Kanwa 緩和 = relief, alleviation, relaxation; *after the <u>Canadian war</u>, I was ready for some <u>relaxation</u>*; cf. related terms listed at anshin

Kanyou 寛容 = tolerance, open-mindedness, forbearance, generosity; *that <u>Canadian yogi</u> shows considerable <u>tolerance</u> and <u>generosity</u>*; cf. houyou = tolerance, magnanimity; cf. houyouryoku = tolerance, broadmindedness; cf. kandai = lenient, generous, broadminded; cf. kanyousa = tolerance, generosity; cf. kanyousei = tolerance

Kanyousa 寛容さ = tolerance, generosity; from kanyou = tolerance, generosity + sa = a suffix that makes a noun from another word; cf. related terms listed at kanyou

Kanyousei 寛容性 = tolerance; from kanyou = tolerance + sei = nature; cf. related terms listed at kanyou

Kanzei 関税 = a customs duty or tariff; from genkan = a front door + zeikin = tax or duty

Kanzen na 完全な = perfect, entire; *the <u>Canadian Zen</u> monk had <u>perfect</u> balance*; cf. related terms listed at kanpeki

Kanzen ni 完全に = perfectly, entirely; from kanzen = perfect, entire

Kanzou 肝臓 = the liver; *a <u>can</u> of <u>Zooey</u>'s beans is good for the <u>liver</u>*; cf. kimo = the liver, courage; cf. other related terms listed at naizou

Kao 顔 = face or look; *that <u>cow</u> has a peaceful <u>face</u>*; cf. egao = a smiling face; cf. jinmen = a human face; cf. negao = a sleeping face

Kaoiro 顔色 = the color of the face; from kao = face + iro = color

Ka'oku (Kaoku) 家屋 = house or building; from ka = house, e.g., kazoku = family; + oku = house; cf. related terms listed at ie and at tatemono

Kaomake 顔負け = being embarrassed or put to shame, e.g., kaomake da = (someone) is put to shame; from kao = face + makeru = to lose

Kaomake da 顔負けだ = (someone) is put to shame; from kaomake = being put to shame; cf. tereru = to be shy or feel embarrassed

Kaori 香り = fragrance, aroma; this can also be spelled 薫り ; *<u>cows</u> in the <u>Orient</u> are associated with certain <u>aromas</u>*; cf. akushuu = a bad smell; cf. houkou = perfume or fragrance; cf. kouryou = fragrance; cf. nioi = fragrance, scent

Kaori takaku 薫り高く = fragrant, aromatic; from kaori = fragrance + takai = high; cf. kanbashii = fragrant

Kappatsu 活発 = active, vivacious; *<u>Karl</u> Marx <u>patted Superman</u> on the back after observing his <u>active</u> pursuit of criminals*; cf. related terms listed at sakan

Kara から = from, since, after, because, therefore; *since the karaoke started after lunch, therefore I can't study*; cf. related terms listed at irai and at node

Kara 殻 = a shell or crust; *since starting karaoke, he has come out of his shell*; cf. related terms listed at koura

Kara 空 = empty, vacant; *I sang karaoke to an empty room*; cf. karappo = empty, hollow

Kara 〜 = to, or from; for example, 3〜4 = (from) 3 to 4

Karaage 唐揚げ = deep-fried food, usually spelled カラアゲ; *one characteristic of the American guest was a fondness for deep-fried food*; cf. related terms listed at tabemono

Karada 体 = body; *after singing karaoke with Darwin, my body is tired*; cf. doutai = body, torso; cf. himantai = an overweight body; cf. itai = a dead body; cf. jinshin = the human body, one's person; cf. jintai = the human body; cf. nakigara = a corpse; cf. nikutai = the human body; cf. mi = body, person; cf. shin = somebody, person, body; cf. shitai = a dead body

Karai 辛い = spicy, hot, harsh; *the captain's rice was spicy*

Karakau からかう = to ridicule or jeer; *in Caracas the cows are ridiculed*; cf. azakeru = to ridicule, mock or scoff

Karamaru 絡まる = to be entwined, to become entangled in; *the character of the master ruined his chances in the election, since he became entangled in scandals*

Karami 辛味 = salty (hot, sharp) taste; from karai = bitter, hot, salty + mi = taste, e.g., shumi = hobby or taste; cf. related terms listed at aji

Karappo 空っぽ = empty, hollow; *it was a caravan of politicians bringing empty promises*; cf. kara = empty, vacant

Karareru かられる = to succumb to, to be driven (by feelings); this can sometimes be spelled 駆られる; *the character of the red rooster often made him succumb to feelings of rage*

Kare 彼 = he, him, boyfriend; *he works at a California restaurant*; cf. related terms listed at aitsu

Kareha 枯れ葉 = dry or withered leaves; from kareru = to wither + ha = a leaf; cf. related terms listed at ha

Karekore かれこれ = roughly, almost, this and that; *if you paint the cabin red correctly, you will be roughly halfway to the end of the job*; cf. related terms listed at yaku

Karera 彼ら = they; from kare = he + ra = a suffix that makes the preceding pronoun plural

Kareru 枯れる = to wither; *after its castration, the red rooster withered away*

Kareshi 彼氏 = boyfriend; from kare = he + shi = mister; *the sheep belongs to the mister*

Kari 狩り = hunting, gathering; from karu = to hunt; cf. shuryou = hunting

Kari ni 仮に = if; *if I carry a needle, you should carry thread*; cf. related terms listed at moshi

Karikari カリカリ = crisp, crunchy; *I carry Caribbean potato chips which are crunchy*; cf. paritto = crisp, crunchy, modern, classy; cf. sakusaku = crisp or crunchy

Kariru 借りる = to borrow or rent; *I borrowed a TV set and carried it to my room*

Karoujite かろうじて = barely; *when I spilled Karo syrup on my jeans in Texas, I was barely able to scrub out the stain*; cf. related terms listed at yatto

Karou 過労 = exhaustion from overwork; *setting up the Christmas carol performance led to exhaustion from overwork*

Karoushi 過労死 = death from overwork; from karou = exhaustion from overwork + shinu = to die; cf. related terms listed at eimin

Karu 刈る = to reap or mow, to cut hair; *Karl Marx made it a rule to cut his hair monthly*; cf. related terms listed at kiru

Karu 狩る = to hunt (animals), to gather (flowers, mushrooms, fruit); *Karl Marx encountered Rudolph when he was hunting reindeer*; cf. related terms listed at atsumeru

Karugaru 軽々 = lightly, easily, carelessly; from karui = light + garui = karui = light; cf. ani = easygoing, lightly, easily; cf. fuwari = softly, gently, lightly; cf. rakuraku = easily; cf. ukkari = carelessly, inadvertently

Karui 軽い = light (weight); *Karl Marx ruined his chances by selecting a light bat when he faced the pitcher*

Kasa 傘 = an umbrella; *people who live in Casablanca rarely need umbrellas*

Kasa 笠 = a bamboo hat or lamp shade; *Casanova sometimes wore a straw hat*; cf. related terms listed at boushi

Kasai 火災 = fire; *the cathedral is silent after the big fire*; cf. related terms listed at kaji

Kasaku 佳作 = a good piece of work, honorable mention; *that cashew sack is a good piece of work*

Kasanaru 重なる = to be piled up, to happen at the same time, to accumulate; *the film Casablanca caused some nasty rumors to pile up about Humphrey Bogart and Ingrid Bergman*; cf. tsumoru = to pile up (intransitive)

Kasaneru 重ねる = to pile up, to stack up (transitive); the transitive form of kasanaru = to be piled up; cf. related terms listed at tsumeru

Kasegu 稼ぐ = to earn (money); *I earned money to buy a cassette tape of goofy jokes*; cf. related terms listed at shutoku suru

Kasei 火勢 = the force of a fire; *the force of the fire declined and the camels were saved*

Kasen 河川 = a river or rivers; *Karl Marx sent his children down the river*; cf. related terms listed at kawa

Kashi 下肢 = a leg; from ka = below + shi = a limb; cf. related terms listed at ude

Kashi 歌詞 = lyrics; *that songwriter is cashing in on her lyrics*; cf. sakushi = writing song lyrics

Kashi 菓子 – see okashi

Kashi 華氏 = degrees Fahrenheit; *I'm cashing in by selling thermometers that read degrees Fahrenheit*; cf. sesshi = degrees Celsius

Kashikoi 賢い = intelligent, wise, clever; *cashing in your old coins is an intelligent move*; cf. josainai = clever, shrewd; cf. kenmei = wise

Kashikomaru かしこまる = to understand humbly, used in the term kashikoma-rimashita = I understand, or I will humbly obey; cf. related terms listed at wakaru

Kashira かしら = I wonder; *I wonder who is cashing the rabbi's checks*

Kasho か所 = a point or place; this can also be spelled 箇所; *at that place there was a cat show*; cf. related terms listed at basho

Kashou 歌唱 = song, singing; *Karl Marx showed us his songs*; cf. bookaru = vocals; cf. dokushou = solo singing; cf. other related terms listed at uta

Kashouhou 歌唱法 = the laws or rules of singing; from kashou = singing + houritsu = law

Kashu 歌手 = a singer; *the singer loves cashew nuts*

Kasoku suru 加速する = to accelerate; *the car hit a puddle, soaked me and then accelerated*; cf. hazumu = to become lively, to accelerate

Kasou 仮想 = imagination, supposition, virtual; *the California soldier has a vivid imagination*; cf. souzou = imagination; cf. katei = a supposition, hypothesis or conjecture; cf. yosoku = a prediction or supposition

Kasou suru 火葬する = to cremate; *the captain and his soldiers cremated their fallen comrades*

Kasou tsuuka 仮想通貨 = a virtual currency; from kasou = virtual + tsuuka = currency

Kassai 喝采 = applause, cheers, acclamation; *my speech on camel psychology was met with applause*; cf. hakushu = applause

Kasshoku 褐色 = dark brown; *after I returned from a tropical vacation, Karl was shocked when he saw my dark brown tan*; cf. related terms listed at cha'iro

Kasu 貸す = to lend or loan; *he casually lends money to strangers*

Kasuka na 微かな = faint or vague; *the carpenter said he had a super camera, but he was vague about the details*; cf. awai = thin, faint, pale, fleeting; cf. bakuzen = obscure, vague; cf. chuushouteki na = abstract or vague; cf. honoka = faint, dim, slight

Kasutera カステラ = castella, a kind of sponge cake; cf. related terms listed at ryouri

Kata 型 = form (e.g., dance), posture, type, mold; *it's important to show the right form when using a catapult*; cf. igata = a mold or cast; cf. kakkou = form, appearance, suitability; cf. keitai = form; cf. shingata = a new model or style; cf. shisei = a stance or posture; cf. taisei = a stance or posture

Kata 形 = shape, form, often used as a suffix, e.g., kamigata = a hair style; *a catapult has a basic shape*; cf. katachi = shape, form

Kata 方 = an honorable person; *that honorable person has cataracts*; cf. related terms listed at hito

Kata 方 = method, direction, e.g., tsukaikata = use method; *he mastered the method for extracting cataracts*; cf. related terms listed at houhou

Kata 潟 = a lagoon; *there was a catastrophe down at the lagoon*; cf. related terms listed at mizuumi

Kata 肩 = shoulder; *the recoil of the catapult hurt my shoulder*

Kata'ude (Kataude) 片腕 = one arm; from katahou = one side + ude = an arm; cf. related terms listed at ude

Katachi 形 = shape, form; *this is the shape of a catapult for firing cheese tubs*; cf. kata = shape, form

Katagami 型紙 = pattern paper (for dressmaking); from kata = form + gami = kami = paper; cf. related terms listed at kami

Katahaba 肩幅 = width of the shoulders; from kata = shoulder + haba = width

Katahiza 片膝 = one knee; from katahou = one side + hiza = knee

Katahou 片方 = one side, the other side; *the catalog I was holding showed prices on one side of the pages*; cf. ippou = one side, the other party, on the other hand, meanwhile; cf. katappashi = one side, one edge

Katai 硬い = hard, firm, stiff; this can also be spelled 固い or 堅い; *the car's tires got hard after I inflated them*; cf. kotai = solid

Kataki 敵 = enemy, rival; *that catapult is the*

key to defeating our enemies; cf. related terms listed at aite

Kataki wo utsu 敵を討つ = to take revenge on an enemy; from kataki = enemy + utsu = to attack (**Note:** this can also be pronounced "teki wo utsu," which has a similar meaning)

Katakori 肩こり = stiff shoulders, muscle tightness in the upper back; this can also be spelled 肩凝り; from kata = shoulder + koru = to become stiff; the cobra on the roof became stiff with the cold

Katakurushii 堅苦しい = overly formal, stiff, rigid; from katai = stiff + kurushii = hard, painful

Katamari 塊 = mass, lump; this can also be spelled 固まり; after the man with cataracts married a woman with good eyesight, she noticed a lump on his arm; cf. kobu = a bump, hump or lump

Katamaru 固まる = to harden, the intransitive form of katameru

Katame 片目 = one eye; from kata = one side; I can only see one side of the catalog; + me = eye

Katameru 固める = to harden, solidify, strengthen; the catapult was described in the meeru (email) as something that would harden our defenses; cf. related terms listed at tsuyomeru

Katamichi 片道 = one-way (trip); from katahou = one side + michi = way; cf. related terms listed at ryokou

Katamuku 傾く = to tilt or incline, to go down; the catamaran hit a patch of muck and inclined onto its side; cf. katayoru = to lean to one side, to be partial to; cf. keisha suru = to tilt or slant

Katana 刀 = a Japanese sword; I bought my Japanese sword from a catalogue store in Nagasaki; cf. mogitou = a fake sword or practice sword; cf. tantou = a dagger; cf. tsurugi = a sword

Katappashi 片っ端 = one side, one edge; the catapult threw the Padre onto the sheep, which fell over onto one side; cf. related terms listed at katahou

Katariau 語り合う = to talk together; from kataru = to talk + au = to come together; cf. related terms listed at hanasu

Kataru 語る = to talk; he talks about how cataracts ruined his life; cf. related terms listed at hanasu

Katawara 傍ら = close by, beside, in addition to, besides; the catalogue of watches ran to 300 pages, in addition to a supplement, and the salesman stood close by as he showed it; cf. related terms listed at ni kuwaete

Katayoru 偏る = to lean to one side, to be partial to; after the catastrophe at Yosemite, the rooster leaned to one side; cf. related terms listed at katamuku

Katayude 固ゆで = hard-boiled; from kata = hard; the catapult was used to harden our defense; + yuderu = to boil

Katazukeru 片づける = to tidy up, finish, settle, get rid of (this is spelled katadukeru in electronic dictionaries); due to a catastrophe at the zoo, my Keds (shoes) were ruined, and later I had to tidy up the mess; cf. related terms listed at osameru

Kate 糧 = food; for some people, caterpillars are a source of food; cf. related terms listed at tabemono

Katei 仮定 = supposition, hypothesis, conjecture; my hypothesis is that the cat's tail helps its balance; cf. kasou = imagination, supposition, virtual; cf. suisoku = an assumption or guess; cf. yosoku = a prediction or supposition

Katei 家庭 = home, household; we have a Catholic tailor in our household; cf. related terms listed at uchi

Katei 過程 = process; the dog caught his tail

in the door while in the <u>process</u> of leaving; cf. related terms listed at kairo

Katsu かつ = breaded, deep-fried cutlet; *the <u>cats</u> were eating the <u>breaded, deep-fried cutlet</u>*; cf. related terms listed at ryouri

Katsu 勝つ = to win; *the <u>cats won</u> the battle against the dogs*; cf. ateru = to hit, touch or win, jushou suru = to win an award or prize; kachinuku = to win through; cf. kachitoru = to win/take; cf. kakutoku suru = to win or obtain; cf. nyuushou suru = to win an award or prize

Katsudon カツ丼 = pork cutlet served on a bowl of rice; from katsu = breaded, deep-fried cutlet + donburi = a porcelain bowl; cf. related terms listed at ryouri

Katsudou 活動 = action, activity; *I eat ton <u>katsu</u> and <u>doughnuts</u> to give me energy for <u>action</u> and <u>activity</u>*; cf. related terms listed at doryoku

Katsudou suru 活動する = to be active; from katsudou = action, activity; cf. related terms listed at ikiru

Katsugu 担ぐ = to carry on one's shoulder; *I have some <u>cats</u> and a <u>goose</u>, and sometimes I <u>carry</u> them <u>on my shoulder</u>*; cf. related terms listed at hakobu

Katsuo カツオ = bonito (fish); *the <u>cats</u> that are <u>old</u> eat <u>bonito</u> every day*; cf. related terms listed at sakana

Katsuobushi かつお節 = bonito flakes; *the <u>cats</u> that are <u>old</u> and <u>bushy</u> eat <u>bonito flakes</u>*

Katsura かつら = a wig; *the man eating ton <u>katsu</u> and <u>ramen</u> is wearing a <u>wig</u>*

Katsuryoku 活力 = energy, vitality; from katsuyaku = activity + ryoku = power; cf. related terms listed at chikara

Katsute かつて = formerly, long ago; *<u>formerly</u> we had <u>cats</u> and <u>Teddy</u> bears in our home*; cf. related terms listed at mukashi

Katsuyaku 活躍 = energetic activity, great efforts, conspicuous service; *the <u>cats</u> belonging to the <u>yakuza</u> exhibited <u>energetic activity</u>*; cf. related terms listed at doryoku

Katsuyaku suru 活躍する = to be active, implying successful or energetic activity; from katsuyaku = activity, great efforts; cf. related terms listed at ikiru

Katsuyou suru 活用する = to make the most of; *the <u>cats</u> like <u>yogurt</u>, and they <u>utilize</u> it whenever possible and <u>make the most</u> of it*; cf. katsyaku suru = to be active; cf. ikasu = to make the most of, to keep alive

Katto suru カットする = to cut

Kattonaru かっとなる = to fly into a rage; *when he was <u>caught</u> on the <u>toll</u> road with a nasty <u>rooster</u>, he <u>flew into a rage</u>*; cf. related terms listed at okoru

Kattou 葛藤 = conflict, friction; *the <u>cat</u> scratched my <u>toe</u> when there was <u>conflict</u> between us*; cf. related terms listed at issen

Kau 買う = to buy; *I will <u>buy a cow</u>*; cf. kounyuu suru = to purchase

Kau 飼う = to keep a pet or raise live-stock, to buy or appreciate; *if you <u>kau</u> (buy) a pet, you have to <u>keep</u> it*

Kau ki 買う気 = an intention to buy; from kau = to buy + kibun = feeling

Kawa 川 = river; *the <u>river</u> supplies water for a <u>car wash</u>*; cf. dakuryuu = a muddy stream; cf. kasen = rivers; cf. keiryuu = a mountain stream; cf. suikei = a water or river system

Kawa 皮 = skin, peel; *the car <u>wash</u> only cleans the outer <u>skin</u> of my car*; cf. related terms listed at hada

Kawa 革 = leather, skin, hide; *I wear <u>leather</u> to the <u>car wash</u>*; cf. related terms listed at hada

Kawagutsu 革靴 = leather shoe; from kawa = leather + gutsu = kutsu = shoe; cf. related terms listed at kutsu

Kawaii 可愛い = cute; *some of the <u>c</u>ars in <u>Hawaii</u> are <u>cute</u>*

Kawaisou かわいそう = pitiful, pitiable; from kawaii = cute + sou = appears to be; cf. related terms listed at ki no doku

Kawakasu 乾かす = to dry, transitive; the transitive form of kawaku = to get dry

Kawaku 乾く = to get dry; *the <u>c</u>aptain visited the <u>w</u>ater <u>c</u>ooler when his throat <u>got</u> <u>dry</u>*

Kawaku 渇く = to be thirsty, usually used in the form 喉が渇く nodo ga kawaku, literally "the throat gets thirsty"; *the <u>c</u>aptain visited the <u>w</u>ater <u>c</u>ooler when he got <u>thirsty</u>*; cf. ueru = to starve, to be thirsty or hungry

Kawara 瓦 = a roof tile; *the <u>c</u>ar's <u>warranty</u> didn't cover damage from falling <u>roof</u> <u>tiles</u>*

Kawari 代わり = a substitute, a second helping of food, an exchange; from kawaru = to take the place of; cf. keisei = formation, repair (plastic surgery), replacement

Kawari ni 代わりに = in place of; *I will call the <u>w</u>arrior's <u>n</u>iece and ask her to service <u>in place of</u> his nephew*

Kawaru 代わる = to take the place of; *the <u>c</u>ar <u>w</u>ash was <u>r</u>uined when the son of the owner <u>took</u> <u>the</u> <u>place</u> <u>of</u> the manager*

Kawaru 変わる = to change, intransitive; *the <u>c</u>ar <u>w</u>ash's <u>roof</u> <u>changed</u> as the years passed*

Kawarugawaru 代わるがわる = alternately, by turns; from kawaru = to take the place of + gawaru = kawaru = to take the place of

Kawasei 革製 = made of leather; from kawa = leather; *I wear my <u>leather</u> shoes to work at the <u>c</u>ar <u>w</u>ash*; + seihin = finished product

Kawatta 変わった = different, unusual, strange, instead of; from kawaru = to change; cf. hibon = unusual, outstanding; cf. hinichijouteki = extraordinary, unusual; cf. ijou = abnormal, bizarre

Kawazoi 川沿い = along the river; from kawa = river + zou = sou = to run along

Kayou 歌謡 = a song or ballad; *the <u>c</u>arpenter <u>y</u>odeled a <u>ballad</u>*; cf. related terms listed at uta

Kayou 通う = to commute; *<u>coyotes</u> <u>commute</u> between hunting grounds*

Kayoukyoku 歌謡曲 = a popular song; from kayou = a song + kyoku = a musical composition; cf. related terms listed at uta

Kayui かゆい = itchy; *in a <u>kayak</u> with <u>y</u>outhful <u>i</u>nsects, I got <u>itchy</u>*

Kazamuki 風向き = wind direction; from kaza = kaze = wind; + muki = direction, from muku = to face toward; cf. similar terms listed at houkou

Kazan 火山 = volcano; from kaji = fire + zan = mountain, e.g. tozan = mountain climbing

Kazaritsuke 飾り付け = decoration, arrangement; from kazaru = to decorate + tsukeru = to attach; cf. soushoku = a decoration

Kazaru 飾る = to decorate; *in <u>Kazakh</u>stan, I heard a <u>rumor</u> that you <u>decorate</u> houses*

Kaze 風 = wind or breeze; *they <u>call</u> him <u>zesty</u> because he rides the <u>wind</u>*; cf. aori = a gust of wind; cf. kyoufuu = a strong wind; cf. shunpu = a spring breeze

Kaze 風邪 = upper respiratory infection; *if you stand in the <u>kaze</u> (wind), you might get an <u>upper</u> <u>respiratory</u> <u>infection</u>*

Kazoeru 数える = to count; *he <u>counted</u> the number of <u>kazoku</u> [family] members that were <u>erudite</u>*

Kazoku 家族 = a family; *the <u>c</u>arnival <u>zone</u> in <u>Ku</u>wait is attractive to <u>families</u>*; cf. ichizoku = family, household, relatives; cf. ikka = a family, a house; cf. kazokutachi =

family members; cf. ryouke = both families; cf. shinseki = a relative; cf. shotai = household, family; cf. uchiwa = family, inner circle

Kazokutachi 家族達 = family members; from kazoku = family + tachi = plural; cf. related terms listed at kazoku

Kazokuteki 家族的 = related to a family, family-like; from kazoku = a family + teki = related to

Kazu 数 = number; *the number of kazoos determines the number of people who can play in the band;* cf. related terms listed at bangou

Kazukazu 数々 = many, various; from kazu = number; cf. iroiro = various, manifold; cf. ironna = various, manifold; cf. moromoro = various things; cf. samazama = various; cf. sho = various, used as a prefix; cf. other related terms listed at takusan

Ke 毛 = hair, fur, wool; *Ken wore a wool coat;* cf. hakuhatsu = grey or white hair; cf. hea = hair; cf. kami = hair; cf. kaminoke = hair; cf. kegawa = fur; cf. shiraga = white or grey hair; cf. youmou = wool

Kebukai 毛深い = bushy or hairy; from ke = hair + bukai = fukai = deep

Kebyou 仮病 = a feigned illness; *Kennedy said that he had B.O. (bacterial overgrowth), but it was a feigned illness;* cf. related terms listed at byouki

Kechi けち = stingy, miserly; *he's stingy and only feeds his family ketchup and cheese*

Kedakai 気高い = noble; from ke = ki = spirit + dakai = takai = high; cf. kouki na (or no) = aristocratic, noble; cf. koushou na = noble, high-brow, refined

Kedo けど = but, however; *he left a keg by the door, but it was gone when I got there;* cf. related terms listed at demo

Kega 怪我 = injury; *a keg of apple juice fell on me and caused an injury;* cf. fushou = an injury or wound; cf. kizu = a scar, injury or wound; cf. kizuato = a scar

Keganin 怪我人 = injured person; from kega = injury + nin = person

Kegawa 毛皮 = fur; *the Kennedys started a gas war, and the fur began to fly;* cf. related terms listed at ke

Kehai 気配 = indication, sign, presence; *Kennedy hired a man to establish a presence on the property, as a sign that it was occupied;* cf. sonzai = an existence or presence; cf. hyouji = an indication, expression, or showing; cf. other related terms listed at zenchou

Keiba 競馬 = horse racing; *I ate some cake in a bar while I watched horse racing*

Keibetsu 軽蔑 = scorn, disdain; *when the caterer bets on the races, she shows disdain for horses that seem slow*

Keibetsu suru 軽蔑する = to scorn or disdain; from keibetsu = scorn, disdain; cf. related terms listed at kirai desu

Keibi 警備 = guard or watch; *canine beasts (i.e., dogs) assist the guard;* cf. ban = a watch (guard) or turn; cf. keikai = vigilance, watch; cf. mihari = guard, lookout, watch-keeping

Keidai 境内 = the grounds of a temple; *the cave where he died is on the grounds of a temple*

Keido 経度 = longitude; *people at that longitude tend to eat cakes and doughnuts at about the same time;* cf. related terms listed at ido

Keiei 経営 = management; *Kay ate a lot of fast food while trying to get into management;* cf. related terms listed at kanri

Keieisha 経営者 = a business manager or owner; from keiei = management + sha = person; cf. kantoku = a director, superintendent, or manager (e.g., of a sports team)

Keigen suru 軽減する = to reduce or alleviate; *the cakes that Genghis ate reduced his stress*; cf. related terms listed at genshou suru

Keigo 敬語 = honorific language; *on Cape Cod, the golfers use honorific language*; cf. related terms listed at gengo

Keihatsu 啓発 = education, edification, inspiration, public awareness; *the cavemen wore hats after they got access to public awareness and education about skin cancer*; cf. related terms listed at kyouiku

Keihou 刑法 = criminal law; from kei = punish, e.g., shikei = death penalty; + houritsu = law; cf. related terms listed at kisoku

Keihou 警報 = warning, alarm; *he received a warning to avoid the cage of hornets*; cf. related terms listed at keikoku

Keii 敬意 = respect; *I feel respect for the caged eagle*; cf. related terms listed at sonkei

Keii wo hyousu 敬意を表す = to pay respect; from keii = respect + hyousu = to express or show; cf. related terms listed at sonkei suru

Keii wo shimesu 敬意を示す = to show respect; from keii = respect + shimesu = to show; cf. related terms listed at sonkei suru

Keiji 刑事 = detective; *that detective is cagey*; cf. sousakan = a police investigator; cf. tantei = a detective

Keiji 慶事 = an auspicious (prosperous or fortunate) event; *the fortune teller was cagey when we asked her if we could expect any auspicious events*

Keiji 掲示 = a written notice or announcement; *the written notice advised us not to eat cake in the Jeep*; cf. related terms listed at sengen

Keijiban 掲示板 = a bulletin board or notice board; from keiji = a written notice + ban = a board, e.g., kanban = a signboard; cf. related terms listed at kokuban

Keika 経過 = passage, expiration, progress, transition; *cakes and cabbages are affected by the passage of time*

Keikai 警戒 = vigilance, watch; *when the cane came flying at the Kaiser, he showed vigilance and ducked*; cf. related terms listed at keibi

Keikai suru 警戒する = to be cautious or watch out; from keikai = vigilance; cf. imashimeru = to admonish, warn, prohibit, be cautious

Keikaku 計画 = a plan, project or schedule; *we have a plan to grow cane and cactus plants*; cf. related terms listed at kikaku

Keikakusho 計画書 = a written plan; from keikaku = a plan, project or schedule; + sho = a document

Keikan 警官 = a police officer; *I always give cake and candy to that policeman*; cf. junsa = patrolman; cf. keisatsukan = a police officer; cf. omawarisan = a policeman

Keiken 経験 = experience; *this dog has experience with cages and kennels*; cf. taiken = experience

Keiken suru 経験する = to experience; from keiken = experience; cf. aru = to exist (used for inanimate objects), to happen, to experience; cf. mimawareru = to experience or undergo; cf. taiken suru = to experience

Keiki 景気 = a business condition, a state or condition; *cake and quiche prices have fallen due to the business condition*; cf. related terms listed at keisei

Keiki 契機 = an opportunity or chance; *I had an opportunity to lock the cage with a key*; cf. related terms listed at kikai

Keiko 稽古 = rehearsal, practice, training; *my dog is in training for the canine corps*; cf. shitami = a preliminary inspection, preview, rehearsal; cf. other related terms listed at kunren

Keikoku 渓谷 = valley, canyon; *the caterer drank some Coke in the canyon*; cf. related terms listed at tani

Keikoku 警告 = warning, caution; *diabetic patients are given a warning not to consume cake or Coke*; cf. chuui = caution, warning; cf. chuuihou = a weather warning; cf. keihou = warning, alarm; cf. youjin = caution

Keikou 傾向 = tendency, inclination, trend; *when cake is kept cold, it has a tendency to last longer*; cf. related terms listed at gachi

Keikou 蛍光 = fluorescence; *the cave was cold, but our black lights revealed fluorescence in its walls*

Keikoutou 蛍光灯 = a fluorescent light; from keikou = fluorescence + dentou = electric light; cf. dentou = electric light

Keimusho 刑務所 = prison; *the cake that the Moonie showed me was going to be smuggled into a prison*; cf. related terms listed at kangoku

Keiniku 鶏肉 = chicken meat; from kei = chicken; *that chicken was raised in a cage*; + niku = meat

Keiri 経理 = management, accounting; *Kay was eating a lot of fast food while she was trying to get into management*; cf. related terms listed at kanri

Keirou 敬老 = respect for the aged; *our country has respect for the aged and supplies them with canes and robots*

Keiryou 計量 = measurement, computation; *let's do a measurement of the cage where Pope Leo was held*; cf. sunpou = measurement

Keiryou suru 計量する = to measure or compute; from keiryou = measurement, computation; cf. related terms listed at hakaru

Keiryuu 渓流 = a mountain stream; from keikoku = valley + ryuu = to flow, e.g., denryuu = electric current; cf. related terms listed at kawa

Keisai suru 掲載する = to publish or print; *I published a paper on canine psychology*; cf. arawasu = to write or publish; cf. hakkou suru = to issue (a publication) or publish; cf. kankou suru = to publish; cf. noseru = to publish, to put on top of; cf. shuppan suru = to publish; cf. suru = to print

Keisan 計算 = calculation; *I did a calculation of the number of caissons that were rolling along*; cf. anzan = mental calculation; cf. kanjou = bill, check, calculation; cf. omowaku = speculation, calculation

Keisatsu 警察 = police; *the guy wearing a cape while reading a satisfying Superman novel works for the police*

Keisatsukan 警察官 = a police officer; from keisatsu = police + kan = a government official, e.g., keikan = a police officer; cf. related terms listed at keikan

Keisatsuken 警察犬 = a police dog; from keisatsu = police + ken = dog; *Ken bought a dog for Barbie*; cf. related terms listed at inu

Keisatsusho 警察署 = a police station; from keisatsu = police + sho = a government office

Keisei 形勢 = situation, condition; *the cake that we bought at Safeway was in good condition*; cf. arikata = the way things are; cf. baai = case or situation; cf. byoujou = a condition related to health; cf. choushi = condition, way, manner, style; cf. furyou = delinquent, poor condition; cf. fuu = appearance, condition, style; cf. genjou = present condition; cf. guai = a condition; cf. ichi = situation; cf. jitai = situation; cf. joutai = condition, circumstances; cf. keiki = a business condition, a state or condition; cf. shoujou = symptoms, condition of a patient; cf. sugata = figure, shape, condition; cf. taichou = a body condition; cf. yousu = condition, state, appearance

Keisei 形成 = formation, repair (plastic surgery), replacement; *the cagey sailors asked about the formation of teams on the ship and how replacements would be selected in case of illness*; cf. kawari = a substitute, a second helping of food, an exchange

Keisei suru 形成する = to form or mold; from keisei = formation

Keisha suru 傾斜する = to tilt or slant; *the cake they served the Shah was tilting to one side*; cf. katamuku = to tilt or incline, to go down

Keisotsu na 軽率な = thoughtless, careless, hasty; *the cape that sotted Superman left at the bar was lost due to his careless behavior*; cf. mubou = reckless, thoughtless; cf. muteppou = reckless; cf. awatadashii = hasty

Keitai 形態 = a form, shape or figure; *the caged tiger had a beautiful form*; cf. related terms listed at kata

Keitai suru 携帯する = to carry; *I bought a cane in Thailand and carried it home*; cf. related terms listed at hakobu

Keitaidenwa 携帯電話 = a cellular phone; from keitai suru = to carry + denwa = phone

Keitou 系統 = system; *the cages and torture were part of a system designed to intimidate the citizens*; cf. kikan = agency or system; cf. seido = system

Keitouteki 系統的 = systematic; from keitou = system + teki = related to

Keiyaku 契約 = a contract; *I signed a contract to build a cage for the yak*

Keiyu 経由 = via, by way of; *to get to my cave in the Yukon, I travel via a forest path*

Keizai 経済 = economy; *the caterer from Zaire (former name of the Congo) understands the economy*

Keizoku 継続 = a continuation; *using cages to house zombies from Kuwait is a continuation of the policies of the previous administration*; cf. tsuzuki = a continuation

Keizokuteki 継続的 = continuous; from keizoku = a continuation + teki = related to

Kekka 結果 = a result or effect; *I put the kettle over a candle, and the result was lukewarm tea*; cf. eikyou = effect, influence; cf. kouka = an effect; cf. kouryoku = an effect

Kekkai 血塊 = a clot of blood; *when Kennedy looked into the kayak, he noticed clots of blood*

Kekkaku 結核 = tuberculosis; *I got tuberculosis, and the kekka (result) was a cure*; cf. related terms listed at byouki

Kekkan 欠陥 = a flaw or defect; *since there was a defect in my stove, I heated the kettle with a candle*; cf. related terms listed at kizu

Kekkan 血管 = blood vessel; from ketsueki = blood + kan = tube; cf. similar terms listed at doumyaku

Kekkon 結婚 = marriage; *Ken asked the conductor to join him in marriage*; cf. kon'in = marriage; cf. yomeiri = marriage

Kekkon iwai 結婚祝い = a marriage celebration, or a wedding gift; from kekkon = marriage + iwai = a celebration or congratulation

Kekkon seikatsu 結婚生活 = married life; from kekkon = marriage + seikatsu = life; cf. related terms listed at inochi

Kekkon suru 結婚する = to get married; from kekkon = marriage; cf. totsugu = to get married (used for women)

Kekkou 結構 = fine, good, rather; *Kennedy's coalition was fine and did rather good work*; cf. related terms listed at ii

Kekkyoku 結局 = after all; *the Kennedys joined the Kyoto Kool-Aid club after all*; cf. douse = anyhow, after all; cf. yappari = as expected, after all, again

Kemono 獣 = an animal; *in Kenya, we saw monotonous herds of wildebeest animals*; cf. related terms listed at doubutsu

Kemuri 煙 = smoke; *I used Kelly-Moore paint to refresh my paint after I had some smoke damage*

Kemutai 煙たい = smoky; *Kelly-Moore says that, in time, your paint will get smoky if you expose it to smoke*

Ken 件 = a matter, case or item; a counter for houses; *Ken and Barbie studied the matter*; cf. jijou = reason, situation, facts, circumstances; cf. jikou = matter, item, facts; cf. monogoto = a matter or thing; cf. youken = a business matter

Ken 券 = a ticket; *Ken bought a ticket for Barbie*; cf. kippu = a ticket

Ken 県 = a prefecture; *Kennedy visited that prefecture*; cf. fu = urban prefecture; cf. ku = a ward or district; cf. todoufuken = the 47 administrative divisions of Japan;

Ken 圏 = a circle, radius or range; *Ken and Barbie hiked in a circle*

Ken 犬 = a dog, used as a word component; *Ken and Barbie have a dog*

Kenbaiki 券売機 = ticket machine; from ken = ticket + hanbai = sales + kikai = machine; cf. related terms listed at kikai

Kenbikyou 顕微鏡 = a microscope; *Ken and Barbara studied beetles in Kyouto using a microscope*; cf. related terms listed at bouenkyou

Kenbutsu 見物 = sightseeing, watching (e.g., sports); *Kennedy's boots sit outside his door while he is watching sports and sightseeing on TV*; cf. kankou = sightseeing

Kenchiku 建築 = architecture, construction; *Ken drinks cheap Kool-Aid while he works on architecture*; cf. konryuu = the act of building (a temple or monument, etc.); cf. related terms listed at kensetsu

Kenchikubutsu 建築物 = buildings; from kenchiku = architecture + butsu = thing; cf. related terms listed at tatemono

Kenchikuka 建築家 = an architect; from kenchiku = architecture + ka = a person

Kencho na 顕著な = conspicuous, remarkable; *Kennedy chose a conspicuous logo for his campaign*; cf. related terms listed at ichijirushii

Kendou 剣道 = Japanese fencing with bamboo swords; *Ken dozed while Barbie practiced Japanese fencing*; cf. budou = martial arts

Ke'nen (Kenen) 懸念 = apprehension, fear; *Ken's energy derives from fear of failure*; cf. related terms listed at osore

Ken'en (Kenen) 犬猿 = dogs and monkeys, used as a metaphor for a bad relationship; from ken = dog; *Ken and Barbie have a dog*; + en = monkey, e.g., ruijien = ape

Ken'etsu (Kenetsu) 検閲 = censorship, inspection; *Ken's etchings of Superman were banned due to censorship*; cf. related terms listed at tenken

Kengai 圏外 = outside the range or orbit; from ken = a radius or circle + gaibu = exterior

Kengaku 見学 = inspection, field trip; *Ken drank a gallon of Kool-Aid after the inspection*; cf. kanshi = monitoring, watching, inspection; cf. tenken = inspection

Ken'i (Keni) 権威 = authority; *some Kennedys in the East, e.g., Boston, had a lot of authority*; cf. kenryoku = authority

Kenjitsu 堅実 = steady, reliable, solid; *Ken got the jittery superstar a reliable guitar*; cf. related terms listed at kakujitsu

Kenjuu 拳銃 = a handgun; *Ken was jubilant when Barbie got him a handgun*; cf. related terms listed at teppou

Kenka けんか = a quarrel or fight; *Ken called Barbie a name, which caused a quarrel*; cf. related terms listed at issen

Kenka suru けんかする = to quarrel or fight; from kenka = a quarrel or fight; cf. related terms listed at arasou

Kenkai 見解 = a viewpoint or opinion; *Senator Kennedy and the Kaiser had different viewpoints*; cf. mikata = a viewpoint; cf. mitoushi = outlook, perspective; cf. shiten = viewpoint; cf. other related terms listed at iken

Kenkei 県警 = prefectural police; from ken = prefecture + keisatsu = police

Kenkou 健康 = health; *Ken's colds got better when his health improved*; cf. sokusai = good health

Kenkyo 謙虚 = modesty; *when the Kennedys visited Kyoto, they noticed the modesty of the residents*; cf. enryo = hesitation, reserve, restraint, modesty; cf. kenkyosa = modesty; cf. kenson = modesty;

Kenkyosa 謙虚さ = modesty; from kenkyo = modesty + sa, a suffix that converts a word to a noun (although kenkyo is already a noun); cf. related terms listed at kenkyo

Kenkyuu 研究 = research, study; *Ken went to Cuba for a study of socialism*; cf. related terms listed at benkyou

Kenkyuujo 研究所 = research institute, laboratory; from kenkyuu = research + jo = place

Kenmei 賢明 = wise; *Ken's maid is wise*; cf. related terms listed at kashikoi

Kenmei 懸命 = eagerness, earnestness; *Kennedy's maid displayed earnestness in her work*

Kenmei ni 懸命に = eagerly, earnestly; from kenmei = eagerness, earnestness; cf. shikiri ni = often, frequently, eagerly

Kenmon 検問 = inspection, examination; *Ken moaned about the number of inspections that he had to conduct*; cf. related terms listed at kensa and tenken

Kenmonjo 検問所 = a checkpoint; from kenmon = inspection + jo = place

Ken'o (Keno) 嫌悪 = hatred, disgust; *Ken owes Barbie an apology for the hatred he expressed*; cf. related terms listed at akui

Kenpou 憲法 = a constitution; *in Kentucky the police enforce the constitution*

Kenri 権利 = right, privilege; *the Kennedys read the Constitution, and they know their rights*; cf. sujiai = right or reason; cf. tokken = privilege

Kenryoku 権力 = authority; from keni = authority + ryoku = force; cf. keni = authority

Kensa 検査 = investigation, examination; *Ken saw to it that Barbie received a careful examination*; cf. chousa = an investigation, survey, analysis; cf. kenmon = an inspection or examination; cf. kentou = an examination, investigation, consideration; cf. kyuumon = an enquiry; cf. sensaku = an inquiry into; cf. shinsa = a hearing or examination; cf. shinsatsu = a medical examination; cf. shirabe = a tune, tone, writing style, investigation, inspection, examination; cf. sousa = a police investigation; cf. sousaku = an investigation or search; cf. tansa = a probe, inquiry or investigation; cf. tansaku = an exploration or investigation

Kensaku 検索 = looking up or retrieval (e.g., words or data); *when Ken needs a sack of cookies, he looks up a retailer on the internet*

Kensaku suru 検索する = to look up (e.g., a word in a dictionary), to retrieve (e.g., data), to search for; cf. kensaku = looking up or retrieval (e.g., words or data); cf. related terms listed at sousaku suru

Kensashitsu 検査室 = a lab where patients' tests are done; from kensa = investigation or examination + shitsu = room; cf. related terms listed at -shitsu

Kensetsu 建設 = construction; *Ken set up a super company for construction work*; cf. kenchiku = architecture, construction; cf. kouji = construction work; cf. kumitate = construction, assembly; cf. tsukuri = a structure or construction

Kensetsuhan 建設班 = a construction group; from kensetsu = construction + han = a group; cf. related terms listed at dantai

Kenshi 剣士 = a swordsman or swordswoman; *Ken carried a shield, since he was a swordsman*; cf. kishi = a knight

Kenshou 懸賞 = an award or prize; *Ken showed us his prize*; cf. related terms listed at houbi

Kenshu 犬種 = a dog breed; from ken = dog; *Ken bought a dog for Barbie*; + shurui = variety, type; cf. related terms listed at shurui

Kenshuu 研修 = training; *Ken's shoes showed the effect of hard training*; cf. related terms listed at kunren

Kenson 謙遜 = modesty; also, kenson na = humble, modest; *the Kennedy sons were known for modesty*; cf. related terms listed at kenkyo

Kentou 見当 = aim, direction, estimate, guess; *he made a guess that Ken's toes were long, like his fingers*

Kentou 検討 = examination, investigation, consideration; *Barbie did an examination of Ken's toes*; cf. related terms listed at hairyo and at kensa

Kentou suru 検討する = to analyze, scrutinize; from kentou = examination, investigation, consideration

Kentou wo tsukeru 見当をつける = to make a guess; from kentou = a guess

Ken'yaku (Kenyaku) 倹約 = thrift; *since Ken owed money to the yakuza, he was forced into thrift*; cf. setsuyaku = economy, thrift

Ken'yaku suru (Kenyaku suru) 倹約する = to save or economize; from ken'yaku = thrift; cf. setsuyaku suru = to economize

Ken'you (Kenyou) 兼用 = multi-use; *Ken designed a yoke that was multi-use, so that Barbie could use it with both oxen and horses*; cf. takinou = multifunction

Keppaku 潔白 = innocence; *a woman was accused of bringing a keg to a party in Kuwait but her innocence was established in court*; cf. related terms listed at mujitsu

Keppeki 潔癖 = fastidious, particular, loving cleanliness; *I bought a kettle in Peking from a seller who was very fastidious*

Keppekishou 潔癖症 = obsession with cleanliness or fastidiousness; from keppeki = fastidious, loving cleanliness; + shoujou = symptom

Keredo けれど = although, but, nevertheless; *Ken wrestled the dolphin in the morning, but he lost the bout*; cf. related terms listed at demo

Keredomo けれども – see keredo

Keru 蹴る = to kick; *my Keds (a brand of shoes) were ruined when I kicked a tarball*; cf. ketobasu = to kick away, to refuse curtly

Kesa 今朝 = this morning; *this morning I had ketchup on my salad*; cf. related terms listed at asa

Kesaki 毛先 = the tips of the hair; from ke = hair + saki = tip

Keshigomu 消しゴム = an eraser; from kesu = to erase + gomu = gum or rubber

Keshiki 景色 = scenery or a view; *Kennedy invited the sheepish king to admire the view*; cf. related terms listed at nagame

Keshitomeru 消し止める = to put out or extinguish; from kesu = to extinguish + tomeru = to stop; cf. synonyms listed at kesu

Keshou 化粧 = cosmetics, makeup; *Ken showed Barbie some cosmetics*; cf. related terms listed at keshouhin

Keshouhin 化粧品 = cosmetics, toilet articles; from keshou = cosmetics + hin = product, e.g., hinshitsu = product quality; cf. keshou = cosmetics, make-up; shiro nuri = white makeup

Kessaku 傑作 = a masterpiece; *Kennedy ate a sack of cookies while admiring his masterpiece*; cf. related terms listed at sakuhin

Kessei 結成 = organization, formation; *Ken saved animals through his work on the formation and organization of the Humane Society*; cf. kyoukai = an association or organization; cf. soshiki = an organization

Kesseki 欠席 = absence; *Kennedy's seki (cough) was the reason for his absence*; cf. related terms listed at fuzai

Kesshin 決心 = a decision or determination; *I made a decision to buy a kettle for the Shinto priest*; cf. related terms listed at handan

Kesshite 決して = never, in no way; *to bring Kentucky sheep to Texas was never going to work*; cf. related terms listed at monoka

Kesshou 結晶 = crystal; *Kennedy showed me his crystal*; cf. related terms listed at suishou

Kesshousen 決勝戦 = final game in a tournament; *Kennedy showed some senators the tournament's final game from his luxury box*

Kesu 消す = to extinguish or turn off, to erase; *I extinguished the fire under the kettle of soup*; cf. keshitomeru = to put out or extinguish; cf. massatsu suru = to obliterate

Keta 桁 = a beam, girder, digit, unit or numerical column (accounting); *Kennedy's tavern had exposed beams in its ceiling, and its cost was in the five-digit range*; cf. related terms listed at ran

Ketobasu 蹴とばす = to kick away, to refuse curtly; from keru = to kick + tobasu = to fly or speed; cf. keru = to kick

Ketsu 血 = blood, used as a word component; *if you put ketchup in your soup, it looks like blood*; cf. related terms listed at ketsueki

Ketsuatsu 血圧 = blood pressure; from ketsu = blood + atsuryoku = pressure; cf. related terms listed at atsuryoku

Ketsuatsukei 血圧計 = blood pressure monitor; from ketsuatsu = blood pressure + kei = to measure, e.g., tokei = clock

Ketsueki 血液 = blood; from ketsu = blood + ekitai = liquid; cf. chi = blood

Ketsueki gata 血液型 = blood type; from ketsueki = blood + gata = kata = form

Ketsugou suru 結合する = to unite; *since we all put ketchup in our soup and keep goats, let's unite*; cf. danketsu suru = to unite or consolidate

Ketsui 決意 = a decision or determination; *when I saw the ketchup in the soup it was easy to make a decision not to eat there*; cf. related terms listed at handan

Ketsui suru 決意する = to decide; *seeing ketchup in the soup made it easy for me to decide not to eat at that restaurant*; cf. related terms listed at kimeru

Ketsujo 欠如 = a deficiency or lack; *we added ketchup to our soup as a joke, but we did face a lack of food choices that day*; cf. fusoku = lack or shortage

Ketsumaku 結膜 = the conjunctiva (white of the eye); *while putting ketchup into my soup in a mall in Kuwait, I spilled some onto my conjunctiva*

Ketsumakuen 結膜炎 = conjunctivitis; from ketsumaku = the conjunctiva + en = inflammation, e.g., haien = pneumonia; cf. related terms listed at byouki

Kettei 決定 = a decision; *I need to make a decision about whether to buy a kettle or a table*; cf. related terms listed at handan

Kettei suru 決定する = to decide; from kettei = a decision; cf. related terms listed at kimeru

Ketten 欠点 = a fault, shortcoming or failure; *Kennedy's tennis game had certain faults*; cf. ayamachi = fault, mistake; cf. ayamari = a mistake; cf. chimeishou = a fatal mistake or injury; cf. dansou = fault, discrepancy; cf. machigai = a mistake; cf. other related terms listed at shippai

Kewashii 険しい = steep, stern; *Ken is washing in a stream next to a steep trail*

Kezureru 削れる = to be shaved or planed; *before putting on your Keds to go to the zoo and see the red rooster, you must be shaved*; cf. related terms listed at yabureru

Kezuru 削る = to shave, sharpen or cut down; the intransitive form of kezuru = to shave, sharpen or cut down; cf. related terms listed at kiru

Ki 忌 = a death anniversary, used as a suffix; *I wore a kimono to the death anniversary ceremony*; cf. related terms listed at shuunen

Ki 木 = a tree, wood; *I planted a tree in Kiev*; cf. jumoku = trees; cf. kigi = trees; cf. koboku = a dead tree; cf. matsu = a pine tree; cf. sakuragi = cherry trees; cf. shin'youju = a conifer or needle-leaved tree; cf. taiboku = a big tree; cf. ueki = a garden plant or tree; cf. yanagi = willow; cf. other related terms listed at shokubutsu

Ki 気 = spirit, soul, feeling, intention, air, inclination; *that quiche lifted my spirits*; cf. related terms listed at kankaku and at seishin

Ki ga kujikeru 気が挫ける = to get dispirited; from ki = spirit + kujikeru = to be discouraged; cf. related terms listed at me'iru

Ki ga kuruu 気が狂う = to go crazy; from ki = spirit + kuruu = to go mad

Ki ga suru 気がする = I have a feeling; from ki = feeling + suru = to do

Ki ga tsuku 気が付く = to notice or become aware of, to regain consciousness; from ki = spirit + tsuku = to attach; cf. related terms listed at satoru

Ki ni iru 気に入る = to like or favor; from ki = spirit + iru = to go in; cf. etsu ni iru = to be gratified or happy; cf. related terms listed at konomu

Ki ni naru 気になる = to worry, care about, to be bothered by; from ki = spirit + naru = to become; cf. related terms listed at kamau and at shinpai suru

Ki ni suru 気にする = to mind, care about or worry; from ki = spirit; cf. related terms listed at kamau and at shinpai suru

Ki ni suru koto nai 気にすることない = nothing to worry about; from ki ni suru = to mind or care about + nai = negation

Ki no doku 気の毒 = pitiful, unfortunate; *the keynote address was read from a document, and it was pitiful*; cf. hisan na = woeful, pitiable, miserable; cf. kawaisou = pitiful, pitiable; cf. mijime na = miserable; cf. nasakenai = miserable, pitiable, shameful

Ki wo otosu 気を落とす = to be discouraged; from ki = spirit + otosu = to decrease; cf. related terms listed at meiru

Ki wo torinaosu 気を取り直す = to completely rethink, to pull one's self together; from ki = spirit + toru = to take + naosu = to correct or repair

Ki wo tsukeru 気を付ける = to be careful, to pay attention; from ki = feeling + tsukeru = to follow or pursue; cf. kizukau = to care for, worry, pay attention

Kiatsu 気圧 = atmospheric pressure; from ki = air or spirit + atsu = pressure; cf. related terms listed at atsuryoku

Kiba 牙 = fang, tusk; *the king of Baghdad wore a necklace of tusks*

Kiban 基盤 = foundation, basis; *I have a key to the bank, so we can go inside and examine its foundation*; cf. kiso = a foundation, base or basis; cf. konkyo = basis or foundation (of a belief, etc.); cf. ne = root, basis

Kibin na 機敏な = nimble, quick; *after eating quiche with beans, he becomes nimble and quick*; cf. related terms listed at hayai

Kibishii 厳しい = stern, rigid, strict, harsh; *if you kibbitz (chat) with Shiites, you will find that they are strict*; cf. genkaku = stern, strict; cf. kakoku = severity, rigor, cruelty (nouns), or harsh (a na adjective)

Kibishisa 厳しさ = strictness, severity; from kibishii = stern or strict + sa = a suffix that makes a noun from an adjective; cf. kakoku = severity, rigor, cruelty (nouns), or harsh (a na adjective)

Kibo 規模 = scale or scope; *the scale of the king's bowling alley was impressive*; cf. daikibo = large-scale; oogakari = large scale

Kibou 希望 = hope or wish; *she has hope of finding the kindergarten's bowling ball*; cf. related terms listed at shomou

Kibou suru 希望する = to hope or wish; from kibou = hope or wish; cf. related terms listed at nozomu

Kibun 気分 = a feeling or mood; *I have a feeling that I gave the key to Daniel Boone*; cf. related terms listed at kankaku

Kicchiri きっちり = precisely, tightly, without fail; *I keep Cheerios in this box and close it tightly without fail*; cf. related terms listed at chanto

Kichi 吉 = good fortune; *we keep that kitschy souvenir for good fortune*; cf. related terms listed at kouun

Kichi 基地 = base; *our base has a kitschy vibe*; cf. fumoto = foot of a mountain, base; cf. honkyochi = headquarters, base; cf. kiso = a foundation, base or basis; cf. kyoten = location, base; cf. moto = base, origin, source

Kichinto きちんと = properly, tidily; *if you kiss her chin and toe when you meet her, you will be behaving properly*; cf. related terms listed at chanto

Kichou 機長 = a pilot; *the king chose a pilot for his plane*; cf. soujuushi = a pilot; cf. other related terms listed at shunou

Kichou 貴重 = valuable, precious; *the kitchen in Margaret Cho's house has a counter made from precious stones*; cf. oshii = unfortunate or regrettable, almost but not quite, precious or valuable; cf. shinsei = holy or sacred; cf. toutoi = sacred, important, valuable

Kichoumen 几帳面 = scrupulous, meticulous; *the king chose his men with meticulous care*; cf. related terms listed at menmitsu

Kidoru 気取る = to put on airs; from ki = spirit or air + doru = toru = to take

Kidou 軌道 = an orbit; *we ate quiche and doughnuts while in orbit*

Kieru 消える = to disappear or extinguish (intransitive); *in Kiev, my dinner was ruined when the lights suddenly extinguished themselves*; cf. related terms listed at bossuru

Kieuseru 消え失せる = to disappear or die; from kieru = to extinguish or disappear + useru = to disappear; cf. related terms listed at bossuru and at shinu

Kifu 寄付 = contribution, donation; *I can keep food in the house, thanks to donations from my friends*; cf. related terms listed at okurimono

Kifu suru 寄付する = to donate; from kifu = contribution, donation; cf. related terms listed at ataeru

Kifukin 寄付金 = a donation; from kifu = a donation + kingaku = a sum of money; cf. related terms listed at okurimono

Kigaeru 着替える = to change one's clothes; from kiru = to wear clothes = gaeru = kaeru = to replace or exchange

Kigane 気兼ね = hesitation, reserve; *I have a key to a garden in the Netherlands, but I feel hesitation to use it*; cf. enryo = hesitation, reserve, restraint, modesty

Kigane wo suru 気兼ねをする = to hesitate; from kigane = hesitation; cf. enryo suru = to hesitate or hold back; cf. mayou = to lose direction, to get lost, to hesitate; cf. shiburu = to hesitate or be reluctant

Kigaru ni 気軽に = freely, readily, cheerfully; from ki = spirit + garui = karui = light + -ni = a suffix that forms an adverb

Kigarui 気軽い = cheerful, lighthearted; from ki = spirit + garui = karui = light; cf. related terms listed at shiawase na

Kigen 期限 = deadline; *the key that Genghis got from the landlord had to be returned by a deadline*; cf. shimekiri = closing, deadline

Kigen 機嫌 = mood, feeling; *the quiche that Genghis ate put him in a good mood*; cf. related terms listed at kankaku

Kigen 紀元 = era, A.D.; *King Genghis Khan ruled during the era called A.D.*; cf. related terms listed at jidai

Kigen 起源 = origin; *the quiche that Genghis ate had its origin in Mongolia*; cf. dengen = electric power source; cf. genin = cause, origin, source; cf. gensan = a place of origin or habitat; cf. hasshou = origin; cf. minamoto = origin, source; cf. moto = base, origin, source; cf. naritachi = origin, structure; cf. yurai = origin, source

Kigenzen 紀元前 = B.C.; from kigen = A.D. + zen = before; cf. seireki = A.D., the Christian era

Kigi 木々 = trees, every tree, many trees; from ki = tree + gi = ki = tree; cf. related terms listed at ki

Kigu 器具 = utensil, apparatus, device; *the king's goose wears a monitoring device*; cf. related terms listed at souchi

Kigurumi 着ぐるみ = a cartoon-character costume; *the king asked his guru for a mirror so that he could see himself in his cartoon-character costume*; cf. yurukyara = a mascot character

Kigyou 企業 = enterprise or company; *our company produces quiche and gyoza*; cf. related terms listed at akinai and at kaisha

Kihada 木肌 = bark of a tree; from ki = tree + hada = skin

Kihon 基本 = basics, basis, foundation, standard; *the key to Honduran cooking is to stick to the basics*

Kihonteki 基本的 = basic; from kihon = basics + teki = related to

Kihou 気泡 = an air bubble; *there's an air bubble in the keyhole*; cf. awa = bubbles, foam

Kiiro 黄色 = yellow; *this key is made of iron, and it's yellow*

Kiiroi 黄色い = yellow; the adjective form of kiiro

Kiji 生地 = material, cloth, texture; *this key for the Jeep has a firm texture*; cf. related terms listed at nuno

Kiji 記事 = an article or news story; *there was an article about a snake that tried to kill Jimmy Carter*; cf. related terms listed at hanashi

Kijun 基準 = a criterion or standard; *the key to jungle survival is to equip yourself according to criteria published by the survival industry*; cf. related terms listed at teido

Kijutsu 記述 = a written description; *this is a written description of your kimono and the way it juts out in the back*; cf. related terms listed at hanashi

Kijutsu suru 記述する = to describe in writing; from kijutsu = a written description; cf. related terms listed at kaku

Kika 幾何 = geometry; *the keys to calculating areas are found in the study of geometry*; cf. kikagaku = geometry

Kikagaku 幾何学 = geometry; from kika = geometry + gaku = study

Kikai 機会 = opportunity; *if he gets the opportunity, he will kick you in the eye*; cf. keiki = an opportunity or chance; cf. ori = occasion, opportunity, time

Kikai 機械 = a machine; *that machine might kick you in the eye*; cf. geemu ki = a game machine; cf. jidouhanbaiki = a vending machine; cf. kenbaiki = a ticket machine

Kikairui 機械類 = machinery, equipment; from kikai = a machine + shurui = variety; cf. related terms listed at setsubi

Kikaku 企画 = project, plan; *there was a plan to purchase a kimono for Karl the Kool-Aid vendor*; cf. an = an idea, plan or proposal; cf. keikaku = project, plan; cf. kouan = conception, design or plan; cf. kousou = a plan or concept; cf. saku = a plan, scheme or device; cf. sekkei = a design or plan; cf. senjutsu = tactics or strategy; cf. taisaku = measures (actions), strategy; cf. yotei = a plan, arrangement or schedule

Kikan 器官 = an organ (body); *the king's cancer spread to his organs*; cf. related terms listed at naizou

Kikan 帰還 = repatriation, return; *please keep this candle until my return*

Kikan 期間 = duration, period; from ki = period, e.g., jiki = season; + kan = interval or space; cf. related terms listed at jikan

Kikan 機関 = engine, system, agency; *the key to curing this cancer is to follow our agency's guidelines and let our engine of knowledge pull you along*; cf. jouki kikan = a steam engine; cf. keitou = system; cf. seido = system; cf. kikansha = a locomotive or engine

Kikansha 機関車 = a locomotive or engine; from kikan = an engine + sha = a car, e.g., jidousha = a car

Kikaseru 聞かせる = to inform, tell, persuade; the causative form of kiku = to hear; cf. related terms listed at shiraseru

Kiken 気圏 = atmosphere; from ki = spirit or air + ken = a radius or circle; cf. related terms listed at kuuki

Kiken 危険 = danger; *in Kiev, Kennedy faced danger*; cf. bouken = adventure, risk; cf. kiki = crisis, danger

Kiken na 危険な = dangerous, risky; from kiken = danger; cf. abunai = dangerous, risky, doubtful, life-threatening; cf. ayaui = dangerous, uncertain, insecure; cf. yabai = dangerous, risky

Kiki 危機 = crisis, danger, risk; *the king had a key to the codes that were to be used in a crisis*; cf. bouken = adventure, risk; cf. kiken = danger

Kikin 基金 = a fund; *the key that the king keeps in his pocket unlocks the safe that contains documents about the fund*; cf. gaku = a sum of money; cf. getsugaku = a monthly sum; cf. kingaku = a sum of money; cf. kougaku = a large sum of money; cf. nenkin = annuity, pension; cf. setsuyaku gaku = an amount of money saved; cf. shihon = capital (finance); cf. shikin = capital, funds; cf. tagaku = a large sum of money; cf. toushishintaku = an investment trust or mutual fund

Kikitori 聞き取り = listening comprehension; from kikitoru = to hear or understand

Kikitoru 聞き取る = to hear or understand;

from kiku = to hear + toru = to take; cf. related terms listed at kiku and at wakaru

Kikkake きっかけ = excuse, catalyst, motive, impetus; *the king's call to Kennedy was the catalyst for the decision*; cf. related terms listed at benkai

Kikoeru 聞こえる = to be audible, to be said to be; from kiku = to hear or listen, to ask or enquire; + koeru = to cross over

Kikoku suru 帰国する = to return to one's own country; from ki = to return, e.g., kitaku = to return home; + koku = country

Kikon 既婚 = already married; *that kinky conductor is already married*

Kikou 気候 = climate; *the climate kills corn plants*; cf. related terms listed at tenki

Kiku 効く = to be effective; *if you kiku (listen) to the doctor's instructions, the medicine will be effective*

Kiku 聞く = to hear or listen, to ask or enquire; *I hear that you like to eat quiche with your Kool-Aid*; cf. kikitoru = to hear or understand; cf. uketamawaru = to hear, to be told, to undertake, to take (a message or reservation), to comply; cf. other related terms listed at tou

Kiku 菊 = chrysanthemum; *the King of Kuwait grows chrysanthemums*; cf. related terms listed at hana

Kikyuu 気球 = a balloon; from ki = air + kyuu = ball

Kimagure 気まぐれ = whimsical, capricious; *he made a whimsical decision to keep a magic goose in his restaurant*

Kimaru 決まる = to be decided, settled or arranged; *it was decided to keep magnets on the roof*

Kimatsu 期末 = end of term (semester); *let's keep these mats until the end of the term*; cf. similar terms listed at shuumatsu

Kimazui 気まずい = awkward, embarrassing; from ki = feeling + mazui = unappetizing; cf. yakkai na = troublesome, awkward; cf. wazurawashii = complicated, troublesome

Kimeru 決める = to decide, determine or arrange; *I decided to keep the medicine in my room*; cf. ketsui suru = to decide; cf. kettei suru = to decide; cf. sadameru = to decide or determine

Kimi 君 = you (used mostly by men and boys); *I keep meeting you*; cf. related terms listed at anata

Kimi 黄身 = an egg yolk; *I will give kimi (you) an egg yolk*; cf. ranou = an egg yolk

Kimo 肝 = the liver, courage; *the doctor lifted my kimono and examined my liver*; cf. kanzou = the liver; cf. other related terms listed at naizou and at yuuki

Kimo wo tsubusu 肝をつぶす = to be frightened out of one's wits, to be amazed; from kimo = courage + tsubusu = to smash; cf. related terms listed at odoroku and at osoreru

Kimochi 気持ち = a feeling; from ki = feeling + motsu = to have; cf. related terms listed at kankaku

Kimochiyoi 気持ちよい = a good feeling, feeling good; from kimochi = feeling + yoi = good; cf. related terms listed at kankaku

Kimono 着物 = a kimono; from kiru = to wear + mono = a tangible thing; cf. related terms listed at fuku

Kimyou 奇妙 = strange; *Kim Jong Un thought that the yogurt looked strange*; cf. fushigi = mysterious, strange; cf. hen = funny, strange, clumsy; cf. myou = odd, unique, strange; cf. okashi na = funny, strange; cf. okashii = funny, strange; cf. kawatta = different, unusual, strange

Kin 金 = gold; this can also be read as kane = money; *the king loved gold*; cf. related terms listed at ougon

Kinako きな粉 = roasted soybean flour; *the king signed an accord to license roasted*

soybean flour; cf. related terms listed at kona

Kinben na 勤勉な = hard-working, diligent; *the kindergarten benches were built by hard-working volunteers*

Kinchou 緊張 = tension, nervousness; *the king chose a psychologist to treat his nervousness*; cf. douyou = uneasiness, agitation; cf. fuan = insecurity, anxiety, uneasiness; cf. fuankan = an uneasy feeling, sense of anxiety; cf. kinchoukan = tension, nervousness

Kinchoukan 緊張感 = tension, nervousness; from kinchou = tension + kanjiru = to feel; cf. related terms listed at kinchou

Kindai 近代 = modern times, present day; from kin = close, e.g., kinjo = neighborhood; + dai = a certain age

Kindaika 近代化 = modernization; from kindai = modern times + ka = a nominalizing suffix (adds the meaning "-ization")

Kin'en (Kinen) 禁煙 = no smoking; from kinjiru = to prohibit + en = smoke; *a train's engine produces smoke*

Ki'nen (Kinen) 記念 = a memorial, memento, or commemoration; *I gave a key to my negative nephew as a memento of his visit*

Kinenhi 記念碑 = a commemorative plaque or stone monument; from kinen = a memorial + hi = a monument, e.g., bohi = a tombstone

Kingaku 金額 = a sum of money; *the king accumulated a sum of money*; cf. related terms listed at kikin

Kin'itsu (Kinitsu) 均一 = uniformity, equality; *each kindergartener eats the same lunch every day, in line with our policy of equality*

Kini'iri (Kiniiri) 気に入り = favorite; from ki ni iru = to like or favor

Kinjiru 禁じる = to prohibit; *after the time when the king's Jeep was ruined, he prohibited everyone from using it*; cf. imashimeru = to admonish, warn, prohibit, be cautious

Kinjo 近所 = neighborhood; *the kindergarten where Jonah worked is in this neighborhood*; cf. related terms listed at fukin

Kinkakuji 金閣寺 = the Golden Pavilion temple in Kyoto; from kin = gold + kaku = tower + jiin = Buddhist temple

Kinko 金庫 = safe; *the king keeps his coat in a safe*

Kinkou 均衡 = balance or equilibrium; *the king was corpulent, but he had good balance*

Kinkou 近郊 = suburb, outskirts; from kin = close, e.g., kinjo = neighborhood; + kougai = suburb; cf. kougai = suburb

Kinkou ga toreru 均衡がとれる = to balance; from kinkou = balance + toreru = to attain, the potential form of toru = to take; cf. kinkou wo hakaru = to balance

Kinkou wo hakaru 均衡をはかる = to balance; from kinkou = balance + hakaru = to measure; cf. kinkou ga toreru = to balance

Kinkyuu 緊急 = emergency; *the king's cute daughter had a medical emergency*; cf. related terms listed at hijou

Kinmotsu 禁物 = a forbidden thing; *to cross the king's moats is a forbidden thing*

Kinmu 勤務 = service, duty, work; *I produce kinky movies at work*; cf. gimu = unlimited duty to the emperor, ancestors and descendants; cf. giri = moral debt, limited duty to the outside world; cf. houshi = service, ministry; cf. ninmu = duty, mission; cf. shokumu = duty, office; cf. other related terms listed at shigoto

Kinnen 近年 = recent years; from kin = close, e.g., kinjo = neighborhood; + nen = year; cf. kinen = no smoking; cf. related terms listed at saikin

Kinniku 筋肉 = muscle; from kin = muscle; *the king and his niece went to Kuwait for muscle training*; cf. shinkin = heart muscle, myocardium

Kinoko きのこ = mushroom; *a mushroom is a ki no (tree's) ko (child)*; cf. related terms listed at yasai

Kinokogari きのこ狩り = mushroom gathering; from kinoko = mushroom + gari = kari = gathering

Kinokorui きのこ類 = several different kinds of mushrooms; from kinoko = mushroom + rui = variety, e.g., shurui = variety; cf. similar terms listed at shurui

Kinomi 木の実 = nut, fruit, berry; from ki = tree + the possessive no + mi = fruit or nut; cf. related terms listed at kudamono

Kinou 昨日 = yesterday; this can also be read sakujitsu, with the same meaning; *yesterday the king of Norway gave a speech*; cf. sakujitsu = yesterday

Kinou 機能 = function; *kimonos in the north serve a function in that they provide warmth*; cf. takinou = multifunction

Kinrin 近隣 = neighborhood, vicinity; *the king rings in the New Year with people from his neighborhood*; cf. related terms listed at fukin

Kinrui = fungus, fungi; *King Louis died of a fungal infection*

Kinsen 金銭 = money; *the king sent me some money*; cf. kahei = money, currency; cf. kane = money; cf. shihei = paper money, bank note; cf. tsuuka = currency

Kinsenmen 金銭面 = money aspect; from kinsen = money + men = mask or face

Kinsenteki 金銭的 = financial; from kinsen = money + teki = related to

Kinshi 禁止 = a prohibition; *there is a prohibition against eating the king's sheep*; cf. kinshirei = a ban or prohibition

Kinshin 謹慎 = penitence, discipline, house-arrest, self-restraint; *the kindergarten at the Shinto temple teaches self-restraint, but one of the teachers is under house arrest*; cf. jishuku = self-restraint, self-discipline

Kinshirei 禁止令 = a ban or prohibition; from kinshi = prohibition + rei = command, e.g., meirei = a command; cf. kinshi = a prohibition

Kintore 筋トレ = muscle training; from kinniku = muscle + toreeningu = training; cf. related terms listed at kunren

Kinu 絹 = silk; *my kimono looks new after I repaired it with silk thread*; cf. related terms listed at nuno

Ki'nyuu (Kinyuu) 記入 = entry, filling in of forms; *we take care of entries for kindergarten youth*; cf. nyuuryoku = computer input, data entry

Kin'yuu (Kinyuu) 金融 = finance, money-lending; *the king has big plans for the Yukon, if finance can be arranged*; cf. zaisei = public finance, financial affairs

Ki'nyuu (Kinyuu) suru 記入する = to write in or enter information; from kinyuu = entry; cf. nyuuryoku suru = to input (data)

Kinzoku 金属 = metal; *the kindergarten serves Zooey's Kool-Aid in metal cups*

Kinzoku 勤続 = continuous service; from kinmu = service + zokushutsu = appearing one after the other

Kioku 記憶 = memory; *I have a memory of eating quiche and oranges in Kuwait*; cf. omoide = memory

Kioku suru 記憶する = to remember; from kioku = memory; cf. related terms listed at oboeru

Kion 気温 = air temperature; from tenki = weather + ondo = temperature; cf. related terms listed at ondo

Kippu 切符 = a ticket; *I try to keep my season tickets*; cf. ken = a ticket

Kirai desu 嫌いです = to hate; *I hate it*

when _kings_ _rise_ up _from_ the _grave_; cf. keibetsu suru = to scorn or disdain; cf. nikumu = to hate or detest

Kirakira hoshi きらきら星 = twinkle twinkle star; from kirakira suru = to glitter or twinkle + hoshi = star

Kirakira suru きらきらする = to glitter or twinkle; _the bottle of_ _tequila_ _glittered_; cf. related terms listed at matataku

Kirei きれい = beautiful, pretty, clean; _in_ _Kiev_ the _ladies_ are _pretty_; cf. related terms listed at seijou and at utsukushii

Kirekire キレキレ = agile; _a regimen of_ _quiche_ and _rest_ _keeps_ _wrestlers_ _agile_

Kireru 切れる = to break, to be cut, to wear out, to expire (time), to be used up or run out (when used as a suffix), to cut well, to get angry, to be disconnected and many other meanings; this looks identical to the potential form of kiru = to cut, but it's actually a different verb; _the king's_ _red_ _rooster_ _was_ _cut_ when it jumped through the _fence_; cf. related terms listed at okoru and at yabureru

Kiri きり = since (after a point in time; this does _not_ = because), used as a suffix; this can also = only or just; _since my_ _kitty_ _left,_ _it's_ _just_ _me_; cf. related terms listed at irai

Kiri 切り = an end or limit; from kiru = to cut; cf. related terms listed at genkai

Kiri 霧 = fog or mist; _my_ _kitty_ got lost in the _fog_; cf. noumu = heavy fog

Kiriageru 切り上げる = to close or finish; from kiru = to cut + ageru = to complete; cf. related terms listed at owaraseru

Kirihiraku 切り開く = to clear land, to open up; from kiru = to cut + hiraku = to open

Kirikaeru 切り替える = to change, convert, switch over; from kiru = to cut + kaeru = to change; cf. related terms listed at kaeru

Kirikiri キリキリ = sharp pain, grinding, chafing; _kitty_ _kitty,_ that knife could cause _sharp_ _pain_; cf. related terms listed at itami

Kirisuto kyou キリスト教 = Christianity; from kirisuto = Christ + shuukyou = a religion

Kiritaosu 切り倒す = to cut down; from kiru = to cut + taosu = to knock down; cf. related terms listed at kiru

Kiritsu suru 起立する = to stand up; _when_ _I wore a tight_ _kimono_ _to the_ _Ritz_ _Hotel, I_ _had to_ _stand up_; cf. tachiagaru = to stand up; cf. tatazumu = to stand a while, to loiter; cf. tatsu = to stand

Kiro キロ kiro = either kilogram or kilometer, i.e., this is an abbreviation of either kiroguramu or kiromeetoru

Kiroku 記録 = a record or document; _I have_ _a_ _key_ to that _robotic_ _Kool-Aid_ dispenser, which keeps _records_ of every transaction; cf. kisai = a record, listing or entry; cf. shiryou = literature, documents; cf. shorui = documents

Kiru 切る = to cut, to turn off, to hang up or stop, to turn a vehicle, to complete an action (when used as a suffix); _the_ _king_ had a _ruby_ _cut_ to his specifications; cf. ashi wo arau = to cut ties with; cf. horu = to engrave, carve or chisel; cf. karu = to reap or mow, to cut hair; cf. kezuru = to shave, sharpen or cut down; cf. kiritaosu = to cut down; cf. kizamu = to cut fine, to shred; cf. setsudan suru = to cut or sever; cf. sogu = to shave off, slice, diminish or spoil; cf. tatsu = to cut (cloth); cf. tatsu = to cut off, discontinue; cf. other related terms listed at mawasu

Kiru 着る = to put on or wear clothes; _King_ _Rudolph_ _puts_ _on_ _clothes_; cf. related terms listed at chakuyou suru

Kiryoku 気力 = willpower, mental energy; from ki = spirit + ryoku = power; cf. related terms listed at ishi

Kisai 記載 = record, listing, entry; *she decided to keep silent about her Wikipedia listing*; cf. related terms listed at kiroku

Kisei 既成 = established, completed, existing; *the quiche will be safe if you send it by an established shipper*

Kisei 規制 = regulations, restrictions; *the quiche sold at Safeway is sold under restrictions, per regulations*; cf. related terms listed at kisoku

Kiseki 奇跡 = miracle, wonder, marvel; *the key to selling quiche is to tell customers that its effects are a marvel*; cf. kyoui = miracle, marvel

Kisen 汽船 = a steam ship; *the kimono for the senator arrived by a steam ship*; cf. related terms listed at fune

Kisetsu 季節 = season; *the king set up a super farm to enjoy during every season*; cf. aki = fall (season), autumn; cf. baiu = rainy season; cf. fuyu = winter; cf. haru = spring (season); cf. jun = season (for specific products); cf. kaki = summer season; cf. natsu = summer; cf. shiki = the four seasons; cf. touki = winter season; cf. tsuyu = rainy season

Kisha 汽車 = a train with a steam locomotive (or an ordinary train); *the key in the shack was used to start the train with a steam locomotive*; cf. related terms listed at densha

Kisha 記者 = a reporter; *the Irish reporter keeps a shamrock in her purse*

Kisha 貴社 = your company; from kichou = precious + kaisha = company; cf. related terms listed at kaisha

Kishi 岸 = a beach; *they keep sheep at the beach*; cf. related terms listed at kaihin

Kishi 棋士 = a shougi or go player; *that shougi player keeps sheep*

Kishi 騎士 = a knight; *if we want to keep our sheep, we should hire a knight as a guard*; cf. kishu = a jockey; cf. kenshi = a swordsman or swordswoman

Kishou 気象 = weather or climate, disposition; from kuuki = atmosphere + inshou = impression; cf. related terms listed at tenki

Kishou 起床 = rising, getting out of bed; *when the king stays by the shore, his rising time is early*

Kishu 騎手 = a jockey; *those kinky shoes belong to a jockey*; cf. kishi = a knight

Kiso 基礎 = a foundation, base or basis; *the king's sofa sits on a high base*; cf. related terms listed at kiban and at kichi

Kisoku 規則 = rules, regulations; *in Kiev he sold Kool-Aid in accordance with regulations*; cf. gensoku = a general rule; cf. houritsu = a law; cf. jourei = an ordinance; cf. keihou = criminal law; cf. kisei = regulations, restrictions; cf. shugi = doctrine, rule, principle

Kisou 競う = to compete with; *the king's soldiers competed with one another*; cf. related terms listed at arasou

Kissaten 喫茶店 = a coffee shop; *I kissed a tennis champion in a coffee shop*; cf. similar terms listed at ryoutei

Kisuu 奇数 = odd number; *I can only kiss you on odd-numbered days*; cf. related terms listed at bangou

Kita 北 = north; *I keep my tapestries on the north side of the house, away from the sun*; cf. similar terms listed at minami

Kitaeru 鍛える = to train or strengthen oneself; *the king has a tall expert in the room to train the basketball team*; cf. related terms listed at shitsukeru

Kitai 期待 = anticipation; *I have anticipation that my kitten's eye will heal*; cf. yosou = expectation; cf. yosoku = prediction

Kitai ni sou 期待に沿う = to meet expectations; from kitai = anticipation + ni

= to + sou = to follow a plan

Kitai suru 期待する = to expect; from kitai = anticipation

Kitaku 帰宅 = returning home; *they were returning home to get more quiche, tap water and Kool-Aid*

Kitanai 汚い = dirty, unjust, indecent; *the kitten goes out at night, and so it's always dirty*; cf. related terms listed at rifujin

Kiteki 汽笛 = a steam whistle; *when I kissed the techie, a steam whistle blew*; cf. fue = a flute or whistle

Kitoku 危篤 = critical condition (health); *in Quito, I drank some Kool-Aid that put me into critical condition*

Kitsu 喫 = to consume, eat, drink or smoke, used as a word component; *I use a kit from Superman to roll cigarettes when I smoke*

Kitsuen 喫煙 = smoking; from kitsu = to smoke + en = smoke

Kitsui きつい = laborious, difficult, tight-fitting, stern, harsh; *the kit from Sweden was difficult to use*; cf. related terms listed at muzukashii

Kitsumon 詰問 = cross-examination, close questioning; *the king's tsuitcase (suitcase) contained a Monet painting, and he had to undergo a cross-examination at the border*

Kitsumon suru 詰問する = to demand; from kitsumon = close questioning; cf. related terms listed at tanomu

Kitte 切手 = a postage stamp; *the kitten ate a postage stamp*

Kitto きっと = for sure, surely, without fail; *I would like to visit Quito without fail*; cf. related terms listed at chanto

Kiui キーウイ = kiwi fruit; cf. related terms listed at kudamono

Kiwameru 極める = to attain or master; *the key to war is to have a merciless ruler who can master his soldiers*; cf. related terms

listed at osaeru

Kiwamete 極めて = extremely; *the quiche and waffles that I ate in a Mexican tent were extremely good*; cf. related terms listed at ooi ni

Kiyoi 清い = clear, pure; *the king is a yogurt eater who likes pure food*; cf. other related terms listed at akiraka and at seijou

Kiyomeru 清める = to purify or cleanse; *the king's yogurt is made in a messy room, but later it is purified*; cf. souji suru = to clean

Kiyomizu 清水 = spring water, pure water; from kiyoi = pure + mizu = water; cf. related terms listed at mizu

Kiyoraka 清らか = clean, pure, chaste; *the king's yogurt lacks calcium, but it is pure*; cf. related terms listed at seijou

Kiyou 起用 = appointment (to a position), being used for a role, promotion; *the king's yogi was used for the role of Santa in the Christmas play*; cf. ninmei = an appointment or nomination

Kizamu 刻む = to cut finely, shred, or carve; *the vegetables that they used in the quiche in that Zambian movie were shredded*; cf. related terms listed at kiru

Kizashi 兆し = sign, omen; *when she kissed Zach's sheep, it moved, which was a sign that it was still alive*; cf. aizu = a sign or signal; cf. hatajirushi = an emblem, slogan or insignia on a flag; cf. maaku = a mark, a sign or symbol; cf. shirushi = a sign or symbol; cf. other related terms listed at zenchou

Kizetsu 気絶 = a faint; *the king's Zen tsuit (suit) was too tight, and he experienced a faint*

Kizoku 貴族 = a noble or aristocrat; from kichou = precious + kazoku = family

Kizu 傷 = scar, wound, injury, defect; *if you get kicked at the zoo, you will probably get some sort of injury*; cf. chimeishou = a fatal mistake or injury; cf. kega = an injury; cf. kekkan = a flaw or defect; cf. fushou = an injury or wound

Kizuato 傷痕 = a scar (this can also be pronounced shoukon, with the same meaning; it can also be spelled 傷跡 or 傷あと); from kizu = a wound + ato = a mark or footprint; cf. related terms listed at kega

Kizukai 気遣い = consideration, concern; from kizukau = to care for, worry, pay attention; cf. related terms listed at hairyo

Kizukare 気疲れ = mental fatigue, worry; from ki = spirit + tsukare = fatigue; spelled kidukare in electronic dictionaries; cf. related terms listed at nayami

Kizukau 気遣う = to care for, worry, pay attention (spelled kidukau in electronic dictionaries); *if you wear your kimono to the zoo and are approached by a cow, pay attention*; cf. ki wo tsukeru = to be careful, to pay attention; cf. other related terms listed at shinpai suru

Kizukiageru 築き上げる = to build up; from kizuku = to establish or build + ageru = to raise; cf. related terms listed at tateru

Kizuku 気づく = to realize or notice, to regain consciousness (this is spelled kiduku in computers or electronic dictionaries); an abbreviation of ki ga tsuku; cf. related terms listed at satoru

Kizuku 築く = to establish, build; *the key to a successful zoo in Kuwait is to build it with air conditioning*; cf. moukeru = to establish or set up; cf. souritsu suru = to establish; cf. sousetsu suru = to establish; cf. other related terms listed at tateru

Kizutsukeru 傷つける = to hurt, injure or damage; from kizu = an injury + tsukeru = to turn on; cf. arasu = to lay waste, damage, devastate, break into, invade; cf. itameru = to injure or cause pain; cf. mushibamu = to spoil or eat away at; cf. sawaru = to harm or annoy; cf. sogu = to shave off, slice, diminish or spoil; cf. sokonau = to injure, mar or spoil; cf. sokoneru = to injure or offend

Kke っけ = I heard it, but forgot; used as a suffix, e.g., itsu deshitakke = when was it again? *I've heard about him, but I've forgotten who Kennedy was*

Kkonai っこない = never can do, used after a potential verb stem; *I never can sleep on cold nights*; cf. related terms listed at monoka

Ko 個 = individual, a counter for eggs and other relatively three-dimensional objects; *I keep a number of eggs in a cold box and enjoy each individual one*

Ko 子 = a child; an abbreviation of kodomo = a child; cf. related terms listed at kodomo

Ko 小 = small, used as a word component, e.g., koneko = a kitten; *this coin is small*

Ko 戸 = a counter for houses; *the corporal bought a house*

Ko 股 = a thigh or crotch, used as a word component; *I have corpulent thighs*; cf. related terms listed at momo

Kobamu 拒む = to refuse or reject; *when the corpulent barber was asked to go to the moon, he refused*; cf. kotowaru = to refuse

Koban 小判 = a small Japanese gold coin, no longer used; *I used my last small Japanese gold coin to buy a cold banana*

Koboku 枯木 = a dead tree; *the corporal made a boat in Kuwait using dead trees*; cf. related terms listed at ki

Kobosu こぼす = to spill; *the co-boss spilled his coffee*

Kobu こぶ = a bump, hump or lump; *I got this lump after drinking too much cold booze*; cf. katamari = mass, lump

Kobun 古文 = ancient writing; from kodai = ancient times + bun = sentence

Kobune 小舟 = a small boat; from ko = small + bune = fune = boat; cf. related terms listed at fune

Kobushi 拳 = a fist; *I paid for that <u>colt</u> with a <u>bushy</u> tail with a <u>fist</u> full of dollars*; cf. genko = a fist

Kocchi こっち – see kochira

Kochira こちら = this person, this place, this way; *the <u>cold cheerful rabbit</u> is <u>this way</u>*

Kochira koso こちらこそ = it is I who should say so, same here; from kochira = this person + koso = for sure

Kochou 誇張 = an exaggeration; *the <u>coach choked</u> when he heard my <u>exaggeration</u>*; cf. related terms listed at iisugi

Kodai 古代 = ancient times; *during <u>ancient times</u>, <u>Korean diets</u> consisted mainly of rice*; cf. related terms listed at mukashi

Kodaijin 古代人 = people from ancient times; from kodai = ancient times + jin = people

Kodakai 小高い = slightly elevated; from ko = small + dakai = takai = high; cf. takai = high, expensive, loud (sound); cf. takame = on the high side

Kodawaru こだわる = to be particular about, to be fixated on; *I am <u>particular about</u> the <u>Kodak warranty</u> for the <u>ruined camera</u>*

Kodoku 孤独 = solitude, isolation; *the <u>co-documentarian</u> lived in <u>solitude</u> and <u>isolation</u>*; cf. hitoribocchi = solitude, loneliness; cf. sabishisa = loneliness

Kodomo 子供 = a child; *the <u>child</u> lived in a <u>cold dormitory</u> in <u>Morocco</u>*; cf. akachan = a baby or infant; cf. akanbou = a baby; cf. chibi = small child, runt, dwarf; cf. jidou = a child; cf. ko = a child; cf. koji = an orphan; cf. shindou = a child prodigy; cf. suekko = the youngest child; cf. taiji = a fetus; cf. youji = a young child

Kodou 古道 = an old road; from kodai = ancient times + douro = a road; cf. related terms listed at michi

Kodou 鼓動 = a beat (drum or heart); from taiko = a drum + dousa = movement

Koe 声 = voice; *that <u>coed</u> has a raspy <u>voice</u>*; cf. onsei = voice; cf. utagoe = a singing voice

Koeda 小枝 = a twig; from ko = small + eda = a branch

Koeru 肥える = to put on weight, to become fertile; *the <u>coed ruined</u> her chances of being selected for the beauty pageant when she <u>put on weight</u>, but then her garden <u>became fertile</u>*; cf. futoru = to gain weight

Koeru 越える = to cross over, to exceed or surpass; this can also be spelled 超える; *a <u>coed</u> named <u>Ruth crossed over</u> from East Berlin*; cf. kosu = to exceed, pass, cross, move (residence); cf. oudan suru = to cross; cf. yogiru = to go by, to cross; cf. other related terms listed at oikosu

Kofun 古墳 = an ancient tomb or burial mound; *the <u>Koreans</u> set up a <u>fund</u> to restore <u>ancient tombs</u>*; cf. related terms listed at bochi

Kogaisha 子会社 = a subsidiary company; from ko = a child + gaisha = kaisha = company; cf. related terms listed at kaisha

Kogasu 焦がす = to scorch or burn; the transitive form of kogeru = to be burned; cf. related terms listed at moyasu

Kogata 小型 = small size; from ko = small + gata = kata = form; cf. related terms listed at chiisai

Kogatasha 小型車 = a compact car; from ko = small + gata = kata = form + sha = a car; cf. related terms listed at kuruma

Kogeru 焦げる = to be scorched or burned; *the <u>Korean guest</u> bumped into the <u>rooster</u> with his cigar, and it got <u>burned</u>*; cf. related terms listed at moeru

Kogitte 小切手 = a check (banking); *the <u>Korean guitarist</u> went on <u>television</u> after*

he received a *check*

Kogoeru 凍える = to be chilled or frozen; *the Korean goalies erupted with joy after the ice in the rink was frozen*; cf. related terms listed at kooru

Kogun 孤軍 = isolated force; *a corrupt goon is using isolated force to extort money from business owners in isolated towns*

Kogun funtou 孤軍奮闘 = fighting alone; from kogun = isolated force + funtou = hard struggle

Kohan 湖畔 = a lake shore or lakeside; *the cobras hang out on the lake shore*; cf. related terms listed at kaihin

Koi 濃い = dark, thick, strong, dense; *this coin is dark, thick, strong and dense*; cf. atsui = thick; cf. futoi = thick, boldface (letters), deep (voice), brazen or rude; cf. other related terms listed at makkura

Koi 恋 = love; *I feel love for my coin collection*; cf. similar terms listed at aijou

Koi wo suru 恋をする = to fall in love; from koi = love + suru = to do

Koibito 恋人 = lover; *the koi (carp) bit off my lover's finger*

Ko'iki (Koiki) 小粋 = stylish, conceited; *this cola is icky, but stylish and conceited people often drink it*

Koimotomeru 恋求める = to beg or request; from kou = to ask + motomeru = to ask, request or buy; cf. related terms listed at tanomu

Ko'ishi (Koishi) 小石 = a pebble or small stone; from ko = small + ishi = a pebble or stone; cf. related terms listed at ishi

Koishii 恋しい = longed for, beloved; *the koi [carp] were separated from the Shiites, and they longed for each other*

Koji 孤児 = an orphan; *the coding genius was an orphan*; cf. related terms listed at kodomo

Kojika 小鹿 = fawn; from ko = small + jika = shika = deer

Kojiki 乞食 = a beggar, or begging; *the corpulent genius gave quiche to the beggar*

Kojin 個人 = individual, private, personal; *for a coder, to wear jeans is a personal decision*; cf. related terms listed at senyou

Kojinteki 個人的 = personal, self-centered; from kojin = personal + teki = related to; cf. koseiteki = unique, individualistic; cf. rikoteki = egotistical, self-centered

Kojou 古城 = old castle; from ko = old; *that koala is old*; + jou = castle; *Joan of Arc stayed in that castle*; cf. related terms listed at shiro

Kokage 木陰 = the shade of a tree; from ko = ki = tree + kage = shade

Kokansetsu 股関節 = the hip joint; from ko = thigh or crotch; *I have corpulent thighs*; + kansetsu = a joint

Koke 苔 = moss, lichen; *the Coke in the kegs was stored under some moss*

Kokka 国家 = nation, country; *people in my country drink Coca Cola*; cf. related terms listed at kuni

Kokkai 国会 = the Diet (legislative body); *some members of the Diet have cockeyed ideas*; cf. gikai = national assembly, Congress or Diet; cf. jouin = an Upper House or Senate;

Kokki 国旗 = national flag; *the corporal from Kiev saluted his national flag*; cf. hata = banner, flag

Kokkyou 国境 = a border; *there is no border between Kobe and Kyouto, since Osaka lies between them*; cf. sakai = boundary, border; cf. kokyou = hometown

Koko ここ = here; *the cold cola is here*

Koko saikin ここ最近 = recent; from koko = here + saikin = recently; cf. related terms listed at saikin

Kokochi 心地 = feeling, sensation, mood; *when I drink cocoa and eat cheese, I get a good feeling*; cf. related terms listed at kankaku

Kokochiyoi 心地良い = comfortable, pleasant; from kokochi = feeling + yoi = good; cf. related terms listed at kokoroyoi

Kokochiyosa 心地良さ = comfort; from kokochiyoi = comfortable, pleasant; cf. ian = consolation, comfort, recreation; cf. igokochi = comfort in a particular ambience; cf. kutsurogi = ease, relaxation, comfort; cf. negokochi = sleep comfort; cf. raku = pleasure, comfort

Kokoro 心 = spirit, heart, mind; *don't throw coconuts at Roy's heart*; cf. futokoro = bosom, heart; cf. kyouchuu = one's heart, mind or intentions; cf. mune = chest, heart; cf. shinzou = the heart (organ)

Kokoro ni 心に = sincerely, from the heart; from kokoro = heart + ni = to

Kokoro wo ubau 心を奪う = to completely fascinate or attract; from kokoro = heart + ubau = to fascinate

Kokoroatari 心当り = some information, a clue; from kokoro = heart + ataru = to hit; cf. related terms listed at jouhou

Kokorobosoi 心細い = downhearted, forlorn; from kokoro = heart + bosoi = hosoi = narrow

Kokorogakeru 心掛ける = to keep in mind; from kokoro = spirit, heart, mind + gakeru = kakeru = to hang; cf. related terms listed at omou

Kokorogamae 心構え = preparedness, readiness, mental attitude; from kokoro = heart + gamau = kamau = to care about

Kokoromi 試み = an attempt or venture; from kokoromiru = to experiment or try; cf. ippatsu = one blow, shot, attempt; cf. misui = a failed attempt

Kokoromiru 試みる = to experiment or try; *they will experiment with coconuts rolling down a mirrored roof in the food-processing plant*; cf. related terms listed at tamesu

Kokoroyoi 快い = pleasant, comfortable, agreeable; *because his kokoro (heart) is yoi (good), he is pleasant, comfortable and agreeable*; cf. kaiteki = pleasant, agreeable, comfortable; cf. kokochiyoi = comfortable, pleasant; cf. yukai = pleasant, cheerful; cf. other related terms at shiawase na

Kokorozashi 志 = kokoroza = ambition, wish, goal; *a man with his kokoro (heart) set on Zambian sheep has an ambition to market wool*; cf. related terms listed at mokuhyou and at shomou

Kokorozasu 志す = to intend or aspire to; from kokorozashi = ambition; cf. related terms listed at nozomu

Kokorozukai 心遣い = thoughtfulness, care and consideration; from kokoro = heart + kizukau = to care for; cf. related terms listed at hairyo and at hogo

Koku 国 = country (used in compound words); *they drink Coke in that country*; cf. related terms listed at kuni

Kokuban 黒板 = blackboard; *Coke is banned from the space near the blackboard*; cf. kanban = a signboard; cf. keijiban = a bulletin board or notice board

Kokuei 国営 = government-run; from koku = country + eigyou = business

Kokufuku suru 克服する = to overcome or conquer; *I drank some Coke in Fukuoka in an attempt to overcome my sleepiness*; cf. related terms listed at seiha suru

Kokugi 国技 = a national sport; from koku = country + gijutsu = skill

Kokuhaku suru 告白する = to confess, acknowledge; *he confessed that the Coke the hackers were drinking had been stolen*; cf. related terms listed at hakujou suru

Kokumei na 克明な = detailed, minute; *the*

corporation in Kuwait mailed us a detailed proposal; cf. related terms listed at menmitsu

Kokumin 国民 = citizen; from koku = country + min = people; cf. related terms listed at shimin

Kokumotsu 穀物 = grain, cereal; *the Coke is near the moats, together with the grain*; cf. related terms listed at mugi

Kokumushou 国務省 = State Department; *I drank Coke at the movie show about the State Department*

Kokunai 国内 = domestic; from koku = country + nai = inside

Kokunaigai 国内外 = domestic and foreign; from kokunai = domestic + gai = foreign, e.g., gaijin = foreigner

Kokunaisen 国内線 = a domestic air route; from kokunai = domestic + sen = a line or track

Kokuou 国王 = king; from koku = country + ou = king; cf. related terms listed at ou

Kokusai 国際 = international; *Coke is advertised on signs in international airports*; cf. kokusaiteki na = international; cf. sekaiteki = gobal, international

Kokusaieiga sai 国際映画祭 = international film festival; from kokusai = international + eiga = movie + sai = festival; *we are having a scientific festival*

Kokusairenmei 国際連盟 = the League of Nations; from kokusai = international + renmei = a league

Kokusaisen 国際線 = an international air route; from kokusai = international + sen = a line or track

Kokusaiteki na 国際的な = international; from kokusai = international + teki = related to; cf. related terms listed at kokusai

Kokusanhin 国産品 = domestic goods; from koku = country + sangyou = industry + hin = goods

Kokuseki 国籍 = nationality; *let's check the nationality of the people who provide Coke to our selfish king*

Kokuso suru 告訴する = to sue or accuse; *they accused him of stealing Coke from soldiers*; cf. semeru = to accuse, reproach, torment

Kokusou 穀倉 = granary; *the Coke that the soldiers drink is stored in the granary*; cf. related terms listed at souko

Kokutei 国定 = state-sponsored, national; from koku = country + shitei = designation

Kokyou 故郷 = hometown (this can also be pronounced furusato, with the same meaning); *people in my hometown add Coke to their yogurt*; cf. related terms listed at furusato

Kokyuu 呼吸 = breath, respiration; *in Korea he found a cure for the problems with his respiration*; cf. iki = breath

Komakai 細かい = small, detailed; *when he was in a coma, the Kaiser looked very small*; cf. related terms listed at chiisai and menmitsu

Komaku 鼓膜 = an eardrum or tympanic membrane; from taiko = a drum + maku = a membrane; cf. related terms listed at maku

Komaru 困る = to be inconvenienced or in trouble; *my prolonged coma ruined my career, and I was in trouble*

Kome 米 = uncooked white rice; *the comedian bought some uncooked white rice*; cf. related terms listed at gohan

Komedawara 米俵 = a bag of rice; from kome = uncooked rice + dawara = tawara = a straw bag; cf. related terms listed at fukuro

Komeru 込める = to put (emotion, effort, etc.) into, to include (tax, etc., in a price); the transitive form of komu = to get crowded

Komezu 米酢 = rice vinegar; this can also be pronounced yonezu; from kome = uncooked rice + zu = su = vinegar; cf. su = vinegar

Komezukuri 米作り = rice cultivation (this is spelled "komedukuri" in electronic dictionaries); from kome = rice + tsukuru = to produce; cf. beisaku 米作 = rice growing; cf. other related terms listed at inasaku

Komiageru 込み上げる = to fill (the heart), to well up (feelings or sensations); from komu = to get crowded + ageru = to raise

Komiau 込み合う = to be crowded; from komu = to get crowded + au = to come together; cf. komu = to get crowded

Komon 顧問 = an advisor or counselor; *my advisor is a corpulent monk*; cf. shidousha = a leader or adviser

Komon bengoshi 顧問弁護士 = a legal advisor; from komon = an advisor + bengoshi = a lawyer; cf. related terms listed at shidousha

Komoru 籠もる = to seclude oneself, to be confined in, usually written こもる; *the cobra moseyed into the room and secluded itself under the bed*; cf. related terms listed at kakureru

Komu 混む = to get crowded (this can also be spelled 込む); *the commune got crowded*; cf. komiau = to be crowded

Komugi 小麦 = wheat; *the Koreans moved the geese away from their wheat*; cf. related terms listed at mugi

Komugiko 小麦粉 = wheat flour; from komugi = wheat + kona = flour; cf. related terms listed at kona

Kon (no) 紺(の) = dark or navy blue; from kon'iro = navy blue; cf. related terms listed at ao

Kona 粉 = flour, powder; *Conan O'Brien cooks with flour*; cf. kinako = roasted soybean flour; cf. komugiko = wheat flour

Konagona 粉々 = in very small pieces; from kona = flour + gona = kona = flour

Konai こない – see Kkonai

Konasu こなす = to digest, to be able to use, to manage, to do completely, to perform or be good at, often used as a suffix, e.g., tsukaikonasu = to be able to use; *Conan O'Brien's supervisor was able to use a computer; Conan O'Brien sued his band leader after he performed some songs poorly, including music that he is usually good at*; cf. related terms listed at enjiru

Konban 今晩 = this evening, tonight; from kono = this + ban = evening, night; cf. konya = tonight; cf. koyoi = this evening

Konbanwa こんばんは = good evening; from konban = this evening + wa = as for

Konchuu 昆虫 = an insect; *those coneheads chew insects for nourishment*; cf. related terms listed at mushi

Kondan 懇談 = a meeting or talk; *Conan O'Brien and the dancer had a good talk*; cf. related terms listed at kaigi

Kondate 献立 = a menu, bill of fare, program; *Conan stared at the dark text on the menu*

Kondo 今度 = this time or next time; from kono = this + do = time; cf. jikai = next time

Kondou 混同 = confusion, mix-up; *there was some confusion about the location of the condo*; cf. konran = confusion, chaos; cf. muchitsujo = chaos, disorder; cf. mayoi = doubt, indecision, hesitation; cf. mecha-kucha = absurd, incoherent, disorder, mess; cf. senka = the turmoil of war; cf. senka = the ravages of war, war damages

Koneko 子猫 = a kitten; from ko = child + neko = cat

Kongan suru 懇願する = to entreat or beg; *the conductor and Gandalf begged for more time to find the bomb on the train*; cf. related terms listed at tanomu

Kongetsu 今月 = this month; from kono = this + getsu = month

Kongo 今後 = hereafter; from kono = this + go = later; cf. ato = after, another (with a number); cf. -go = after; cf. ikou = hereafter, thereafter, since; cf. igo = hereafter, thereafter, since; cf. nochihodo = afterward, later

Kongou 混合 = a mixture; *the economy of the Congo is based on a mixture of hunting, agriculture and mining*

Kongou suru 混合する = to mix, mingle or blend; from kongou = a mixture; cf. related terms listed at mazeru

Kon'in (Konin) 婚姻 = marriage; *Conan was insane to embark on that marriage*; cf. related terms listed a kekkon

Kon'iro (Koniro) 紺色 = navy blue; from kon = dark blue; *the conductor ironed his dark blue suit*; cf. related terms listed at ao

Konjaku 今昔 = past and present; *Conan and Jack Nicholson talked about the past and present*

Konkai 今回 = this time, now, lately; from kono = this + kai = times

Konkatsu 婚活 = searching for a marriage partner; from kekkon = marriage + katsudou = activity

Konkurabe 根比べ = a test of endurance; *Conan O'Brien wanted to kuraberu (compare) himself to his rival, so he set up a test of endurance*

Konkyo 根拠 = basis or foundation (of a belief, etc.); *Conan O'Brien went to Kyoto and discovered a basis for the rumor*; cf. related terms listed at kiban

Konkyuu 困窮 = poverty; *Conan and his Cuban friends suffered from poverty*; cf. related terms listed at binbou

Konkyuu suru 困窮する = to be poor; from konkyuu = poverty

Konmori こんもり = thickly, densely; *Conan O'Brien visited the mori (forest) to see trees that grew thickly*

Konna こんな = this kind of, such; *Conan O'Brien is this kind of person*; cf. anna = that kind over there, that sort over there, such; cf. koushita = such; cf. sonna = that kind of, such, that

Kkonai っこない = something can never occur, used after a potential verb stem, e.g., taberarekkonai = I can never eat; *I can never wear this coat at night*

Konnan 困難 = difficult, difficulty, distress; *Conan O'Brien performed a difficult stunt*; cf. related terms listed at muzukashii

Konnendo 今年度 = this year, this fiscal or school year; from kono = this + nen = year + do = time; cf. kotoshi = this year

Konnichiwa こんにちは = hello (morning or afternoon); from kono = this + nichi = day + wa = as for; cf. moshimoshi = hello (usually on the phone)

Kono この = this; *this is a correct Norwegian*

Kono mae この前 = recently; from kono = this + mae = before

Konoha 木の葉 = foliage, leaves of trees; from ko = ki = tree + the possessive no + ha = a leaf; cf. related terms listed at ha

Konomi 好み = liking, taste; from konomu = to prefer; cf. shumi = hobby, taste; cf. related terms listed at aijou

Konomu 好む = to like or prefer; *Superman liked the way the women hid their cold noses on the moon*; cf. daisuki desu = to like a lot; cf. ki ni iru = to like or favor; cf. suki desu = to like

Konran 混乱 = confusion, chaos; *Conan O'Brien ran away in the confusion*; cf.

Kondou = confusion, mix-up; cf. muchitsujo = chaos, disorder; cf. mechakucha = absurd, incoherent, disorder, mess

Konryuu 建立 = the act of building (a monument or temple); *the Coneheads reused their old cones to construct walls as they were building a temple*; cf. related terms listed at kenchiku

Konseki 痕跡 = traces, vestiges; *in the Congo, the selfish king found traces of gold*; cf. related terms listed at ato

Konshuu 今週 = this week; from kono = this + shuu = week

Konsui 昏睡 = coma, stupor; *the woman from the Congo drank the Swedish potion and fell into a coma*

Konya 今夜 = tonight; from kono = this + ya = night; cf. related terms listed at konban

Kon'yaku (Konyaku) 婚約 = an engagement (to be married); from kekkon = marriage + yakusoku = a promise

Konzatsu 混雑 = crowdedness, congestion; *a conehead lost Zach's tsuitcase (suitcase) in the congestion of the airport*; cf. juutai = gridlock (traffic)

Konzetsu 根絶 = eradication, extermination; *the contractor put on a Zen tsuit (suit) and thought about how to achieve the eradication of construction waste*; cf. related terms listed at satsujin

Koori 氷 = ice; *in Corinth people put ice in their drinks*; cf. hyou = ice

Kooru 凍る = to freeze; *when it's cold in the room, we freeze*; cf. kogoeru = to be chilled or frozen; cf. reitou suru = to freeze

Kooto コート = a coat; cf. uwagi = jacket, outer clothes

Kore hodo これ程 = so much, this much; from kore = this + hodo = about; cf. kakumo = so

Kore kara これから = from now on; from kore = this + kara = from

Kore これ = this, now; *this is correct*

Korera これら = these; from kore = this + ra = a suffix that makes the preceding pronoun plural

Koriru 懲りる = to learn a lesson or get sick of, usually written こりる; *she damaged some Corinthian ruins and learned a lesson*; cf. related terms listed at akiru

Koro 頃 = goro = approximate time, used as a suffix; *that was the approximate time when I got coronavirus*

Korobu 転ぶ = to fall over, to stumble; *after trying to treat the coronavirus with booze, I fell over*; cf. related terms listed at ochiru

Korogaru 転がる = to roll, fall over, lie down; from korobu = to fall over + garu = to show signs of doing something, e.g., ikitagaru = to show signs of wanting to go; cf. related terms listed at ochiru and at yoko ni naru

Koromo 衣 = coating or breading (food), clothes; *the Corolla's motor had a coating of mud after the journey*

Koroshiau 殺し合う = to kill each other; from korosu = to kill + au = to come together

Korosu 殺す = to kill; *the corporation's robots attacked Superman and tried to kill him*; cf. koroshiau = to kill each other

Koru 凝る = to become stiff, to be absorbed in; *the cobra on the roof was absorbed in watching the mouse, but then it became stiff in the cold*

Kosa 濃さ = consistency, darkness, thickness, density; from koi = dark, thick, dense + sa = a suffix that makes a noun from an adjective; cf. ikkan = consistency, coherence, integration; cf. noudo = concentration; cf. noukou = density, concentration

Kosei 個性 = individuality, personality; from kojin = individual, private, personal +

seikaku = personality; cf. jinkaku = personality, character; cf. seikaku = personality

Koseiteki 個性的 = unique, individualistic; from kosei = individuality + teki = related to; cf. kojinteki = personal, self-centered; cf. dokuji = original, unique; cf. dokutoku = unique, original, characteristic; cf. myou = odd, unique, strange; cf. yuiitsu = only, sole, unique

Koseki 戸籍 = a family register; *the corporal showed the selfish king his family register*

Kosekishouhon 戸籍抄本 = an official copy of a family registry extract; from koseki = a family register + shouhon = an extract

Koshi 腰 = low back, waist, hip; *a cobra bit the Shiite on his low back*; cf. senaka = back (of the body)

Koshi wo sueru 腰を据える = to settle down, to settle in, to concentrate all of one's energy; from koshi = low back, waist or hip + sueru = to place or set up

Koshitsu suru 固執する = to be persistent; *he was persistent in tucking in the corners of his sheets*

Koshitsu 個室 = a private or single room; from kojin = individual + shitsu = room; cf. related terms listed at -shitsu

Koshou 故障 = a breakdown, malfunction or failure; *the Korean show was interrupted by a malfunction in equipment*; cf. related terms listed at shippai

Koso こそ = for sure, used for emphasis, e.g., kochira koso = it is I who should say so, same here; *let's drink cold soda, for sure*

Kossetsu suru 骨折する = to break a bone; *a corporation settled with Superman after he broke a bone when he slipped on a wet floor*; cf. related terms listed at kowasu

Kosu 越す = to exceed, pass, cross, move (residence); *the co-supervisor crossed a line when he ridiculed the boss*; cf. koeru = to cross over; cf. oudan suru = to cross; cf. yogiru = to go by, to cross; cf. other related terms listed at hikkosu, oikosu, and sugiru

Kosui 湖水 = lake water; *I like cold sweet lake water*; cf. related terms listed at mizu

Kosureru 擦れる = to be rubbed; the intransitive form of kosuru = to rub or scrub

Kosuru 擦る = to rub or scrub; *the co-superintendent ruined the shirt by scrubbing it too hard*; cf. momu = to massage or rub; cf. naderu = to rub or stroke; cf. sureru = to rub against, to wear down, to become jaded; cf. surimuku = to abrade or scrape

Kotae 答え = a reply or solution; from kotaeru = to answer; cf. henji = a reply; cf. kaitou = a reply;

Kotaeru 応える = to respond or affect; *the co-eds in the tavern were erudite and responded to our questions*; cf. related terms listed at oujiru

Kotaeru 答える = to answer; *the co-ed in the tavern was erudite and answered the questions*; cf. iikaesu = to talk or answer back, to say repeatedly

Kotai 固体 = solid; *the Korean tiger had solid muscles*

Kotatsu こたつ = a table with a heater under it, surrounded by a hanging quilt; *since it was cold and I was wearing a tattered suit, I sat at the heated table with a hanging quilt*

Kotchi こっち – see kochira

Kotei suru 固定する = to rivet, fix, stabilize; *Koreans use tape to stabilize their furniture*

Koten 古典 = classical work, classic; *the Colombian tennis player was reading a classic*

Kotenteki 古典的 = classical, old-fashioned; from koten = classic + teki = related to; cf.

dentouteki = traditional

Koto 事 = intangible thing, matter, affair, occurrence; *Colombian tonal music is an intangible thing*

Koto 琴 = a Japanese harp; *this Japanese harp has cold tonal qualities*

Koto desu (or koto da) ことです = one should do something, e.g., benkyou suru koto desu = one should study; cf. related terms listed at seneba

Koto ga aru ことがある = sometimes people do things or sometimes things occur; from koto = intangible thing + aru = to exist

Koto kara ことから = because, on the basis that; from koto = intangible thing + kara = because; cf. related terms listed at node

Koto mo nai こともない = possibly, when used after a plain negative verb, e.g., kawanai koto mo nai = I will possibly buy it; from nai = not + koto = tangible thing + nai = not, creating a double negative that means "possibly"

Koto naku ことなく = without, e.g., akirameru koto naku = without giving up; from koto = intangible thing + naku = the adverbial form of nai = negation; cf. related terms listed at naki

Koto ni 殊に = especially, moreover, what is more (usually spelled ことに); *moreover, and especially, my cold toes need socks*; cf. koto ni wa = unless, when used after a plain negative verb; cf. related terms listed at toku ni

Koto ni naru ことになる = to be scheduled or arranged; from koto = intangible thing + ni = to + naru = to become

Koto ni suru ことにする = to decide to, to make a practice of doing; from koto = intangible thing + ni = to + suru = to do

Koto ni wa ことには = unless, when used after a plain negative verb, e.g., minai koto ni wa = unless I see; this is also used after positive verbs to emphasize emotion; *unless the koto (Japanese harp) gets to my niece in Washington, I won't pay for it*; cf. koto ni = especially, moreover, what is more

Koto no hoka 殊の外 = exceedingly, unusually; *I got cold toes in Norway while holding a cat, and they were exceedingly blue*

Koto wa arimasen ことはありません – see koto wa nai

Koto wa nai ことはない = it isn't necessary, e.g., kaisha ni iku koto wa nai = it isn't necessary to go to the company; from koto = intangible thing + nai = doesn't exist; cf. koto wa arimasen = it isn't necessary; cf. hitsuyou wa arimasen = it isn't necessary; cf. ni wa oyobanai = it isn't necessary

Kotoba 言葉 = language, word; *I left my koto (Japanese harp) at the bar while I had a word with her*; cf. goi = vocabulary; cf. hitokoto = a single word, a brief comment; cf. hitokuchi = a mouthful, one word; cf. tango = a word; cf. other related terms listed at gengo

Kotobazukai 言葉遣い = speech customs, word use; from kotoba = word + kizukau = to care for

Kotonaru 異なる = to differ; *the koto (Japanese harp) that the nanny ruined differed from the one that she didn't touch*; cf. chigau = to differ (verb) or different, wrong (adjective)

Kotori 小鳥 = a small bird; from ko = small + tori = bird; cf. related terms listed at tori

Kotoshi 今年 = this year; from kono = this + toshi = year; cf. konnendo = this year, this fiscal or school year

Kotowaru 断る = to refuse; *since the koto (Japanese harp) was ruined, he refused to accept it*; cf. kobamu = to refuse or reject

Kotozuke 言付け = a message (usually expressed as otokozuke; this is spelled kotoduke in electronic dictionaries); this is usually spelled 言づけ or ことづけ; from kotozukeru = to send a message; cf. dengon = a message

Kotozukeru 言付ける = to send a message, to make an excuse (this is spelled kotodukeru in electronic dictionaries); this can also be spelled 言づける; *when I left my koto (Japanese harp) at the zoo, Ken and Rudolph sent messages to the zookeeper about it*

Kotsu 骨 = skeleton, bone, used as a word component; *I wear two coats to keep my bones warm*; cf. related terms listed at hone

Kotsu コツ = a knack; *she has a knack for designing coats*; cf. related terms listed at waza

Kotsukotsu コツコツ = tapping, clicking, steadily; *they were making coats and coats steadily, and their needles were clicking*

Kotsutsubo 骨壷 = funerary urn; from kotsu = bone; *I wear two coats to keep my bones warm*; + tsubo = urn; cf. related terms listed at tsubo

Kotsuzumi 小鼓 (こつづみ) = a small hand drum, spelled kotsudumi in electronic dictionaries; from ko = small + tsuzumi = a drum; cf. 小包 (こづつみ) kozutsumi = a package, spelled kodutsumi in electronic dictionaries; cf. related terms listed at taiko

Kou こう = like this; *the cobra is like this*

Kou 公 = public, used as a word component, e.g., kouen = a public park; *the corporal serves the public*

Kou 請う = to beg or ask; *he asked for a coat*; cf. related terms listed at tanomu

Kou 甲 = a shell (e.g., of a tortoise), armor, back (of the hand), top (of the foot), the former; *the former visitor poured cola on the turtle's shell*; cf. related terms listed at koura

Kou no 甲の = the first, the former; from kou = the former + the possessive no; cf. otsu no = the second, the latter

Kouan 考案 = a conception, design, or plan; *he developed a design for a Korean ant farm*; cf. related terms listed at kikaku

Koubai 勾配 = a slope or incline; *although I was climbing a steep slope, I was cold on my bike*; cf. related terms listed at shamen

Kouban 交番 = a police box or small station; from kousaten = traffic intersection + ban = watch

Koubutsu 好物 = favorite food; from kou = to like; *I like cola*; + butsu = thing; cf. aiyou = favorite thing, habitual use; cf. okiniiri = a favorite thing or person; cf. related terms listed at tabemono

Koubutsu 鉱物 = mineral; from kouzan = a mine + butsu = thing

Koucha 紅茶 = black tea; *the corporal took a chance and ordered black tea*; cf. related terms listed at cha

Kouchi 拘置 = arrest, confinement; *he was subject to arrest for stealing the corporation's cheese*; cf. taiho = arrest, apprehension, capture

Kouchisho 拘置所 = a jail or detention center; from kouchi = confinement + sho = a place; cf. related terms listed at kangoku

Kouchou 校長 = a school principal; from gakkou = school + chou = chief; cf. related terms listed at shunou

Koudai 広大 = vast; *the Korean dike is vast*; cf. related terms listed at ookii

Koudo 高度 = high-level, advanced; *the Korean door maker uses advanced methods*; cf. koukyuu = high class or quality

Koudou 行動 = behavior, action; *one of his actions was to make a Korean door*; cf. related terms listed at furumai

Koudou 講堂 = an auditorium; from kougi = lecture + dou = a hall

Kouei 光栄 = honor or glory; *the cold aviator received honor and glory after his long flight*; cf. eikou = glory, eminence; cf. homare = honor or distinction; cf. meiyo = honor or glory

Kouen 公園 = a public park; *Leonard Cohen went to the public park*; cf. teien = a garden or park

Kouen 公演 = public performance; from kou = public + enjiru = to perform; cf. related terms listed at shutsuen

Kouen 講演 = a speech or lecture; *Leonard Cohen gave a lecture*; cf. related terms listed at enzetsu

Koufuku 幸福 = happiness; *the cola I drank in Fukuoka brought me happiness*; cf. related terms listed at shiawase

Koufuku na 幸福な = happy; from koufuku = happiness; cf. related terms listed at shiawase na

Koufuku suru 降伏する = to surrender; *when the corporal reached Fukuoka, he surrendered*; cf. kuppuku suru = to surrender; cf. kussuru = to bend or yield to

Koufun 興奮 = excitement; *playing with koalas is fun and leads to excitement*

Kougai 郊外 = suburb; *the cold guy lives in the suburbs*; cf. kinkou = suburb, outskirts

Kougaku 高額 = a large sum of money; from kou = high, e.g., koukou = high school; + kingaku = a sum of money; cf. related terms listed at kikin

Kougeki 攻撃 = attack, criticism; *after a corporal found a guest key to the enemy's castle, we launched an attack*; cf. related terms listed at hihan and shuugeki

Kougeki suru 攻撃する = to attack or criticize; from kougeki = attack, criticism; cf. related terms listed at hihan suru and at osou

Kougi 抗議 = a protest; *I will join a protest against the treatment of Korean geese*; cf. related terms listed at kujou

Kougi 講義 = a lecture; *the lecture was about Korean geese*; cf. related terms listed at enzetsu

Kougou 皇后 = an empress; *the Korean gold belonged to the empress*; cf. related terms listed at joou

Kougou heika 皇后陛下 = Her Majesty the Empress; from kougou = empress + heika = Your Majesty; cf. related terms listed at joou

Kougu 工具 = a tool; *I use this tool to split coconuts for the goose*; cf. related terms listed at souchi

Kougyou 工業 = industry; *in that industry, the workers get cold gyoza for lunch*; cf. sangyou = industry, occupation; cf. seikougyou = steel industry; cf. yousangyou = the sericulture (silkworm) industry; cf. other related terms listed at akinai

Kougyouka 工業化 = industrialization; from kougyou = industry + ka = a nominalizing suffix

Kouhai 後輩 = junior (in age or rank); *the corporation hides its junior members in cubicles*

Kouhan 後半 = the latter half; *the corporal was handsome, but he typically came to work during the latter half of the day*; cf. chuujun = around the middle of a month; cf. shojun = the first ten days of a month; cf. other related terms listed at han

Kouhan'i (Kouhani) 広範囲 = extensive; from koudai = vast + han'i = area; cf. related terms listed at habahiroi

Kouhi 后妃 = a queen; *the queen likes to*

drink *koohii (coffee*; cf. related terms listed at joou

Kouhinshitsu 高品質 = high product quality; from kou = high, e.g., koukou = high school; + hinshitsu = quality; cf. related terms listed at hinshitsu

Kouho 候補 = a candidate; *the candidate came from a cohort of politicians who banded together*; cf. kouhosha = a candidate

Kouhosha 候補者 = a candidate; from kouho = candidate + sha = person; cf. kouho = a candidate

Kouhou 広報 = public relations, publicity, information; *the Korean hotel was good at public relations*; cf. senden = advertising, publicity; cf. other related terms listed at jouhou

Kouhou 後方 = behind, in the rear; *my cohorts followed in the rear*; cf. related terms listed at ushiro

Kouhouka 広報課 = a public relations department; from kouhou = public relations + ka = section, e.g., kachou = section manager

Kouhyou 好評 = favorable review, good reception; from kou = to like, e.g., koubutsu = favorite food; + hyouban = reputation; cf. related terms listed at hyouban

Kouhyouka 高評価 = highly rated, well-liked; from kouhyou = high reputation + kachi = value

Koui 行為 = deed, action; *I went to Colombia at Easter to try to do some good deeds*; cf. related terms listed at furumai

Kouin 工員 = a factory worker; from koujou = factory + in = member, e.g., kaishain = company employee; cf. related terms listed at roudousha

Kouji 工事 = construction work; *coalition Jeeps were diverted to construction work*; cf. related terms listed at kensetsu and at shigoto

Koujitsu 口実 = an excuse or pretext; *since it was cold the jittery superstar used the weather as an excuse for cancelling the concert*; cf. related terms listed at benkai

Koujo 控除 = a deduction or subtraction; qKoujo 控除 = a deduction or subtraction; *when it was cold in her apartment, Josephine would take a deduction from her rent check*

Koujou 向上 = improvement; *the corn that Joan was eating was an improvement over the seeds that she was eating before*; cf. related terms listed at kaizen

Koujou 工場 = a factory; *in Cologne, Joan of Arc worked in a factory*

Koujou 荒城 = a ruined castle; from kouya = wilderness + jou = a castle; cf. related terms listed at shiro

Koujouchou 工場長 = a factory manager; from koujou = factory + chou = a chief; cf. related terms listed at shunou

Koujousen 甲状腺 = the thyroid gland; *since she was always cold, Joan of Arc sensibly went to get her thyroid gland tested*

Koujoushin 向上心 = ambition, desire to improve oneself; from koujou = improvement + shin = heart

Kouka 効果 = an effect; *the cold car had an effect on the children*; cf. eikyou = effect, influence; cf. kekka = an effect or result; cf. kouryoku = an effect

Kouka 硬貨 = coins; *I buy Coca Cola with coins*; cf. kozeni = coin, small change

Kouka 高価 = expensive; *Korean cattle are expensive*; cf. takai = high, expensive, loud (sound)

Koukai 公会 = a public meeting; from kou = public + kaigi = a meeting

Koukai 公開 = opening, or releasing to the public; *the corporation kindly released information to the public and opened its facilities to them*

Koukai 後悔 = regret; *he poured Coke into his eye, and now he has regrets*; cf. hansei = scrutiny, self-scrutiny, regret; cf. ikan = regret; cf. kui = regret

Koukai 航海 = sailing, voyage; *the Coast Guard escorted the Kaiser on his voyage*; cf. hansou = sailing; cf.shuppan = sailing, departure

Koukaidou 公会堂 = a town hall or public hall; from koukai = a public meeting + dou = a hall or public chamber

Koukan suru 交換する = to exchange; *I want to exchange this Coke can for a Pepsi*; cf. hikikaeru = to exchange or convert; cf. irekaeru = to replace, to shift or change places; cf. kaeru = to replace or exchange; cf. torikaeru = to exchange or replace

Koukan = a high-ranking official; from koukyuu = high class + kan = a government official, e.g., keikan = a policeman; cf. kanryou = a government official or bureaucrat

Koukateki 効果的 = effective; from kouka = effect + teki = related to; cf. yuukou = valid, effective

Koukei 光景 = scene or sight; *the koala wearing a cape was an amusing sight*; cf. related terms listed at bamen

Koukeisha 後継者 = a successor; *we will consume cola and cake, and then the Shah will name his successor*; cf. kounin = a successor or replacement

Kouken 貢献 = a contribution; *the corpulent Kennedy made a contribution to obesity research*; cf. related terms listed at okurimono

Kouketsuatsu 高血圧 = high blood pressure; from kou = high, e.g., koukou = high school; + ketsuatsu = blood pressure

Kouki 光輝 = brightness, splendor; *the corporal polished the key to the prescribed level of brightness*

Kouki 後期 = second half (of a period);); *I eat cold quiche in the second half of the day*; cf. related terms listed at han

Kouki na (or no) 高貴な = aristocratic, noble; from saikou = the best + kichou = precious; cf. related terms listed at kedakai

Koukishin 好奇心 = curiosity; *I plan to wear a coat over my kimono when I visit the Shinto shrine, but I feel curiosity about what other people will wear*

Koukoku 広告 = advertisement; *the advertisement was for cold Coke*; cf. shi emu = commercial or advertisement; cf. senden = advertising, publicity

Koukou 孝行 = filial piety; *the Korean coach exhibited filial piety*; cf. oyakoukou na = reverent to parents

Koukou 高校 = a high school; from koudo = high-level + gakkou = school

Koukou suru 航行する = to sail; *the cold coders sailed against the wind*

Koukuu 航空 = aviation, flying; *we ship Coke and Kool-Aid by aviation*; cf. hikou = aviation, flight

Koukuubin 航空便 = air mail; from koukuu = aviation + bin = service; *we provide bingo chips as a service*

Koukyo 皇居 = the Imperial Palace; *the court in Kyoto was held in an Imperial Palace*; cf. related terms listed at kyuuden

Koukyou 公共 = public or communal; *when it's cold in Kyouto, people go to public or communal bathhouses*; cf. kyoudou no = cooperative, communal; cf. other related terms listed at kouritsu

Koukyuu 恒久 = permanence; *corruption in Cuba has acquired permanence*

Koukyuu 高級 = high class or quality; *the*

coach's cute house was of *high quality*; cf. koudo = high-level, advanced; cf. other related terms listed at hinshitsu

Koukyuuteki 恒久的 = permanent; from koukyuu = permanence + teki = related to

Koumei 高名 = fame; from koudo = high-level + na = name or fame; cf. related terms listed at chimeido

Koumu 公務 = official or public business; *as part of my official business, I have to commute to the moon*; cf. related terms listed at akinai

Koumuin 公務員 = a public employee; from koumu = public business + in = a group member; cf. related terms listed at seishain

Kounetsu 高熱 = a high fever; from kou = high, e.g., koukou = high school; + netsu = fever

Kounin 公認 = (publicly) authorized or approved; *the corpulent ninja was authorized to carry out the mission*

Kounin 後任 = successor, replacement; *the Korean ninja is the successor to the Japanese one*; cf. koukeisha = a successor

Kounyuu 購入 = a purchase; *a coach in Nyuuyooku (New York) made a purchase*; cf. kaitori = a purchase or sale

Kounyuu suru 購入する = to purchase; from kounyuu = a purchase; cf. kau = to buy

Koura 甲羅 = a shell; *she poured cola on the turtle's shell*; cf. kara = a shell or crust; cf. kou = a shell

Koura yaki 甲羅焼き = baked in the shell; from koura = shell + yaku = to bake

Kourei 恒例 = customary; *in this area, cold rain is customary*; cf. related terms listed at taitei

Kourei 高齢 = elderly; from kou = high, e.g., koukou = high school; + rei = age, e.g., nenrei = age; cf. toshiue = senior, older

Koureika 高齢化 = aging; from kourei = elderly + ka = a nominalizing suffix; cf. rouka = aging

Ko'uri (Kouri) 小売り = retail; from ko = small + uru = to sell

Kouritsu 公立 = public; *the corporation received a written suggestion that it allow public access to some of its facilities*; cf. koukyou = public or communal; cf. koushuu = the public; cf. taishuu = the general public

Kouritsu 効率 = efficiency; *when it's cold, I go to the Ritz Hotel with Sue, and she praises my efficiency in finding a place to get warm*; cf. seinou = performance, efficiency

Kouron 口論 = argument, quarrel; *in Korea, Ronald Reagan got into a quarrel*; cf. related terms listed at issen

Kouryo 考慮 = consideration; *a corporation asked Pope Leo for his consideration in reducing their taxes*; cf. related terms listed at hairyo

Kouryo suru 考慮する = to consider; from kouryo = consideration; cf. related terms listed at omou

Kouryoku 効力 = an effect; *when the corporation hired Pope Leo to advertise Kool-Aid, it had an effect on sales*; cf. eikyou = effect, influence; cf. kekka = an effect or result; cf. kouka = an effect

Kouryou 香料 = fragrance; *the cologne that Pope Leo uses has a nice fragrance*; cf. related terms listed at kaori

Kouryuu 興隆 = a rise, prosperity; *the corporal reused many household items, and gradually he achieved prosperity*; cf. related terms listed at han'ei

Kouryuu suru 興隆する = to prosper or flourish; from kouryuu = prosperity; cf. related terms listed at sakaeru

Kousa 交差 = crossing, intersection;

commuting salarymen wait at intersections; cf. kousaten = a traffic intersection

Kousa 黄砂 = yellow dust from the Yellow River region, which blows to Japan; *after I left it outside, my corn salad was covered with yellow dust*

Kousaku 耕作 = cultivation (of land); *I eat corn from a sack during the cultivation of my land*; cf. baiyou = cultivation, nurture, culture; cf. inasaku = rice cultivation, rice crop; cf. saibai = cultivation

Kousaten 交差点 = a traffic intersection; *they were selling Korean sardines for ten dollars at the intersection*; cf. kousa = crossing, intersection

Kousatsu 絞殺 = strangulation; *the court found that the satisfied supervisor died from strangulation*

Kousei 構成 = structure, composition; *the composition of the crew is Korean sailors*; cf. naritachi = origin, structure

Kousei busshitsu 抗生物質 = an antibiotic; from teikou = opposition + sei = life + busshitsu = a substance

Kouseki 功績 = achievement; *the cornea transplant performed for the selfish king was a real achievement for the doctors*; cf. related terms listed at seiseki

Kousha 校舎 = a school building; *that Colombian shack used to be a school building*

Koushi 孔子 = Confucius; *Confucius sometimes slept between cold sheets*; cf. jukyou = Confucianism

Koushi 格子 = a lattice work or grill; *the coats of the sheep were dyed in a lattice work pattern*

Koushi 講師 = a lecturer or instructor; *she's a lecturer on the topic of Korean sheep*; cf. related terms listed at sensei

Koushiki 公式 = a formula; *in Korea I often used the shift key when I typed formulas*

Koushiki na (or no) 公式な = official; *in Korea, using a shift key is official policy*; cf. seishiki na (or no) = formal or official

Koushin 更新 = renewal, improvement; *in Kobe, many shingles were changed during urban renewal*; cf. related terms listed at kaizen

Koushin 行進 = a march; *wearing a coat of shingles, I joined the march*; cf. related terms listed at sanpo

Koushita こうした = such; from kou = like this + shita = did; cf. related terms listed at konna

Koushou 交渉 = negotiation, bargaining, contact; *my coach showed me how to conduct a negotiation*

Koushou na 高尚な = noble, high-brow, refined; *that Korean show is rather high-brow*; cf. related terms listed at jouhin and at kedakai

Koushuu 公衆 = the public; *I got cold shoes while waiting for that public phone*; cf. related terms listed at kouritsu

Koushuukai 講習会 = classes, lessons, a course; *when she learned that I had cold shoes, the kind teacher invited me in to listen to her lessons*; cf. related terms listed at jugyou

Kouso 酵素 = an enzyme; *the corn was soaked in a vat of enzymes*

Kousoku 拘束 = a restraint or restriction; *we have restrictions against cobras soaking in our baths*

Kousoku 梗塞 = a stoppage, tightness or block, an infarction; *when he jumped into the icy water for a cold soak, he sustained an infarction*; cf. shinkin kousoku = a heart attack or myocardial infarction; cf. other related terms at chuushi

Kousoku 高速 = high speed; from koudo = high level + sokudo = speed; cf. kaisoku =

express, high speed, mobility

Kousoku douro 高速道路 = a highway or freeway; from kousoku = high speed + douro = a road; cf. related terms listed at michi

Kousou 構想 = a plan or concept; *the Korean soldiers had a plan*; cf. gainen = a concept or general idea; cf. other related terms listed at kikaku

Kousou 高層 = multi-storied, high-rise; *the Korean soldier lived in a high-rise*

Kousui 香水 = perfume; *coeds in Sweden use perfume*

Ko'uta (Kouta) 小唄 = a ballad; from ko = small + uta = a song with samisen; cf. related terms listed at uta

Koutai 交代 = alternation, shift; *since we only have one coat and tie, my brother and I wear them in shifts*

Koutaku 光沢 = luster; *cold tap water and Kool-Aid will put the luster back into your silverware*; cf. tsuya = luster, glaze, polish

Koutei 公邸 = official residence; from koukyou = public + teitaku = mansion; cf. related terms listed at teitaku

Koutei 皇帝 = an emperor; *this Korean table once belonged to an emperor*; cf. related terms listed at ou

Koutei 肯定 = positive, affirmation; *the coat that the tailor made earned him affirmation*

Koutei suru 肯定する = to affirm, answer positively or admit; from koutei = affirmation; cf. mitomeru = to recognize, admit or allow

Kouteiteki 肯定的 = affirmative, positive; from koutei = affirmation + teki = related to; cf. related terms listed at maemuki

Kouten 好天 = good weather; from kou = to like, e.g., koubutsu = favorite food; + tenki = weather; cf. related terms listed at tenki

Kouten suru 好転する = to improve; *the cold weather tends to improve in April*; cf. related terms listed at ryouyou suru

Koutetsu 鋼鉄 = steel; *the cold tetanus shot that Superman got was delivered via a steel needle*; cf. related terms listed at tetsu

Koutokuten 高得点 = a high score; from kou = high, e.g., koukou = high school; + tokuten = marks or score; cf. related terms listed at seiseki

Koutsuu 交通 = traffic, transportation, exchange (of ideas, etc.); *he wore a coat and suit as he faced the traffic*; cf. related terms listed at ourai

Koutsuuryou 交通量 = traffic volume; from koutsuu = traffic + ryou = quantity; cf. related terms listed at ryou

Kouun 幸運 = good luck; *it was good luck that the koala was under the bridge when the train came*; cf. fuku = good luck; cf. fuun = bad luck; cf. kichi = good fortune; cf. un = luck, fortune; cf. unmei = fate or destiny

Kouya 荒野 = wilderness, the wild; *the coat of a yak is adapted to wilderness life*

Kouyou 公用 = public business, official business; from kou = public, e.g., kouen = public park; + youji = errand

Kouyou 紅葉 (this can also be pronounced momiji) = autumn colors, fall leaves; if pronounced momiji, this refers to maple trees or their leaves; *when the autumn colors peaked, it was cold, and we practiced yoga; we had a momentary meeting in the Jeep under the maple tree leaves*; cf. momiji = autumn leaves

Kouza 口座 = an account (e.g., bank); *I took money from my account to buy a colt in Zambia*

Kouza 講座 = an academic course or lecture; *I attended a lecture about coconut palms in Zambia*; cf. related terms listed at jugyou

Kouzan 鉱山 = a mine; *that <u>corporation</u> operates in <u>Zan</u>zibar, where it has a <u>mine</u>*

Kouzan 高山 = high mountains; *if you think it's <u>cold</u> in <u>Zan</u>zibar, you should come up to the <u>high mountains</u> where we live*; cf. related terms listed at yama

Kouzetsu 口舌 = way of speaking, words, lip service; *when the <u>corporal</u> put on a <u>Zen</u> <u>tsuit</u> (suit), his <u>way of speaking</u> seemed to change*

Kouzui 洪水 = a flood; *a <u>Colombian zoo</u> in the <u>east</u> was affected by a <u>flood</u>*

Kouzuru 講ずる = to take measures, to work out a plan, to lecture, to read aloud, to confer; *she will <u>take measures</u> to ensure that the <u>cold zoo</u> gets a <u>roof</u>*

Kowagaru 怖がる = to be afraid of; from kowai = afraid + -garu = appears to be; cf. osoreru = to be afraid or apprehensive

Kowai 怖い = afraid; *the <u>koala</u> saw the evil <u>eye</u> and was <u>afraid</u>*; cf. okubyou na = timid

Kowarekakaru 壊れかかる = to begin to break down; from kowareru = to break (intransitive), + kakaru = to start doing something

Kowareru 壊れる = to break, the intransitive form of kowasu = to break; cf. related terms listed at yabureru

Kowasu 壊す = to break or destroy; *when the <u>koala</u> visited <u>Sudan</u>, he <u>broke</u> some plates*; cf. hakai suru = to destroy; cf. kossetsu suru = to break a bone; cf. kudaku = to break or smash; cf. oru = to break or fold; cf. torikowasu = to tear down; cf. waru = to break glass or wood; cf. yaburu = to break, tear or violate; cf. other related terms listed at horobosu

Koya 小屋 = cabin, hut; from ko = small + ya = house or store; cf. related terms listed at ie

Koyoi 今宵 = this evening; from ko = now, e.g., kotoshi = this year; + yoi = evening;

cf. related terms listed at konban

Koyomi 暦 = a calendar; *a <u>calendar</u> was used to schedule a <u>coyotes'</u> <u>meeting</u>*; cf. reki = a calendar or almanac; cf. taiyoureki = a solar calendar

Kozeni 小銭 = coin, small change; *the <u>coins</u> that the <u>Zen</u> monks spend when they <u>eat</u> out are <u>small change</u>*; cf. kouka = coins

Kozou 小僧 = a boy or a novice priest; from ko = small + zou = sou = priest; cf. related terms listed at otoko

Kozutsumi 小包 (こづつみ) = a package, spelled kodutsumi in electronic dictionaries; from ko = small + tsutsumu = to wrap up; cf. 小鼓 (こつづみ) kotsuzumi = a small hand drum, spelled kotsudumi in electronic dictionaries

Ku 区 = a ward or district; *<u>Ku</u>wait is divided into areas or <u>districts</u>*; cf. similar terms listed at ken

Ku 句 = a phrase or haiku; *some <u>phrases</u> found in <u>haiku</u> are <u>cool</u>*; cf. related terms listed at shi

Kubi 首 = a neck; *he stuck his <u>neck</u> out over the top of his <u>cubicle</u>*

Kubi 首 = dismissal, firing from a job; from kubi wo kiru = to cut the neck; cf. related terms listed at kaiko

Kubitsuri 首吊り = hanging by the neck; from kubi = neck + tsurusu = to hang up

Kuchi 口 = mouth; *his <u>mouth</u> was full of <u>Kool-Aid</u> and <u>cheese</u>*

Kuchi ni suru 口にする = to taste, eat, speak of; literally "to do to the mouth"; cf. ajiwau = to taste, savor, relish; cf. mimi ni suru = to hear

Kuchi wo kiku 口を利く = to speak; from kuchi = mouth + kiku = to be effective; cf. related terms listed at hanasu

Kuchiatari 口当たり = taste; from kuchi = mouth + atari = a hit or success; cf. related terms listed at aji

Kuchibashi くちばし = beak, bill; *the part of a woodpecker's kuchi (mouth) that it uses for bashing holes in trees is called its beak*

Kuchibiru 唇 = the lips; *when using my kuchi (mouth) to drink biiru (beer) from a broken bottle, I cut my lip*

Kuchibue 口笛 = whistling; from kuchi = mouth + bue = fue = a whistle

Kuchihige 口ひげ = a mustache; from kuchi = a mouth + hige = a beard

Kuchikomi 口コミ = word of mouth; from kuchi = mouth + komyunikeeshon = communication

Kuchiku 駆逐 = expulsion; *in Kuwait, selling cheap Kool-Aid is grounds for expulsion*; cf. related terms listed at tsuihou

Kuchiru 朽ちる = to rot or decay; *the Kuwaiti cheese was ruined when it rotted*; cf. fuhai suru = to decay or rot

Kuchizuke 口づけ (spelled kuchiduke in electronic dictionaries) = a kiss; from kuchi = mouth + tsukeru = to attach

Kuchou 口調 = tone of voice, verbal expression; from kuchi = mouth + choushi = condition

Kuda 管 = tube, pipe; *my cool dad is a plumber and fixes pipes*; cf. gesuikan = a sewer pipe; cf. kan = a pipe or tube

Kudakeru 砕ける = to be broken or smashed; the intransitive form of kudaku = to break; cf. related terms listed at yabureru

Kudaku 砕く = to break or smash; *my cool Dad went to Kuwait to smash stones*; cf. related terms listed at kowasu

Kudamono 果物 = fruit; *my cool dad has a monotonous diet of fruit*; cf. budou = grapes; cf. kajitsu = fruit; cf. kaki = a persimmon; cf. kinomi = nut, fruit, berry; cf. kiui = kiwi fruit; cf. mi = fruit or nut; cf. mikan = a mandarin orange; cf. momo = a peach; cf. nashi = pear tree, or a pear; cf. ringo = an apple; cf. ume = a plum

Kudaranai 下らない = ridiculous, stupid, worthless, petty; *since he kudaranai (doesn't descend) from that tree, he seems ridiculous*

Kudarisen 下り線 = the down line or the outbound line; from kudaru = to descend + sen = line

Kudarizaka 下り坂 = a downward slope; from kudaru = to go down + saka = hill; cf. related terms listed at shamen

Kudaru 下る = to descend; *the Kuwaiti damsel wore rubies when she descended the staircase*; cf. related terms listed at oriru

Kudasai 下さい = please; the imperative form of kudasaru = to give to me; cf. choudai = please, used to address children; cf. kure = please (used in less polite situations)

Kudasaru 下さる = to give to someone in the speaker's in-group, by someone outside the group who has equal or greater age or status; *when the Kuwaiti damsel saw my roommate's predicament, she gave her some money*; cf. related terms listed at ataeru

Kudasu 下す = to hand down (orders), to lower, to do by oneself; an abbreviation of kudasaru = to give

Kufuu 工夫 = ingenuity; *it was a cooler full of food, packed with considerable ingenuity*

Kufuu suru 工夫する = to work hard to find a solution; from kufuu = ingenuity

Kugi 釘 = a nail or peg; *I used nails to build a shed for my cool geese*

Kugizuke ni naru 釘付けになる = to be unable to take one's eyes from; from kugi = nail + tsuku = to adhere + ni naru = to become

Kuguru くぐる = to go under, pass through; *that cool guru can pass through concrete barriers*; cf. related terms listed at tooru

Kui 悔い = regret; *he has cool ears, but he felt regret after he had them pierced*; cf. related terms listed at koukai

Kuitomeru 食い止める = to hold back or check; from kuu = to eat + tomeru = to stop; cf. related terms listed at yameru

Kuji くじ = a lottery; *I won a cool Jeep in the lottery*; cf. related terms listed at takarakuji

Kujikeru 挫ける = to lose heart, be dispirited; *the cool jeans that Kennedy ruined were his favorite pants, and he lost heart*; cf. related terms listed at me'iru

Kujira 鯨 = a whale, usually spelled くじら; *the Kuwaiti genius ran a whale-watching business*; cf. related terms listed at sakana

Kujou 苦情 = a complaint; *although it was cool, Job had complaints about the heat*; cf. butsubutsu = grunt, grumble, complaint; cf. fufuku = dissatisfaction, complaint; cf. gamigami = nagging, griping; cf. guchi = a complaint; cf. kougi = a protest; cf. monku = a complaint

Kujou wo iu 苦情を言う = to complain; from kujou = a complaint + iu = to say; cf. boyaku = to grumble or complain

Kukaku 区画 = a sector, block or division; *if you want to see cool cars in Kuwait, visit that sector*

Kuki 茎 = a stalk or stem; *my cookie has a plant stem in it*

Kukkiri くっきり = clearly; *my cool kitty clearly enjoys attention*; cf. hakkiri = clearly

Kukuru 括る = to bind or bundle; *the hotel had bundled some cool Kuwaiti rooms together, and we rented them for our stay*; cf. matomeru = to conclude or settle, bundle together, compile, summarize

Kuma 熊 = a bear; *I saw a bear at a Kuwaiti mall*

Kumade 熊手 = a rake or fork; from kuma = bear + de = te = hand (or paw)

Kumi 組 = group, team, school class; *my class drinks Kool-Aid with its meals*; cf. related terms listed at dantai

Kumiawaseru 組み合わせる = to match; from kumu = to partner with + awaseru = to combine or harmonize

Kumitate 組み立て = construction, assembly; from kumitateru = to assemble or build; cf. related terms listed at kensetsu

Kumitateru 組み立てる = to assemble or build; from kumu = to assemble + tateru = to build or put upright; cf. related terms listed at tateru

Kumo クモ = a spider; *the Kool-Aid that Moses drank had a spider in it*; cf. related terms listed at mushi

Kumo 雲 = a cloud; *Governor Cuomo saw a cloud hanging over his political future*

Kumoru 曇る = to become cloudy, to be in a gloomy mood; *Governor Cuomo heard a rumor that it would become cloudy the next day*

Kumu くむ = to ladle or scoop water; *in that cool movie the actors scooped water*; cf. sukuu = to scoop up or ladle

Kumu 組む = to fold arms or cross legs, to assemble, to make a plan, to partner with; *under a cool moon, we assembled, folded our arms and made a plan*; cf. related terms listed at tateru

Kun 君 = a suffix used after the names of young people, friend or colleagues (instead of -san or -sama); *my young friend is cunning*

Kuni 国 = a country (or province); *there are cunning people in that country*; cf. gaikoku = a foreign country; cf. kakkoku = each country; cf. kokka = nation, country; cf. koku = a country; cf. nangoku = southern countries; cf. ryoukoku = both countries; cf. shokoku = various countries; cf. taikoku = a big country; cf. takoku = a foreign country, another country; cf. other related terms listed at sokoku

Kunou 苦悩する = agony, anguish, suffering; when <u>Kool</u>-Aid went up my <u>nose</u>, I was in <u>agony</u>; cf. related terms listed at itami

Kunren 訓練 = training; the <u>cunning rent</u> collector came while the soldier was in <u>training</u>; cf. ikusei = training; cf. keiko = rehearsal, practice, training; cf. kenshuu = training; cf. kintore = muscle training; cf. mourenshuu = hard training; cf. renshuu = practice, exercise, drill; cf. shugyou = training, apprenticeship; cf. tanren = training, tempering, forging, hardening, disciplining; cf. tokkun = intensive training; cf. toreeningu = training

Kunrensei 訓練性 = trainability; from kunren = training + sei = nature

Kunrin 君臨 = reigning; the <u>cunning ringleader</u> wanted to start <u>reigning</u> over the country

Kunsei 薫製 = smoked food; the <u>cunning sailor</u> brought plenty of <u>smoked food</u>; cf. related terms listed at tabemono

Kunshou 勲章 = a medal or decoration; the <u>cunning Shougun</u> gave out a lot of <u>medals</u>

Kuppuku suru 屈服する = to surrender; the <u>cooped</u>-up <u>ukulele</u> players were forced to <u>surrender</u>; cf. related terms listed at koufuku suru

Kura 蔵 = a storehouse; I keep <u>kuuraas</u> (coolers, or air-conditioners) in my <u>storehouse</u>; cf. related terms listed at souko

Kuraberu 比べる = to compare; the <u>kuuraa</u> (air-conditioner) looks <u>better</u> on the <u>roof</u>, <u>compared</u> to installing it on the ground; cf. taihi suru = to compare, contrast

Kuragari 暗がり = darkness; that <u>Kuwaiti rabbit</u> helps <u>Garry</u> stave off the <u>darkness</u>; cf. related terms listed at yami

Kurai (or -gurai) くらい = about, approximately, almost, something like, used as a suffix; this tastes <u>approximately</u> like <u>Kuwaiti rice</u>; cf. related terms listed at yaku

Kurai 位 = rank; due to his <u>rank</u>, he can eat <u>Kuwaiti rice</u> every day; cf. chi'i = rank, status, position; cf. -i = rank or place, used as a suffix; cf. joui = high rank; cf. kaikyuu = class, rank, caste; cf. mibun = social status or position

Kurai 暗い = dark, gloomy, depressing; I store <u>Kuwaiti rice</u> in a <u>dark</u> cupboard; cf. related terms listed at makkura

Kuramu 眩む = to be blinded or dazzled; the <u>curator</u> of the <u>moon</u> rocks was <u>dazzled</u> by the amount of money that he was offered for them

Kurashi 暮らし = living, life; from kurasu = to live or make a living; cf. related terms listed at inochi

Kurashimuki 暮らし向き = life direction; from kurashi = life + muki = direction; cf. related terms listed at houkou

Kurasu 暮らす = to live or make a living; I <u>make</u> a <u>living</u> by teaching <u>kurasu</u> (classes); cf. related terms listed at ikiru

Kurau 食らう = to receive (a blow), to eat or drink; in <u>Kuwait</u>, <u>Raul Castro ate</u> too much and <u>received</u> a blow as a result; cf. related terms listed at taberu

Kurayami 暗闇 = darkness; from kurai = dark + yami = darkness; cf. related terms listed at yami

Kure くれ = please; the imperative form of kureru = to give to a member of the speaker's in-group; cf. related terms listed at kudasai

Kure 暮れ = year-end, nightfall; at <u>nightfall</u>, we went to a <u>Kuwaiti restaurant</u>; cf. higure = nightfall, dusk

Kureru くれる = to give to a member of the speaker's in-group, by someone in the group or by someone outside the group who has equal or inferior status; *my daughter gave me a cool red rooster*; cf. related terms listed at ataeru

Kurihirogeru 繰り広げる = to unfold, to open; from kurikaesu = to repeat + hirogeru = to unfold; cf. aku = to open or start (intransitive), to come to an end

Kurikaesu 繰り返す = to repeat, to do something over again; *when he gives me curry, I kaesu (give it back), and then we repeat this behavior*

Kuro 黒 = black; the noun form of kuroi = black

Kuroi 黒い = black; *in Kuwait, Roy Rogers wore a black hat*

Kuroji 黒字 = being in the black (i.e., making a profit); from kuroi = black + ji = character

Kuromitsu 黒蜜 = brown sugar syrup; from kuroi = black + mitsu = honey, e.g., hachimitsu = honey

Kurou 苦労 = hardship; *they are cool robots, but they are taking away jobs and causing hardship*; cf. related terms listed at meiwaku

Kurouto 玄人 = an expert or professional; *that cool rototiller must be handled by a professional*; cf. kyoshou = a master or a preeminent person; cf. shirouto = an amateur; cf. tatsujin = expert, master; cf. senmonka = a specialist or expert

Kuru 来る = to come; *he came to buy a Kuwaiti ruby*; cf. irassharu = to come, go or exist honorably; cf. mairu = to come or go humbly

Kuruma 車 = a car; *in Kuwait they have room at the malls for cars*; cf. chuukosha = a used car; cf. jidousha = a car; cf. kogatasha = a compact car; cf. kuusha = a free (available) taxi; cf. shinsha = a new car

Kurushii 苦しい = difficult, painful; *when Madam Curie rushed the Shiites, she sustained a painful injury*; cf. tsurai = painful; cf. other related terms listed at muzukashii

Kurushimi 苦しみ = suffering, pain, hardship; from kurushimu = to suffer; cf. related terms listed at itami and at meiwaku

Kurushimu 苦しむ = to suffer, to be worried; *after our Kool-Aid was ruined by sheepish Moonies, we suffered and worried*; cf. related terms listed at shinpai suru

Kurushisa 苦しさ = pain, suffering; from kurushii = painful + sa, a suffix that makes a noun from another word; cf. related terms listed at itami

Kuruu 狂う = to go mad; *the Kuwaiti rooster went mad*; cf. ki ga kuruu = to go crazy

Kusa 草 = grass; *the cool saxophone players played on the grass*

Kusabana 草花 = flowering plants, flower; from kusa = grass + bana = hana = flowers; cf. related terms listed at hana and at shokubutsu

Kusai 臭い = smelly, stinking, suspicious; *the cub scout sighed as he approached the smelly outhouse*; cf. hana wo tsuku = to be smelly or stink

Kusaki 草木 = plants, vegetation; from kusa = grass + ki = a tree; cf. related terms listed at shokubutsu

Kusari 鎖 = a chain; *I like to wear a chain with my cool sari*

Kusaru 腐る = to rot, spoil, be corrupted; *I started to eat a cool salad with rhubarb, but it was spoiled*

Kuse 癖 = a habit or characteristic; *the Kool-Aid seller has a habit of drinking Kool-Aid*; cf. tokuchou = a characteristic or special feature; cf. tokushuu = a feature or special edition; cf. other related terms listed at shuukan

Kuse ni くせに = and yet, in spite of; *in spite of the fact that the Kool-Aid seller stabilized it on his knee, the glass spilled*

Kushami くしゃみ = a sneeze; *in Kuwait, the Shah asked about the meaning of his sneezes*

Kushi 串 = a skewer; *in my cushy job, I insert skewers into vegetables*

Kushi くし = a comb; *someone should use a comb on that cool sheepdog*

Kussuru 屈する = to bend or yield to; *the cooped-up Superman ruined our cause when he yielded to the demands of our opponents*; cf. kagameru = to bend or stoop; cf. other related terms listed at koufuku suru

Kusuri 薬 = medicine, pill, drug, ointment, a good lesson; *in Kuwait you can surely get some medicine*; cf. chintsuuzai = a pain medicine; cf. chiryouhou = a remedy or cure

Kusuriya 薬屋 = a pharmacy; from kussuri = medicine + ya = store; cf. yakkyoku = a pharmacy

Kutakuta くたくた = exhausted, mushy; *after looking at cool tapestries all day and then drinking Kool-Aid in a tavern, I was exhausted*; cf. tsukareta = tired

Kutouten 句読点 = punctuation marks; *kooky Tolstoy tended to use too many punctuation marks*

Kutsu 靴 = a shoe; *those shoes were so tight that they cut Superman's feet*; cf. geta = Japanese clogs; cf. kawagutsu = a leather shoe; cf. zouri = Japanese sandals

Kutsugaeru 覆る = to be overturned; the intransitive form of kutsugaesu = to overturn; cf. tenpuku suru = to capsize or overturn (intransitive)

Kutsugaesu 覆す = to overturn or overthrow; *when a king cut Superman's guy's suit, Superman tried to overthrow him*; cf. hikkurikaesu = to turn over, to knock over; cf. kaesu = to return something, to overturn or retaliate

Kutsujoku 屈辱 = humiliation, disgrace; *he cut Superman and made a joke about it, which led to his disgrace*

Kutsurogi くつろぎ = ease, relaxation, comfort; *take off your kutsu (shoes), roll up your gear, and enjoy some relaxation*; cf. related terms listed at kokochiyosa

Kutsurogu くつろぐ = to relax or make oneself at home; *I take off my kutsu (shoes) and roll around with my goose when I want to relax*; cf. hotto suru = to relax or feel relief; cf. kanwa suru = to relax or alleviate; cf. nagomu = to be softened, to calm down; cf. ochitsuku = to relax or be settled; cf. shizumaru = to become calm or quiet

Kutsushita 靴下 = socks; from kutsu = shoes + shita = below; cf. shirotabi = white Japanese socks; cf. tabi = Japanese socks with a separate compartment for the big toe

Kutsuu 苦痛 = pain, agony; *after they cut Superman, he was in agony*; cf. related terms listed at itami

Kutsuzoko 靴底 = the sole of a shoe; from kutsu = shoe + zoko = soko = bottom

Kuttsuku くっつく = to adhere to, keep close to; from kutsu = shoe + tsuku = to adhere; cf. haritsuku = to cling to; cf. shigamitsuku = to cling; cf. tsuku = to adhere to, to be added, to come along with, to be connected

Kuu 食う = to eat (rough speech); *she eats cookies*; cf. related terms listed at taberu

Kuuchuu 空中 = mid-air; from kuu = sky, e.g., kuukou = airport; + chuu = inside; cf. joukuu = the sky, upper air

Kuufuku 空腹 = hunger; *the Kool-Aid pitcher in Fukuoka was empty, which worsened our hunger*; cf. related terms listed at ue

Kuukan 空間 = a space; *the Kool-Aid and candies belong in this space*; cf. kuuran = a blank space; cf. okiba = a storage space; cf. yochi = room or space

Kuuki 空気 = air or atmosphere; *that kooky guy is trying to fly in the air*; cf. kiken = atmosphere; cf. taiki = air, atmosphere; cf. taikiken = the atmosphere

Kuuki ga yomeru 空気が読める = to be able to read the air, i.e., to be able to assess the situation; from kuuki = air + yomeru = to be able to read

Kuukou 空港 = an airport; *I shared my Kool-Aid with my co-worker at the airport*

Kuuran 空欄 = a blank space; from kuukan = space; + ran = a column; cf. related terms listed at kuukan

Kuusha 空車 = a free (available) taxi; *the kooky Shah got into a free taxi*; cf. related terms listed at kuruma

Kuuso na 空疎な = insubstantial, vain, futile; *the Kuwaiti soldier's efforts to escape were futile*

Kuwadateru 企てる = to attempt or plot; *when she attempted to water a hanging plant, the cool water that my daughter used fell onto the television and ruined it*; cf. related terms listed at tamesu

Kuwaeru 加える = to add or include; *when they visit Kuwait, erudite people include the library in their itineraries*; cf. tsukekuwaeru = to add; cf. fukumu = to contain or include; cf. tasu = to add (numbers)

Kuwashii 詳しい = detailed, fully explained, versed, knowledgeable; *the cool washing machine featured a detailed painting on its front panel*; cf. related terms listed at menmitsu

Kuwawaru 加わる = to be added to, to participate, to join in; the intransitive form of kuwaeru = to add or include; cf. nakamairi suru = to join a group; cf. sanka suru = to participate; cf. shutsujou suru = to appear (e.g., on a stage), to participate (e.g., in a tournament)

Kuyakusho 区役所 = a ward office; from ku = a ward or district + yaku = service + sho = place; cf. shiyakusho = city hall

Kuyamu 悔やむ = to regret, repent; *I gave Kool-Aid to the yaks to improve their mood, but now I regret doing so*

Kuyashii 悔しい = vexing, mortifying; *the cure of the yak was done by Shiites, which was mortifying to the Sunnis*

Kuzu 葛 = arrowroot (known as kudzu in English); *arrowroot grows inside the Kuwaiti zoo*

Kuzumochi 葛餅 = a Japanese jelly-like dessert made with kuzu and resembling mochi; from kuzu = arrowroot + mochi = Japanese rice cake; cf. related terms listed at ryouri

Kuzureochiru 崩れ落ちる = to tumble down, to fall in; from kuzureru = to collapse + ochiru = to fall; cf. related terms listed at ochiru

Kuzureru 崩れる = to collapse, be destroyed, lose shape; *the cool zucchinis were attacked by a red rooster, and they collapsed*; cf. kuzureochiru = to tumble down, to fall in

Kuzusu 崩す = to dismantle, pull down or destroy, to throw off balance, to change money; *the cool zucchinis that Superman grew were destroyed by rats*; cf. torihazusu = to dismantle, detach or take something away; cf. other related terms listed at horobosu

Kyacchi suru キャッチする = to catch

Kyakkan 客観 = object (vs. subject); *the object I saw in the water was a kayak from Canada*; cf. related terms listed at shugo

Kyakkanteki 客観的 = objective; from kyakkan = object + teki = related to

Kyaku 客 = a customer or guest; *the guest is a kayaker who loves Kool-Aid*; cf. jouren = a regular customer; cf. okyakusama = very honorable customer; cf. raihin = a guest or visitor; cf. raikyaku = a visitor or caller; cf. riyoukyaku = a using customer

Kyakuhon 脚本 = a script or screenplay; *the kayaker was in Honduras when she write her script*

Kyakuhonka 脚本家 = a scriptwriter; from kyakuhon = a script + ka = a person

Kyakuma 客間 = parlor, drawing room; *the kayaker and his ma (mother) are in the parlor*; cf. related terms listed at -shitsu

Kyodai 巨大 = huge; *the Kyoto diet club is huge*; cf. kyoudai = siblings; cf. related terms listed at ookii

Kyogi 虚偽 = a deception or lie; *in Kyoto the geek told a lie*; cf. kyougi = a discusson; cf. related terms listed at uso

Kyohi 拒否 = rejection, refusal; *I received a rejection from the Kyoto healer*; cf. hitei = a rejection or denial

Kyojin 巨人 = a giant; *the Kyoto gingerbread man is a giant*

Kyoka 許可 = permission, approval; *I have permission to drive a Kyoto car*; cf. shoudaku = compliance, approval, consent; cf. shounin = approval, recognition, sanction; cf. zenin = approval

Kyoku 局 = a bureau or office; *the Kyoto Kool-Aid Club was started by employees of a bureau*; cf. kaisha = a company, corporation or office; cf. kanchou = a government office; cf. honsha = a head or main office; cf. shibu = a subdivision or branch office; cf. shikyoku = a branch office; cf. shisha = a branch office; cf. shiten = a branch office or store; cf. soudanjo = a consultation office or bureau

Kyoku 曲 = a musical composition, a song; *I wrote a song about the Kyoto Kool-Aid Club*; cf. related terms listed at uta

Kyokuchi 局地 = a locality or limited area; *the Kyoto Kool-Aid Club serves cheese in that locality*; cf. related terms listed at basho

Kyokuchiteki 局地的 = local; from kyokuchi = a locality + teki = related to; cf. jimoto = local, hometown

Kyokuryoku 極力 = as much as possible, to the best of one's ability; *after drinking Kyoto Kool-Aid, Pope Leo bakes cookies to the best of his ability*; cf. related terms listed at narubeku

Kyonen 去年 = last year; *Kyoto welcomed my negative nephew last year*; cf. kyuunen = last year; cf. sakunen = last year; cf. zennen = the previous year

Kyori 距離 = distance; *the Kyoto soldiers retreated some distance*

Kyorokyoro きょろきょろ = looking around restlessly; *the Kyoto rogues looked around restlessly*

Kyosei 去勢 = castration; *in Kyoto the sailor was sentenced to castration*

Kyoshou 巨匠 = a master or a preeminent person; *the master went to Kyoto to show his work*; cf. related terms listed at kurouto

Kyoten 拠点 = position, location, base, point; *the Kyoto tennis club is at this location*; cf. related terms listed at kichi and at basho

Kyou 今日 = today; *today we're going to Kyouto*; cf. honjitsu = today, this day

Kyouaku 凶悪 = brutal, inhuman; *I thought that my Kyouto acupuncturist was brutal for inserting so many needles*; cf. related terms listed at ranbou

Kyouakusei 凶悪性 = atrocity, heinous nature; from kyouaku = brutal + sei = nature

Kyouchou suru 強調する = to emphasize; *in Kyouto, he chose to emphasize his love of Japanese food*; cf. related terms listed at tsuyomeru

Kyouchuu 胸中 = one's heart, mind or intentions; *in Kyouto, I chewed my food while I asked about her intentions*; cf. related terms listed at kokoro and at seishin

Kyoudai 兄弟 = brothers and sisters; *my brothers and sisters are on a Kyouto diet*; cf. ane = older sister; cf. ani = older brother; cf. imouto = younger sister; cf. oneesan = older sister; cf. oniisan = older brother; cf. otouto = younger brother

Kyoudan 教壇 = a podium or platform; *in Kyouto the dancers stood on a platform*; cf. related terms listed at dai

Kyoudou 協同 = cooperation, sharing; *in Kyouto, dough (money) can buy cooperation*; cf. icchi = agreement, coincidence, conformity, cooperation; cf. kyouryoku = cooperation

Kyoudou no 共同の = cooperative, communal; from kyoudou = cooperation, sharing; cf. koukyou = public or communal

Kyoufu 恐怖 = fear, dread, horror; *in Kyouto I met a fool who filled me with dread*; cf. related terms listed at osore

Kyoufushou 恐怖症 = morbid fear, phobia; from kyoufu = dread + shoujou = symptoms; cf. related terms listed at osore

Kyoufuu 強風 = a strong wind; from kyou = strong, e.g., saikyou = the strongest; + fuu = wind, e.g., taifuu = a typhoon; cf. related terms listed at kaze

Kyougi 協議 = discussion, conference; *we had a discussion about Kyouto geese*; cf. kyogi = a lie; cf. related terms listed at rikutsu

Kyougi 競技 = athletic competition; *in Kyouto, I carried my guitar during an athletic competition*; cf. related terms listed at issen

Kyouguu 境遇 = circumstances, environment; *in Kyouto, the goose enjoyed good circumstances*; cf. kankyou = environment; cf. other related terms listed at jitai

Kyouhaku 脅迫 = threat, blackmail; *in Kyouto I sold Hawaiian Kool-Aid, and I received threats from cola sellers*; cf. kyoui = a threat, peril, menace; cf. kyoukatsu = blackmail or extortion; cf. odokashi = a threat

Kyouhon 教本 = a textbook; from kyouiku = education + hon = a book; cf. related terms listed at kyoukasho

Kyoui 脅威 = a threat, peril, menace; *some Kyouto eagles are a menace*; cf. kyouhaku = threat, blackmail

Kyoui 驚異 = miracle, marvel; *in Kyouto, the eagles are a marvel*; cf. kiseki = miracle, marvel, wonder

Kyouiku 教育 = education; *in Kyouto I came down with ear cooties as I pursued my education*; cf. keihatsu = education, edification, inspiration, public awareness; cf. kyouyou = education, learning

Kyouiteki 驚異的 = marvelous, miraculous; from kyoui = marvel, miracle + teki = related to; cf. related terms listed at idai

Kyoujin 狂人 = a lunatic; from kyouki = lunacy + jin = a person

Kyouju 教授 = a professor; *the professor served on a Kyouto jury*; cf. related terms listed at sensei

Kyouju suru 享受する = to enjoy; *the Kyouto jeweler enjoyed making bracelets*; cf. tanoshimu = to enjoy

Kyoujuu ni 今日中に = by the end of today; from kyou = today + juu = throughout + ni = at

Kyouka suru 強化する = to strengthen, fortify; *in Kyouto, calcium tablets are fortified with Vitamin D*; cf. related terms listed at tsuyomeru

Kyoukai 協会 = association, organization; from kyouryoku = cooperation + kaisha = company; cf. kessei = an organization or formation; cf. soshiki = an organization

Kyoukai 教会 = a church; *in Kyouto, the Kaiser visited a church*

Kyoukan 共感 = sympathy; *in Kyouto, if you have cancer, you get sympathy*; cf. related terms listed at doujou

Kyoukasho 教科書 = a textbook; *I read my textbook during the Kyoto car show*; cf. kyouhon = a textbook; tekisuto = a textbook

Kyoukatsu 恐喝 = blackmail or extortion; *due to extortion, I had to hand over my Kyouto cats*; cf. kyouhaku = threat, blackmail

Kyouki 凶器 = a lethal weapon; *in Kyouto, a king was attacked with a lethal weapon*; cf. related terms listed at buki

Kyouki 狂気 = lunacy, madness; *during a bout of madness, he wandered around Kyouto in a kimono*

Kyoukoku 峡谷 = a canyon or ravine; *in Kyouto we bought Coke to take to the canyon*; cf. related terms listed at tani

Kyoukou na 強硬な = firm, stable; *the cities of Kyouto and Kobe enjoy a firm and stable friendship*

Kyoukun 教訓 = moral, teaching, lesson; *in Kyouto, my cunning teacher taught me a lesson*; cf. related terms listed at jugyou

Kyoukyuu 供給 = supply or provision; *in Kyouto, they store cucumbers as a provision for the winter*; cf. nounyuu = payment of taxes, etc, supply (of goods, etc.), delivery

Kyoukyuu suru 供給する = to supply or provide; from kyoukyuu = supply or provision; cf. hokyuu suru = to supply or supplement; cf. shikyuu suru = to supply or provide; cf. sonaetsukuru = to provide, equip or install; cf. teikyou suru = to offer, provide or sponsor

Kyoumi 興味 = interest; *I have an interest in Kyouto meat*; cf. kanshin = concern, interest

Kyoumi shinshin 興味津々 = very interesting; from kyoumi = interest + shinshin = flowing; cf. related terms listed at omoshiroi

Kyoumibukai 興味深い = very interesting; from kyoumi = interest + bukai = fukai = deep; cf. related terms listed at omoshiroi

Kyouraku 享楽 = pleasure; from kyouju suru = to enjoy + raku = pleasure; cf. related terms listed at shiawase

Kyouretsu na 強烈な = intense, powerful; from kyouryoku = powerful + mouretsu = fervent; cf. related terms listed at tsuyoi

Kyouri 郷里 = hometown; *is Kyouto really your hometown?* cf. related terms listed at furusato

Kyouryoku 協力 = cooperation; *when I do Kyouto ryokou [travel] to a cool temple, I need cooperation from a taxi driver*; cf. icchi = agreement, coincidence, conformity, cooperation; cf. kyoudou = cooperation, sharing

Kyouryoku na 強力な = powerful; *in Kyouto, Pope Leo made Kool-Aid for his powerful friends*; cf. related terms listed at tsuyoi

Kyouryoku suru 協力する = to cooperate; from kyouryoku = cooperation

Kyouryuu 恐竜 = a dinosaur; *at the Kyouto reunion, I discussed my dinosaur research*

Kyousan 共産 = communism; from kyoudou no = cooperative or communal + seisan = production; cf. kyousanshugi = communism

Kyousanshugi 共産主義 = communism; from kyousan = communism + shugi = a doctrine; cf. shihonshugi = capitalism

Kyousei 矯正 = a correction; *the city of Kyouto employs a sage to make corrections to its ordinances*; cf. teisei = a correction

Kyousei suru 矯正する = to correct; from kyousei = a correction; cf. related terms listed at shuuri suru

Kyoushi 教師 = teacher (classroom); *the Kyouto sheep farmer became a teacher*; cf. related terms listed at sensei

Kyoushinshou 狭心症 = angina (pain due to narrowing of the heart arteries), heart attack; from kyoushou = narrow + shin = heart + shoujou = symptoms; cf. shinkin kousoku = a heart attack or myocardial infarction; cf. shinzou hossa = heart attack

Kyoushitsu 教室 = a classroom; from kyouiku = education + shitsu = room; cf. related terms listed at -shitsu

Kyoushoku 教職 = the teaching profession; from kyoushitsu = classroom + shokugyou = occupation

Kyoushou 狭小 = cramped, narrow, confined; *in Kyouto, they showed me a cramped apartment*; cf. related terms listed at semai

Kyoushuku 恐縮 = gratitude or embarrassment; *after my Kyouto friends gave me shoes from Kuwait, I felt gratitude and embarrassment*; cf. touwaku = embarrassment, bewilderment; cf. other related terms listed at kansha

Kyoushuu 郷愁 = nostalgia, homesickness; *I feel homesickness when I look at these Kyouto shoes*; cf. satogokoro = homesickness, nostalgia

Kyousou 競争 = competition; *in Kyouto, soldiers engage in competition*; cf. related terms listed at issen

Kyousoukyoku 協奏曲 = a concerto; from kyoudou = cooperation + ensou = a musical performance + kyoku = a song

Kyoutei 協定 = a pact or agreement; *the Kyouto tailor had an agreement to make a suit*; cf. related terms listed at shouchi

Kyouto 教徒 = adherent (of a religion); *the adherents met in Kyouto*; cf. fushinsha = a person who doesn't believe, an unbeliever

Kyoutsuu no 共通の = common, mutual; *in Kyouto, everyone wears nice tsuits (suits) by mutual consent*; cf. related terms listed at tagai

Kyouyou 共用 = common use; *in Kyouto, yoga studios are in common use*

Kyouyou 教養 = education, learning; *I came to Kyouto to study with a yogi and complete my education*; cf. related terms listed at chishiki and at kyouiku

Kyuu 急 = urgent, sudden, unexpected, steep; *my trip to Cuba was urgent and sudden*; cf. related terms listed at ikinari

Kyuu 球 = a ball; *this ball is from Cuba*

Kyuu 級 = class, level, grade; *those cute girls are middle class*; cf. bumon = category, class, section; cf. kaikyuu = class, rank, caste; cf. saidaikyuu = the largest class or top category; cf. sou = a layer, stratum, social class, story (of a building); cf. toukyuu = grade, ranking

Kyuu 旧 = old times, used as a prefix; *I remember the old times in Cuba*; cf. related terms listed at mukashi

Kyuu ni 急に = swiftly, suddenly, immediately; from kyuu = urgent, sudden, unexpected + -ni = a suffix that forms an adverb; cf. battari = with a thud, unexpectedly, suddenly; cf. futo = accidentally, suddenly, casually; cf. ichiyaku = suddenly, overnight; cf. isshun de = in an instant; cf. nukiuchi = drawing a sword and striking in the same stroke, suddenly, without warning; cf. sassoku = immediately, at once, sudden; cf. satto quickly (actions) or suddenly (esp. rain and wind); cf. other related terms listed at sokkoku

Kyuuai 求愛 = courting; *the cute ice cream salesman was courting me*

Kyuuban 吸盤 = suction cup, sucker; *the Cuban used a suction cup to attach a cross* to his windshield

Kyuuchi 窮地 = plight, adversity, dilemma; *the Cuban cheese company faced adversity*

Kyuuchi ni tatasu 窮地に立たす = to get into trouble; from kyuuchi = adversity + tatasu = to raise or rouse

Kyuuden 宮殿 = palace; *the cute dentist lives in a palace*; cf. koukyo = the Imperial Palace; cf. miya = a palace or shrine; cf. oukyuu = a royal palace; cf. rikyuu = an imperial villa

Kyuudou 弓道 = archery; *in Cuba, there is a domed building devoted to archery*

Kyuuen 救援 = rescue; *a Cuban engineer was responsible for my rescue*; cf. related terms listed at kyuujo

Kyuugeki 急激 = abrupt or rapid; from kyuu = sudden + geki = intense; cf. related terms listed at ikinari

Kyuujitsu 休日 = a holiday or day off; *in Cuba, the jittery superstar enjoyed a holiday*; cf. related terms listed at yasumi

Kyuujo 救助 = rescue or relief; *a Cuban joke is to fall down and call for rescue*; cf. hosa = aid, help; cf. kyuuen = rescue; cf. kyuusai = help, rescue, relief; cf. sukui = help, hope; cf. tasuke = help, support; cf. tetsudai = help or helper

Kyuujou 球場 = a baseball stadium; from yakyuu = baseball + kaijou = venue;

Kyuuka 休暇 = holiday, day off; *I rented a cute car to use during my holiday*; cf. related terms listed at yasumi

Kyuukaku 嗅覚 = sense of smell; *that cute guy named Karl the Kool-Aid vendor has a good sense of smell*

Kyuukangokutou 旧監獄塔 = a former prison tower; from kyuu = former, e.g., kyuunen = last year; + kangoku = prison + tou = tower

Kyuukei 休憩 = a rest or break; *I took a break in a Cuban cave*; cf. related terms listed at yasumi

Kyuuketsusei 吸血性 = blood-sucking; from kyuu = to suck, e.g., kyuuban = a suction cup; + ketsu = blood + sei = nature or personality

Kyuukou 休校 = closing classes temporarily; *since Madame Curie had a cold, her classes were closed temporarily*

Kyuukou 急行 = an express train; *I wore my cute coat on the express train*; cf. related terms listed at densha

Kyuukyuu 救急 = first aid, emergency (aid); *we sent some cucumbers to Cuba as part of an emergency aid package*

Kyuukyuusha 救急車 = ambulance; from kyuukyuu = first aid, emergency (aid) + sha = vehicle

Kyuumon 糾問 = an enquiry; *they conducted an enquiry into the influence of Cuban money in the election*; cf. related terms listed at kensa

Kyuumonteki 糾問的 = inquisitorial; from kyuumon = an enquiry + teki = related to

Kyuunen 旧年 = last year, used in formal writing; from kyuu = old times + nen = year; cf. related terms listed at kyonen

Kyuuryou 給料 = salary or wages; *I use my salary to buy curios*; cf. related terms listed at chin

Kyuusai 救済 = help, rescue, relief; *Cuban scientists have organized a rescue effort*; cf. related terms listed at kyuujo

Kyuusei 旧姓 = maiden name, former name; *Madame Curie would always say that her maiden name was Sklodowska*; cf. related terms listed at namae

Kyuusei no 急性の = acute or sudden; *the Cuban sailor had an acute emergency*; cf. related terms listed at ikinari

Kyuusen 休戦 = a cease-fire or truce; from kyuuka = a holiday + sensou = war

Kyuushamen 急斜面 = steep slope; *in Cuba, the Shah's men climbed a steep slope*; cf. related terms listed at shamen

Kyuushoku suru 求職する = to look for work; from kyuushoku = looking for work; cf. related terms listed at shigoto suru

Kyuushoku 求職 = looking for work; *the Cuban got a shock when he was looking for work*; cf. shuushoku = employment

Kyuushougatsu 旧正月 = lunar New Year, or Chinese New Year; from kyuu = old times + shougatsu = New Year; cf. related terms listed at shougatsu

Kyuushutsu suru 救出する = to rescue or extricate; from kyuusai = help, rescue + shutsu = to put out, e.g., gaishutsu suru = to go out; cf. related terms listed at tasukeru

Kyuushuu suru 吸収する = to absorb or digest; *on Kyuushuu island, I watched a sponge absorb a bowl of water*; cf. shouka suru = to digest; cf. suitoru = to absorb

Kyuusoku 急速 = rapidly, promptly; *the Cuban soldiers drank the Kool-Aid rapidly*; cf. hiyakuteki ni = rapidly; cf. kyuusoku ni = rapidly, promptly; cf. satto = quickly (actions) or suddenly (esp. rain and wind)

Kyuusoku ni 急速に = rapidly, promptly; a variation of kyuusoku = rapidly, promptly; cf. related terms listed at kyuusoku

Kyuuyou 休養 = rest, recuperation, recreation; *the Cuban yogi advised recuperation and rest*; cf. related terms listed at kaifuku and at yasumi

Kyuuyuu 旧友 = old friend; from kyuu = old times + yuujin = friend; cf. related terms listed at tomodachi

Kyuuyuu 級友 = a classmate; *that cute youth is my classmate*; cf. doukyuusei = a classmate

Kyuuzou 急増 = sudden increase; from kyuu = ni = suddenly + zou = to increase, e.g., baizou suru = to double; cf. related terms listed at zouka

Maa まあ = oh, my, well; *well, you've mastered it*

Maaku マーク = a mark, a sign or symbol; cf. related terms listed at kizashi and at shouchou

Maamaa まーまー = so-so, passable; *the guy that Ma married was passable*

Maboroshi 幻 = illusion, vision; *a mariner got into a boat and was rowing some sheep across a lake when he saw a vision*; cf. genkaku = hallucination; cf. gensou = fantasy, illusion

Mabushii 眩しい = dazzling, blinding; *after drinking Massachusetts booze with some Shiites, I went out into the dazzling sun*; cf. hanayaka = dazzling, gorgeous

Mabusu まぶす = to cover or sprinkle with; *the Massachusetts booze that Superman spilled covered the floor*; cf. kakeru = to expend or spend (e.g., time, money, love), to hang (a picture), to make (a call), to multiply, to put on (glasses), to pour or sprinkle onto, to sit down, among many other meanings

Maccha 抹茶 = powdered green tea for ceremonies; from massatsu = erasure, suggesting that most color has been erased from green tea; + cha = tea; cf. related terms listed at cha

Machi 町 = a town, village, block or street; *that town is matching donations for earthquake relief*; cf. related terms listed at shi

Machi 街 = boulevard, avenue, town; *we wore matching outfits on the boulevard*; cf. machi = a town; cf. related terms listed at michi

Machiawase 待ち合わせ = an appointment; machiawaseru = to arrange to meet; cf. related terms listed at yakusoku

Machiawaseru 待ち合わせる = to rendezvous, to arrange to meet; from matsu = to wait + awaseru = to match, join together, combine

Machibuseru 待ち伏せる = to ambush; from matsu = to wait + buseru = fuseru = to lie down; cf. related terms listed at osou

Machidooshi 待ち遠し = eagerly awaited; from matsu = to wait + dooi = tooi = far

Machigaeru 間違える = to make a mistake; from ma = interval, e.g., maniau = to be on time; + chigaeru = to make a mistake; cf. ayamaru = to make a mistake; cf. machigau = to make a mistake; cf. torimachigaeru = to take something by mistake

Machigai 間違い = a mistake; from machigau = to make a mistake; cf. related terms listed at ketten

Machigau 間違う = to make a mistake; from ma = interval, e.g., maniau = to be on time; + chigaeru = to make a mistake; cf. related terms listed at machigaeru

Machijikan 待ち時間 = waiting time; from matsu = to wait + jikan = time; cf. related terms listed at jikan

Machikado 街角 = street corner; from machi = street + kado = corner; cf. related terms listed at kado

Machikaneru 待ち兼ねる = to wait eagerly for (literally, to be unable to wait); from matsu = to wait + kaneru = to be unable to do something; cf. matsu = to await, anticipate

Machinami 街並み = a townscape, the look of houses and stores; from machi = town + narabu = to line up + miru = to see; cf. related terms listed at nagame

Machiokoshi 町興し = a town renewal project; from machi = town + okosu = to revive or raise up

Machiya 町屋 = a townhouse, or a tradesman's house; from machi = a town + ya = a shop; cf. related terms listed at ie

Mada まだ = still, not yet; *the marvelous damsel still hasn't come*; cf. imada = as yet, still, not yet finished; cf. imada ni = even now, still, until this very day; cf. madamada = still more to come, not yet

Madamada まだまだ = still more to come, not yet; from mada = still, not yet; cf. related terms listed at mada

Made まで = until, as far as, up to; *the mad dentist drilled as far as the bone, until I made him stop*

Made ni までに = by, not later than, before; from made = until + ni = at

Mado 窓 = a window; *the magic dolphin jumped out a window*; cf. madoguchi = a ticket window; cf. shasou = a train or car window

Madobe 窓辺 = the window place, next to the window; from mado = window + be = place; *a beggar is standing in that place*

Madoguchi 窓口 = a ticket window; from mado = a window + guchi = kuchi = mouth; cf. related terms listed at mado

Madowasu 惑わす = to delude or seduce; *outside the mado (window) was Superman, trying to delude me*; cf. damasu = to trick, cheat or deceive; cf. uragiru = to betray or deceive

Mae 前 = front, before, ago; *the maestro moved to the house in front of mine a year ago*; cf. related terms listed at saki ni

Mae no 前の = former, facing; from mae = front, before, ago + the possessive no; cf. related terms listed at saki ni

Maeba 前歯 = a front tooth; from mae = front + ha = ba = tooth; cf. related terms listed at mushiba

Maemotte 前もって = in advance; from mae = before + motsu = to have; cf. related terms listed at saki ni

Maemuki 前向き = facing forward, positive; from mae = front + muku = to face toward; cf. kouteiteki = affirmative, positive; cf. sekkyoku = positive, progressive; cf. yousei no = cheerful, positive

Mafuraa マフラー = a muffler or scarf

Magarikado 曲がり角 = a street corner or a bend in the road; from magaru = to turn + kado = corner; cf. related terms listed at kado

Magaru 曲がる = to turn; *I turned around and saw a magazine in the room*; cf. related terms listed at mawaru

Mageru 曲げる = to twist, bend or falsify; *the magician gets the rooster to twist its head around*; cf. related terms listed at tatamu

Magirawashii 紛らわしい = confusing or misleading; *the magical rascal started washing the floor, and that was confusing to the cops*

Mago 孫 = a grandchild; *my grandchild scored a magnificent goal*; cf. magomusuko = a grandson; cf. magomusume = a granddaughter

Magomusuko 孫息子 = a grandson; from mago = grandchild + musuko = son; cf. similar terms listed at mago and at musuko

Magomusume 孫娘 = a granddaughter; from mago = grandchild + musume = daughter; cf. similar terms listed at mago and at musume

Magukappu マグカップ = a mug; from mug + cup

Maguro マグロ = tuna; *the magic goose rode on a tuna*; cf. related terms listed at sakana

Mahou 魔法 = magic, witchcraft; *this magnificent horse was created through magic*

Mahou no 魔法の = magical; from mahou = magic; cf. gensouteki = fantastic, magical

Mai 枚 = a counter for thin, flat items, used as a suffix; *the miser hoarded dollar bills which are thin and flat*

Mai 毎 = each, every; *he visited every mine*

Maiasa 毎朝 = every morning; from mai = every + asa = morning

Maichiru 舞い散る = to dance down (leaves, petals, etc.); from mau = to dance + chiru = to fall or scatter

Maido 毎度 = each time, every time, always; from mai = each, every + do = time (frequency); cf. tabi ni = every time, whenever

Maigetsu 毎月 – see maitsuki

Maigo 迷子 = lost person; *I might go look for that lost person*

Maiko 舞妓 = an apprentice geisha, a dancing girl; *a miner from Kobe met an apprentice geisha*; cf. related terms listed at geisha

Maiku マイク = a microphone

Mainichi 毎日 = every day; from mai = every + nichi = day

Maioriru 舞い降りる = to swoop down on, to alight; from mau = to dance + oriru = to get down from a vehicle; cf. chakuriku suru = to land

Maipeesu マイペース = my pace = doing things one's own way

Mairu 参る = to come or go humbly; *he humbly came a mairu (mile) and then humbly went back*; cf. iku = to go; cf. kuru = to come; cf. irassharu = to come, go or exist honorably

Maisou 埋葬 = burial; *the mighty soldier received a burial*

Maitoshi 毎年 = every year; from mai = each + toshi = year

Maitsuki 毎月 = every month (maigetsu is a

less-common pronunciation); from mai = every + tsuki = month

Maji マジ = serious, an abbreviation of majime = diligent, serious, earnest; cf. genshuku na = solemn or serious; cf. honkaku = serious, genuine, original method or procedure; cf. shinkoku = serious, grave; cf. other related terms listed at majime (na) and at seijitsu

Majieru 交える = to mix (transitive); *she mixed magical erudite expressions into her writing*; cf. related terms listed at mazeru

Majika まじか = proximity, soon, nearby; *a magic car is nearby and will arrive soon*; cf. related terms listed at chikai

Majime (na) 真面目 = sincere, honest, industrious, serious; *the people selling this magic medicine are sincere, honest and industrious*; cf. related terms listed at maji, at seijitsu and at shoujiki

Majiru 混じる, or 交じる, = to be mixed or blended with (intransitive); *the magical roosters were mixed with hens in the cage*

Majiwaru 交わる = to keep company or mingle with, to have a sexual relationship with; cf. tsukiau = to associate with, to keep company

Majo 魔女 = a witch; *in Massachusetts, Jonah met a witch*

Makaseru 任せる = to entrust; *I put the macaroni in the secretary's room and entrusted her with its care*; cf. taku suru = to entrust; cf. yudaneru = to entrust

Makasu 負かす = to defeat; the transitive form of makeru = to lose; cf. taosu = to throw down or knock down, to defeat

Make 負け = a defeat; from makeru = to lose

Makeru 負ける = to lose; *if the mackerels ruin the pond, we will all lose*; cf. yabureru = to lose or be defeated

Maki 薪 = firewood, usually spelled まき; *here is the master key to the firewood shed*

Makijaku 巻尺 = a tape measure; *the length of the mackintosh (raincoat) that Jack wore was measured by Jill, using a tape measure*

Makikomu 巻き込む = to involve or entangle in; *I entangled the Mackintosh (raincoat)-wearing Communist in a plot to overthrow the government*

Makimono 巻物 = a scroll painting; from makikomu = to entangle in + mono = a tangible thing

Makitsukeru 巻きつける = to twine around; from maku = to wind + tsukeru = to attach

Makka 真っ赤 = bright red; from ma = truth, e.g., majime = sincere + akai = red

Makki (or Matsugo) 末期 = the hour of death; *Ma (Mother) praised the king at the hour of his death*; this can also be pronounced "matsugo"; *Matsumoto will go see him at the hour of his death*

Makkura 真っ暗 = pitch dark; from makoto = truth + kurai = dark; cf. insei = negative, gloomy; cf. kurai = dark, gloomy, depressing; cf. koi = dark, thick, strong, dense

Makkuro 真っ黒 = jet black; from makoto = truth + kuroi = black; cf. masshiro = pure white

Makoto 真 = sincerity, truth (this can also be spelled 誠); *when Ma (mother) plays the koto (Japanese harp), I feel her sincerity and truth*; cf. seii = sincerity; cf. seishin = sincerity; cf. other related terms listed at hontou

Makoto ni 真に = really, truly (this can also be spelled 誠に); *to see Ma's koto (Mother's Japanese harp) being played by my niece was truly wonderful*; cf. related terms listed at zehi

Maku 巻く = to roll or wind, to envelope, to move ahead; *the machine in Kuwait was rolling* string *into balls*; cf. makuru = to roll up (e.g., sleeves)

Maku 幕 = theater curtain, act of a play; *we bought a theater curtain at a mall in Kuwait*

Maku 膜 = a membrane or film; *magic cookies can stimulate your membranes*; cf. komaku = an eardrum or tympanic membrane; cf. nenmaku = a mucous membrane

Maku まく = to sow, sprinkle, scatter; *after the farmer got macular degeneration, he could no longer sow his fields*; cf. furikakeru = to sprinkle; cf. ueru = to plant, grow, raise (transitive)

Maku no uchi 幕の内 = literally, between the curtains ("no" is understood); from maku = theater curtain + uchi = inside; this refers to a kind of lunch box originally served during intermissions at sumo matches

Makura まくら = a pillow; this can also be spelled 枕; *a magical Kuwaiti rabbit slept on my pillow*

Makuru まくる = to roll up (e.g., sleeves); *she rolled up her sleeves and drew a map of the Kuwaiti ruins*; cf. maku = to roll or wind

Mama まま = as is; *his mama thinks he's fine as is*

Mama ni ままに = as, wherever; from mama = as is + ni = a suffix that creates an adverb

Mame 豆 = bean; *mad men (i.e., people who work on Madison Ave) love beans*; cf. ingen = beans; cf. ingenmame = green bean, string bean

Mamedeppou 豆鉄砲 = a pea shooter; from mame = beans + deppou = teppou = a gun

Mamonaku まもなく = before long; *the mammoth drank some nasty Kool-Aid, and before long it will get sick*; cf. ima ni mo = soon, at any time; cf. izure = which, soon, someday, in the end; cf. mou = already, before long, another, more; cf. sorosoro = before long, slowly, quietly, gradually; cf. sugu = soon; cf. yagate = before long, soon

Mamorinuku 守り抜く = to hold fast or protect to the end; from mamoru = to protect + nuku = to surpass

Mamoru 守る = to protect, to observe (rules) or keep (promises); *I will keep my promise to protect the bones of the mammoth in that room*; cf. genshu suru = to observe strictly (regulations, etc.); cf. mamorinuku = to hold fast or protect to the end; cf. mimamoru = to watch over, watch attentively

Manabu 学ぶ = to study or learn; *the manager of the booze factory was studying at night*; cf. related terms listed at benkyou suru

Manazashi 眼差し = a look or gaze; *when our manager went to Zambia, some sheep caught his attention, and he directed a look in their direction*; cf. shisen = a gaze

Manbennaku 満遍なく = equally, thoroughly, uniformly, all over; *the man asked Ben to pour nasty Kool-Aid all over his body*

Manchou 満潮 = high tide; *the man chose to surf at high tide*; cf. related terms listed at shio

Mane 真似 = imitation, mimicry; *the man from the Netherlands is selling imitation goods*; cf. mogi = imitation, mock; cf. mohou = imitation; cf. ruijihin = imitation, or similar, article

Mane suru 真似する (an abbreviation of mane wo suru) = to imitate or copy; *I copied a map of the Netherlands*

Maneku 招く = to invite, ask, or beckon; *the mannequin was rather cool when I invited her to the party*; cf. related terms listed at shoutai suru and at tanomu

Manga 漫画 = cartoon; *the man in the*

garden is reading <u>cartoons</u>

Mangaka 漫画か = a cartoonist; from manga = cartoon + ka = a person

Mangekyou 万華鏡 = kaleidoscope; *the* <u>mantel</u> *at the* <u>guesthouse</u> *in* <u>Kyouto</u> *held a* <u>kaleidoscope</u>

Maniau 間に合う = to be on time, to suffice; from ma = interval; *the* <u>magazine</u> *comes out at certain* <u>intervals</u>; + au = match or agree with

Man'ichi (Manichi) 万一 = unlikely event, by some possibility; from man = 10,000 + ichi = one, suggesting odds of 1 in 10,000

Man'in (Manin) 満員 = full house, no vacancy; *the* <u>man</u> *who works at this* <u>inn</u> *says that there is* <u>no vacancy</u>; cf. manseki = full house

Man'in (Manin) onrei 満員御礼 = a banner of thanks for a full house (seen at concerts, tournaments, etc.); from manin = full house + onrei = gratitude

Mankai 満開 = in full bloom; from man = full, e.g., manpuku = a full stomach; + kaika = flowers blooming

Mankitsu 満喫 = fully enjoying, having enough food and drink; *the* <u>man</u> *who was engaged in* <u>kitsuen</u> *(smoking) was* <u>fully enjoying</u> *himself*; cf. related terms listed at manzoku

Manmaru まん丸 = a perfect circle; from manjitsu = truth + maru = circle; cf. related terms listed at maru

Mannaka 真中 = center, middle; *he* <u>manages</u> *a car dealership in the* <u>middle</u> *of town*; cf. related terms listed at chuubu

Manpuku 満腹 = a full stomach; *since that* <u>man</u> *is* <u>poor</u>, *he drinks* <u>Kool-Aid</u> *until he has a* <u>full stomach</u>; cf. onaka ga ippai = I'm full

Manrui 満塁 = bases loaded; from man = full, e.g., man'in = a full house + rui = a base; cf. related terms listed at rui

Mansei 慢性 = chronic; *the* <u>manager</u> *for Safeway has* <u>chronic</u> *problems*

Manseki 満席 = full house, all seats occupied; from manin = full house + seki = seat

Manshin 慢心 = pride, self-conceit; *the* <u>mansion's</u> <u>shingles</u> *were a source of* <u>pride</u>; cf. related terms listed at hokori

Manshon マンション = a condominium or apartment; from the English "mansion"

Manugareru 免れる = to be exempted from, to avoid; *the* <u>manual</u> *that the* <u>gambler</u> *wrote about* <u>red</u> <u>roosters</u> <u>avoided</u> *the topic of sex*; cf. kaihi suru = to avoid; cf. sakeru = to avoid

Manzoku 満足 = satisfaction; *the* <u>man</u> *who drank* <u>Zooey's</u> <u>Kool-Aid</u> *reported* <u>satisfaction</u>; cf. mankitsu = fully enjoying, having enough food and drink; cf. tannou = 1) skillful, or 2) enjoyment/satisfaction

Mappiruma 真っ昼間 = broad daylight; *in the* <u>magnificent</u> <u>piano</u> <u>room</u>, *the* <u>master</u> *was snoring in* <u>broad</u> <u>daylight</u>

Maru 丸 = a circle, a whole; *I was* <u>marooned</u> *on an island shaped like a* <u>circle</u>; cf. manmaru = a perfect circle; cf. saakuru = a circle; cf. wa = round shape (ring, circle etc.)

Maru de まるで = absolutely, entirely, completely; from maru = a circle + de = of; cf. related terms listed at zenzen

Marui 丸い = round; from maru = circle; this can also be spelled 円い

Marunomi 丸呑み = swallowing whole; from maru = circle + nomu = to drink

Masa ni まさに = exactly, naturally, duly, certainly, on the verge; *after she* <u>massaged</u> *my* <u>knee</u>, *which she did* <u>exactly</u> *as expected, she was* <u>certainly</u> <u>on the</u> <u>verge</u> *of massaging my foot*; cf. shizen ni = naturally, spontaneously; cf. umare nagara = by nature, naturally, by birth; cf. other related terms listed at choudo and at tashika ni

Masaka まさか = something expected, an emergency, by no means, never; *when I massaged the cat, I got something unexpected (i.e., a scratch) which caused an emergency that I never thought would happen*; cf. related terms listed at igai, at hijou, and at monoka

Masashiku 正しく = undoubtedly, evidently; this is more commonly read as tadashiku = correctly; there is *no* adjective form, e.g. ~~masashii~~; *undoubtedly, the master's sad sheep is from Kuwait*

Masatsu 摩擦 = friction, rubbing; *Ma's (Mother's) satisfying Superman novel, which she carried in her pocket, was responsible for rubbing the fabric of her jeans*; cf. massatsu = erasure

Masatsumen 抹殺面 = friction surface; from masatsu = friction + men = surface; cf. related terms listed at men

Masayume 正夢 = a dream come true; from masa = duly + yume = a dream; cf. related terms listed at yume

Mashi まし = better, preferable, e.g., hou ga mashi da = it's better; *it's better to keep mashing potatoes*

Massaki ni 真っ先に = first of all; *first of all, let's massage the king's knees*; cf. mazu = first of all

Massatsu 抹殺 = erasure, denial, ignoring (an opinion); *Ma (Mother) spends her time reading satisfying Superman novels because she is in denial about her problems*; cf. masatsu = friction; cf. related terms listed at hitei

Massatsu suru 抹殺する = to obliterate; from massatsu = erasure; cf. synonyms listed at kesu

Masshiro 真っ白 = pure white; from makoto = truth + shiro = white; cf. makkuro = jet black

Massugu 真っすぐ = straight; *after drinking the magic soup, Goofy could walk straight*

Massugu ni 真っすぐに = directly or straight; from massugu = straight + -ni = a suffix that forms an adverb; cf. chokusetsu = directly

Masu 升 = a small square measuring box, sometimes used for sake; *I poured mango soup into the small square measuring box*; cf. related terms listed at hako

Masui 麻酔 = anesthesia; *that man chose Sweden for his anesthesia training*

Masumasu ますます = increasingly, more and more; this can also be spelled 益々; *he is learning mas y mas (more and more, in Spanish)*; cf. iyoiyo = more and more, increasingly, at last; cf. other related terms listed at tsui ni

Mata 又 = again, also, and, as well as; *the matador won the tournament again*; cf. related terms listed at aratamete

Mata 股 = a thigh or groin; *the matador had muscular thighs*; cf. related terms listed at momo

Mata wa 又は = or, either … or; *let's visit the magic tawaa (tower) or stay home*; cf. related terms listed at soretomo

Mataataku 瞬く = to blink or twinkle; *the master tatami maker drank some Kool-Aid as his eyes twinkled*; cf. kirakira suru = to glitter or twinkle; cf. tenmetsu suru = to go on and off, to blink

Matataku ma ni 瞬く間に = in an instant; from matataku = to blink + ma = interval + -ni = a suffix that forms an adverb; cf. atto iu ma ni = in the blink of an eye

Matenrou 摩天楼 = a skyscraper; *in Manhattan, I counted ten rows of skyscrapers*

Mato 的 = target, center of attention; *after I stepped on Ma's toes, I was the center of attention*; cf. hyouteki = target

Matomaru まとまる = to be collected or settled, to be in order; the intransitive form of matomeru = to settle or conclude

Matomeru まとめる = to conclude or settle, bundle together, compile, summarize; *we plan to bundle the magnificent toads and the Mexican roosters, sell them in one lot, and conclude the sale*; cf. kukuru = to bind or bundle; cf. soukatsu suru = to generalize or summarize; cf. youyaku suru = to summarize; cf. other related terms listed at osameru and owaraseru

Matomete まとめて = all together, all at once; *the magnificent toads left for Mexico and Texas all together and all at once*; cf. related terms listed at issho ni

Matsu 待つ = to await, anticipate; *we sat on mats as we awaited the parade*; cf. machikaneru = to wait eagerly for

Matsu 松 = a pine tree; *they put mats under the pine tree*; cf. related terms listed at ki

Matsuri 祭り = a festival; from matsuru = to pray, worship, celebrate

Matsuru 祭る = to pray, worship, celebrate; *the mat that Superman put in the room is a good cushion to kneel on when worshipping one's ancestors*; cf. inoru = to pray; cf. iwau = to celebrate or congratulate

Matsuzaka gyuu 松坂牛 = a type of wagyu beef produced in Mie prefecture; from matsu = pine tree + zaka = saka = hill + gyuunyuu = beef; cf. related terms listed at gyuuniku

Mattaku 全く = really, utterly, completely; *the matador's Kool-Aid was really good*; cf. related terms listed at zehi

Mau 舞う = to dance; *Mao Tse Tung liked to dance*; cf. furumau = to behave; cf. odoru = to dance

Mawari 周り = surroundings; from mawaru = to turn or spin; cf. kankyou = environment, surroundings; cf. shuui = surroundings

Mawaridasu 回り出す = to begin to turn; from mawaru = to turn + dasu = to emerge; cf. related terms listed at mawaru

Mawaru 回る = to turn or spin (intransitive); *Ma's washing machine was ruined when it spun too fast*; cf. kaiten suru = to revolve or rotate; cf. magaru = to turn; cf. mawaridasu = to begin to turn

Mawasu 回す = to turn (transitive); *the marine warrior and Superman turned the valve and released the water*; cf. kiru = to cut, to turn off, to hang up or stop, to turn a vehicle; cf. tenjiru = to turn or shift

Mayaku 麻薬 = a narcotic; *that mansion is where the yakuza keep their narcotics*

Mayoi 迷い = doubt, indecision, hesitation; from mayou = to lose direction; cf. related terms listed at kondou and at utagai

Mayou 迷う = to lose direction, to get lost, to hesitate; *I got lost in the mayonnaise factory*; cf. enryo suru = to hesitate or hold back; cf. kigane wo suru = to hesitate; cf. shiburu = to hesitate or be reluctant

Mayowazu 迷わず = mayowazuni = mayowanai de = not getting lost; from mayou = to get lost

Mayu 眉 = eyebrows; *I married a youth without eyebrows*; cf. mayuge = eyebrows

Mayu wo hisomeru 眉をひそめる = to frown or scowl; from mayu = eyebrow + hisomeru = to knit

Mayuge 眉毛 = eyebrows; from mayu = eyebrows + ge = ke = fur

Mazeru 混ぜる = to mix (transitive); this can also be spelled 交ぜる; *in the mansion's Zen room, we mix our potions*; cf. kongou suru = to mix, mingle or blend; cf. majieru = to mix (transitive); cf. najimaseru = to make fit in, to blend or mix in thoroughly

Mazu 先ず = first of all; *first of all, let's look*

at a <u>map</u> of the <u>zoo</u>; cf. massaki ni = first of all

Mazui まずい = unappetizing; *on this <u>map</u> of the <u>zoo</u>, to the <u>east</u>, you can see an <u>unappetizing</u> restaurant*

Mazushii 貧しい = poor; *we give <u>maps</u> of the <u>zoo</u> and other <u>sheets</u> of paper to <u>poor</u> people*

Me 目 = eye, counter for numbers in a series, e.g., futatsu me = second; *the <u>mermaid</u> has big <u>eyes</u>*; cf. akame = a red eye; cf. katame = one eye; cf. medama = eyeball

Me ga sameru 目が覚める = to wake up; from me = eyes + sameru = to wake up; cf. related terms listed at samasu

Me ni amaru 目に余る = to be intolerable; from me ni = to the eyes + amaru = to be in excess; literally "to the eyes to be in excess"; cf. tamaranai = intolerable or irresistable

Me ni hairu 目に入る = to catch sight of; from me = eye + hairu = to enter; cf. mikakeru = to catch sight of

Me ni kakaru 目にかかる = to meet humbly; from me = eyes + ni = to + kakaru = to take (time); cf. related terms listed at deau

Me ni suru 目にする = to see or observe; literally, to do to the eyes; cf. related terms listed at miru

Me ni tsuku 目につく = to be noticeable, to notice; from me = eyes + tsuku = to be attached; cf. medatsu = to stand out

Me wo kakeru 目をかける = to gaze at, to favor; from me = eye + kakeru = to spend; cf. related terms listed at miru

Me wo kugizukeru 目をくぎづける = to attract attention; from me = eyes + kugi = nail + zukeru = tsukeru = to adhere; cf. kugizuke ni naru = to be unable to take one's eyes from

Me wo samasu 目を覚ます = to wake up; this has the same meaning as me ga sameru, but it has a more active nuance, suggesting that I *make* myself wake up, or get up; from me = eyes + samasu = to awake; cf. related terms listed at samasu

Me wo toosu 目を通す = to scan or look over; from me = eyes + toosu = to force or let through; cf. related terms listed at miorosu

Meate 目当て = prospect, aim, goal, intention; *the <u>men</u> bought <u>a tent</u> with the <u>aim</u> of using it for a fishing trip*; cf. related terms listed at mokuhyou

Mebae 芽生え = budding, awakening; *the <u>Mexican</u> <u>barber</u> feels <u>energy</u> when he sees the <u>budding</u> of new leaves*; cf. hatsuga = budding

Mebaeru 芽生える = to bud or sprout; the verb form of mebae = budding; cf. related terms listed at haeru

Mechakucha めちゃくちゃ = absurd, incoherent, disorder, mess; *after taking the <u>medicine</u>, Prince <u>Charles</u> started his <u>Kool</u>-Aid <u>chants</u>, which were generally <u>incoherent</u>*; cf. kondou = confusion, mix-up; cf. konran = confusion, chaos; cf. muchitsujo = chaos, disorder; cf. rifujin = unfair or absurd

Medama 目玉 = eyeball; from me = eye + dama = tama = ball; cf. related terms listed at me

Medatsu 目立つ = to stand out; from me = eye + datsu = tatsu = to stand up; cf. me ni tsuku = to be noticeable, to notice

Meekaa メーカー = maker or manufacturer

Meetoru メートル = a meter

Megami 女神 = goddess, female deity; from me = female; *I know a <u>female</u> in <u>Mexico</u>*; + gami = kami = god; cf. kami = good

Megane 眼鏡 = eyeglasses (this can also be read "gankyou," with the same meaning); *the <u>megalomaniac's</u> <u>neck</u> supported his*

eyeglasses; cf. gankyou = eyeglasses

Megumareru 恵まれる = to be endowed with, to abound with; the passive form of megumu = to bestow; cf. sazukaru = to be endowed with or blessed with; cf. sonawaru = to be furnished, equipped or endowed with; cf. tomu = to get rich, to abound with; cf. yuu suru = to own or be endowed with

Megumu 恵む = to bless, show mercy, give money, bestow a favor, etc.; the *Mexican goose in the movie was able to bestow favors*; cf. related terms listed at ataeru

Meguri 巡り = circumference, tour, circulation; the noun form of meguru = to go around; cf. junkan = circulation, circular movement

Meguru 巡る = to go or come around, to surround; *the Mexican guru came around and surrounded us with his followers*; cf. related terms listed at kakomu

Megutte めぐって – see wo megutte

Mei 名 = a counter for people, e.g., nimei = two people; *people serve as maids*

Meian 名案 = a good idea; *mailing ants is a good idea*; cf. related terms listed at omoi

Meibo 名簿 = a directory or list of names; the *mayor boasted about his list of names*; cf. related terms listed at namae

Meibutsu 名物 = famous or special product, specialty; from mei = name, e.g., yuumei = famous; + butsu = tangible thing; cf. related terms listed at tokuchou

Meigara 銘柄 = a brand name; *the mayonnaise in the garage carries a brand name*; cf. related terms listed at name

Meigen 名言 = a wise or famous saying; *the mayor quoted Genghis' wise sayings*; cf. in'you = a quotation or citation

Meihou 名峰 = famous mountain; *the maid had a home on a famous mountain*; cf. related terms listed at yama

Meijiki 明治期 = the Meiji era; from Meiji + ki = time, e.g., jiki = time or season

Meijiru 命じる = to command or appoint; *in the Meiji era, people spread rumors about whom the emperor might appoint to high office*; cf. shimei suru = to appoint or nominate; cf. other related terms listed at meirei suru

Meijou 名城 = a famous castle; from mei = famous, e.g., yuumei = famous; + jou = a castle; cf. related terms listed at shiro

Meimei めいめい = each, individual; *the mayor mailed thank-you notes to each person who contributed to his campaign*; cf. related terms listed at goto ni

Meimon 名門 = a noted family or prestigious school; from yumei = famous + mon = a gate

Meirei 命令 = a command or order; *the major rated his men according to how well they responded to his commands*; cf. gourei = a command or order; cf. sashizu = direction, command, order

Meirei suru 命令する = to command or order; from meirei = a command or order; cf. meijiru = to command; cf. sashizu suru = to command or direct

Me'iru (Meiru) 滅入る = to feel depressed; *when I see that these men iru (exist) outside my house, I feel depressed*; cf. ki ga kujikeru = to get discouraged; cf. ki wo otosu = to be discouraged; cf. kujikeru = to lose heart, be dispirited; cf. shizumu = to set (sun or moon), to sink (intransitive), to feel depressed

Meiryou na 明瞭な = obvious, clear; *from the mail that Pope Leo was getting, it was obvious that some people disliked him*; cf. related terms listed at akiraka na

Meiryousa 明瞭さ = clarity; from meiryou na = clear + sa = a suffix that creates a noun

Meisaku 名作 = a masterpiece; from yuumei

= famous + sakuhin = a creation; cf. related terms listed at shouhin

Meishi 名刺 = a business card; *the mayor met the Shiites and gave them her business card*

Meishi 名詞 = a noun; *the maid says that "sheet" is a noun*; cf. related terms listed at shugo

Meishin 迷信 = a superstition; *maybe Shintoism is based on superstition*

Meisho 名所 = a famous place; from yuumei = famous + basho = place; cf. related terms listed at basho

Meishou 名勝 = a place of scenic beauty; *in the month of May, they showed me several places of scenic beauty*; cf. related terms listed at basho

Meishou 名称 = name, title; *the major came on the show and revealed his name*; cf. related terms listed at namae

Meisui 名水 = a famous spring or mineral water; *the maid from Sweden drank the famous mineral water*; cf. related terms listed at mizu

Meiwaku 迷惑 = trouble, annoyance; *the way that May walks spells trouble*; cf. kurou = hardship; cf. kurushimi = suffering, pain, hardship; cf. mendou = annoyance, trouble, care; cf. tema = a lot of time or trouble

Meiyo 名誉 = honor or glory; *I have the honor of delivering the mail at Yosemite*; cf. related terms listed at kouei

Memai めまい = dizziness; *my memories of Ireland include a bout of dizziness*

Men 綿 = cotton; *my mentor wears cotton shirts*; cf. related terms listed at momen

Men 面 = mask, face, surface, or aspect; *men who rob banks wear masks*; cf. fukumen = a mask; cf. gaikan = surface, exterior; cf. gamen = an (electronic) screen or picture; cf. hyou = a surface, chart or diagram; cf. hyoumen = surface, exterior; cf. masatsumen = friction surface; cf. noumen = a Noh mask; cf. omote = surface, front; cf. sokumen = a side or aspect; cf. uramen = the back side; cf. zenmen = whole surface, entire

Men 麺 = noodles; *men love noodles*; cf. related terms listed at soba

Men suru 面する = to face on, to look out on; from men = a surface; cf. related terms listed at miru

Mendou 面倒 = annoyance, trouble, care; *those men at the door will cause trouble*; cf. related terms listed at meiwaku

Mendoukusai 面倒くさい = annoying, tiresome; from mendou = annoyance + kusai = smelly

Men'eki (Meneki) 免疫 = immunity; *she was exposed to meningitis at the eki (station), but she has immunity*; cf. meneki ryoku = immunity

Men'eki (Meneki) ryoku 免疫力 = immunity; from meneki = immunity + ryoku = power

Menjo 免除 = an exemption, exoneration, discharge; *the men asked Jonah to help them get an exemption from military service*; cf. menzei = a tax exemption; cf. shakuhou = release, liberation, or acquittal

Menjou 免状 = diploma, license; *the men joked that their diplomas were written with disappearing ink*; cf. menkyo = license

Menkai 面会 = an interview; *the men visited the Kaiser for an interview*; cf. kaiken = a meeting or interview; cf. mensetsu = an interview

Menkyo 免許 = license; *the men went to Kyoto to get a license*; cf. menjou = diploma, license

Menmitsu 綿密 = detailed, meticulous; *the men will meet Superman to show him their detailed plan*; cf. kichoumen = scrupulous, meticulous; cf. kokumei na = detailed, minute; cf. komakai = small, detailed; cf.

kuwashii = detailed, fully explained, versed, knowledgeable; cf. neniri = elaborate, meticulous

Menseki 面積 = an area; *the <u>men</u>tor of the <u>s</u>elfish <u>k</u>ing showed him how to calculate the <u>area</u> of the land he owned*; cf. hirosa = a width, expanse or area; cf. tsubo = a unit of area comprising 3.3 square meters, or 2 tatami mats

Mensetsu 面接 = an interview; *the <u>men set</u> <u>Sue</u> aside during the <u>interview</u>*; cf. kaiken = a meeting or interview; cf. menkai = an interview

Menzei 免税 = a tax exemption; from menjo = exemption + zeikin = taxes; cf. menjo = an exemption; cf. other related terms listed at zeikin

Meshi 飯 = rice, food or a meal (male speech); *this <u>rice</u> is <u>messy</u>*; cf. related terms listed at tabemono

Meshiagaru 召し上がる = to eat honorably; *he has been <u>mesh</u>ing the gears of his truck <u>again</u>st the <u>rules</u> in order to be able to get home faster and <u>eat honorably</u>*; cf. related terms listed at taberu

Mesu 雌 = a female (animal), often spelled メス; *the <u>me</u>dical <u>su</u>pervisor had a <u>female</u> cat*; cf. osu = a male animal

Metsubou 滅亡 = downfall, destruction; *I <u>met</u> Superman in the <u>bowling</u> alley just before its <u>destruction</u>*

Metta ni 滅多に = rarely, seldom; *I give <u>Me</u>xican <u>t</u>affy to my <u>niece rarely</u>*

Me'ue (Meue) 目上 = superior or senior; from me = eye + ue = up

Mezamashii 目覚ましい = outstanding, striking; *he's up in the <u>mezzanine mash</u>ing potatoes and doing an <u>outstanding</u> job*; cf. related terms listed at joutou

Mezameru 目覚める = to wake up; an abbreviation of me ga sameru = to wake up; cf. related terms listed at samasu

Mezashi 目指し = aim, goal or purpose; this can also be spelled 目差し; from mezasu = to aim at; cf. related terms listed at mokuhyou

Mezasu 目指す = to aim at; this can also be spelled 目差す; *sitting in the <u>mezz</u>anine of the theater, <u>Sue</u> decided to <u>aim at</u> a career in the opera*; cf. mokuhyou suru = to aim at; cf. nerau = to aim

Mezawari 目ざわり = an eyesore or an unpleasant sight; from me = eyes + zawari = sawari = harm

Mezurashii 珍しい = unusual, rare; *at the <u>Me</u>xican <u>zoo</u>, I met a <u>radical Shii</u>te with <u>unusual</u> opinions*; cf. hibon = unusual, outstanding; cf. hinichijouteki = extraordinary, unusual; cf. kawatta = different, unusual, strange

Mi 実 = fruit or nut; *we eat <u>fruit or nuts</u> with every <u>meal</u>*; cf. related terms listed at kudamono

Mi 身 = body, person, e.g., hitori mi = one person; *the <u>body</u> is made out of <u>meat</u>*; cf. related terms listed at karada

Mi み = a nominalizing suffix used after the stems of some i adjectives, e.g., itai = painful, itami = pain; omoi = heavy, omomi = weight; atsui = thick, atsumi = thickness

Mi ga hairu 身が入る = to make one's best effort; from mi = body + hairu = to enter

Mi ni tsukeru 身に付ける = to wear (clothes, etc.) or carry, to learn or acquire knowledge; from mi = body or person + tsukeru = to wear; cf. related terms listed at benkyou suru and at chakuyou suru

Miageru 見上げる = to look up, raise one's eyes; from miru = to look + ageru = to raise; cf. related terms listed at miru

Miai 見合い = an arranged marriage meeting; from miru = to look + au = to match

Miataru 見当たる = to be found; from miru = to see + ataru = to hit; cf. related terms listed at mitsukaru

Miawaseru 見合わせる = to exchange glances, to postpone, to refrain from doing something; from miru = to look + awaseru = to put together, to harmonize; cf. enki suru = to postpone; cf. nobasu = to extend or postpone; cf. tsutsushimu = to be discreet, to refrain from

Mibae 見栄え = pretensions, ostentation, appearance; *I've been meaning to go to Bali to escape all of this ostentation*; cf. related terms listed at mitame

Mibun 身分 = social status or position; from mi = person + bun = a share; cf. related terms listed at kurai

Mibunshoumeishou 身分証明書 = an identification card; from mibun = social status + shoumei = proof or identification + sho = a document

Michi 道 = street, road, way; *I live along a road in Michigan*; cf. doori = a street or way; cf. douro = a road; cf. jarimichi = a gravel path; cf. kaidou = a highway or path; cf. kodou = an old road; cf. kousoku douro = a highway or freeway; cf. machi = boulevard, avenue, town; cf. sakamichi = an uphill path; cf. toori = street, avenue, way

Michibata 道端 = the roadside; *in Michigan, I found a bag of tapestries on the roadside*

Michibiku 導く = to guide, direct, lead; *on a Michigan beach, a Kool-Aid vendor guided me to the best swimming spot*; cf. hikiiru = to lead

Michigaeru 見違える = to be beyond recognition or very different; from miru = to look + chigaeru = to change

Michiru 満ちる = to become full; *in Michigan I ruined my appetite when I became full of potato chips*

Midara na 淫らな = indecent, obscene; *King Midas was a rascal who told obscene jokes*; cf. related terms listed at mittomonai

Midareru 乱れる = to become chaotic, disrupted or windblown (hair); *during my meal with Darwin, his red rooster caused our conversation to become disrupted*

Midori 緑 = green; *her miniature dory is green*

Midori yutaka 緑豊か = lushly green, verdant; from midori = green + yutaka = rich or abundant

Midori'iro (Midoriiro) 緑色 = green; the adjective form of midori = green; from midori = green + iro = color

Mieru 見える = to be visible, to appear or seem; *the meaning of that erudite inscription is barely visible, but it appears to be positive*; cf. related terms listed at mitai

Miesuku 見え透く = to be transparent, to be obvious; from mieru = to be visible + suku = to become transparent; cf. related terms listed at sumu

Migaki 磨き = polish or burnishing; from migaku = to brush or polish

Migaki 身欠き = the process of removing poison from fugu fish; *there was a meeting between Gandalf and the king about the process of removing poison from fugu*

Migaku 磨く = to brush, shine or polish; *after the mediator drank a gallon of Kool-Aid, she brushed her teeth*

Migi 右 = the right-hand side; *there are some mean geese on the right side*; cf. higashi = the left-hand side

Migoro 見頃 = the best time to see; from miru = to see + goro = koro = approximate time

Migoto 見事 = wonderful; *the mediator's goal was to tone down the rhetoric, and he did a wonderful job*; cf. related terms listed at idai

Migurushii 見苦しい = unsightly, shameful; from miru = to look + gurushii = kurushii = difficult or painful; cf. minikui = ugly; cf. other related terms listed at mittomonai

Mihakkutsu 未発掘 = not yet excavated; from mirai = future + hakkutsu = excavation

Mihari 見張り = guard, lookout, watch-keeping; *if you want to meet Prince Harry, you have to figure out how to get past the guard*; cf. related terms listed at keibi

Mihiraku 見開く = to open one's eyes wide; from miru = to look + hiraku = to open

Mihon 見本 = a sample or example; *our meals in Honduras consisted of samples from a big box store*; cf. rei = an example or precedent; cf. tatoe = an example

Mihon'ichi (Mihonichi) 見本市 = a sample show or trade fair; from mihon = sample + ichiba = market

Mijika ni 身近に = close at hand, closely related; from mi = body or person + jika = chika = close + -ni = a suffix that forms an adverb; cf. related terms listed at chikai

Mijikai 短い = short (object); *the missionary bought a Jeep car at Easter, and it's short, compared to other cars*; cf. hikui = low, small (sound), short (person)

Mijime na 惨めな = miserable; *the miniature Jeep from Mexico broke down, and we had a miserable time*; cf. related terms lised at ki no doku

Mikado 帝 = the Emperor of Japan; *I checked my reflection in the mirror on the car door before going in to see the Emperor of Japan*; cf. related terms listed at ou

Mikai 未開 = primitive, undeveloped, uncivilized; *I will meet the Kaiser in a primitive village*; cf. mikaitaku = undeveloped; cf. yaban na = barbarous, uncivilized

Mikaitaku 未開拓 = undeveloped; from mikai = undeveloped + kaitaku suru = to develop; cf. related terms listed at mikai

Mikake 見かけ = outward appearance; from mikakeru = to catch sight of; cf. related terms listed at mitame

Mikakeru 見かける = to catch sight of; from mi = to see + kakeru = to begin to do something; cf. me ni hairu = to catch sight of

Mikan ミカン = a mandarin orange; *during my meal with the Canadians, we ate mandarin oranges*; cf. related terms listed at kudamono

Mikaneru 見かねる = to be unable to look, or unable to let pass unnoticed; from miru = to look + kaneru = to be unable to do

Mikata 味方 = a supporter or ally; *if we meet during a catastrophe, I will be your ally*; cf. shijisha = a supporter or adherent

Mikata 見方 = a viewpoint; from miru = to look + kata = a direction; cf. related terms listed at kenkai

Mikata suru 味方する = to take someone's side; from mikata = a supporter or ally + suru = to do

Mikeiken 未経験 = inexperienced; from mi = yet; *the meeting has yet to start;* + keiken = experience

Mikeneko 三毛猫 = calico cat, a cat with three colors of fur; from mittsu = three + ke = hair or fur + neko = cat

Miki 幹 = tree trunk; *Mickey Mouse can climb tree trunks*

Mikkai 密会 = secret meeting; *when I meet the Kaiser, it's always a secret meeting*; cf. related terms listed at kaigi

Mikomi 見込み = prospects; *if you meet that commie (communist), you will see that he has excellent prospects to rise in the party*

Mikon 未婚 = unmarried; from mi = yet; *the meeting has yet to start;* + kekkon = marriage; cf. dokushin = single, unmarried

Mimai 見舞い = visiting a sick person; *if you visit your sick friend in the mouse hospital, you might meet Mighty Mouse*

Mimamoru 見守る = to watch over, watch attentively; from miru = to watch + mamoru = to protect; cf. related terms listed at mamoru

Miman 未満 = under, less than, used as a suffix; *the meterman is less than five feet tall*; cf. ika = below, less than, the following, the rest; cf. inai = within, inside of, less than; cf. ni suginai = no more than, merely; cf. tatta = only, merely, but, no more than

Mimawareru 見舞われる = to experience or undergo; *you will meet a magical wacky red rooster which has experienced many hardships*; cf. related terms listed at keiken suru

Mimi 耳 = an ear; *if you mimic a sound, my ear can hear it*

Mimi ni suru 耳にする = to hear; from mimi = ear + suru = to do; cf. kuchi ni suru = to taste, eat or speak of

Miminari 耳鳴り = ear ringing; from mimi = ears + naru = to ring

Mimoto 身元 = identity, lineage; *the median age of those motorcars tells you something about their lineage*

Mimuki mo sezu 見向きもせず = mimuki mo shinai = taking no notice, ignoring; from mimuku = to look around + mo = even + sezu = shinai de = not doing

Mimuku 見向く = to look around; from miru = to look + muku = to face toward; cf. related terms listed at miru

Min 民 = people, nation, subjects; *the people in this nation are mean*

Mina 皆 – see minna

Minami 南 = south; *my minature amigo (friend in Spanish) goes south for the winter*; cf. higashi = east; cf. kita = north; cf. nishi = west

Minamoto 源 = origin, source; *concern about Minasota (Minnesota) motorcycle injuries was the origin of a law requiring riders to wear helmets*; cf. related terms listed at kigen

Minaosu 見直す = to re-examine or reconsider, to correct the view; from miru = to look + naosu = to correct

Minarau 見習う = to follow another's example; from miru = to watch + narau = to learn

Minato 港 = a harbor or port; *mighty NATO uses this harbor for its warships*

Mine 峰 = mountain peak; *there are some minerals near the mountain peak*; cf. related terms listed at choujou

Minikui 醜い = ugly; from miru = to look + nikui = difficult to do; cf. migurushii = unsightly, shameful

Minna 皆 = mina = all, everyone, everything; *all of them live in Minnasota (Minnesota), where they have everything*

Minna de みんなで = all together, all told, in sum; from minna = all, everyone, everything + de = of; cf. related terms listed at issho ni

Minogasu 見逃す = to overlook, to turn a blind eye to; *the mean old gas station owner overlooked the boy's shoplifting*; cf. okotaru = to be lazy, to overlook or neglect; cf. orosoka ni suru= to neglect; cf. other related terms listed at mushi suru

Minori 実り = a harvest; from minoru = to bear fruit or ripen; cf. related terms listed at sakumotsu

Minori'ooi (Minoriooi) 実り多い = fruitful, successful; from minori = a harvest + ooi =

numerous; cf. related terms listed at sakan

Minoru 実る = to bear fruit, ripen; *the minotaur stood on the roof and waited for the fruit to ripen*; cf. naru = to bear (fruit); cf. other related terms listed at jukusu

Minshu 民主 = democracy, democratic; from shimin = citizen + shujin = master; cf. minshushugi = democracy

Minshushugi 民主主義 = democracy; from minshu = democracy + shugi = doctrine or rule; cf. minshu = democracy

Min'you (Minyou) 民謡 = a folk song; *the minister yodeled as we sang folk songs*; cf. related terms listed at uta

Minzoku 民族 = an ethnic group or race; from min = people, e.g., shimin = citizen; + zoku = family or tribe, e.g., kazoku = family; cf. related terms listed at buzoku

Miokuru 見送る = to see off (e.g., to an airport), to let pass or postpone, to wait and see; from miru = to look + okuru = to spend time; cf. related terms listed at enki suru

Miorosu 見下ろす = to overlook (scenery); *the mean old rogue sued after he happened to overlook his neighbor trampling on his shrubs*; cf. me wo toosu = to scan or look over; cf. miwatasu = to look over (a scene); cf. nozomu = to attend (e.g., a function), to appear (e.g., in court), to deal with, to look out upon

Mirai 未来 = future; *mirrors will be made of ice in the future*; cf. shourai = future

Mirin みりん = a sweet rice wine used in cooking; *when I meet Ringo, I will offer him some sweet rice wine*; cf. related terms listed at sake

Miru 見る = to look, see, watch; *I watched the mean rooster torment the hens*; cf. aogu = to look up, look up to, ask for advice, depend on; cf. goran ni naru = to see, look or watch honorably; cf. haiken suru = to see or read humbly; cf. me ni suru = to see or observe; cf. me wo kakeru = to gaze at, to favor; cf. men suru = to face on, to look out on; cf. miageru = to look up, raise one's eyes; cf. mimuku = to look around; cf. mitsu-meru = to gaze at; cf. mokugeki suru = to witness or observe; cf. nagameru = to gaze at; cf. shinsa suru = to examine, inspect or review; cf. sukasu = to look through; cf. ukagau = to observe or watch

Miryoku 魅力 = attractiveness, charm; *after my meal, I drank some of Pope Leo's Kool-Aid and was delighted by its charm*; cf. apiiru = appeal, in the sense of being attractive to people

Miryokuteki 魅力的 = fascinating, charming; from miryoku = charm + teki = related to

Miryou 魅了 = fascination, charm; *if you meet Leo, you will understand my fascination with him*; cf. uruoi = charm, profit, moisture

Misaki 岬 = a cape or promontory; *a miserable Achilles lived in a tent at the cape*

Mise 店 = a store, shop or restaurant; *this is a miserable store*; cf. baiten = stall, booth, kiosk; cf. gofukuya = a dry goods store, a kimono store; cf. heiten = a closed store; cf. honya = a bookstore; cf. fukuyasan = a clothing store; cf. honten = a main store or head office; cf. senmonten = a specialty shop; cf. shiten = a branch office or store; cf. ten = a shop or store, used as a word component; cf. tenpo = a shop or store; cf. touten = this store; cf. yatai = a cart (e.g., selling food), stall or stand; cf. other related terms listed at ryoutei

Miseba 見せ場 = highlight, high point; *visiting this miserable bar is the high point of my day*

Miseinensha 未成年者 = a minor; *the meek sailor and his negative nephew live in a shack by themselves, and the nephew is a minor*

Miserareru 魅せられる = to be enchanted or fascinated; *the miserable red rooster is fascinated* by the hens

Miseru 見せる = to show; *he showed me his miserable room*; cf. arawasu = to reveal or show; cf. hagu = to strip (the skin) from something, to reveal; cf. hyousu = to express or show; cf. oshieru = to teach, show or tell; cf. shimesu = to show or point out

Miso みそ = fermented bean paste; *when we meet the soldiers, let's give them some fermented bean paste*

Misu ミス = a mistake or failure; from the English "miss"; cf. related terms listed at shippai

Misui 未遂 = a failed attempt; *Miss Sweden entered the Miss Universe contest, but it was a failed attempt*; cf. related terms listed at kokoromi

Misumacchi ミスマッチ = mismatch

Misuterii ミステリー = mystery; cf. shinpi = mystery

Mitai みたい = resembling, seeming, used as a suffix; *this mirror from Thailand seems to be good*; cf. mieru = to be visible, to appear or seem; cf. -sou = seems to be; cf. -rashii = seems or appears to be; cf. -you = appearing, seems to be, way to, method of, form or style, like or similar to

Mitame 見た目 = appearance; from mita = saw + me = eyes; cf. furi = pretense or appearance; cf. gaiken = appearance; cf. kakkou = form, appearance, suitability; cf. mibae = pretensions, ostentation, appearance; cf. mikake = outward appearance; cf. youbou = face, features, looks; cf. youshi = appearance, looks; cf. yousu = condition, state, appearance

Mite morau 診てもらう = to consult a doctor; similar to mite morau = to be seen and receive

Mitomeru 認める = to recognize, admit or allow; *I admit that a good mediator can tomeru [stop] a strike*; cf. koutei suru = to affirm, answer positively or admit

Mitooshi 見通し = outlook, perspective; *mitochondria shield this cell's nucleus, from our perspective*; cf. kenkai = viewpoint; cf. shiten = viewpoint

Mitsu 蜜 = honey, nectar, molasses; *when I meet Superman, I give him honey*

Mitsukaru 見つかる = to be found or caught; the intransitive form of mitsukeru = to find out or locate; cf. hamaru = to fall into or be caught, to fit in or into (intransitive); cf. hasamaru = to get between, to get caught in; cf. miataru = to be found; cf. tsukamaru = to be caught

Mitsukedasu 見つけ出す = to find out, discover, locate; from mitsukeru = to find + dasu = to put out; cf. related terms listed at mitsukeru

Mitsukeru 見つける = to find out, discover or locate; from miru = to look + tsukeru = to attach; cf. hakken suru = to discover; cf. horiateru = to find or strike (gold, etc.); cf. mitsukedasu = to discover, to locate; cf. saguriateru = to find out; cf. tsukitomeru = to find out, located, ascertain

Mitsumeru 見つめる = to gaze at; from miru = to look + tsumeru = to pack into or stuff; cf. related terms listed at miru

Mittomonai みっともない = shameful, disgraceful; *when Mitt Romney used his tomography machine to scan his neighbors at night, it was disgraceful*; cf. asai = shallow, superficial, frivolous, wretched, shameful; cf. gehin = vulgar, coarse, indecent; cf. hitogiki warui = disgraceful, disreputable; cf. midara na = indecent, obscene; cf. migurushii = unsightly, shameful; cf. nasakenai = miserable, pitiable, shameful; cf. zoku na = mundane, vulgar, common

Miugoki 身動き = moving about; from mi = body + ugoku = to move

Miwake 見分け = a distinction; from miru = to see + wake = a division

Miwakeru 見分ける = to distinguish; the

verb form of miwake = a distinction

Miwatasu 見渡す = to look over (a scene); from miru = to look + watasu = to carry across; cf. related terms listed at miorosu

Miya 宮 = palace or shrine; *she will <u>meet</u> the Yankees in a <u>palace</u>*; cf. related terms listed at jinja and at kyuuden

Miyabita 雅びた = gracious, elegant, refined; *the <u>mirror</u> that the <u>yakuza</u> gave to <u>beefy</u> <u>Tarzan</u> was <u>elegant</u>*; cf. related terms listed at jouhin

Miyako 都 = a capital; *the <u>meeting</u> of <u>yak</u> owners was held in the <u>capital</u>*

Miyoumimane 見よう見まね = learning by imitation; from miyou = shall look + miru = to look + mane suru = to imitate or copy; cf. related terms listed at chishiki

Mizo 溝 = a ditch, groove or gap; *that <u>ditch</u> is a <u>meeting</u> <u>zone</u> for raccoons*; cf. related terms listed at unga

Mizu 水 = water; *the <u>mediator's</u> <u>zucchini</u> plants need a lot of <u>water</u>*; cf. deisui = muddy water, red-light district; cf. dobumizu = ditch water; cf. gesui = sewage; cf. kaisui = sea water; cf. kiyomizu = spring water; cf. kosui = lake water; cf. meisui = a famous spring or mineral water; cf. nettou = boiling water; cf. onsui = warm water; cf. oyu = honorable hot water; cf. senjousui = wash water; cf. suibun = moisture, water; cf. tansui = fresh water; cf. wakimizu = spring water; cf. yu = hot water

Mizuasobi 水遊び = playing in water; from mizu = water + asobu = to play

Mizugi 水着 = a bathing suit; from mizu = water + giru = kiru = to wear clothes

Mizukara 自ら = for one's self, personally; *the <u>mizu</u> (water) that I brought to the <u>karaoke</u> party was <u>for myself</u>*; cf. related terms listed at jibun de

Mizumizushii みずみずしい = juicy; from mizu = water + mizu = water + shii = a common ending for adjectives; cf. juushii = juicy

Mizumore 水漏れ = a leak (of water); from mizu = water + moreru = to leak; cf. more = a leak

Mizushigen 水資源 = water resources; from mizu = water + shigen = resources; cf. shigen = resources

Mizuumi 湖 = a lake; *some of the <u>mizu</u> (water) in the <u>umi</u> (ocean) comes from lakes*; cf. ike = a pond; cf. kata = a lagoon

Mo も = also, even; *he <u>even</u> has a <u>motorcycle</u> <u>also</u>*

Mo 藻 = algae, seaweed; *<u>Moses</u> collects <u>seaweed</u>*; cf. kaisou = seaweed

Mo 喪 = mourning, used as a word component; *she went into <u>mourning</u> after her <u>mole</u> died*

Mo daijoubu も大丈夫 – see te mo ii

Mo ii もいい – see te mo ii

Mo kamaimasen もかまいません – see te mo ii

Mo yoroshii もよろしい – see te mo ii

Mochi 餅 = Japanese rice cake; *I want <u>more</u> <u>cheese</u> to eat with my <u>Japanese</u> <u>rice</u> <u>cakes</u>*; cf. okaki = mochi cut thin and then dried, baked or fried

Mochiageru 持ち上げる = to elevate, raise up, flatter; from motsu = to hold + ageru = to raise; cf. related terms listed at ageru

Mochidasu 持ち出す = to bring up, to carry out, to run away with, to mention something; from motsu = to hold + dasu = to put out; cf. related terms listed at hakobu

Mochigome 餅米 = glutinous rice; from mochi = Japanese rice cake + gome = kome = uncooked rice; cf. related terms listed at gohan

Mochiifu モチーフ = a motif

Mochiiru 用いる = to use; *I give more cheese to the eager rooster because I want to use him in a poultry show*; cf. related terms listed at riyou suru

Mochikaeru 持ち帰る = to bring back; from motsu = to hold + kaeru = to return; cf. related terms listed at mottemairu

Mochikomu 持ち込む = to bring in; from motsu = to have + komu = to crowd in; cf. ireru = to insert or let in, to make coffee or tea; cf. sounyuu suru = to insert; cf. toriireru = to harvest, take in, adopt, incorporate

Mochinushi 持ち主 = an owner; from motsu = to hold + nushi = a master; cf. jinushi = a land owner; cf. shujin = a master, owner or husband; cf. teishu = a husband or owner; cf. tenshu = a shop owner

Mochiron もちろん = of course, naturally; *to add more cheese is wrong, but of course he will do it anyway*

Modaeru もだえる = to be in agony, to worry; *Moses and his dad are erudite, and they tend to worry about grammatical errors*; cf. related terms listed at shinpai suru

Modoru 戻る = to return; *he returned to his moldy dorm room*; cf. kaeru = to go back or return, to go home

Modosu 戻す = to put back, to give back; the transitive form of modoru = to return

Moe 萌 = feelings of affection directed at certain anime or manga characters, who are called "moe characters"; *I feel more energy when I watch moe characters*; cf. related terms listed at kankaku

Moeru 燃える = to burn (intransitive); *in the morning the volcano erupted, and then the forest burned*; cf. enjou suru = to blaze up or burn; cf. kogeru = to be scorched or burned; cf. shoushi suru = to burn to death; cf. zenshou suru = to burn completely (intransitive)

Moeru 萌える = to sprout or bud; *Moses was erudite and knew when the trees would bud*; cf. related terms listed at haeru

Mofuku 喪服 = mourning dress; from mo = mourning + fuku = clothing

Mogi 模擬 = imitation, mock; *Moses had a guitar made from imitation wood*; cf. related terms listed at mane

Mogitou 模擬刀 = a fake sword or practice sword; from mogi = imitation + tou = a sword, e.g., tantou = a dagger; cf. related terms listed at katana

Mogura モグラ = a mole; *the mole thought that the moaning goose might be rabid*

Mogurazuka モグラ塚 = a mound created by a mole; from mogura = mole; + zuka = tsuka = mound; cf. tsuka = a mound

Moguru 潜る = to dive or hide; *the mogul's guru taught him to hide from people*; cf. related terms listed at kakusu and at tobu

Mohan 模範 = an example or model; *this is an example of a motorcycle handlebar*; cf. related terms listed at rei

Mohaya もはや = by now or (with negative sentences) any longer; *Moses has a yacht by now, but soon he won't have one any longer*; cf. related terms listed at mou

Mohou 模倣 = imitation; *this motorhome is paneled with imitation wood*; cf. related terms listed at mane

Moji 文字 = character, letter; *my motorcycle and my Jeep have characters painted on them*; cf. related terms listed at ji

Moku 木 = wood, used as a word component, e.g., mokusei = made of wood; *I stayed in a motel in Kuwait that was made of wood*

Mokuba 木馬 = a wooden horse; from moku = wood + ba = horse; cf. similar terms listed at uma

Mokugeki 目撃 = witnessing, observing; *as he was observing the game, he drank more*

Kool-Aid and played with his guest key

Mokugeki suru 目撃する = to witness or observe; from mokugeki = witnessing, observing; cf. related terms listed at miru

Mokuhyou 目標 = aim, goal; *when the Lone Ranger saw that more Kool-Aid had arrived, he said "Hi-yo Silver," since his goal was to serve everyone, including his horse*; cf. kokorozashi = kokoroza = ambition, wish, goal; cf. meate = prospect, aim, goal, intention; cf. mezashi = aim, goal or purpose; cf. mokuteki = purpose, goal; cf. shibou = ambition, wish, goal; cf. shushi = purpose, gist, tenor

Mokusei 木星 = Jupiter; *there's more Kool-Aid in the Safeway stores on Jupiter*

Mokusei 木製 = made of wood; from moku = wood + seihin = a product; cf. mokuzou = wooden construction; cf. takesei = made from bamboo

Mokuteki 目的 = purpose, goal; *on mokuyoubi (Thursday), the techie achieved his goal*; cf. related terms listed at mokuhyou

Mokutekichi 目的地 = destination; from mokuteki = goal + chi = ground or soil; cf. shukuhakusaki = a lodging destination; cf. taizaisaki = a lodging destination

Mokuzou 木造 = wooden construction; from moku = wood + seizou = manufacturing; cf. related terms listed at mokusei

Momen 木綿 = cotton; *the moment that cotton prices went up, I sold my stock*; cf. men = cotton; cf. wata = cotton; cf. other related terms listed at nuno

Momiji 紅葉 = autumn leaves; cf. kouyou = autumn colors, fall leaves

Momimomi もみもみ = massage; *he adds more meat to my food if I give him a massage*

Momo 桃 = a peach; *most motorists like peaches*; cf. related terms listed at kudamono

Momo 股 = a thigh; this can also be pronounced mata = a thigh or groin; *I spilled moldy molasses on my thigh*; cf. ko = thigh or crotch, used as a word component; cf. mata = a thigh or groin

Momu もむ = to rub or massage; *when Moses was in the mood, he would massage his wife*; cf. related terms listed at kosuru

Mon 門 = a gate, a counter for cannons; *the monk waited by the gate*

Mondai 問題 = a question or problem; *Monet's diet was a problem*; cf. shomondai = various problems

Mongen 門限 = curfew; *the monks under Genghis had a strict curfew*

Monka もんか – see monoka

Monku 文句 = complaint, phrase, words; *the monk had a complaint*; cf. related terms at kujou

Monmon 悶々 = worry, agony, worrying endlessly; *I moan and moan due to worry*; cf. related terms listed at nayami

Mono 物 = a tangible thing or object; this can imply "since" or "because"; *this molasses on my nose is a tangible thing*

Mono 者 = a humble person; *that humble person is monogamous*; cf. related terms listed at hito

Mono da ものだ = an expression of emotion, e.g., hayai mono da = time flies! this can also = "because"; also, see mono desu; from mono = tangible thing + da = it is

Mono dearu のである – see mono desu

Mono desu のです (or mono da, or mono dearu) = one should do something; this can also = "because"; from mono = tangible thing + desu = it is; cf. related terms listed at seneba

Mono desu ka ものですか = never; from mono = a tangible thing + desu ka = is it? cf. related terms listed at monoka

Mono nara ものなら = if possible, when used after a plain-speech potential verb, e.g., ikeru mono nara = if it were possible to go; mono nara can also mean "if," when used after a "shall" or "let's" verb; from mono = thing + nara = if, or in case

Monogatari 物語 = story; *the monotonous gambler tarried in order to tell a story*; cf. related terms listed at hanashi

Monogataru 物語る = to tell or indicate; the verb associated with monogatari = story; cf. related terms listed at hanasu

Monogoto 物事 = a matter or thing; from mono = thing + goto = koto = thing; cf. busshitsu = material, substance; cf. other related terms listed at ken

Monoka ものか = never, i.e., the opposite is true; *the monorail car falls off the rail? never!* cf. kesshite = never, in no way; cf. -kkonai = never can do, used after a potential verb stem; cf. masaka = something expected, an emergency, by no means, never; cf. monka = never; cf. mono desu ka = never

Monono ものの = but, although; *he plays monotonous notes, but he's considered a musician*

Monotarinai 物足りない = unsatisfying; from mono = a tangible thing + the negative form of tariru = to be sufficient

Monouri 物売り = a peddler; from mono = a tangible thing + uru = to sell

Mooru モール = a mall

Moppara 専ら = exclusively, chiefly; *Moses and his Pa (father) met a rabbi who focused on Talmudic studies exclusively*

Morasu 漏らす = to let out, to omit; *Moses was a rascal from Sudan who let out the dogs and omitted feeding them*; cf. dasu = to take out, put out; cf. habuku = to omit or to cut down (cost)

Morau もらう = to receive; *I received a mole from Raul Castro*; cf. itadaku = to receive humbly, to eat or drink humbly; cf. ukeru = to receive, to take (a class, etc.), to be affected or suffer from, to catch or get

More 漏れ = a leak; from moreru = to leak; cf. mizumore = a leak (of water)

Moreru 漏れる = to leak; *after Moses bought the red rooster, the barn began to leak*

Mori 森 = a forest or woods; *Maureen spent time in the forest*; cf. chikurin = a bamboo grove; cf. hayashi = a grove; cf. nettairin = a tropical forest; cf. shinrin = a forest

Moriagaru 盛り上げる = to swell, rise, get excited; from moru = to fill or pile up + agaru = to rise; cf. chi ga sawagu = to get excited; cf. hareru = to swell up

Moridakusan 盛りだくさん = many, varied; from moru = to fill or pile up + dakusan = takusan = many; cf. related terms listed at takusan

Moromoro 諸々 = various things, large number of people; *those morose Moroccans are worried about various things*; cf. related terms listed at kazukazu

Moru 盛る = to fill or pile up; *Moses ruined the pool when he filled it with dirt*; cf. related terms listed at tsumeru

Moshi もし = if, in case, providing; *if we need more shingles, we'll buy them*; cf. dattara = if it's the case; cf. kari ni = if; cf. moshimo = if; cf. nara = if, in case; cf. naraba = if, in case; cf. sai ni = in case of, at that time

Moshikashitara もしかしてら = perhaps, maybe; from moshi = if + ka = question mark + shitara = if it does; cf. related terms listed at kamoshiremasen

Moshikashite もしかして – see moshikashitara

Moshikasuruto もしかすると – see moshikashitara

Moshimo もしも = if; a variation of moshi; cf. related terms listed at moshi

Moshimoshi もしもし = hello (usually on the phone); *hello, I need more sheets for my mopy sheep*; cf. konnichiwa = hello (morning or afternoon)

Motarasu もたらす = to bring about, to bring or take; *Moses was in the tavern with some other rascals drinking soup and planning how to bring about a rebellion*; cf. shoujiru = to occur or bring about

Moto 元 = formerly; this can also = base, origin, source, principal (money); *formerly I rode a motorcycle*; cf. related terms listed at kichi and at kigen

Moto de もとで – see moto ni

Moto ni もとに = on the basis of; this can also be expressed as moto de; from motozuku = to be based on + ni = a suffix that forms an adverb; cf. related terms listed at motozuku

Moto no のとの = original, former; from moto = formerly

Motomeru 求める = to ask, request or buy, to pursue (pleasure); *the motormen made it a rule to ask passengers for payment*; cf. related terms listed at tanomu

Motomoto 元々 = originally, from the outset; from moto = origin

Motomu 求む = to seek or demand; *the motor-mouthed movie star demanded higher wages*; cf. related terms listed at tanomu

Motorikishi 元力士 = ex-wrestlers; from moto = origin + rikishi = wrestler; cf. rikishi = a sumo wrestler

Motozuku 基づく = to be based on; *that motorized zoo coops up its animals efficiently based on its automated gates*; cf. moto de = on the basis of; cf. moto ni = on the basis of; cf. ni motozuite = based on, according to; cf. no koto dakara = based on

Motsu 持つ = to have or own; *the king owns these moats*; cf. hoyuu suru = to own; cf. you suru = to have or possess, to embrace; cf. yuu suru = to own or be endowed with

Motteiku 持っていく = to take, to carry away; from motsu = to have + iku = to go; cf. related terms listed at mottemairu

Mottekuru 持ってくる = to bring; from motsu = to have + kuru = to come; cf. related terms listed at mottemairu

Mottemairu 持ってまいる = to bring or take humbly; from motsu = to have + mairu = to come or go humbly; cf. mochikaeru = to bring back; cf. motteiku = to take, to carry away; cf. mottekuru = to bring

Motto もっと = more; *my motto is "play games more"*; cf. mou = already, before long, another, more

Mottomo もっとも = the most; *those motorcycles on that motorway are the most expensive*; cf. dai ichi = number one, i.e., the most, the best or the first; cf. daibubun = the major part, the majority; cf. daitasuu = a majority; cf. kahansuu = a majority; cf. taihan = the majority; cf. tasuu = a large number, a majority

Mou もう = already, before long, another, more; *Moses and another guy already called, and they will be here before long*; cf. mohaya = by now or (with negative sentences) any longer; cf. motto = more; cf. sude ni = already, too late; cf. other related terms listed at hoka and at mamonaku

Mou 猛 = fierce, strong, used as a prefix; *the mole is fierce*

Mou 網 = netting or network, used as a word component; *Moses manages our network*

Mou ii もういい = that's enough! from mou = already + ii = good

Mou sugu もうすぐ = pretty soon; from mou = before long + sugu = soon

Moubenkyou 猛勉強 = studying extra hard; from mou = fierce, strong; *the mole is fierce*; + benkyou = study; cf. related terms listed at benkyou

Mouchou 盲腸 = an appendix (a blind pouch in the intestine); from moumoku = blindness + chou = intestines; cf. related terms listed at naizou

Moude 詣で = a temple or shrine visit; from mouderu = to visit a temple or shrine; cf. similar terms listed at houmon

Mouderu 詣でる = to make a pilgrimage or visit a temple or shrine; *Moses and his dentist ruined their clothes when they visited a temple and fell into a pond*

Moudouken 盲導犬 = a guide dog; *they train guide dogs in a moldy dorm in Kentucky*; cf. related terms listed at inu

Moufu 毛布 = blanket; *Moses looks foolish with that blanket over his head*

Mouhitsu 毛筆 = a writing or painting brush; *Moses hits you with a writing brush when you talk in class*; cf. fude = a writing brush

Mouja 亡者 = a person who is money mad; *he's money mad and keeps his cash in molasses jars*

Moukaru もうかる = to make a profit; *Moses calculated that his roosters would make a profit*

Mouken 猛犬 = savage dog; from mou = fierce, strong; *the mole is fierce*; + ken = dog; *Ken and Barbie have a dog*; cf. related terms listed at inu

Moukeru 設ける = to set up, establish; *we fed mostly ketchup to the rooster while we set up the chicken coop*; cf. kizuku = to establish, build; cf. souritsu suru = to establish; cf. sousetsu suru = to establish; cf. other related terms listed at settei suru

Moumoku 盲目 = blindness; *due to his blindness, Moses asked for more Kool-Aid, even though his glass was half-full*

Moura 網羅 = comprising, including; *he mowed the ranch, including the pasture*; cf. wo hajime = including, as well as, not to mention

Mourenshuu 猛練習 = hard training; from mou = fierce, strong; *the mole is fierce*; + renshuu = practice; cf. related terms listed at kunren

Mouretsu 猛烈 = fierce, fervent; *when he made a fervent speech, Moses wore a retro suit*; cf. hageshii = fierce, tempestuous, crowded (traffic), frequent (change)

Moushiageru 申し上げる = to say, speak or tell humbly; from mousu = to say, speak or tell humbly + ageru = to give; cf. related terms listed at hanasu

Moushide 申し出 = a proposal; from moushideru = to offer or volunteer; cf. related terms listed at teian

Moushideru 申し出る = to offer or volunteer; from mousu = to speak humbly + deru = to emerge; cf. sashidasu = to hold out, offer, send; cf. teikyou suru = to offer, provide or sponsor

Moushikomi 申込書 = an application; from moushikomu = to apply; cf. gaitou = application, correspondence; cf. hutsugan = an application; cf. oubo = application, subscription

Moushikomisho 申込書 = an application form; from moushimomi = an application + sho = a document

Moushikomu 申し込む = to apply for; from mousu = to speak humbly + komu = to crowd in; cf. shigan suru = to volunteer, to apply for; cf. shinsei suru = to apply for or request

Moushiwake 申し訳 = an apology or excuse; from mousu = to speak humbly + wake = reason; cf. shazai = an apology; cf. other related terms listed at benkai

Mousho 猛暑 = fierce heat, heat wave; *Moses showed the people of Israel how to* survive a _heat_ _wave_ in the wilderness; cf. kanpa = a cold wave; cf. related terms listed at atsusa

Mousou 妄想 = a fantasy or delusion; _Moses_ _went_ to _Somalia_ to pursue his _fantasies_ and _delusions_; cf. related terms listed at gensou

Mousu 申す = to say, speak or tell, or to be called, humbly; _he_ _humbly_ _says_ that he wants _more_ _soup_; cf. related terms listed at hanasu

Moyasu 燃やす = to burn; _as the house_ _burned_, he drank _more_ _yak_ _soup_; cf. kogasu = to scorn or burn (transitive); cf. taku = to burn (wood)

Moyooshi 催し = an event or meeting; from moyoosu = to hold an event; cf. gyouji = an event or function; cf. other related terms listed at kaigi

Moyoosu 催す = to hold an event; _a_ _motormouth_ _yogi_ _opened_ _a_ _supermarket_ _and_ _held_ _an_ _event_ to mark the occasion; cf. kaisai suru = to hold a meeting or open an exhibition

Moyou 模様 = design, pattern; _the_ _mold_ _on_ _the_ _yogurt_ _seems_ to _be_ _forming_ _a_ _design_; cf. sekkei = a design or plan

Mu 無 = negation, used as a word component; _my_ _mood_ is one of _negation_; cf. fu = negation; cf. nai = negation

Mubou 無謀 = reckless, thoughtless; _the way he drove the Mooneys' boat was reckless_; cf. related terms listed at keisotsu

Mubyou 無病 = in perfect health; from mu = negation + byouki = illness; cf. related terms listed at genki

Muchitsujo 無秩序 = chaos, disorder; from mu = negation + chitsujo = order; cf. kondou = confusion, mix-up; cf. konran = confusion, chaos; cf. mechakucha = absurd, incoherent, disorder, mess

Muchuu 夢中 = daze, trance, engrossment; _after the_ _movie_ _star_ _chewed_ _on the tablet, she fell into a_ _trance_

Muda 無駄 = useless, wasteful; _to_ _mo_ve _the_ _dam_ would be _wasteful_

Muda ni suru 無駄にする = to waste, to not make good use of, to render futile; from muda = useless, wasteful; cf. rouhi suru = to waste

Mudaboe 無駄吠え = wasteful barking, or barking in vain; from muda = wasteful + boeru = hoeru = to bark

Mudan de 無断で = without permission; _don't_ _move_ _the_ _dandelions_ _without_ _permission_

Mudenchuuka 無電柱化 = the process of removing utility poles; from mu = negation + denchuu = utility pole + ka = a nominalizing suffix

Mugai 無害 = harmless; from mu = negation + gai = harm

Mugamuchuu 無我夢中 = losing oneself in, being absorbed; from mu = negation; + ga = self; _my_ _self_ _has the gift of_ _gab_; + mu = dream; _I_ _dream_ _about the_ _moon_; + chuu = inside

Mugen 無限 = eternal, infinite, endless; from mu = negation + genkai = limit; cf. fuhen no = constant, unchanging, eternal; cf. fukyuu no = eternal, immortal; cf. fumetsu no = immortal, eternal; cf. yuukyuu no = eternal

Mugi 麦 = barley, wheat; _we had to_ _move_ _our_ _gear to make room for the_ _barley_; cf. gokoku = the five grains (wheat, rice, beans, awa and kibi); cf. kokumotsu = grain, cereal; cf. komugi = wheat; cf. oomugi = barley

Mugon 無言 = silent, speechless; _when he awoke, the_ _moon_ _was_ _gone_, _and he was_ _speechless_; cf. related terms listed at odayaka

Muhon 謀反 = a mutiny or rebellion; _some_ _Moonies_ _in_ _Honduras_ _attempted a_ _mutiny_; cf. related terms listed at hangyaku

Muimi 無意味 = meaningless; from mu = negation + imi = meaning

Mujaki 無邪気 = innocence; *that movie shows Jackie Kennedy's innocence*; cf. related terms listed at mujitsu

Mujin eki 無人駅 = unmanned station; from mu = negation + jin = person + eki = station; cf. mujintou = an uninhabited island

Mujintou 無人島 = an uninhabited island; *I examine the moon, drink gin and stretch my toes on my uninhabited island*; cf. mujin eki = unmanned station; cf. other related terms listed at shima

Mujitsu 無実 = innocence or innocent; *I saw a movie in which a jittery superstar proclaimed his innocence*; cf. keppaku = innocence; cf. mujaki = innocence; cf. muzai = innocent

Mujun 矛盾 = an inconsistency or contradiction; *there was an inconsistency between her mood in June and her mood in July*

Mukae 迎え = greeting, welcome; from mukaeru = to meet/welcome; cf. related terms listed at eshaku

Mukaeru 迎える = to meet/welcome; *on the moon, cars full of erudite people are sent to meet/welcome new arrivals*; cf. related terms listed at deau

Mukamuka むかむか = feeling sick or nauseous; *watching movies in the car with a Moonie named Karl made me feel nauseous*

Mukamuka suru むかむかする = to feel nauseated or disgusted; from mukamuka = feeling sick or nauseous

Mukanshin 無関心 = indifference; from mu = negation + kanshin = concern or interest

Mukashi 昔 = old days, ancient times; *that movie is cashing in on ancient times*; cf. katsute = formerly, long ago; cf. kodai = ancient times; cf. kyuu = old times, used as a prefix; cf. oomukashi = ages ago; cf. touji = those days, old days

Mukashibanashi 昔話 = legends, reminiscences, old stories; from mukashi = olden times + banashi = hanashi = story; cf. related terms listed at hanashi

Mukau 向かう = to face, to go towards; *the moody cow is facing the barn and going toward the farmer*; cf. muku = to look or face toward

Muke 向け = intended for, aimed at; *this movie about Kennedy is intended for an older audience*; cf. muki = direction, suitability, tendency

Mukeru 向ける = to direct, point, turn towards; the transitive form of muku = to face toward; cf. related terms listed at sasu

Muki 向き = direction, suitability, tendency; *this movie about quiche has a suitability for foodies*; cf. muke = intended for, aimed at; cf. other related terms listed at gachi

Mukidasu むきだす = to show or bare (the teeth); *after swimming in the mucky pool, Dad threatened to sue the swim club and bared his teeth to show that he was serious*

Mukou 向こう = the other side; *the moon is colder on the other side*; cf. related terms listed at hou = direction or side

Mukou 無効 = invalidity; *we had to move the court date due to the invalidity of our attorney's license*

Mukougawa 向こう側 = the other side; from mukou = the other side + gawa = a side; cf. related terms listed at hou = direction or side

Muku 剥く = to peel or skin, usually written むく; *when I moved to Kuwait, I learned to peel vegetables*

Muku 向く = to look or face toward; *the movie was cool, and we all faced toward the screen*; cf. mukau = to face, to go towards

Mukuchi 無口 = taciturn, reticent; from mu = negation + kuchi = mouth

Mumei 無名 = anonymous, unknown; from mu = negation + mei = name, e.g., yuumei = famous; cf. fumei = unknown, uncertain

Munage 胸毛 = chest hair; *the moon animals and their guests all had chest hair*

Munashii 空しい = empty, fruitless; *under the moon, a Shiite farmer planted fruitless seeds*

Mune 宗 = a religion or sect; *in our sect, we welcome moon experts*; cf. related terms listed at shuukyou

Mune 胸 = chest, heart; *the moon expert puffed out his chest*; cf. related terms listed at kokoro

Mura 村 = a village or town; *there's a mural in that village*; cf. related terms listed at shi

Murabito 村人 = a village person; from mura = village + bito = hito = person; cf. related terms listed at hito

Muragaru 群がる = to flock or throng; *people flocked to see the mural that the gambler ruined*; cf. related terms listed at shuugou suru

Murasaki 紫 = purple; *the mural of the sacking of Rome depicted torn purple robes*

Murasakiji 紫地 = a purple background; from murasaki = purple + ji = chi = ground; cf. related terms listed at haikei

Murasawa gyuu 村沢牛 = a type of wagyu beef produced in Nagano prefecture; from mura = village + sawa = swamp + gyuunyuu = beef; cf. related terms listed at gyuuniku

Mure 群れ = herd, crowd, group; *I saw a movie about red roosters that lived in a group*; cf. related terms listed at dantai

Muri 無理 = impossible, unreasonable; *Muriel is impossible and unreasonable*; cf. fukanou = impossible; cf. wake ni wa ikanai = impossible to do

Muri ni 無理に = by force; from muri = unreasonable + ni = by

Muriyari 無理やり = forcibly, against one's will; from muri = unreasonable + yaru = to do

Muryou 無料 = free of charge; from mu = negation + -ryou = fee or charge

Musekinin 無責任 = irresponsible; from mu = negation + sekinin = responsibility; cf. iikagen = unreliable, irresponsible, perfunctory, careless

Musekininsa 無責任者 = irresponsibility; from musekinin = irresponsible + sa = a suffix that makes a noun from another word

Musen 無線 = wireless; from mu = negation + sen = a line

Musen kyoku 無線局 = a radio station; from musen = wireless + kyoku = an office

Mushi 虫 = an insect or worm; *there were insects and worms in the mushy soil*; cf. hae = housefly; cf. hotaru = a firefly; cf. ka = a mosquito; cf. konchuu = an insect; cf. kumo = a spider; cf. saikin = bacterium, germ

Mushi nuno 蒸し布 = a cloth for steaming; from mushiatsui = hot and humid + nuno = a cloth; cf. related terms listed at nuno

Mushi suru 無視する = to disregard or ignore; *I heard a mushy story about a person who disregarded warnings*; cf. minogasu = to overlook, to turn a blind eye to; cf. socchinoke = to ignore one thing for another

Mushiatsui 蒸し暑い = hot and humid; from musu = to steam + atsui = hot; cf. related terms listed at atsui

Mushiba 虫歯 = a decayed tooth; from mushi = an insect or worm + ba = ha = tooth; cf.

ha = a tooth; cf. hanarabi = a row or set of teeth; cf. maeba = front tooth

Mushibamu むしばむ = to be eaten by worms, to spoil or ruin, to affect adversely; from mushi = an insect or worm + bamu = a suffix indicating that something is in the state of the preceding noun; cf. related terms listed at kizutsukeru

Mushimegane 虫眼鏡 = a magnifying glass; from mushi = insect + megane = reading glasses; cf. related terms listed at bouenkyou

Mushimushi むしむし = hot and humid; from mushiatsui = hot and humid; cf. related terms listed at atsui

Mushiro むしろ = rather; *the mushi (insect) roams on land rather than water*; cf. kaette = conversely, rather, all the more

Musu 蒸す = to steam, to be hot and humid; *in the movie, Superman steamed his food*; cf. related terms listed at niru

Musubu 結ぶ = to bind, connect, tie, conclude, organize, close tightly (mouth); *I bound the moody supervisor's bootlaces together*; cf. related terms listed at osameru and tsunagu

Musuko 息子 = a son; *my son is a musical Uber driver in Korea*; cf. chakunan = an heir or oldest son; cf. chounan = oldest son; cf. jinan = a second son; cf. magomusuko = a grandson; cf. sannan = a third son

Musume 娘 = a daughter; *my daughter works at a museum in the summer*; cf. choujo = an eldest daughter; cf. magomusume = a granddaughter

Musumemuko 娘婿 = a son-in-law; from musume = a daughter + hanamuko = a bridegroom; cf. related terms listed at hanayome

Musuu 無数 = countless; from mu = negation + suuji = number; cf. related terms listed at takusan

Muteppou 無鉄砲 = reckless; *influenced by the moon in Texas, the pope became reckless*; cf. teppou = gun; cf. related terms listed at keisotsu

Mutonchaku 無頓着 = nonchalant, indifferent; from mu = negation + tonchaku suru = to care about; cf. reitan na = cool, indifferent; cf. other related terms listed at nanigenai

Mutsumajii 睦まじい = harmonious, happy, affectionate; *those mutts (dogs) are magical in the way they create a harmonious atmosphere and make me happy*; cf. related terms listed at shiawase na

Mutto むっと = sullenly, angrily; *the movie star greeted Tony Blair sullenly*

Muzai 無罪 = innocent; *after she was found innocent, she moved to Zaire (former name of the Congo)*; cf. yuuzai = guilty; cf. other related terms listed at mujitsu

Muzan na 無惨な = heartless, tragic (usually spelled 無残な); *the moon in Zanzibar illuminated a tragic scene*; cf. related terms listed at kanashii

Muzukashii 難しい = difficult; *when we see museums in Zurich cashing in on body parts, it's difficult to defend them*; cf. fukuzatsu = complicated, difficult; cf. kitsui = laborious, difficult, tight-fitting, stern, harsh; cf. konnan = difficult; cf. kurushii = difficult, painful; cf. -nikui = difficult to do, used as a suffix; cf. shinan no = extremely difficult; cf. taihen = difficult, terrible, extremely

Muzumuzu むずむず = to feel itchy, to be impatient or eager to do something; *while at the museum, you want to visit the zoo; why are you so impatient?* cf. aseru = to be in a hurry or impatient, to be flustered; cf. hayaru = to be impatient or hotblooded

Myaku 脈 = pulse or vein; *after drinking a lot of Miami Kool-Aid, my pulse was throbbing*; cf. related terms listed at doumyaku

Myou 妙 = strange, odd, unique; *it's me, oh Lord, I cried, when I saw the strange light* from wa = harmony or Japanese style, e.g., washoku = Japanese food; cf. related terms listed at kimyou and at yuiitsu

Myougonichi 明後日 = the day after tomorrow; this can also be pronounced asatte, with the same meaning; *the meowing ghost will meet Nietzche on the day after tomorrow*

Myouji 名字 = a family name or surname; *when you meet the yogi, check his Jeep, since his family name is painted on it*; cf. related terms listed at namae

Myoujin 明神 = a gracious deity; from myou = bright; *the cat meows in the bright sun*; + jin = god, e.g., jinja = a Shinto shrine

Myounichi 明日 = tomorrow; *tomorrow you will hear meowing from the niches where I plan to lock the cats*; cf. related terms listed at ashita

Myuujikaru akuto ミュージカルアクト = musical act

Na な = don't (do), e.g., taberu na = don't eat; *don't be nasty*

Na 名 = name or fame; from namae = name; cf. related terms listed at chimeido and at namae

Nabe 鍋 = pot, pan; *our Nanny won a bet and bought herself a pot*; cf. related terms listed at tsubo

Nadakai 名高い = famous; from namae = name + dakai = takai = high; cf. chimei = famous; cf. chomei = famous; cf. yuumei = famous

Naderu 撫でる = to rub or stroke; *Ralph Nader ruined the cake when he stroked it*; cf. kosuru = to rub or scrub; cf. sureru = to rub against, to wear down, to become jaded

Nado など = etcetera, for instance, such as; this can also = such a thing, things like, something like (usually in a derogatory context); *they sell nasty doughnuts, etcetera*; cf. nadonado = etcetera; cf. tari = etcetera, used as a suffix after the past plain speech stems of verbs or the past stems of i adjectives; cf. toka = etcetera; cf. ya = etcetera; cf. yara = etcetera

Nadonado 等々 = etcetera; cf. related terms listed at nado

Nae 苗 = a seedling; *the nasty eggplant grew from a seedling*

Naeru 萎える = to lose strength, to become weak, to wither or droop; *our nanny is erudite, but she is losing strength*

Nagai 長い = long; *Nagaina was a long cobra*; cf. hosonagai = long and narrow; cf. nagame = longish

Nagai aida 長い間 = a long time; from nagai = long + aida = interval; cf. choujikan = a long time; cf. choukikan = a long time

Naga'iki (Nagaiki) 長生き = longevity, long life; from nagai = long + ikiru = to live

Nagame 眺め = a view or scene; from nagameru = to gaze at; cf. choubou = a view; cf. fuukei = a view or scenery; cf. keshiki = a view or scenery; cf. machinami = a townscape, the look of houses and stores; cf. shiya = scope, field of vision, view; cf. zekkei = a superb view; cf. other related terms listed at bamen

Nagame 長め = longish; from nagai = long; cf. related terms listed at nagai

Nagameru 眺める = to gaze or look at; *Nagaina checks her meeru (e-mail) and gazes at it*; cf. related terms listed at miru

Nagara ながら = while, at the same time; *Nagaina ran after the bird at the same time she was chasing the squirrel*; cf. -chuu = in the middle of, in the process of, during, among; cf. -juu = throughout; cf. noni = in spite of the fact, in order to, while, if only; cf. tsuide ni = incidentally, while doing something; cf. -tsutsu (used after a verb stem) = while, even though; cf. tsuujite=

through, throughout, by way of; cf. other related terms listed at douji ni

Nagarekomu 流れ込む = to flow into; from nagareru = to flow + komu = to crowd into

Nagareru 流れる = to flow; *when Nagaina chased the red rooster, it jumped across a ditch which had water flowing through it*; cf. nagarekomu = to flow into; cf. tsuujiru = to lead to, reach by phone, communicate, flow, be knowledgeable; cf. other related terms listed at wakideru

Nagaretsuku 流れ着く = to drift to, to be washed ashore; from nagarareru = to flow + tsuku = to arrive; cf. tadayou = to drift

Nagasa 長さ = length; from nagai = long + sa, a suffix that makes a noun from an adjective; cf. setake = height, stature; cf. shinchou = a person's height; cf. takasa = height; cf. take = size or height; cf. tate = length or height; cf. zenchou = overall length or span

Nagashi 流し = flowing; also = kitchen sink; from nagasu = to flush, drain, pour, wash away; cf. shinshin = flowing, everlasting

Nagashidai 流し台 = a sink; from nagasu = to flush + dai = platform

Nagasode 長袖 = a long-sleeved garment; from nagai = long + sode = a sleeve; cf. related terms listed at sode

Nagasu 流す = to flush, drain, pour, wash away; *Nagaina sued her husband for flushing her wedding ring*; cf. related terms listed at sosogu

Nagatabi 長旅 = a long trip; from nagai = long + tabi = trip; *I brought a tabby cat along on the trip*; cf. related terms listed at ryokou

Naga'uta (Nagauta) 長唄 = a long epic song; from nagai = long + uta = a song with samisen; cf. related terms listed at uta

Nagekakeru 投げかける = to throw at, to cast; from nageru = to throw + kakeru = to extend; cf. related terms listed at nageru

Nageki 嘆き = sorrow; from nageku = to grieve; cf. related terms listed at kanashimi

Nageku 嘆く = to lament, grieve; *I nag my guests to drink Kool-Aid and grieve when they refuse*; cf. goukyuu suru = to cry aloud, lament; cf. nakidasu = to burst into tears; cf. naku = to cry or weep (human)

Nageru 投げる = to throw; *I nagged the erudite person to throw me a book*; cf. hourikomu = to throw into; cf. nagekakeru = to throw at, to cast; cf. toujiru = to throw into or invest; cf. touka suru = to throw down or drop; cf. tounyuu suru = to throw into or invest

Nagetaosu 投げ倒す = to throw a person down; from nageru = to throw + taosu = to knock down; cf. taosu = to throw down or knock down, to defeat

Nagomu 和む = to be softened, to calm down; *the nagging ghost was in a mood to calm down*; cf. related terms listed at kutsurogu

Nagori なごり = traces, remnants; *the nanny saw gory traces and called the police*; cf. related terms listed at ato

Nagoyaben 名古屋弁 = Nagoya dialect; from Nagoya + ben = dialect

Nagoyaka 和やか = peaceful, gentle; *in Nagoya I met a cat who was peaceful and gentle*; cf. related terms listed at odayaka

Naguritaosu 殴り倒す = to knock down or knock out; from naguru = to punch + taosu = to knock down; cf. related terms listed at taosu

Naguru 殴る = to beat up, punch or slap; *the nagging guru would beat up his disciples*; cf. related terms listed at utsu

Nagusameru 慰める = to console or divert; *the nag's goofiness made Sam erupt in laughter and served to divert and console him*

Nai ない = inside or within, used as a suffix;

I keep my knife inside the house; cf. related terms listed at naka

Nai ない = no, not, negation, does not exist; *we have no knives*; cf. related terms listed at mu

Naibu 内部 = inside; from nai = inside + bu = part or section; cf. naisou = interior, interior design; cf. oku = heart, interior; cf. other related terms listed at ichibu

Naichi 内地 = inland area, mainland area of Japan, i.e., Honshu, Shikoku and Kyushu, as viewed from Hokkaido and Okinawa; from nai = inside + chi = ground or soil; cf. related terms listed at tairiku

Naika 内科 = internal medicine; *the internal medicine doctor was on night call*; cf. related terms listed at gankagaku

Naikai 内科医 = an internal medicine specialist; from naika = internal medicine + isha = doctor

Naikaku 内閣 = the Cabinet; *the nice prime minister invited Karl the Kool-Aid vendor to join the Cabinet*

Naiseimen 内政面 = domestic affairs, internal administration; *some nice sailing men are in charge of domestic affairs*

Naisho 内緒 = secret; *the night show is a secret*; cf. himitsu = secret

Naisou 内装 = interior, interior design; *the nice socialist was interested in interior design*; cf. related terms listed at naibu

Naiyashu ken 内野手兼 = doubling as an infielder; from naiyashu = infielder + kenyou = multi-use

Naiyashu 内野手 = an infielder; from nai = inside + yakyuu = baseball + senshu = athlete

Naiyou 内容 = content, substance; *I stuck a knife in the yogurt to see if it had any content or substance*; cf. ganyuu = content; cf. nakami = contents

Naizou 内臓 = internal organ, intestines; from nai = inside + zou = organ; cf. chou = intestines, bowel; cf. daichou = the large intestine; cf. ichou = the stomach and intestines; cf. jinzou = a kidney; cf. kanzou = the liver; cf. kikan = an organ (body); cf. kimo = the liver, courage; cf. mouchou = an appendix (a blind pouch in the intestine); cf. shinzou = the heart (organ); cf. zouki = an internal organ

Naizou shikkan 内臓疾患 = an internal disease; from naizou = an internal organ + shikkan = a disease; cf. related terms listed at byouki

Najimaseru なじませる = to make fit in, to blend or mix in thoroughly; *the narco's Jeep matched the settler's rooster, since its paint had been blended throughly to make it fit in*; cf. related terms listed at mazeru

Najimu なじむ = to get used to or adapt; *I got used to wearing these nasty jeans when I worked on the moor*; cf. nareru = to become accustomed to

Naka 中 = inside or middle; *there is a nasty cat inside that house*; cf. -inai = within, inside of, less than, used as a suffix; cf. nai = inside or within, used as a suffix; cf. uchi = inside, within, among, middle, center, while; cf. other related terms listed at chuubu

Naka 仲 = relationship; *I have a relationship with a nasty cat*; cf. related terms listed at kanrensei

Nakaba 半ば = middle, half-way, in-between; from naka = middle + basho = a place; cf. related terms listed at chuubu

Nakagoro 中頃 = about the middle; from naka = middle + goro = approximate time; cf. related terms listed at chuubu

Nakama 仲間 = colleague or buddy; *my colleague bought a nasty cat at the mall*; cf. aibou = a buddy or partner; cf. douryou = a pal, colleague or coworker; cf. doushi = peer, comrade, each other; cf. hanryo = a spouse or companion

Nakamairi 仲間入り = joining a group;

from nakama = a colleague + iri = entering, e.g., iriguchi = an entrance; cf. related terms listed at sanka

Nakamairi suru 仲間入りする = to join a group; from nakamairi = joining a group; cf. related terms listed at kuwawaru

Nakami 中身 = contents; from naka = inside + mi = body; cf. ganyuu = content; cf. naiyou = content, substance

Nakanaka なかなか = not easily or readily (with negative constructions), quite or considerably (with positive constructions); *I got the nasty cat out of the National Cathedral, but not easily*; cf. related terms listed at kanari

Nakayoshi 仲良し = close friend; *my close friend works at the National Cathedral, and he eats yogurt made from sheep milk*; cf. related terms listed at tomodachi

Naki なき = lacking, less, without, used as a suffix; *the nasty king is lacking subjects*; cf. fusoku = lack or shortage; cf. koto naku = without; cf. nashi de = without; cf. nuki ni = without

Nakidasu 泣き出す = to burst into tears; from naku = to cry + dasu = to put out; cf. related terms listed at nageku

Nakigara 亡骸 = a corpse; *the Nazi had a key to the garage where the corpses were kept*; cf. related terms listed at karada

Nakigoe 泣き声 = a human cry, weeping; from naku = to cry + goe = koe = voice; cf. related terms listed at tooboe

Nakigoe 鳴き声 = an animal cry, howl, chirp; from naku = to bark, chirp or cry + goe = koe = voice; cf. related terms listed at tooboe

Naku 泣く = to cry or weep (human); *this nasty Kool-Aid makes me cry*; cf. synonyms listed at nageku

Naku 鳴く = to chirp, bark or cry (animal sounds); *in Narnia the Kool-Aid is so tasteless that it makes the animals cry*; cf. hoedasu = to bark; cf. hoeru = to bark, howl, roar, cry; cf. unaru = to groan or roar

Nakunaru 亡くなる = to die; *after Nancy went to Kuwait, I heard a nasty rumor that she had died*; cf. related terms listed at shinu

Nakunaru 無くなる = to run out or disappear; from naku, the adverbial form of nai = not + naru = to become; cf. related terms listed at bossuru

Nakusu 無くす = to lose (an item); *a nanny in Kuwait sued her employer after he lost her passport*; cf. related terms listed at okiwasureru

Nakutemo なくても = even if not, even without, used as a suffix; from nai = negation + temo = even if

Nama 生 = raw, uncooked; *Joe Namath likes raw vegetables*

Namae 名前 = a name; *Nancy's maestro knows her name*; cf. aishou = a pet name; cf. chimei = a place name; cf. jinmei = a person's name; cf. kyuusei = a maiden name, former name; cf. meibo = a directory or list of names; cf. meigara = a brand name; cf. meishou = a name or title; cf. myouji = a family name or surname; cf. na = name or fame; cf. sei = a family name or surname; cf. seimei = a full name; cf. shimei = a full name; cf. tenmei = a name of a store; cf. tsuushou = a nickname or alias, popular name; cf. tsuushoumei = a nickname or alias; cf. yobina = a name or alias

Namakeru 怠ける = to be lazy; *the nasty man staying in Ken's room is lazy*; cf. okotaru = to be lazy, to overlook or neglect

Namari 鉛 = lead (an element); *the narco named Mario uses lead bullets*; cf. related terms listed at tanso

Nameraka 滑らか = mellow, smooth; *my nanny from Mexico is a rock artist, and she is mellow, with smooth skin*; cf. enkatsu = smooth, harmonious; cf. tsurutsuru = smooth, slippery

Nami 波 = a wave; *a tsu<u>nami</u> is a big <u>wave</u>*

Namida 涙 = tears; *when the <u>Na</u>zis broke her <u>mir</u>ror, my <u>daughter</u> shed <u>tears</u>*

Namidagumu 涙ぐむ = to be moved to tears; from namida = tears + gumu = kumu = to ladle or scoop water

Nan なん = a softener, e.g., dame nan desu = it's bad; cf. no = a softener

Nan 何 = what; *<u>what</u> is <u>Nan</u>cy wearing?*

Nan 南 = south, used as a word component, e.g., nankyoku = the South Pole; *our <u>nann</u>y is from <u>South</u> America*

Naname no 斜めの = diagonal, oblique; *<u>Nan</u>cy's <u>nan</u>ny <u>messed</u> up by allowing her to draw <u>diagonal</u> lines on the wall*

Nanban 何番 = what number; from nani = what + bangou = number

Nanboku sensou 南北戦争 = the American Civil War; from nan = south, e.g., nanbei = South America; + boku = hoku = north, e.g., hokubu = northern parts; + sensou = a war

Nanbonka 何本か = a few long thin objects; from nan = what + bon = hon = counter for long thin objects + ka = question marker

Nanbu 南部 = southern parts; from nan = south + bubun = a part of something; cf. related terms listed at ichibu

Nanchaku mo 何着も = trying on clothes many times even; from nan = what + chakuyou suru = to put clothes on + mo = even; cf. shichaku = trying on clothes

Nanda 何だ = is this all? what do you mean? do you mean to say? or it's nothing! from nani = what + da = it is

Nandaka なんだか = a little, somewhat, somehow; *when the <u>nan</u>ny took <u>Dar</u>win for a ride in the <u>car</u>, they fooled around <u>a little</u>*; cf. chottoshita = somewhat, quite; cf. ikubun = somewhat, somehow, to some extent; cf. ikuraka = somewhat, a little

Nandatte なんだって = anyone, anything; what? *<u>Nan</u>cy opens her <u>daughter</u>'s <u>ten</u>nis court to <u>anyone</u>*; cf. nandemo = every thing, anything

Nande なんで = why?, what for?, how? from nan = what + de = from; cf. related terms listed at naze

Nandemo なんでも = everything, anything; from nani = what + demo = any or even; cf. nandatte = anyone, anything

Nandoka 何度か = several times, once or twice; from nando = how many times + ka (ka adds the meaning "some" when it follows a question word, e.g., nanika = something, dokoka = somewhere); cf. related terms listed at nandomo

Nandomo 何度も = many times; from nani = what + do = times + mo = even; cf. nandoka = several times, once or twice; cf. saisan = many times, again and again

Nangoku 南国 = southern countries; from nan = south + goku = koku = country; cf. related terms listed at kuni

Nani 何 = what; *<u>what</u> is the <u>nann</u>y wearing?*

Nan'i (Nani) 南緯 = southern latitude; from nan = south + ido = latitude

Nani shiro 何しろ = at any rate, anyhow; *our <u>nan</u>ny wears <u>sheepskin</u> <u>rob</u>es, but they are clean, <u>at</u> <u>any</u> <u>rate</u>*; cf. related terms listed at tonikaku

Nanigashi 某 = so-and-so, one, that person, usually spelled なにがし; *our <u>nann</u>y was <u>gashing</u> herself with <u>so-and-so</u>'s <u>knives</u>*; cf. related terms listed at aitsu

Nanige ni 何気に = inadvertently, without knowing; *the <u>nanny</u>'s <u>guest</u> didn't see my <u>niece</u> and <u>inadvertently</u> stepped on her <u>foot</u>*; cf. related terms listed at ukkari

Nanigenai 何気ない = casual, nonchalant; *I will ask him in a <u>casual</u> <u>nonchalant</u> way <u>nani</u> (what) he <u>gets</u> from the refrigerator at <u>night</u>*; cf. heiki = unconcerned, nonchalant, calmness; cf. mutonchaku = nonchalant, indifferent; cf. nonki = easygoing, nonchalant

Nanigoto 何事 = what, something, everything, nothing (with negatives), something or other; from nani = what + goto = koto = intangible thing; cf. related terms listed at banji

Nanika 何か = something; from nani = what + ka = question marker

Nanika ni tsukete 何かにつけて = one way or another; from nanika = something + ni = to + tsukeru = to follow

Nanimo 何も = nothing (with negative constructions); from nani = what + mo = even

Nanimokamo 何もかも = everything; from nani = what + mo = even + kamoshiremasen = possibly; cf. related terms listed at banji

Naniyori (mo) 何より(も) = more than anything; from nani = what + yori = compared to + mo = even

Nanji 何時 = what time; from nan = what + ji = time

Nanjikan 何時間 = how many hours; from nani = what + jikan = hour

Nanjuu 何十 = several tens; from nani = what + juu = ten

Nanka なんか = something like, somehow, things like, such a thing; from nani = thing + ka = question marker

Nankai 何回 = how many times; from nani = what + kai = times

Nankai 難解 = difficult to understand; *the nanny and the Kaiser are difficult to understand when they speak in German*

Nankaimo 何回も = many times; from nankai = how many times + mo = even; cf. related terms listed at nandomo

Nankyoku 南極 = the Antarctic or South Pole; *my nanny drank Kyoto Kool-Aid when she went to the Antarctic*

Nankyoku 難局 = a difficult situation; *that nanny wants to join the Kyoto Kool-Aid club, but she's involved in a difficult situation and may not be accepted*

Nanmin 難民 = refugee; from nan = difficult, e.g., konnan = difficult; + shimin = citizen

Nanninka 何人か = some people; from nannin = how many people + ka = question marker

Nanpa suru ナンパする = to hit on, to pick up a woman on the street; from nanpa = seducer, playboy; *the nanny's Pa (father) is a playboy*

Nanseibu 南西部 = the southwestern part; from nan = south + sei = west, e.g., sei'ou = Western Europe; + bu = part or section; cf. related terms listed at ichibu

Nante なんて = such a thing, something; *Nancy's tennis ball fell into the river, such a thing*

Nanto なんと = what, how, whatever; *what a treasure our nanny's tomatoes are*

Nanto shitemo 何としても = by any means necessary; from nanto = whatever + shitemo = if we do

Nantoka 何とか = somehow or something, somehow or other, something or other; from nani = what + toka = etecetera

Nantomo なんとも = quite or extremely, in positive constructions; not at all, in negative constructions; *Nancy says that tomorrow is an extremely good days; regarding other days, she is not at all sure*; cf. related terms listed at ooi ni and at zenzen

Nantonaku なんとなく = somehow or other, for some reason or another; from nan = something + to = if + naku = adverbial form of nai = not; so this could be understood as, "if something, not" or "maybe yes, maybe no"; cf. douyara = somehow or other; cf. douka = please, somehow or other; cf. nazeka = somehow

Nao 尚 = further, in addition, still; this is usually spelled なお; *in addition, Naomi will still be joining us*; cf. related terms listed at ni kuwaete

Naoru 治る = to be cured or get well; *go to Naomi's room if you want to be cured*

Naoru 直る = to be corrected or repaired; *Naomi's ruined bicycle was repaired*

Naosu 治す = to cure or heal; *Naomi's soup can cure the common cold*; cf. iyasu = to heal, cure, quench (thirst)

Naosu 直す = to correct or repair; *Naomi's supervisor repaired her chair*; cf. related terms listed at shuuri suru

Nara なら = if, in case; *in case you narrate the story, please speak slowly*; cf. related terms listed at moshi

Naraba ならば = if, in case; *in case you narrate badly, I will help you*; cf. related terms listed at moshi

Naraberu 並べる = to line up (transitive); *in Nara, I took my best rubies and lined them up*

Narabu 並ぶ = to line up (intransitive); *in Nara, the firefighters' boots were lined up*

Naranai ならない = must not (when used after te wa); cannot help (doing); one must (e.g., when used after nakute wa, nakereba or nai to); the past tense of naru, this means, literally, "will not become"; cf. ikemasen = ikenai = bad, unacceptable, prohibited

Narasu 鳴らす = to ring or sound; the transitive form of naru = to ring or sound

Narau 習う = to learn or study; *a nanny told Raul Castro to study more*; cf. related terms listed at benkyou suru

Nareru 慣れる = to become accustomed to; *the nasty red rooster became accustomed to the farmer*; cf. najimu = to get used to or adapt

Nari なり = or, or something; *she is trying to be naughty or something*; cf. related terms listed at soretomo

Nari ni なりに = in a person's own way or style; *the nanny reads to my niece in her own way*

Narikiru なりきる = to turn completely into, to become completely; from naru = to consist of + kiru = to cut

Naritachi 成り立ち = origin, structure, the way something came about; from naritatsu = to materialize; cf. kousei = structure, composition; cf. other related terms listed at kigen

Naritatsu 成り立つ = to consist of, to materialize; *the buildings at Narita that tatsu (stand up) consist of concrete and steel*; cf. naru = to consist of

Naru なる = to become, to turn out or result in; *the nasty rumor became a reality*

Naru 成る = to consist of; *after something naru (becomes) it consists of whatever it has become*; cf. naritatsu = to consist of, to materialize

Naru 生る = to bear (fruit); *when fruit naru (becomes), a tree bears fruit*; cf. minoru = to bear fruit, ripen

Naru 鳴る = to chime, ring or sound; *the nanny asked Rudolph to ring the door bell*

Narubeku なるべく = as much as possible; *the nanny's ruined the beggar's Kool-Aid when she added as much sugar as possible*; cf. kyokuryoku = as much as possible, to the best of one's ability; cf. dekiru dake = as much as possible

Naruhodo なるほど = I see, that's right; *there's a nasty rumor that I hold the door only for people I like; I see*

Nasa 無さ = absence, nonexistence; from nai = not + sa = a suffix that makes a noun from other words; cf. related terms listed at fuzai

Nasai なさい = do; the stem form of nasaru = to do honorably; used as a suffix after the stem form of a verb, in order to form commands, e.g., tabenasai = eat!

Nasakenai 情けない = miserable, pitiable, shameful, regrettable; *when NASA shot Ken into the sky at night, it was shameful*; cf. related terms listed at ki no doku and at mittomonai

Nasaru なさる = to do honorably; *while working at NASA, Ruth did things honorably*; cf. related terms listed at suru

Nashi 梨 = pear tree, or a pear; *when he saw that pear, he started gnashing his teeth*; cf. related terms listed at kudamono

Nashi de 無しで = without; *I can do without your teeth gnashing*; cf. related terms listed at naki

Nashieru なし得る = to be capable of doing (this can also be pronounced nashiuru); *he started gnashing his teeth when he realized that the erudite guy was capable of doing the work*

Nashitogeru 成し遂げる = to accomplish or complete; *after gnashing their teeth together with Rudolph all night, they completed the job*; cf. related terms listed at hatasu

Nasu ナス = eggplant; *the nasty surprise was an eggplant*; cf. related terms listed at yasai

Nasu 成す = to achieve or effect; *the nasty supervisor achieved his goal*

Natsu 夏 = summer; *gnats bothered the supervisor during the summer*; cf. related terms listed at kisetsu

Natsu gentei de 夏限定で = exclusively in the summer; from natsu = summer + gentei = restriction + de = of

Natsukashii 懐かしい = nostalgic, evocative of times past; *I think of the natsu (summer) when I was cashing in my stocks, and I feel nostalgic*

Natsuku なつく = to become emotionally attached; *I got emotionally attached to my natty suit with Kool-Aid stains on it*; cf. related terms listed at ai suru

Nattoku suru 納得する = to acquiesce, agree; *the Nazis were totally cool with the idea and agreed to it*; cf. related terms listed at sansei suru

Nawa 縄 = rope; *narco warlords use rope to tie up their opponents*; cf. tsuna = rope

Nawatobi 縄跳び = skipping rope; from nawa = rope + tobu = to jump

Nayamasu 悩ます = to annoy or worry; this is the transitive form of nayamu = to be troubled or worried; *when I was taking a nap in the yard, my master's soup boiled, and that annoyed me*; cf. sawaru = to harm or annoy

Nayami 悩み = distress, worry; from nayamu = to be troubled or worried; cf. kizukare = mental fatigue, worry; cf. monmon = worry, agony, worrying endlessly; cf. shinpai = anxiety, worry

Nayamu 悩む = to be troubled or worried; this is the intransitive form of nayamasu = to annoy or worry; *while I was taking a nap in the yard, the earth moved, and I got worried*; cf. related terms listed at shinpai suru

Naze なぜ = why or how; *why is Nancy so zesty?* cf. doushite = why or how; cf. nande = why?, what for?, how?

Nazeka なぜか = somehow; from naze = why or how + ka = question marker; cf. related terms listed at nantonaku

Nazenara なぜなら = because, the reason is; from naze = why + nara = case

Nazo 謎 = an enigma, puzzle or riddle; *there are puzzles and riddles in the narco zone*; cf. nazonazo = an enigma, puzzle or riddle

Nazonazo 謎々 = an enigma, puzzle or riddle; from nazo = an enigma, puzzle or riddle

Nazukeru 名付ける = to name or christen (this is spelled nadukeru in electronic dictionaries); from namae = name + tsukeru = to attach

Ne 値 = cost or price; *Netflix prices are rising*; cf. related terms listed at nedan

Ne 根 = root, basis; *in the Netherlands, the root of our social structure is fraternal love*; cf. related terms listed at kiban

Nebarinuku 名張抜く = to stick it out or see through it to the end; *when the negative barber was recycling nuclear waste, he saw it through to the end*; cf. related terms listed at tsuzukeru

Nebaru 粘る = to persist, to be sticky; *the nectar they served at the bar room was sticky*; cf. related terms listed at tsuzukeru

Nebou 寝坊 = sleeping in late; this can also be spelled 寝ぼう; *after hurting my neck while bowling, I slept in late*

Necchuu suru 熱中する = to be absorbed in, to be enthusiastic about; *Netflix chooses movies for me, and I am absorbed in them*; cf. harikiru = to be in high spirits, enthusiastic, eager

Nedan 値段 = cost or price; *the Netherland's dance studios are raising prices*; cf. atai = value, price; cf. bukka = prices (in general); cf. kakaku = price; cf. hi = cost or expense, used as a suffix; cf. hiyou = cost; cf. ne = price; cf. ryoukin = a price, fare or fee

Nefuda 値札 = price tag; *in the Netherlands, my foolish daughter changed the price tags on some merchandise*; cf. related terms listed at fuda

Negaeru 寝返る = to betray; *the negative erudite guy betrayed us*; cf. uragiru = to betray or deceive

Negai 願い = a hope, prayer or request; from negau = to ask, hope, pray or request; cf. related terms listed at shomou

Negao 寝顔 = a sleeping face; from neru = to sleep + gao = kao = face; cf. related terms listed at kao

Negau 願う = to ask, hope, pray or request; *the negative Australian requested help*; cf. related terms listed at tanomu

Negi ネギ = a green onion; *in the Netherlands, they eat geese with green onions*; cf. related terms listed at yasai

Negokochi 寝心地 = sleep comfort; from neru = to sleep + gokochi = kokochi = feeling or mood; cf. related terms listed at kokochiyosa

Ne'iro (Neiro) 音色 = timbre; from ne = sound; *the neighbors are making a sound*; + iro = color

Nekasu 寝かす = to put to sleep; the transitive form of neru = to sleep

Nekki 熱気 = hot air, intensity, zeal; *the couple was necking with some intensity*; cf. related terms listed at nesshin

Neko 猫 = a cat; *that cat is owned by a negative coder*; cf. koneko = a kitten

Nemui 眠い = sleepy; from nemuru = to sleep

Nemuke 眠気 = sleepiness; from nemui = sleepy + ke = ki = feeling

Nemuri 眠り = sleep; from nemuru = to sleep; cf. suimin = sleep

Nemuru 眠る = to sleep; *my nephew moved the rooster so that he could sleep*; cf. related terms listed at neru

Nen 年 = year; *my negative nephew has been waiting a year for help to arrive*; cf. banzai = 10,000 years; cf. dounen = that year, the same year, the same age; cf. nendo = fiscal year, school year, etc.; cf. nenkan = the whole year, annual; cf. reinen = an average or normal year; cf. sai = age, years old; cf. suunen = several years; cf. toshi = year

Nen 念 = sense or feeling; *my negative nephew has a feeling of hopelessness*; cf. related terms listed at kankaku

Nendai 年代 = age, generation, period; from nen = year + jidai = era; cf. related terms listed at jidai

Nendo 年度 = fiscal year, school year, etc.; from nen = year + do = time; cf. related terms listed at nen

Nendo 粘土 = clay; *my negative nephew built a dome out of clay*; cf. related terms listed at aka

Nendo 粘度 = viscosity; from nen = sticky; *my negative nephew uses dough with high viscosity for baking*

Nengajou 年賀状 = a New Year's card; from nen = year + gajou = New Year's card; cf. gajou = a New Year's card

Nengou 年号 = name of an era, a year number; from nen = year + gou = number, e.g., bangou = number; cf. related terms listed at bangou

Nen'iri (Neniri) 念入り = elaborate, meticulous; *my negative nephew irritates people with his elaborate arguments*; cf. related terms listed at menmitsu

Nenjuugyouji 年中行事 = an annual event; from nen = year + juu = chuu = inside + gyouji = event

Nenkan 年間 = the whole year, annual; from nen = year + kan = interval or space; cf. related terms listed at nen

Nenkin 年金 = annuity, pension; from nen = year + kingaku = a sum of money; cf. related terms listed at kikin

Nenmaku 粘膜 = a mucous membrane; *my negative nephew has magic cookies that stimulate mucous membranes*; cf. related terms listed a maku

Nenmatsu 年末 = end of the year; from nen = year + matsu = end, e.g., shuumatsu = weekend; cf. similar terms listed at shuumatsu

Nennen 年々 = year by year, annually; from nen = year

Nenpou 年俸 = an annual salary; *my negative nephew's pony cost more than my annual salary*; cf. related terms listed at chin

Nenrei 年齢 = age; *as the nen (years) race by we begin to show our age*; cf. rourei = advanced age

Nenryou 燃料 = fuel; *my negative nephew sold Pope Leo some fuel*

Nenza 捻挫 = a sprain; *when my negative nephew went to Zambia, he got a sprain*

Nerau 狙う = to aim; *she aimed the gun at the necklace that Raul Castro was wearing*; cf. mezasu = to aim at; cf. mokuhyou suru = to aim at

Neri 練り = paste; from neru = to knead

Neru 寝る = to sleep or go to bed; *my nephew's room is a good place to sleep*; cf. jukusui suru = to sleep well; cf. nemuru = to sleep

Neru 練る = to knead or plan carefully; *negative Ruth kneads bread dough*

Nesshin 熱心 = enthusiasm; *the doctor had enthusiasm for treating diseases of the neck and the shin*; cf. jounetsu = enthusiasm; cf. nekki = hot air, intensity, zeal

Nessuru 熱する = to heat; from netsu = heat + suru = to do

Netami 妬み = jealousy, usually written ねたみ; from netamu = to be jealous; cf. senbou = envy; cf. shitto = jealousy; cf. urayamashii = envious

Netamu 妬む = to be jealous, to envy, usually written ねたむ; *I envy your*

Netflix amusements

Netchuu suru 熱中する – see necchuu suru

Netsu 熱 = heat, fever; *Netflix showed a Superman movie, but I couldn't watch because I had a fever*; cf. binetsu = a slight fever; cf. other related terms listed at atsusa

Netsuretsu na 熱烈な = passionate, vehement; *his passionate performance in the movie netted Superman a retro suit*

Nettai 熱帯 = the tropics; *I threw a net over a tiger in the tropics*

Nettairin 熱帯林 = a tropical forest; from nettai = the tropics + shinrin = a forest; cf. related terms listed at mori

Nettou 熱湯 = boiling water; *my neighbor cooks tofu in boiling water*; cf. related terms listed at mizu

Neyou tto 寝ようっと = I shall sleep! From neyou = I shall sleep + tto = a suffix used for emphasis

Nezumi ねずみ = a rat or mouse; *that mouse has a lot of nerve, zooming around the house*

Nezuyoi 根強い = firmly rooted; from ne = root; + tsuyoi = strong

Ni に = a suffix that forms an adverb from the preceding word, e.g., shinsetsu ni = kindly

Ni に = at, by, for, from, in, on, to, per, for the purpose of; cf. de = at, in (space), on, in (time), by (means), from, of, because of, and; cf. e = to, for, toward

Ni atatte にあたって = at the time of; from ni = at + ataru = to hit; cf. ni saishite = at the time of

Ni chigainai に違いない = no doubt, certainly; from chigau = to differ; literally this means "not to differ" or "there is no discrepancy"; cf. related terms listed at tashika ni

Ni chikai に近い = almost; from chikai = close; cf. related terms listed at ayauku

Ni hoka naranai に他ならない = is due to nothing but, is none other than; from ni = to + hoka naranai = nothing but; cf. shikanai = have no choice, there's nothing but, no more than

Ni kagiru に限る = it's limited to, or there's nothing better; from ni = to + kagiru = it's limited to

Ni kagitte に限って = particularly when; from ni kagiru = it's limited to; cf. related terms listed at toku ni

Ni kakawarazu にかかわらず – see kakawarazu

Ni kakete にかけて = for, over or through (a period of time); *my niece carried Kennedy's tennis rackets for years*

Ni kuwaete に加えて = in addition; from kuwaeru = to add or include; cf. katawara = close by, beside, in addition to, besides; cf. nao = further, in addition, still; cf. oyobi = and, in addition; cf. sonota (or sono hoka) = otherwise, besides, in addition, the rest

Ni made にまで = as far as; from ni = to + made = as far as

Ni mo kakawarazu にもかかわらず = nevertheless, in spite of, regardless; *the needy moping cabbie carries the warrant to the zoo regardless of whether he is authorized to do so*; cf. related terms listed at kakawarazu

Ni motozuite に基づいて = based on, according to; from motozuku = to be based on; cf. ni yotte = according to, by means of, due to; cf. other related terms listed at motozuku

Ni mukete に向けて = towards, for the purpose of; from ni = to + mukeru = to direct or turn towards

Ni naru になる = to become, to do honorably; *my niece heard nasty rumors that she was becoming lazy, and she started to do things more honorably*; cf. to naru = to become, to amount to

Ni oite において = at or in, regarding; *my niece oiled her tennis racket at the gym*; cf. related terms listed at ni tsuite

Ni okeru における = in, at, on, as for, regarding; *my niece acts OK when Ruth talks to her regarding things she doesn't understand*; cf. related terms listed at ni tsuite

Ni oujite に応じて = depending on; from ni = to + oujiru = to respond or comply with; cf. related terms listed at ni yotte

Ni saishite に際して = at the time of; from ni = at + sai = when + shite = doing; cf. ni atatte = at the time of

Ni shiro にしろ = even though; *my niece wears sheepskin robes even though she has nice clothes*; cf. noni = in spite of the fact, in order to, while, if only; cf. -tsutsu (used after a verb stem) = while, even though

Ni shitara にしたら – see ni totte

Ni shite wa にしては = for (e.g., she dances well for a child), considering it's; *when niece and the Shiite techie walk to town, they make good time, considering how often they stop to look at flowers*

Ni shitemo にしても – see sore ni shitemo

Ni sotte に沿って = in accordance with, along; *since my niece is a socialist, the television programs she watches are in accordance with her views*; cf. douri ni = rightly, in accordance with; cf. zoi = along

Ni suginai に過ぎない = no more than, merely; from suginai = does not exceed; cf. related terms listed at miman

Ni sureba にすれば – see ni totte

Ni suru にする = to make A into B, to raise a person to a position, to decide (see koto ni suru); from ni = to + suru = to do

Ni tai shite に対して = against, toward, as against, as compared with, in contrast to, with respect to, in regard to; from tai suru = to face toward, to confront, to be related to

Ni totte にとって (or ni shitara, or ni sureba) = regarding, concerning, to, for; *my niece totes eggs, and that's all I know concerning her job*; cf. related terms listed at ni tsuite

Ni tsuite について = concerning, regarding; *we had a conversation regarding my niece's tsuite (sweet) tooth*; cf. kan shite = concerning, regarding; cf. kan suru = to be related to, concerning; cf. ni oite = regarding, at, in; cf. ni okeru = regarding, in, at, on, as for; cf. ni shitara = regarding, concerning, to, for; cf. ni sureba = regarding, concerning, to, for; cf. ni totte = regarding, concerning, to, for; cf. ni tsuki = per, apiece, because of, regarding; cf. to kitara = regarding, concerning; cf. wo megutte = in regard to, concerning (disputes)

Ni tsukete につけて (or ni tsuke) – see nanika ni tsukete

Ni tsuki につき = per, apiece, because of, regarding; *when my niece went to the tsuki (moon), they charged $10 million apiece because of the expense*; cf. atari = per, apiece; cf. other related terms listed at ni tsuite and at tame

Ni tsumaru に詰まる = to be at a loss; *my niece had only one tsuitcase (suitcase) when she was marooned, and she was at a loss*

Ni tsure につれ = as X, then Y; an abbreviation of ni tsurete

Ni tsurete につれて = accordingly; from ni = to + tsureru = to lead

Ni tsuzuite に続いて = following, subsequently, after; from ni = by + tsuzuku = to be continued; cf. related terms listed at tsugi

Ni wa oyobanai には及ばない = it isn't necessary; from ni = to + the negative form of oyobu = to reach or extend, suggesting that an obligation doesn't extend very far;

cf. related terms listed at koto wa nai

Ni yori により – see ni yotte

Ni yoru による – see ni yotte

Ni yotte によって = according to, by means of, due to; this is the gerund, or "-ing" form of ni yoru = according to, by means of, due to; it is equivalent to ni yori, which is the stem form of ni yoru; *I have to kneel for yoga and tennis lessons due to my bad feet*; cf. ni motozuite = based on, according to; cf. ni oujite = depending on; cf. ni totte = to, for, concerning, regarding; cf. shidai de = depending on

Niau 似合う = to suit or become (as in clothing); *the needlework that the owl is wearing suits it*

Nibui 鈍い = dull, dim-witted, slow; *the dim-witted guy wore knee-high boots at Easter*; cf. donkusai = slow, stupid, irritating

Niburu 鈍る = to become dull, blunt or weak; the verb form of nibui = dull, dim-witted or slow

Nicchuu 日中 = daytime, during the day; from nichi = day + chuu = during; cf. related terms listed at hiru

Nichi 日 = day, date; *Nietzche said to make every day count*; cf. hi = sun, sunlight, day; cf. related terms listed at yokujitsu

Nichibotsu 日没 = sunset; *Nietzsche took his friends out in boats to see the sunset*; cf. yuuyake = sunset

Nichiji 日時 = a date; from nichi = day + ji = time; cf. related terms listed at hinichi

Nichijou 日常 = ordinary, usual; *Nietzche and Joan of Arc visited their usual restaurant which was ordinary*; cf. related terms listed at taitei

Nidatsu 煮立つ = to boil; from niru = to boil + datsu = tatsu = to stand up; cf. related terms listed at niru

Nieru 煮える = to be cooked or boiled; this is the intransitive form of niru = to cook; cf. futtou suru = to boil; cf. gutsugutsu nieru = to simmer; cf. takeru = to be boiled or cooked; cf. waku = to grow hot, to boil (intransitive), to get excited

Nifuda 荷札 = tag, label, sign; *while kneeling, my foolish daughter changed the labels on some merchandise*; cf. related terms listed at fuda

Nigai 苦い = bitter; *since he can't get help for his broken foot, the kneeling guy is bitter*

Nigata 二型 = type two; from ni = two + gata = kata = form or style

Nigate 苦手 = a weak point; *as I kneel in the garden to repair my tent, I realize that sewing is one of my weak points*; cf. tokui = a strong point; cf. yowami = a weak point

Nigeru 逃げる = to escape or run away; *the Nigerian rooster ran away*; cf. nogareru = to escape; cf. hashirisaru = to run away; cf. nigesaru = to take flight or disappear; cf. nigetsuzukeru = to contine to run away; cf. nogareru = to escape

Nigesaru 逃げ去る = to take flight or disappear; from nigeru = to escape or run away + saru = to leave; cf. other related terms listed at bossuru and at nigeru

Nigetsuzukeru 逃げ続ける = to contine to run away; from nigeru = to run away + tsuzukeru = to continue; cf. related terms listed at nigeru

Nigiri 握り = grasping, a handful, a rice ball; from nigiru = to grasp or hold tight

Nigirishimeru 握りしめる = to grasp tightly; from nigiru = to grasp + shimeru = to tighten; cf. related terms listed at tsukamu

Nigiru 握る = to grasp or hold tight; *my niece grabbed the geese and the rooster and held tight*; cf. related terms listed at tsukamu

Nigiyaka にぎやか = lively, crowded; *my niece chased the geese while the Yankee* chased the <u>cat</u>, and it was a <u>lively</u> scene

Nigoru 濁る = to be muddy, cloudy or unclear; *the <u>kneeling golfer ruined</u> his pants because the grass <u>was muddy</u>*

Nihiki 二匹 = two small animals or bolts of cloth; from hiki = a counter for small animals or bolts of cloth

Nihon hen 日本円 = Japanese edition; from nihon = Japan + henshuu = editing

Nihonfuu 日本風 = Japanese style; from nihon = Japan + fuu = appearance, condition, style

Nihonga 日本画 = a Japanese painting; from nihon = Japan + kaiga = painting; cf. related terms listed at e

Nihongo 日本語 = the Japanese language; from nihon = Japan + go = language, word

Nihonjin 日本人 = a Japanese person; from nihon = Japan + jin = a person; cf. related terms listed at hito

Nihonsan 日本産 = made in Japan; from nihon = Japan + sangyou = industry; cf. nihonsei = made in Japan

Nihonsei 日本製 = made in Japan; from nihon = Japan + seihin = a product; cf. nihonsan = made in Japan

Nihonzaru 日本猿 = Japanese macaque; from nihon = Japan + zaru = saru = monkey; cf. related terms listed at saru

Niji 虹 = a rainbow; *I <u>needed</u> a <u>Jeep</u> to drive out and look for <u>rainbows</u>*

Nijoujou 二条城 = Nijou Castle; from ni = two + jouken = condition + jou = castle, e.g., meijou = famous castle

Nijuu 二重 = double; *my <u>niece</u> buys <u>juice</u> in <u>double</u> packs*; cf. baigaku = double the amount; cf. baizou = double

Nijuujinkaku 二重人格 = split personality; from nijuu = double + jinkaku = personality

Nijuukakoku 20ケ国 = 20 countries; this small ka can often be seen in counting words, e.g., nikagetsu = 2 months

Nikka 日課 = daily lesson or routine; from nichi = day + ka = a lesson; cf. related terms listed at jugyou

Nikkapokka ニッカポッカ = knickerbockers (men's baggy trousers); cf. zubon = pants or trousers

Nikki 日記 = a diary; *my <u>niece keeps</u> a <u>diary</u>*

Nikkou 日光 = sunlight, also a town and national park in Japan; *my <u>niece</u> went to <u>Colombia</u> to enjoy the <u>sunlight</u>*; cf. taiyoukou = sunlight

Nikkyuu 日給 = daily wage; from nichi = day + kyuuryou = salary, wages; cf. related terms listed at chin

Nikomu 煮込む = to cook together; from niru = to cook + komu = to crowd in; cf. related terms listed at niru

Nikoniko suru にこにこする = to smile; *when St. <u>Nicholas</u> reaches for his <u>nicotine</u>, he <u>smiles</u>*; cf. related terms listed at warau

Niku 肉 = meat or flesh; *we ate some <u>meat</u> when we were <u>near Kuwait</u>*

Nikui にくい = difficult to do, used as a suffix, e.g., tabenikui = difficult to eat; this is sometimes written 難い; *my <u>niece</u> in <u>Kuwait</u> tried to catch an <u>eagle</u>, but it was <u>difficult</u> <u>to do</u>*; cf. related terms listed at muzukashii

Nikujuu 肉汁 = gravy; from niku = meat + juu, which reminds us of juice; cf. related terms listed at shiru

Nikumiau 憎み合う = to hate each other; from nikumu = to hate + au = to come together

Nikumu 憎む = to hate or detest; *my <u>niece</u> in <u>Kuwait</u> saw a <u>movie</u> that she <u>detested</u>*; cf. related terms listed at kirai desu

Nikushoku 肉食 = meat-eating, carnivorous; from niku = meat + shokuji = meal

Nikushokujuu 肉食獣 = a carnivore; from nikushoku = meat-eating + yajuu = a wild animal

Nikutai 肉体 = the human body; from niku = meat + tai = body; cf. related terms listed at karada

Nikutaiteki 肉体的 = material, corporeal; from nikutai = the human body + teki = related to

Nimotsu 荷物 = luggage; *I left my luggage near the moats outside the castle*

Nin 人 = a person, used as a suffix, e.g., sannin = three people; *the ninja is a person*; cf. related terms listed at -sha

Ninau 担う = to carry or bear; *my niece now carries a lot of responsibility*; cf. related terms listed at hakobu

Ninchi 任地 = a post or appointment; *the ninja's chief assigned him to that post*

Ninensei 二年制 = a two-year system; from ninen = two years + seido = system; cf. related terms listed at seido

Ningen 人間 = a human being; *the ninjas that Genghis hired were human beings*; cf. related terms listed at hito

Ningyo 人魚 = a mermaid; from nin = a person + gyo = fish, e.g., gyogyou = a fishing business; cf. ningyou = a doll

Ningyou 人形 = a doll; *after the ninja ate his gyoza, his mother gave him a doll*; cf. hina = a doll

Ninja 忍者 = a spy or secret agent; *the ninny spread jam on the floor while trying to catch a ninja (spy)*

Ninjin にんじん = a carrot; *the ninja's jeans had carrot stains on them*; cf. related terms listed at yasai

Ninki 人気 = popularity; *the ninja's quiche acquired some popularity*; cf. hyouban = reputation, popularity, rumor

Ninkiburi 人気ぶり = so popular; from ninki = popularity + buri = "it's like; cf. buri ni = after an interval

Ninkimono 人気者 = a popular person, a favorite; from ninki = popularity + mono = a person

Ninmei 任命 = an appointment or nomination; *the ninja and the mayor received appointments to the committee*; cf. kiyou = appointment (to a position), being used for a role, promotion

Ninmu 任務 = duty, mission; *the ninja on the moon do their duty and attempt missions*; cf. gimu = unlimited duty to the emperor, ancestors and descendants; cf. giri = moral debt, limited duty to the outside world; cf. kinmu = service, duty, work

Ninpu 妊婦 = a pregnant woman; *the pregnant woman was married to a ninja who was poor*; cf. related terms listed at onna

Ninshiki 認識 = awareness, recognition, knowledge; *that ninja has sheep in Kiev, and he demonstrates awareness and knowledge of them*; cf. ishiki = consciousness; cf. other related terms listed at chishiki

Ninshin 妊娠 = pregnancy; *the ninja consulted a Shinto priest about his wife's pregnancy*

Nintai 忍耐 = patience; *the ninja treats his tiger with patience*; cf. gaman = patience, endurance; cf. gamanzuyosa = patience, perseverance; cf. shinbou = endurance, patience; cf. taikyuu = endurance

Nintairyoku 忍耐力 = fortitude; from nintai = patience + ryoku = force

Nintoku 仁徳 – see jintoku

Ninzuu 人数 = number of people; *number of nin (people) at the zoo is 50*; cf. related terms listed at bangou

Nioi 匂い = fragrance, scent; from niou = to smell of; cf. related terms listed at kaori

Niou 仁王 = two fierce guardians of Buddha whose statues stand at the entrance of many Buddhist temples; *the two fierce guardians of Buddha kneeled before the ocean*

Niou 匂う = to smell of; *that knee oil that you are applying smells of vinegar*

Niru 似る = to resemble; *Nietsche and Rousseau resembled each other*

Niru 煮る = to boil or cook; *my niece ruins food when she cooks*; cf. iru = to roast or toast; cf. itameru = to cook or fry; cf. musu = to steam, to be hot and humid; cf. nidatsu = to boil; cf. nikomu = to cook together; cf. senjiru = to boil; cf. taku = to cook (rice, etc.); cf. wakasu = to boil, to heat (transitive); cf. yaku = to bake, burn, roast, grill, toast; cf. yuderu = to boil

Nise 偽 = a falsehood or lie; *my niece sent me a letter that contained a lie*; cf. related terms listed at uso

Nisemono 偽物 = a counterfeit or fake; from nise = a lie + mono = a tangible thing

Nishi 西 = west; *there are some needy sheep to the west*; cf. similar terms listed at minami

Nishiki 錦 = brocade, fine dress; *she wore brocade while kneeling in front of a Shiite king*; cf. related terms listed at fuku

Nisou 尼僧 = a nun or priestess; *my niece lived a solo life until she became a nun*; cf. ama = a nun

Nite にて = at (a location) or for (a category, speaking of a prize); this is equivalent to the particle "de"; *my niece's teddy Bear was at home when it was considered for a prize in the cuteness category*

Nite iru 似ている = resembling; from niru = to resemble

Nitou 二等 = second class or place; from ni = two + toukyuu = a ranking

Niwa 庭 = a garden or yard; *in order to have a nice garden, we will need water*; cf. rakuen = paradise, or pleasure garden; cf. saien = a vegetable garden; cf. shokubutsuen = a botanical garden; cf. teien = a garden or park

Niwatori 鶏 = chicken; *the niwa (garden) contains a tori (bird) which is a chicken*; cf. related terms listed at tori

No = a *possessive particle*, e.g., watashi no = mine; a *question marker*, e.g., iku no = will you go? a *nominalizer* that forms nouns, e.g., miru no ga suki desu = I like looking, or, takai no = the expensive one; a *softener*, e.g., ame ga furidashita no yo = it started to rain for sure; cf. nan = a softener

No koto dakara のことだから = based on; from the possessive no + koto = intangible thing + dakara = therefore; cf. related terms listed at motozuku

No kuse ni のくせに – see kuse ni

No moto (ni) のもと(に) = in front of or underneath a person, on the basis of; from moto = base, implying that the location of a person is his or her "base"

Nobasu 伸ばす = to grow long, to lengthen, extend, smooth out, stretch, develop, expand (transitive); *since there is no basu (bus), I will extend my stay*; cf. related terms listed at shiku

Nobasu 延ばす = to extend or postpone; *since there was no bus, I postponed my departure*; cf. related terms listed at miawaseru

Noberu 延べる = to lengthen or stretch (transitive); *since there is no bedroom, we will lengthen this wall to make a partition*; cf. related terms listed at shiku

Noberu 述べる = to tell or state; *if you can state the results of your research clearly, you might win a Nooberu (Nobel) prize*; cf. related terms listed at hanasu

Nobeyuka menseki 延床面積 = total floor

area; from noberu = nobiru = to lengthen or stretch + yuka = floor + menseki = area

Nobiru 伸びる = to lengthen or stretch, to be postponed or prolonged (intransitive); (this is sometimes spelled 延びる) since there is *no biiru* (beer), the party will be *postponed*; cf. hirogaru = to spread out, to extend (intransitive)

Nobori 上り = an ascent; from noboru = to rise or ascend; cf. joushou = rising, ascending, climbing

Noborisen 上り線 = the up line or the inbound line; from noboru = to rise + sen = line

Noborizaka 上り坂 = uphill slope; from noboru = to climb + zaka = saka = hill; cf. related terms listed at shamen

Noboru 上る = to rise or ascend (used for most situations apart from sunrise and moonrise); *nobody saw the rooster rise into Heaven*; cf. related terms listed at agaru

Noboru 昇る = to rise (used for sunrise and moonrise); *nobody was on the roof to see the sun rise*; cf. related terms listed at agaru

Noboru 登る = to climb; *when I climbed the mountain, nobody was rooting for me*; cf. agaru = to climb, go up, rise (prices), enter a house; cf. touchou suru = to climb to the summit; cf. tsutau = to go along, to climb up or down; cf. yojinoboru = to scramble up

Nochihodo 後ほど = afterward, later; *now there's no cheese, but the host will dole some out later*; cf. related terms listed at kongo

Node ので = because; *we have no dentist because the previous one retired*; cf. dake atte = because; cf. dake ni = because; cf. de = at, in (space), on, in (time), by (means), from, of, because, and; cf. datte = because, something is reportedly true, well; cf. kara = from, since, after, because, therefore; cf.

koto kara = because, on the basis that

Nodo 喉 = throat; *I have no dough (money) to buy medicine for my throat*

Nogareru 逃れる = to escape; *since he had no gas, he had to walk to town, and while he was gone, his red rooster escaped*; cf. related terms listed at nigeru

Nogasu 逃す = to let go, to allow to escape; *because he had no gas, the policeman allowed the speeder to escape*

Nohara 野原 = a field; *there is no harassment allowed in my fields*; cf. related terms listed at hara

Nokeru 退ける = to move something or put it out of the way; *since I could see no ketchup for Ruth, I moved the mayonnaise out of the way*; cf. idou suru = to move (an object); cf. iten suru = to move (a business, etc.); cf. ugokasu = to move something

Noki 軒 = eaves; *since it was raining and I had no key, I waited under the eaves*

Nokori 残り = remainder, balance, remnant; from nokoru = to remain; cf. iseki = ruins, remains; cf. other related terms listed at ato

Nokoru 残る = to stay behind, remain; *since we had no coconuts in our room, I stayed behind to harvest some*; cf. amaru = to be left over, to remain

Nokosu 残す = to leave behind; the transitive form of nokoru = to stay behind or remain; cf. okiwasureru = to mislay or leave behind

Nomi のみ = only, nothing but; *since there's no meat, we eat only vegetables*; cf. related terms listed at dake

Nomikomu 飲み込む = to swallow; from nomu = to swallow + komu = to get crowded

Nomimono 飲み物 = a beverage; from nomu = to drink + mono = thing; cf. inryou = a beverage

Nomu 飲む = to drink, swallow, take pills, smoke; *nomads on the moon drink a lot*

Nonbaabaru ノンバーバル = non-verbal

Nonbiri のんびり = carefree, at leisure, relaxed; *the juice had a non-beery taste, and it made me feel relaxed and carefree*

Noni のに = in spite of the fact, in order to, while, when, if only, too bad; *in spite of the fact that he has no knees, he runs the race in order to get exercise*; cf. related terms listed at nagara, at ni shiro and at tame

Nonki のんき = easygoing, nonchalant; *that nonchalant kid is easygoing*; cf. related terms listed at nanigenai

Nonoshiru 罵る = to revile, abuse or swear at, usually written ののしる; *he took no notice of the sheep in the room and started reviling the sheepdogs*; cf. related terms listed at ijimeru

Nooto ノート = a notebook

Norikaeru 乗り換える = to transfer (trains); from noru = to board a vehicle + kaeru = to exchange; cf. furikomu = to transfer

Norikiru 乗り切る = to get through (adversity), to overcome, to ride across; from noru = to ride a vehicle + kiru = to cut; cf. norikoeru = to overcome, to surpass, to ride across; cf. oshikiru = to overcome resistance

Norikoeru 乗り越える = to overcome, to surpass, to ride across; from noru = to ride a vehicle + koeru = to cross over, to exceed or surpass; cf. related terms listed at oikosu and norikiru

Norikosu 乗り越す = to ride past, to miss a train stop; from noru = to ride on + kosu = to pass or exceed

Norimono 乗り物 = a vehicle, transportation; from noru = to ride on + mono = a tangible thing

Noritsugu 乗り継ぐ = to connect (to a different flight, train, etc.); *Noriko tsued (sued) the goofballs at the airline when they didn't allow her to connect to a flight*

Noroi 呪い = a curse; *in Norway, Roy Rogers was greeted with curses*

Noroi korosu 呪い殺す = to put a deadly curse on; from noroi = a curse + korosu = to kill

Noru 乗る = to get on or ride in; *I tried to get on the bus, but there was no room*

Noru 載る = to be printed or placed on; *it's normal for rumors to be printed in that newspaper, and it's normal for such rumors to be placed on my desk*

Noseru 乗せる = to carry, load, transport; the transitive form of noru = to get on or ride in; cf. tsumikomu = to load (goods, etc.), to put on board

Noseru 載せる = to publish, to put on top of; the transitive form of noru = to be printed or placed on; cf. related terms listed at keisai suru

Noshigami のし紙 = gift-wrapping paper; *the nomad's sheets and the gambler's mirror were wrapped in gift-wrapping paper*; cf. related terms listed at kami

Noshikakaru のしかかる = to lean on, to weigh on; *in Norway, sheep meat kakaru (costs) more if the butcher leans on the meat while weighing it*; cf. yoriakaru = to lean on

Nou 能 = Noh, old-style Japanese theater; cf. kabuki = a form of traditional Japanese drama

Nou 脳 = a brain; *Alfred Nobel had a good brain*; cf. related terms listed at atama

Noudo 濃度 = concentration; *the Norwegian bread dough has a high concentration of sugar*; cf. kosa = consistency, darkness, thickness, density; cf. noukou = density, concentration

Nouen 農園 = a farm; from nougyou = agriculture + en = a park, e.g., kouen = a park; cf. related terms listed at noujou

Noufu 農夫 = farmer; *that farmer is no fool*; cf. related terms listed at hyakushou

Nougyou 農業 = agriculture; *the workers in agriculture received no gyoza*; cf. related terms listed at inasaku

Noujou 農場 = a farm; from nougyou = agriculture + jou = place; cf. bokujou = a stock farm, ranch, pasture; cf. nouen = a farm

Nouka 農家 = farmer, farmhouse; *the Norwegian carpenter became a farmer*; cf. related terms listed at hyakushou

Noukan suru 納棺する = to place a body in a coffin; *the nose of the kangaroo protruded when they put its body in a coffin*

Noukon 濃紺 = dark blue; *the nosy conductor wore a dark blue uniform*; cf. related terms listed at ao

Noukou 濃厚 = density, concentration; *North Korea has a high concentration of poverty*; cf. kosa = consistency, darkness, thickness, density; cf. noudo = concentration

Noumen 能面 = a Noh mask; from Nou = Noh (old-style Japanese theater) + men = mask; cf. related terms listed at men

Noumu 濃霧 = heavy fog; *due to heavy fog no moon was visible*; cf. kiri = fog or mist

Nounai 脳内 = inside the brain, intracerebral; from nou = brain + nai = inside

Nounyuu 納入 = payment of taxes, etc, supply (of goods, etc.), delivery; *if there is no nyuusu (news), we always have a supply of stories about cats and dogs, or we can explain the payment of taxes*; cf. kyoukyuu = supply or provision

Nouryoku 能力 = ability, competence, skill; *in Norway, Pope Leo made Kool-Aid, demonstrating his ability, competence and skill*; cf. gijutsu = skill, technique, technology; cf. tegiwa = skill, performance, tact; cf. waza = skill, technique

Nousakumotsu 農作物 = agricultural crops; from nougyou = agriculture + sakumotsu = crops; cf. related terms listed at sakumotsu

Nousanbutsu 農産物 = agricultural produce; from nougyou = agriculture + sangyou = industry + butsu = thing; cf. related terms listed at sakumotsu

Noushuyou 脳腫瘍 = a brain tumor; from nou = a brain + shuyou = a tumor; cf. related terms listed at byouki

Nousocchuu 脳卒中 = a stroke; *the Norwegian soldier started chewing his fingernails after he had a stroke*; cf. related terms listed at byouki

Noutan 濃淡 = shade (of color, flavor, etc.); *the Norwegian tank was painted in shades of green*

Nozokikomu 覗き込む = to peer into; from nozoku = to snoop + komu = to crowd in

Nozoku 覗く = to peek or snoop; *I parked in the No Zone outside the Kool-Aid factory so that I could snoop on the activities inside*; cf. nozokikomu = to peer into

Nozoku 除く = to remove; *in the No Parking zone, a Kool-Aid truck was parked, but a tow truck removed it*; cf. related terms listed at hazusu

Nozomi 望み = hope, dream, wish; *in the Norwegian zone, they have plenty of meat, and my hope is to visit there*; cf. related terms listed at shomou

Nozomu 望む = to hope, dream or wish; *I parked in the No Zone at the movie theater and hoped that I wouldn't get towed*; cf. kibou suru = to hope or wish; cf. kokorozasu = to intend or aspire to

Nozomu 臨む = to attend (e.g., a function or class), to appear (e.g., in court), to deal with, to look out upon; *I parked in the No Parking zone under the moon when I attended the wedding*; cf. related terms listed at shori suru and at shusseki suru

Nugu 脱ぐ = to remove clothing; *when I went back into the swamp, I got new goop on my pants and had to remove my clothing*; cf. related terms listed at hazusu

Nuguu 拭う = to wipe; *I have to wipe up after that neutered goose*; cf. fuku = to wipe or mop

Nuiawaseru 縫い合わせる = to sew together; from nuu = to sew + awaseru = to join together; cf. related terms listed at nuu

Nuitsukeru 縫い付ける = to sew on; from nuu = to sew + tsukeru = to attach; cf. related terms listed at nuu

Nukeru 抜ける = to come out or come off, to fall out, to escape, to be missing; *the new kettle was ruined when it fell out of the box*; cf. hageru = to come off or peel off

Nuki (ni) 抜き = without, or omitting; *you can't be nuking my niece without permission*; cf. related terms listed at naki

Nukiuchi 抜き打ち = drawing a sword and striking in the same stroke; suddenly, without warning; from nuku = to extract + utsu = to strike; cf. related terms listed at kyuu ni

Nuku 抜く = to extract, omit, outrun or surpass, to do something to the end (if used as a suffix); *if I nuke you, that will extract all of your corks*; cf. toridasu = to extract; cf. other related terms listed at oikosu

Nukumori 温もり = warmth; *the nutritious Kool-Aid that Maureen served provided some warmth*; cf. related terms listed at atsusa

Numa 沼 = a swamp; *this new machine pumps swamp water*; cf. doronuma = a marsh, bog or swamp; cf. numachi = swampland

Numachi 沼地 = swampland; from numa = swamp + chi = ground; cf. doronuma = a marsh, bog or swamp; cf. numa = a swamp; cf. other similar terms listed at basho

Nuno 布 = cloth; *to put cloth on your head when you go out is the new normal*; cf. gofuku = cloth (for Japanese clothes), textile; cf. kiji = material, cloth, texture; cf. kinu = silk; cf. mushi nuno = a cloth for steaming; cf. nunoji = cloth or fabric; cf. orimono = textiles; cf. tanmono = cloth, textile; cf. zoukin = a dust cloth or cleaning cloth; cf. other related terms listed at momen

Nunoji 布地 = cloth or fabric; *since my new nose attracts jeers, I'm covering it with fabric*; cf. related terms listed at nuno

Nureru ぬれる = to get wet; *my new red roof got wet*

Nurikaeru 塗り替える = to repaint, rewrite; from nuru = to paint + kaeru = to replace or exchange

Nuru 塗る = to paint, plaster, spread, smear; *I painted my new roof*; cf. egaku = to draw, paint, depict, describe

Nurui ぬるい = lukewarm; *the nuclear reactor was ruined when they poured lukewarm water on it*

Nushi 主 = a master, used as a suffix, e.g., jinushi = a land owner; *the master had new shingles installed*

Nusumidasu 盗み出す = to steal (from a person); from nusumu = to steal + dasu = to take out; cf. related terms listed at nusumu

Nusumigiki 盗み聞き = eavesdropping; from nusumu = to steal + giku = kiku = to hear

Nusumu 盗む = to steal; *after a nuclear souvenir was moved into the garden, a guy stole it*; cf. nusumidasu = to steal (from a person); cf. ubaitoru = to snatch or plunder; cf. ubau = to rob or fascinate

Nuu 縫う = to sew; *the hangman sewed a noose for his victim*; cf. nuiawaseru = to sew together; cf. nuitsukeru = to sew on

Nyou 尿 = urine; *the neo-Nazi threw urine at his opponent*

Nyoubou 女房 = one's wife; *when we need yogurt for our boy, my wife buys some*; cf. related terms listed at kanai

Nyuu 入 = entering, used as a word component, e.g., nyuugaku = entering school; *I am entering Nyuuyooku (New York)*

Nyuudan 入団 = enrollment; from nyuu = entering + dantai = group; cf. touroku = registration, enrollment

Nyuugaku 入学 = entering school; from nyuu = entering + gaku = study, learning; cf. shuugaku = attending school; cf. tsuugaku = commuting to school

Nyuugakushiki 入学式 = school entrance ceremonies; from nyuugaku = entering school + shiki = ceremony

Nyuugan 乳癌 = breast cancer; from nyuu = milk, e.g., gyuunyuu = cow's milk; + gan = cancer; cf. related terms listed at byouki

Nyuuin 入院 = hospitalization; *in Nyuuyoku (New York) an infection led to his hospitalization*

Nyuuin suru 入院する = to be hospitalized; from nyuuin = hospitalization

Nyuujou 入場 = admission (to a theater, etc.); from nyuu = entering + jou = place

Nyuuryoku 入力 = computer input, data entry; from nyuu = entering + ryoku = power; cf. ki'nyuu = entry, filling in of forms

Nyuuryoku suru 入力する = to input (data); from nyuuryoku = computer input, data entry; cf. kinyuu suru = to write in or enter information

Nyuuseihin 乳製品 = dairy products; from nyuu = milk, e.g., gyuunyuu = cow's milk; + seihin = a product

Nyuusha 入社 = entering a company; from nyuu = entering + kaisha = company

Nyuushou suru 入賞する = to win an award or prize; *at the Nyuuyooku (New York) show, I won a prize*; cf. related terms listed at katsu

Nyuuyoku suru 入浴する = to take a bath; *I took a bath in nyuuyoku (New York)*; cf. abiru = to bathe, to receive (praise or attention) abundantly

O お = an honorific or humble prefix; *this is an honorable oak tree*; cf. go = an honorific or humble prefix

O 小 = small, used as a word component, e.g., ogawa = a brook; *these oats are small*

Oba 伯母 = an aunt, often spelled おば; *my aunt likes old bananas*; cf. oji = an uncle

Obaasan お祖母さん = a grandmother, an old lady; *my grandmother had an old banana and an apple for lunch*; cf. related terms listed at sofubo

Obasan 伯母さん = an aunt, an old woman, ma'am; often spelled おばさん; from oba = aunt + san = a honorific suffix

Obi 帯 = a kimono sash; *after Oprah drank beer, her kimono sash was too short*

Obiyakasu 脅かす = to menace or threaten; *the oily beast approached the yak, which assumed that it was an enemy and turned to threaten it*; cf. odokasu = to threaten; cf. odosu = to threaten

Oboeru 覚える = to memorize or remember; *those old boys are erudite, and they remember the things they memorize*; cf. kioku suru = to remember; cf. omoiataru = to come to mind or recall; cf. omoidasu = to remember; cf. omoiukabu = to come to mind

Obon お盆 = a Buddhist summer festival when ancestors are worshipped; *we visit our ancestor's old bones at a temple during the Buddhist summer festival*

Oboreru 溺れる = to drown, or to indulge in,

usually spelled おぼれる; *the old boys had a red rooster, but it drowned*; cf. botsu = to drown, sink, disappear, or die

Ocha お茶 = tea, usually green; from the honorific "o" + cha = tea; cf. related terms listed at cha

Ochiba 落ち葉 = fallen leaves; from ochiru = to fall + ba = ha = leaf; cf. related terms listed at ha

Ochichi お乳 – see chichi

Ochiiru 陥る = to fall into, to be trapped in; *I was eating old cheese at Easter with Ruth when I realized that we had fallen into a trap*; cf. related terms listed at ochiru

Ochikomi 落ち込み = a decline; from ochiru = to fall + komu = to crowd into; cf. related terms listed at genshou

Ochiru 落ちる = to fall, fail, go downhill; *the old chief ruined his knee when he fell*; cf. korobu = to fall over, to stumble; cf. korogaru = to roll, fall over, lie down; cf. kuzureochiru = to tumble down, to fall in; cf. ochiiru = to fall into, to be trapped in; cf. taoreru = to fall or faint, to become bankrupt; cf. tenraku suru = to fall or decline; cf. tsuiraku suru = to fall or crash; cf. other related terms listed at hazureru

Ochitsuki 落ち着き = composure, calmness, serenity; from ochitsuku = to relax; cf. related terms listed at heiki and at reisei

Ochitsuku 落ち着く = to relax or be settled; ochitsuku = to relax or be settled; *I have some old cheese in my tsuitcase (suitcase) and some Kool-Aid, so please relax*; cf. related terms listed at kutsurogu

Ochuugen 御中元 = an honorable mid-summer gift; from the honorific prefix "o" + chuugen = a midsummer gift; cf. related terms listed at okurimono

Odaijini お大事に = take care of yourself, said to a sick person; usually preceded by douzo = go ahead; from the honorific "o" + daiji = precious + -ni = a suffix that forms an adverb; so douzo odaijini means literally "go ahead, preciously"

Odayaka 穏やか = calm, peaceful, gentle, quiet; *when my older daughter sat in the yard and lit candles, we all felt calm and peaceful*; cf. heion na = peaceful, calm; cf. kansei na = quiet (neighborhood); cf. mugon = silent, speechless; cf. nagoyaka = peaceful, gentle (nagoyaka is used to refer to atmosphere or situations, while odayaka refers to people or weather); cf. shizuka = quiet, silent, calm; cf. yuuyuu = quiet, calm, leisurely

Odokashi 脅かし = a threat; from odokasu = to threaten; cf. related terms listed at kyouhaku

Odokasu 脅かす = to startle or threaten; *the odor that Karl Marx and Superman smelled startled and threatened them*; cf. obiyakasu = to threaten; cf. odosu = to threaten

Odori 踊り = a dance; from odoru = to dance; cf. buyou = dancing or dance

Odoriko 踊り子 = a dancer (usually female); from odoru = to dance + ko = child

Odorokaseru 驚かせる = to surprise or frighten; the causative form of odoroku = to be astonished

Odoroki 驚き = a surprise; from odoroku = to be astonished

Odoroku 驚く = to be astonished; *I was astonished at the odorous Kool-Aid that they served*; cf. akireru = to be disgusted or astonished; cf. gyouten suru = to be astounded; cf. kantan suru = to admire or be astonished; cf. kimo wo tsubusu = to be frightened out of one's wits, to be amazed

Odorokubeki 驚くべき = surprising, remarkable; from odoroku = to be astonished + beki = should; cf. susamajii = amazing, horrible; cf. other related terms listed at ichijirushii

Odoru 踊る = to dance; *some of the odors in Uruguay made me want to dance*; cf. mau = to dance

Odosu 脅す = to threaten; *the odor Superman smelled was threatening*; cf. obiyakasu = to threaten; cf. odokasu = to threaten

Oeru 終える = to finish; this is the transitive form of owaru = to finish; cf. related terms listed at owaraseru

Ofuro お風呂 – see furo

Ofuse お布施 = honorable alms or offerings (e.g., given to monks); *the old food seller gave an offering to the monk*

Ogawa 小川 = a brook; from o = small + gawa = kawa = river

Oginau 補う = to supplement or compensate for; *an old guitar is now being offered to compensate him for his work*; cf. hokyuu suru = to supply or supplement; cf. tsugunau = to compensate

Ohaka お墓 = a graveyard; see haka

Ohakamairi お墓参り = visit to a grave; from the honorific "o" + haka = graveyard + mairu = to go humbly; cf. similar terms listed at houmon

Ohayou (gozaimasu) おはよう(ございます) = good morning; *when I met an old hacker in Yosemite, I said, "good morning"*

Ohitaki matsuri お火焚き祭 = a Kyoto-area festival, held during the 11th lunar month, in which bonfires are burned at shrines; from ohi = honorable fire + taku = to burn wood + matsuri = festival

Oi おい – see ooi

Oide = おいで honorable coming, going or being, e.g., oide ni narimasu = he is there, he will come or he will go; oide kudasai = either please come or please go; *the oily dentist honorably went to see his oil wells*

Oideyasu おいでやす = welcome (used in shops); from oide = honorable coming or going + yasuragu = to feel at peace; cf. related terms listed at youkoso

Oiharau 追い払う = to drive someone or something away; from oikakeru = to chase + harau = to pay or brush away; *when we harass that Uruguayan kid, he just brushes us away*; cf. oikomu = to herd or drive into

Oikakeru 追い掛ける = to pursue or chase after; from ou = to chase + kakeru = to run; cf. ou = to chase; cf. tsuikyuu suru = to pursue a goal, to chase

Oikomu 追い込む = to herd or drive into; from ou = to chase + komu = to crowd in; cf. oiharau = to drive someone or something away

Oikosu 追い越す = to overtake or surpass; from ou = to chase + kosu = to exceed or pass; cf. hiideru = to excell or surpass; cf. hikihanasu = to separate, surpass or outrun; cf. koeru = to cross over, to exceed or surpass; cf. kosu = to exceed, pass, cross, move (residence); cf. norikoeru = to overcome, to surpass, to ride across; cf. nuku = to extract, omit, outrun or surpass; cf. oitsuku = to overtake or catch up to; cf. uwamawaru = to surpass or exceed; cf. other related terms listed at hikkosu

O'inarisan (Oinarisan) お稲荷さん = the god of harvests and wealth; from the honorific "o" + inari = the god of harvests and wealth; *the god of harvests and wealth forbids inappropriate reading on the job*; + the honorific "san"

O'iru (Oiru) 老いる = to grow old; *when he grew old, he kept old eagles in his room*; cf. fukeru = to age or lose one's youthful appearance

Oisha お医者 – see isha

Oishigeru 生い茂る = to grow thickly; from ou = to grow, used as a word component; *as kids get older, they grow*; + shigeru = to grow thickly; cf. related terms listed at haeru

Oishii おいしい = delicious; this can also be spelled 美味い (identical to one spelling for umai); *when I eat <u>delicious</u> food in bed, I get <u>oily</u> <u>sheets</u>*; cf. umai = skillful, delicious (used by men), successful

Oitsuku 追いつく = to overtake or catch up to; *if I <u>oil</u> the wheels of my <u>tsu</u>itcase (suitcase) from <u>Kuwait</u>, I will be able to drag it faster and <u>catch up</u>*; cf. related terms listed at oikosu

Oiwai お祝い – see iwai

Oji 伯父 = an uncle, often spelled おじ; *my <u>uncle</u> drives an <u>old Jeep</u>*; cf. oba = an aunt

Ojigi お辞儀 = a bow (polite gesture); *when he saw the <u>old jeep</u> carrying <u>geese</u>, he <u>bowed</u> to the driver*; cf. eshaku = a bow, salute, greeting, nod

Ojiisan お祖父さん = grandfather, old man; *my <u>grandfather</u> says that his <u>old Jeep</u> is <u>easy</u> to drive*; cf. related terms listed at sofubo

Ojisan 伯父さん = uncle, old man, mister, often spelled おじさん; *that <u>old</u> <u>man</u> drives an <u>old Jeep</u>*

Ojousan お嬢さん = a young girl, someone else's daughter; from the honorific "o" + jou = girl; *<u>Jo</u>an of Arc was a <u>girl</u>*; + the honorific "san"; cf. related terms listed at onna

Oka 丘 = a hill; this can also be spelled 岡; *<u>occasionally</u> I climb the <u>hill</u> behind my house*; cf. related terms listed at yama

Okaasan お母さん = mother; *<u>Mother</u> makes me eat <u>old cauliflower</u> and <u>apples</u>*; cf. related terms listed at haha

Okage de おかげで = thanks to, owing to, because; *<u>Op</u>rah <u>called</u> a <u>guest</u> in <u>Denmark</u>, <u>thanks to</u> modern technology*; this can also be expressed as "okage sama de"

Okaki おかき = mochi cut thin and then dried, baked or fried; *<u>occasionally the king</u> likes to eat <u>mochi cut thin and then baked</u>*; cf. mochi = Japanese rice cake

Okamainaku お構いなく = not bothering about me; from the honorific "o" + kamainaku = not minding (from kamau = to mind)

Okami 女将 = mistress, landlady, proprietress, hostess; *an <u>old</u> <u>Cambodian</u> immigrant is the <u>hostess</u>*; cf. onna shujin = a female owner; cf. yanushi = landlord or landlady

Okane お金 – see kane

Okashi お菓子 = honorable sweets, cake, etc.; *I'm <u>cashing</u> in my stocks so that I can buy more <u>honorable sweets</u>*

Okashi na おかしな – see okashii

Okashii おかしい = funny, strange; *<u>occasionally sheets</u> are twisted into <u>strange</u> shapes that are <u>funny</u>*; cf. related terms listed at kimyou

Okasu 侵す = to invade; *<u>occasionally</u> <u>Superman</u> <u>invades</u> countries with bad rulers*; cf. semeru = to attack or invade

Okasu 冒す = to brave or risk, to face or venture; *<u>occasionally Superman risks</u> injury*

Okasu 犯す = to violate, to commit (a crime); *<u>occasionally Superman violates</u> the speed limit*

Okazu おかず = side dish; *<u>occasional zoos</u> serve <u>side dishes</u>*; cf. related terms listed at ryouri

Oki 沖 = open sea, off the coast; *the <u>old king</u> swam in the <u>open sea</u>*

Oki ni おきに = repeated every other interval (day, week, etc.; this means every 3rd day, but every *other* month, year or other specified interval; *the <u>old king</u> and his <u>niece</u> spoke on the phone <u>every other</u> month*

Okiba 置き場 = storage space; from oku =

to place + basho = place; cf. related terms listed at kuukan

Okiniiri お気に入り = a favorite thing or person, from the honorific "o" + ki ni iru = to like or favor; cf. aiyou = favorite thing, habitual use; cf. koubutsu = favorite food

Okiru 起きる = to occur, to get up, to wake up; *the Okinawa rooster caused the accident to occur*; cf. okoru = to occur; cf. other related terms listed at hassei suru and at samasu

Okiwasureru 置き忘れる = to mislay or leave behind; from oku = to place + wasureru = to forget; cf. funshitsu suru = to lose (something); cf. nakusu = to lose (an item); cf. nokosu = to leave behind; cf. otosu = to drop (transitive), to lose, to decrease; cf. ushinau = to lose something; cf. wasureru = to forget or leave behind

Okiya 置屋 = geisha house; *the old king's yacht was being used as a geisha house*

Okonai 行い = act, behavior; from okonau = to conduct or perform; cf. related terms listed at furumai

Okonau 行う = to conduct or perform, to do, to carry out; *I'm going to Oklahoma now to perform a show*; cf. furumau = to behave, to treat to food or drink; cf. toriokonau = to hold a ceremony; cf. other related terms listed at enjiru

Okoriuru 起こりうる = to be possible to occur; from okoru = to originate or happen + ariuru = arieru = is possible; cf. related terms listed at kanou

Okoru 怒る = to get angry or upset; *when the old coder ruined my computer, I got upset*; cf. hara ga tatsu = to become angry; cf. kattonaru = to fly into a rage; cf. kireru = to break, to be cut, to wear out, to expire, to be used up, to cut well, to get angry, and many other meanings

Okoru 起こる = to happen, to originate, to break out; *the old coder ruined my computer, but stuff happens*; cf. related terms listed at hassei suru

Okosan お子さん = another person's child; from the honorific o + ko = child + san = an honorific suffix

Okosaseru 起こさせる = to cause to wake up; the causative form of okosu = to raise, to cause, to wake someone

Okoshi お越し = honorable coming or going; from the honorific "o" + kosu = to exceed, pass, cross or move (residence)

Okoshi 興し = revitalization; from okosu = to revive or raise up; cf. similar terms listed at kaisou

Okoshiyasu おこしやす = welcome (used in shops); from the honorific o + kosu = to cross, e.g., hikkoshimasu = to move one's residence; + yasuragu = to feel at peace; cf. related terms listed at youkoso

Okosu 興す = to revive, to raise up; *Oklahoma Sue can raise up the dead*; cf. sosei suru = to revive; cf. yomigaeru = to revive or raise from the dead

Okosu 起こす = to raise, to cause, to wake someone; *Oklahoma Sue woke me up and caused my sleepiness*; cf. related terms listed at ageru and at hikiokosu

Okotaru 怠る = to be lazy, to overlook or neglect; *the woman threw an old coat over the tan rooster and then neglected it*; cf. namakeru = to be lazy

Okotozuke お言づけ – see kotozuke

Oku 奥 = heart, interior; *the orange Kool-Aid is in the interior of the refrigerator*; cf. related terms listed at naibu

Oku 置く = to place, to leave as it is, to do in advance; *I will place the orange Kool-Aid in the refrigerator in advance*; cf. hameru = to put on, to fit or mold; cf. sueru = to place or set up

Oku 屋 = a roof, house or shop, used as a word component; *my house is made of oak*

Okubyou mono 臆病者 = a coward; from okubyou = timid + mono = a person; cf.

yowamushi = a coward or weakling

Okubyou na 臆病な = timid; *as he pursued occult studies, the bee owner became timid*; cf. kowai = afraid

Okugai 屋外 = outdoors; *this oak tree guide is meant to be used outdoors*; cf. related terms listed at soto

Okureru 遅れる = to be late or delayed; *the occult museum invited the red rooster, but its visit was delayed*

Okurimono 贈り物 = a gift; from okuru = to give a present + mono = thing; cf. kifu = a contribution, donation; cf. kifukin = a donation; cf. kouken = a contribution; cf. ochuugen = an honorable mid-summer gift; cf. oseibo = an honorable year-end gift; cf. purezento = a present or gift

Okurimukae 送り迎え = dropping people off and then picking them up later; from okuru = escort someone + mukaeru = to meet/welcome

Okuru 贈る = to give a present; *I will give her a present consisting of a trip to some old Kuwaiti ruins*; cf. related terms listed at ataeru

Okuru 送る = to spend time, live one's life, send a thing, escort a person; *Oprah's Kool-Aid is rumored to help people live their lives with more zest, and I send it to my friends*; cf. related terms listed at ikiru and sugosu

Okusan 奥さん = another person's wife, a married woman; *your wife wants to occupy a house in San Francisco*; cf. related terms listed at kanai

Okuyami お悔やみ = condolences; *in the oaken yacht's meeting room, I offered condolences*; cf. aitou = condolences; cf. aitou no i = condolences; cf. chouji = a message of condolence or a memorial address

Okyakusama お客様 = very honorable customer; from the honorific "o" + kyaku = customer + sama = an honorific suffix; cf. related terms listed at kyaku

Omae お前 = you (informal men's speech); *you will find Omaha entertaining*; cf. related terms listed at anata

Omaera お前ら = you (plural); from omae = you + ra = a suffix that makes the preceding pronoun plural

Omairi お参り = a humble visit to a shrine, grave, etc; from mairu = to go humbly; cf. similar terms listed at houmon

Omake ni おまけに = besides, on top of that; *on top of that, in Omaha Kennedy met my niece*; cf. related terms listed at oyobi

Omatase shimashita お待たせしました = I humbly made you wait (an apology); from the humble "o" + matasu = the causative form of matsu = to wait; + shimashita = I did

Omawarisan お巡りさん = a policeman; *people in Omaha are wary of policemen*; cf. related terms listed at keikan

Ome ni kakaru お目にかかる – see me ni kakaru

Omedetai おめでたい = special, auspicious, happy; from omedetou = congratulations

Omedetou おめでとう = congratulations; *the old men who grew the dentist's tomatoes deserve congratulations*

Omedetou gozaimasu おめでとうございます = congratulations; from omedetou = congratulations + gozaimasu = to exist humbly

Omiai お見合い = marriage interview; from the honorific "o" + miru = to see + au = to meet

Omimai お見舞い – see mimai

Omiyage お土産 = a souvenir or present; *the old mean Yankee's guest bought a lot of souvenirs*

Omiyamairi お宮参り = shrine visit; from o = honorable + miya = palace or shrine + mairu = to go humbly; cf. similar terms listed at houmon

Omo na 主な = main, chief; *that old motorcycle is my chief means of transportation*; cf. oote = major; cf. shuyou = chief, major

Omo ni 主に = mainly, primarily; from omo na = main or chief + -ni = a suffix that forms an adverb

Omocha おもちゃ = a toy; *to him, old mobile phones and chandeliers are toys*

Omochabako おもちゃ箱 = toybox; from omocha = toy + bako = hako = box

Omoeru 思える = to seem or appear likely; the potential form of omou = to think or feel

Omoi 思い = idea, thought, sentiment, love; from omou = to feel, think, intend; cf. an = idea, plan, proposal; cf. kangae = thinking, thought; cf. meian = a good idea; cf. senken = a shallow view or superficial idea; cf. shikou = thought or consideration; cf. shisou = a thought or idea

Omoi 重い = heavy; *when oats are moist, they are heavy*; cf. buatsui = bulky, heavy

Omoiataru 思い当たる = to come to mind or recall; from omou = to think + ataru = to hit; cf. oboeru = to memorize or remember; cf. omoidasu = to remember; cf. omoiukabu = to come to mind

Omoidasu 思い出す = to remember; from omou = to think + dasu = to put out; cf. kangaetsuku = to think of; cf. oboeru = to memorize or remember; cf. omoiataru = to come to mind or recall; cf. omoiukabu = to come to mind

Omoide 思い出 = memory; from omou = think + deru = to go out; cf. kioku = memory

Omoidoori 思い通り = as one expects or wants; from omou = to think + doori = way

Omoigakenai 思いがけない = unexpected; *I had an omoi (thought) that gallant Ken's eyes might open unexpectedly*; cf. related terms listed at igai

Omoigakezu 思いがけず = unexpectedly; from omoigakezuni = omoigakenai de = unexpectedly

Omoikiru 思い切る = to cut off thought, i.e., to take the plunge and do something; from omou = to think + kiru = to cut

Omoiukabu 思い浮かぶ = to come to mind; from omou = to think/feel + ukabu = to float; cf. oboeru = to memorize or remember; cf. omoiataru = to come to mind or recall; cf. omoidasu = to remember

Omoiwazurau 思い煩う = to worry about; from omou = to think + wazurau = to worry about

Omoiyari 思いやり = consideration, compassion, empathy; from omoiyaru = to be considerate, to sympathize or empathize

Omoiyaru 思いやる = to be considerate, to sympathize or empathize; from omoi = a thought + yaru = to give

Omomi 重み = weight; from omoi = heavy + mi = a nominalizing suffix used after the stems of some i adjectives; cf. related terms listed at omosa

Omomuki ga aru 趣がある = tasteful; *you often chase old mosquitoes in mucky swamps, but the decoration of your home is quite tasteful*

Omomuku 赴く = to go, to tend toward; *the old motel clerk watching the moon in Kuwait went out to see it because he tended toward romanticism*; cf. related terms listed at chikazuku

Omoni 重荷 = a burden; from omoi = heavy + nimotsu = luggage; cf. futan = responsibility, burden; cf. jama = burden, disturbance

Omosa 重さ = weight; from omoi = heavy + sa = a suffix that makes a noun from an adjective; cf. omomi = weight; cf. taijuu = body weight

Omoshiroi 面白い = interesting, enjoyable, funny; *the old motorcycle that the Shiite rode on Easter was interesting*; cf. kyoumibukai = very interesting; cf. kyoumi shinshin = very interesting; cf. tanoshii = enjoyable, fun

Omote 表 = surface, front; *the surface of the old motel was white*; cf. gaikan = surface, exterior; cf. hyoumen = surface, exterior; cf. men = mask, face, surface or aspect

Omotemuki 表向き = openly, publicly, officially, ostensibly; from omote = surface + muki = direction

Omou 想う = to imagine or contemplate; this is similar to omou = to feel or think

Omou 思う = to think, feel or intend; *the owner mowed the lawn as he thought about his problems*; cf. kangaeru = to think or consider; cf. kokorogakeru = to keep in mind; cf. kouryo suru = to consider; cf. zonjiru = to know, think or feel humbly

Omowaku 思惑 = speculation, calculation; *his speculation was that an old motorcycle would be useful in the war against the Kool-Aid industry*; cf. suiri = speculation, inference; cf. other related terms listed at keisan

Omowazu 思わず = unintentionally, involuntarily; from omowazuni = omowanai de = not thinking

On 恩 = indebtedness, obligation, gratitude; *I feel gratitude to the owner of my apartment building for keeping the rent low*; cf. related terms listed at kansha and at gimu

On 音 = a sound or noise (this can also be read as oto, with the same meaning); *my only complaint about my apartment is the noise*; cf. related terms listed at oto+

Onaji 同じ = same, equivalent to; unlike other na adjectives, this is *not* usually followed by na when modifying a noun, e.g., onaji mise = the same store; *these old nasty jeans are the same ones I wore yesterday*; cf. dou = the same; cf. douyou = similar, same; cf. gotoshi = like, as if, the same as; cf. ruiji no = similar to

Onaka お腹 = honorable stomach; *my old nasty cat was suffering from honorable stomach problems*; cf. fukubu = abdomen, stomach; cf. hara = stomach, abdomen; cf. i = stomach; cf. ichou = the stomach and intestines

Onaka ga ippai お腹がいっぱい = I'm full; from onaka = stomach + ippai = full; cf. manpuku = a full stomach

Onaka ga suku お腹がすく = to become hungry; from onaka = stomach + suku = to become empty; cf. hara ga heru = to become hungry; cf. hara ga suku = to be hungry; cf. onaka ga sukaseru = to get hungry; cf. ueru = to starve, to be thirsty or hungry

Onaka wo sukaseru お腹を空かせる = to get hungry; from onaka = stomach + sukaseru = the causative form of suku = to become empty; cf. related terms listed at onaka ga suku

Ondo 温度 = temperature; *this is the only dolphin with a high temperature*; cf. kion = air temperature; cf. teion = a low temperature; cf. taion = body temperature

Ondokei 温度計 = a thermometer; from ondo = temperature + kei = to measure or count, e.g., tokei = clock; cf. taionkei = a clinical thermometer

Ondori 雄鳥 = a rooster (this can also be spelled オンドリ); *I'll use my own dough (money) to repay you for the rooster*; cf. related terms listed at tori

Oneesan お姉さん = older sister; *my older sister makes me eat old nectarine sandwiches*; cf. similar terms listed at kyoudai

Onga 温雅 = graceful, affable; *the owner of*

that <u>gas</u> station is <u>affable</u>; cf. related terms listed at jouhin

Ongaeshi 恩返し = returning a favor; from on = indebtedness + gaesu = kaesu = to return something

Ongaku 音楽 = music; *I traded my <u>only</u> gallon of <u>Kool</u>-Aid for an hour of <u>music</u>*

Ongyoku 音曲 = songs with samisen accompaniment; from ongaku = music + gyoku = kyoku = a musical composition; cf. related terms listed at uta

Oni 鬼 = a devil, or a cruel person; *that <u>devil</u> is <u>owning</u> a cow*; cf. akuma = a devil or evil spirit

Onigiri おにぎり = a rice ball; from the honorific "o" + nigiru = to grasp or hold tight; cf. related terms listed at ryouri

Oniisan お兄さん = older brother; *my <u>older</u> brother has a passion for <u>owning</u> books*; cf. similar terms listed at kyoudai

Onkei 恩恵 = a favor or benefit; *I <u>only</u> make cakes, but I'll do you a <u>favor</u> and bake you a pie*

Onna 女 = a woman, female; *an <u>old</u> <u>nasty</u> taskmaster is forcing a <u>woman</u> to work*; cf. bijin = a beautiful woman; cf. fujin = a woman; cf. josei = a woman or girl, female; cf. joshi = a woman or girl; cf. ninpu = a pregnant woman; cf. ojousan = a young girl, someone else's daughter; cf. onna no hito = a woman; cf. onna no ko = a girl; cf. otome = a maiden; cf. rouba = an old woman; cf. roufujin = an old woman; cf. shoujo = a girl; cf. shukujo = a lady

Onna no hito 女の人 = a woman; from onna = female + hito = person; cf. related terms listed at onna

Onna no ko 女の子 = a girl; from onna = female + the possessive no + ko = a child; cf. related terms listed at onna

Onna shujin 女主人 = a female owner; from onna = female + shujin = master or owner; cf. related terms listed at okami

Onnen 怨念 = a grudge, malice, hatred; *my <u>only</u> <u>negative</u> <u>nephew</u> carries a <u>grudge</u>*; cf. related terms listed at akui

Onore 己 = self; *my <u>self</u> was the <u>honoree</u> at the banquet*; cf. related terms listed at jibun

Onpa 音波 = sound wave; *my <u>only</u> <u>parent</u> is studying <u>sound</u> <u>waves</u>*

Onrei 御礼 = thanks, gratitude; an alternative way of saying orei; cf. related terms listed at kansha

Onryou 音量 = sound volume; from ongaku = music + ryou = quantity; cf. related terms listed at ryou

Onsei 音声 = voice; *the <u>only</u> <u>sailor</u> who showed up for choir practice had a good <u>voice</u>*; cf. related terms listed at koe

Onsen 温泉 = a hot spring; *he is the <u>only</u> senator to visit this <u>hot</u> <u>spring</u>*; cf. izumi = a spring or fountain

Onsui 温水 = warm water; from on = warm, e.g., onsen = hot spring; + sui = water; cf. related terms listed at mizu

Onyoku 温浴 = a warm bath; from on = warm, e.g., onsen = hot spring; + yoku = to bathe; cf. related terms listed at furo

Ooame 大雨 = a heavy rain; from ooi = numberous + ame = rain; cf. related terms listed at ame

Oogakari 大がかり = large scale; *<u>Oprah</u> and the <u>gambler</u> <u>carried</u> debt on a <u>large</u> <u>scale</u>*; cf. related terms listed at kibo and at ookii

Oogata 大型 = large size; from ookii = large + gata = kata = form; cf. related terms listed at ookii

Oogesa 大袈裟 = exaggerated; *<u>Obama</u> <u>guessed</u> he had 10 <u>apples</u>, but it was an <u>exaggerated</u> estimate*

Ooi おおい = hey! (informal speech); *<u>hey!</u> there's <u>oil</u> on the floor*

Ooi 多い = numerous, the majority; *at this zoo, old eagles are numerous*; cf. related terms listed at takusan

Ooi ni 大いに = very much, greatly, a lot of; from ooi = numerous + -ni = a suffix that forms an adverb; cf. amari = surplus, remainder, more than, very much, not very (with negative constructions); cf. goku = quite, extremely, very; cf. hijou ni = extremely; cf. kiwamete = extremely; cf. nantomo = quite or extremely, in positive constructions; not at all, in negative constructions; cf. shigoku = extremely; cf. sugoku = very, awfully; cf. taihen = difficult, terrible, extremely; cf. taisou = very; cf. totemo = very; cf. tottemo = terribly, extremely, completely; cf. unto = greatly, very much; cf. zuibun = very; cf. zutto = always, all the while, all the way, very much, far more

Ookami オオカミ = a wolf; *the old can of meat was eaten by wolves*

Ookii 大きい = big, large, loud (sound); *these old keys are big*; cf. bakudai = enormous; cf. boudai na = huge, enormous, gigantic; cf. -dai = big, serious, very; cf. daikibo = large-scale; cf. dekai = huge; cf. hiroi = wide, spacious; cf. hiroihiroi = very big; cf. koudai = vast; cf. jindai = very great, enormous, serious; cf. kyodai = huge; cf. oogakari = large scale; cf. oogata = large size; cf. ookina = big, great; cf. oomori = a large serving; cf. oosa = a large number or volume; cf. tai = big; cf. tadai na (or no) = enormous

Ookina 大きな = big, great; an abbreviation of ookii = big + na, indicating a na adjective; cf. related terms listed at ookii

Ookina osewa 大きなお世話 = none of your business; from ookina = big + osewa = honorable assistance

Ooku 多く = most or mainly, many; the adverbial form of ooi = numerous; cf. related terms listed at taitei

Ooku ni 多くに = mostly; an adverbial form of ooku = most or mainly; cf. related terms listed at taitei

Oomori 大盛り = a large serving; from ookii = big + moru = to fill or pile up; cf. related terms listed at ookii

Oomugi 大麦 = barley; from ookii = big + mugi = barley; cf. related terms listed at mugi

Oomukashi 大昔 = ages ago; from ooi ni = very much + mukashi = ancient times; cf. related terms listed at mukashi

Oosa 多さ = a large number or volume; from ooi = many + sa, a suffix that makes a noun from an adjective; cf. related terms listed at ookii

Oosawagi 大騒ぎ = a big fuss, uproar; from ookii = big + sawagu = to make a fuss

Oosugiru 多すぎる = to be too much, or too numerous; from ooi = numerous + sugiru = to be too much; cf. related terms listed at sugiru

Oote 大手 = major; *my major source of income is selling old teddy bears*; cf. related terms listed at omo na

Ootsubu 大粒 = large drop, large grain; from ookii = big + tsubu = drop or grain; cf. related terms listed at tsubu

Oou 覆う = to cover, conceal, wrap, disguise; *I covered the oak furniture*; cf. kakusu = to hide or cover up; cf. tsutsumu = to wrap up

Ooyoso おおよそ – see oyoso

Ooyuki 大雪 = heavy snowfall; from ooi = numerous + yuki = snow; cf. related terms listed at yuki

Oozappa 大雑把 = rough, broad, sketchy; *o (the honorable) Frank Zappa was rough, broad, and sketchy*; cf. arai = violent, rough, rude

Oozei 大勢 = many, a crowd of people; *Oprah acted zany in front of the crowd*; cf. related terms listed at dantai and at takusan

Opushon オプション = option, optional

Oranda オランダ = Holland

Orareru おられる = to exist honorably; this is the passive form of oru = to exist humbly and is used as an honorific verb to refer to people outside one's in-group; cf. related terms listed at aru

Ore 俺 = I, me (used by men and boys); *I live in Oregon*; cf. related terms listed at watashi

Ore 折れ = breakage; from oreru = to be broken

Orei お礼 = gratitude, thanks; *the old racer felt gratitude toward his fans*; cf. related terms listed at kansha

Orera 俺ら = we; from ore = I + ra = a suffix that makes the preceding pronoun plural; cf. related terms listed at watashi

Oreru 折れる = to be broken or folded; the intransitive form of oru = to break or fold; cf. related terms listed at yabureru

Ori おり = a cage or cell; *when I was in a prison cell, I ate Oreo cookies*; cf. kago = basket or cage

Ori 折り = occasion, opportunity, time; *orientation week is an occasion to learn*; cf. tabi = a time or occasion; cf. other related terms listed at kikai

Origami 折り紙 = Japanese paper folding; from oru = to break or fold + gami = kami = paper

Orikata 折り方 = origami instructions; from oru = to fold + kata = a method

Orimageru 折り曲げる = to bend or fold down; from oru = to break or fold + mageru = to twist; *the magician gets the rooster to twist his head around*; cf. related terms listed at tatamu

Orimono 織物 = textiles; from oru = to weave + mono = things; cf. related terms listed at nuno

Oriru 降りる = to get down from a vehicle, to descend (e.g., a mountain), to precipitate frost, dew or mist (but not rain or snow); *when I got down from the train, frost was precipitating, and I found an oriental ruby on the platform*; cf. kudaru = to descend; cf. sagaru = to hang (intransitive), go down, step backward, drop; cf. other related terms listed at furu

Orizuru 折り鶴 = a folded paper crane; from oru = to fold + zuru = tsuru = a crane (this is spelled oriduru in electronic dictionaries)

Oroka na 愚かな = foolish; *it's foolish to drive that old robotic car*

Oroshi 卸 = wholesale; from orosu = to sell wholesale

Oroshiuri ichiba 卸売市場 = wholesale market; from oroshi = wholesale + uru = to sell + ichiba = market (as a place)

Orosoka 疎か = neglect, negligence, not to mention, needless to say; *needless to say, she took her old robe from Somalia to California but then lost it due to negligence*; cf. iu made mo naku = needless to say; cf. other related terms listed at taiman and at wo hajime

Orosoka ni suru 疎かにする = to neglect; from orosoka = negligence + ni suru = to decide; cf. related terms listed at minogasu

Orosu 下ろす = to let someone out of a vehicle, to take something down, to fillet (e.g, a fish), to withdraw money; *after I took it down from the ship, I used an old rowboat to take my supervisor to the shore, where I let her out*

Orosu 卸す = to sell wholesale; *I bought ordinary robot in a supermarket, and they sold it to me wholesale*; cf. related terms listed at uru

Oru おる = to exist humbly, the humble equivalent of iru; *I exist humbly in my own room*; cf. related terms listed at aru

Oru 折る = to break or fold (transitive);

Oprah ruined the photo when she folded it; cf. related terms listed at kowasu and at tatamu

Oru 織る = to weave; *she weaves cloth in an open room*

Osaeru 抑える = to suppress or control;
Osama used his erudite mind to control his followers; cf. related terms listed at shori suru

Osaeru 押さえる = to press down or master, to apprehend or comprehend; *Osama's erudite mind helped him to master his followers*; cf. kiwameru = to attain or master; cf. osameru = to learn or master; cf. shuutoku suru = to master (a subject or skill); cf. tsukaikonasu = to handle (men), to master (a tool or a language)

Osaki ni お先に – see saki ni

Osamaru 治まる = to be settled or solved; *when Osama married Ruth, all of his problems were solved*; cf. related terms listed at tokeru

Osameru 修める = to learn or master; *Osama's men ruined his kitchen when they tried to master cooking*; cf. related terms listed at osaeru

Osameru 収める = to put away (in a closet), conclude, pay a bill; **Note:** this can also be spelled 納める; *when Osama met Ruth, he was putting away the dishes and paying the bills*; cf. katazukeru = to tidy up, finish, settle, get rid of; cf. matomeru = to conclude or settle, bundle together, compile, summarize; cf. musubu = to bind, connect, tie, conclude, organize; cf. shimau = to put away or close, or (when used as a suffix) to finish doing something

Osameru 治める = to reign or administer; *Osama meant to rule the kingdom and to administer its judicial processes*

Osanai 幼い = childish, very young; *Osama's nightmares were childish*; cf. wakai = young, immature; cf. youchi = childish, puerile

Osananajimi 幼なじみ = childhood friend; from osanai = childish + najimu = to get used to; cf. related terms listed at tomodachi

Osechi ryouri お節料理 = food served during the New Year's holidays; from the honorific prefix "o" + sechi = season; *we sell cheese during that season*; + ryouri = cuisine

Oseibo お歳暮 = an honorable year-end gift; *the old sailor got off the boat to give me my year-end gift*; cf. related terms listed at okurimono

Osen 汚染 = pollution; *Oprah sensed that pollution was increasing in the environment*

Osewa お世話 – see sewa

Oshaberi おしゃべり = chatting; from the honorific "o" + shaberu = to chat; cf. related terms listed at kaiwa

Oshare おしゃれ = stylish; *OSHA (the Occupational Safety and Health Administration) told the referees to dress stylishly*; cf. related terms listed at kakko ii

Oshiageru 押し上げる = to boost or push up; from osu = to push + ageru = to lift; cf. related terms listed at ageru and at osu

Oshie 教え = a teaching, dogma or doctrine; from oshieru = to teach; cf. shinnen = a belief

Oshiekomu 教え込む = to train or give an idea; from oshieru = to teach + komu = to crowd in; cf. related terms listed at shitsukeru

Oshieru 教える = to teach, show or tell; *the old sheepherder was erudite and taught me a lot*; cf. shikomu = to train, to teach, to stock merchandise; cf. other related terms listed at miseru and at shiraseru

Oshii 惜しい = unfortunate or regrettable, almost but not quite, precious or valuable;

the old Shiite had a precious, valuable clock that was almost but not quite on time, and this was unfortunate and regrettable; cf. related terms listed at kichou and at zannen

Oshiire 押し入れ = a closet; from osu = to push + ireru = to insert

Oshiiru 押し入る = to push in; from osu = to push + iru = to go in; cf. related terms listed at osu

Oshikiru 押し切る = to overcome resistance; from osu = to push + kiru = to cut; cf. related terms listed at norikiru

Oshikko おしっこ = urination; the old sheep along the coast have urination issues; cf. related terms listed at hi'nyou

Oshikko suru おしっこする = to urinate; from oshikko = urination

Oshiri お尻 = honorable buttocks; the o (honorable) sheep had a reason to put their buttocks under a lean-to

Oshokujidokoro お食事処 = a restaurant (Japanese style); from oshokuji = honorable meal + dokoro = tokoro = a place; cf. related terms listed at ryoutei

Osoi 遅い = late, slow; she was late and slow in replacing the old soy sauce; cf. osome = late, slow; cf. yurui = lax, loose, slow; cf. yuuchou = leisurely, slow, deliberate, easy-going

Osome 遅め = late, slow; from osoi = late, slow; cf. related terms listed at osoi

Osoraku 恐らく = probably, perhaps; the old soldier and the racoon will probably get along; cf. doumo = thank you, somehow or somewhat, probably; cf. tabun = perhaps, probably

Osore 恐れ = fear; from osoreru = to fear; cf. gakuzen = shock, astonishment, terror; cf. ke'nen = apprehension, fear; cf. kyoufu = fear, dread, horror; cf. kyoufushou = morbid fear, phobia

Osoreirimasu 恐れ入ります = I'm overwhelmed, i.e., I'm sorry; from osore = fear + iru = irimasu = to go in; cf. related terms listed at sumimasen

Osoreru 恐れる = to be afraid or apprehensive; the old soldier looked at the red rooster and was afraid; cf. kimo wo tsubusu = to be frightened out of one's wits, to be amazed; cf. kowagaru = to be afraid of

Osoroi お揃い = matching, going together; when the old soldier sang duets with Roy Rogers, they wore matching outfits

Osoroshii 恐ろしい = frightening, terrible; the old soldier rose from his seat and gave the Shiite general a terrible look

Osoru osoru 恐る恐る = timidly; the old soldier stayed in his room timidly

Osou 襲う = to attack; the old soldier wanted to attack; cf. kougeki suru = to attack; cf. machibuseru = to ambush; cf. semeru = to attack or invade; cf. shuugeki suru = to attack; cf. totsugeki suru = to attack; cf. tsuku = to strike or attack; cf. utsu = to shoot at or attack

Osowaru 教わる = to be taught; the intransitive form of oshieru = to teach

Ossharu おっしゃる = to say or tell honorably, to be called honorably (by a name); OSHA (the Occupational Safety and Health Administration) has a rule that managers must say things honorably; cf. related terms listed at hanasu

Osu 押す = to push; that old supervisor pushed me; cf. oshiageru = to boost or push up; cf. oshiiru = to push in; cf. tsukidasu = to push out, to thrust out

Osu 推す = to recommend, to infer or conclude, to ponder deeply; for a more casual look, I recommend that you open your suit; cf. related terms listed at susumeru

Osu 雄 = a male animal, often spelled オス;

in <u>Oosutorariya</u> (Australia), I kept a <u>male animal</u> as a pet; cf. mesu = a female animal

Otaku お宅 = your honorable home or organization, honorable you; from the honorific prefix "o" + taku = home; cf. related terms listed at uchi

Otama お玉 = a ladle; *the <u>old</u> <u>taxidermist's</u> <u>master</u> attacked me with a <u>ladle</u>*

Otera お寺 – see tera

Oto 音 = sound; *the <u>old</u> <u>torpedo</u> made a loud <u>sound</u> when it exploded*; cf. hibiki = echo, repercussion, sound; cf. on = a sound or noise

Otoko 男 = a male or a man; *that <u>man</u> is wearing an <u>Ottoman</u>-era <u>coat</u>*; cf. bocchan = another person's son, a boy; cf. dansei = male, a man; cf. danshi = a boy, male; cf. kozou = a boy or a novice priest; cf. otoko no hito = a man; cf. otoko no ko = a boy; cf. seinen = a young man; cf. shounen = a boy

Otoko no hito 男の人 = a man; from otoko = male + hito = person; cf. related terms listed at otoko

Otoko no ko 男の子 = a boy; from otoko = male + the possessive no + ko = a child; cf. related terms listed at otoko

Otokode 男手 = male help, man's handwriting; from otoko = male + de = te = hand

Otome 乙女 = a maiden; *<u>Otto</u> Preminger <u>met</u> a <u>maiden</u> and cast her in a movie*; cf. related terms listed at onna

Otona 大人 = an adult; *the <u>otoscope</u> that <u>Nancy</u> is playing with is designed for <u>adults</u>*

Otonashii おとなしい = obedient, docile, quiet; *the <u>otolaryngologist</u> was <u>gnashing</u> his teeth, but he was <u>quiet</u>, <u>docile</u> and <u>obedient</u>*; cf. sunao = obedient, meek, honest

Otoroeru 衰える = to become infirm, to decline; *he <u>opened</u> a <u>toll</u> <u>road</u> and was considered <u>erudite</u> in his day, but now his cognition <u>declines</u> steadily*; cf. related terms listed at genshou suru

Otoru 劣る = to be inferior, to fall behind; *the <u>old</u> <u>Toyota's</u> <u>roof</u> is <u>inferior</u>*

Otosata 音沙汰 = news, letter; from oto = sound + sata = communication; cf. related terms listed at jouhou

Otosu 落とす = to drop (transitive), to lose, to decrease; *I <u>dropped</u> my <u>otoscope</u> in the <u>soup</u>*; cf. touka suru = to throw down or drop; cf. other related terms listed at genshou suru and at okiwasureru

Ototoi おととい = the day before yesterday; *<u>the</u> <u>day</u> <u>before</u> <u>yesterday</u>, I threw away my old <u>Toyota</u> <u>toys</u>*

Ototoshi おととし = the year before last; *the <u>year</u> <u>before</u> <u>last</u> I wrapped my <u>otoscope</u> in a <u>torn</u> <u>sheet</u> for safekeeping*

Otousan お父さん = father; *<u>Father</u> makes me eat <u>old</u> <u>tomatoes</u>*; cf. chichi = father; cf. chichioya = a father; cf. oyaji = one's father

Otouto 弟 = younger brother; *my <u>younger</u> <u>brother</u> eats only <u>organic</u> <u>tomatoes</u>*; cf. similar terms listed at kyoudai

Otowazu – see towazu

Otozure 訪れ = a visit or arrival; from otozureru = to visit or arrive; cf. related terms listed at houmon and at touchaku

Otozureru 訪れる = to visit or arrive; *he <u>visited</u> me in order to return the <u>otoscope</u> that I left at the <u>zoo</u> in the cage with the <u>red</u> <u>roosters</u>*; cf. houmon suru = to visit; cf. tazuneru = to visit; cf. ukagau = to visit or ask; cf. other related terms listed at tsuku

Otsu no 乙の = the second, the latter; *the <u>latter</u> customer ordered <u>oats</u>*; cf. dainiji = the second; cf. kou no = the first, the former

Otsumami おつまみ = an appetizer; from the honorific "o" + tsumamu = to pick up or eat with fingers; cf. related terms listed at ryouri

Otsuri お釣り = change (balance in a money transaction), usually written おつり; from the honorific "o" + tsuri = fishing, perhaps suggesting that change is like small fish

Otto 夫 = husband; *Otto Preminger was a good husband*; cf. related terms listed at shujin

Ou おう = let's do, or I shall do; used as a suffix after the root of the plain speech form of a u verb, e.g., nomou = let's drink; *let's open the window*; cf. related terms listed at -shou

Ou 王 = a king; *the king was old*; cf. heika = the Emperor, Your Majesty; cf. kokuou = a king; cf. koutei = an emperor; cf. mikado= the emperor of Japan; cf. ousama = a king; cf. tennou = the emperor of Japan

Ou 負う = to be injured, to take responsibility, to owe; *Oprah was injured in the accident, for which she had to take responsibility, and then she owed money*

Ou 追う = to chase; *Ahab chased the whale across the ocean*; cf. related terms listed at oikakaeru

Ou 央 = center or middle, used as a word component; *we are sailing in the middle of the ocean*; cf. related terms listed at chuubu

Oubei 欧米 = Europe and the U.S., the West; *there are some old bakeries in Europe and the U.S.*; cf. related terms listed at oushuu

Oubo 応募 = application, subscription; *he completed an application to work on Oprah's boat*; cf. related terms listed at moushikomi

Oudan suru 横断する = to cross; *the old dancer crossed the stage*; cf. kakaru= to span; cf. koeru = to cross over; cf. kosu = to exceed, pass, cross, move (residence); cf. wataru = to cross (e.g., a bridge); cf. yogiru = to go by, to cross

Oudou 黄銅 = brass; *the old door is made of brass*; cf. similar terms listed at dou

Ouen 応援 = support; *the older engineers give support to the younger ones*; cf. related terms listed at enjo

Ouendan 応援団 = a cheering squad; from ouen = support + dantai = a group of people

Ouenka 応援歌 = a cheering song; from ouen = support + ka = song, e.g., kashu = singer; cf. related terms listed at uta

Oufuku 往復 = a round trip; *the old Fukuoka resident took a round trip*; cf. related terms listed at ryokou

Ougi 扇 = a folding fan; *I took feathers from some old geese to make that folding fan*; cf. related terms listed at sensu

Ougon 黄金 = gold; *that old gong is made of gold*; cf. junkin = pure gold; cf. kin = gold; cf. related terms listed at tanso

Ouhei na 横柄な = arrogant; *sending the orchestra hate mail is arrogant*; cf. gouman na = insolent, arrogant

Ouhi 王妃 = queen; *the queen is an old healer*; cf. related terms listed at joou

Oui 王位 = throne, crown; from ou = king + i = rank, e.g., dai ichi i = first place; cf. kanmuri = a crown; cf. oukan = a royal crown

Ouji 王子 = a prince; *the prince drives an old Jeep*

Ouji 皇子 = an imperial prince; *the imperial prince drives an old Jeep*

Oujiru 応じる = to respond or comply with; *the old genius and his rooster responded to my invitation*; cf. kanaeru = to grant or answer a request, to meet requirements; cf. kotaeru = to respond or affect

Oujo 王女 = a princess; from ou = king + josei = female; cf. hime = a princess

Oukan 王冠 = a royal crown; from ou = a king + kanmuri = a crown; cf. related terms listed at oui

Oukyuu 王宮 = royal palace; from ou = king + kyuuden = palace; cf. related terms listed at kyuuden

Ourai 往来 = traffic; *the old rice truck was stuck in traffic*; cf. hansou = transportation, conveyance, delivery; cf. koutsuu = traffic, transportation; cf. tsuukou = passage, traffic; cf. unpan = carriage, transport

Ousama 王様 = king; from ou = king; *the king is old*; + sama = very honorable; cf. related terms listed at ou

Ousei na 旺盛な = flourishing, active, high, full of vim and vigor; *the old saint is flourishing and has a high energy level*; cf. related terms listed at sakan

Oushin 往診 = a doctor's house call; *that old Shinto doctor makes house calls*

Oushitsu 王室 = royal family; from ou = king + shitsu = room

Oushuu 欧州 = Europe; *I got these old shoes in Europe*; cf. chuuou = central Europe; cf. hokuou = northern Europe; cf. oubei = Europe and the U.S., the West; cf. seiou = western Europe

Owakare お別れ = a farewell; from the honorific "o" + wakare = a separation

Owaraseru 終わらせる = to cause to finish; this is the causative form of owaru = to finish or end, often used as a transitive verb meaning to finish something; cf. ageru = to finish; cf. kanryou suru = to finish; cf. kansei suru = to finish, accomplish, complete; cf. kiriageru = to finish; cf. matomeru = to conclude or settle, bundle together, compile, summarize; cf. oeru = to finish; cf. shiageru = to finish; cf. sumaseru = to finish; cf. sumasu = to finish; cf. uchiageru = to wash up (ashore), to dash (waves), to launch or shoot off, to finish or close (a performance)

Owari 終わり = the end; from owaru = to finish or end; cf. saigo = last, end, conclusion, most recent; cf. sue = tip, end, future

Owaru 終わる = to finish or end (intransitive); *my lunch ended when the ocean water ruined my sandwich*; cf. agaru = to finish; cf. shuuryou suru = to finish or end; cf. sumu = to finish

Oya おや = my!, an expression of mild surprise; *my, that's an old yak*

Oya 親 = parent; *the old yak missed his parents*; cf. fubo = parents; cf. hogosha = parent or guardian; oyago = another person's parents; cf. ryoushin = parents

Oyadori 親鳥 = a bird parent; from oya = bird + dori = tori = bird

Oyago 親御 = another person's parents; *the old yakuza played golf with another person's parents*; cf. related terms listed at oya

Oyaji 親父 = one's father; from oya = parent + ji = father; cf. related terms listed at otousan

Oyakata 親方 = master, boss; from oya = parent + kata = honorable person; cf. related terms listed at shujin

Oyako 親子 = parent and child; from oya = parent + ko = child

Oyakodon 親子丼 = chicken and egg on rice in a bowl (this can also be pronounced oyakodonburi); from oya = parent + ko = child (since a chicken is a parent and an egg is a child) + donburi = a porcelain bowl; cf. related terms listed at ryouri

Oyakoukou na 親孝行な = reverent to parents; from oya = parent + koukou = filial piety

Oyasuminasai お休みなさい = good night; from the honorific "o" + yasumi = a rest + nasai = do

Oyatsu おやつ = between-meal snack; *we had some o (honorable) yak tsoup (soup)*

as a *snack*; cf. related terms listed at shokuji

Oyobi 及び = and, in addition; cf. ni kuwaete = in addition; cf. omake ni = besides, on top of that; cf. sonota (or sono hoka) = otherwise, besides, in addition, the rest; cf. sore ni shitemo = besides, moreover

Oyobigoshi 及び腰 = bent back, timidity; from oyobu = to reach or extend + goshi = koshi = low back

Oyobu 及ぶ = to reach or extend to; *the old yogi's boots extended across the floor of the closet*; cf. itaru = to lead to, reach, result in; cf. tassuru = to reach or become; cf. todoku = to reach, to be received

Oyogi 泳ぎ = swimming; from oyogu = to swim; cf. suiei = swimming

Oyogu 泳ぐ = to swim; *Oprah eats yogurt with Goofy before she swims*

Oyoso およそ = an estimate or outline, approximately; this can also be spelled and pronounced ooyoso; *the old yogurt that the soldiers ate was approximately a month past its expiration date*; cf. gaisan = a rough estimate; cf. rinkaku = an outline, contour or summary; cf. other related terms listed at yaku

Oyu お湯 = honorable hot water; from the honorific prefix "o" + yu = hot water; cf. related terms listed at mizu

Ozen お膳 = a four-legged tray for festive food; from the honorific "o" + zen = a counter for bowls of cooked rice; cf. bon = a tray

Paati パーティー = a party; cf. enkai = a party or banquet

Pai 杯 – see hai

Paki パキッ = twig-snapping sound; *when I was packing my suitcase, I heard some twig-snapping sounds*

Pakku パック = a pack

Pakkuri ぱっくり = gaping (mouth); *Pac-Man waited for his curry with a gaping mouth*

Pan パン = bread; *Peter Pan liked bread*; cf. shokupan = Japanese milk bread

Panku パンク = a puncture or flat tire

Paritto パリッと = crisp, crunchy, modern, classy; *in Pari (Paris), the toast is crisp*; cf. related terms listed at karikari

Patsu 発 – see hatsu

Pekopeko ペコペコ = very hungry, starving; *all I've had for nourishment is pekoe tea, pekoe tea, and I'm starving*

Penki ペンキ = paint; *he scratched the car's paint with a pen and a key*; cf. enogu = artist's paint

Penkie (Penki'e) ペンキ絵 = a picture painted with oil paint, especially a mural in a public bath; from penki = paint + e = picture; cf. related terms listed at e

Perapera ペラペラ = fluent; *my pet rabbit and my pet rat must be fluent in their own languages*

Perori to ぺろりと = eating up quickly; *when that person visited the Orient with Tony Blair, he ate his meals quickly*

Pikapika ぴかぴか = glitter, sparkle; *Picasso's pickax had a certain sparkle*

Pikapika suru ぴかぴかする = to sparkle or glisten; from pikapika = glitter, sparkle; cf. related terms listed at teru

Pittari ぴったり = tightly, exactly, ideally; *the pittance that they're giving you for retiring is exactly what you deserve*; cf. related terms listed at choudo

Poppu ポップ = pop, e.g., pop music

Ppanashi っぱなし = to leave something unfinished, i.e., an action or its result continues, used after a verb stem; *although he has panache, he leaves things unfinished*

Ppoi っぽい = a suffix meaning "-ish" or "-like"; *poison is like a toxin*

Ppon 本 – see hon

Pun 分 – see fun

Purasuchikku プラスチック = plastic

Purezento プレゼント = a present or gift; cf. related terms listed at okurimono

Puutaroo プータロー = freeloader, unemployed person, vagrant; *that poor talented rogue is a vagrant*

Ra ら = a suffix that makes the preceding pronoun plural; *we have more than one rat*

Raamen ラーメン = Chinese-style noodles in broth; *the radical men were eating Chinese-style noodles in broth*; cf. related terms listed at soba

Rachi 拉致 = kidnapping, taking captive; *during my kidnapping, I had to eat rancid cheese*; cf. yuukai = an abduction

Rai 来 = next, used as a word component, e.g., raishuu = next week; *next we will serve rice*

Raigetsu 来月 = next month; from rai = next + getsu = month

Raihin 来賓 = a guest or visitor; *a rhyming Hindu was our guest for dinner*; cf. related terms listed at kyaku

Raijou 来場 = attendance; from rai = to come, e.g., rainichi suru = to come to Japan; + kaijou = the site of an event

Raikyaku 来客 = visitor or caller; from rai = to come, e.g., rainen = the coming year, + kyaku = customer; cf. related terms listed at kyaku

Raimei 雷鳴 = thunder; *I was riding in a mail truck when I heard thunder*; cf. kaminari = thunder or lightning

Rainen 来年 = next year; from rai = next + nen = year

Rainichi 来日 = a visit to Japan; *he ate rice with Nietzsche during a visit to Japan*; cf. similar terms listed at houmon

Raishuu 来週 = next week; from rai = next + shuu = week; cf. raigetsu = next month; cf. rainen = next year; cf. yokujitsu = the next day

Raisu ライス = rice; cf. related terms listed at gohan

Raiten 来店 = coming to a store; from rai = coming, e.g., rainichi suru = to come to Japan; + ten = store, e.g., tennin = store clerk

Raitoappu ライトアップ = light up, or lit up, e.g., architectural floodlighting

Rakkan 楽観 = optimism; *the rabbi faced his cancer with optimism and said "rock on!"*; cf. rakuten = optimism

Rakkanteki 楽観的 = optimistic; from rakkan = optimism + teki = related to; cf. rakutenki = optimistic; cf. yousei no = cheerful, positive

Raku 楽 = pleasure, comfort; *the raccoon enjoyed pleasure and comfort*; cf. related terms listed at kokochiyosa and at shiawase

Rakuda ラクダ = a camel; *the barracudas ate a camel*

Rakuen 楽園 = paradise, or pleasure garden; from raku = pleasure; *the lack of Kool-Aid affects my pleasure*; + en = park, e.g., kouen = park; cf. related terms listed at niwa

Rakugo 落語 = a comic story; *the raccoon refused to go, and it made for a comic story*

Rakugoka 落語家 = a comic story teller; from rakugo = a comic story + ka = a person

Rakunou 酪農 = dairy farming; *raccoons are sticking their noses into our dairy farming business*; cf. related terms listed at inasaku

Rakunou seihin 酪農製品 = dairy products; from rakunou = dairy farming + seihin = a product; cf. related terms listed at tabemono

Rakuraku 楽々 = easily; from raku = pleasure, comfort; cf. related terms listed at karugaru

Rakutan 落胆 = disappointment, dejection, discouragement; *when the raccoon tangled with the coyote, the encounter led to disappointment on both sides*; cf. related terms listed at gakkari

Rakuten 楽天 = optimism; *he feels optimism about the upcoming racketball and tennis tournaments*; cf. rakkan = optimism

Rakutenteki 楽天的 = optimistic; from rakuten = optimism + teki = related to; cf. related terms listed at rakkanteki

Ramen – see raamen

Ran 欄 = a column (newspaper); *our ranch was featured in a newspaper column*; cf. bikouran = a remarks column; cf. keta = a beam, girder, unit or numerical column (accounting)

Ran 蘭 = an orchid, sometimes used as a proper noun; *I grow orchids on my ranch*; cf. related terms listed at hana

Ranbou na 乱暴な = violent, disorderly; *violent men ransacked the bowling alley*; cf. arai = violent, rough, rude; cf. hidoi = inhuman, cruel, painful, violent, terrible; cf. kyouaku = brutal, inhuman; cf. sobou = wild, rude, violent

Ran'ou (Ranou) 卵黄 = an egg yolk; *he ran over an egg yolk*; cf. kimi = an egg yolk

Ranran らんらん = blazing, fiery, glaring; *he ran and ranted in the blazing sun*

Ransou 卵巣 = an ovary; *the ranking soldier had her ovaries removed*; cf. seisou = a testicle

Ran'you (Ranyou) suru 乱用する = to abuse, misuse; *he misused a key to unlock a door and ransacked the yogurt store*; cf. related terms listed at ijimeru

Rashii らしい = seems or appears to be, used as a suffix; *the rabbit that the Shiite caught seems to be healthy*; cf. related terms listed at mitai

Rashin 羅針 = a compass needle; *the rabbit hunter asked a Shinto priest for a compass needle*

Rashinban 羅針盤 = a compass; from rashin = a compass needle + ban = a disk, e.g., enban = a disk; cf. jishaku = magnet or compass

Ratai no 裸体の = naked; *a ranch in Thailand caters to naked people*

Reen レーン = a lane

Rei 例 = an example or precedent; *racing is an example of a sporting activity*; cf. mihon = a sample or example; cf. mohan = an example or model; cf. tatoe = an example

Rei 零 = zero, often written and pronounced ゼロ zero; *the number of raisins in my lunchbox is zero*

Rei 霊 = soul or ghost; *after he died of rabies, his ghost came back to haunt us*; cf. related terms listed at yuurei

Reibou 冷房 = air conditioning; *the racer boasted about his air conditioning*

Reido 零度 = zero degrees; from rei = zero + do = degrees; cf. reika = below zero

Reigai 例外 = exception; *that racist guy is an exception in my school*

Reigi 礼儀 = civility, etiquette; *when it rained on the geeks, she had the civility to invite them inside*

Reigi tadashii 礼儀正しい = polite, well-mannered; from reigi = etiquette + tadashii = correct; cf. related terms listed at teinei

Reihai 礼拝 = worship; *after the rain, Heidi went to worship*

Reiji 零時 = midnight; from rei = zero + ji = o'clock

Reika 零下 = below zero; from rei = zero + ka = below; cf. reido = zero degrees

Reikai 霊界 = the spiritual world; from rei = soul + sekai = world

Reikoku na 冷酷な = cruel, heartless, inhuman; *it was cruel of you to put the rabies virus in my Coke*

Reikon 霊魂 = a soul or spirit; *that racer is controlled by a fiery spirit*; cf. related terms listed at seishin

Reinen 例年 = an average or normal year; from rei = example + nen = year; cf. related terms listed at nen

Reisei 冷静 = calm, composure; *the racing sailors kept their composure*; cf. heiki = unconcerned, nonchalant, calmness; cf. ochitsuki = composure, calmness, serenity

Reitan na 冷淡な = cool, indifferent; *I am indifferent to the spectacle of racing tanks*; cf. mutonchaku = nonchalant, indifferent

Reitou suru 冷凍する = to freeze; *we raise tomatoes and freeze them*; cf. related terms listed at kooru

Reitouko 冷凍庫 = a freezer; *when it rains, we eat toast and corn from the freezer*

Reizouko 冷蔵庫 = refrigerator; *I raced Zooey to get a cola from the refrigerator*

Reji レジ = cash register

Reki 暦 = a calendar or almanac, used as a word component; *you're wrecking that calendar by writing all over it*; cf. similar terms listed at koyomi

Rekishi 歴史 = history; *according to history, he was seen wrecking a sheep pen*; cf. enkaku = history, development; cf. yuisho = history, pedigree, lineage, fame

Rekizen 歴然 = evident, clear, distinct; *it is clear that the process of wrecking the Zen temple has begun*; cf. related terms listed at akiraka

Remon jiru レモン汁 = lemon juice; from lemon + jiru = shiru = soup; cf. related terms listed at shiru

Ren'ai (Renai) 恋愛 = romantic love; *if you are sharing your rent and your ice cream, that's a sign of romantic love*; cf. related terms listed at aijou

Renchuu 連中 = a group of people, a crowd; *that group of people believes that renters should choose our leaders*; cf. related terms listed at dantai

Renga レンガ = a brick; *my rented garage is made from bricks*

Rengou 連合 = alliance, federation, coalition; *our coalition is renting goats to keep the grass short*; cf. doumei = an alliance, league or union; cf. gappei = a merger, combination or union; cf. renpou = a federation

Renkon 蓮根 = lotus root; *I rented a condo with a pond where I can harvest lotus root*; cf. related terms listed at yasai

Renkou suru 連行する = to take someone to the police, to drag someone away; *let's rent a corporal to help us take that guy to the police*

Renmei 連盟 = a league or alliance; from renraku = communication + mei = an alliance, e.g., doumei = an alliance

Renpou 連峰 = a mountain range; *I will rent a pony and explore that mountain range*; cf. related terms listed at yama

Renpou 連邦 = a federation; *some federations allow people to rent police to provide security at concerts*; cf. related terms listed at rengou

Renraku 連絡 = contact or communication; *the rental car racked up so many miles that*

I had to initiate some communication *with the rental agency*; cf. tsuushin = communication

Renshuu 練習 = practice, exercise, drill; *the rented shoes were used for soccer practice*; cf. related terms listed at kunren

Rensou suru 連想する = to associate or be reminded of; *collecting rent from the soldier reminded me of my military service*

Renzoku 連続 = a series; *I rented Zooey's Kool-Aid stand for a series of two weeks*; cf. ichiren = a series

Renzoku shite 連続して = consecutive; from renzoku suru = to occur in succession; cf. related terms listed at tsugitsugi ni

Renzoku suru 連続する = to occur in succession; from renzoku = a series

Ressha 列車 = train; from retsu = line + sha = vehicle; cf. related terms listed at densha

Retsu 列 = line or row; *I stand in line wearing my retro suit*; cf. related terms listed at gyou

Rettou 列島 = an archipelago or chain of islands; from retsu = a line + tou = island; cf. related terms listed at shima

Rieki 利益 = profit, advantage, interests; *the reason that Edward the King made a profit was that he kept his expenses low*; cf. rijun = a profit; cf. saisan = profit, surplus; cf. toku = profit; cf. uruoi = charm, profit, moisture

Rifujin 理不尽 = unfair or absurd; *her reason for throwing food at the genius was absurd and unfair*; cf. futou = unjust or unfair; cf. kitanai = dirty, unjust, indecent; cf. mechakucha = absurd, incoherent, disorder, mess

Rijun 利潤 = a profit; *in that sales region, we are making a profit*; cf. related terms listed at rieki

Rikai 理解 = understanding; *reading the Kaiser's writings, I achieved understanding*; cf. related terms listed at shouchi

Rikai suru 理解する = to understand; from rikai = understanding; cf. related terms listed at wakaru

Riki 力 = power, used as a word component; *Ricky has a lot of power*

Rikishi 力士 = a sumo wrestler; *Ricky gave a sheepdog to the sumo wrestler*; cf. motorikishi = ex-wrestler

Rikon 離婚 = divorce; *an incident on a reef in the Congo led to my divorce*

Rikoshugi 利己主義 = egotism, selfishness; *that person who is rico (rich, in Spanish) and has nice shoes and lots of guitars displays some egotism*

Rikoteki 利己的 = egotistical, self-centered; *that rico (rich, in Spanish) techie seems to be egotistical*; cf. kojinteki = personal, self-centered

Riku 陸 = land; *real Kool-Aid comes from a far-away land*; cf. related terms listed at basho

Rikugun 陸軍 = an army; from riku = land + gunjin = soldier; cf. related terms listed at guntai

Rikutsu 理屈 = argument, theory, pretext; *the reason that I cut Superman was to test the theory that he is vulnerable to certain blades;* cf. giron = discussion, controversy, argument; cf. kyougi = a discussion or conference; cf. riron = a theory; cf. rongi = a discussion; cf. ryouron = both arguments; cf. setsu = a theory or opinion; cf. shingi = a discussion or scrutiny; cf. touron = a debate or discussion

Rikyuu 離宮 = an imperial villa; from ri = to separate, e.g., rikon = divorce; + kyuuden = palace; cf. related terms listed at kyuuden

Rimokon リモコン = remote control

Rinen 理念 = an ideal or doctrine; *the reason my negative nephew quit school was that he adopted a doctrine of noncomformity*; cf. genri = a principle; cf. risou = an ideal; cf. shugi = a doctrine, rule or principle

Ringo リンゴ = an apple; *Ringo likes apples*; cf. related terms listed at kudamono

Rinia リニア = linear

Rinji 臨時 = temporary, extraordinary, emergency; *the band used Ringo's Jeep in extraordinary situations and in emergencies, as a temporary expedient*; cf. zantei = tentative, temporary; cf. other related terms listed at hijou and at hinichijouteki

Rinkaku 輪郭 = an outline, contour or summary; *the rink where Karl the Kool-Aid vendor skates has an oval outline*; cf. oyoso = an estimate or outline, approximately

Rinne 輪廻 = samsara, cycle of death and rebirth; *he rewound the Netflix movie to watch the part about samsara*

Rinri 倫理 = ethics; *Ringo revised the Beatles' code of ethics*; cf. related terms listed at doutoku

Rinrigaku 倫理学 = ethics (a branch of philosophy); from rinri = ethics + gaku = study; cf. related terms listed at doutoku

Rippa 立派 = splendid, impressive; *although there is a rip in your pants, your outfit is splendid*; cf. related terms listed at inshouteki

Ririku suru 離陸する = to take off (flight); from ri = to separate, e.g., rikon = divorce; + riku = land; cf. chakuriku suru = to land

Ririshii りりしい = manly, dignified, gallant; *the reason that I retreated from the Shiites is that they all looked so manly*; cf. isagiyoi = unhesitating, manly, wholehearted, sportsmanlike

Riron 理論 = theory; *the reason that Ronald Reagan believed in his economic theory is that he thought it would allow him to pay fewer taxes*; cf. related terms listed at rikutsu

Risou 理想 = an ideal; *when I prepare risotto, I strive toward an ideal in Italian cuisine*; cf. related terms listed at rinen

Risoushugi 理想主義 = idealism; from risou = ideal + shugi = rule or principle

Risu りす = a squirrel; *the retired supervisor likes to feed squirrels*

Ritou 離島 = isolated island; *I returned the tortoise to its isolated island*; cf. related terms listed at shima

Ritsu 率 = percentage, proportion, rate; *at the Ritz Hotel, a supervisor added a percentage to my bill*

Ritsudai 立大 = private university; from kiritsu = to stand + daigaku = university; cf. related terms listed at daigaku

Ritsuzou 立像 = standing statue; from kiritsu suru = to stand up; + zou = image or shape, e.g., butsuzou = statue or image of Buddha; cf. related terms listed at zou

Riyou 利用 = use, utilization; *I reminded the yogi about the utilization of electricity*; cf. shiyou = use, employment

Riyou suru 利用する = to use; from riyou = use, utilization; cf. mochiiru = to use; cf. shoumou suru = to consume, use up or deplete; cf. tsukaikiru = to use up, to exhaust, to wear out; cf. tsukau = to use

Riyoukyaku 利用客 = a using customer; from riyou = use + kyaku = customer; cf. related terms listed at kyaku

Riyousha 利用者 = user; from riyou = utilization + sha = person

Riyuu 理由 = reason, excuse; *the reason that I reuse plastic bottles is to help the environment*; cf. jijou = reason, situation, facts, circumstances; cf. sujiai = right or reason; cf. wake = reason, meaning; cf. other related terms listed at benkai

Ro 炉 = a fireplace or furnace; *I roasted chestnuts in the fireplace*; cf. danro = a fireplace or stove

Rojou 路上 = the surface of the road; from douro = a road + jou = above, e.g., jouzu = skillful

Roku 録 = a record or recording; *the robotic Kool-Aid dispenser makes a recording of each transaction*

Rokujou 六畳 = six tatami mats; from roku = six + jou = a counter for tatami mats; cf. tatami = a tatami mat

Rokuon 録音 = a sound recording; from roku = a recording + on = sound, e.g., ongaku = music; cf. shuuroku = compilation or recording

Romanchisuto ロマンチスト = romanticist

Romen 路面 = a road surface; from douro = a road + men = a surface

Romen densha 路面電車 = a streetcar; from romen = a road surface + densha = a train

Ronbun 論文 = essay, research paper, thesis; *Ronald Reagan studied Daniel Boone and wrote a thesis about his life*; cf. related terms listed at sakuhin

Rongi 論議 = discussion; *Ronald Reagan brought his guitar to the discussion*; cf. related terms listed at rikutsu

Ronjiru 論じる = to discuss or argue; *Ronald jeered at Rudolph as they were arguing*; cf. related terms listed at hanasu

Rosen 路線 = route (transportation); *the robots are sent on their routes*

Rouba 老婆 = an old woman; *an old woman was on the road to Barcelona*; cf. related terms listed at onna

Rouden 漏電 = electric short circuit; *the robotic dental assistant developed a short circuit*

Roudou 労働 = manual labor; *when we use robots to make doors, we save a lot of manual labor*; cf. related terms listed at shigoto

Roudousha 労働者 = laborer; from roudou = manual labor + sha = person; cf. kouin = a factory worker; cf. sagyouin = a laborer

Roufujin 老婦人 = an old woman; from rourei = advanced age + fujin = a woman; cf. related terms listed at onna

Rougan 老眼 = farsightedness due to aging; *robots assist Gandalf as he treats farsightedness due to aging*

Rouhi 浪費 = waste, extravagance; *building another road through the Himalayas is an extravagance*

Rouhi suru 浪費する = to waste; from rouhi = waste, extravagance; cf. muda ni suru = to waste, to not make good use of, to render futile

Roujin 老人 = elderly person; *an elderly person may become a low jin (short person)*; cf. toshiyori = an elderly person

Rouka 廊下 = corridor or hallway; *the robotic car raced down the corridor*

Rouka 老化 = aging; from roujin = elderly person + ka = a nominalizing suffix; cf. koureika = aging

Rounin 浪人 = wandering samurai without a master, a person waiting for another chance to take a university exam; *a roaming nin (person) is like a wandering samurai*

Rourei 老齢 = advanced age; *his advanced age causes him to roam in the rain*; cf. nenrei = age

Rousoku ろうそく = a candle; *I'm on the road with our soldiers in Kuwait, writing this by the light of a candle*

Rousui 漏水 = water leak; *our roses smelled*

sweeter this year, since they benefited from a <u>water</u> <u>leak</u> in the sprinkler system

Rousui 老衰 = senility; some <u>robots</u> in <u>Sweden</u> assist people with <u>senility</u>

Rufu 流布 = dissemination, circulation; <u>Rudolph</u> <u>foolishly</u> approved the <u>circulation</u> of his book before Santa had cleared it

Rui 塁 = a base (baseball); King <u>Louis</u> ran to first <u>base</u>; cf. manrui = bases loaded; cf. sanrui = third base; cf. tourui = a stolen base

Ruiji no 類似の = similar to; <u>Luigi</u> is <u>similar</u> <u>to</u> Mario; cf. related terms listed at onaji

Ruijihin 類似品 = imitation, or similar, article; from ruiji = similar + hin = merchandise; cf. related terms listed at mane

Ruijin'en (Ruijinen) 類人猿 = an ape; <u>Luigi's</u> <u>nephew</u> <u>entertained</u> the <u>apes</u>; cf. related terms listed at saru

Ruiseki 累積 = an accumulation; in <u>Louisiana</u>, the <u>selfish</u> <u>king</u> had an <u>accumulation</u> of debts; cf. related terms listed at shuushuu

Rusu 留守 = absence, being away from home; my <u>absence</u> was due to my visit to a <u>ruined</u> <u>supermarket</u>; cf. related terms listed at fuzai

Rusu ni suru 留守にする = to be absent, or away from home; from rusu = absence

Rusuden 留守電 = an answering machine, phone messages; from rusu = absence + denwa = phone

Ryaku 略 = an abbreviation or omission; when <u>Leah</u> made the <u>Kool</u>-Aid, she left the sugar out due to an <u>omission</u>; cf. shouhon = an excerpt, abstract or abbreviated transcript; cf. shouryaku = an abbreviation or omission; cf. tanshuku = a shortening or abbreviation; cf. tanshukukei = an abbreviation or shortened form

Ryokan 旅館 = a Japanese inn; from ryokou = travel + kan = a large building; cf. yado = an inn or lodging

Ryoken 旅券 = a passport; from ryokou = travel + ken = a ticket

Ryokou 旅行 = travel or trip; Pope <u>Leo</u> and his <u>court</u> took a trip; cf. ian ryokou = a pleasure trip, a company recreational trip; cf. katamichi = one-way (trip); cf. nagatabi = a long trip; cf. oufuku = a round trip; cf. shucchou = a business trip; cf. tabi = trip, travel; cf. yakou = night travel

Ryokousha 旅行社 = traveler; from ryokou = travel + sha = person

Ryoku 力 = power, used as a suffix; drinking <u>Leo's</u> <u>Kool</u>-Aid gives me <u>power</u>; cf. related terms listed at chikara

Ryokucha 緑茶 = green tea; from ryoku = green; Pope <u>Leo</u> drinks <u>Kool</u>-Aid that is <u>green</u>; + cha = tea; cf. related terms listed at cha

Ryou 両 = both, used as a prefix; an abbreviation of ryouhou = both

Ryou 寮 = a dormitory; when Pope <u>Leo</u> was in seminary, he lived in a <u>dormitory</u>

Ryou 料 = fee or charge, used as a suffix, eg. muryou = free of charge; Pope <u>Leo</u> charged <u>fees</u> for indulgences

Ryou 漁 = fishing; Pope <u>Leo</u> likes to go <u>fishing</u>

Ryou 量 = quantity; Pope <u>Leo</u> has a <u>quantity</u> of carnations; cf. koutsuuryou = traffic volume; cf. onryou = sound volume; cf. shouhiryou = amount of consumption; cf. tairyou = large amount

Ryouashi 両足 = both feet; from ryouhou = both + ashi = foot; cf. related terms listed at ude

Ryoudo 領土 = territory; while Pope <u>Leo</u> was <u>dozing</u>, the enemy invaded his <u>territory</u>; cf. related terms listed at chitai

Ryougae 両替 = money exchange, making

change; from ryouhou = both sides + gaeru = kaeru = to replace or exchange

Ryouhou 両方 = both, both sides; *Pope Leo's horses are both big*; cf. related terms listed at hou

Ryouiki 領域 = area, domain, field; *Pope Leo and an Eastern king fought a war over a domain*; cf. related terms listed at fukin and at hara

Ryoukai 了解 = agreement, consent, understanding; *Pope Leo and the Kaiser reached an agreement*; cf. related terms listed at shouchi

Ryoukai suru 了解する = to agree, consent or understand; from ryoukai = agreement, consent, understanding; cf. related terms listed at sansei suru and at wakaru

Ryouke 両家 = both families; from ryouhou = both + ke = family, e.g., souke = head of family

Ryoukin 料金 = a price, fare or fee; *Pope Leo charged the king a price for his advice*; cf. related terms listed at nedan

Ryoukoku 両国 = both countries; from ryouhou = both + koku = country; cf. related terms listed at kuni

Ryoukokukan 両国間 = between both countries; from ryoukoku = both countries + kan = interval or space

Ryoukou 良好 = favorable, satisfactory; *Pope Leo says the cold weather is favorable for our hike*; cf. related terms listed at daijoubu

Ryoumen 両面 = both sides; from ryouhou = both + men = surface; cf. related terms listed at hou

Ryouri 料理 = cooking, cuisine; *Pope Leo and Ringo like fine cuisine*; cf. botamochi = azuki bean mochi; cf. ippin ryouri = a la carte; cf. kamameshi = a rice, meat and vegetable dish served in a pot; cf. kasutera = castella, a kind of sponge cake; cf. katsu = breaded, deep-fried cutlet; cf. katsudon = pork cutlet served on a bowl of rice; cf. kuzumochi = a Japanese jelly-like dessert made with kuzu; cf. okazu = side dish; cf. onigiri = a rice ball; cf. otsumami = an appetizer; cf. oyakodon = chicken and egg on rice in a bowl; cf. sashimi = raw sliced fish; cf. sushi = raw sliced fish on rice; cf. tamagoyaki = a rolled omelet; cf. tekka maki = raw tuna sushi wrapped in seaweed; cf. tenpura = Japanese deep-fried food; cf. teppanyaki = food grilled on an iron griddle; cf. teriyaki = meat or fish marinated in sweet soy sauce and broiled; cf. tonkatsu = pork cutlet, breaded and fried; cf. tonkotsu = a Japanese dish made with simmered pork belly, vegetables, etc.; cf. toro = fatty tuna (sushi); cf. yakitori = chicken grilled on a skewer; cf. other related terms listed at chouri, at soba, and at tabemono

Ryourinin 料理人 = a chef or cook; from ryouri = cuisine + nin = person; cf. chourishi = a chef

Ryouron 両論 = both arguments; from ryouhou = both + kouron = argument; cf. related terms listed at rikutsu

Ryousha 両社 = both companies; from ryou = both + kaisha = company

Ryousha 両者 = both people, both things; from ryouhou = both + sha = person

Ryoushi 猟師 = hunter; *Pope Leo lent his sheepdog to the hunter*

Ryoushin 両親 = parents; *Pope Leo ordered new shingles for his parents*; cf. related terms listed at oya

Ryoushitsu 良質 = fine quality; *Pope Leo uses sheets of fine quality*; cf. related terms listed at hinshitsu

Ryoushou 了承 = understanding, acknowledgment; *Pope Leo showed them his deep understanding*; cf. related terms listed at shouchi

Ryoushou suru 了承する = to understand or acknowledge; from ryoushou = understanding, acknowledgment; cf.

related terms listed at wakaru

Ryoushuusho 領収書 = receipt; *Pope Leo went to a shoe show and saved his receipt*; cf. denpyou = a receipt, bill or slip; cf. suitou = receipts and disbursements

Ryoute 両手 = both hands; from ryouhou = both + te = hand; cf. related terms listed at te

Ryoutei 料亭 = a traditional Japanese restaurant; *Pope Leo likes the taste of the food at that traditional Japanese restaurant*; cf. izakaya = a pub or bar; cf. kissaten = a coffee shop; cf. mise = a store, shop or restaurant; cf. oshokujidokoro = a restaurant (Japanese style); cf. suteeki ten = a steak restaurant

Ryouyou 療養 = recovery, recuperation; *Pope Leo used yoga to accelerate his recovery*; cf. related terms listed at kaifuku

Ryouyou suru 療養する = to recuperate or receive medical treatment; from ryouyou = recovery, recuperation; cf. kaifuku suru = to recover from illness, to improve; cf. kouten suru = to improve; cf. zenkai suru = to recover completely

Ryukku リュック = an abbreviation of ryukkusakku = rucksack, or backpack

Ryukkusakku リュックサック = a rucksack, or backpack

Ryuugaku 留学 = study abroad; *I wore reused garments in Kuwait during my study abroad*; cf. related terms listed at benkyou

Ryuuki 隆起 = a protuberance or rising; *we were reunited in Kiev on a protuberance that was part of a cliff*

Ryuukou 流行 = vogue, fashion; *reused corn cobs are in fashion as hair ornaments*

Ryuusan'en (qRyuusanen) 硫酸塩 = sulfate; *the reused Santa toy that entertained me as a child fell into a bath of magnesium sulfate (Epsom salt)*

Ryuushi 粒子 = a particle or grain; *we reuse our sheets after removing every particle of dirt from them*; cf. related terms listed at tsubu

Ryuutsuu 流通 = distribution; *we encourage the distribution of reused tsuits (suits)*; cf. haifu = distribution; cf. haitatsu = delivery or distribution

Sa さ = a suffix that makes a noun from other words, e.g., hirosa = width, expanse, area; sa can also be used to show emphasis

Saakuru サークル = circle; cf. related terms listed at maru

Sabaku 捌く = to handle or process, to prepare (meat or fish) for cooking, to sell out (stock); *before the Sabbath, the Kool-Aid often sells out, and I have to prepare our food without it, but I can handle that*; cf. related terms listed at shori suru

Sabaku 砂漠 = a desert; *we visited the desert on a Sabbath in Kuwait*

Sabetsu 差別 = discrimination; from sa = gap, e.g., jisa = time difference; + betsu = separate

Sabishii 寂しい = lonely; *after the salaryman's favorite beerhall was closed by the Shiites, he was lonely*

Sabishisa 寂しさ = loneliness; from sabishii = lonely + sa, a suffix that makes a noun from an adjective; cf. related terms listed at kodoku

Sabu'ado (Sabuado) サブアド = a sub-address, i.e., a secondary email address; this is an abbreviation of sabu'adoresu

Sacchi suru 察知する = to perceive; *I perceive that this satchel is made from cheap materials*; cf. kanjiru = to feel or sense

Sadameru 定める = to decide or determine; *when my sad dad met Ruth, he decided to ask her to marry him, and that determined his fate*; cf. related terms listed at kimeru

Sadou 作動 = operation, functioning; *the sagacious doorman supervised the operation of the elevators*; cf. related terms listed at sousa

Sadou 茶道 = the tea ceremony; from sa = tea, e.g., kissaten = a café; + dou = way

Sae さえ (or de sae) = even, if only (implying that that's all one needs), as long as, the only thing needed; *Saruman believes in education as long as it supports his regime*; cf. desae = even, but, however; cf. sura = as long as, even, if only

Saegiru 遮る = to block or interrupt; *the sad entertainer with a guitar ruined my party when he interrupted it to play a sad song*

Sagaru 下がる = to hang (intransitive), go down, step backward, drop; *in the saga that Ruth told, she dropped off a cliff and hung from a tree*; cf. kakaru = to start doing something, used as a suffix; cf. tareru = to hang, droop, dangle, sag, lower, drip, ooze; cf. taresagaru = to hang; cf. other related terms listed at oriru

Sagasu 捜す = to look for or search, usually referring to police activities; *the police are looking for a sad gasu (gas) station attendant*; cf. related terms listed at sousaku suru

Sagasu 探す = to search or look for; *the sad gasu (gas) station attendant looked for his wallet*; cf. related terms listed at sousaku suru

Sageru 下げる = to hang (transitive), lower, reduce, remove; the transitive form of sagaru = to hang; cf. kakeru = to expend or spend (e.g., time, money, love), to hang (a picture), to make (a call), to multiply, to put on (glasses), to pour or sprinkle onto, to sit down, among many other meanings; cf. tsuriageru = to lift up or suspend; cf. tsurisageru = to suspend from; cf. tsuru = to suspend or hang up; cf. tsurusu = to suspend or hang up; cf. other related terms listed at genshou suru

Sagesumu 蔑む = to look down on, to scorn or despise; *the sagacious guest from Sudan watched a movie and despised it*; cf. related terms listed at anadoru

Sagi サギ = a heron; *that heron has sagging feathers*; cf. related terms listed at tori

Sagi 詐欺 = a fraud or hoax; *my roof is sagging because the installer committed fraud*; cf. related terms listed at tsumi

Sagishi 詐欺師 = a swindler; from sagi = fraud + shi = an expert, e.g., kyoushi = a teacher; cf. related terms listed at hannin

Saguriateru 探り当てる = to find out; from saguru = to probe, grope, look for + ateru = to hit, touch or win; cf. related terms listed at mitsukeru

Saguru 探る = to grope, look for, probe; *the sad guru groped around in his wallet for money*

Sagyou 作業 = work, operations, manufacturing; *this sack of gyoza is the result of our work*; cf. seisaku = manufacture, production; cf. seisan = production; cf. seizou = manufacturing, production; cf. other related terms listed at shigoto

Sagyouin 作業員 = a laborer; from sagyou = work + in = a group member; cf. related terms listed at roudousha

Sahodo さほど = not so, not particularly, not very, not that much; *the satisfaction she gets when I hold the door for her is not that much*; cf. amari = surplus, remainder, more than, very much, not very (with negative constructions)

Sai 歳 = age, years old; *the scientist lived to an advanced age*; cf. related terms listed at nen

Sai 際 = when, verge, time; *when I have nothing to say, I am silent*

Sai ni 際に = in case of, at that time; *in case you study science with my niece, behave yourself at that time*; cf. touji = those days, at that time, old days; cf. other related terms listed at moshi

Saiaku 最悪 = the worst; from sai = the most, e.g., saikou = the best; + aku = bad, e.g., akui = ill will; cf. related terms listed at warui

Saibai 栽培 = cultivation; *the scientists buy seeds for cultivation*; cf. inasaku = rice cultivation, rice crop; cf. kousaku = cultivation

Saiban 裁判 = trial or judgment; *the silent banker did not testify at his trial*; cf. related terms listed at handan

Saibanchou 裁判長 = a presiding judge; from saibankan = a judge + chou = a chief; cf. related terms listed at saibankan and at shunou

Saibankan 裁判官 = a judge; from saiban = judgment + kan = government official, e.g., keikan = police officer; cf. hanji = a judge; cf. saibanchou = a presiding judge

Saibansho 裁判所 = a court of law; from saiban = judgment + sho = a place; cf. houtei = a court of law

Saibou 細胞 = a cell (biology); *that scientist's bones are full of cells*

Saibu 細部 = details; *I'm learning the details of the science behind boomerangs*; cf. shousai = details

Saichuu 最中 = in the midst of, during; *the scientist chewed gum during the meeting*; cf. aida ni = during

Saidai 最大 = biggest, maximum; *the science of dieting helps the biggest people*; cf. saidaigen = maximum

Saidaigen 最大限 = maximum; *the science of dikes under Genghis reached its maximum*; cf. saidai = biggest, maximum

Saidaikyuu 最大級 = the largest class or top category; from saidai = biggest or maximum + kyuu = order or class, e.g., koukyuu = high class or category; cf. related terms listed at kyuu

Saien 菜園 = a vegetable garden; *the scientist had a vegetable garden*; cf. related terms listed at niwa

Saifu 財布 = a wallet or purse; *the scientist foolishly lost her purse*

Saigai 災害 = a disaster; *the scientific guy is prepared for disaster*; cf. sainan = a disaster; cf. sounan = an accident or disaster; cf. tensai = a natural disaster; cf. wazawai = a calamity or disaster; cf. yaku = misfortune, disaster

Saigen suru 再現する = to reproduce, replicate; *the scientist that Genghis hired was able to reproduce the results of the experiment*

Saigo 最後 = last, end, conclusion, most recent; *the scientists' golf game lasted until the last hole*; cf. owari = the end; cf. saishin = latest or newest; cf. saishuu = last

Saihou 裁縫 = sewing; *the silent hostess returned to her sewing*; cf. harishigoto = sewing, needlework

Saihousou 再放送 = a re-broadcast; from sai = again; *the scientists performed the experiment again*; + housou = broadcast

Saikai suru 再会する = to meet again; *the scientists and the Kaiser will meet again*; cf. related terms listed at deau

Saikai suru 再開する = to reopen or resume; *the sign says that the kite show will resume*

Saikaibi 再開日 = reopening day; from saikai suru = to reopen + bi = hi = day; cf. shonichi = first or opening day

Saiken 債券 = bonds (finance); *the silent Kennedy kept his money in bonds*

Saikin 最近 = recently, nowadays; *the science underlying kindling fires has recently improved*; cf. chikagoro = recently, lately, nowadays; cf. kinnen = recent years; cf. koko saikin = recent

Saikin 細菌 = bacterium, germ; *scientists*

visited the <u>kindergarten</u> to investigate the <u>bacteria</u> living there; cf. related terms listed at mushi

Saikou 最高 = the best or highest; <u>Psycho</u> was <u>the best</u> movie; cf. dai ichi = number one, i.e., the most, the best or the first; cf. saizen = the best

Saikousai 最高裁 = the Supreme Court; the <u>psycho</u> <u>scientist</u> took his case to the <u>Supreme</u> <u>Court</u>

Saikousaibansho 最高裁判所 = the Supreme Court (as a location); the <u>psycho</u> <u>scientist</u> was <u>banned</u> from <u>showing</u> his injuries outside the <u>Supreme</u> <u>Court</u>

Saikyou 最強 = the strongest; the <u>silent</u> guy from <u>Kyouto</u> is the <u>strongest</u>; cf. related terms listed at tsuyoi

Saimu 債務 = debt; she went into <u>debt</u> to make that <u>silent</u> <u>movie</u>; cf. related terms listed at fusai

Sainan 災難 = misfortune, disaster; the <u>scientist's</u> <u>nanny</u> caused the <u>disaster</u>; cf. related terms listed at saigai

Sainou 才能 = talent; he has a <u>talent</u> for <u>sighing</u> through his <u>nose</u>

Saisan 再三 = many times, again and again; the <u>scientist</u> ate a <u>sandwich</u> while she performed the experiment <u>again</u> <u>and</u> <u>again</u>; cf. related terms listed at aratamete and at nandomo

Saisan 採算 = profit, surplus; by reducing the <u>size</u> of its <u>sandwiches</u>, the deli was able to make a <u>profit</u>; cf. rieki = profit, advantage, interests; cf. toku = profit; cf. other related terms listed at yoyuu

Saisei 再生 = recycling, rebirth, regeneration, playback or view (of a sound or video track); a video in which <u>scientists</u> <u>say</u> that <u>recycling</u> is good for the environment has received a lot of <u>playbacks</u>

Saiseki 砕石 = rubble, broken stone; the <u>silent</u> <u>selfish</u> <u>king</u> gazed at the <u>rubble</u> where his palace had been; cf. jari = gravel

Saishin 最新 = latest or newest; the <u>sign</u> outside the <u>Shinto</u> shrine uses the <u>latest</u> technology; cf. saigo = last, end, conclusion, most recent

Saisho 最初 = first, beginning; the <u>science</u> <u>show</u> was the <u>first</u> one we saw; cf. related terms listed at hajime and at hajime ni

Saishu 採取 = picking, gathering, harvesting; the <u>scientist</u> put on her <u>shoes</u> before going outside and <u>gathering</u> data

Saishu suru 採取する = to pick or gather; from saishu = picking, gathering, harvesting; cf. related terms listed at shuukaku suru

Saishuu 採集 = a collection; I have a <u>collection</u> of <u>scientifically</u> designed <u>shoes</u>; cf. related terms listed at shuushuu

Saishuu 最終 = last; the <u>silent</u> <u>shooter</u> was on his <u>last</u> legs; cf. saigo = last, end, conclusion, most recent

Saishuubi 最終日 = the last or final day; from saishuu = last + bi = hi = day

Saishuukai 最終回 = the last time, the final episode; from saishuu = last + kai = times; the <u>kites</u> rotate many <u>times</u>

Saisoku 最速 = fastest; from sai = the most, e.g., saikou = the best; + soku = fast; e.g., sokutatsu = express mail; cf. related terms listed at hayai

Saitakane 最高値 = the highest price; from saidai = the maximum + takai = high + nedan = price

Saitei 最低 = minimum, worst; the <u>silent</u> <u>table</u> is where there is a <u>minimum</u> of conversation, and it's <u>the</u> <u>worst</u>; cf. saiteigen = minimum

Saiteigen 最低限 = minimum; the <u>science</u> of <u>tasers</u> under <u>Genghis</u> was at its <u>minimum</u>; cf. saitei = minimum, worst

Saiten 採点 = grading, marking; the <u>psychology</u> student was <u>tense</u> as he waited for the <u>grading</u> of his paper

Saiwai 幸い = lucky, happy; *the <u>scientist's</u> <u>wife</u> was <u>happy</u>*; cf. related terms listed at shiawase na

Saiyou 採用 = adoption, acceptance, employment; *the <u>science</u> of <u>yogurt</u> is gaining more <u>acceptance</u> and contributing to the <u>adoption</u> of milk products and the <u>employment</u> of more people*; cf. related terms listed at shouchi

Saiyou suru 採用する = to adopt, accept or employ; from saiyou = adoption, acceptance, employment; cf. related terms listed at yatou

Saiyuusen 最優先 = maximum priority; from saidai = maximum + yuusen = priority

Saizen 最善 = the best; *the <u>scientist</u> thought that <u>Zen</u> was <u>the</u> <u>best</u> religion*; cf. related terms listed at saikou

Saka 坂 = slope, hill; *we play <u>sakkaa</u> (soccer) on that <u>hill</u>*; cf. other related terms listed at shamen and at yama

Sakadateru 逆立てる = to stand on end or bristle (referring to hair); from sakarau = to oppose or disobey + dateru = tateru = to build or put upright

Sakaeru 栄える = to prosper or thrive; *he sets up <u>sakaa</u> games for <u>erudite</u> people, and he is <u>thriving</u>*; cf. hanei suru = to prosper; cf. kouryuu suru = to prosper or flourish; cf. sakan desu = is thriving

Sakai 境 = boundary, border; *a policeman will <u>sock</u> you in the <u>eye</u> if you cross the <u>border</u>*; cf. kokkyou = a border

Sakamichi 坂道 = uphill path; from saka = hill + michi = path; cf. related terms listed at michi

Sakan 盛ん = active, enthusiastic, energetic, thriving; *drinking <u>sake</u> from a <u>can</u> is a <u>thriving</u> custom, and people who do it tend to be <u>active</u> and <u>enthusiastic</u>*; cf. kappatsu = active, vivacious; cf. minoriooi = fruitful, successful; cf. ousei na = flourishing, active, high; cf. seidai = grandiose, pompous, thriving, successful

Sakan desu 盛んです = is thriving; cf. related terms listed at sakaeru

Sakana 魚 = fish; *I bought a <u>sack</u> of <u>Canadian</u> <u>fish</u>*; cf. fugu = a blowfish or puffer fish; cf. iruka = dolphin; cf. katsuo = bonito (fish); cf. kujira = whale; cf. maguro = tuna; cf. sake = salmon; cf. sanma = Pacific saury; cf. tara = codfish

Sakarau 逆らう = to oppose or disobey; *at the game, the <u>sakkaa</u> (soccer) fans were <u>rowdy</u> and <u>disobeyed</u> the security staff*; cf. han suru = to oppose; cf. taikou suru = to oppose or fight

Sakasama no さかさまの = reverse, upside-down, topsy-turvy; *at the <u>sakkaa</u> (soccer) game, Samantha stood on her head and watched the game <u>upside</u>-<u>down</u>*

Sakatsubo 酒壺 = sake jar; from saka = sake + tsubo = jar; cf. related terms listed at tsubo

Sakazuki wo suru 盃をする = to share a cup of sake; *after I play <u>sakkaa</u> (soccer) with the <u>zoo</u> <u>keeper</u>, we <u>share</u> <u>a</u> <u>cup</u> <u>of</u> <u>sake</u>*

Sake サケ = salmon; *I drink <u>sake</u> when I eat <u>salmon</u>*; cf. related terms listed at sakana

Sake 酒 = Japanese rice wine, alcoholic beverage; *<u>sad</u> <u>Ken</u> was drinking too much <u>Japanese</u> <u>rice</u> <u>wine</u>*; cf. happoushu = sparkling wine, low-malt beer; cf. mirin = a sweet rice wine used in cooking

Sakebigoe 叫び声 = a scream; from sakebu = to scream + koe = goe = voice; cf. related terms listed at kakegoe

Sakebu 叫ぶ = to shout, yell, scream; *after drinking <u>sake</u> and other <u>booze</u>, he started to <u>scream</u>*; cf. donaru = to shout or yell; cf. himei wo ageru = to scream

Sakeru 裂ける = to split or tear (intransitive); *the <u>sake</u> was <u>ruined</u> when the side of its cask <u>split</u> open*; cf. related terms listed at yabureru

Sakeru 避ける = to avoid; *there was sake in the room, but I avoided drinking it*; cf. kaihi suru = to avoid; cf. manugareru = to avoid or be exempted from

Sakezuki 酒好き = a drinker, someone who likes sake; from sake + zuki = suki = to like; cf. similar terms listed at honzuki

Saki 先 = tip, point, future, former, destination, end, ahead; *the sack of quiche is located at the point of this arrow*; cf. sentan = vanguard, tip, end; cf. sue = tip, end, future

Saki ni 先に = ahead, formerly, before, beyond; from saki = tip, point, future, destination + -ni = a suffix that forms an adverb; cf. chokugo ni = immediately after or behind; cf. chokuzen = just before; cf. izen = ago (suggesting a long time), before; cf. jizen = in advance, prior; cf. mae = front, before, ago; cf. mae no = former, facing; cf. maemotte = in advance; cf. zen = former, before, in front of

Sakihodo 先ほど = some time ago, just now; from saki = former + hodo = approximate time; cf. sakki = some time ago, just now

Sakimawari 先回り = going on ahead; from saki = tip + mawaru = to turn

Sakka 作家 = a writer; *the writer writes about sakkaa (soccer)*; cf. chosha = writer; cf. hissha = writer

Sakkaku 錯覚 = an illusion or misunderstanding; *there was a misunderstanding about the salary of Karl the Kool-Aid vendor*; cf. related terms listed at genkaku and at kanchigai

Sakki さっき = some time ago, just now; *I remembered just now that some time ago, I was sacking an employee*; cf. sakihodo = some time ago, just now

Sakkin 殺菌 = sterilization, pasteurization; *in Sapporo kindergartens, they serve milk that has been treated with pasteurization*

Sakkyoku 作曲 = composition (music); *in this sack, the Kyoto Kool-Aid club keeps its musical compositions*; cf. related terms listed at sakuhin

Sakoku 鎖国 = national isolation, exclusion of foreigners; *the sad Coke drinkers could no longer get their favorite drink due to national isolation*

Saku 冊 = a volume; *I have two volumes of the book in this sack*; cf. satsu = a counter for books

Saku 咲く = to blossom or flower; *Saruman went to Kuwait when the trees were flowering*

Saku 柵 = a fence; *I keep my fence posts in a sack*; cf. related terms listed at kakine

Saku 策 = a plan, scheme or device; *I have plans for that sack of Kool-Aid*; cf. related terms listed at kikaku

Saku 裂く = to split or rip (transitive); *I ripped up the salty Kool-Aid packages*; cf. hikisaku = to tear off or separate; cf. yaburu = to break, tear or violate

Saku 作 = a work or production; an abbreviation of sakuhin = a creation, or of sakubun = a composition

Sakuban 昨晩 = last night; *I ate a sack of bananas last night*; cf. related terms listed at sakuya

Sakubun 作文 = a composition (writing); *after using up a sack of Kool-Aid, Daniel Boone completed his composition*; cf. related terms listed at sakuhin

Sakugen 削減 = a curtailment or reduction; *the sack of cookies that Genghis ordered this week was a reduction, compared to his usual orders*; cf. related terms listed at genshou

Sakugo 錯誤 = a mistake or error; *I made a mistake when I gave salty cookies to that golfer*; cf. related terms listed at shippai

Sakuhin 作品 = creation, production, composition; *the sack the Hindu carried* contained his *composition*; cf. bun = sentence, composition; cf. bunshou = sentence, composition, writing; cf. eisakubun = English composition; cf. kessaku = a masterpiece; cf. meisaku = a masterpiece; cf. ronbun = essay, research paper, thesis; cf. sakkyoku = a composition (music); cf. sakubun = a composition (writing); cf. souzou = creation

Sakuin 索引 = index; *that salaryman spilled Kool-Aid and ink on the index of this book*

Sakujitsu 昨日 = yesterday; this can also be read kinou, with the same meaning; *yesterday they sacked (fired) the jittery superstar*; cf. kinou = yesterday; cf. related terms listed at yokujitsu

Sakujo 削除 = a deletion, cancellation or erasure; *the sack of cookies that Job ordered didn't arrive due to an accidental cancellation and deletion of the order*

Sakumotsu 作物 = crops; *after harvesting crops near the castle, I ate a sack of cookies between the moats*; cf. beisaku = rice growing, rice crop; cf. gokoku houjou = a bumper crop; cf. fusaku = a poor harvest; cf. houjou = good harvest; cf. housaku = a good harvest or bumper crop; cf. inasaku = rice cultivation, rice crop; cf. minori = a harvest; cf. nousakumotsu = agricultural crops; cf. nousanbutsu = agricultural produce; cf. shuukaku = harvest, crop

Sakunen 昨年 = last year; from saku = previous, e.g., sakuban = last night; + nen = year; cf. related terms listed at kyonen

Sakura 桜 = cherry; this can also be spelled 櫻; *the salaryman turned off his kuuraa (cooler, or air conditioner) before going out to see the cherry blossoms*

Sakura 櫻 = cherry, sometimes used as a component of proper nouns; this can also be spelled 桜; *the salaryman turned off his kuuraa (cooler, or air conditioner) before going out to see the cherry blossoms*

Sakuragi 桜木 = cherry trees; from sakura = cherry + gi = ki = a tree; cf. related terms listed at ki

Sakusaku サクサク = crisp or crunchy; *he has sacks and sacks of crunchy potato chips*; cf. related terms listed at karikari

Sakusei suru 作成する = to draw up (document), prepare, write, make, produce; *the sad Kool-Aid salesman made his final plans and drew up his will*; cf. related terms listed at kaku = to write and at tsukuru

Sakushi 作詞 = (writing) song lyrics; *I have this sack of sheets of paper that I use for writing song lyrics*; cf. kashi = lyrics

Sakushu 搾取 = exploitation; *due to exploitation, the sad Kuwaiti shoe salesman had barely enough to eat*; cf. related terms listed at kaihatsu

Sakuya 昨夜 = last night; *I drank sake and Kool-Aid in the yard last night*; cf. sakuban = last night; cf. yuube = evening, yesterday evening

Sakyuu 砂丘 = a sand dune; *the sad Cuban was living on a sand dune*

Sama 様 = a very honorific suffix used to indicate Mr., Mrs., Ms, etc.; *Very Hononorable Samantha came to visit*

Samasu 冷ます = to cool (transitive), to let cool; *the Good Samaritan assumed that the motel would cool his room*; cf. hiyasu = to cool or chill, transitive

Samasu 覚ます = to wake up; *the Samsung executives assumed that their engineers would wake up in time*; cf. me ga sameru = to wake up; cf. me wo samasu = to wake up; cf. okiru = to occur, to get up, to wake up; cf. sameru = to wake up

Samatageru 妨げる = to hinder or obstruct; *the Good Samaritan talked the guest into staying in my room where she obstructed my access to the exit*; cf. soshi suru = to obstruct or hinder

Samazama 様々 = various; *the Good Samaritan and his Zambian friend Max were involved in various plans*; cf. related terms listed at kazukazu

Sameru 冷める = to become cool; *after the salaryman met Ruth, his lover for his wife became cool*; cf. hieru = to get cold or chilly, intransitive

Sameru 覚める = to wake up or become sober, to understand; *Samsung's erudite engineer woke up*; cf. related terms listed at samasu and at wakaru

Samui 寒い = cold, chilly (atmosphere); *the samurai's ears were cold*; cf. tsumetai = cold (object)

Samuke 寒気 = a chill, the shivers; from samui = cold + ke = ki = feeling

Samurai 侍 = a Japanese warrior; *I'm sad because a Moonie took my rice and gave it to a Japanese warrior*; cf. bushi = a warrior or samurai

San さん = a suffix used to indicate Mr., Mrs., Ms, etc.; *Mr. Sandman came to visit*

Sanbashi 桟橋 = a wharf, bridge, jetty or pier; *Santa was bashing some cans on the wharf, getting ready to recycle them*; cf. hatoba = a pier or wharf

Sanbun 散文 = prose; *Santa asked Daniel Boone to stick to prose (after reading his poems)*; cf. inbun = poetry

Sanbutsu 産物 = product; from sangyou = industry + butsu = thing; cf. buppin = article, things, goods; cf. fukusanbutsu = a byproduct; cf. henpin = returned goods; cf. seihin = a product, manufactured goods; cf. shina = goods, article, quality; cf. shinamono = merchandise, article; cf. shinseihin = a new product; cf. shouhin = commodity, merchandise; cf. shusanbutsu = a main product; cf. suisanbutsu = marine products

Sanbyoushi 三拍子 = triple time (music); from san = three + hyoushi = byoushi = rhythm

Sanchuu 山中 = in the mountains; from san = mountain + chuu = inside

Sandou suru 賛同する = to approve or endorse; *Santa's doughnuts were approved by everyone*; cf. kaketsu suru = to approve or pass (legislation)

Sangaku 山岳 = mountains; *Santa drank a gallon of Kool-Aid as he climbed the mountains*; cf. related terms listed at yama

Sangakuchi 山岳地 = mountain lands; from sangaku = mountains + chi'iki = area; cf. related terms listed at chitai

Sango サンゴ = coral; *Santa paid in gold for that coral necklace*

Sangoshou サンゴ礁 = coral reef; from sango = coral + ganshou = reef

Sangyou 産業 = industry, occupation; *that industry produces sanitary gyoza*; cf. related terms listed at kougyou

Sanka 参加 = participation; *I will participate in drinking Sanka*; cf. kamei = participation, joining; cf. nakamairi = joining a group; cf. shutsujou = appearance, participation (e.g., in a tournament)

Sanka 産科 = obstetrics; from san = to produce, e.g., sangyou = industry; + kagaku = science

Sanka suru 参加する = to participate; from sanka = participation; cf. related terms listed at kuwawaru

Sanka'i (Sankai) 産科医 = an obstetrician; from sanka = obstetrics + isha = a physician

Sankaku 三角 = a triangle; from san = three + kaku = a corner

Sankakusu 三角州 = a delta; from sankaku = a triangle + su = sandbank; *Superman flew over the sandbank*

Sankan 山間 = among the mountains; a shortened version of sankanchi = a place among the mountains

Sankanchi 山間地 = a place among the mountains; from san = mountain + kan = interval or space + chi = ground or soil

Sankasha 参加者 = participant; from sanka suru = to participate + sha = person; cf. shussekisha = attendee

Sankei shinbun 産経新聞 = the Sankei newspaper in Japan; from sangyou = industry + keizai = economics + shinbun = newspaper

Sanma さんま = Pacific saury (a kind of fish); *the Sandman likes Pacific saury*; cf. related terms listed at sakana

Sanmyaku 山脈 = mountain range; *Santa appeared in a commercial for Miami Kool-Aid, standing in front of a mountain range*; cf. related terms listed at yama

Sannan 三男 = a third son; *Santa's nanny had a third son*; cf. similar terms listed at musuko

Sanpi 賛否 = yes and no, for and against; *the reaction to Santa's piano playing was yes and no*

Sanpo 散歩 = a walk; *Santa and the pope went for a walk*; cf. hokou = walking; cf. koushin = a march; cf. toho = walking, going on foot

Sanpo suru 散歩する = to walk; from sanpo = a walk; cf. related terms listed at aruku

Sanran 産卵 = egg-laying, spawning; from san = products, e.g., seisan = production + ran = egg; *I got these eggs at the ranch*

Sanretsu suru 参列する = to attend or participate in; *Santa wore a retro suit when he attended the wedding*; cf. related terms listed at shusseki suru

Sanrinsha 三輪車 = tricycle; from san = three + rin = wheel; *Ringo has cool wheels*; + sha = vehicle

Sanroku 山麓 = the base of a mountain; *the base of the mountain is covered with sand and rocks*; cf. related terms listed at fumoto

Sanrui 3塁 = third base; from san = three + rui = a base; cf. related terms listed at rui

Sansei 賛成 = agreement; *when I met Santa at Safeway, he signed an agreement with me*; cf. related terms listed at shouchi

Sansei 酸性 = acidity; *Santa saved some oranges because he liked their acidity*

Sansei suru 賛成する = to agree; from sansei = agreement; cf. nattoku suru = to acquiesce, agree; cf. ryoukai suru = to agree, consent or understand

Sanshou suru 参照する = to browse (e.g., the internet), to refer to (e.g., notes) or to consult (e.g., a dictionary); *before Santa visited the shore, he browsed the internet to find the best beaches*; cf. hiku = to pull, to attract, to look up, to subtract, to subside, to draw a line, to install utilities (e.g., gas)

Sanshutsu suru 産出する = to yield or produce, to compute or calculate; *Santa shoots off fireworks when the elves produce lots of toys, a habit derived from his New Year's celebrations*; cf. related terms listed at tsukuru

Sanso 酸素 = oxygen; *Santa's soda is infused with oxygen*; cf. related terms listed at tanso

Sanson 山村 = a mountain village; *Santa's son lives in that mountain village*; cf. related terms listed at shi

Sansuu 算数 = arithmetic; *Santa sued his dwarves due to their poor arithmetic*; cf. suugaku = mathematics

Sanzan 散々 = devastatingly, severely; the adverbial form of sanzan na = devastating

Sanzan na 散々な = devastating, terrible; *when Santa visited Zanzibar, he had a terrible time*; cf. related terms listed at hidoi

Sara 皿 = a dish, plate or saucer; *I cover my dishes with Saran wrap*

Sara ni 更に = again, furthermore; *you put Saran wrap on your knee again*; cf. sono ue = furthermore, on top of; cf. tsuzuite = continuing, next, furthermore; cf. other related terms listed at aratamete

Saraigetsu 再来月 = the month after next; from sa = again; *I was sad that it happened again*; + raigetsu = next month

Sarainen 再来年 = the year after next; from sa = again; *I was sad that it happened again*; + rainen = next year

Saraishuu 再来週 = the week after next; from sa = again; *I was sad that it happened again*; + raishuu = next week

Sarasu さらす = to expose; *when I removed the Saran wrap from the soup, I exposed our food to the air*

Sareru される = to have done to, or to do honorably; the passive form of suru = to do

Saru 去る = to leave; *Saruman left Middle Earth forever*; cf. related terms listed at deru

Saru 猿 = a monkey; *Saruman kept a monkey as a pet*; cf. nihonzaru = Japanese macaque; cf. ruijinen = an ape

Sasae 支え = support; from sasaeru = to support; cf. related terms listed at enjo

Sasaeau 支え合う = to support each other; from sasaeru = to support + au = to come together; cf. related terms listed at seien suru

Sasaeru 支える = to support; *the sad salaryman is erudite and supports his company*; cf. related terms listed at seien suru

Sasayaka na ささやかな = small, modest; *the sad salaryman's yard held a cat that was small*; cf. related terms listed at chiisai

Sasayaku ささやく = to whisper; *my co-worker whispered that she had served a salty sandwich to the yakuza customer*

Sasen 左遷 = a demotion; *the salaryman is sensitive about his demotion*

Sashiageru 差し上げる = to give humbly; *when the sad sheep ageru (give), they give humbly*; cf. related terms listed at ataeru

Sashidasu 差し出す = to hold out, offer, send; from sashiageru = to give humbly + dasu = to put out; cf. related terms listed at moushideru

Sashie 挿絵 = an illustration; *it was an illustration of satisfied sheep entering their pen*; cf. related terms listed at e

Sashikakaru 差し掛かる = to come near or approach; *the sassy card-carrying roofer approached us*; cf. chikazuku = to approach

Sashikomu 差し込む = to shine in or flow in, to insert or plug in; *the sad sheep komu (crowd in) when they flow into their pens at the end of the day*; cf. related terms listed at teru

Sashimi 刺身 = raw sliced fish; *I slept on satin sheets and had a meal of raw sliced fish*; cf. related terms listed at ryouri

Sashitsukae 差支え = hindrance, impediment; from sashitsukaeru = to interfere

Sashitsukaeru 差し支える = to interfere or hinder; *the satisfied sheep drag tsuitcases (suitcases) and kaeru (return) to their pens where they interfere with the shepherd's work*

Sashizu 指図 = direction, command, order; *the sad Shiite visited the zoo in accordance with his the sad Shiite visited the zoo in accordance with his orders and commands*; cf. gourei = a command or order; cf. meirei = a command or order

Sashizu suru 指図する = to command or direct; from sashizu = direction, command, order; cf. related terms listed at meirei suru

Sasori サソリ = a scorpion; *the salaryman is sorry that he put a scorpion in your shoe*

Sasou 誘う = to invite, entice, encite; *she invited me to hear a saxophone solo*; cf. related terms listed at shoutai suru

Sassa to さっさと = immediately, promptly; *in Sapporo, I saw a tote bag and purchased it immediately*; cf. related terms listed at sokkoku

Sasshi 冊子 = a booklet or pamphlet; *this is a pamphlet about Sapporo sheep*; cf. zasshi = a magazine; cf. related terms listed at hon

Sassoku 早速 = immediately, at once, sudden; *if you sass that old Kool-Aid vendor, I will reprimand you immediately*; cf. related terms listed at kyuu ni and at sokkoku

Sasu 差す = to hold up (e.g., an umbrella), to rise, to fill or insert; *I held up an umbrella to protect my salty soup from the rain*; cf. related terms listed at kakageru

Sasu 刺す = to stab, sting or bite (insect); *in Sapporo the superintendent was bitten by mosquitoes*

Sasu 指す = to point; *Saturn is super, he said, as he pointed at the sky*; cf. mukeru = to direct, point, turn towards; cf. shimesu = to show or point out; cf. shiteki wo suru = to point out; cf. yubisasu = to point to (with finger)

Sasuga ni さすがに = indeed, as expected; *he sacked up Superman's garbage on his knees, as expected*; cf. yappari = as expected, after all, again

Sata 沙汰 = information, communication, command, affair; *I received information that you have salty tap water*; cf. related terms listed at jouhou

Sate さて = well, now, then; *well, here is a sad teddy bear*

Sateoki さておき = setting aside, leaving to one side; *I'm satisfied with the television station's report on Okinawa, so I'm setting that aside*

Sato 里 = hometown, village; *there is a satellite tower in the village*; cf. related terms listed at furusato

Satogokoro 里心 = homesickness, nostalgia (used with tsuku, e.g., satogokoro ga tsuku = to get homesick); from sato = hometown + gokoro = kokoro = heart; cf. kyoushuu = nostalgia, homesickness

Satori 悟り = enlightenment, comprehension; from satoru = to realize

Satoru 悟る = to realize, fathom, become enlightened; *after the satellite tower ruined my view, I realized that it didn't matter*; cf. ki ga tsuku = kizuku = to realize or notice, to regain consciousness

Satosu 諭す = to warn or advise; *I warn you against serving salty tortillas to Superman*; cf. related terms listed at iikikaseru

Satou 砂糖 = sugar; *the salaryman eats toast with sugar on it*

Satsu 冊 = a counter for books; *I have many satisfying Superman books*; cf. saku = a volume

Satsu 札 = a bill (paper currency); *the satisfied supervisor counted his twenty-dollar bills*

Satsuei 撮影 = filming, photographing; *our next job is filming the satisfied supervisor's ape*; cf. shashin satsuei = photography

Satsujin 殺人 = murder; *the satisfying Superman novel described how some stained jeans helped to solve the murder*; cf. ansatsu = assassination; cf. konzetsu = eradication, extermination; cf. satsujinzai = the crime of murder; cf. satsushobun = culling or euthanizing unwanted animals; cf. taiji = extermination, suppression

Satsujinki 殺人鬼 = killer, cutthroat; *I read a satisfying Superman novel about a genius who used a skeleton key to uncover evidence about a killer*

Satsujinzai 殺人罪 = the crime of murder; from satsujin = murder + zaiaku = a crime; cf. related terms listed at satsujin

Satsushobun 殺処分 = culling or euthanizing unwanted animals; from satsujin = murder + shobun = disposal; cf. related terms listed at satsujin

Satto サット = quickly (actions) or suddenly (esp. rain and wind); *the satellite tower fell down quickly after the wind blew suddenly*; cf. sotto = softly, gently; cf. related terms listed at kyuu ni and at kyuusoku

Sattou suru 殺到する = to rush at or surge; *the sad-looking toads rushed into the pond*

Sawa 沢 = a swamp; *I saw water in the swamp*

Sawagu 騒ぐ = to make noise, to make a fuss; *when he saw the wagon carrying his goose, he made a fuss*

Sawari 障り = a hindrance, obstacle or harm; from sawaru = to harm; cf. daisongai = great damage; cf. gai = harm; cf. higai = damage or loss; cf. songai = harm or loss; cf. sonshou = damage or injury; cf. other related terms at shougai

Sawaru 触る = to touch or feel, usually intentional; *the salad was ruined when that guy touched it*; cf. related terms listed at fureru

Sawaru 障る = to harm or annoy; *Saruman put the walrus in my room to annoy me*; cf. nayamasu = to annoy or worry; cf. other related terms listed at kizutsukeru

Sayoku 左翼 = left wing (politics); *the saxophone player guy played yoku (well) and favored left wing politics*; cf. uyoku = right wing (politics)

Sayounara さようなら = goodbye; *after I saw the yogi in Nara, I said goodbye*

Sayuu 左右 = left and right; *the sad youth did not know left from right*

Sazukaru 授かる = to be endowed with or blessed with; *the Sapporo zoo has a kangaroo that is endowed with powerful legs*; cf. related terms listed at megumareru

Sazukeru 授ける = to give or grant; *I gave the Sapporo zoo a Kenyan rooster*; cf. related terms listed at ataeru

Se 背 = height, stature; *he is sensitive about his stature*; cf. sei = height, stature

Sebiro 背広; often written セビロ = a business suit; *when I sell beer in Rome, I wear a business suit*; cf. similar terms listed at fuku

Secchi 設置 = establishment, installation; *they sell cheese in that establishment*; cf. sougyou = establishment (e.g., of business)

Sei せい = fault, responsibility; *it's my responsibility to keep the baby safe, and it's my fault that he fell*; cf. related terms listed at tsutome

Sei 姓 = a family name or surname; *the sailor was addressed by his surname*; cf. related terms listed at namae

Sei 性 = gender, sex, nature, personality; *the sailor's gender was male*; cf. related terms listed at seikaku

Sei 生 = life, a living thing or person, often used as a suffix, e.g., sensei = a teacher; *that sailor is a living person who is full of life*; cf. related terms listed at inochi

Sei 精 = a spirit; vigor, energy; *the saint listened to a spirit that had a lot of energy*; cf. related terms listed at seishin

Sei 背 = height, stature; *the sailor's height is six feet*; cf. se = height, stature

Seibu 西部 = the western parts; from sei = west, e.g., seiou = Western Europe; + bubun = a part of something; cf. related terms listed at bu

Seibun 成分 = ingredient, component; *the sailor asked Daniel Boone to reveal the ingredients in his recipe*; cf. sozai = ingredient; cf. zairyou = ingredient; cf. other related terms listed at youso

Seibutsu 生物 = a living creature; from seikatsu = life + butsu = thing; cf. related terms listed at doubutsu

Seibutsushu 生物種 = species; from seibutsu = a living creature + shurui = type; cf. related terms listed at shurui

Seichou 成長 = growth; *the Safeway corporation chose a leader who promised growth*; cf. hatsuiku = development or growth

Seichou suru 成長する = to grow; from seichou = growth; cf. related terms listed at haeru

Seidai 盛大 = grandiose, pompous, thriving, successful; *the sailors built a dike that was grandiose and successful*; cf. related terms listed at sakan

Seido 制度 = system or regime; *that sailor's doughnuts are made using a special system*; cf. getsugakusei = a monthly payment system; cf. keitou = system; cf. kikan = agency or system; cf. ninensei = a two-year system

Seidou 青銅 = bronze; *the sailor's door was made of bronze*; cf. similar terms listed at dou

Seiei 精鋭 = elite; *the sailors under honest Abe's leadership were an elite team*

Seien 声援 = support, cheering, encouragement; *the sailors' enthusiasm could be seen in their cheering*; cf. related terms listed at enjo and at gekirei

Seien suru 声援する = to cheer or support (this can also be expressed as seien wo okuru); from seien = support, cheering, encouragement; cf. hagemasu = to cheer or encourage; cf. sasaeau = to support each other; cf. sasaeru = to support

Seifu 政府 = government; *the government tries to ensure safe food*; cf. taisei = a power, government or socioeconomic structure

Seifuku 制服 = a uniform; from seido = system + fuku = clothes; cf. hakui = a white uniform

Seifuku 征服 = conquest; *he sailed to Fukuoka, bent on conquest*

Seigen 制限 = limit, restriction; *Carl Sagan put restrictions on his family's credit card use*; cf. related terms listed at genkai

Seigo 生後 = since birth; *the saint pursued his goals since birth*

Seigyo 制御 = control, governing, checking; *the sailors made gyoza under the control of their captain*; cf. kankatsu = jurisdiction or control; cf. touchi = governing; cf. other related terms listed at kanri

Seiha suru 制覇する = to conquer, dominate or rule; *he carries a saber and a hacksaw in order to dominate other people*; cf. kokufuku suru = to overcome or conquer; cf. shiri ni shiku = to dominate

Seihin 製品 = a product, manufactured goods; *sailing Hindus carry products around the world*; cf. related terms listed at sanbutsu

Seihinka 製品化 = making into a product; *the sailing Hindu bought calcium for making into a product*

Seii 誠意 = sincerity; *the saint who was honored on Easter was known for his sincerity*; cf. related terms listed at makoto

Seiippai 精一杯 = the best of one's ability, with all one's might; from sei = energy + ippai = full of; cf. related terms listed at zenryoku

Seijaku 静寂 = silence, stillness; *in the Safeway store, Jack Nicholson assumed a stony silence*; cf. chinmoku = silence; cf. gobusata = a long silence, not contacting for a while

Seiji 政治 = politics, administration, government; *thanks to our politics, this country ensures safe Jeeps for the public*

Seijika 政治家 = a politican; from seiji = politics + ka = a person

Seijin 聖人 = a saint; *let's save our jeans and give them to that saint*; cf. zennin = a good person

Seijitsu 誠実 = sincere or faithful; *they say that the jittery superstar is sincere*; cf. majime (na) = sincere, honest, industrious, serious; cf. maji = serious; cf. shinken = earnest, sincere; cf. other related terms listed at shoujiki

Seijou 正常 = normal; *to tell only safe jokes on government-run TV shows is normal*; cf. seiki = regular, normal, legitimate

Seijou 清浄 = pure or clean; *Saint Joan had a pure heart*; cf. junsui na (or no) = pure, pure-blooded, genuine; cf. kirei = beautiful, pretty, clean; cf. kiyoi = clear, pure; cf. kiyoraka = clean, pure, chaste; cf. seiketsu = clean; cf. toumei = transparent, clean

Seijuku 成熟 = maturity, ripeness; *the sailor's jukebox reflected the maturity of audio technology*

Seikai 政界 = the political world; from seikai = politics + sekai = the world; cf. related terms listed at sekai

Seikai 正解 = correct answer; *a sage told the Kaiser the correct answer*

Seikaku 性格 = personality, disposition; *when sane people kaku (write), their writing reflects their personalities*; cf. jinkaku = personality, character; cf. kosei = individuality, personality; cf. sei = gender, sex, nature, personality; cf. taishitsu = disposition, nature, constitution (physical)

Seikaku 正確 = precise, accurate, exact, truthful; *when sane people kaku [write], their writing is accurate and exact*; cf. seizen = orderly, tidy, regular, accurate, well-organized; cf. tannen = precise, meticulous

Seikakusa 正確さ = accuracy; from seikaku = accurate + sa = a suffix that makes a noun from an adjective

Seikatsu 生活 = livelihood, life (daily existence); *my livelihood is saving cats*; cf. related terms listed at inochi

Seikatsu hi 生活費 = living costs; from seikatsu = livelihood; *my livelihood is to cook safe ton katsu*; + hiyou = cost

Seikatsu suru 生活する = to maintain a lifestyle; cf. related terms listed at ikiru

Seiken 政権 = political power, reign, government; from seifu = government + ken'i = authority

Seiketsu 清潔 = clean; *the sailor cleaned the ketchup from his suit, and now it's clean*; cf. related terms listed at seijou

Seiki 世紀 = century; *the sail was the key to naval exploration during that century*

Seiki 正規 = regular, normal, legitimate; *the sailors' quiche is made in accordance with regular and normal procedures*; cf. seijou = normal

Seikou 成功 = success; *the Safeway corporation is a success*; cf. seikyou = success

Seikougyou 製鋼業 = steel industry; from 製品 seihin = a finished product + 鋼鉄 koutetsu = steel + 工業 kougyou = industry; cf. related terms listed at kougyou

Seikyo 逝去 = death; *the saint from Kyoto experienced death at an early age*; cf. related terms listed at eimin

Seikyo suru 逝去する = to die; from seikyo = death; cf. related terms listed a shinu

Seikyou 盛況 = success, prosperity; *the Safeway store in Kyouto is a success*; cf.

seikou = success; cf. other related terms listed at hanei

Seikyuu 請求 = a demand or request; *there was demand for a safe cure for cancer*; cf. irai = a request or commission; cf. juyou = a demand or request; cf. shomou = a desire, wish or request; cf. youkyuu = a request or demand

Seikyuu suru 請求する = to demand or request; from seikyuu = a demand or request; cf. related terms listed at tanomu

Seikyuusho 請求書 = invoice; from seikyuu = demand + sho = a document

Seimei 声明 = declaration, statement; *she made a statement saying that she wanted to save the mayonnaise for later*; cf. related terms listed at sengen

Seimei 姓名 = a full name; *the sailor told the major his full name*; cf. related terms listed at namae

Seimei 生命 = life or existence; *the sailor and the mailman both enjoyed life*; cf. seizon = existence, survival; cf. other related terms listed at inochi

Seinen 青年 = a young man; *the sailor's negative nephew was a young man*; cf. related terms listed at otoko

Seinou 性能 = performance, efficiency; *sane old people demonstrate good performance and efficiency on our tests*; cf. kouritsu = efficiency

Seiou 西欧 = Western Europe; *the sailor owned a house in Western Europe*; cf. related terms listed at oushuu

Seireki 西暦 = A.D., the Christian era; *the saints have been wrecking idols since the start of the Christian era*; cf. kigenzen = B.C.

Seiri suru 整理する = to arrange, put in order; *to ensure a safe retirement, she arranged her investments*; cf. soroeru = to arrange, prepare, put in order, make uniform; cf. totonoeru = to put in order, to prepare

Seiriseiton 整理整頓 = keeping things neat and tidy; from seiri suru = to arrange and put in order + seiton = orderliness

Seiritsu 成立 = establishment, coming into existence; *the sailor received a written suggestion that he help in the establishment of a center for maritime study*

Seiryoku 精力 = energy, vigor, vitality; from sei = vigor or energy + ryoku = power; cf. related terms listed at chikara

Seisai 制裁 = a punishment or sanction; *he received a punishment for sailing to Cyprus*; cf. related terms listed at bakkin

Seisaku 制作 = manufacture, production; *they save sacks in Uganda and use them in the manufacture of curtains*; cf. sagyou = work, operations, manufacturing; cf. seisan = production; cf. seizou = manufacturing, production

Seisaku 政策 = a policy; *our policy is to save the old sacks and re-use them*; cf. houshin = policy, principle, direction

Seisan 清算 = an adjustment (financial); *a sailor delivered the sand, and we made an adjustment to the account*

Seisan 生産 = production; *we're involved in the production of safe and sanitary products*; cf. sagyou = work, operations, manufacturing; cf. seisaku = manufacture, production; cf. seizou = manufacturing, production

Seisan suru 清算する = to settle (an account) or clear (a debt); from seisan = an adjustment

Seisan suru 生産する = to produce; from seisan = production; cf. related terms listed at tsukuru

Seisansha 生産者 = producer; from seisan suru = to produce + sha = person

Seisei せいせい = feeling refreshed or

relieved; *after the sailors saved me, I felt relieved*

Seisei suru せいせいする = to feel refreshed or relieved; from seisei = feeling refreshed or relieved; cf. sukkiri suru = to feel refreshed

Seiseki 成績 = achievement, school grades; *I wrote a report about a saint and a selfish king and received a good grade*; cf. gyouseki = accomplishments, results, performance (business); cf. jisseki = accomplishment, achievement; cf. koutokuten = a high score; cf. kouseki = an achievement; cf. tensuu = score, marks, points; cf. tokuten = marks or score

Seishain 正社員 = regular employee, permanent employee; from seiki = regular, normal, legitimate + shain = employee; cf. kaishain = a company employee; cf. koumuin = a public employee; cf. shain = a company employee; cf. shuugyouin = an employee

Seishiki 正式 = formal or official; *the saint kept the shift key pressed when he typed official reports*; cf. koushiki na (or no) = official

Seishin 精神 = mind, soul, spirit; *if you say Shinto prayers, you can improve your mind, soul and spirit*; cf. ikioi = force, power, energy, spirit; cf. ki = spirit, soul, feeling, intention, inclination; cf. kyouchuu = one's heart, mind or intentions; cf. reikon = a soul or spirit; cf. sei = a spirit; vigor, energy; cf. tamashii = a soul or spirit

Seishin 誠心 = sincerity; *when I say Shinto prayers, I employ sincerity*; cf. related terms listed at makoto

Seishinbunseki 精神分析 = psychoanalysis; from seishin = mind, soul or spirit + bunseki = analysis

Seishinteki 精神的 = spiritual, mental; from seishin = mind or spirit + teki = related to

Seishitsu 性質 = character or nature; *the sailor's sheets have a threadbare character*; cf. related terms listed at etai

Seisho 聖書 = the Bible; *when the sailor reached shore, he kissed his Bible*

Seishoku 生殖 = reproduction, procreation; *the saints were shocked when procreation was discussed during the church service*; cf. hanshoku = breeding, proliferation

Seisoku 生息 = habitation; *the sailor soaks in the tub inside his habitation*; cf. hitozato = human habitation

Seisoku suru 生息する = to reside; from seisoku = habitation; cf. related terms listed at ikiru

Seisou 清掃 = cleaning; *sailors and soldiers do a lot of cleaning*; cf. souji = cleaning

Seisou 精巣 = a testicle; *the sailor sold one of his testicles*; cf. ransou = an ovary

Seito 生徒 = a student; *the student saved a tortoise*; cf. related terms listed at gakusei

Seiton 整頓 = orderliness; *the sailor used tongs to maintain the orderliness of the logs in the fire*; cf. chitsujo = order

Seitou 政党 = a political party; *the sailors heard Tony Blair speak and decided to join his political party*

Seitsuu 精通 = acquaintance, being expert; *watching the sailor pack his tsuitcase (suitcase), I could observe his acquaintance with the details of travel*

Seiyaku 誓約 = a vow or pledge; *the sailor cared for the yak in accordance with his pledge*; cf. seiyakusho = a written vow or pledge; cf. sensei = an oath or vow; cf. yakusoku = an appointment, promise or agreement

Seiyakusho 誓約書 = a written vow or pledge; from seiyaku = a written vow or pledge + sho = a document; cf. related terms listed at seiyaku

Seiza 星座 = a constellation; *that sage from Zambia knows all the constellations*

Seizen 整然 = orderly, tidy, regular, accurate,

well-organized; *the sailor said that Zen helped him to be more tidy and well-organized*; cf. related terms listed at seikaku

Seizon 生存 = existence, survival; *in the safe zone, our chances of survival are greater*; cf. seimei = life or existence

Seizonsha 生存者 = a survivor; from seizon = survival + sha = a person

Seizou 製造 = manufacturing, production; *we conduct manufacturing in a safe zone*; cf. sagyou = work, operations, manufacturing; cf. seisaku = manufacture, production; cf. seisan = production

Seizoukatei 製造過程 = manufacturing process; from seizou = manufacturing + katei = process; cf. related terms listed at kairo

Sekai 世界 = world, society; *the selfish Kaiser toured the world*; cf. chikyuu = the Earth, the globe; cf. seikai = the political world; cf. tenka = realm, world, nation; cf. yo = world, era, age; cf. yo no naka = the world, society, life

Sekaichuu 世界中 (this can also be pronounced sekaijuu) = throughout the world; from sekai = world + chuu = in the middle of

Sekaiteki 世界的 = gobal, international; from sekai = world + teki = related to; cf. related terms listed at kokusai

Seken 世間 = society, other people, the way of the world; *the selfish Kennedys were members of high society*; cf. seken = society, other people, the way of the world; cf. shakai = society; cf. yo no naka = the world, society, life

Seki せき = a cough; *the selfish king had a cough*

Seki 席 = a seat; *the selfish king took a seat*; cf. benza = a toilet seat; cf. isu = a chair; cf. shiteiseki = a reserved seat; cf. za = a seat or position; cf. zaseki = a seat (transportation or theater)

Seki 石 = a stone, used as a word component; *the selfish king sat on the best stone*; cf. related terms listed at ishi

Seki 隻 = a counter for ships, one of a pair; *the selfish king keeps track of how many ships he has*

Sekidou 赤道 = the equator; *we sell quiche and doughnuts near the equator*

Sekijitsu 昔日 = old times; *in old times, the selfish king was friendly with the jittery superstar*

Sekijuuji 赤十字 = the Red Cross; from seki = red; *the selfish king wore a red robe*; + juu, which is shaped like a cross, + ji = a character

Sekinin 責任 = responsibility; *I had a seki (cough) when I was near that nin (person), so I have a responsibility for his illness*; cf. related terms listed at tsutome

Sekinin ga aru 責任がある = is responsible; from sekinin = responsibility;

Sekininkan 責任感 = sense of responsibility; from sekinin = responsibility + kanjiru = to feel

Sekininsha 責任者 = a person in charge; from sekinin = responsibility + sha = person; cf. tantousha = a person in charge

Sekisho 関所 = checkpoint; *I had a seki (cough) when I went to the show, and they stopped me at a health checkpoint outside the theater*

Sekitan 石炭 = coal; *our selfish king got tangled up in a coal scandal*

Sekitsui 脊椎 = the spine; *the selfish king tsuitely (sweetly) asked to have his spine adjusted*; cf hone = a bone

Sekitsuikotsu 脊椎骨 = a vertebra; from sekitsui = the spine + kotsu = bone; cf. related terms listed at hone

Sekiyu 石油 = petroleum; *the selfish king visited the Yukon to look for petroleum*

Sekkaku せっかく = with much trouble, kindly; *the settlers asked Karl the Kool-Aid vendor to sell them the beverages that he had collected with much trouble*; cf. shinmi ni = kindly; cf. shinsetsu ni = kindly

Sekkei 設計 = design or plan; *they are selling cakes with innovative designs*; cf. moyou = design, pattern; cf. other related terms listed at kikaku

Sekkeisha 設計者 = a designer; from sekkei = a design or plan + sha = a person

Sekken 石けん = soap; *Senator Kennedy always washed with soap*

Sekkin suru 接近する = to approach; *the selfish king approached his palace*; cf. semaru = to come close, to urge; cf. yoru = to gather, approach, drop in

Sekkyoku 積極 = positive, progressive; *he sells Kyoto Kool-Aid in a positive and progressive way*; cf. maemuki = facing forward, positive; cf. yousei no = cheerful, positive

Sekkyokuteki ni 積極的に = aggressively, positively; from sekkyoku = positive, progressive + teki = related to + -ni = a suffix that forms an adverb

Semai 狭い = narrow, small; *he sells mice in a narrow store*; cf. hosoi = narrow, thin, fine; cf. hosonagai = long and narrow; cf. kyoushou = cramped, narrow, confined; cf. usui = thin or light (color); cf. other related terms listed at chiisai

Semaru 迫る = to come close, to urge; *he came close and urged me to sell magazines about roosters*; cf. sekkin suru = to approach; cf. yoru = to gather, approach, drop in; cf. unagasu = to urge

Seme no 攻めの = aggressive, offensive; from semeru = to attack + the possessive no; cf. kageki = aggressive, radical

Semeru 攻める = to attack or invade; *the cemetery's rooster attacked his rival*; cf. okasu = to invade; cf. other related terms listed at osou

Semeru 責める = to accuse, reproach, torment; *at the cemetery, Ruth reproached me*; cf. kokuso suru = to sue or accuse

Semete せめて = at least; *at this cemetery, at least six of my ancestors are buried*; cf. related terms listed at dake wa

Sen 先 = previous, used as a word component, e.g., senshuu = last week; *I will send you the previous article*

Sen 栓 = a bottle cap, cork or stopper; *the senator sniffed the cork before tasting the wine*; cf. futa = a cover, bottle cap or lid

Sen 線 = a line or track; *the senator crossed the line*; cf. related terms listed at gyou

Sen 腺 = a gland; *glands send out hormones to regulate metabolism*; cf. koujousen = the thyroid gland

Sen wo suru 栓をする = to stopper or plug (a bottle); from sen = a cork or bottle cap + suru = to do

Senaka 背中 = back (of the body); *the Senator carried her child on her back*; cf. koshi = low back, waist, hip

Senbei 煎餅 = a rice cracker; *after the senator bathes, he wants a rice cracker*

Senbou 羨望 = envy; *I feel envy that you have sen (1,000) boats*; cf. related terms listed at netami

Sencha 煎茶 = green tea; *the senator's cha (tea) is green tea*; cf. related terms listed at cha

Senchi センチ = a centimeter

Senden 宣伝 = advertising, publicity; *the sensational dentist garnered a lot of publicity which amounted to free advertising*; cf. kouhou = public relations, publicity, information; cf. other related terms listed at koukoku

Sendou 先導 = guidance, leadership; *Senator*

Dole gave me *guidance*; cf. annai = information, guidance; cf. senshin = advance, leadership, seniority; cf. shidou = guidance; cf. shudouken = leadership, domination

Seneba せねば = ought to do, must do; when I visited the *Senegal bar*, I *felt obliged* to drink alcohol; cf. -beki = must, should (social respon-sibility); cf. -hazu = should, ought, surely; cf. koto da = one should do something; cf. koto desu = one should do something; cf. mono da = one should do something; cf. mono desu = one should do something; cf. seneba naranai = ought to do, must do, feel obliged to do

Seneba naranai せねばならない = ought to do, must do; this is an alternative way of saying shinakereba naranai = one must do; cf. related terms listed at seneba

Sen'en (Senen) satsu 千円札 = 1,000-yen bill; from sen'en = 1,000 yen + satsu = bill; *I paid for a satisfying Superman novel with a 1,000-yen bill*

Sengen 宣言 = a declaration or announce-ment; *the senator helped Genghis to prepare a declaration*; cf. chinjutsu = a statement, an oral report; cf. genkou = a draft or manuscript; cf. happyou = an announce-ment or publication, a statement; cf. hatsugen = a statement or remark; cf. hirou = an announcement or demonstration; cf. hyoumei = a declaration or announcement; cf. keiji = a written notice or announce-ment; cf. seimei = a declaration or statement; cf. shuchou = assertion, claim; cf. soukou = a draft or manuscript; cf. toukou = a post or written contribution (e.g., to a journal)

Sengetsu 先月 = last month; from sen = previous + getsu = month

Sengyou 専業 = principal occupation, specialty; from senmon = specialty + gyou = business, e.g., kougyou = industry; cf. related terms listed at senmon

Sen'i (Seni) 繊維 = fiber; *the senator said it was easy to include fiber in his diet*

Senjiru 煎じる = to boil; *the senator's jeep was ruined when the radiator boiled over*; cf. related terms listed at niru

Senjitsu 先日 = yesterday, the other day; *the senator met the jittery superstar yesterday*; cf. related terms listed at yokujitsu

Senjou 洗浄 = washing, laundering; *the Senator asked Joan to help with the washing*; cf. sentaku = laundry

Senjousui 洗浄水 = wash water; from senjou = washing + sui = water; cf. related terms listed at mizu

Senjutsu 戦術 = tactics or strategy; from sensou = war + gijutsu = technique; cf. related terms listed at kikaku

Senka 戦渦 = the turmoil of war; *the sensible captain had survived the turmoil of war*; cf. related terms listed at kondou

Senka 戦禍 = the ravages of war, war damages; *the senator's car showed the ravages of war*; cf. related terms listed at kondou

Senkai 旋回 = rotation, turning; *the sensational kite was turning in the air*; cf. related terms listed at kaiten

Senken 浅見 = a shallow view or superficial idea; *Senator Kennedy had a superficial idea*; cf. related terms listed at omoi

Senkoku 宣告 = a sentence or judgment; *the senator drank a Coke as he awaited his sentence*; cf. related terms listed at handan

Senkou 専攻 = major subject, specialty; *the sensible course of action is to choose a major subject early*; cf. related terms listed at senmon

Senkou 線香 = an incense stick; *the senator traded coal for incense sticks*

Senkusha 先駆者 = originator, pioneer; *the senator lived in a cool shack with some pioneers*; cf. kaitakusha = a pioneer

Senkyo 選挙 = an election; *the senator from*

Kyoto faced another election

Senkyou 宣教 = missionary work; *they set up a center in Kyouto for their missionary work*

Senkyou 戦況 = war situation; from sensou = war + kyou = situation, e.g., joukyou = circumstance

Senkyoushi 宣教師 = a missionary; from senkyou = missionary work + shi = an expert, e.g., ishi = a physician

Senmei 鮮明 = bright, clear, vivid; *the senator's maid wore a bright colored dress*; cf. related terms listed at akarui and at akiraka

Senmen 洗面 = washing the face; *the Senator's men washed their faces*

Senmenjo 洗面所 = bathroom; from senmen = washing the face + jo = place; cf. furoba = a bathroom (for bathing); cf. yokujou = a bath, bathtub, bathhouse, bathroom; cf. yokushitsu = a bathroom

Senmon 専門 = specialty; *the sensational Monet painting was authenticated by a woman with a specialty in Impressionism*; cf. sengyou = principal occupation, specialty; cf. senkou = major subject, specialty

Senmonka 専門家 = specialist or expert; from senmon = specialty + ka = a person; cf. related terms listed at kurouto

Senmonten 専門店 = a specialty shop; from senmon = specialty + ten = store, e.g., tennin = a store clerk; cf. related terms listed at mise

Sennen suru 専念する = to concentrate or focus on; *my sensitive negative nephew focused on building self-esteem*; cf. shuuchuu suru = to concentrate

Sennyuukan 先入観 = prejudice, preconception, bias; *a senator from Nyuu Yooku (New York) with cancer encountered prejudice in the health care system*

Senpai 先輩 = a senior, elder, predecessor; *the senator's pipe is held by a senior staffer*; cf. related terms listed at joushi

Senpatsu 洗髪 = having a shampoo, washing one's hair; from sen = to wash with water, e.g., sentaku = laundry; + patsu = hatsu = hair, e.g., hakuhatsu = grey hair

Senpuuki 扇風機 = an electric fan; *after the senator finished puking, he turned on an electric fan*

Senran 戦乱 = war, strife; from sensou = war + ranbou = violent; cf. related terms listed at issen

Senritsu 旋律 = a melody; *the senator's staff was given a written suggestion to play a happy melody whenever the senator entered a room*; cf. related terms listed at uta

Senro 線路 = railway track; from sen = track + douro = road

Senryuu 川柳 = a satiric poem; *the senator reused some old jokes in his satiric poem*; cf. related terms listed at shi

Sensai 繊細 = fragile, sensitive, delicate; *the senator was silent about his delicate health*; cf. related terms listed at binkan

Sensaku 詮索 = an inquiry into; *she made an enquiry into the whereabouts of the senator's sack of cookies*; cf. related terms listed at kensa

Sensei 先生 = teacher, master, physician, title used for lawyers, politicians, etc.; *the sensible sailor became a teacher*; cf. koushi = a lecturer or instructor; cf. kyouju = a professor; cf. kyoushi = a teacher

Sensei 宣誓 = an oath or vow; *he made a vow to set up a center for sailors*; cf. related terms listed at seiyaku

Senshin 先進 = advance, leadership, seniority; *the sensible Shinto priest was promoted to a leadership role*; cf. related terms listed at sendou

Senshu 選手 = an athlete or player in a game; *athletes are sensual*

Senshuken 選手権 = championship; from senshu = athlete + kenri = right or privilege; cf. related terms listed at shouri

Senshutsu 選出 = a choice or selection; from sentaku = a selection + shutsu = emerging, e.g., shutsujou = appearance or participation; cf. related terms listed at sentaku

Senshuu 先週 = last week; from sen = previous + shuu = week

Sensou 戦争 = war; *my sensory organs were overwhelmed by the chaos of war*; cf. related terms listed at issen

Sensu 扇子 = a folding fan; *touching that folding fan is a sensual experience*; cf. ougi = a folding fan; cf. uchiwa = a nonfolding hand-held fan

Sensui 潜水 = diving; *the senator went to Sweden for a diving excursion*

Sentaku 洗濯 = laundry; *sensible Tarzan went to Kuwait to do his laundry*

Sentaku 選択 = selection, choice; *the senator said that Tarzan's cookies were his choice for snacks*; cf. senshutsu = a choice or selection; cf. sentakushi = a choice, alternative or option; cf. sentei = selection

Sentaku suru 洗濯する = to wash laundry; from sentaku = laundry; cf. related terms listed at arau

Sentaku suru 選択する = to choose; from sentaku = selection, choice; cf. related terms listed at erabu

Sentakushi 選択肢 = a choice, alternative or option; from sentaku = a selection or choice + shi = a limb (arm or leg); cf. related terms listed at sentaku

Sentan 先端 = vanguard, tip, end; *the senator's tan put him in the vanguard of his colleagues*; cf. related terms listed at saki

Sentei 選定 = selection; *the senator taped arrows on his selections*; cf. related terms listed at sentaku

Sentou 先頭 = vanguard, first; from sen = before, e.g., sensei = teacher; + tou = head; cf. related terms listed at hajime ni

Sentou 銭湯 = a public bath; *the senator soaked his toes in a public bath*; cf. related terms listed at furo

Sen'you (Senyou) 専用 = exclusive, private; from sen = exclusive + you = use; *the senator practiced yoga at an exclusive club*; cf. kojin = individual, private, personal; cf. shiyou = private

Senzai 洗剤 = detergent; *after retiring, the senator went to Zaire (former name of the Congo) to sell detergent*; cf. shokkiyou senzai = dish detergent

Senzai 潜在 = potentiality, latency; *the senator from Zaire saw the potentiality of his country*

Senzaiteki na 潜在的な = latent, potential; from senzai = potentiality + teki = related to

Senzo 先祖 = an ancestor; *the central zone of the cemetery is where my ancestors are buried*; cf. gosenzosama = very honorable ancestor; cf. sosen = an ancestor;

Seou 背負う = to carry on one's back, to shoulder a burden; *the settlers owned some plows, which they carried on their backs*; cf. related terms listed at hakobu

Seri 競り = an auction; *an auction is for selling stuff*

Sesshi 摂氏 = degrees Celsius; *I'm selling a sheep so that I can buy a thermometer that measures degrees Celsius*; cf. kashi = degrees Fahrenheit

Sesshu 摂取 = intake, absorption, assimilation; *when I was selling shoes, my aim was the absorption of the best sales techniques*

Sessuru 接する = to border on, adjoin or encounter; *the selfish supervisor ruined the creek which adjoined his property*; cf. related terms listed at deau

Setake 背丈 = height, stature; *the senator was a tall Kennedy whose height was remarkable*; cf. related terms listed at nagasa

Setogiwa 瀬戸際 = brink, critical moment; *they sent torpedos to the geeky warriors at the critical moment in the battle*

Setomono 瀬戸物 = pottery, chinaware; *they sell tobacco on monotonous chinaware trays*; cf. touki = chinaware, pottery; cf. yakimono = earthenware, chinaware

Setsu 説 = theory, opinion; *the settlement's super pioneers had theories about agriculture*; cf. related terms listed at iken and at rikutsu

Setsu 雪 = snow, used as a word component; *our settlement's super pioneers are good at handling snow*

Setsubi 設備 = equipment, facility; *let's set up a super bee hive in that facility*; cf. kikai'rui = machinery, equipment; cf. shitsetsu = equipment, facility; cf. soubi = equipment; cf. souchi = equipment

Setsudan suru 切断する = to cut or sever; *after we set up a super dance party, we had to cut the list of invited guests*; cf. related terms listed at kiru

Setsugou 接合 = fusing or linking; *after they set up Superman's golf course, there was a linking of its ponds via a canal*; cf. yuugou = fusion, adhesion, blending

Setsumei 説明 = an explanation or illustration; *the explanation as to why I set up a super mailbox is that someone was stealing my mail*; cf. kaishaku = an explanation or interpretation

Setsumei suru 説明する = to explain or illustrate; from setsumei = an explanation or interpretation; cf. kaisetsu suru = to explain, comment or interpret

Setsuyaku 節約 = economy, thrift; *I settled Sue and her yak in a cottage for the sake of economy*; cf. ken'yaku = thrift

Setsuyaku gaku 節約額 = an amount of money saved; from setsuyaku = economy + gaku = a sum of money; cf. related terms listed at kikin

Setsuyaku suru 節約する = to economize; from setsuyaku = economy; cf. ken'yaku suru = to save or economize

Setsuzoku 接続 = connection, attachment, link, conjunction; *if you set Sue up in a commercial zone with a Kool-Aid stand, she will make connections*; cf. kankei = relationship, connection

Settei suru 設定する = to set up; *they set the table and then set up the Christmas tree*; cf. moukeru = to set up or establish; cf. setto suru = to set up or place; cf. tateru = to build or put upright

Setto suru セットする = to set up or place; cf. related terms listed at settei suru

Settou 窃盗 = theft; *police are investigating the theft of the secretary's toaster*; cf. related terms listed at tsumi

Sewa 世話 = looking after, assistance, usually expressed as osewa; *I can sell a lot of washing machines with your assistance*; cf. related terms listed at enjo

Sezu せず – an abbreviation of sezuni

Sezuni せずに = shinai de = not doing; from shimasu + zuni = not doing (the use of the prefix "se" rather than "shi" before zuni is an exception unique to this verb)

Sha 者 = a person, used as a suffix; *the Shah was a person*; cf. -jin = a person; -ka = a person; cf. -nin = a person; cf. other related terms listed at hito

Sha 車 = a car or wheeled vehicle, used as a suffix, e.g., jitensha = a bicycle; *the Shah owned many wheeled vehicles*

Sha 社 = a company; an abbreviation of kaisha; cf. related terms listed at kaisha

Shaberi しゃべり = talk, chat; from shaberu = to talk or chat

Shaberu しゃべる = to talk or chat; *the Shah's bedroom was a good place to chat*; cf. related terms listed at hanasu

Shachou 社長 = a company president; from kaisha = company + chou = leader or chief; cf. related terms listed at shunou

Shadan 遮断 = an interruption; *there was an interruption in the Shah's dance*

Shain 社員 = a company employee; from kaisha = company + in = a group member; cf. related terms listed at seishain

Shakai 社会 = society; *the Shah and the Kaiser worked to improve society*; cf. shakou = social life; cf. seken = society, other people, the way of the world; cf. yo no naka = the world, society, life

Shakaijin 社会人 = a working adult; from shakai = society + jin = person

Shakkin 借金 = debt; *the Shah was a king with a lot of debt*; cf. related terms listed at fusai

Shako 車庫 = garage; *a shack near the coast served as our garage*

Shakou 社交 = social life; from shakai = society + kou = crossing or mingling, e.g., kousa = crossing, intersection; cf. related terms listed at shakai

Shakouteki 社交的 = social, sociable; from shakou = social life + teki = related to; cf. aiso ga ii = sociable

Shakudo 尺度 = criterion, measure; *the shack's residents thought that getting a door installed would be a measure of progress*; cf. related terms listed at teido

Shakuhachi 尺八 = a Japanese bamboo flute; *the shack contained hachi (eight) Japanese bamboo flutes*

Shakuhou 釈放 = release, liberation, or acquittal; *the shackles will hold them until their release*; cf. houmen = a release (from custody), discharge, setting free; cf. menjo = an exemption, exoneration, discharge

Shakuhou suru 釈放する = to release; from shakuhou = release, liberation, or acquittal; cf. related terms listed at tokihanatsu

Shaku'i (Shakui) 爵位 = peerage, court rank; *she lived in a shack, but at Easter she went out to see the peerage dressed in their fine clothes*; cf. related terms listed at kaikyuu

Shamen 斜面 = slope, slanting surface; *the Shah's men ran up the slope*; cf. koubai = a slope or incline; cf. kudarizaka = a downward slope; cf. kyuushamen = a steep slope; cf. noborizaka = an uphill slope; cf. saka = a slope or hill

Shanai 社内 = inside a company; from kaisha = company + nai = inside or within

Shanai 車内 = inside a train or car; from densha = train + nai = inside

Shari しゃり = rice prepared for sushi; *my neighbor and I are sharing our sushi rice*; cf. related terms listed at gohan

Sharin 車輪 = wheel; *I am sharing a bicycle wheel with my brother*

Sharyou 車両 = a railroad car; *the Shah visited Pope Leo in his railroad car*

Shashin 写真 = a photograph; *I took this photograph which I'm sharing with my Shinto friends*

Shashin satsuei 写真撮影 = photography; from shashin = photo + satsuei = photographing; cf. satsuei = filming, photographing

Shashinka 写真家 = a photographer; from shashin = a photograph + ka = a person

Shashinshuu 写真集 = a collection of photos, a photo album; from shashin = photograph + shuushuu = a collection; cf. related terms listed at shuushuu

Shashinten 写真展 = a photography exhibit; from shashin = photograph + tenji = exhibition; cf. related terms listed at tenji

Shashou 車掌 = a bus or train conductor; *the Shah showed the conductor his ticket*

Shasou 車窓 = a train or car window; from densha = train + sou = window; *I saw a soaring cowbird through the window*; cf. related terms listed at mado

Shataku 社宅 = company-owned housing; from kaisha = company + taku = a house; cf. related terms listed at uchi

Shazai 謝罪 = an apology; *the Shah visited Zaire (the former name of the Congo) to make an apology*; cf. moushiwake = an apology or excuse

Shi し = and, used at the end of a clause, implying an explanation; *the sheep were giving me trouble, and (implying that's why I was late)*; cf. related terms listed at soshite

Shi 市 = city; *Shiites live in the city*; cf. daitoshi = a large city; cf. machi = town; cf. mura = village; cf. sanson = a mountain village; cf. shichouson = cities, towns, villages; cf. tokai = city; cf. toshi = city

Shi 死 = death; *the death of the sheep affected me*; cf. related terms listed at eimin

Shi 氏 = mister; *the sheep belongs to the mister*

Shi 肢 = a limb (arm or leg), used as a word component; *a sheep has four limbs*; cf. related terms listed at ude

Shi 詩 = a poem; *I wrote a poem about sheep*; cf. haiku = a style of Japanese poetry, or a poem written in this style; cf. inbun = verse or poetry; cf. ku = a phrase or haiku; cf. senryuu = a satiric poem

Shi 師 = an expert or teacher, used as a word component; *that sheep farmer is an expert in his field*

Shi emu シーエム = commercial or advertisement; an abbreviation commonly used in Japan for TV commercials; cf. related terms listed at koukoku

Shiageru 仕上げる = to finish or complete (transitive); *the Shiites will ageru (give) the rice when they finish cooking it*; cf. related terms listed at owaraseru

Shiai 試合 = a competition or game; *the sheep on the ice affected the hockey game*; cf. related terms listed at issen

Shiai suru 試合する = to compete; from shiai = a competition; cf. related terms listed at arasou

Shiawase 幸せ = happiness; *the Shiite got an award for selling merchandise, and it brought him happiness*; cf. etsu = ecstasy, joy, rapture; cf. kanki = exhilaration, joy; cf. koufuku = happiness; cf. kyouraku = pleasure; cf. raku = pleasure, comfort; cf. shifuku = supreme bliss; cf. tanoshimi = enjoyment; cf. yorokobi = joy, delight

Shiawase mono 幸せ者 = fortunate person, lucky fellow; from shiawase = happiness + mono = person

Shiawase na 幸せな = happy; from shiawase = happiness; cf. kigarui = cheerful, lighthearted; cf. koufuku na = happy; cf. mutsumajii = harmonious, happy, affectionate; cf. saiwai = lucky, happy; cf. ureshii = happy, glad, pleased, pleasant; cf. youki = merry, happy-go-lucky; cf. other related terms at kokoroyoi

Shiba 芝 = a lawn or turf; an abbreviation of shibafu = a lawn or turf; cf. shibau = a lawn

Shibafu 芝生 = a lawn; *the Queen of Sheba fooled around on her lawn*; cf. shiba = a lawn or turf

Shibaraku しばらく = a short time; this can also be spelled 暫く ; this can also mean "it's been a long time (since I've seen you, etc.)," when followed by desu; *the Queen of Sheba had a raccoon for a short time*; cf. related terms listed at hisashiburi ni

Shibaru 縛る = to tie or bind; *the Queen of Sheba used that room for tying up her rivals*; cf. related terms listed at tsunagu

Shibashiba しばしば = frequently; *the Queen of Sheba had a shield from Babylon which she polished frequently*; cf. shikiri ni = often, frequently, eagerly

Shibasu 市バス = city bus; from shi = city, e.g., shichou = mayor; + basu = bus

Shiboridasu 絞り出す = to squeeze out or wring out; from shiboru = to wring + dasu = to put out

Shiboru 搾る = to wring, squeeze or narrow down (this is usually spelled 絞る, # 1739); *the Shiite was bored on the roof and began to wring his hands*; cf. shiboridasu = to squeeze out or wring out

Shibou 志望 = ambition, wish, goal; *when the first sheep was born, my ambition was to raise a large herd*; cf. related terms listed at mokuhyou and shomou

Shibou 脂肪 = fat; *the sheep meat that we ate on the boat contained a lot of fat*; cf. abura = fat

Shibu 支部 = a subdivision or branch office; from shisha = a branch office + bubun = a part of something; cf. related terms listed at kyoku

Shibui 渋い = astringent, chic, sullen; *Shiites and Buddhists eat astringent foods*

Shiburu 渋る = to hesitate or be reluctant; *I'm reluctant to wear my Shiite boots on the roof*; cf. enryo suru = to hesitate or hold back; cf. kigane wo suru = to hesitate; cf. mayou = to lose direction, to get lost, to hesitate

Shichaku 試着 = trying on clothes; *the sheep farmer drank champagne and Kool-Aid while trying on clothes*; cf. nanchaku mo = trying on clothes many times even

Shichikaiki 七回忌 = the 6th anniversary of a death; this can also be pronounced nanakaiki; from shichi = seven + kai = a counter for occurrences + ki = a death anniversary; cf. isshuuki = the first anniversary of a death; cf. sankaiki = the second anniversary, and so forth

Shichou 市長 = mayor; from shi = city, e.g., toshi = city; + chou = chief; cf. related terms listed at shunou

Shichouson 市町村 = cities, towns, villages; from shi = city, e.g., toshi = city + chou = town; *I chose to live in this town*; + son = village; *my son lives in that village*; cf. related terms listed at shi

Shidai de 次第で (or shidai desu) = depending on; *if she dies, the debt will be paid, depending on her brother*; cf. related terms listed at ni yotte

Shidai ni 次第に = gradually; *if she dies, my niece will gradually take over the business*; cf. dandan = gradually; cf. jojo ni = gradually, step by step; cf. sorosoro = before long, slowly, quietly, gradually; cf. yukkuri (to) = slowly, leisurely

Shidou 指導 = guidance, coaching; *I received coaching on how to make a shield from a door*; cf. annai = information, guidance; cf. sendou = guidance, leadership

Shidousha 指導者 = leader or adviser; from shidou = guidance + sha = person; cf. komon = an advisor or counselor; cf. komon bengoshi = a legal advisor; cf. other related terms listed at shunou

Shien 支援 = support; *the Shiites encouraged me, and I appreciated their support*; cf. related terms listed at enjo

Shifuku 至福 = supreme bliss; *when I was reunited with my sheepdog in Fukuoka, it was a moment of supreme bliss*; cf. related terms listed at shiawase

Shigaisen 紫外線 = ultraviolet rays; *the Shiite guy sent me some information about ultraviolet rays*

Shigamitsuku しがみつく = to cling; *the*

sheep that the gambler meets tsuku (adhere) to him and cling to him tenaciously; cf. related terms listed at kuttsuku

Shigan suru 志願する = to volunteer, to apply for; *the Shiite asked Gandalf to volunteer for the Fellowship of the Ring*; cf. related terms listed at moushikomu

Shigeki 刺激 = stimulation; *the sheep at Gettysburg eat quiche for stimulation*

Shigemi 茂み = a bush; from shigeru = to grow thickly + mi = body; cf. related terms listed at shokubutsu

Shigen 資源 = resources; *the sheep that Genghis owned were resources*; cf. mizushigen = water resources

Shigeru 繁る = to grow luxuriantly or thickly; *the sheep at Gettysburg ruined the grass that grew luxuriantly*; cf. related terms listed at haeru

Shigoku 至極 = extremely; *the sheep and the goats like Kool-Aid, but it makes them extremely fat*; cf. related terms listed at ooi ni

Shigoto 仕事 = work; *she goes to work every day*; cf. arubaito = part-time work; cf. baito = part-time work; cf. juuroudou = heavy labor; cf. kinmu = duty, service, work; cf. kouji = construction work; cf. roudou = manual labor; cf. sagyou = work, operations, manufacturing; cf. tesagyou = manual labor; cf. zangyou = over-time work

Shigoto suru 仕事する = to work; from shigoto = work; cf. hataraku = to labor; cf. juuji suru = to work or engage in (a profession); cf. kyuushoku suru = to look for work; cf. shukkin suru = to go to work; cf. shussha suru = to go to one's office, attend work; cf. shuushoku suru = to find employment

Shigotoba 仕事場 = a workshop, construction site; from shigoto = work + basho = place

Shigusa しぐさ = gesture, mannerism; *that sheep farmer and those goofy saxophone players have some strange mannerisms*

Shiharai 支払い = a payment; from shiharau = to pay; cf. hensai = repayment, reimbursement

Shiharau 支払う = to pay; *the Shiites hacked Raul Castro and made him pay a ransom*; cf. harau = to brush away, to pay (money or attention)

Shihei 紙幣 = paper money, bank note; *my sheep eat hay, which I pay for with paper money*; cf. related terms listed at kinsen

Shihon 資本 = capital (finance); *I need capital for my sheep farm in Honduras*; cf. related terms listed at kikin

Shihonshugi 資本主義 = capitalism; from shihon = capital + shugi = a doctrine; cf. kyousanshugi = communism

Shiiku 飼育 = breeding, raising, rearing; *sometimes our sheep suffer from ear cooties while we are breeding them*

Shiikuin 飼育員 = a caretaker at a zoo or aquarium; from shiiku = to raise an animal + in = member; cf. shokuin = staff, personnel

Shiin 子音 = a consonant; *the sheepish intellectual avoided using hard consonants*; cf. boin = a vowel

Shiireru 仕入れる = to replenish stock; *after the Shiites eat their red roosters, they have to replenish stock*

Shiitageru 虐げる = to persecute or oppress; *the sheep from Italy in the guest room were persecuted by their previous owner*; cf. dan'atsu suru = to oppress or suppress

Shiji 指示 = instructions, directions; *the instructions were to transport the sheep in a Jeep*; cf. related terms listed at houhou

Shiji 支持 = support; *there is support for the concept of a Shinto Jeep*; cf. related terms listed at enjo

Shijin 詩人 = poet; *the Shiite genius is a poet*

Shijisha 支持者 = a supporter or adherent; from shiji = support + sha = a person; cf. mikata = a supporter or ally

Shijou 史上 = historical; *this shield designed by Joan of Arc has historical significance*

Shijou 市場 = market (as an abstract idea); *she jokes about the stock market*; cf. 市場 ichiba = market (as a physical place)

Shijuku 私塾 = a private school (in a house); from shiyou = private + juku = a private school; cf. related terms listed at gakkou

Shika しか = except for only, used as a suffix; *except for only a rabbit, the Shiite caught nothing*; cf. related terms listed at dake

Shika 歯科 = dentistry, dental clinic; *the sheep herder took a cab to a dental clinic*; cf. related terms listed at gankagaku

Shika 鹿 = deer; *the sheep in California are friendly with the deer*

Shikaeshi 仕返し = revenge; from shiyou = a method + kaesu = to retaliate

Shikai 司会 = a presenter, host, or master of ceremonies; *she is kind to agree to be master of ceremonies*

Shikai 歯科医 = a dentist; from shika = dentistry + i = medicine, e.g., isha = doctor

Shikaku 四角 = a square or rectangle; from shi = four + kaku = corner

Shikaku 資格 = credentials, qualifications; *when my sheep bumped into the cactus, I found a veterinarian with good credentials*

Shikamo しかも = moreover, nevertheless, and yet; *the sheep was camouflaged; nevertheless the wolf found it*; cf. related terms listed at kakawarazu

Shikan 士官 = a military officer; *the Shiite Canadian became a military officer*; cf. chuui = a first lieutenant; cf. gunsou = a sergeant; cf. hei'in = military personnel; cf. joukan = a superior officer; cf. shougun = a general, the head of the Samurai government (Shogun); cf. shousa = a major; cf. taichou = a commanding officer; cf. taisa = a colonel; cf. teitoku = an admiral; cf. taii = a captain; cf. other related terms listed at heishi

Shikanai しかない = have no choice, there's nothing but, no more than; used as a suffix; from shikata ga nai = it can't be helped; cf. ni hoka naranai = is due to nothing but, is none other than

Shikaru 叱る = to scold, usually written しかる; *I scolded the sheepish cat on the roof*; cf. related terms listed at hihan suru

Shikashi しかし = however, but; *she's cashing the checks, but she doesn't acknowledge them*; cf. related terms listed at demo

Shikata 仕方 = way (of doing), method; from shimasu = to do + kata = method; cf. related terms listed at houhou

Shikata ga nai 仕方がない = it can't be helped, I can't stand it; from shikata = way or method + ga nai = it doesn't exist

Shikei 死刑 = death penalty; *he got the death penalty for killing a sheepish caterer*

Shiken 試験 = an exam or test; *the test asked us to calculate the number of sheep in Kentucky*

Shikenteki 試験的 = experimental, provisional; from shiken = a test + teki = related to

Shiki 四季 = the four seasons; from shi = four + kisetsu = season; cf. related terms listed at kisetsu

Shiki 式 = a ceremony or rite, a style; *the sheepish king attended the ceremony*; cf. gishiki = ritual, ceremony, formality

Shiki 指揮 = conducting, direction, command; *the sheepish king took command of the army*

Shikichi 敷地 = location or site; *the Shiites put on a kitschy play at that location*; cf. related terms listed at basho

Shikikan 指揮官 = a commander; from shiki = command + kan = government official, e.g., keikan = policeman; cf. shikisha = a conductor or commander

Shikin 資金 = capital, funds; *I'm trying to raise capital to build a shield around the kindergarten*; cf. related terms listed at kikin

Shikiri ni しきりに = often, frequently, eagerly; *the sheep and the kitty come around often*; cf. kenmei ni = eagerly; cf. shibashiba = frequently; cf. other related terms listed at itsumo

Shikiru 仕切る = to divide or partition; from shiyou = means or method + kiru = to cut; cf. buntan suru = to share; cf. wakeru = to divide or share

Shikisai 色彩 = color, hue; *the Shiite king was silent when he saw the color of his new robes*; cf. iro = color

Shikisha 指揮者 = a musical conductor or commander; from shiki = command + sha = person; cf. shikikan = a commander

Shikkaku 失格 = disqualification, elimination; *the Shiite carried Kool-Aid in the race, causing his disqualification*

Shikkan 疾患 = a disease; *sheep cancer is a disease*; cf. related terms listed at byouki

Shikkari しっかり = firmly, tightly, strongly, well; *she carries her responsibilites strongly*

Shikke 湿気 = dampness, humidity; *the sheep farmer keeps the kettle boiling to increase the humidity in this room*

Shikkei 失敬 = impudent, rude; *to hide the shift key in a cave was rude*; cf. arai = violent, rough, rude; cf. atsukamashii = impudent, shameless; cf. sobou = wild, rude, violent

Shikki 漆器 = lacquerware; *the sheep belonging to the king eat from lacquerware*; cf. urushi = lacquer, lacquerware

Shikko しっこ – see oshikko

Shikko suru しっこする – see oshikko suru

Shikkou suru 執行する = to carry out or execute; *please execute the plan to feed the sheep corn*; cf. related terms listed at hatasu

Shikkyaku suru 失脚する = to fall from power; *after he bragged about his chic kayak, the mayor fell from power*

Shikomu 仕込む = to train, to teach, to stock merchandise; *she communicates with people when she trains them to stock merchandise*; cf. oshieru = to teach, show or tell; cf. other related terms listed at shitsukeru

Shikou 思考 = thought, consideration; *he puts a lot of thought into protecting his sheep from the cold*; cf. omoi = idea, thought, sentiment, love; cf. shisou = a thought or idea; cf. other related terms listed at hairyo

Shikou 施行 = execution, enforcement; *the sheep are cold because of a lack of enforcement of the "warm pens" law*; cf. related terms listed at jitsugen

Shikou 歯垢 = dental plaque; *this sheep drinks too much cola and suffers from dental plaque*

Shikou 試行 = making an attempt, a trial run; *during the trial run of the enclosure system, the sheep got into the corn*

Shikou suru 試行する = to make an attempt; from shikou = making an attempt; cf. related terms listed at tamesu

Shiku 敷く = to lay out, spread or take a position; *the sheep food and the Kool-Aid packages have been laid out in the pantry*; cf. haru = to stretch, spread, or put up (e.g., a tent); cf. hirogeru = to spread, expand or unfold; cf. nobasu = to grow long, to lengthen, extend, stretch, develop, expand (transitive); cf. noberu = to lengthen or stretch (transitive)

Shikushiku しくしく = with a dull pain, upset, weeping; *after the sheep drank the Kool-Aid, their stomachs were upset*; cf. related terms listed at itami

Shikyo 死去 = death; *sheep in Kyoto sometimes confront death*; cf. related terms listed at eimin

Shikyoku 支局 = a branch office; *she asked the Kyoto Kool-Aid Club to open a branch office*; cf. related terms listed at kyoku

Shikyuu 子宮 = uterus; *we took our sheep to Cuba to have surgery done on its uterus*

Shikyuu 至急 = immediately, urgently; *the sheep were cute, but I had to go to the bathroom urgently*; cf. related terms listed at sokkoku

Shikyuu suru 支給する = to supply or provide; *the sheep in Cuba supply wool and milk*; cf. related terms listed at kyoukyuu suru

Shima 島 = an island; *she married that guy on an island*; cf. mujintou = an uninhabited island; cf. rettou = an archipelago or chain of islands; cf. ritou = an isolated island; cf. shimajima = islands; cf. tou = an island

Shimai 姉妹 = sisters; *that Shiite mine is owned by two sisters*

Shimajima 島々 = islands; from shima = island + jima = shima = island; cf. related terms listed at shima

Shimaru 締まる = to tighten (intransitive); the intransitive form of shimeru = to fasten

Shimaru 閉まる = to close; the intransitive form of shimeru = to close

Shimatta しまった = oops! or damn! from shimaru = to close (intransitive); cf. shimeta = all right!

Shimau しまう = to put away or close, or (when used as a suffix) to finish doing something; *I always put away my sheets in Maui before leaving*; cf. related terms listed at osameru

Shimei 氏名 = a full name; *she made up a full name and gave it to the police*; cf. related terms listed at namae

Shimei suru 指名する = to appoint or nominate; *the sheepish maid was appointed to the night watch*; cf. meijiru = to command or appoint

Shimekiri 締切 = closing, deadline; from shimeru = to strangle + kiru = to cut; cf. heien = a closing (park, etc.); cf. heisa = closing, shutdown; cf. kigen = a deadline

Shimeru 占める = to occupy; *the sheep and the Mexican rooster occupied the barn*

Shimeru 湿る = to get damp; *the sheep and the Mexican rooster got damp in the rain*; cf. urumu = to moisten, to be blurred; cf. uruou = to become moist, to profit;

Shimeru 締める = to fasten (seatbelt), tie (necktie), strangle, constrict, tighten (transitive); this can also be spelled 絞める; *when I fly my plane and look at the shimmering roofs below, I involuntarily constrict my chest muscles*; cf. related terms listed at tsunagu

Shimeru 閉める = to close or shut; *I closed the store after the sheep and the Mexican rooster got in*; cf. fusagu = block, to stop up, close; cf. habamu = to block or stop; cf. heisa suru = to close down; cf. soshi suru = to obstruct or hinder; cf. tojiru = to close or shut

Shimesu 湿す = to wet or moisten; the transitive form of shimeru = to get damp

Shimesu 示す = to show or point out; *I pointed out that she had made a mess*; cf. related terms listed at miseru and at sasu

Shimeta しめた = I've got it!, or all right! *when the sheepherders met Tarzan, they said "all right!"*; cf. shimatta = oops! or damn!

Shimi 染み = a stain; from shimiru = to penetrate; cf. yogore = dirt or a stain

Shimikomu 染み込む = to soak into or penetrate; from shimiru = to penetrate + komu = to get crowded; cf. shimiru = to pierce or penetrate, to soak in

Shimin 市民 = a citizen; *the Shiites mean to provide education to citizens*; cf. kokumin = a citizen; cf. shinmin = a royal subject

Shiminken 市民権 = citizenship; from shimin = citizen + kenri = right or privilege

Shimiru 染みる = to pierce or penetrate, to soak in; *the sheep meat ruined the tablecloth when it penetrated it*; cf. shimikomu = to soak into or penetrate; cf. tsuranuku = to penetrate, to accomplish, to carry out

Shimo 霜 = frost; *the sheep were moaning from the frost and the cold*

Shimon 指紋 = a fingerprint; *Shimon Peres had fingerprints on file at the FBI*

Shin no 真 = true, genuine, real; *I thought that Shinto was the true religion*; cf. hontou no = real, true, geniuine; cf. jitsu no = real, biological

Shin 心 = core, heart, mind, center; *my heart is drawn to the Shinto faith*

Shin 新 = new, used as a word component, e.g., shingata = a new model; *those shingles look new*; cf. related terms listed at atarashii

Shin 芯 = a wick or core; *the Shinto priest makes wicks for his candles*

Shin 身 = somebody, person, body; *the sheen on that person's body is from the oil spill*; cf. related terms listed at karada

Shin 針 = a needle, used as a word component; *the Shinto priest gave me a needle*; cf. hari = a needle

Shina 品 = goods, article, quality; *the sheets that Nancy sews are goods for sale*; cf. related terms listed at sanbutsu

Shinai 市内 = within a city; from toshi = a city + nai = inside

Shinamono 品物 = merchandise, article; from shina = goods, article + mono = tangible thing; cf. related terms listed at sanbutsu

Shinan no 至難の = extremely difficult; *the sheets that the nanny had torn were extremely difficult to repair*; cf. related terms listed at muzukashii

Shinboku 親睦 = friendship; *I enjoy a friendship with a Shinto priest who was born in Kuwait*; cf. related terms listed at yuujou

Shinboru シンボル = symbol; cf. related terms listed at shouchou

Shinbou 辛抱 = endurance, patience; *the Shinto boy showed endurance and patience*; cf. gaman = patience, endurance; cf. nintai = patience; cf. taikyuu = endurance

Shinbouzuyoi 辛抱強い = patient; from shinbou = patience + zuyoi = tsuyoi = strong

Shinbun 新聞 = a newspaper; *since the Shinto priest lived in the boondocks, he was happy when he could read a newspaper*; cf. choukan = a morning newspaper; cf. yuukan = an evening newspaper

Shinchou 慎重 = careful, prudent; *the Shinto priest did his chores early, since he is prudent*; cf. chuuibukai = attentive, cautious, careful; cf. other related terms listed at teinei

Shinchou 身長 = a person's height; *the Shinto priest and Margaret Cho are the same height*; cf. related terms listed at nagasa

Shindafuri 死んだふり = pretending to be dead; from shinda = died + furi = pretense

Shindan 診断 = diagnosis; *the Shinto dancer received a diagnosis of ankle sprain*

Shindo 震度 = seismic intensity; from shin = to tremble, e.g., jishin = earthquake + do = time, e.g, kondo = this time

Shindou 振動 = vibration, quaking, oscillation; *the Shinto doorman noticed quaking in his building*

Shindou 神童 = a child prodigy; *the shingles covering the dome were designed by a child prodigy*; cf. related terms listed at kodomo

Shindousuu 震度数 = frequency; *the Shinto doorman was sued with frequency*; cf. hindo = frequency of occurrence; cf. kaisuu = frequency

Shingata 新型 = a new model or style; from shin = new + gata = kata = form or style

Shingi 審議 = discussion, scrutiny; *the Shinto shrine's geese are coming under scrutiny and discussion*; cf. hansei = scrutiny, self-scrutiny, regret; cf. other related terms listed at rikutsu

Shingou 信号 = a traffic signal; *the Shinto golfer stopped at the traffic signal*

Shinjin 新人 = a newcomer; from shin = new + jin = person; cf. related terms listed at hito

Shinjiru 信じる = to believe; *I believe that a Shinto genius will rule the country*; cf. shinkou suru = to believe (a religion)

Shinjitsu 真実 = truth, reality; *the Shinto priest told the jittery superstar the truth*; cf. related terms listed at hontou

Shinju 真珠 = a pearl; *I visited a pearl store in Shinjuku*

Shinka 進化 = progress, evolution; *the Shinto caravan made progress*; cf. related terms listed at hattatsu

Shinka suru 進化する = to evolve or progress; from shinka = progress, evolution

Shinkan 新刊 = a new publication; from shin = new + kankou suru = to publish; cf. related terms listed at shuppan

Shinkansen 新幹線 = bullet train; from shin = new + kan = trunk or main; *Canada is our main export market*; + sen = line; cf. related terms listed at densha

Shinkansho 新刊書 = a new publication; from shinkan = a new publication + sho = a document; cf. related terms listed at shuppan

Shinkei 神経 = nerves, sensitivity; *shingles is a case of illness in which a nerve is inflamed*; cf. kanjusei = sensitivity

Shinkeikabin 神経過敏 = overly sensitive; from shinkei = nerves + kabin na = overly sensitive

Shinkeishou 神経症 = a nervous disorder or neurosis; from shinkei = nerves + shoujou = symptoms

Shinken 真剣 = earnest, sincere; *the Shinto priest named Ken was earnest and sincere*; cf. related terms listed at seijitsu

Shinkin 心筋 = heart muscle, myocardium; from shin = heart + kinniku = muscle

Shinkin 親近 = a relative, familiarity; *my relatives all attended that Shinto kindergarten, and we have a familiarity with it*

Shinkin kousoku 心筋梗塞 = a heart attack or myocardial infarction; from shinkin = heart muscle + kousoku = an infarction; cf. related terms listed at kyoushinshou

Shinkinkan 親近感 = a feeling of intimacy; from shinkin = familiarity + kanji = feeling

Shinkoku 深刻 = serious, grave; *if you see a sheen on your Coke, it's a sign of grave contamination*; cf. related terms listed at maji

Shinkou 信仰 = a belief or religion; *that Shinto coalition is working to strengthen religion and religious beliefs*; cf. related terms listed at shuukyou

Shinkou suru 信仰する = to believe (a religion); from shinkou = a belief or religion; cf. shinjiru = to believe

Shinme 新芽 = a bud or sprout; from shin = new + mebae = budding

Shinmi ni 親身に = kindly; *the Shinto priest fed me a meal kindly*; cf. sekkaku = with much trouble, kindly; cf. shinsetsu ni = kindly

Shinmin 臣民 = a royal subject; from shin = subject; *the Shinto priest was a loyal subject of the emperor*; + min = citizen; cf. related terms listed at shimin

Shinmitsu na 親密な = intimate, close; *the Shinto priest meets his intimate friends*; cf. shitashii = intimate, friendly

Shinmitsusa 親密さ = intimacy, friendship; from shinmitsu = intimate + sa = a suffix that makes a noun from an adjective; cf. related terms listed at yuujou

Shinnen 信念 = a belief; *the Shinto that my negative nephew follows promotes strange beliefs*; cf. oshie = a teaching, dogma or doctrine

Shinnen 新年 = New Year; from shin = new + nen = year; cf. related terms listed at shougatsu

Shinnenkai 新年会 = a New Year's party; from shinnen = New Year + kaigi = a meeting

Shinnyuu 侵入 = an invasion; *the Shinto youth were recruited for an invasion*

Shinnyuu 新入 = newly entered, used as a word component, e.g., shinnyuu shain = a newly hired employee; from shin = new + nyuu = entering

Shinobikomu 忍び込む = to creep in or steal in; from shinobu = to conceal oneself + komu = to crowd in

Shinobu 忍ぶ = to endure, to conceal oneself; *after the sheep from Norway drank booze they were hard to endure, and we concealed ourselves from them*; cf. kakureru = to conceal oneself; cf. taeru = to endure

Shinpai 心配 = anxiety, worry; *I feel worry about the shingles made of pine wood*; cf. related terms listed at nayami

Shinpai suru 心配する = to be anxious, to worry; from shinpai = anxiety, worry; cf. ki ni naru = to worry, care about, to be bothered by; cf. ki ni suru = to mind, care about or worry; cf. kizukau = to care for, worry, pay attention; cf. kurushimu = to suffer, to be worried; cf. modaeru = to be in agony, to worry; cf. nayamu = to be troubled or worried; cf. wazurau = to worry about, to have trouble doing

Shinpan 審判 = an umpire or referee; *the referee hits offending players with a shiny pan*

Shinpi 神秘 = a mystery; *the Shinto priest peeked into the room in an effort to unravel the mystery*; cf. misuterii = mystery

Shinpiteki 神秘的 = mysterious; from shinpi = mystery + teki = related to; cf. fushigi = mysterious, strange

Shinpu 新婦 = a bride; *the Shinto woman, who was poor, became a bride*; cf. related terms listed at hanayome

Shinrai 信頼 = trust, confidence, reliance; *I have confidence in Shinto rice*; cf. shinyou = trust or faith; cf. tayori = reliance

Shinrin 森林 = a forest; *I lost my Shinto ring*

in the *forest*; cf. related terms listed at mori

Shinrou 新郎 = a bridegroom; *the Shinto guy roamed around until he became a bridegroom*; cf. related terms listed at hanayome

Shinryaku 侵略 = aggression, invasion; *the shingles were carried from Riyadh to Kuwait during an invasion*

Shinryoku 新緑 = new green leaves; from shin = new + ryoku = green, e.g., ryokucha = green tea; cf. related terms listed at ha

Shinsa 審査 = a hearing or examination; *the Shinto guy's salary was increased after the hearing, where there was an examination of his projects*; cf. related terms listed at kensa

Shinsa suru 審査する = to examine, inspect or review; from shinsa = a screening or examination; cf. related terms listed at miru

Shinsai 震災 = a great earthquake; *the shingles at the scientist's house fell during the great earthquake*; cf. related terms listed at jishin

Shinsatsu 診察 = a medical examination; *the Shinto doctor wore a satin suit during the medical examination*; cf. related terms listed at kensa

Shinsei 神聖 = holy or sacred; *this shingle from the saint's home is sacred*; cf. related terms listed at kichou

Shinsei suru 申請する = to apply for or request; *the Shinto sailor requested shore leave*; cf. moushikomu = to apply for; cf. other related terms listed at tanomu

Shinseihin 新製品 = a new product; from shin = new + seihin = a product; cf. related terms listed at sanbutsu

Shinseki 親戚 = a relative; *the Shinto priest and the selfish king are relatives*; cf. related terms listed at kazoku

Shinsen 新鮮 = fresh; *the Shinto shrine sent me some fresh fruit*; cf. related terms listed at atarashii

Shinsetsu 親切 = kind(ness), gentle(ness); *the Shinto priest sets you up in business because he's kind*; cf. yasashisa = kindness, gentleness; cf. other related terms listed at yasashii

Shinsetsu ni 親切に = kindly; from shinsetsu = kindness + -ni = a suffix that forms an adverb; cf. sekkaku = with much trouble, kindly; cf. shinmi ni = kindly

Shinsha 新車 = a new car; from shin = new + sha = a car; cf. related terms listed at kuruma

Shinshi 紳士 = a gentleman; *the shiny ship belongs to a gentleman*

Shinshin 津々 = flowing, everlasting; *the Shinto priest used shingles to protect his shrine from flowing rain water*; cf. nagashi = flowing

Shinshitsu 寝室 = a bedroom; *we have shiny sheets in our bedroom*; cf. related terms listed at -shitsu

Shinshu 新種 = new species or variety; from shin = new + shurui = type; cf. related terms listed at shurui

Shinshutsu 進出 = advance, expansion, emerging; *if that Shinto priest shoots you, there will be an expansion of the charges against him and an advance in his trial date*; cf. kakuchou = expansion, enlargement; kakudai = magnification, enlargement

Shinshutsu suru 進出する = to progress, expand or branch out into; from shinshutsu = advance, expansion, emerging; cf. susumu = to advance or make progress

Shinsou 真相 = truth, real situation; *the Shinto soldier sought the truth*; cf. related terms listed at hontou

Shinsui suru 浸水する = to be flooded; *a Shinto shrine in Sweden was flooded*

Shintaku 信託 = a trust (finance); from shinjiru = to believe + taku suru = to entrust

Shintou 神道 = a Japanese religion based on animism; *the <u>sheen</u> on that <u>tortoise</u> shell reminds me of a <u>Japanese religion based on animism</u>*

Shinu 死ぬ = to die; *when <u>she</u> heard the news, she <u>died</u>*; cf. bossuru = to sink, go down, to set, to pass away, to die, to disappear; cf. botsu = to drown, sink, disappear, or die; cf. eimin suru = to die; cf. horobiru = to perish or be ruined; cf. kieuseru = to disappear or die; cf. nakunaru = to die; cf. seikyo suru = to die

Shinya 深夜 = dead of night; *the <u>Shinto yak</u> got up in the <u>dead</u> of <u>night</u>*; cf related terms listed at tetsuya

Shinyou 信用 = trust or faith; *the <u>Shinto</u> priest and the <u>yogi</u> had <u>trust</u> in one another*; cf. shinrai = trust, confidence, reliance; cf. tayori = reliance

Shinyoudo 信用度 = a level of trust or confidence; from shinyou = trust + do = degree, e.g., hyakudo = 100 degrees

Shin'youju (Shinyouju) 針葉樹 = a conifer or needle-leaved tree; *the <u>Shinto</u> priest and the <u>yogi</u> drank <u>juice</u> under a <u>conifer</u> tree*; cf. related terms listed at ki

Shinzou hossa 心臓発作 = a heart attack; from shinzou = heart + hossa = attack or fit; *when the <u>horse saw</u> the snake, he had a <u>fit</u>*; cf. kyoushinshou = angina (pain due to narrowing of the heart arteries), heart attack

Shinzou 心臓 = the heart (organ); from shin = heart + zou = organ; *<u>zou</u> (elephants) have big internal <u>organs</u>*; cf. related terms listed at kokoro and at naizou

Shinzui 真髄 = essence or gist; *the <u>shiny</u> feathers on the <u>zooming eagle</u> seemed to embody the <u>essence</u> of style*

Shio 塩 = salt; *the <u>sheep's owner</u> gives it <u>salt</u>*

Shio 潮 = the tide; *the <u>sheep</u> went to the <u>ocean</u> to see the <u>tide</u>*; cf. hikishio = low tide; cf. manchou = high tide; cf. shiohi = low tide

Shiohi 潮干 = low tide; *the <u>sheep</u> can <u>only</u> <u>hear</u> me at <u>low tide</u>*; cf. related terms listed at shio

Shiohigari 潮干狩り = shell gathering, clamming; from shiohi = low tide + garu = karu = to gather fruit, etc.

Shippai 失敗 = a failure or mistake; *when I <u>shipped</u> the <u>pies</u>, I <u>made a mistake</u>*; cf. fuseiritsu = a failure; cf. ketten = a fault, shortcoming or failure; cf. koshou = a breakdown, malfunction or failure; cf. misu = a mistake or failure; cf. sakugo = a mistake or error; cf. zasetsu = a failure or setback

Shippai suru 失敗する = to fail or make a mistake; from shippai = a failure or mistake; cf. related terms listed at hazureru

Shippo しっぽ = a tail (animal); *the <u>sheet</u> covered most of the <u>pony</u> but not its <u>tail</u>*

Shirabe 調べ = a tune, tone, writing style, investigation, inspection, examination; *the <u>sheep</u> and the <u>rabbits</u> were <u>betting</u> that the <u>investigation</u> would clear them, and they played a happy <u>tune</u> when it did*; cf. related terms listed at kensa, at tenken and at uta

Shiraberu 調べる = to investigate, check, look up, consult; *he will <u>investigate</u> the <u>sheep</u> <u>ranch</u> near <u>Beirut</u>*; cf. related terms listed at sousaku suru

Shiraga 白髪 = white or grey hair; *the <u>sheep</u> <u>ranch's garage</u> was full of <u>white hair</u>*; cf. related terms listed at ke

Shirase 知らせ = notification, news; from shiraseru = to notify or inform; cf. related terms listed at jouhou

Shiraseru 知らせる = to notify or inform; *I <u>informed</u> him that the <u>sheep ranch</u> is <u>selling roosters</u>*; cf. happyou suru = to announce, publish or reveal; cf. kikaseru = to inform, tell, persuade; cf. oshieru = to teach, show or tell; cf. tsugeru = to tell, inform or announce; cf. tsutaeru = to inform, to hand down or transmit

Shiri ni shiku 尻にひく = to dominate, usually one's husband; from shiri = buttocks + shiku = to lay out, spread or sit, so this suggests that someone sits on her husband; cf. seiha suru = to conquer, dominate or rule

Shiriai 知り合い = an acquaintance; from shiriau = to meet; cf. related terms listed at tomodachi

Shiriau 知り合う = to meet; from shiru = to know + au = to meet; cf. related terms listed at deau

Shiriizu シリーズ = a series

Shiritsu no 市立の = municipal, related to a city; *the sheet contained a written suggestion that I purchase municipal bonds*

Shirizoku 退く = to retreat; *the sheep were reading the signs of the Zodiac and drinking Kool-Aid when they had to retreat from a wolf*

Shiro しろ – see ni shiro

Shiro 城 = a castle; *the sheep are roaming among the ruins of that castle*; cf. jou = a castle, used as a suffix; cf. kojou = an old castle; cf. koujou = a ruined castle; cf. meijou = a famous castle

Shiro 白 = white; the noun form of shiroi = white; cf. masshiro = pure white

Shiro nuri 白塗り = white makeup; from shiro = white + nuru = to paint; cf. related terms listed at keshouhin

Shiroi 白い = white; *the sheets that Roy is washing are white*

Shiroji 白地 = a white background; from shiroi = white + ji = chi = ground; cf. related terms listed at haikei

Shirotabi 白足袋 = white Japanese socks; from shiroi = white + tabi = Japanese socks; cf. related terms listed at kutsushita

Shirouto 素人 = an amateur; *using sheepdogs and rope to tow the truck was the idea of an amateur*; cf. similar terms listed at kurouto

Shiru 汁 = soup; *I drank soup with a Shinto ruler*; cf. kajuu = fruit juice; cf. nikujuu = gravy; cf. remon jiru = lemon juice; cf. tsukejiru = a sauce

Shiru 知る = to know; *the Shinto ruler knows his subjects*; cf. gozonji desu = honorably knows; cf. wakaru = to understand, know or recognize; cf. zonjiru = to know, think or feel humbly

Shirushi 印 = sign, symbol, indication; *the Shiites were rushing to remove the symbols of Saddam from Iraq*; cf. related terms listed at kizashi and at shouchou

Shirusu 記す = to record or write; *the reporter wrote a story about some sheep that ruined a supermarket*; cf. related terms listed at kaku

Shiryoku 視力 = eyesight; *the sheep that were fed Pope Leo's Kool-Aid developed better eyesight*

Shiryou 資料 = literature, documents; *I read some literature about the sheep of Pope Leo*; cf. related terms listed at kiroku

Shisa 示唆 = an implication or suggestion; *he made a suggestion to provide the sheep with salt licks*; cf. imiai = nuance, implication

Shisei 姿勢 = a posture, stance; *the sheepdog in the Safeway store adopted a threatening stance*; cf. kata = form (e.g., dance), posture, style; cf. taisei = a stance or posture

Shiseikatsu 私生活 = private life; from shiyou = private + seikatsu = life; cf. related terms listed at inochi

Shisen 視線 = a gaze; *I avoided the gaze of the sheepish senator*; cf. manazashi = a look or gaze

Shisetsu 施設 = a facility, institution, or equipment; *the Shiites set up a super institution*; cf. setsubi = equipment, facility; cf. soubi = equipment; cf. souchi = equipment

Shisha 使者 = an emissary or messenger; from shiyou suru = to use + sha = person; cf. taishi = an embassador

Shisha 支社 = a branch office; from shi = branch or support; *we use spreadsheets at that branch to support our finances*; + sha = company; cf. related terms listed at kyoku

Shisha 死者 = dead people; from shinu = to die + sha = a person

Shishutsu 支出 = expenditures; *she shoots her gun all day, increasing our expenditures for ammunition*; cf. related terms listed at shouhi

Shison 子孫 = a descendant; *that Shiite who works for Sony has several descendants*

Shisou 思想 = a thought or idea; *the Shiite soldier had a good idea*; cf. omoi = idea, thought, sentiment, love; cf. shikou = thought or consideration

Shisseki 叱責 = a reprimand or rebuke; *the sheepdog hid behind the selfish king after its rebuke*; cf. related terms listed at hihan

Shita 下 = below, inferior; *my sheep tattoo is below my snake tattoo*; cf. chokka = directly under; cf. ika = below, less than, the following, the rest

Shita 舌 = a tongue; *the sheep licked the taffy with their tongues*

Shitagatte したがって = accordingly or therefore; this can sometimes be spelled 従って; from shitagau = to follow; cf. related terms listed at dakara

Shitagau 従う = to obey or follow; *she tagged the Australian cattle, following them around and obeying her orders*; cf. fukujuu suru = to obey or submit; cf. other related terms listed at tadoru

Shitagi 下着 = underwear; from shita = below + giru = kiru = to wear clothes; cf. hadagi = underwear

Shitai 死体 = a dead body; from shinu = to die + tai = body, e.g., taijuu = body weight; cf. related terms listed at karada

Shitajunbi 下準備 = a preliminary preparation; from shita = below + junbi = preparation; from shita = inferior + junbi = preparation; cf. related terms listed at youi

Shitaku 支度 = preparations; *we are making preparations for our sheep to be tattooed in Kuwait*; cf. related terms listed at youi

Shitamawaru 下回る = to be less than; from shita = below + mawaru = to turn or spin, suggesting that something is rotating below a given level

Shitami 下見 = a preliminary inspection, preview, rehearsal; from shita = below + miru = to look; cf. keiko = rehearsal, practice, training; cf. other related terms listed at tenken

Shitashii 親しい = intimate, friendly; *I got a sheep tattoo from a Shiite who was friendly*; cf. shinmitsu na = intimate, close

Shitashimu 親しむ = to be intimate with; the verb form of shitashii = intimate

Shitatariochiru 滴り落ちる = to trickle down; from shitataru = to drip + ochiru = to fall

Shitataru 滴る = to drip; *when I got a sheep tattoo in the tattoo room, my tears dripped onto the floor*; cf. shitatariochiru = to trickle down; cf. tareru = to hang, droop, dangle, sag, lower, drip, ooze

Shitau 慕う = to adore or yearn for; *I adore my sheets and towels*; cf. akogareru = to admire, to long for

Shitei 指定 = designation, assignment; *the Shiite tailor received a designation as a hero*; cf. haizoku = assignment or attachment (of a person or animal)

Shiteiseki 指定席 = reserved seat; from shitei = a designation + seki = seat; cf. related terms listed at seki

Shiteki 指摘 = pointing out, identification; *the Shiite techie was responsible for the identification of the computer virus*

Shiteki wo suru 指摘をする = to point out; from shiteki = pointing out; cf. related terms listed at sasu

Shiten 支店 = a branch office or store; *in that branch store, they sell sheets and tents*; cf. related terms listed at kyoku and at mise

Shiten 視点 = viewpoint, point of view; *the sheep on the tennis court have their own point of view*; cf. kenkai = viewpoint; cf. mitoushi = outlook, perspective

Shitoshito しとしと = gently (raining); *the sheep toy got damp when it rained gently*; cf. related terms listed at sotto

Shitsu 室 = a room, used as a suffix; *I keep sheets in this room*; cf. boushitsu = a room, a bedroom of a married couple, atrium or ventricle (heart); cf. chikashitsu = a basement; cf. heya = a room; cf. ima = a living room; cf. kensashitsu = a lab where patients' tests are done; cf. koshitsu = a private or single room; cf. kyakuma = a parlor or drawing room; cf. kyoushitsu = a classroom; cf. shinshitsu = a bedroom; cf. yokushitsu = a bathroom; cf. zashiki = a Japanese-style room with tatami flooring

Shitsu 質 = quality; *these sheets are of high quality*; cf. related terms listed at hinshitsu

Shitsudo 湿度 = humidity level; *due to the humidity level, I have to hang my sheets on the door in order to dry them*

Shitsugyou 失業 = unemployment; *due my unemployment, I'm wearing sheets and eating only gyoza*

Shitsukeru しつける = to train or to teach manners; *I'm going to train you how to iron the sheets that are kept in that room*;

cf. kitaeru = to train or strengthen oneself; cf. oshiekomu = to train or give an idea; cf. shikomu = to train, to stock merchandise; cf. tanren suru = to train

Shitsumon 質問 = a question or enquiry; *I have a question about the sheets for the monks*; cf. related terms listed at utagai

Shitsunai 室内 = indoor, inside the room; from shitsu = a room + naibu = inside

Shitsurei 失礼 = rudeness, discourtesy; *to leave the sheets out in the rain was rude*; cf. bujoku = insult, contempt, disrespect

Shitsurei shimasu 失礼します = excuse me, or I must be going; from shitsurei = rudeness, discourtesy; cf. related terms listed at sumimasen

Shitsuren 失恋 = unrequited love, lost love; *I keep sheets in the rental car and sleep outside her house, but I have unrequited love*; cf. related terms listed at aijou

Shitsuryou 質量 = mass; from shitsu = contents, e.g., busshitsu = substance; + ryou = quantity

Shitto 嫉妬 = jealousy; *I feel jealousy because you have so many sheep and tortoises*; cf. related terms listed at netami

Shitto bukai 嫉妬深い = deeply jealous; from shitto = jealousy + bukai = fukai = deep

Shiwa しわ = wrinkle; *she washed her face every night to prevent wrinkles*

Shiya 視野 = scope, field of vision, view, outlook; from shiryoku = eyesight + ya = a field, e.g., yakyuu = baseball; cf. related terms listed at nagame

Shiyakusho 市役所 = city hall; from shi = city + yaku = service + sho = place; cf. kuyakusho = a ward office

Shiyou 仕様 = a means or method; *they know the means for using sheep milk to produce yogurt*; cf. related terms listed at houhou

Shiyou 使用 = use, employment; *one use for*

sheep yogurt is in the treatment of burns; cf. riyou = use, utilization

Shiyou 私用 = private; *our sheep yogurt is for private consumption*; cf. related terms listed at senyou

Shizen 自然 = nature; *both Shinto and Zen favor the preservation of Nature*; cf. etai = nature or character; cf. shizenkai = nature, the natural world

Shizen ni 自然に = naturally, spontaneously; from shizen = nature + ni, a suffix that makes an adverb from a noun or an adjective; cf. related terms listed at masa ni

Shizenkai 自然界 = nature, the natural world; from shizen = nature + kai = world, e.g., sekai = the world; cf. etai = nature or character; cf. shizen = nature

Shizenkou 自然光 = natural light; from shizen = nature + nikkou = sunlight; cf. related terms listed at hikari

Shizuka 静か = quiet, silent, calm; *the sheep at the zoo in California were quiet*; cf. related terms listed at odayaka

Shizuku しずく = a drip or drop; *when the sheep at the zoo drink Kool-Aid, they don't waste a drop*; cf. related terms listed at tsubu

Shizumaru 静まる = to become calm or quiet; from shizuka = quiet + maru = round, completely; cf. damaru = to keep silent; cf. other related terms listed at kutsurogu

Shizumeru 沈める = to sink or submerge (transitive); *the sheep from the zoo in Mexico ruined the boat and sank it*

Shizumeru 鎮める = to alleviate or suppress, to calm; *we are letting the sheep at the zoo sleep in the men's room to alleviate crowding*; cf. related terms listed at genshou suru

Shizumu 沈む = to set (sun or moon), to sink (intransitive), to feel depressed; *the sheep from the zoo watched the moon as it set*; cf. related terms listed at bossuru and at meiru

Sho 所 = a place, used as a suffix; *let's hold our show at that place*

Sho 書 = a document, used as a suffix, e.g., jisho = a dictionary; *show me the document*

Sho 諸 = various, used as a prefix; *being short leads to various problems*; cf. related terms listed at kazukazu

Sho 署 = a government office, used as a suffix; *the short guy works at a government office*

Shobun 処分 = disposal, expulsion, punishment; *I showed Daniel Boone how to arrange for the expulsion of rats from his house and their disposal*; cf. related terms listed at tsuihou

Shochou 初潮 = first menstruation; *after I had my first menstruation, I went to a show starring Margaret Cho*

Shodou 書道 = calligraphy; *I showed the doorman my calligraphy*

Shohou 処方 = prescription, formulation; *she showed me the hotel where prescriptions are sold*; cf. shohousen = a prescription (medical)

Shohousen 処方箋 = a prescription (medical); *if you show that horse to the senator, she might be able to help you get a prescription for it*; cf. shouhou = prescription, formulation

Shojun 初旬 = the first ten days of a month; from sho = to begin, e.g., saisho = the beginning; + jun = season; cf. chuujun = around the middle of a month; cf. kouhan = the latter half

Shoki 初期 = a beginning or initial stage; *the beginning of the play was shocking*; cf. related terms listed at hajime ni

Shokkan 食感 = texture of food; from shokuji = meal + kanjiru = to feel

Shokki 食器 = tableware; *this tableware was shocking the child who was inserting it into* an electric outlet

Shokkidana 食器棚 = a cupboard; from shokki = tableware + dana = tana = shelf

Shokkiyou senzai 食器用洗剤 = dish detergent; from shokki = tableware + you = a use + senzai = detergent

Shokoku 諸国 = various countries; from sho = various; *being short leads to various issues*; + koku = countries; cf. related terms listed at kuni

Shoku 職 = job; *my job is to shock people*

Shokuba 職場 = workplace; from shoku = job + basho = place

Shokubou 嘱望 = expectation, hoping for; *showing Kool-Aid is boring, but I have an expectation that someone will buy some*; cf. yosou = an expectation

Shokubunka 食文化 = food culture; from shokuji = a meal + bunka = culture; cf. bunka = culture

Shokubutsu 植物 = plant, vegetation; *he felt a shock in his boots when he stepped on the wire hidden in some vegetation*; cf. bonsai = a miniature potted plant; cf. hachiue = a potted plant; cf. ine = a rice plant; cf. kusabana = flowering plants; cf. kusaki = plants, vegetation; cf. shigemi = a bush; cf. ueki = a garden plant or tree, a potted plant; cf. other related terms listed at ki

Shokubutsuen 植物園 = a botanical garden; from shokubutsu = plant, vegetation + en = park, e.g., kouen = a park; cf. related terms listed at niwa

Shokudou 食堂 = a dining hall or cafeteria; from shokuji = a meal + dou = a hall

Shokugyou 職業 = occupation; *my occupation is to show Kuwaiti people how to make gyoza*

Shokuhin 食品 = food products; from shokuji = meal + seihin = product; cf. related terms listed at tabemono

Shokuin 職員 = staff, personnel; from shokugyou = occupation + in = group member; cf. shiikuin = a caretaker at a zoo or aquarium

Shokuji 食事 = a meal; *we were shocked that the genius took his meals in bed*; cf. asagohan = breakfast; cf. bangohan = the evening meal; cf. choushoku = breakfast; cf. chuushoku = lunch; cf. hirugohan = lunch; cf. oyatsu = between-meal snack; cf. yuugohan = the evening meal; cf. yuuhan = the evening meal; cf. yuushoku = the evening meal

Shokumotsu 食物 = food; *does it shock you that I'm fishing in the moats for food?* cf. shokubutsu = vegetation; cf. related terms listed at tabemono

Shokumu 職務 = duty, office; from shokugyou = occupation + kinmu = service, duty; cf. related terms listed at kinmu

Shokunin 職人 = a craftsperson or artisan; from shokugyou = occupation + nin = person; cf. takumi = an artisan, workman or carpenter

Shokupan 食パン = Japanese milk bread; from shokuji = a meal + pan = bread

Shokuryou 食料 = food; this can also be spelled 食糧; from shokuji = meal + ryouri = cuisine; cf. related terms listed at tabemono

Shokuryouhin 食料品 = groceries; from shokuryou = food + hin = goods; cf. related terms listed at tabemono

Shokuseikatsu 食生活 = eating habits; from shokuji = a meal + seikatsu = life

Shokutaku 嘱託 = commission, entrusting, a temporary employee; *we were shocked that we could only get tap water and Kool-Aid, and we set up a commission of temporary employees to investigate*

Shokutaku 食卓 = a dining table; *I showed her the Kool-Aid which I made by combining tap water and Kool-Aid powder at the dining table*

Shokuyoku 食欲 = appetite (for food); from shokuji = a meal + yokubari = greed

Shokuzai 食材 = an ingredient (food); from shokuji = a meal + zairyou = an ingredient; cf. related terms listed at seibun

Shomei 署名 = signature; *please show the mayor your signature*; cf. chouin = signature, sealing

Shomin 庶民 = common people, the masses; *the Shogun was mean to the masses*; cf. related terms listed at hito

Shomondai 諸問題 = various problems; from sho = various; *being short leads to various issues*; + mondai = problem

Shomou 所望 = desire, wish, request; *my desire is that you show me your motor-cycle*; cf. bonnou = worldly desire; cf. hoshii = want, yearn for; cf. inori = prayer; cf. kibou = hope or wish; cf. kokorozashi = kokoroza = ambition, wish, goal; cf. negai = a hope, prayer or request; cf. nozomi = hope, dream, wish; cf. shibou = ambition, wish, goal; cf. yokkyuu = desire; cf. yoku = greed, desire; cf. other related terms listed at seikyuu

Shomu 庶務 = general affairs; *the Shogun was in a mood to discuss general affairs*; cf. gyoumu = business, affairs

Shomuka 庶務課 = the general affairs section of a company; from shomu = general affairs + ka = a section; cf. gyoumuka = general affairs section of a company

Shonichi 初日 = first or opening day; from sho = to begin, e.g., saisho = the beginning; + nichi = day; cf. saikaibi = reopening day

Shoppai しょっぱい = salty; *I'm shopping for pies, especially salty ones*

Shori suru 処理する = to deal with, handle, eliminate; *Shorty deals with our garbage*; cf. atsukau = to deal with or deal in, to take care of; cf. ayatsuru = to control, manipulate, handle; cf. nozomu = to attend (e.g., a function), to appear (e.g., in court), to deal with, to look out upon; cf. osaeru = to suppress or control; cf. sabaku = to handle or process; cf. taisho suru = to deal with, implying that one solves a problem; cf. tegakeru = to manage or handle; cf. toriatsukau = to handle or treat; cf. torikumu = to deal with, wrestle with; cf. yokusei suru = to control or curb

Shorui 書類 = documents; *they showed King Louis the documents*; cf. related terms listed at kiroku

Shosai 書斎 = a library (home) or study; *that short scientist is working in his home library*; cf. related terms listed at toshokan

Shoseki 書籍 = a book; *you should show the selfish king your book*; cf. related terms listed at hon

Shosen 所詮 = after all; *after all, if the show is sensational, they will come*; cf. related terms listed at tonikaku

Shotai 世帯 = household, family; *our household keeps a short tiger as a pet*; cf. related terms listed at ie and at kazoku

Shotou 諸島 = an archipelago or group of islands; *I showed Tony Blair the group of islands*

Shou しよう = let's do, or I shall do; this replaces the su at the end of a masu verb, e.g., tabemashou = let's eat; *let's go to a show*; cf. -ou = let's do, or I shall do; cf. you = let's do, or I shall do

Shou 晶 = a crystal; *the crystals put on a show in the sun*; cf. related terms listed at suishou

Shou 章 = a chapter; *the next chapter is about the shoreline*; cf. ka = a chapter, lesson or section, a counter for chapters of a book

Shou 賞 = a prize; *I'll show you my prize*; cf. related terms listed at houbi

Shou ga nai しょうがない – see shikata ga nai

Shouaku suru 掌握する = to hold or seize; *the Shogun's acupuncturist seized a needle*; cf. related terms listed at taiho suru

Shoubai 商売 = business, commerce; *I show bicycles in my business*; cf. related terms listed at akinai

Shoubou 消防 = firefighting; *he showed me the bonus that he got for firefighting*

Shouboushi 消防士 = a firefighter; from shoubou = firefighting + shinshi = a gentleman

Shoubousho 消防署 = a fire station; from shoubou = firefighting + sho = a government office

Shouchi 承知 = acceptance, consent, understanding; *with her consent, I only showed the cheap merchandise*; cf. doui = the same opinion, agreement; cf. goui = consent or agreement; cf. icchi = agreement, coincidence, conformity, cooperation; cf. kyoutei = a pact or agreement; cf. rikai = understanding; cf. ryoukai = agreement, consent, understanding; cf. ryoushou = an understanding or acknowledgment; cf. saiyou = adoption, acceptance, employment; cf. sansei = agreement; cf. shoudaku = compliance, approval, consent; cf. shounou = acceptance

Shouchi suru 承知する = to understand; from shouchi = acceptance, consent, understanding; cf. related terms listed at wakaru

Shouchou 象徴 = symbol; *the shore was choked with plastic waste, a symbol of consumerism*; cf. maaku = a mark, a sign or symbol; cf. shinboru = symbol; cf. shirushi = sign, symbol, indication

Shouchuu 焼酎 = a Japanese spirit distilled from sweet potatoes, rice, etc.; *showpeople choose to drink shouchuu*; cf. jouryuushu = distilled liquor;

Shoudaku 承諾 = compliance, approval, consent; *my short daughter in Kuwait has approval to play outside the house*; cf. related terms listed at kyoka and at shouchi

Shoudou 衝動 = an impulse; *on an impulse, I went to the shore to see the dolphins*

Shouga しょうが = ginger; *the Shougun's garden contained ginger plants*

Shougai 生涯 = one's lifetime or career; *that short guy had a career as a submarine captain*; cf. related terms listed at isshou

Shougai 障害 = an obstacle, disability or disorder; *the short guy is an obstacle to my plans*; cf. bougai = an interference, disturbance, intrusion or obstacle; cf. jama = a burden, hindrance or disturbance; cf. sogai = an obstruction or inhibition; cf. related terms listed at sawari

Shougakkou 小学校 = an elementary school; from shou = small, e.g., shoujo = a girl; + gakkou = school; cf. related terms listed at gakkou

Shougakkukin 奨学金 = a fellowship, scholarship or stipend; from shourei = encouragement + gaku = learning + kingaku = a sum of money

Shougaku 小学 = elementary school, a variant of shougakkou = an elementary school; cf. related terms listed at gakkou

Shougatsu 正月 = New Year or New Year's Day; from shou = correct, e.g., shoujiki = honest; + gatsu = getsu = month; cf. ganjitsu = New Year's Day; cf. kyuu shougatsu = lunar New Year; cf. shinnen = New Year

Shougeki 衝撃 = impact, shock; *I felt a shock when he showed me his guest key, since I hadn't known that he was staying with us*

Shougen 証言 = testimony; *the testimony showed that Genghis was at the scene of the crime*; cf. related terms listed at shouko

Shougi 将棋 = Japanese chess; *we showed*

the geeks how to play Japanese chess

Shougou 照合 = comparison, collation; *I will show you my goats, and you can make comparisons among them*; cf. hikaku = a comparison

Shougun 将軍 = a general, the head of the Samurai government (Shogun); *the general always liked to show his gun*; cf. related terms listed at shikan

Shouhi 消費 = consumption, expenditure; *the shoulder healed, thanks to my expenditures for physical therapy*; cf. shishutsu = expenditures; shouhiryou = amount of consumption; cf. shoumou = exhaustion, consumption, waste; cf. shuppi = expenditures

Shouhin 商品 = commodity, merchandise; *I will show the Hindus the merchandise*; cf. related terms listed at sanbutsu

Shouhin hatsu 商品発 = a product launch; from shouhin = merchandise + hatsu = a departure

Shouhiryou 消費量 = amount of consumption; from shouhi = consumption + ryou = quantity; cf. related terms listed at ryou

Shouhisha 消費者 = a consumer; from shouhi = consumption + sha = a person

Shouhon 抄本 = an excerpt, abstract or abbreviated transcript; *the Shougun went to Hong Kong to see an excerpt of the report*; cf. bassui = an excerpt or extract; cf. other related terms listed at ryaku

Shoujiki 正直な = honest; *since I believe that you're honest, I will show you the Jeep keys*; cf. majime (na) = sincere, honest, industrious, serious; cf. socchoku = frank, candid, straightforward; cf. sunao = obedient, meek, honest, frank; cf. other related terms listed at seijitsu

Shoujikisa 正直さ = honesty; from shoujiki = honest + sa = a suffix that makes a noun from an adjective

Shoujin 精進 = concentration, devotion; *I can show you a genius with remarkable concentration and devotion*

Shoujin ryouri 精進料理 = vegetarian cuisine, as eaten by Buddhist monks; from shoujin = concentration, devotion + ryouri = cuisine

Shoujiru 生じる = to arise or occur; to bring about; *let's show the geniuses ruling the country what can occur if they don't change their ways*; cf. motarasu = to bring about; cf. other related terms listed at hassei suru

Shoujo 少女 = a girl; from shousuu = a few + josei = woman; cf. shounen = a boy; cf. related terms listed at onna

Shoujou 症状 = symptoms, condition of a patient; *I will show Joan of Arc my list of symptoms*; cf. choukou = a symptom or sign; cf. other related terms listed at keisei

Shouka 消化 = digestion (food or information); *I showed Karl Marx the fiber supplement that I take for digestion*

Shouka suru 消化する = to digest; from shouka = digestion; cf. related terms listed at kyuushuu suru

Shoukai 紹介 = introduction; *a showman and the Kaiser received an introduction*; cf. dounyuu = introduction, leading in

Shoukaijou 紹介状 = letter of introduction; *although she showed it to the Kaiser, Joan didn't expect much from the letter of introduction*; cf. related terms listed at tegami

Shoukaisaki 紹介先 = reference; *I showed the Kaiser a sack of quiche when he asked for my references as a cook*

Shoukan suru 召喚する = to summon; *we summoned the short Canadian*; cf. yobidasu = to summon

Shouki 笑気 = laughing gas or nitrous oxide; *the short king got high on laughing gas*

Shoukibo 小規模 = small-scale; from shou = small, e.g., shoujo = a girl; + kibo = scale; cf. related terms listed at chiisai

Shouko 証拠 = evidence, proof, testimony; the *short Colombian* gave *testimony* about the *evidence* and provided *proof*; cf. akashi = proof, certificate; cf. shougen = testimony; cf. shoumei = proof, identification

Shoumei 証明 = proof, identification; I *showed* the *mayor* my *identification* card which is a *proof* of my identity; cf. akashi = proof, certificate; cf. shouko = evidence, proof, testimony

Shoumou 消耗 = exhaustion, consumption, waste; we *showed Moses* how to work efficiently, to reduce his *exhaustion* and his *waste* of resources; cf. related terms listed at shouhi

Shoumou suru 消耗する = to consume, use up or deplete; from shoumou = consumption; cf. related terms listed at riyou suru

Shounen 少年 = a boy; from shousuu = a few + nen = years; cf. shoujo = a girl; cf. related terms listed at otoko

Shounika 小児科 = pediatrics; I *showed* my *knee cap* to the doctor in the *pediatrics* clinic; cf. related terms listed at gankagaku

Shounin 商人 = merchant, shopkeeper; from shouhin = merchandise + nin = person; cf. related terms listed at gyousha

Shounin 承認 = approval, recognition, sanction; the *short ninja* indicated his *approval* of the mission; cf. kyoka = permission, approval; cf. zenin = approval

Shouninzuu 少人数 = few people; from shousuu = few + ninzuu = number of people

Shounou 笑納 = acceptance, as in goshounou kudasai = please accept (a gift); *show no fear* at the time of your *acceptance* of the traffic ticket; cf. related terms listed at shouchi

Shourai 将来 = future; I will *show* you my *rice* in the *future*; cf. mirai = future

Shourei 奨励 = encouragement or promotion; the *short racer* needed *encouragement*; cf. related terms listed at gekirei

Shouri 勝利 = victory, triumph; I will *show* the *wreath* that I received for my *victory*; cf. senshuken = championship; cf. yuushou = a victory

Shourou 鐘楼 = a bell tower; he wants to *show* the *Romans* how to build a *bell tower*

Shouryaku 省略 = abbreviation, omission; when I *showed Leah* the *Kool*-Aid, she tasted it and noticed the *omission* of sugar; cf. related terms listed at ryaku

Shousa 少佐 = a major; I *showed* my *saxophone* to the *major*; cf. related terms listed at shikan

Shousai 詳細 = details; please *show* the *scientists* the *details* of your experiment; cf. saibu = details

Shousan 賞賛 = exhaltation, praise; we *show Santa* our esteem by giving him *praise*

Shousan suru 賞賛する = to praise, admire, commend; from shousan = praise; cf. homeru = to praise, admire or speak well of; cf. zessan suru = to praise highly

Shousetsu 小説 = a novel; in his *novel* about the theatre, he *shows* how *sets* are built; cf. related terms listed at hon

Shoushi suru 焼死する = to burn to death; he *showed* us how the *sheep burned to death*; cf. related terms listed at moeru

Shoushin 昇進 = promotion (rising in rank); the *short Shinto* priest was due for *promotion*

Shoushitsu 焼失 = being destroyed by fire; she *showed* us the *sheets* that she rescued from her home as it was *being destroyed by fire*

Shoushitsu suru 焼失する = to be destroyed by fire; from shoushitsu = being destroyed by fire

Shoushou 小々 = a little, just a moment; this is a humble version of chotto = a little, just a moment; *she showed us the shore for just a moment*; cf. related terms listed at ittan

Shoushuu 消臭 = deodorization; *the Shougan's shoes required regular deodorization*

Shousoku 消息 = whereabouts, news; *the whereabouts of the Shougun's socks are unknown*; cf. yukue = whereabouts; cf. other related terms listed at jouhou

Shousuu 少数 = a few; *I showed the supervisor a few of my drawings*; cf. related terms listed at tarinai

Shoutai 招待 = an invitation; *show your tie if you want an invitation*; cf. shoutaijou = a written invitation

Shoutai suru 招待する = to invite; from shoutai = an invitation; cf. maneku = to invite, ask, or beckon; cf. sasou = to invite, entice, encite

Shoutaijou 招待状 = a written invitation; *show your tie, Joe, if you want a written invitation*; cf. shoutai = an invitation

Shouten 焦点 = focus or central issue; *I will show ten slides that highlight the central issue or focus of my talk*; cf. chuushin = center, core, focus; cf. chuushinteki = central

Shouten wo ateru 焦点を当てる = to focus on; from shouten = a focus + ateru = to hit

Shoutotsu 衝突 = a crash, collision or conflict; *the Shougun totes a heavy sword that he uses during conflicts, and we hear a crash when he drops it*

Shoutotsu kon 衝突痕 = an impact mark; from shoutotsu = a collision + konseki= a vestige

Shoutotsu suru 衝突する = to collide or conflict; from shoutotsu = a collision

Shoutou 消灯 = lights out time; *I was ready to show my toys, but it was lights out time*

Shouwa jidai 昭和時代 = the Showa era (1926-1989); *I will show you some washing machines from the Showa era*

Shouyo 賞与 = a reward or bonus; *I will show the yodeler his bonus*; cf. related terms listed at houbi

Shouyou 商用 = business; *in my business, I show yogurt samples to retailers*; cf. related terms listed at akinai

Shouyu しょう油 = soy sauce; *let's show the youths how to make soy sauce*

Shouzou 肖像 = a portrait; *let's show Zooey her portrait*; cf. shouzouga = a portrait

Shouzouga 肖像画 = a portrait; from shouzou = a portrait + kaiga = a painting

Shoyuu 所有 = ownership, possession; *we need to show our youth that they have an ownership in this country*; cf. hoyuu = possession, ownership

Shozoku suru 所属する = to belong to (e.g., to a group); *the short person drinking Zooey's Kool-Aid belongs to a Kool-Aid club*; cf. zoku suru = to belong to

Shucchou 出張 = a business trip; *he tried to shoot Margaret Cho during his business trip*; cf. related terms listed at ryokou

Shuchou 主張 = assertion, claim; *the shoes were chosen based on the claim that they were more durable*; cf. related terms listed at sengen

Shuchou suru 主張する = to advocate, assert or claim; from shuchou = assertion, claim; cf. tonaeru = to advocate or recite

Shudan 手段 = means, way; *I found a way to get shoes for the dancer*; cf. related terms listed at houhou

Shudouken 主導権 = leadership, domination; *he found some shoes behind a door in Kenya and wore them in his leadership role*; cf. sendou = guidance, leadership

Shufu 主婦 = housewife; *that housewife will shoot you in the foot*; cf. related terms listed at kanai

Shugi 主義 = doctrine, rule, principle; *I shoot geese in accordance with the doctrine that the strong eat the weak*; cf. houshin = policy, principle, direction; cf. kisoku = rules, regulations; cf. other related terms listed at rinen

Shugo 主語 = a subject (grammar); from shujin = master + tango = word; cf. buttai = an object or body (in physics); cf. doushi = a verb; cf. hinshi = part of speech; cf. kyakkan = an object (vs. subject); cf. meishi = a noun; cf. shutai = a core, nucleus, protagonist, subject (vs. object); cf. taishou = an object (of study, etc.)

Shugyou 修業 = training, apprenticeship; *the shoe salesmen were fed gyoza during their training*; cf. related terms listed at kunren

Shuin 朱印 = a red seal (calligraphy); *as I was about to apply a red seal to my work, the master started shooing me away*

Shujin 主人 = a master, owner, or husband; *the master bought new shoes and jeans*; cf. daimyou = a samurai lord; cf. danna = a husband or master; cf. dannasan = male customer, master; cf. otto = husband; cf. oyakata = a master or boss; cf. teishu = a husband or owner; cf. tono = a lord or master; cf. tonosama = daimyo, feudal lord; cf. yanushi = landlord or landlady

Shujinkou 主人公 = hero, heroine, protagonist, lead; *you will need to change your shoes, jeans and coat before you can play the lead in this drama*; cf. related terms listed at eiyuu

Shujutsu 手術 = surgery; *your shoe juts out, suggesting that you have a bunion requiring surgery*; cf. geka = surgery

Shuken 主権 = sovereignty; from shujin = master + ken'i = authority

Shukka 出荷 = shipping, shipment; *the shoes and calendars will be sent out in today's shipping*; cf. unsou = shipping, shipment, transportation

Shukkin 出勤 = work attendance; *while we are in work attendance, we are shucking corn*

Shukkin suru 出勤する = to go to work; from shukkin = work attendance; cf. related terms listed at shigoto suru

Shukudai 宿題 = homework, assignment; *my homework is to research shoes from Kuwait that stop on a dime*

Shukuga 祝賀 = a celebration; *during the celebration, we will shoot off fireworks and drink Kool-Aid in the garden*; cf. related terms listed at iwai

Shukugakai 祝賀会 = a celebration; from shukuga = celebration + kaigi = meeting; cf. related terms listed at iwai

Shukuhaku 宿泊 = lodging; *I can order shoes from Kuwait and Hawaiian Kool-Aid from my lodging*; cf. yado = an inn or lodging

Shukuhakusaki 宿泊先 = a lodging destination; from shukuhaku = lodging + saki = destination; cf. related terms listed at mokutekichi

Shukujitsu 祝日 = a national holiday; *I gave some shoes from Kuwait to the jittery superstar to wear on national holidays*; cf. related terms listed at yasumi

Shukujo 淑女 = a lady; *a lady bought shoes from Kuwait and joked that they made her taller*; cf. related terms listed at onna

Shukushou 縮小 = a reduction or cutback; *due to a reduction in income, I'm cutting back on shoes, Kool-Aid and shows*; cf. related terms listed at genshou

Shumi 趣味 = hobby, taste; *he shooed me away because he didn't like my hobby*; cf.

konomi = liking, taste

Shun 旬 = season (for specific products); this can also be pronounced jun; *the autumn clothes were shunned after the Fall season*

Shun no sakana 旬の魚 = fish in season; from shun = jun = season + sakana = fish

Shuniku 朱肉 = red ink used for seals; from shuin = a red seal + niku = meat; cf. related terms listed at bokujuu

Shunin 主任 = a foreman or director; *surely the ninja will serve as a foreman*; cf. related terms listed at shunou

Shunkan 瞬間 = moment; *I shun candy because it only provides a moment of satisfaction*; cf. ikkoku = a moment, an instant; cf. isshun = one moment or instant; cf. tsuka no ma = a moment

Shunkanteki ni 瞬間的に = momentarily; from shunkan = moment + teki = related to + -ni = a suffix that forms an adverb

Shunou 首脳 = a leader or top executive; *the shoes that Alfred Nobel wore marked him as a leader and a top executive*; cf. buchou = a division manager; cf. hanchou = a squad or group leader; cf. kachou = a section manager; cf. kaichou = chairman of the board; cf. kakarichou = an assistant section chief; cf. kanbu = an executive; cf. kichou = a pilot; cf. kouchou = a school principal; cf. koujouchou = a factory manager; cf. saibanchou = a presiding judge; cf. shachou = a company president; cf. shichou = a mayor; cf. shidousha = a leader or adviser; cf. shunin = a foreman or director; cf. taichou = a commanding officer; cf. tenchou = a store manager; cf. synonyms for prime minister listed at souri

Shunpu 春風 = a spring breeze (this can also be pronounced "harukaze," with the same meaning); *since he's focused on the spring breeze, he shuns the poor children who are gathering around*; cf. related terms listed at kaze

Shuppan 出帆 = sailing, departure; *I have to buy some shoes and pants before the sailing*; cf. related terms listed at koukai

Shuppan 出版 = publication; *this is a publication about shoes and pants*; cf. shinkan = a new publication; cf. shinkansho = a new publication

Shuppan suru 出版する = to publish; from shuppan = publication; cf. related terms listed at keisai suru

Shuppansha 出版社 = publisher; from shuppan = publication + kaisha = company

Shuppatsu 出発 = a departure, a start; *prior to your departure for school, your mother surely pats you on the back*

Shuppatsu suru 出発する = to depart or start out; from shuppatsu = a departure; cf. related terms listed at deru

Shuppi 出費 = expenditures; *I often shoot peas at my cats, and my expenditures from this are minimal*; cf. shouhi = consumption, expenditure

Shurui 種類 = variety, type; *the shoes that Louie wears are of several types*; cf. isshu no = a kind of, a type of; cf. kenshu = a dog breed; cf. kinokorui = several different kinds of mushrooms; cf. shinshu = a new species or variety; cf. seibutsushu = a species; cf. tenkei = type, model, representative

Shuryou 狩猟 = hunting; *when we go hunting, I'm careful not to shoot Pope Leo*; cf. kari = hunting or gathering

Shusai 主催 = sponsorship, promotion, hosting; *we have taken on the promotion and sponsorship of shoe science*; cf. hansoku = a sales promotion; cf. sokushin = propagation, promotion

Shusai 主宰 = supervision, chairmanship; *shoe science has advanced under the supervision of that researcher*

Shusanbutsu 主産物 = a main product; from shu = main, e.g., shujin = master; + sanbutsu = product; cf. related terms listed at sanbutsu

Shushi 趣旨 = purpose, gist, tenor; this can also be spelled 主旨); *the gist of the discussion was that we should put shoes on our sheep*; cf. youshi = the gist or main idea; cf. other related terms listed at mokuhyou

Shushoku 主食 = main food; from shu = main, e.g., shujin = master; + shokuji = meal; cf. related terms listed at tabemono

Shushou 首相 = prime minister; *I met the prime minister at a shoe show*; cf. related terms listed at souri

Shusseki suru 出席する = to attend or be present; *we bought new shoes for the selfish king to wear when he attends the wedding*; cf. deru = to come out, go out, leave, attend or participate; cf. nozomu = to attend (e.g., a function), to appear (e.g., in court), to deal with, to look out upon; cf. sanretsu suru = to attend or participate in

Shussekisha 出席者 = attendee; from shusseki suru = to attend + sha = person; cf. sankasha = a participant

Shussha suru 出社する = to go to one's office, attend work; *even though his shoes are shabby, he goes to the office*; cf. related terms listed at shigoto suru

Shusshin 出身 = birthplace, hometown, alma mater, alumnus; *at my alma mater, I majored in shoe shining*; cf. related terms listed at furusato

Shutai 主体 = core, nucleus, protagonist, subject (as opposed to object); *the protagonist, who is at the core of the movie, will shoot a tiger*; cf. chuuken = mainstay, nucleus, main body, middle standing, center field (baseball); cf. other related terms listed at shugo

Shutaiteki 主体的 = independent, responsible; *his shoes are always tied, and that techie is an independent and responsible employee*; cf. dokuritsu shite iru = is independent

Shutchou 出張 – see shucchou

Shuto 首都 = capital city; from shu = neck or chief, e.g., shushou = prime minister; + toshi = city; cf. shutoken = the capital city

Shutoken 首都圏 = the capital city, often Tokyo, typically denoting the portion within a 50-km radius around the center; from shuto = capital city + ken = a radius or circle; *Ken and Barbie hiked in a circle*; cf. shuto = capital city

Shutoku 取得 = acquisition, obtaining; *his shoes are totally cool, but his acquisition of them was difficult*

Shutoku suru 取得する = to acquire or obtain; from shutoku = acquisition, obtaining; cf. eru = to get, earn, understand, receive something undesirable (like a punishment); cf. kakutoku suru = to win or obtain; cf. kasegu = to earn (money); cf. te ni hairu = to obtain or get one's hands on; cf. te ni ireru = to obtain; cf. toriageru = to take up or feature, to adopt, to take away, to pick up; cf. toru = to get, take, or pick up

Shutsuen 出演 = a performance; from shutsu = to put out, e.g., gaishutsu suru = to go out; + enjiru = to perform; cf. engi = a performance (stage); cf. ensou = a musical performance; cf. ensoukai = concert or recital; cf. geinou = entertainment, performance; cf. kouen = a public performance

Shutsugan 出願 = an application; *he mentioned on his job application that he sometimes shoots gangsters*; cf. related terms listed at moushikomi

Shutsugen suru 出現する = to appear; *in the play, the assassin appears and shoots Genghis*; cf. related terms listed at arawareru

Shutsujou 出場 = appearance, participation (e.g., in a tournament); from shutsu = to go out, e.g., gaishutsu suru = to go out; + jou = place; cf. related terms listed at sanka

Shutsujou suru 出場する = to appear (e.g., on a stage), to participate (e.g., in a tournament); from shutsujou = appearance, participation; cf. related terms listed at kuwawaru

Shuu 周 = a lap or a round; *after walking a lap around the town, my shoes are worn out*

Shuu 週 = week; *those shoes lasted only a week*

Shuu 州 = a state or province; *I wore out my shoes walking through every state*

Shuubun 醜聞 = a scandal; *if you shoot Daniel Boone, that will cause a scandal*; cf. fushouji = scandal;

Shuuchaku 執着 = attachment, persistence; *he showed persistence in shooting at champagne bottles in Kuwait*

Shuuchi 周知 = well known; *as is well known, those shoes are cheap*

Shuuchuu suru 集中する = to concentrate; *when the shooter is choosing a target, she concentrates*; cf. sennen suru = to concentrate

Shuudan 集団 = a group; *the shooter turned out to be a dancer from our group*; cf. related terms listed at dantai

Shuudatsu 収奪 = plundering, exploitation; *I keep my shoes in my Datsun to prevent thieves from plundering them*; cf. related terms listed at kaihatsu

Shuugaku 就学 = attending school; *my parents gave me shoes and a gallon of Kool-Aid for attending school*; cf. related terms listed at nyuugaku

Shuugeki 襲撃 = an attack; *her attack consisted of throwing her shoes and her guest key at her husband*; cf. hangeki = a counterattack; cf. kougeki = attack, criticism; cf. totsugeki = assault, charge, attack

Shuugeki suru 襲撃する = to attack; from shuugeki = an attack; cf. related terms listed at osou

Shuugou suru 集合する = to gather or assemble; *the top shooters in the golf club assembled*; cf. atsumaru = to meet or assemble; cf. muragaru = to flock or throng; cf. sorou = to be complete, to be equal, to be the same, to assemble, to have everything at one's disposal

Shuugyou 就業 = employment; *if I find employment, I will be able to buy new shoes and eat more gyoza*; cf. shuushoku = employment

Shuugyouin 就業員 = an employee; from shuugyou = employment + in = a group member; cf. related terms listed at seishain

Shuuhen 周辺 = neighborhood, vicinity; *I throw shoes at the hens in this vicinity*; cf. related terms listed at fukin

Shuui 周囲 = surroundings; *I shoo eagles away if they appear in my surroundings*; cf. kankyou = environment, surroundings; cf. mawari = surrounding

Shuujin 囚人 = a prisoner; *if you shoot the genius, we will make you our prisoner*; cf. related terms listed at horyo

Shuujitsu 終日 = all day, for a whole day; *the shoes of the jittery superstar sat outside his room for a whole day*

Shuukaku 収穫 = harvest, crop; *put on your shoes and help Karl the Kool-Aid vendor with the harvest*; cf. related terms listed at sakumotsu

Shuukaku suru 収穫する = to harvest; from shuukaku = harvest, crop; cf. saishu suru = to pick or gather; cf. toriireru = to harvest, take in, adopt, incorporate

Shuukan 習慣 = a custom or habit; *I have a custom of keeping my shoes in a can*; cf. akuheki = a bad habit; cf. akushuu = a bad habit, evil practice; cf. -heki = a habit or mannerism; cf. kanshuu = a usual custom; cf. kuse = a habit or characteristic; cf. waruguse = a bad habit

Shuukanshi 週刊誌 = weekly magazine; *a shoe can shield your foot better than a weekly magazine*; cf. related terms listed at zasshi

Shuukou 舟航 = sailing, navigation; *when I'm sailing, my shoes can get cold*

Shuukyou 宗教 = a religion; *the shoes I bought in Kyouto are required by my religion*; cf. mune = a religion or sect; cf. shinkou = a belief or religion; cf. zenshuu = Zen Buddhism

Shuukyoukan 宗教感 = religious feelings; from shuukyou = religion + kanjiru = to feel; cf. shuukyoushin = piety, religious feeling

Shuukyoushin 宗教心 = piety, religious feeling; from shuukyou = religion + shin = heart or mind; cf. shuukyoukan = religious feelings

Shuumatsu 週末 = weekend; *on the weekend, we take off our shoes and sit on mats*; cf. getsumatsu = end of a month; cf. kimatsu = end of a term (semester); cf. nenmatsu = end of a year

Shuunen 周年 = an anniversary; from shuu = lap, e.g., isshuu = one lap; + nen = year; cf. isshuuki = the first anniversary of a death; cf. ki = a death anniversary, used as a suffix; cf. shichikaiki = the 7th anniversary of a death

Shuunin 就任 = inauguration, assumption of office; from shuushoku suru = to find employment + ninmu = duty

Shuunyuu 収入 = income; *people shun you if your income is low*; cf. related terms listed at chin

Shuuri 修理 = repairs; *that shoe repair shop does all of the repairs on my shoes*; cf. shuuzen = a repair

Shuuri suru 修理する = to repair; from shuuri = repairs; cf. kyousei suru = to correct; cf. naosu = to correct or repair; cf. tsukurou = to mend or repair

Shuuritsudai 州立大 = state university; from shuu = large area or state, e.g., Kyuushuu = an island in Japan; + ritsudai = private university; cf. related terms listed at daigaku

Shuuroku 収録 = compilation or recording; *the reason that I've been slow to complete the compilation and recording is that my shoe has a rock in it*; cf. rokuon = a sound recording

Shuuryou 終了 = ending, termination; *if you shoot Pope Leo, that will cause a termination of our relationship*

Shuuryou suru 終了する = to finish or end (intransitive); from shuuryou = a termination; cf. related terms listed at owaru

Shuusai 秀才 = an outstanding student or an able person; *if you shoot the scientist, you will hurt an outstanding student and an able person*; cf. related terms listed at gakusei

Shuuseki 集積 = accumulation; *the shoes of the selfish king were covered by an accumulation of mud*; cf. related terms listed at shuushuu

Shuushi 終始 = beginning and ending, from beginning to end; *these shoes were worn by sheep from the beginning of the race to the end*; cf. related terms listed at hajime; cf. related terms listed at hajime ni

Shuushoku 就職 = employment; *when your shoes shock you, they are telling you to find employment*; cf. shuugyou = employment

Shuushoku suru 就職する = to find employment; from shuushoku = employment; cf. related terms listed at shigoto suru

Shuushou 愁傷 = grief, sorrow; *I feel sorrow after my shoe designs were rejected at the shoe show*; cf. related terms listed at kanashimi

Shuushuu 収集 = a collection; *the shooter's shoes were combined into a collection*; cf. ruiseki = an accumulation; cf. saishuu = a collection; cf. shashinshuu = a collection of photos, a photo album; cf. shuuseki = accumulation; cf. taiseki = a pile or accumulation; cf. zousho = a book collection or library

Shuutoku 習得 = learning, acquisition, mastery; *he is working on the acquisition of knowledge about shoes in the Tokugawa era*

Shuutoku suru 習得する = to master a subject or skill; from shuutoku = learning; cf. related terms listed at osaeru

Shuuyou suru 収容する = to accommodate or take in; *when he saw the shooting star, the yogi decided to accomodate us*; cf. toriireru = to harvest, take in, adopt, incorporate

Shuuzen 修繕 = a repair; *when I took off my shoes at the Zen center, I saw that they were in need of repair*; cf. shuuri = repairs

Shuwa 手話 = sign language; from shu = hand, e.g., akushu = a handshake; + kaiwa = conversation

Shuyou 主要 = chief, major; *the shoes that the yogi sold were his major source of income*; cf. related terms listed at omo na

Shuyou 腫瘍 = a tumor; *the shoe of the yogi was modified to accommodate the tumor on his foot*

Shuzei 酒税 = a liquor tax; from shu = alcohol, e.g., nihonshu = Japanese sake; + zeikin = a tax; cf. related terms listed at zeikin

Shuzeihou 酒税法 = a liquor tax law; from shuzei = a liquor tax + houritsu = a law

Shuzou 酒造 = sake brewing; *I bought some shoes in the Canal Zone, and then I learned sake brewing*; cf. jouzou = brewing, distilling

Shuzoujou 酒造場 – see shuzousho

Shuzousho 酒造所 = a brewery, distillery (usually pronounced shuzoujou); from shuzou = sake brewing; + basho = place; cf. tsukurizakaya = a sake brewery;

Soaku na 粗悪な = crude, coarse, inferior; *soil accumulates in this crude hotel*; cf. related terms listed at somatsu

Soba そば = buckwheat noodles; *these buckwheat noodles aren't so bad*; cf. men = noodles; cf. raamen = Chinese-style noodles in broth; cf. soumen = thin white noodles; cf. tsukemen = cold Chinese noodles with soup for dipping; cf. udon = Japanese noodles; cf. other related terms listed at ryouri

Soba 側 = neighborhood, vicinity, usually written そば; *a socialist barber works in this vicinity*; cf. related terms listed at fukin

Soba ni 側に = close to, beside; from soba = vicinity + ni = at; cf. related terms listed at chikai

Sobieru そびえる = to tower over; *the sobieto (Soviet) ruins towered over us*

Sobieto renpou ソビエト連邦 = the Soviet Union; from sobieto = Soviet + renpou = a federation

Sobo 祖母 = grandmother; *my grandmother is so bold*; cf. related terms listed at sofubo

Soboku na 素朴な = simple, naïve, unpretentious; *the Soviet boat's cooling system was simple*

Sobokusa 素朴さ = simplicity, naivete; from soboku = simple + sa = a suffix that makes a noun from another words

Sobou 粗暴 = wild, rude, violent, hard; *those soldiers are bowling in a wild, rude and violent way*; cf. related terms listed at ranbou and at shikkei

Socchi そっち – see sochira

Socchinoke そっちのけ = to ignore one thing for another; *the <u>so</u>da is <u>cheap</u>, and they have <u>no</u> <u>ketchup</u>, so I <u>ignore</u> the absence of ketchup and drink the soda*; cf. related terms listed at mushi suru

Socchoku 率直 = frank, candid, straightforward; *the <u>so</u>ldier <u>choked</u> up after hearing the <u>candid</u> story*; cf. related terms listed at shoujiki

Sochi 措置 = an action; *he <u>sold</u> <u>cheese</u>, among other <u>actions</u>*; cf. souchi = equipment

Sochira そちら = you, there; *the <u>sober</u> <u>cheerful</u> <u>rabbit</u> is <u>there</u>*

Sodateru 育てる = to bring up, raise or nurture; *as I <u>bring up</u> my kids, I tell them that <u>soda</u> is <u>terrible</u> and will <u>ruin</u> their teeth*; cf. related terms listed at yashinau

Sodatsu 育つ = to grow up or be brought up; *I was <u>brought up</u> to put <u>soda</u> in my <u>tsoup</u> (soup)*; cf. related terms listed at haeru

Sode 袖 = a sleeve; *that white coat had long <u>sleeves</u>, and we <u>sold</u> it to a <u>dentist</u>*; cf. hansode = short sleeves; cf. nagasode = a long-sleeved garment

Soeru 添える = to attach to, to garnish a dish, to help or support; *in the <u>So</u>viet Union, <u>erudite</u> people <u>supported</u> the less educated ones*; cf. haru = to paste, stick or attach; cf. tsukeru = to attach, install, and many other meanings; cf. other related terms listed at tasukeru

Sofu 祖父 = grandfather; *my <u>grandfather</u> eats <u>soul</u> <u>food</u>*; cf. related terms listed at sofubo

Sofubo 祖父母 = grandparents; *my <u>grandparents</u> eat <u>soul</u> <u>food</u> in their <u>boat</u>*; cf. obaasan = a grandmother, an old lady; cf. ojiisan = grandfather, old man; cf. sobo = grandmother; cf. sofu = grandfather

Sogai 阻害 = an obstruction or inhibition; *the <u>So</u>viet <u>guy</u> put <u>obstructions</u> in our path*; cf. related terms listed at shougai

Sogu 削ぐ = to shave off, slice, diminish or spoil; *when he <u>shaved</u> all his hair, he looked <u>so</u> <u>goofy</u>, and he seemed <u>diminished</u>*; cf. related terms listed at kiru and at kizutsukeru

Sokkoku 即刻 = immediately; *he <u>sold</u> me some <u>Coke</u> <u>immediately</u>*; cf. kyuu ni = swiftly, suddenly, immediately; cf. sassa to = immediately, promptly; cf. sassoku = immediately, at once; cf. shikyuu = immediately, urgently; cf. sokuza ni = immediately; cf. tadachi ni = immediately

Sokkuri そっくり = just like, entirely; *the <u>So</u>viet <u>curry</u> was <u>identical</u> to the Pakistani curry*

Soko そこ = there; *the <u>so</u>ldier's <u>cola</u> is <u>there</u>*

Soko 底 = the bottom; *I <u>sold</u> my <u>coal</u> when the price reached the <u>bottom</u>*; cf. donzoko = the depths; cf. kaitei = the bottom of the sea

Sokoku 祖国 = one's native country; from so = ancestral, e.g., sofu = grandfather; + koku = country; cf. bokoku = one's native country; cf. wagakuni = one's country; cf. other related terms listed at kuni

Sokonau 損なう = to injure, mar or spoil, or (if used as a suffix) to fail to do something; *that <u>So</u>mali <u>cobra</u> is <u>now</u> about to <u>injure</u> us; the <u>So</u>mali <u>cobra</u> is <u>now</u> <u>failing</u> to catch a mouse*; cf. related terms listed at kizutsukeru

Sokoneru 損ねる = to injure or offend; *when I <u>sold</u> <u>coal</u> from my <u>nephew's</u> <u>room</u>, I <u>offended</u> him*; cf. related terms listed at kizutsukeru

Sokubaku 束縛 = a restraint, restriction, or confinement; *there are <u>restrictions</u> on the time you may spend <u>soak</u>ing your <u>back</u> in our hot springs, and you are subject to <u>confinement</u> if you exceed them*; cf. related terms listed at genkai

Sokudo 速度 = speed; *the <u>So</u>viets used <u>Kool</u>-Aid and <u>doughnuts</u> to entice their athletes to greater <u>speed</u>*; cf. jisoku = speed

Sokujitsu 即日 = the same day; *after I soaked the jittery superstar, he fired me the same day*; cf. related terms listed at yokujitsu

Sokumen 側面 = a side or aspect; *that wave soaked the men on the right side of the boat*; cf. related terms listed at men

Sokusai 息災 = good health; *as I soak in the tub, I sigh and wish for good health*; cf. related terms listed at kenkou

Sokushin 促進 = propagation, promotion; *I soaked my shingles in a water-repellant coating after I saw a promotion for it*; cf. hansoku = a sales promotion; cf. shusai = sponsorship, promotion, hosting

Sokushin suru 促進する = to promote or propagate; from sokushin = propagation, promotion; cf. hiromeru = to publicize, propagate, spread

Sokutatsu 速達 = express, special delivery; *after I accidentally soaked my tattered suit, I sent it to the dry cleaners by express mail*

Sokutei suru 測定する = to measure; *the rain soaked the tailor, but he kept on measuring his cloth*; cf. related terms listed at hakaru

Sokuza ni 即座に = immediately; *if you soak Zach's knee, he will dry it immediately*; cf. related terms listed at sokkoku

Somaru 染まる = to be dyed or stained, to be influenced (intransitive); *the Somali carpet in the room was dyed black*; cf. someru = to dye (transitive)

Somatsu na 粗末な = cheap, crude, shabby; *the soldiers' mats were cheap and shabby*; cf. arai = coarse, rugged; cf. furyou = delinquent, poor condition; cf. soaku = crude, coarse, inferior

Someru 染める = to dye; the transitive form of somaru = to be dyed

Son 損 = a loss; an abbreviation of songai = harm, loss; cf. soushitsu = loss

Son 村 = a village, used as a word component; *my son lives in that village*

Sonae 備え = preparation, provision; from sonaeru = to prepare, to equip with

Sonaeru 備える = to equip with, to prepare; *when sonar was introduced, erudite people made sure that warships were equipped with it, as they prepared for war*; cf. related terms listed at toritsukeru

Sonaetsukeru 備え付ける = to provide, equip, install; from sonaeru = to be equip with + tsukeru = to attach; cf. related terms listed at kyoukyuu suru and toritsukeru

Sonawaru 備わる = to be furnished, equipped or endowed with; the intransitive form of sonaeru = to equip with; cf. megumareru = to be endowed with; cf. yuu suru = to own or be endowed with

Sonchou suru 尊重する = to respect or value; *the Sony corporation chose to value its employees*; cf. related terms listed at sonkei suru

Songai 損害 = harm, loss; *the Sony guy who came to fix our TV caused harm*; cf. related terms listed at sawari and at shonshitsu

Sonkei 尊敬 = respect; *the Sony corporation gives its employees cakes to show respect*; cf. ikei = awe and respect, reverence; cf. keii = respect

Sonkei suru 尊敬する = to respect; from sonkei = respect; cf. hyouka suru = to value, to appreciate; cf. keii wo hyousu = to pay respect; cf. keii wo shimesu = to show respect; cf. sonchou suru = to respect or value; cf. toutobu = to respect or value; cf. uyamau = to respect or venerate

Sonna そんな = that kind of, such, that; *a sonata is that kind of musical piece*; cf. related terms listed at konna

Sono その = that, those; *that is a sober Norwegian*

Sono mama そのまま = as it is or was,

without change; from sono = that + mama = as is

Sono uchi そのうち = before long, soon, sooner or later; from sono = that + uchi = while

Sono ue その上 = furthermore, on top of; from sono = that + ue = above; cf. related terms listed at sara ni

Sonota その他 = otherwise, besides, in addition, the rest; **Note:** this is often pronounced sono hoka; from sono = that + ta = others, e.g., ta'nin = other people; cf. ni kuwaete = in addition; cf. oyobi = and, in addition; cf. sore ni = besides, moreover

Sonshitsu 損失 = loss; *the damage to Sony's spreadsheets from the hack resulted in a significant loss*; cf. higai = damage or loss; cf. songai = harm, loss

Sonshou 損傷 = damage or injury; *my son showed me his injury*; cf. related terms listed at sawari

Sonzai 存在 = existence, presence; *Sony opened an office in Zaire (former name of the Congo) in order to have a presence there*; cf. kehai = indication, sign, presence

Sonzai suru 存在する = to exist; from sonzai = existence; cf. related terms listed at aru

Sonzoku 存続 = duration, continuance; *that song about Zooey's Kool-Aid has a short duration*; cf. related terms listed at jikan

Sonzoku suru 存続する = to continue; from sonzoku = continuance

Sooseeji ソーセージ = sausage

Sora 空 = sky, weather; *the solitary rabbit looked up at the sky*; cf. chuu = space or sky; cf. joukuu = the sky, upper air; cf. ten = heavens, sky; cf. uchuu = universe, cosmos, space; cf. yozora = night sky

Sorasu 逸らす = to dodge, to turn away; *we sold the ram from Sudan and turned away before it was eaten*

Soratobu enban 空飛ぶ円盤 = flying saucer; from sora = sky + tobu = to fly + en = round; *ichien (one yen) is round*; + ban = shallow bowl; *I mash bananas in this shallow bowl*

Sore それ = that; *that is so red*

Sore de それで = and, because of that; from sore = that + de = and (or because of)

Sore de wa それでは = well then, in that case; from sore = that + de = because of + wa = as for; cf. sore ja = well then, in that case; cf. sore nara = in that case; cf. sureba = if so, in that case

Sore ja それじゃ – see sore dewa

Sore kara それから = and then, after that; from sore = that + kara = after; cf. related terms listed at irai and at soshite

Sore nara それなら = in that case; from sore = that + nara = in that case; cf. related terms listed at sore de wa

Sore ni それに = besides, moreover; *besides your sore red knee, did you sustain other injuries?* cf. related terms listed at oyobi and at sonota

Sore ni shitemo それにしても (this can be abbreviated as ni shitemo) = nevertheless, at any rate; from sore ni = besides + shitemo = doing even; cf. related terms listed at kakawarazu

Soredokoro それどころ = not that much, used before a negative verb; *if you ask what proportion of soldiers from the Red Army own Corollas, I would say not that much*

Soredokoroka それどころか = on the contrary; *on the contrary, the typical soldier from the Red Army eats his doughnuts in a Corolla car*; cf. related terms listed at dokoroka

Soren ソ連 = the Soviet Union; from sobieto = Soviet + rengou = an alliance

Sorera それら = those; from sore = that + ra

= a suffix that makes the preceding pronoun plural

Soretomo それとも = or; from sore = that + to = if + mo = also; cf. ka = or; cf. mata wa = or, either … or; cf. nari = or, or something

Sorezore それぞれ = each, respectively, severally; from sore = that + zore = sore = that; cf. related terms listed at goto ni

Sorikaeru 反り返る = to bend back or warp; *after you bent back my finger, I was sorry that I called you erudite*

Soroban 算盤 = an abacus; *in my sorrow after the bank fired me, I took up the abacus*

Soroeru 揃える = to arrange, prepare, put in order, make uniform; *the sorrowful erudite guy arranges things*; cf. seiri suru = to arrange, put in order; cf. totonoeru = to put in order, to prepare

Sorosoro そろそろ = before long, slowly, quietly, gradually; *the Soviet robot moved slowly*; cf. related terms listed at mamonaku and at shidai ni

Sorou 揃う = to be complete, to be equal, to be the same, to assemble, to have everything at one's disposal; *when my family assembles, we are equal, but we feel sorrow that we are poor*; cf. related terms listed at shuugou suru

Soryasou da そりゃそうだ = sore wa sou da = as for that, it's so = of course it's true

Sosei suru 蘇生する = to revive (transitive); *the Soviet sailor revived his comrade*; cf. okosu = to revive or raise up; cf. yomigaeru = to revive or raise from the dead

Sosen 祖先 = an ancestor; *my ancestors were so sensitive to social class*; cf. related terms listed at senzo

Soshi suru 阻止する = to obstruct or hinder; *the solo sheep hindered our passage*; cf. samatageru = to hinder or obstruct; cf. other related terms listed at shimeru

Soshiki 組織 = an organization; *the people in that organization are so chic*; cf. kessei = an organization or formation; cf. kyoukai = an association or organization; cf. other related terms listed at dantai

Soshite そして = and, and then; *he sold sheets and textiles, and then he retired*; cf. shi = and, used at the end of a clause, implying an explanation; cf. sore kara = and then, after that; cf. to = and, with, if, when

Soshou 訴訟 = a lawsuit; *that sordid show led to a lawsuit*

Sosogu 注ぐ = to pour, to devote; *when you pour juice and spill it, the carpet gets so soggy and gooey*; cf. kakeru = to pour or sprinkle onto, among many other meanings; cf. nagasu = to flush, drain, pour, wash away

Sosuu 素数 = prime number; *the Soviet superintendent was researching prime numbers;* cf. related terms listed at bangou

Soto 外 = exterior, outside, outdoors; *why don't you soak your toes outside?* cf. gai = outside, used as a word component; cf. gaibu = the outside world, exterior; cf. okugai = outdoors; cf. sotogawa = the outside

Sotogawa 外側 = the outside; from soto = outside + gawa = side; cf. related terms listed at soto

Sotsugyou 卒業 = graduation; *sotted Superman feasted on gyoza after his graduation*

Sotsugyousei 卒業生 = a graduate; from sotsugyou = graduation + sei = a person; cf. gakushi = a university graduate

Sotto そっと = softly, gently, quietly; this reminds us of sotto voce (Italian), referring to soft music; cf. fuwari = softly, gently, lightly; cf. shitoshito = gently (raining)

Sou そう = like that, what you just mentioned; *a soldier is like that*

Sou そう = so, yes, seems to be (when used as a suffix); *your solar panel seems to work, and I admit that you said so*; cf. related terms listed at -mitai

Sou 僧 = a monk or priest; *that monk is usually sober*; cf. related terms listed at juushoku

Sou 層 = a layer, stratum, social class, story (of a building); *socialites belong to a privileged social class*; cf. bumon = category, class, section; cf. kaikyuu = class, rank, caste; cf. kyuu = class, level, grade

Sou 沿う = to run along, to follow a plan; *the soldiers followed the plan*; cf. related terms listed at tadoru

Soubetsukai 送別会 = farewell party; *sober Betsy kindly came to my farewell party*

Soubi 装備 = equipment; *the soda and beer were dispensed by some equipment*; cf. setsubi = equipment, facility; cf. shitsetsu = equipment, facility; cf. related terms listed at souchi

Souchi 装置 = equipment, device; *he sold cheap equipment*; cf. sochi = an action; cf. dougu = a tool, appliance, utensil; cf. kigu = utensil, apparatus, device; cf. kougu = a tool; cf. setsubi = equipment, facility; cf. shitsetsu = equipment, facility; cf. soubi = equipment

Souchou 早朝 = early morning; *the soldiers chose to attack in the early morning*; cf. related terms listed at asa

Soudai 壮大 = magnificent, imposing; *the Soviet diver was magnificent*; cf. related terms listed at idai

Soudan 相談 = consultation, advice; *I drank soda with a dancer while we engaged in consultation*; cf. chuukoku = advice or admonition; cf. kaidan = a consultation, conversation or conference; cf. kankoku = recommendation, advice; cf. susume = advice, suggestion

Soudanjo 相談所 = a consultation office or bureau; from soudan = consultation + jo = place; cf. related terms listed at kyoku

Sougaku 総額 = total amount; *I sold a gallon of Kool-Aid for a total amount of $5*; cf. goukei = sum, total

Sougen 草原 = grasslands, prairie, meadow; *when he was sober, Genghis would ride on the prairie*

Sougi 葬儀 = a funeral; *the soldier played his guitar at the funeral*; cf. soushiki = a funeral

Sougo 相互 = mutual, reciprocal; *the soldiers and the ghosts kept a reciprocal watch on each other*; cf. related terms listed at tagai

Sougo ni 相互に = mutually; from sougo = each other, mutuality + -ni = a suffix that forms an adverb; cf. tagai ni = mutually

Souguu suru 遭遇する = to encounter; *the soldier's goose encountered a fox*; cf. related terms listed at deau

Sougyou 創業 = establishment (e.g., of a business); *after the establishment of that restaurant, he sold gyoza*; cf. secchi = establishment, installation

Souji 掃除 = cleaning; *using soap and wearing my jeans, I do cleaning*; cf. seisou = cleaning

Souji suru 掃除する = to clean; from souji = cleaning; cf. kiyomeru = to purify or cleanse

Soujiki 掃除機 = vacuum cleaner; from souji = cleaning + kikai = machine

Soujite 総じて = in general, on the whole; *sombreros and jeans are accepted attire in Texas, in general*; cf. futsuu = ordinary, usual, general, average

Soujuu 操縦 = management, handling, operation; *he is charged with the management and handling of the soprano's jewels*; cf. taiou = handling, treatment; cf.

other related terms listed at kanri and at sousa

Soujuu suru 操縦する = to fly (a plane), to manage, handle or operate; from soujuu = management, handling, operation; cf. sousa suru = to operate (a machine); cf. ugokasu = to operate (a machine); cf. un'ei suru = to manage or operate

Soujuushi 操縦士 = a pilot; *the orange that the pilot ate was so juushii (juicy)*; cf. kichou = a pilot

Soujuushitsu 操縦室 = a cockpit or control room; from soujuu = operation + shitsu = a room

Soukai 爽快 = refreshing, exhilarating; *the soap that the Kaiser gave me has a refreshing smell*; cf. sugasugashii = refreshing

Soukai 総会 = general meeting; from soujite = in general + kaigi = meeting; cf. related terms listed at kaigi

Soukan na 壮観な = spectacular, magnificent; *that's a magnificent soda can*; cf. related terms listed at idai

Soukatsu suru 総括する = to generalize or summarize; *to summarize, she sold cats for a living*; cf. matomeru = to conclude or settle, bundle together, compile, summarize

Souke 宗家 = head of family, originator; *the sober Kennedy is the head of the family*

Souko 倉庫 = a warehouse; *the soldiers' coats were kept in a warehouse*; cf. kokusou = a granary; cf. kura = a storehouse

Soukou 草稿 = a draft or manuscript; *it was so cold, we burned our manuscripts for fuel*; cf. related terms listed at sengen

Soukou 走行 = running a wheeled vehicle; from sou = to run; *people used to run in the Soviet Union*; + kou = to go, e.g., ryokou = trip

Soumen そうめん = thin white noodles; *the Soviet men ate white noodles*; cf. related terms listed at soba

Sounan 遭難 = accident, disaster, being stranded; *our sober nanny prevented a disaster*; cf. related terms listed at saigai

Sounyuu suru 挿入する = to insert; *a soldier from Nyuuyooku (New York) inserted himself into the conversation about the band Sonic Youth*; cf. related terms listed at mochikomu

Souon 騒音 = noise; *the Soviet owner of that car said that it makes very little noise*; cf. zatsuon = noise

Souri 総理 = prime minister; *the prime minister was targeted by a Soviet ring of spies*; cf. daijin = a Cabinet minister; cf. souridaijin = prime minister; cf. shushou = prime minister; cf. synonyms for leader listed at shunou

Souridaijin 総理大臣 = prime minister; *the prime minister was sorry that he had dyed his jean*; cf. related terms listed at souri

Souritsu suru 創立する = to establish; *the soldiers received a written suggestion to establish a base*; cf. kizuku = to establish, build; cf. moukeru = to establish or set up; cf. sousetsu suru = to establish

Souryo 僧侶 = a monk or priest; *when sober, Pope Leo behaved like a good monk*; cf. related terms listed at juushoku

Souryou 送料 = postage, shipping charges; *we sold Pope Leo a Bible, and we will pay for the postage*

Sousa 捜査 = a police investigation; *I was so sad to learn of the police investigation*; cf. related terms listed at kensa

Sousa 操作 = operation (of a machine); *I'm so sad that I have to waste my time on the operation of this machine*; cf. sadou = operation, functioning; cf. soujuu = management, handling, operation; cf. unkou = operation, revolution (planet), transportation; cf. unten = operation of a car or machinery

Sousa suru 操作する = to operate (a machine); from sousa = operation; cf. soujuu suru = to operate or handle; cf. ugokasu = to operate (a machine); cf. unei suru = to manage or operate; cf. unten suru = to drive a car or operate a machine

Sousakan 捜査官 = a police investigator; from sousa = a police investigation + kan = government official, e.g., keikan = a police officer; cf. related terms listed at keiji

Sousaku 捜索 = an investigation or search; *the soldier took my sack and conducted a search of it*; cf. related terms listed at kensa

Sousaku suru 捜索する = to investigate or search; from sousaku = an investigation or search; cf. ginmi suru = to check in detail, to examine; cf. kensaku suru = to look up (e.g., a word in a dictionary), to retrieve (e.g., data), to search for; cf. sagasu = to look for or search; cf. shiraberu = to investigate, check, look up, consult; cf. tankyuu suru = to pursue or search for

Sousetsu suru 創設する = to found, establish; from souzou = creation + shisetsu = facility or institution; cf. kizuku = to establish, build; cf. moukeru = to establish or set up; cf. souritsu suru = to establish

Sousha 奏者 = an instrumentalist or player; from ensou = a musical performance + sha = a person

Soushiki 葬式 = a funeral; *a sophisticated Shiite king attended the funeral*; cf. sougi = a funeral

Soushitsu 喪失 = a loss; *I took a loss when I sold my sheets*; cf. son = disadvantage, loss, damage

Sousho 草書 = cursive or "grass" script; from sou = grass, e.g., sougen = grasslands; + sho = a document; cf. related terms listed at kaisho

Soushoku 草食 = plant-eating, herbivorous; from sougen = grasslands + shokuji = meal

Soushoku 装飾 = decoration; *I was so shocked when the decoration exploded*; cf. kazaritsuke = decoration, arrangement

Soutoku 総督 = governor general, governor, viceroy; *the governor general thought that his soldiers were totally cool*

Soutou 相当 = appropriate, considerable, very large; *I have considerable pain from my sore toe*; cf. related terms listed at tekitou

Soutousuu 相当する = a considerable number; from soutou = considerable + suuji = numeral; cf. related terms listed at bangou

Souzoku 相続 = succession, inheritance; *when I lived in the Soviet zone, Kool-Aid was the only inheritance that I could expect*; cf. isan = inheritance, legacy, heritage

Souzoku suru 相続する = to inherit; from souzoku = succession, inheritance; cf. related terms listed at tsugu

Souzou 創造 = creation; *in the Soviet zone, scientists were assigned the creation of new weapons*; cf. related terms listed at sakuhin

Souzou 想像 = imagination; *most people who lived in the Soviet zone could get rich only in their imaginations*; cf. kasou = imagination, supposition, virtual

Souzoujou no 想像上の = imaginary; from souzou = imagination + jou = above, e.g., joukuu = the sky

Souzouryoku 想像力 = powers of imagination; from souzou = imagination + ryoku = power

Souzoushii 騒々しい = noisy; *a solo (isolated) zou (elephant) was living with some Shiites, and it was very noisy*; cf. urusai = noisy, annoying

Sozai 素材 = material, ingredient; *the soap in*

Zaire (former name of the Congo) had some unusual ingredients; cf. seibun = ingredient; cf. zairyou = ingredient

Sozei 租税 = taxation; *this sofa is zany, but it's subject to taxation*

Su 巣 = nest, animal habitat, cobweb, honeycomb, den; *Superman protected the nest*; cf. horaana = cave, den

Su 酢 = vinegar; *he puts vinegar in his soup*; cf. komezu = rice vinegar

Subarashii 素晴らしい = wonderful, superb, excellent; *the sub's Arab captain was a Shiite, and he was wonderful*; cf. related terms listed at idai and also at joutou

Subayai 素早い = nimble, speedy; *subatomic particles in yaks eating ice are speedy and nimble fast*; cf. related terms listed at hayai

Subeki すべき = an abbreviation of suru beki = should do; from suru = to do + beki = should

Suberu 滑る = to slide or slip, to fail an exam; *when submarines erupt from under the water, fish slide off the sides*; cf. related terms listed at hazureru

Subesube suru すべすべする = to feel smooth and sleek; from suberu = to slide

Subete 全て = everything, all, the whole, entirely; *the subeditor tells me everything*; cf. related terms listed at banji

Sude 素手 = barehanded; *since Superman cannot acquire infections, Superman's dentist works barehanded*

Sude ni すでに = already, too late; this is sometimes spelled 既に; *Superman and the dentist's niece already got married*; cf. mou = already, before long, another, more

Sue 末 = tip, end, future; *in the end, I bought a suede jacket*; cf. saki = tip, point, future, former, destination, end, ahead; cf. other related terms listed at owari

Suekko 末っ子 = the youngest child; *on the Suez Canal, cola is served only to the youngest children*; cf. related terms listed at kodomo

Sueru 据える = to place or set up; *Suez Canal rules require ship captains to place flags on their vessels*; cf. related terms listed at oku

Sugasugashii すがすがしい = refreshing; *if you add sugar and sugar to their tea, the Shiites will find it refreshing*; cf. soukai = refreshing, exhilarating

Sugata 姿 = figure, shape, condition; *the sugar in that tavern is in the shape of cubes*; cf. related terms listed at keisei

Sugi 杉 = Japanese cedar tree; *Superman's geese gathered under some Japanese cedar trees*

Sugiru 過ぎる = to exceed, to be too much, to pass through, often used as a suffix; *after the supervisor's gears were ruined, he couldn't exceed ten miles per hour*; cf. kosu = to exceed, pass, cross, move (residence); cf. oosugiru = to be too much;

Sugoi すごい = great, wonderful, terrific, terrible; this is sometimes spelled 凄い; *Superman said that the goy (Gentile) he met was terrific*; cf. related terms listed at idai and at inshouteki

Sugoku すごく = very, awfully; the adverbial form of sugoi = great, wonderful, terrific; cf. related terms listed at ooi ni

Sugoshikata 過ごし方 = a way of spending time; from sugosu = to spend + kata = method

Sugosu 過ごす = to spend or pass time; *the Sudanese golfer and Sue spend time together*; cf. kakeru = to expend or spend (e.g., time, money, love); cf. okuru = to spend time, live one's life, send a thing, escort a person; cf. tsuiyasu = to spend time or money

Sugu (ni) すぐ(に) = soon, immediately, very (e.g., sugusoba = very near); this can also be spelled 直ぐに; *Superman's goose will arrive soon*; cf. related terms listed at mamonaku

Sugureru 優れる = to excell; *Superman's goofy red rooster excells at crowing*; cf. hiideru = to excell or surpass

Sugureta 優れた = excellent; from sugureru = to excell; cf. related terms listed at joutou

Sugusoba すぐそば = very near; from sugu = very + soba = vicinity; cf. related terms listed at chikai

Suiatsu 水圧 = water pressure; *the Swede staying at Superman's house complained about the water pressure*; cf. related terms listed at atsuryoku

Suibun 水分 = moisture, water; from sui = water, e.g., suiei = swimming + bun = a share or quantity; cf. related terms listed at mizu

Suichoku 垂直 = vertical, perpendicular; *the swing choked me when its vertical rope got caught on my scarf*; cf. tate = length or height, vertical, e.g., tate no sen = a vertical line

Suichuu 水中 = under water; from sui = zui = water, e.g, kouzui = flood; + chuu = middle

Suiei 水泳 = swimming; *the sweet Asian girl was fond of swimming*; cf. oyogi = swimming

Suifu 水夫 = a sailor; *sailors like sweet food*

Suigou 水郷 = riverside or lakeside location; *there are some sweet goats at the lakeside location*

Suihanki 炊飯器 = rice cooker; *I left my Swedish hankie (handkerchief) in the rice cooker*

Suijaku suru 衰弱する = to become weak; *when he visited Sweden, Jack Nicholson became weak*

Suijouki 水蒸気 = water vapor; from sui = water, e.g., suiei = swimming; + jouki = vapor; cf. jouki = vapor, steam

Suijun 水準 = a standard or level; *the Swedish junior had high standards*; cf. related terms listed at teido

Suikei 水系 = a water or river system; from sui = water, e.g., onsui = warm water; + keitou = a system; cf. related terms listed at kawa

Suikomu 吸い込む = to inhale or absorb; from suu = to inhale + komu = to get crowded

Suimasen すいません = an abbreviation of sumimasen = sorry, excuse me

Suimen 水面 = surface of the water; *the Swedish men appeared at the surface of the water*

Suimenka 水面下 = below the surface of the water; from suimen = surface + ka = below

Suimin 睡眠 = sleep; *Swedish people are mean when they don't get enough sleep*; cf. nemuri = sleep

Suiri 推理 = speculation, inference; *there is speculation that he has a new sweety (sweetheart)*; cf. omowaku = speculation, calculation

Suiri shousetsu 推理小説 = a mystery or detective novel; from suiri = speculation + shousetsu = novel

Suisaiga 水彩画 = a watercolor painting; *the Swedish scientist bought Gandalf a watercolor painting*; cf. related terms listed at e

Suisanbutsu 水産物 = marine products; from sui = water, e.g., suiei = swimming; + sanbutsu = product; cf. related terms listed at sanbutsu

Suisei 水生 = aquatic, water based; from sui = water, e.g., suiei = swimming; + sei = life

Suisen suru 推薦する = to recommend; *a Swedish senator recommended tax cuts*; cf. related terms listed at susumeru

Suishou 水晶 = crystal; *I found this crystal on a Swedish shore*; cf. kesshou = a crystal; cf. shou = a crystal

Suishoutai 水晶体 = the crystalline lens (of the eye); from suishou = a crystal + tai = a body

Suiso 水素 = hydrogen; *the Swiss and the Soviets agreed that hydrogen could be a good energy source*; cf. related terms listed at tanso

Suisoku 推測 = an assumption or guess; *when I was on the swing and felt myself getting soaked, I made an assumption that it was raining*; cf. related terms listed at katei

Suisou 水槽 = a water tank; *the Swedish soldier soaked in a water tank*

Suitoru 吸い取る = to absorb; from suu = to suck + toru = to take; cf. related terms listed at kyuushuu suru

Suitou 出納 = receipts & dispersements; *we are in the sweet toast business, and these are my receipts and dispersements*; cf. denpyou = a receipt, bill or slip; cf. ryoushuusho = a receipt

Suitou 水筒 = a water bottle; from sui = water, e.g., kosui = lake water; + entou = a cylinder

Suizokukan 水族館 = an aquarium; from sui = water, e.g., suiei = swimming; + kazoku = family + kan = a large building

Suji 筋 = streak (line), fiber, muscle, tendon, story line, logic, lineage; *the suit that the genius wore had streaks on it*; cf. related terms listed at gyou

Sujiai 筋合い = right, reason; *she had her reasons, and she was right to drive the super Jeep on icy roads*; cf. kenri = right, privilege; cf. other related terms listed at riyuu

Sukasu 透かす = to look through; the transitive form of suku = to become transparent; cf. related terms listed at miru

Sukeroku 助六 = an assortment of inari and maki sushi; from suke = to help; *Superman and the Kennedys are here to help*; + roku = six

Suki (desu) 好き(です) = to like, a liking; *I like to ski*; cf. related terms listed at konomu

Suki 隙 = gap, opening, carelessness, inattentiveness; *there is a gap in the wall at the sukiyaki restaurant*; cf. fuchuui = carelessness; cf. other related terms listed at dansou

Sukima 隙間 = gap, hole; from suki = gap + ma = between; cf. related terms listed at ana and at dansou

Sukimakaze 隙間風 = a draft (air current); from suki = gap + ma = between + kaze = wind

Sukitootta 透き通った = transparent, clear; from suku = to become transparent + tooru = to pass through; cf. related terms listed at akiraka

Sukiyaki すき焼き = thin slices of beef boiled with vegetables; *the superior king was yakking (talking) about thin slices of beef boiled with vegetables*

Sukkari すっかり = thoroughly, completely; *Superman carries out his duties completely*; cf. related terms listed at zenzen

Sukkiri suru すっきりする = to feel refreshed; *after Superman washed the kitty, it felt refreshed*; cf. seisei suru = to feel refreshed or relieved

Sukoshi 少し = a small amount, a little bit, slightly, for a short time; *the super coder shielded his eyes from the sun for a short time*; cf. chotto = a little, just a moment; cf. tashou = a little

Sukoyaka 健やか = vigorous, healthy, sound; *the super coder, who had a yacht and a car, was vigorous and healthy*; cf. related terms listed at genki

Suku 空く = to become empty; *when Superman visited Kuwait, his stomach became empty*

Suku 透く = to become transparent, to thin out; *when Superman visited Kuwait, he became transparent*; cf. related terms listed at sumu

Sukui すくい = scooping; from sukuu = to scoop up

Sukui 救い = help, hope; from sukuu = to rescue; cf. related terms listed at kyuujo

Sukumeru すくめる = to shrug (shoulders), duck (head) or draw back (body); *when she learned about succulent plants via meeru (e-mail), she shrugged her shoulders*

Sukunai 少ない = few, scarce, insufficient; *the soup from Kuwait was nice, but it was insufficient as a meal*; cf. related terms listed at tarinai

Sukuu すくう = to scoop up or ladle; *Superman went to the Kool-Aid pitcher and scooped up a drink*; cf. kumu = to ladle or scoop water

Sukuu 救う = to rescue; *by suing the Kool-Aid industry, we hope to rescue some sugar addicts*; cf. related terms listed at tasukeru

Sumaho スマホ = a smart phone

Sumaseru 済ませる = to finish (transitive); the transitive form of sumu = to finish; cf. related terms listed at owaraseru

Sumasu 済ます = to finish something (transitive); *superior managers supervise workers to make sure that they finish their work*; cf. related terms listed at owaraseru

Sumi 墨 = ink stick, black ink; *the souvenir the mediator purchased was an ink stick*; cf. related terms listed at bokujuu

Sumi 炭 = charcoal; *they sued me for burning charcoal*

Sumi 隅 = an inside corner; *Sumisu-san (Mr. Smith) sat in the corner*; cf. related terms listed at kado

Sumibi 炭火 = a charcoal fire; from sumi = charcoal + bi = hi = fire; cf. related terms listed at kaji

Sumigama 炭窯 = a charcoal kiln; from sumi = charcoal + gama = kama = a kiln

Sumikko 隅っこ = a corner, nook or recess; *sumisu-san (Mr. Smith) looked cozy in his chair in the corner*; cf. related terms listed at kado

Sumimasen すみません = I'm sorry, excuse me, thank you; *I'm sorry that you want to sue me and the mad senator*; cf. gomen (nasai) = I'm sorry, excuse me; cf. osoreirimasu = I'm sorry; cf. shitsurei shimasu = excuse me, or I must be going; cf. other related terms listed at arigatou

Sumitsuku 住み着く = to settle in; from sumu = to reside + tsuku = to arrive

Sumou 相撲 = sumo wrestling

Sumoubeya 相撲部屋 = a sumo stable or training center; from sumou = sumo + beya = heya = room

Sumu 住む = to reside; *I will soon move and reside in a new town*; cf. related terms listed at ikiru

Sumu 済む = to finish (intransitive), to result in something less severe than expected; *after I finished the Superman movie, I decided that it was less awful than I expected*; cf. related terms listed at owaru

Sumu 澄む = to become clear or transparent; *after Superman moved the tree next door, our view of the ocean became clear*; cf. hanmei suru = to prove to be, to become clear; cf. miesuku = to be transparent, to be obvious; cf. suku = to become transparent

Suna 砂 = sand; *soon arguments broke out on*

the <u>sand</u>; cf. dosha = earth and sand

Sunahama 砂浜 = sandy beach; from suna = sand + hamabe = beach; cf. related terms listed at kaihin

Sunao 素直 = obedient, meek, honest, frank; <u>Superman</u> and <u>Naomi</u> are <u>frank</u> with one another; cf. otonashii = obedient, docile; cf. other related terms listed at shoujiki

Sunawachi すなわち = or, that is, namely, in other words; *I'm always on my guard; <u>in other words</u>, I know that my <u>superior nanny</u> is <u>watching</u> me*; cf. tsumari = that is to say, in other words

Sunpou 寸法 = measurement; *<u>soon</u> the <u>police</u> will come and take <u>measurements</u>*; cf. keiryou = measurement, computation

Sunzen 寸前 = just before, on the verge; *I'm <u>on the verge</u> and will <u>soon</u> attain <u>Zen</u> enlightenment*; cf. chokuzen = just before

Supeingo スペイン語 = the Spanish language; from supein = Spain + go = language

Suppai 酸っぱい = sour; *the <u>supervisor's</u> <u>pie</u> was <u>sour</u>*

Suppori すっぽり = completely, entirely; *the <u>supervising policeman completely</u> forgot to turn on his body camera*; cf. related terms listed at zenzen

Sura すら = even, if only (a variation of sae, implying that that's all one needs), as long as; *<u>Superman</u> will buy a <u>ranch</u>, <u>as long as</u> he can get some cattle*; cf. related terms listed at sae

Suraido suru スライドする = to slide, i.e., to change in value proportionally

Sure 擦れ = a scrape; from sureru = to rub against

Sureba すれば = if so, in that case; the eba form of suru = to do; literally, this = if one does; cf. related terms listed at sore de wa

Surechigau すれ違う = to pass by one another, to miss each other; from sure = a scrape + chigau = to differ

Sureru 擦れる = to rub against, wear down, become jaded; *the <u>supervisor's</u> <u>red</u> <u>rooster</u> <u>rubs</u> <u>against</u> the wires of his cage*; cf. kosuru = to rub or scrub; cf. naderu = to rub or stroke; cf. suriorosu = to grate or scrape off

Suri スリ = pickpocket; *<u>surely</u> we can eliminate <u>pickpockets</u>*

Surikireru 擦り切れる = to wear out; *<u>Superman</u> <u>realized</u> that the <u>key</u> to the <u>red</u> <u>rooster's</u> cage was <u>worn</u> <u>out</u>*

Surimuku 擦りむく = to abrade or scrape; *<u>Superman</u> <u>realized</u> that he should <u>move</u> the <u>coop</u> when he saw that the rabbits were <u>abrading</u> their skins on it*; cf. related terms listed at kosuru

Suriorosu すり下ろす = to grate or scrape off; from sureru = to wear down + orosu = to fillet; cf. related terms listed at sureru

Suriyoru すり寄る = to draw close, to cuddle with; *<u>Superman</u> <u>reads</u> in the <u>yoru</u> (night), <u>cuddled</u> with Lois Lane*

Suru する = to do, to turn into, to cause to become, to serve as, to wear (clothes, facial expression, etc), to view as being, to think of as, to use as, to decide on, to choose; *if you <u>do</u> as I say, you will have a <u>superior</u> <u>roof</u>*; cf. itasu = to do humbly; nasaru = to do honorably; cf. yaru = to give to someone of equal or lower status or to a member of the speaker's in-group, to do, to get along

Suru 刷る = to print; *<u>Superman</u> <u>rumors</u> are often <u>printed</u> in the newspaper*; cf. related terms listed at keisai suru

Suru ki wa nai する気はない = I don't have the desire (or intention) to do it; from suru = to do + ki = feeling

Surudoi 鋭い = acute, sharp, insightful, keen; *finding <u>super</u> <u>Rudolph</u> was <u>easy</u>, since my dog has an <u>acute</u> sense of smell*

Surume スルメ = dried shredded squid;

soon my roommate will bring me some dried shredded squid; cf. ika = squid

Susamajii 凄まじい = amazing, horrible, usually written すさまじい; that amazing shop sells superior sandwiches made with magical ingredients; cf. related terms listed at odorokubeki

Sushi 寿司 = raw sliced fish on rice; cf. related terms listed at ryouri

Suso 裾 = a hem or cuff, the foot or base of a mountain; you have soup and soda stains on the cuffs of your sleeves

Susume 勧め = advice, suggestion; from susumeru = to advise; cf. related terms listed at soudan

Susumeru 勧める = to advise or recommend; this can also (less frequently) be spelled 薦める; I advise Sue to attend summer school to get erudite; cf. osu = to recommend; cf. suisen suru = to recommend

Susumeru 進める = to advance or promote, transitive; the transitive form of susumu

Susumu 進む = to advance or make progress, intransitive; Superman's summer music program is advancing; cf. shinshutsu suru = to progress, expand or branch out into

Sutajio スタジオ = studio

Sutareru 廃れる = to become obsolete, to decline; Superman and Tarzan had a red rooster, but its health began to decline; cf. related terms listed at genshou suru

Suteeki ten ステーキ店 = steak restaurant; from steak + ten = store, e.g., ten'in = store clerk; cf. related terms listed at ryoutei

Suteki 素敵 = great, wonderful; Superman and the techies make a wonderful team; cf. related terms listed at idai

Suteru 捨てる = to throw away or abandon; this can also be spelled 棄てる; Superman's terrible roommate threw away his cape; cf. houridasu = to expel, abandon, neglect; cf. houru = to throw away or neglect

Suu 吸う = to smoke, to inhale, to suck; I smoke superior cigarettes

Suu 数 = a number, used as a word component, e.g., suugaku = mathematics; what is the number of suits that you want cleaned? cf. related terms listed at bangou

Suubyou 数秒 = several seconds; from suu = a number + byou = a second

Suuchi 数値 = numerical value or reading; Superman cheated by understating the numerical reading on the odometer

Suudai 数台 = several units; from suuji = numeral + dai = unit, e.g., nidai = 2 cars, etc.

Suugaku 数学 = mathematics; I will sue that gakusei (student) if he keeps talking about mathematics; cf. sansuu = arithmetic

Suugakuteki 数学的 = mathematical; from suugaku = mathematics + teki = related to

Suuhai 崇拝 = adoration, worship; Superman hides to avoid the adoration of his fans; cf. related terms listed at aijou

Suuji 数字 = numeral, figure; the super genius saw numerals wherever she looked; cf. related terms listed at bangou

Suukai 数回 = a few times; from suuji = numeral + kai = time

Suukasho 数箇所 = several places; from suuji = numeral + kasho = a place; cf. tokorodoko = here and there, several places

Suunen 数年 = several years; from suuji = numeral + nen = years; cf. related terms listed at nen

Suunichikan 数日間 = a few days; from suuji = number + nichi = day + kan =

interval or space

Suunin 数人 = several people; from suuji = number + nin = people

Suuseki no fune 数隻の船 = several boats; from suu = number + seki = a counter for ships + the possessive no + fune = a ship or boat

Suusen 数千 = thousands; from suuji = numeral + sen = thousand

Suwaru 座る = to sit; *Superman went to the war room and sat on a cushion*; cf. kakeru = to sit

Suzu 鈴 = a small bell; *after I sued the zoo, I got a small bell*; cf. chaimu = a chime or doorbell; cf. fuurin = a wind chime; cf. kane = a bell, gong or chimes; cf. yobirin = a doorbell or buzzer

Suzushii 涼しい = cool; *when Superman went to the zoo, he met some Shiites who were there to keep cool*; cf. hinyari = cool, chilly

Ta 田 = a rice field; *let's talk in the rice field*; cf. related terms listed at hara

Taba 束 = a bundle; *the tattered bags were tied into a bundle*; cf. fusa = a bunch, cluster, tassel; cf. ichiwa = a bundle or bunch

Tabegoro 食べごろ = good for eating, in season; from taberu = to eat + goro = approximate time

Tabehoudai 食べ放題 = all-you-can-eat; from taberu = to eat + houdai = without restriction

Tabemono 食べ物 = food; from taberu = to eat + mono = tangible thing; cf. agemono = deep-fried food; cf. esa = animal food or bait; cf. gochisou = a delicacy; cf. joushoku = staple food; cf. karaage = deep-fried food; cf. kate = food; cf. koubutsu = favorite food; cf. kunsei = smoked food; cf. meshi = rice, food or a meal (male speech); cf. rakunou seihin = dairy products; cf. shokuhin = food products; cf. shokumotsu = food; cf. shokuryou = food; cf. shokuryouhin = groceries; cf. shushoku = main food; cf. washoku = Japanese food; cf. youshoku = Western food; cf. other related terms listed at gohan, at ryouri and at yasai

Taberu 食べる = to eat; *Tarzan goes to the bedroom to eat*; cf. itadaku = to receive humbly, to eat or drink humbly; cf. kurau = to receive (a blow), to eat or drink; cf. kuu = to eat (rough speech); cf. meshiagaru = to eat honorably

Tabete iku 食べていく = to make a living; from taberu = to eat + iku = to go; cf. related terms listed at ikiru

Tabi 度 = a time or occasion; *tacky bees attacked us on that occasion*; cf. ori = occasion, opportunity, time

Tabi 旅 = trip, travel; *I bring my tabby cat on my travels*; cf. related terms listed at ryokou

Tabi 足袋 = Japanese socks with a separate compartment for the big toe; *a tacky bee stung me through my Japanese socks*; cf. related terms listed at kutsushita

Tabi ni 度に = every time, whenever; from tabi = an occasion + ni = on; cf. maido = each time, every time, always

Tabidatsu 旅立つ = to begin a trip, to pass away; from tabi = trip + datsu = tatsu = to stand

Tabun 多分 = perhaps, probably; *I will probably tackle Daniel Boone*; cf. related terms listed at osoraku

Tachi 達 = a suffix denoting that the preceding noun is plural; often spelled たち; *I am attaching more than one file to this message*

Tachiagaru 立ち上がる = to stand up; from tatsu = to stand + agaru = to rise; cf. related terms listed at kiritsu suru

Tachiageru 立ち上げる = to start

something, to start up; from tatsu = to stand + ageru = to give; cf. related terms listed at hajimeru

Tachiba 立場 = position, situation; from tachimasu = to stand + basho = a place

Tachiiru 立ち入る = to enter, meddle, be nosy; from tatsu = to stand + ireru = to insert; cf. related terms listed at hairu

Tachinoki 立ち退き = eviction; from tachinoku = to evacuate

Tachinoku 立ち退く = to evacuate, vacate; *we were attaching a nose to our cool snowman when we were told to evacuate the snowfield*; cf. related terms listed at deru

Tachiyoru 立ち寄る = to drop in for a short visit; from tatsu = to stand + yoru = to drop in; cf. yoru = to gather, to approach, to drop in at

Tada ただ = only, merely, simply, free of charge; *my tallest daughter is only five feet tall*; cf. related terms listed at dake

Tadachi ni 直ちに = immediately; *a taxi dashed up and delivered the cheese immediately*; cf. related terms listed at sokkoku

Tadai na (or no) 多大な = enormous; *Tarzan's dike was enormous*; cf. related terms listed at ookii

Tadaima ただいま = right now, also used to say "I'm home!"; from tada = simply + ima = now

Tadashii 正しい = correct; *the tall dashing Italian guy was usually correct*

Tadayou 漂う = to drift; *when my tall daughter visited Yosemite, she drifted down the river on a raft*; cf. nagaretsuku = to drift to, to be washed ashore

Tadoritsuku 辿り着く = to find one's way to a place at last, to struggle on; from tadoru = to trace or follow + tsuku = to arrive

Tadoru 辿る = to follow or trace; *that tan doe on the roof followed me here*; cf. shitagau = to obey or follow; cf. sou = to run along, to follow a plan; cf. tsukeru = to attach, install, follow or pursue, make an entry, to turn on, and many other meanings

Taemanai 絶え間ない = incessant, constant; from taeru to discontinue or cease + ma = duration of time, e.g., hiruma = daytime; + nai = negation; cf. related terms listed at fuhen no

Taemanaku 絶え間なく = incessantly; the adverbial form of taemanai; cf. taezu = constantly, continually

Taenaru 妙なる = exquisite; *the tapestries and etchings in the nanny's room were exquisite*; cf. related terms listed at utsukushii

Taeru 絶える = to discontinue or cease; *the tall expert ruined the evidence, forcing the police to discontinue their investigation*; cf. related terms listed at yameru

Taeru 耐える = to endure; *the tall erudite woman endured my ignorant questions*; cf. shinobu = to endure, to conceal oneself

Taezu 絶えず = constantly, continually; from taeru = to discontinue or cease; this is an abbreviation of taenai de = taezuni = not ceasing; cf. taemanaku = incessantly

Tagai 互い = mutual, reciprocal, each other; *if you both speak Tagalog, it will be easy to communicate with each other*; cf. doushi = fellow, mutual, companion; cf. kyoutsuu no = common, mutual; cf. sougo = mutual, reciprocal

Tagai ni 互いに = with each other, mutually, reciprocally; from tagai = each other + -ni = a suffix that forms an adverb; cf. sougo ni = mutually

Tagaku 多額 = a large sum of money; from ta = many, e.g., takinou = multi-function; + gaku = a sum of money; cf. related terms listed a kikin

Tagaru たがる – see -garu

Tagayasu 耕す = to plow or cultivate; *a Tagalog farmer drinks yak soup before he plows his land*; cf. tsuchikau = to nourish or cultivate; cf. yashinau = to feed, nourish, support or cultivate

Tahata 田畑 = field (crops); *Tarzan paid the harbor tax for the crops from his field*; cf. related terms listed at hara

Tahatsu 多発 = a repeated occurrence; *sighting people in tall hats is a repeated occurrence in my neighborhood*

Tai たい = want to do, used after a verb stem, e.g., tabetai desu = wants to eat; *he wants to visit Thailand*; cf. aritai = I want (something) to exist

Tai 体 = a body, used as a word component; *that tiger has a big body*

Tai 大 = big, used as a word component; *the tiger is big*; cf. related terms listed at ookii

Tai shite 対して – see ni tai shite

Tai suru 対する = to face toward, to confront, to be related to; *the Thai soldier confronted his enemy*; cf. chokumen suru = to face or be involved with, to confront with; cf. taiketsu suru = to confront

Taiboku 大木 = a big tree; *the Thai bowler drank Kool-Aid under a big tree*; cf. related terms listed at ki

Taichou 体調 = body condition; from tai = body + choushi = condition; cf. related terms listed at keisei

Taichou 隊長 = a commanding officer; *the commanding officer was tired of his chores*; cf. related terms listed at shikan and at shunou

Taida 怠惰 = laziness; *the tired dancer was accused of laziness*

Taida na 怠惰な = lazy; from taida = laziness

Taido 態度 = attitude; *the Thai doorman has a good attitude*

Taifuu 台風 = a typhoon; cf. arashi = a storm

Taigan 対岸 = the opposite shore; from taishite = as opposed to + kaigan = a beach or coast; cf. related terms listed at kaihin

Taiguu 待遇 = treatment (of customer), salary and benefits; *the treatment of the Thai goose was fair*; cf. taiou = handling, treatment; cf. other related terms listed at chin

Taihan 大半 = the majority; from tai = big + han = half; cf. related terms listed at mottomo

Taihen 大変 = difficult, terrible, extremely; *a tiger and a hen are extremely different, and they make a terrible team*; cf. related terms listed at muzukashii and at ooi ni

Taihi suru 対比する = to compare, contrast; *the Thai hero compared his options*; cf. kuraberu = to compare

Taiho 逮捕 = arrest, apprehension, capture; *the Thai hostess captured a mouse*; cf. kouchi = arrest, confinement

Taiho suru 逮捕する = to arrest; from taiho = arrest; cf. shouaku suru = to hold or seize; cf. toraeru = to arrest, capture, understand; cf. toriosaeru = to capture or arrest; cf. toru = to catch; cf. tsukamaeru = to capture, catch or seize

Taihou 大砲 = a cannon; *I'm tired of holding onto this cannon*

Taii 大尉 = a captain; *the captain is tired of eels for dinner*; cf. related terms listed at shikan

Taiji 胎児 = a fetus; *the tired genius was carrying a heavy fetus in her womb*; cf. related terms at kodomo

Taiji 退治 = extermination, suppression; *we are using a Thai Jeep in our suppression efforts*; cf. related terms listed at satsujin

Taijuu 体重 = body weight; *the Thai guy's juice consumption affects his body weight*; cf. related terms listed at omosa

Taikai 大会 = convention, tournament, rally; from tai = big + kaigi = meeting; cf. related terms listed at kaigi

Taiken 体験 = experience; *Thailand and Kenya are places to enjoy the experience of ocean fishing*; cf. keiken = experience

Taiken suru 体験する = to experience; from taiken = experience; cf. related terms listed at keiken suru

Taiketsu suru 対決する = to confront; *the Thai general poured ketchup in his soup as he confronted his subordinates*; cf. chokumen suru = to face or be involved with, to confront with; cf. tai suru = to face toward, to confront

Taiki 大気 = air or atmosphere; an abbreviation of taikiken = atmosphere; cf. related terms listed at kuuki

Taikiken 大気圏 = the atmosphere; from tai = big + kiken = atmosphere; cf. related terms listed at kuuki

Taiko 太鼓 = a drum; *the tyrant grabbed a coconut and beat it like a drum*; cf. tsuzumi = a drum; cf. kotsuzumi = a small hand drum

Taikoku 大国 = big country; from tai = big, e.g., taihen = terrible; + koku = country; cf. related terms listed at kuni

Taikou suru 対抗する = to oppose or fight; *the Thai corporations oppose our plan*; cf. related terms listed at arasou and at sakarau

Taikutsu 退屈 = boredom; *since these Thai kutsu (shoes) are all the same, they are contributing to my boredom*

Taikyuu 耐久 = endurance; *the Thais and the Cubans showed endurance*; cf. gaman = patience, endurance; cf. nintai = patience; cf. shinbou = endurance, patience

Taikyuuryoku 耐久力 = durability; from taikyuu = endurance + ryoku = force; cf. taikyuusei = durability

Taikyuusei 耐久性 = durability; from taikyuu = endurance + sei = nature; cf. taikyuuryoku = durability

Taiman 怠慢 = negligence; *the tired man fell asleep and was accused of negligence*; cf. orosoka = neglect, negligence, not to mention, needless to say; cf. yudan = negligence, inattentiveness

Taimen 体面 = a reputation; from nikutai = the human body + men = a surface or mask; cf. related terms listed at hyouban

Tainai 体内 = inside the body; from nikutai = the human body + nai = inside

Tainou 滞納 = delinquency (failure to pay); *the time to send the renters a notice about their delinquency*; cf. hasan = bankruptcy

Taion 体温 = body temperature; *the tiger's owner has a high body temperature*; cf. related terms listed at ondo

Taionkei 体温計 = a clinical thermometer; from taion = body temperature + kei = to measure or count, e.g., tokei = clock; cf. ondokei = a thermometer

Taiou 対応 = handling, treatment; *I'm tired of the owner's handling of my complaints*; cf. soujuu = management, handling, operation; cf. taiguu = treatment (of customer), salary and benefits

Taiou suru 対応する = to address (a problem); from taiou = handling; cf. taisho suru = to deal with

Taira 平 = flat, level; *the tiger ran across the level ground*; cf. hira = even, flat, peace; cf. hiratai = flat, simple

Tairiku 大陸 = continent, mainland (China); from tai = big + riku = land; cf. hondo = mainland; cf. naichi = inland area, mainland area of Japan

Tairyoku 体力 = stamina; from tai = body, e.g., taijuu = body weight; + ryoku =

strength, e.g., nouryoku = ability

Tairyou 大量 = large amount; from tai = big + ryou = quantity; cf. related terms listed at ryou

Taisa 大佐 = a colonel; *the Thai salaryman dreamed of becoming a colonel*; cf. related terms at shikan

Taisaku 対策 = measures (actions), strategy; *the Thai guy buys sacks of cookies as part of a strategy to gain weight*; cf. related terms listed at furumai and at kikaku

Taisei 体制 = a power, government or socioeconomic structure; *the Thai sage suggested a strong government built on a structure he designed*; cf. seifu = government

Taisei 態勢 = stance, posture; *the Thai sailor assumed a defensive stance*; cf. kata = form (e.g., dance), posture, style; cf. shisei = a stance or posture

Taiseki 堆積 = a pile or accumulation; *the tired selfish king had a pile of work to do*; cf. related terms listed at shuushuu

Taisekibutsu 堆積物 = sediment, deposit; from taiseki = an accumulation + butsu = thing

Taisen 対戦 = competition; from tai suru = to confront + sensou = war; cf. related terms listed at issen

Taisetsu 大切 = important, beloved; *the Thai guy set up a super farm which was important to him*; cf. related terms listed at juuyou

Taisetsu ni suru 大切にする = to value or treasure, to take good care of; from taisetsu = important + ni suru = to make A into B; cf. related terms listed at hyouka suru

Taisha 代謝 = metabolism, renewal; *the tired Shah had a slow metabolism*

Taishi 大使 = an ambassador; *that tired sheepdog belongs to the ambassador*; cf. shisha = an emissary or messenger

Taishita 大した = considerable, great, important; *the Thai sheets that Tarzan bought were great*; cf. related terms listed at idai and juuyou

Taishite 対して = against, in contrast to, as opposed to, toward; from tai suru = to confront

Taishitsu 体質 = disposition, nature, constitution (physical); *the Thai sheets have a durable constitution*; cf. related terms listed at seikaku

Taisho suru 対処する = to deal with, implying that one solves a problem; *at the Thai show, I had to deal with many problems*; cf. taiou suru = to address; cf. related terms listed at shori suru

Taishoku 退職 = retirement from office, resignation; *the Thai people were shocked by the prime minister's resignation*; cf. jihyou = a written resignation

Taishoku suru 退職する = to retire from office; from taishoku = retirement + suru = to do; cf. related terms listed at jishoku suru

Taishou 大賞 = a grand prize; from tai = big + shou = a prize; cf. related terms listed at houbi

Taishou 対称 = symmetry; *the tiger showed off its symmetry*; cf. taishousei = symmetry

Taishou 対象 = an object (of study, etc.); *the tigers living by the shore were the objects of the hunt*; cf. related terms listed at shugo

Taishousei 対称性 = symmetry; *the tiger showed the sailors its symmetry*; cf. taishou = symmetry

Taishouteki 対称的 = symmetrical; from taishou = symmetry + teki = related to

Taishouteki ni 対照的に = diametrically opposite; *the tiger showed the techie a diametrically opposite way of solving the problem*; cf. related terms listed at dokoroka

Taishuu 大衆 = general public; *the general public knows how to tie their shoes*; cf. related terms listed at kouritsu

Taisou たいそう = very; *the Thai soldier was very young*; cf. related terms listed at ooi ni

Taisou 体操 = gymnastics, exercise; *the Thai soldiers worked on gymnastics*; cf. undou = exercise, sport, action, movement

Taitei 大抵 = usually, mostly, probably; usually written たいてい; *the Thai tailor usually works on weekends*; cf. bon'you na = mediocre, commonplace; cf. daitai = approximately, about, general; cf. fudan = usual, casual, everyday; cf. futsuu = ordinary, usual, general, average; cf. gaishite = generally, for the most part; cf. heibon = ordinary; cf. higoro = usual, everyday; cf. ippan ni = usually; cf. ippanteki ni = commonly, generally, usually; cf. kourei = customary; cf. nichijou = ordinary, usual; cf. ooku = most or mainly; cf. ooku ni = mostly; cf. tsuujou = usual; cf. zenmenteki = all-out, general, extensive, full-scale, over-all, complete; zoku ni = commonly (slang)

Taiyou 大洋 = ocean; *the Thai yogi lives beside the ocean*; cf. related terms listed at umi

Taiyou 太陽 = the sun; *when I'm tired of yodeling, I lie in the sun*; cf. hi = sun, sunlight, day; cf. yuuhi = evening sun, setting sun

Taiyoukei 太陽系 = the solar system; from taiyou = the sun + keitou = system

Taiyoukou 太陽光 = sunlight; from taiyou = the sun + kouki = brightness; cf. nikkou = sunlight

Taiyoureki 太陽暦 = a solar calendar; from taiyou = the sun + reki = a calendar; cf. similar terms listed at koyomi

Taizai suru 滞在する = to stay (at a hotel, etc.); *when I got tired in Zaire (former name of the Congo), I stayed at a hotel*; cf. todomaru = to stay, remain or stop; cf. tomaru = to stay overnight (house or hotel)

Taizaisaki 滞在先 = a lodging destination; from taizai suru = to stay (at a hotel) + saki = destination; cf. related terms listed at mokutekichi

Taka タカ = a hawk; *Tarzan visited California to see the hawks*; cf. related terms listed at tori

Takai 高い = high, expensive, loud (sound); *that tall kite is expensive, but it flies high*; cf. kouka = expensive; cf. other related terms listed at kodakai

Takamaru 高まる = to rise; the intransitive form of takameru = to raise; cf. related terms listed at agaru

Takame 高め = on the high side; from takameru = to raise; cf. related terms listed at kodakai

Takameru 高める = to raise; from takai = high; cf. related terms listed at ageru

Takara 宝 = treasure; *Tarzan's caravans carried treasure*

Takarakuji 宝くじ = a lottery; from takara = treasure + kuji = a lottery or raffle; *I won a cool Jeep in the lottery*; cf. chuusen = a lottery or raffle; cf. kuji = a lottery

Takasa 高さ = height; from takai = high + sa, a suffix that turns an adjective into a noun; cf. related terms listed at nagasa

Takatobikomi 高飛び込み = a high dive; from takai = high + tobikomu = to dive

Take 丈 = size, height; *this guy drinks a tall keg every day, which might explain his size*; cf. related terms listed at nagasa

Take 竹 = bamboo; *that tavern's kegs are made of bamboo*; cf. chiku = bamboo, used as a suffix

Takenawa たけなわ = in full swing, at full height; *the competition between the tall Kennedys and the narco warlords was in full* *swing*

Takenoko 竹の子 = a bamboo shoot; from take = bamboo + the possessive no + ko = a child

Takeru 炊ける = to be boiled or cooked; the intransitive form of taku = to cook; cf. related terms listed at nieru

Takesei 竹製 = made from bamboo; from take = bamboo + seihin = finished product; cf. related terms listed at mokusei

Taki 滝 = waterfall, cascade; *we were talking about a waterfall*

Takibi 焚き火 = a bonfire; *that tacky bee flew into the bonfire*; cf. related terms listed at kaji

Takikomi gohan 炊き込みご飯 = rice seasoned and cooked with various ingredients; from taku = to cook + komu = to crowd in + gohan = cooked rice

Takinou 多機能 = multifunction; *the tacky gnome in my garden is multi-functional*; cf. kenyou = multi-use; cf. kinou = function

Takkyuu 卓球 = pingpong; *some tacky youths are playing pingpong*

Tako 凧 = kite; *I eat tacos while flying my kite*

Takoku 他国 = a foreign country, another country; from ta'nin = other people + koku = country; cf. related terms listed at kuni

Taku 宅 = a house or home; *the tall Kuwaiti invited me to his home*; cf. related terms listed at uchi

Taku 炊く = to cook (rice, etc.); *Tarzan drinks Kool-Aid while he cooks rice*; cf. related terms listed at niru

Taku 焚く = to burn (wood); *Tarzan drinks Kool-Aid while he burns wood*; cf. related terms listed at moyasu

Taku suru 託する = to entrust; *I entrusted the tall Kuwaiti guy with important responsibilities*; cf. related terms listed at makaseru

Takuhaibin 宅配便 = a home delivery service; from taku = a home + haitatsu = delivery + bin = service, e.g., yuubin = the mail; cf. demae = a (food) delivery or catering service

Takumashii たくましい = strong, dependable; *when he is using tap water to make Kool-Aid and mashing potatoes, my husband seems strong and dependable*; cf. related terms listed at tsuyoi

Takumi 匠 = an artisan, workman or carpenter; *the artisan serves tap water and Kool-Aid in meetings with his customers*; cf. shokunin = a craftsperson or artisan

Takumi na 巧みな = skillful; *those talented Kuwaiti mediators are skillful*; cf. related terms listed at jouzu

Takusan たくさん = many, much; *the tap water and Kool-Aid that Santa served satisfied many people*; cf. kazukazu = many, varied; cf. moridakusan = many, varied; cf. ooi = numerous; cf. oozei = many, a crowd of people; cf. musuu = countless

Takuwaeru 蓄える = to store or save; *I saved money to buy a talking Kuwaiti watch for my erudite friend*; cf. tameru = to save (money)

Tama 弾 = bullet; *the tall marathon runner dodged a bullet*; cf. dangan = a bullet

Tama 玉 = a ball, bead, jewel or bullet; a coin (if used as a suffix and pronounced dama); this can also be read as gyoku = jewel; *after I eat my tamale, I'm going to play ball*; cf. tama = a jewel, bead, or drop

Tama 珠 = a jewel, bead, or drop; *I found a jewel in my tamale*; cf. tama = a ball, bead, jewel or bullet

Tama ni たまに = occasionally; *occasionally I eat the tamales that my niece makes*; cf. toki ni = occasionally, by the way; cf. toki to shite = sometimes; cf. tokidoki = sometimes, now and then; cf. tokiori = once in a while

Tamago 卵 = an egg; *I eat eggs with tamales and goat cheese*

Tamagoyaki 卵焼き = a rolled omelet; from tamago = egg + yaku = to grill; cf. related terms listed at ryouri

Tamanegi 玉ねぎ = an onion; from tama = a ball + negi = a green onion; cf. related terms listed at yasai

Tamaranai たまらない = intolerable or irresistable; *the tall marathon runner knifed me, and it was intolerable*; cf. me ni amaru = to be intolerable

Tamashii 魂 = a soul or spirit; *a tamale was given to the Shiite by an evil spirit*; cf. related terms listed at seishin

Tamatama たまたま = unexpectedly, by chance; from tama ni = occasionally; cf. related terms listed at igai

Tame (ni) 為(に) = in order to, because of; *the tavern in Mexico hired my niece in order to serve their tables*; cf. ni tsuki = per, apiece, because of, regarding; cf. noni = in spite of the fact, in order to, while, if only

Tame'iki (Tameiki) ため息 = a sigh; *the tall Mexican released his iki (breath) suddenly, and the result was a sigh*; cf. to'iki = a sigh

Tameru ためる = to accumulate; this is sometimes spelled 溜める, using a kanji that we don't teach; *the talented Mexicans had a room where they accumulated corn*

Tameru 貯める = to save (money); *after buying a tapestry in Mexico, Ruth had to save money again*; cf. takuwaeru = to store or save

Tamesu 試す = to attempt or try out, to test; *the tall Mexican supervisor attempted to shoot a basket*; cf. chousen suru = to challenge or attempt; cf. hakaru = to plot or attempt; cf. idomu = to challenge or contend for; cf. kuwadateru = to attempt or plot; cf. kokoromiru = to experiment or try;

cf. shikou suru = to make an attempt; cf. to suru = to try to

Tamotsu 保つ = to keep or maintain; *the tavern outside the moats of the castle is maintained by a tavern keeper*; cf. related terms listed at azukaru

Tan 淡 = thin, faint, pale; *my skin tan is faint*

Tan kasshoku 淡褐色 = light brown; from tan = faint + kasshoku = dark brown; cf. related terms listed at chairo

Tana 棚 = shelf; *we keep our tangy apples on this shelf*

Tana kara botamichi da 棚からぼた餅だ = it's azuki bean mochi from the shelf = it's good luck

Tanbo 田んぼ = a rice field; *that tanned boy works in the rice fields*; cf. related terms listed at hara

Tanchou タンチョウ = Japanese crane; *a tanned Margaret Cho announced a campaign to protect the Japanese crane*; cf. related terms listed at tori

Tane 種 = seed; *I keep my seeds in tan eggshells*

Tango 単語 = a word; *when I asked her to dance the tango, she answered with one word*; cf. related terms listed at kotoba

Tan'i (Tani) 単位 = credit (school) or unit; *my school gives credit for tanning classes, and I received two units for the one I took*

Tani 谷 = valley; *there is a tanning booth in the valley*; cf. keikoku = valley, canyon; cf. kyoukoku = a canyon or ravine

Ta'nin (Tanin) 他人 = a stranger, or other people; *I met a stranger in the tanning booth*; cf. tasha = other people

Tanjou suru 誕生する = to be born; *the tanner joked that he was born at the tannery*; cf. umareru = to be born

Tanjoubi 誕生日 = birthday; from tanjou suru = to be born + bi = hi = day

Tanjun 単純 = simple; *sorting through this tan junk is simple, since most of it is discarded khaki uniforms*; cf. related terms listed at kantan

Tanka 担架 = a stretcher; *if you tangle with that captain, you might end up on a stretcher*

Tanken 探検 = exploration, expedition; *I drove a tank in Kenya during my expedition*; cf. ensei = an expedition; cf. tansaku = exploration, investigation

Tankenka 探検家 = an explorer; from tanken = exploration + ka = a person

Tanki 短期 = short-term; *my tan kimono is suitable for short-term vacations*; cf. chouki = long-term

Tankoubon 単行本 = special book, separate volume; *I sat in a tank of cold water and chewed a bone while I read a special book*; cf. related terms listed at hon

Tankyuu suru 探究する = to pursue or search for; *the tanned Cubans searched for gold*; cf. related terms listed at sousaku suru

Tanmono 反物 = cloth, textile; *the decor in the tanning booth was monotonous until I added some cloth on the walls*; cf. related terms listed at nuno

Tannaru 単なる = mere; *in Montana, roosters make up a mere fraction of the animals*

Tannen 丹念 = precise, meticulous; *my tanned negative nephew was meticulous about the time he spent in the tanning booth*; cf. related terms listed at seikaku

Tanni 単に = merely, only; from tanjun = simple + ni, a suffix that converts an adjective to an adverb; cf. tani = school credit; cf. related terms listed at dake

Tannou 堪能 = 1) skillful, or 2) enjoyment/satisfaction; *the tank driver in Norway was skillful and performed to the satisfaction and enjoyment of his commander*; cf. related terms listed at jouzu and at manzoku

Tanomigoto 頼み事 = a favor, something requested; from tanomu = to request + goto = koto = intangible thing

Tanomoshii 頼もしい = reliable, trustworthy; *this tan old motorcycle that a Shiite sold me is reliable*; cf. related terms listed at kakujitsu

Tanomu 頼む = to ask or request; *I requested his tangle of old movie film stock*; cf. chuumon suru = to request or order; cf. kitsumon suru = to demand; cf. koimotomeru = to request or beg; cf. kongan suru = to entreat or beg; cf. kou = to ask or beg; cf. maneku = to ask, invite or beckon; cf. motomeru = to ask or request; cf. motomu = to seek or demand; cf. negau = to ask, hope, pray or request; cf. seikyuu suru = to claim, demand, or request; cf. shinsei suru = to request or apply for; cf. youkyuu suru = to request or demand

Tanoshii 楽しい = enjoyable, fun; *the talented nobleman wore a sheet to the Halloween party, and it was enjoyable*; cf. omoshiroi = interesting, enjoyable, funny

Tanoshimi 楽しみ = enjoyment; from tanoshimu = to enjoy; cf. related terms listed at shiawase

Tanoshimu 楽しむ = to enjoy; *the tall Norwegian plays from sheet music, and we enjoy listening*; cf. kyouju suru = to enjoy

Tanpaku たんぱく = egg white, protein; *he had a tantrum at a party in Kuwait because someone put egg white, which is rich in protein, in his hair*

Tanpaku shitsu たんぱく質 = protein; from tanpaku = protein + shitsu = quality

Tanpen 短編 = short story or film; *the tank driver penned a short story about the war*; cf. related terms listed at hanashi

Tanren 鍛錬 = training, tempering, forging, hardening, disciplining; *this water tank* that I <u>rented</u> is for diving <u>training</u>; cf. related terms listed at kunren

Tanren suru 鍛錬する = to train; from tanren = training; cf. related terms listed at shitsukeru

Tansa 探査 = probe, inquiry, investigation; when the <u>tank</u> got stuck in the <u>sand</u>, an <u>investigation</u> was conducted; cf. related terms listed at kensa

Tansaku 探索 = exploration, investigation; riding in a <u>tank</u> with a <u>sack</u> of <u>cookies</u>, we set off on our <u>exploration</u>; cf. other related terms listed at kensa and at tanken

Tansei 丹精 = diligence, working earnestly; the <u>tanned sailor</u> showed <u>diligence</u> in applying sunscreen

Tanshuku 短縮 = a shortening or abbreviation; the <u>tank</u> driver wore <u>shoes</u> from <u>Kuwait</u>, and his name tag contained the <u>abbreviation</u> "Sgt."; cf. related terms listed at ryaku

Tanshukukei 短縮形 = an abbreviation or shortened form; from tanshuku = a shortening or abbreviation + keitai = a form; cf. related terms listed at ryaku

Tanso 炭素 = carbon; from tan = carbon, e.g., sekitan = coal; + genso = an element; cf. aen = zinc; cf. chisso = nitrogen; cf. dou = copper; cf. gin = silver; cf. iou = sulfur; cf. namari = lead (an element); cf. ougon = gold; cf. sanso = oxygen; cf. suiso = hydrogen; cf. tetsu = iron

Tansu タンス = a chest of drawers or dresser; I keep my <u>tan suit</u> in the <u>dresser</u>

Tansui 淡水 = fresh water; that <u>tank</u> from <u>Sweden</u> carries a supply of <u>fresh water</u>; cf. related terms listed at mizu

Tansuikabutsu 炭水化物 = carbohydrates; from tanso = carbon + sui = water, e.g., suiei = swimming; + ka = a nominalizing suffix + butsu = a thing

Tantei 探偵 = a detective; the <u>detective</u> unwound the <u>tangled tape</u> that he found at the crime scene; cf. related terms listed at keiji

Tantou 担当 = charge (duty); <u>Tonto</u> is in <u>charge</u>; cf. related terms listed at tsutome

Tantou 短刀 = a dagger; when I had a <u>tantrum</u> in <u>Toukyou</u>, I pulled out my <u>dagger</u>; cf. related terms listed at katana

Tantou suru 担当する = to be responsible or in charge; from tantou = charge; cf. hikitoru = to take back, take over, claim, take charge of; cf. hikiukeru = to take charge of, to undertake

Tantousha 担当者 = a person in charge; from tantou = charge + sha = person; cf. sekininsha = a person in charge

Taoreru 倒れる = to fall or faint, to become bankrupt; I threw a <u>towel</u> over the <u>red rooster</u>, and it <u>fainted</u>; cf. related terms listed at ochiru

Taosu 倒す = to throw down or knock down, to defeat; the <u>towel</u> that <u>Superman</u> threw <u>knocked down</u> the criminal; cf. makasu = to defeat; cf. nagetaosu = to throw a person down; cf. naguritaosu = to knock down or knock out

Tara たら = codfish; the <u>codfish</u> ate a <u>tarantula</u>; cf. related terms listed at sakana

Tareru 垂れる = to hang, droop, dangle, sag, lower, drip, ooze; after the <u>talented red</u> <u>roosters</u> ran through the swamp, their feathers were <u>drooping</u>; cf. shitataru = to drip; cf. other related terms listed at sagaru

Taresagaru 垂れ下がる = to hang; from tareru = to hang + sagaru = to hang down; cf. related terms listed at sagaru

Tari たり = etcetera, used as a suffix after the past plain speech stems of verbs or the past stems of i adjectives; we're paying for high <u>tariffs</u>, <u>etcetera</u>; cf. related terms listed at nado

Tarinai 足りない = insufficient; from taru = to be sufficient + nai = negation; cf. hanpa = insufficient, incomplete, insincere;

cf. shousuu = a few; cf. sukunai = few, scarce, insufficient; cf. toboshii = scarce

Tariru 足りる = to be sufficient; an alternative spelling of taru = to be sufficient; *the tariffs on rubies should be sufficient*

Taru たる = that which is, those who are, in the capacity of; *those who are here will talk to Rudolph*

Taru 足る = to be sufficient (this can also be spelled tariru); *the tavern's rooms are sufficient for our gathering*

Tasha 他者 = other people; from ta'nin = a stranger, other people + sha = a person

Tashika ni 確かに = for sure, certainly; *if you take a takushii (taxi) and bring a camera to my niece, she will certainly be able to take some photos*; cf. kakujitsu ni = certainly; cf. masa ni = exactly, naturally, certainly; cf. ni chigainai = no doubt, certainly

Tashikameru 確かめる = to ascertain or confirm; *if you take a takushii (taxi) and bring a camera, you can take photos of the rooster & ascertain its qualities*; cf. related terms listed at kakunin suru

Tashizan 足し算 = addition (mathematics); from tasu = to add + zan = to count, e.g., anzan = mental calculation

Tashou 多少 = a little; *the taxidermy show was a little too long*; cf. related terms listed at sukoshi

Tassei 達成 = an achievement; *when Tarzan saved that person, it was regarded as a great achievement*

Tassei suru 達成する = to accomplish; from tassei = an achievement; cf. related terms listed at hatasu

Tassuru 達する = to reach or become; *after Tarzan gave soup to Rudolph, they became friends and reached their goals*; cf. related terms listed at oyobu

Tasu 足す = to take care of business, to add numbers, to add something; *after putting on a tan suit, I took care of my business*; cf. related terms listed at azukaru and at kuwaeru

Tasukaru 助かる = to be rescued or helped; the intransitive form of tasukeru = to help or rescue

Tasuke 助け = help, support; from tasukeru = to help or rescue; cf. related terms listed at kyuujo

Tasukeau 助け合う = to help each other, cooperate; from tasukeru = to help + au = to come together, match or suit; cf. related terms listed at tasukeru

Tasukeru 助ける = to help or rescue; *the tall superintendent's Keds (a brand of shoes) were ruined when he rescued the drowning child*; cf. kyuushutsu suru = to rescue; cf. soeru = to help or support, and other meanings; cf. sukuu = to rescue; cf. tasukeau = to help each other, cooperate; cf. tetsudau = to help

Tasuu 多数 = a large number, a majority; from ta = many, e.g., takinou = multi-function; + suuji = a numeral or figure; cf. related terms listed at bangou and at mottomo

Tatakau 戦う = to fight, make war; this can also be spelled 闘う; *the tall taxi driver will kau [buy] a weapon before he fights*; cf. related terms listed at arasou

Tataku たたく = to beat or strike; *when the tall taxi driver ran out of Kool-Aid, he began to beat his head against his car*; cf. related terms listed at utsu

Tatami 畳 = tatami mat; from tatamu = to fold; cf. rokujou = six tatami mats; cf. yojouhan = 4 ½ tatami mats

Tatamu 畳む = to fold; *the tall talented movie star is folding origami*; cf. mageru = to twist, bend or falsify; cf. orimageru = to bend or fold down; cf. oru = to break or fold

Tatasu 立たす = to help a person stand, to raise or rouse; an abbreviation of tataseru, the causative form of tatsu = to stand

Tatazumu たたずむ = to stand a while, to loiter; *as the tall talented zookeeper watched the moon, he loitered on the sidewalk*; cf. related terms listed at kiritsu suru

Tate 盾 = a shield; *the talented tennis player used her racket as a shield*

Tate 縦 = length or height, vertical, e.g., tate no sen = a vertical line; *the tall techie had a height of seven feet when he assumed a vertical position*; cf. suichoku = vertical; cf. other related terms listed at nagasa

Tate no sen 縦の線 = a vertical line; from tate = vertical + sen = line

Tatejiku 縦軸 = a vertical axis; from tate = vertical + jiku = an axis; cf. related terms listed at jiku

Tatemono 建物 = a building; from tateru = to raise or put up + mono = thing; cf. betsumune = separate building, outbuilding; cf. biru = a building; cf. hondou = a main temple building; cf. kaoku = a house or building; cf. kenchikubutsu = buildings

Tatenaosu 建て直す = to rebuild or reconstruct; from tateru = to build + naosu = to repair; cf. related terms listed at tateru

Tateru 建てる = to build or put upright; *my neighbor built a tall tent and ruined my view*; cf. kizukiageru = to build up; cf. kizuku = to establish or build; cf. kumitateru = to assemble or build; cf. kumu = to assemble, make a plan, partner with, to fold arms or cross legs; cf. tatenaosu = to rebuild or reconstruct

Tateru 立てる = to raise, to put up, to treat with respect, to give someone their due, to set up or develop, to make (a noise), among many other meanings; *Tarzan has a Texas rooster, and we treat it with respect*; cf. related terms listed at kakageru and at settei suru

Tatoe 例え = example, supposing; an abbreviation of tatoeba = for example; cf. mihon = a sample or example; cf. rei = an example or precedent

Tatoeba 例えば = for example; *I often take risks; for example, I got this tattoo from an eccentric barber*

Tatsu 建つ = to be built; the intransitive form of tateru = to build

Tatsu 断つ = to cut off, discontinue; *when he wants to cut off a conversation, he tatsu (stands up)*; cf. kiru = to cut, to turn off, to hang up or stop, to turn a vehicle; cf. other related terms listed at yameru

Tatsu 立つ = to stand, to find oneself in (a difficult position); *he stood all day in his tattered suit*; cf. related terms listed at kiritsu suru

Tatsu 竜 = a dragon; *this tattered souvenir is supposed to be a model of a dragon*

Tatsu 経つ = to pass or elapse; *time has passed since I last wore my tattered suit*

Tatsu 裁つ = to cut (cloth); *she cut some cloth from a tattered suit*; cf. kiru = to cut, to turn off, to hang up or stop, to turn a vehicle

Tatsujin 達人 = expert, master; *the master wore tattered suits and jeans*; cf. related terms listed at kurouto

Tatsumaki 竜巻 = a tornado; *the tornado carried off my tattered suit with my master keys*

Tatta たった = only, merely, but, no more than; tatta is often used with numbers; *the tacky tavern is only five minutes away*; cf. related terms listed at dake and at miman

Tatte たって – see te mo ii

Taue 田植え = rice planting; from tanbo = rice paddy + ueru = to plant

Tawamureru 戯れる = to play, to be amused (with something); *when the tall warrior was in the right mood, he saw the red rooster and was amused*; cf. asobu = to play

Tawara 俵 = a straw bag; *I keep my tax warrants in a straw bag*; cf. related terms listed at fukuro

Tawashi タワシ = a scrubbing brush; *Tarzan was washing the dog with a scrubbing brush*; cf. related terms listed at fude

Tayori 便り = news, letter; *the tall Yorkshire man is reading his letters*; cf. related terms listed at tegami and at jouhou

Tayori 頼り = reliance; from tayoru = to rely on; cf. shinrai = trust, confidence, reliance; cf. shinyou = trust or faith

Tayoru 頼る = to rely or depend on; *a tax on yogurt is rumored, since the government has to rely on taxes for revenue*

Tazuna 手綱 = a bridle or reins (this is spelled taduna in electronic dictionaries); *Tarzan went to the zoo riding a nag equipped with a bridle*

Tazuneru 尋ねる = to ask, inquire or look for; *Tarzan went to the zoo after hearing the negative rumor and asked if it were true*; cf. related terms listed at ukagau

Tazuneru 訪ねる = to visit; *I visit the tall zookeeper when he neru (sleeps)*; cf. related terms listed at ukagau

Tazusaeru 携える = to carry with; *the tall zookeeper from Sapporo was erudite and he always carried an electronic dictionary with him*; cf. related terms listed at hakobu

Tazusawaru 携わる = to engage (in); *the tall zookeeper from Sapporo kept wasps in his room and was engaged in the science of entomology*

Te 手 = a hand; *I use my right hand to play tennis*; cf. teashi = hands and feet; cf. ryoute = both hands

Te mo daijoubu desuても大丈夫です – see te mo ii

Te mo ii てもいい = it's OK, used as a suffix incorporating the te or de form of a *positive* verb, e.g., tabete mo ii = it's OK to eat; this can also be expressed as te mo yoroshii, te mo daijoubu desu, or te mo kamaimasen

Te mo ii てもいい = something is not necessary, used as a suffix incorporating a *negative* verbal phrase ending in naku (like tabenaku) and followed by ii, yoi, kamawanai, kamaimasen or daijoubu, e.g., tabenakute mo ii = it isn't necessary to eat; sometimes this can be replaced by *tatte*, e.g., tabenakutatte ii desu = it isn't necessary to eat

Te mo kamaimasen てもかまいません – see te mo ii

Te mo yoroshii てもよろしい – see te mo ii

Te ni hairu 手に入る = to obtain or get one's hands on; from te = hand + ni = to + hairu = to enter; cf. related terms listed at shutoku suru

Te ni ireru 手に入れる = to obtain; from te = hand + ni = to + ireru = to insert or let in; cf. related terms listed at shutoku suru

Te ni kakaru 手にかかる = to be in someone's hands; from te = hand + kakaru = to hang, to be caught in, and other meanings

Te no kou 手の甲 = back of the hand; from te = hand + the possessive no + koura = shell

Te okure 手遅れ = occurring too late; from te = hand + okureru = to be delayed, suggesting that a hand was employed too late

Te wo furu 手を振る = to wave or shake the hand; from te = hand + furu = to wave; cf. related terms listed at furu

Te wo tazusaete 手を携えて = hand in hand; from te = hand + tazusaeru = to carry with

Teashi 手足 = hands and feet, limbs; from te = hand + ashi = foot or leg; cf. related terms listed at te

Teate 手当 = medical treatment; from te = hand + ateru = to touch; cf. related terms listed at chiryou

Tebukuro 手袋 = gloves; from te = hand + bukuro = fukuro = a bag

Techou 手帳 = pocket notebook; from te = hand + chou = notebook; *Margaret Cho writes her jokes in a notebook*; cf. related terms listed at hon

Teema テーマ = theme

Tegakeru 手がける = to manage or handle; *I will manage the Texas gas station that Kennedy ruined*; cf. related terms listed at shori suru

Tegami 手紙 = a letter; *while Ted was gaming, a letter arrived*; cf. shoukaijou = a letter of introduction; cf. tayori = news, letter

Tegaru 手軽 = easy, informal, cheap, quick; from te = hand + garui = karui = light weight; cf. related terms listed at kantan

Tegiwa 手際 = skill, performance, tact; *Tennessee geese swim on water and have skill in catching fish*; cf. gijutsu = skill, technique, technology; cf. nouryoku = skill, ability, competence; cf. waza = skill, technique

Tegoro 手頃 = handy, affordable; *Ted Kennedy rode on the merry-go-round because it was handy and affordable*; cf. benri = convenient, handy; cf. other related terms listed at yasui

Teguchi 手口 = a method or trick; *I learned a method for making textiles for Guchi bags*; cf. related terms listed at houhou

Tehai 手配 = arrangements, preparations; *we are making arrangements to buy a Teddy bear for Heidi*; cf. related terms listed at youi

Tehon 手本 = a copybook, a model or pattern; from te = hand + hon = book; cf. tenkei = type, model, representative

Tei 丁 = counter for guns, tools, leaves or cakes of something; *I attach a piece of tape to my desk as a counter after I complete ten tasks*

Teian 提案 = proposal; *the tape that Queen Anne sent contained her proposals*; cf. an = an idea, plan or proposal; cf. gen'an = the original proposal or plan; cf. moushide = a proposal

Teiban 定番 = a standard, routine, or staple; *the tailor's bandana was a standard size*

Teibou 堤防 = an embankment or dike; *the tailor's boat was tied up to a dike*; cf. tsutsumi = an embankment or dike

Teiden 停電 = power failure; *during the power failure, the tailor and the dentist started kissing*

Teido 程度 = criterion, standard, extent, degree, amount; *the taste of the dough met the baker's standard*; cf. kijun = criterion, standard; cf. shakudo = criterion, measure; cf. suijun = a standard or level

Teien 庭園 = a garden or park; *the tailor enjoyed the garden*; cf. kouen = a park; cf. other related terms listed at niwa

Teigi 定義 = a definition; *a definition of tame geese is "geese that let me hold them"*

Teihyou 定評 = reputation, notoriety; *the tailor's healing yogurt had a good reputation*; cf. related terms listed at hyouban

Teika suru 低下する = to decrease; *if you use tasers on the cats, their numbers will decrease*; cf. related terms listed at genshou suru

Teikei 定型 = a fixed form; *the tailor made the cape according to a fixed form*

Teikeishi 定型詩 = poetry with a fixed form; from teikei = a fixed form + shi = a poem

Teiki 定期 = routine, regularity; *my routine is to taste quiche before serving it*

Teikiteki ni 定期的に = at fixed intervals; from teiki = routine + teki = related to + -ni = a suffix that forms an adverb

Teikoku 帝国 = an empire; *when I get back to the empire, I want to taste Coke again*

Teikou 抵抗 = resistance, opposition; *the tailor and his co-workers are leading the resistance*; cf. related terms listed at hantai

Teikouryoku 抵抗力 = power of resistance; from teikou = resistance + ryoku = power; cf. related terms listed at hantai

Teikyou suru 提供する = to offer, provide or sponsor; *I will take you to Kyouto if you will provide our meals*; cf. related terms listed at kyoukyuu suru and at moushideru

Teinei 丁寧 = polite, courteous, careful; *be careful not to catch your tail on a nail*; cf. reigi tadashii = polite, well-mannered; cf. shinchou = careful, prudent

Teion 低温 = a low temperature; from teika suru = to decrease + ondo = temperature; cf. related terms listed at ondo

Te'ire (Teire) 手入れ = care; from te = hand + ireru = to insert; cf. related terms listed at hogo

Te'ire (Teire) wo suru 手入れをする = to take care of; from teire = care; cf. related terms listed at azukaru

Teisei 訂正 = a correction; *we can make a correction to the boat by taping the sails*; cf. kyousei = a correction

Teisha 停車 = stopping (a vehicle); *when the taser was fired at the Shah, it resulted in a stopping of his vehicle*; cf. related terms listed at chuushi

Teisha eki 停車駅 = scheduled train stop; from teisha = stopping (vehicle) + eki = station

Teishi 停止 = stoppage or suspension; *the tame sheep caused a stoppage of traffic*; cf. related terms listed at chuushi

Teishu 亭主 = a husband or owner; *the owner, who is my husband, has good taste in shoes*; cf. related terms listed at shujin

Teishutsu suru 提出する = to hand in or submit; *if that taser shoots me, I will submit my resignation*

Teitaku 邸宅 = mansion, residence; *the tailor had tap water and Kool-Aid flowing from the faucets in his mansion*; cf. daiteitaku = a mansion; cf. koutei = official residence; cf. yashiki = an estate, mansion or residence; cf. other related terms listed at ie

Teitoku 提督 = an admiral; *the admiral sitting at that table is totally cool*; cf. similar terms listed at shikan

Teitou 抵当 = mortgage; *the tailor toiled to pay off his mortgage*

Teki 敵 = enemy, opponent; *that techie is my enemy*; cf. related terms listed at aite

Teki 滴 = a drop; *that techie doesn't drink a drop of alcohol*; cf. related terms listed at tsubu

Teki 的 = related to, used as a suffix; *the techie is responsible for issues related to software*

Teki wo utsu 敵を討つ – see kataki wo utsu

Tekido 適度 = moderate; *that techie eats doughnuts in moderate quantities*

Tekigi 適宜 = suitable, appropriate; *the techie thought that the geese were suitable*; cf. related terms listed at tekitou

Tekinin 適任 = competent, suitable, qualified; *the techie and the ninja were competent*; cf. yuunou = competent; cf. other related terms listed at tekitou

Tekiou 適応 = adaptation, accommodation; *that techie is old, but he has skills in adaptation and accommodation to the needs of others*; cf. junnou = adaptation

Tekiou ryoku 適応力 = adaptability; from tekiou = adaptation + ryoku = strength or force, e.g., doryoku = effort

Tekisetsu 適切 = proper, fitting; *the techie set Superman's password in a proper way*; cf. related terms listed at tekitou

Tekisuto テキスト = a textbook; cf. related terms listed a kyoukasho

Tekitou na 適当な = appropriate, suitable, reasonable; *that techie's toes are suitable for typing on a keyboard*; cf. atarimae = natural, reasonable; cf. datou na = right, appropriate, reasonable; cf. soutou = appropriate, considerable, very large; cf. tekigi = suitable, appropriate; cf. tekinin = competent, suitable, qualified; cf. tekisetsu = proper, fitting; cf. tennen = natural; cf. touzen = justly, natural

Tekka maki 鉄火巻 = raw tuna sushi wrapped in seaweed; *in Texas and California, people are making raw tuna sushi wrapped in seaweed*; cf. related terms listed at ryouri

Tekkou 鉄鉱 = iron ore; from tetsu = iron + koubutsu = mineral

Tekkou 鉄鋼 = steel; *the tent poles were cold because they were made of steel*; cf. related terms listed at tetsu

Tekkyou 鉄橋 = iron bridge, railroad bridge; from tetsu = iron + kyou = bridge; *a bridge was built in Kyouto*

Tekubi 手首 = a wrist; from te = hand + kubi = neck

Tema 手間 = a lot of time or trouble; from te = hand + ma = duration, e.g., mamonaku = before long; cf. related terms listed at meiwaku

Temae 手前 = before, this side; from te = hand + mae = before; cf. similar terms listed at hou

Temo (demo, tomo) ても = even if, even though, no matter how; this is a suffix formed by adding mo to an adjective's te form, or by adding temo or demo to a verb stem, or by using demo after a na adjective or a noun; when used with some adjectives expressing amount, temo = "at the very most or least, etc."

Temoto 手元 = at hand, nearby; *Ted Kennedy kept his motorcycle nearby*; cf. related terms listed at chikai

Ten 天 = heavens, sky; *we play tennis under the sky*; cf. related terms listed at sora

Ten 店 = a shop or store, not used by itself but as a word component, e.g., shiten = a branch store; *that store sells tennis equipment*; cf. related terms listed at mise

Ten 点 = a point, a spot, a decimal point; *to prove her point, she lived in a tent*

Tenchou 店長 = a store manager; from ten = a shop or store + chou = a chief or leader; cf. related terms listed at shunou

Tengoku 天国 = heaven, paradise; from ten = sky, e.g., tenki = weather; + goku = koku = country

Ten'in (Tenin) 店員 = a store clerk; from ten = a shop or store + in = a group member

Tenji 展示 = a display or exhibition; *there are ten Jeeps in this display*; cf. chinretsu = a display; cf. hakki = an exhibition, display, manifestation; cf. shashinten = a photography exhibit; cf. tenjikai = an exhibition; cf. tenrankai = an exhibition

Tenjihin 展示品 = display goods; from tenji = display + hin = goods, e.g., seihin = a product

Tenjikai 展示会 = exhibition; from tenji = display + kaigi = meeting; cf. related terms listed at tenji

Tenjiru 転じる = to turn or shift; *the tenacious genius who ruled over the factory decided to shift its production to electric cars*; cf. related terms listed at mawasu

Tenjou 天井 = ceiling; *the tent that Joan of Arc slept in had a low ceiling*

Tenka 天下 = realm, world, nation; from ten = heaven + ka = below; cf. related terms listed at sekai

Tenka 添加 = an addition; *the Tennessee cabin will have an addition built*; cf. tsuika = addition, supplement

Tenkabutsu 添加物 = an additive (e.g., to food); from tenka = addition + butsu = thing

Tenkai 展開 = development; *the tenacious Kaiser insisted on further development*; cf. related terms listed at hattatsu

Tenkei 典型 = type, model, representative; *these ten canines are representative of the dog species*; cf. tehon = a copybook, a model or pattern; cf. other related terms listed at shurui

Tenkeiteki 典型的 = typical; from tenkei = representative + teki = related to; cf. tokuyuu = characteristic (of), peculiar (to)

Tenken 点検 = inspection; *ten Kennedys conducted the inspection*; cf. etsuran = inspection, reading, browsing (e.g., the web); cf. kanshi = monitoring, watching, inspection; cf. ken'etsu = censorship, inspection; cf. kengaku = inspection, field trip; cf. kenmon = an inspection or examination; cf. shirabe = a tune, tone, writing style, investigation, inspection, examination; cf. shitami = a preliminary inspection, preview, rehearsal

Tenki 天気 = weather; *the tennis player keeps checking the weather forecast*; cf. akutenkou = bad weather; cf. hideri = dry weather, drought; cf. kanbatsu = a drought; cf. kikou = climate; cf. kishou = weather or climate; cf. kouten = good weather; cf. tenkou = weather; cf. tenkou furyou = bad weather

Tenkin 転勤 = a job transfer; *ten kings agreed to his job transfer*

Tenkou 天候 = weather; *thanks to the weather, we have tender corn this year*; cf. related terms listed at tenki

Tenkou furyou 天候不良 = bad weather; from tenkou = weather + furyou = poor condition; cf. related terms listed at tenki

Tenmei 店名 = a name of a store; from ten = a store + meishou = a name; cf. related terms listed at namae

Tenmetsu suru 点滅する = to go on and off, to blink; *when the tennis coach met Superman, the lights in the house began to blink*; cf. related terms listed at matataku

Tennai 店内 = store interior; from tennin = store clerk + nai = inside

Tennen 天然 = natural; *ten nen [years] ago, this was all a natural forest*; cf. related terms listed at tekitou

Tennentou 天然痘 = smallpox; *ten nen (years) ago, my toes showed signs of smallpox*; cf. related terms listed at byouki

Tennin 店員 = a store clerk; *there are ten ninjas in line and only one store clerk to wait on them*

Tennou 天皇 = the Emperor of Japan; *the Emperor of Japan played tennis in Osaka*; cf. related terms listed at ou

Tenohira 掌 = the palm of the hand; from te = hand + the possessive no + hira = flat

Tenpo 店舗 = shop, store; *you can buy tent poles in that shop*; cf. related terms listed at mise

Tenpu 添付 = an attachment or appendix; *the tennis court and pool are attachments to the house*

Tenpu suru 添付する = to attach or

append; from tenpu = an attachment or appendix; cf. related terms listed at tsukeru

Tenpuku suru 転覆する = to capsize or overturn (intransitive); *after ten days of puking from seasickness, his boat capsized*; cf. utsugaeru = to be overturned

Tenpura 天ぷら = Japanese deep-fried food; *after playing tennis with Putin, the rascal enjoyed some deep-fried food*; cf. related terms listed at ryouri

Tenraku suru 転落する = to fall or decline; *since ten raccoons fell off a cliff, their population has declined*; cf. related terms listed at ochiru and at genshou suru

Tenrankai 展覧会 = an exhibition; *a tennis player ran into a kite during an athletic exhibition*; cf. related terms listed at tenji

Tensai 天才 = genius; *ten scientists said that he is a genius*

Tensai 天災 = natural disaster; from tennen = natural + sainan = disaster; cf. related terms listed at saigai

Tenshaku 天爵 = true merit, natural nobility; *that tennis player lives in a shack, but she has true merit*

Tenshi 天使 = angel; from ten = sky, e.g., tenki = weather; + shi = servant, e.g., taishi = ambassador

Tenshou 転生 = reincarnation; *the ten shows that I watched were about reincarnation*

Tenshu 店主 = shop owner; from tennin = store clerk + shujin = master; cf. related terms listed at mochinushi

Tensuu 点数 = score, marks, points; *when we play tennis, Superman keeps score*; cf. related terms listed at seiseki

Tenteki 点滴 = an intravenous infusion; *after playing tennis, the techie needed an intravenous infusion to rehydrate*

Tenui 手縫い = hand-sewn; from te = hand + nuu = to sew

Teppai 撤廃 = abolition; *they worked toward the abolition of terrible pies*

Teppanyaki 鉄板焼き = food grilled on an iron griddle; from tetsu = iron + pan = plank or plate; *that pan is made from metal plates*; + yaku = to cook; cf. related terms listed at ryouri

Teppen てっぺん = top, summit; *I carried a Teddy bear and a pen to the summit*; cf. related terms listed at choujou

Teppou 鉄砲 = a gun; *in Texas, the police carry guns*; cf. juu = a gun; cf. kenjuu = a handgun

Tera 寺 = a temple; *there is a terrace outside the temple*; cf. bukkaku = a Buddhist temple; cf. jiin = a Buddhist temple

Terasu 照らす = to illuminate or light; *the terrarium looks super when I illuminate it*

Tereru 照れる = to be shy or feel embarrassment; *I feel embarrassed about eating that tender red rooster*; cf. kaomake da = (someone) is put to shame

Teriyaki 照り焼き = meat or fish marinated in sweet soy sauce and broiled; from teru = to shine + yaku = to grill; cf. related terms listed at ryouri

Teru 照る = to shine; *the television in my room shines all night*; cf. haeru = to shine or look attractive; cf. hikaru = to shine, glitter or stand out; cf. kagayaku = to shine, glitter, sparkle; cf. pikapika suru = to sparkle or glisten; cf. sashikomu = shine in, flow in

Tesagyou 手作業 = manual labor; from te = hand + sagyou = work, operations; cf. related terms listed at shigoto

Tessaku 鉄柵 = iron fence; from tetsu = iron + saku = fence; cf. related terms listed at kakine

Tesuu 手数 = pains or trouble; from te = hand + suu = numeral

Tesuuryou 手数料 = a handling fee or

comission; from tesuu = trouble + ryoukin = fee

Tetsu 鉄 = iron; *the tetanus shot that Superman gave was administered via an iron needle*; cf. koutetsu = steel; cf. tekkou = steel; cf related terms listed at tanso

Tetsu 哲 = philosophy, used as a word component; *a guy who works in a tetracycline factory in Sudan reads philosophy*; cf. tetsugaku = philosophy

Tetsudai 手伝い = help or helper, maid; from tetsudau = to help; cf. related terms listed at kyuujo

Tetsudau 手伝う = to help; *the tetanus shot that Superman gave my daughter helped her*; cf. related terms listed at tasukeru

Tetsudou 鉄道 = railroad, railway; from tetsu = iron + dou = way

Tetsugaku 哲学 = philosophy; from tetsu = philosophy + gaku = learning

Tetsugakusha 哲学者 = a philosopher; from tetsugaku = philosophy + sha = person

Tetsuki 手つき = manner of using the hands; from te = hand + tsukau = to use

Tetsuya 徹夜 = all night; *the tetracycline factory in Sudan was run by yakuza (gangsters), and it operated all night*; cf. ichiya = one evening, all night; cf. shinya = the dead of night; cf. yakan = at night; cf. yonaka = the middle of the night; cf. yodooshi = throughout the night

Tetsuzuki 手続き = procedure; *the tetsu (iron) is inspected by the zookeeper according to a specific procedure*

Tettai 撤退 = evacuation, withdrawal, retreat; *after giving tetanus shots to Thai students, we had to conduct an evacuation*

Tettei 徹底 = thoroughness, completeness; *the tetanus vaccine was wrapped in tape in a display of thoroughness*

Tewatasu 手渡す = to hand to or submit; from te = hand + watasu = to hand over; cf. related terms at hakobu

Tezawari 手触り = touch, feel; from te = hand + zawaru = sawaru = to touch or feel

To と = a quotation marker, used before a quotation

To と = and, with, if, when; cf. related terms listed at soshite

To 戸 = door; *I caught my toe in the door*; cf. related terms listed at doa

To ikenai kara といけないから = literally, "if, since bad"; used after a clause describing a possible activity in order to suggest a resulting course of action, e.g., yuki ga furu to ikenai kara hayaku kaetta hou ga ii = if it snows, since bad, it would be better to return early

To itte mo ii と言ってもいい = it's all right to say; from to = quotation marker + iu = to say + te mo ii = it's OK

To itte mo ii hodo desu と言ってもいいほどです = it's all right to say to that degree, or you could go so far as to say; from to itte mo ii = it's all right to say + hodo = extent

To iu という = called, named, about (e.g., to iu monogatari = a story about); from to = a quotation marker + iu = to say

To iu koto da ということだ (or tte iu koto da) – see to iu koto desu

To iu koto desu ということです (or to iu koto da, or tte iu koto desu) = therefore, or something is reported to be true; from to = a quotation marker + iu = to say + koto = intangible thing + desu = it is; cf. related terms listed at dakara

To iu koto wa ということは (or tte iu koto wa) = that is to say, so that means, because; from to = a quotation marker + iu = to say + koto = an intangible thing; cf. to iu no wa (or tte iu no wa) = as for the one called, that is to say, because; cf. to wa =

as for the one called; cf. tte = something is reportedly true, speaking of, as for the one called, because

To iu no wa というのは (or tte iu no wa) = as for the one called, that is to say, because; from to = a quotation marker + iu = to say + no = a nominalizer (converts iu into the noun phrase "said thing") + wa = as for; cf. related terms listed at to iu koto wa

To iu wake desu という訳です (or to iu wake da) = therefore or as a result; from to = a quotation marker + iu = to say + wake = reason + desu = it is; cf. related terms listed at dakara

To kitara ときたら = regarding, concerning; this is equivalent to "ni tsuite," but "to kitara" is used when a speaker is expressing negative feelings about a topic; *we received a complaint concerning the fact that Tolstoy keeps talking about rats*; cf. related terms listed at ni tsuite

To naru となる = to become, to amount to; from to = with + naru = to become; cf. ni naru = to become, to do honorably

To sareru とされる = is considered to be, is required, is claimed, seems to be; from to = if + sareru = the passive form of suru = to do, so this can be understood literally as "if it is done on"

To shite として = as (in the role of), for (from the viewpoint of), apart from (used to change the topic), not even (with a negative verb), thinking that, trying to; this is the te form of to suru = to take as, to regard as, to look or feel like

To suru とする = to take as, to regard as, to look or feel like; this also = to try to do, to be about to do, and several other meanings; *I regarded as excellent the toaster that Superman ruined, and its destruction felt like a major loss*; cf. related terms listed at tamesu

To wa とは = as for the one called; from to = a quotation marker + wa = as for; cf. tte = something is reportedly true, speaking of, as for the one called, because; also used to indicate insistence or certainty; cf. related terms listed at to iu koto wa

To wa kagiranai とは限らない = not necessarily so, is not always true; see kagiranai

Tobaku 賭博 = gambling; *while engaged in gambling, I smoked tobacco in Kuwait*; cf. related terms listed at bakuchi

Tobasu 飛ばす = to fly, speed, skip over; *Tony Blair's basu (bus) was speeding*; cf. tobu = to fly

Tobiagaru 跳びあがる = to jump up; from tobu = to fly + agaru = to rise; cf. related terms listed at tobu

Tobibako 跳び箱 = a vaulting box; from tobu = to jump + bako = hako = box

Tobidasu 飛び出す = to jump out or fly out; from tobu = to fly + dasu = put out; cf. related terms listed at tobu

Tobihaneru 飛び跳ねる = to hop; from tobu = to fly + haneru = to hop; cf. related terms listed at tobu

Tobikakaru 飛びかかる = to leap at, to swoop down on; from tobu = to fly + kakaru = to hang; cf. related terms listed at tobu

Tobikoeru 飛び越える = to jump over; from tobu = to fly + koeru = to go across; cf. related terms listed at tobu

Tobikomu 飛び込む = to jump or dive in; from tobu = to fly + komu = to crowd in; cf. related terms listed at tobu

Tobinoru 飛び乗る = to jump onto a moving object; from tobu = to fly + noru = to board a vehicle; cf. related terms listed at tobu

Tobiokiru 飛び起きる = to jump to one's feet; from tobu = to fly + okiru = to get up; cf. related terms listed at tobu

Tobioriru 飛び降りる = to jump down; from tobu = to fly + oriru = to exit a vehicle; cf. related terms listed at tobu

Tobira 扉 = a front door, a title page; *when I came out of the <u>front</u> <u>door</u>, I encountered a <u>tortoise</u> and a <u>beaming</u> <u>rabbit</u> and guessed who had won their race*; cf. related terms listed at doa

Tobitatsu 飛び立つ = to jump up, to fly away, to take off; from tobu = to fly + tatsu = to stand up; cf. related terms listed at tobu

Tobitsuku 飛びつく = to jump at; from tobu = to fly + tsuku = to adhere; cf. related terms listed at tobu

Toboshii 乏しい = scarce; <u>toboggans</u> in <u>Shiite</u> country are <u>scarce</u>; cf. related terms listed at tarinai

Tobu 跳ぶ = to jump or leap; *Tony Blair wears <u>boots</u> when he <u>jumps</u>*; cf. haneru = to jump or hop; cf. moguru = to dive or hide; cf. tobiagaru = to jump up; cf. tobidasu = to jump out or fly out; cf. tobihaneru = to hop; cf. tobikakaru = to leap at, to swoop down on; cf. tobikoeru = to jump over; cf. tobikomu = to jump or dive in; cf. tobiokiru = to jump to one's feet; cf. tobinoru = to jump onto a moving object; cf. tobioriru = to jump down; cf. tobitatsu = to jump up, to fly away, to take off; cf. tobitsuku = to jump at; cf. tsukkomu = to thrust into or jump into

Tobu 飛ぶ = to fly; *after a few <u>toasts</u> of <u>booze</u>, I felt that I could <u>fly</u>*; cf. tobasu = to fly, speed, skip over

Tochi 土地 = land, place; *<u>tomatoes</u> are <u>cheap</u> in this <u>place</u>*; cf. related terms listed at basho

Tochuu 途中 = halfway; *<u>Tolstoy</u> <u>chewed</u> gum when he was <u>halfway</u> to school*

Tochuu de 途中で = en route, in the middle; from tochuu = halfway; cf. chuuto = in the middle, half-way; cf. douchuu = along the way; cf. toorisugari = on the way, passing

Todana 戸棚 = cupboard; from to = door + dana = tana = shelf

Todoke 届 = a notification, registration or report; from todokeru = to report or deliver

Todokeru 届ける = to deliver, to report; the transitive form of todoku = to reach, to be received

Todokooru 滞る = to stagnate, be delayed, be left undone; *the trial <u>was</u> <u>delayed</u> after a <u>tornado</u> blew a <u>door</u> off a <u>courtroom</u>*

Todoku 届く = to reach, to be received; *<u>Tolstoy's</u> <u>document</u> <u>reached</u> a large audience after it was finally <u>received</u> by his <u>publisher</u>*; cf. related terms listed at oyobu

Todomaru とどまる = to stay, remain or stop; *we <u>told</u> the <u>doorman</u> who was <u>marooned</u> to <u>remain</u> where he was*; cf. related terms listed at taizai suru

Todoufuken 都道府県 = the 47 administrative divisions of Japan; *Tony Blair gave some <u>dough</u> (money) and <u>food</u> to <u>Ken</u> for memorizing the <u>administrative</u> <u>divisions</u> of <u>Japan</u>*; cf. similar terms listed at ken

Todouji ni と同時に = at the same time, as well; from to = and + douji ni = at the same time; cf. related terms listed at douji ni

Toge 刺 = thorn (this is usually spelled とげ); *we have to accept <u>thorns</u> <u>together</u> with roses*

Togeru 遂げる = to accomplish; *Santa told his reindeer, "If you work <u>together</u> with <u>Rudolph</u>, you can <u>accomplish</u> the deliveries"*; cf. related terms listed at hatasu

Togiageru 研ぎ上げる = to finish sharpening; from togu = to sharpen + ageru = to finish

Togu 研ぐ = to sharpen, to wash rice; *he used his <u>toes</u> to hold the <u>goose</u> while he <u>sharpened</u> his knife*; cf. togiageru = to finish sharpening

Toho 徒歩 = walking, going on foot; *<u>Tolstoy</u> went <u>home</u> <u>walking</u>*; cf. related terms listed at sanpo

Toi 問い = a question; from tou = to ask or enquire; cf. related terms listed at utagai

To'iki (Toiki) 吐息 = a sigh; *the toilet was icky, and he let out a sigh*; cf. tame'iki = a sigh

Tojikomeru 閉じ込める = to confine or shut up; from tojiru = to close + komeru = to put into

Tojimari 戸締まり = fastening doors; from to = door + jimari = shimari = fastening

Tojiru 閉じる = to close or shut; *I told the genius and Ruth to close the door*; cf. heisa suru = to close down; cf. shimeru = to close

Toka とか = etcetera; *I totaled my car, etcetera*; cf. related terms listed at nado

Tokai 都会 = city; *Tolstoy advised the Kaiser to expand his cities*; cf. related terms listed at shi

Tokareru 解かれる = to get solved or untied; the passive form of toku = to untie, solve, undo, work out, dispel; cf. synonyms listed at tokeru

Tokasu 溶かす = to melt or dissolve (transitive); *I used a torch to light a candle in Sudan in order to melt wax*

Tokasu とかす = to comb; *I sit on a tomato can with Superman while we comb our hair*

Tokehajimeru 溶け始める = to begin to melt; from tokeru = to melt + hajimeru = to start something

Tokei 時計 = a watch or clock; *when the tornado came, I glanced at my watch*

Tokekomu 溶け込む = to blend in or adjust; from tokeru = to melt or dissolve + komu = to crowd in

Tokeru 溶ける = to melt or dissolve (intransitive); *the butter in the toy kettle in my room melted*; cf. torokeru = to melt, to be charmed (intransitive)

Tokeru 解ける = to be solved or untied (intransitive); *the toys that Kennedy kept in his room were tied up in bundles, and they got untied*; cf. osamaru = to be settled or solved; cf. tokareru = to get solved or untied

Toki 時 = time; *at that time a toad was the king of this pond*; cf. related terms listed at jikan

Toki ni 時に = occasionally, by the way; from toki = time + ni = by; cf. related terms listed at tama ni

Toki to shite 時として = sometimes; from toki = time + to shite = in the role of; cf. related terms listed at tama ni

Tokidoki 時々 = sometimes, now and then; from toki = time + doki = toki = time; cf. related terms listed at tama ni

Tokihanatsu 解き放つ = to release; from toku = to undo or solve + hanatsu = to release; *Hannah's tsuitcase (suitcase) was released by Customs*; cf. hanasu = to release, loosen; cf. houmen suru = to acquit, release or let loose; cf. kaihou suru = to emancipate, liberate or release; cf. shakuhou suru = to release

Tokikata 解き方 = manner of solving; from tokeru = to be solved + kata = method

Tokiori 時折り = once in a while; from toki = time + ori = occasion; cf. related terms listed at tama ni

Tokken 特権 = privilege; *the king's crown is a token of his privilege*; cf. kenri = right, privilege

Tokku ni とっくに = a long time ago, already; *Tony from Kuwait met my niece a long time ago*

Tokkumiai 取っ組み合い = a scuffle; *during the scuffle, Tolstoy's Kool-Aid got into the mediator's eye*; cf. related terms listed at issen

Tokkun 特訓 = intensive training; from toku ni = especially + kunren = training; cf. related terms listed at kunren

Tokkyuu 特急 = limited express (train); from toku = special + kyuu = urgent; cf. related terms listed at densha

Toko 床 = a bed or floor; *after Tony Blair had a coronary, he spent a lot of time in bed or on the floor*; cf. yuka = a floor

Tokoro ところ = circumstance, time, moment; *Tony's coronary occurred at that moment*

Tokoro ところ = just (about to), just (when), just (finished), in the process of; used as a suffix and often followed by da or desu; *Tony's coronary might happen just when he is making a speech and is on the point of discussing the budget*; cf. totan ni = just as

Tokoro 所 = a place or a part; *Tony Blair had a coronary at this place*; cf. related terms listed at basho and at ichibu

Tokoro de ところで = by the way, even if, no matter what; *by the way, Tony had a coronary, even if he took his medicine correctly*; cf. chinami ni = in passing, incidentally

Tokorodoko 所々 = here and there, several places; from tokoro = place + dokoro = tokoro = place; cf. suukasho = several places

Tokoya 床屋 = barbershop; *Tony Blair drinks cola with his Yankee friends at the barbershop*

Toku 得 = gain, profit; *it's totally cool that I will make a profit*; cf. rieki = profit; cf. saisan = profit, surplus

Toku 特 = special; *Tony Blair thought that Kuwait was special*; cf. related terms listed at tokubetsu

Toku 解く = to untie, unfasten, solve; *he solved the problem by mixing tomato juice and Kool-Aid*; cf. related terms listed at hogureru

Toku ni 特に = especially, particularly; *after Tolstoy spilled Kool-Aid on his knee, he seemed especially anxious to go home*; cf. betsu ni = particularly; cf. koto ni = especially, moreover, what is more; cf. ni kagitte = particularly when

Tokubai 特売 = a special sale; from tokubetsu = special + baibai = buying and selling; cf. related terms listed at uriage

Tokubetsu 特別 = special, exceptional; *it's totally cool that you bet on Superman, since he's an exceptional guy*; cf. irei = exceptional, unprecedented, single; cf. toku = special; cf. tokushu na = unique, peculiar, special

Tokuchou 特徴 = a characteristic or special feature; *totally cool chores usually include special features, such as opportunities for snacking*; cf. kuse = a habit or characteristic; cf. meibutsu = famous or special product, specialty; cf. tokushuu = a feature or special edition; cf. zokusei = an attribute

Tokui 得意 = pride, strong point; *my French toast cuisine is my strong point*; cf. choushou = merit, a strong point; cf. other related terms listed at hokori

Tokumei 匿名 = anonymity; *Tolstoy used a Kuwaiti mailing address to preserve his anonymity*

Tokushu na 特殊な = unique, peculiar, special; *these totally cool shoes are unique*; cf. related terms listed at dokuji and at tokubetsu

Tokushuu 特集 = a feature, a special edition; *totally cool shoes are a feature of their costumes*); cf. kuse = a habit or characteristic; cf. tokuchou = a characteristic or special feature

Tokutei 特定 = particular, specific; *it's totally cool that the tailor created a specific design for you*

Tokuten 得点 = marks or score; *the totally*

cool *tennis* player received good *marks*; cf. related terms listed at seiseki

Tokuyuu 特有 = characteristic (of), peculiar (to); *it's totally cool that the Yukon has so many characteristic features*; cf. tenkeiteki = typical

Tomadou 戸惑う = to be bewildered or perplexed; *when someone threw tomatoes at my door, I was bewildered*

Tomaru 止まる = to stop (intransitive); *the tomatoes were ruined when it stopped raining*; cf. yamu = to stop (intransitive)

Tomaru 泊まる = to stay overnight (house or hotel); *in exchange for the tomatoes in that room, you can stay overnight*; cf. related terms listed at taizai suru

Tomeru 止める = to stop or turn off, to park a car; the transitive form of tomaru = to stop; cf. related terms listed at yameru

Tomi 富 = wealth; from tomu = to get rich; cf. bunkazai = cultural assets; cf. yuufuku = wealth; cf. zaisan = assets, fortune, property; cf. zenzaisan = everything one owns

Tomo とも – see temo

Tomo ni 共に = together; *we are going to have tomograms of our knees done together*; cf. related terms listed at issho ni

Tomodachi 友達 = a friend; *tomorrow I will give some dark cheese to my friend*; cf. chijin = an acquaintance or friend; cf. kyuuyuu = an old friend; cf. nakayoshi = a close friend; cf. osananajimi = a childhood friend; cf. shiriai = an acquaintance; cf. yuujin = a friend

Tomonau 伴う = to take with, to be accompanied by; *if I am getting my tomogram now, I want to be accompanied by my mother*

Tomu 富む = to get rich, to abound with; *Tony Blair's mood improved when he got rich*; cf. related terms listed at megumareru

Tomurau 弔う = to mourn, to hold a funeral; *Tony Blair moved Raul Castro's chair when they held a funeral*

Tonaeru 唱える = to advocate, recite, advance or insist; *the tonal quality of the erudite attorney's voice impressed us as she advocated for justice*; cf. shuchou suru = to advocate, assert or claim

Tonari 隣 = neighboring, the house next door; *Tobias of Narita lives in the neighboring house*

Tonari doushi 隣同士 = nextdoor neighbor; from tonari = neighbor + doushi = comrade, peer, each other

Tonaru となる – see to naru

Tonchaku suru 頓着する = to care about; *his tongue craves champagne and Kool-Aid, and that's what he cares about*; cf. related terms listed at kamau

Tondemonai とんでもない = unthinkable, unexpected, not at all; *Tony Blair and the debutante moaned about ghosts at night, but it was unthinkable to take them to the psych ward*; cf. related terms listed at igai

Tonikaku とにかく = anyhow, in any case; *I didn't win the Tony Award, but I will kaku [write] a book, in any case*; cf. douse = anyhow, after all; cf. nani shiro = at any rate, anyhow

Tonkatsu 豚カツ = pork cutlet, breaded and fried; *I stuck my tongue out at the cats that were eating pork cutlet*; cf. related terms listed at ryouri

Tonkotsu 豚骨 = a Japanese dish made with simmered pork belly, vegetables, etc.; *Tony Blair removed his coats before eating a Japanese dish made with simmered pork belly, vegetables, etc.*; cf. related terms listed at ryouri

Tono 殿 = lord, master; *that lord is totally normal*; cf. related terms listed at shujin

Tonokoto とのこと = I'm told, (someone) was informed, I'm passing on a message; from to, a quotation marker, + no = from + koto = intangible thing

Tonosama 殿様 = daimyo, feudal lord; from tono = lord; + sama = very honorable; cf. related terms listed at shujin

Tooboe 遠吠え = howling; from tooi = far + boeru = hoeru = to bark; cf. nakigoe = an animal cry, howl, chirp; cf. nakigoe = a human cry, weeping;

Tooi 遠い = far; *my toys are far from here*

Tooku 遠く = far away, a distant place; the adverbial form of tooi = far

Toonoku 遠のく = to become distant, to recede; from tooi = far + tachinoku = to evacuate

Toori 通り = street, avenue, way; *the Tory lives on this street*; cf. related terms listed at michi

Toorikakaru 通りかかる = to happen to pass by; *the Tories called the captain into their room when he happened to pass by*; cf. related terms listed at tooru

Toorinukeru 通り抜ける = to pass through; from tooru = to pass through + nukeru = to go through; cf. related terms listed at tooru

Toorisugari 通りすがり = on the way, passing; *the Tory drank sugary drinks on the way to Parliament*; cf. related terms listed at tochuu de

Toorisugiru 通り過ぎる = to pass through; from tooru = to pass through + sugiru = to pass through; cf. related terms listed at tooru

Tooru 通る = to pass through, to pass an exam; *Tony Blair was in the room when I passed through*; cf. kuguru = to go under, pass through; cf. toorikakaru = to happen to pass by; cf. toorinukeru = to pass through; cf. toorisugiru = to pass through

Toosu 通す = to lead (into a house), to show in, to force or let through, to go through, to persist in, to penetrate, to proceed logically; the transitive form of tooru = to pass through

Toppa suru 突破する = to break through; *the Tory party broke through and won the election*

Tora 虎 = tiger; *Tony Blair ran away from the tiger*

Toraeru 捕える = to arrest, capture or understand; *he has studied the Torah and is quite erudite, so we cannot hope to capture him*; cf. taiho suru = to arrest; cf. toriosaeru = to capture or arrest; cf. toru = to catch; cf. tsukamaeru = to capture, catch or seize; cf. other related terms listed at wakaru

Torawareru 捕らわれる = to be caught; the intransitive form of torareru = to capture; cf. other related terms listed at tsukamaru

Toreenaa トレーナー = trainer

Toreeningu トレーニング = training; cf. related terms listed at kunren

Toreru 取れる = to come off, to be removed, to disappear; the potential form of toru = to take

Tori 鳥 = a bird; *the Tory keeps a bird in a cage*; cf. ahiru = a duck; cf. hakuchou = a swan; cf. ichiwa = one bird; cf. kotori = a small bird; cf. niwatori = a chicken; cf. ondori = a rooster; cf. sagi = a heron; cf. taka = a hawk; cf. tanchou = Japanese crane; cf. tsuru = a crane; cf. washi = eagle

Toriaezu とりあえず = for now, for the time being; *the Tories are going to visit the art exhibit at the zoo, for the time being*; cf. ichiou = more or less, tentatively, for the time being; cf. toubun = for the moment, for awhile; cf. zantei = tentative, temporary

Torigeru 取り上げる = to take up or feature, to adopt, to take away, to pick up;

from toru = to take + ageru = to raise; cf. related terms listed at hirou and at shutoku suru

Toriatsukau 取り扱う = to handle or treat; from toru = to take + atsukau = to take care of; cf. related terms listed at shori suru

Toriawase 取り合わせ = assortment, combination; from toru = to take + awaseru = to harmonize or put together

Toridasu 取り出す = to extract; from toru = to take + dasu = to take out; cf. nuku = to extract, omit, outrun or surpass

Torie 取り柄 = merit or good point; *he helped the Tories escape, so that was his good point*; cf. related terms listed at hokori

Torihazusu 取り外す = to dismantle, detach or take something away; from toru = to take + hazusu = to remove or take off; cf. kuzusu = to dismantle, pull down or destroy, to throw off balance, to change money

Torihiki 取引 = business deal; *if you do business deals with birds, you may get a tori (bird) hickey*

Toriireru 取り入れる = to harvest, take in, adopt, incorporate; from toru = to take + ireru = to put in; cf. shuuyou suru = to accommodate or take in; cf. other related terms listed at mochikomu and at shuukaku suru

Torikaeru 取り替える = to exchange or replace; from toru = to take + kaeru = to replace or exchange; cf. related terms listed at koukan suru

Torikago 鳥かご = bird cage; from tori = bird + kago = basket; *we use baskets to carry our cargo*; cf. related terms listed at kago

Torikakaru 取り掛かる = to begin or set out, to launch or start; from toru = to take + kakaru = to start doing something; cf. uchiageru = launch or shoot off, to finish or close (a performance); cf. other related terms listed at hajimeru

Torikakomu 取り囲む = to surround; from toru = to take + kakomu = to surround; cf. related terms listed at kakomu

Torikkusutaa トリックスター = a trickster

Toriko 虜 = captive, prisoner; *the Tory corporal captured a prisoner*; cf. related terms listed at horyo

Torikowasu 取り壊す = to tear down; from toru = to take + kowasu = to destroy; cf. related terms listed at kowasu

Torikumi 取り組み = initiative, effort, dealing with; from torikumu = to deal with; cf. related terms listed at doryoku

Torikumu 取り組む = to deal with, wrestle with; from toru = to take + kumu = to assemble or make a plan; cf. related terms listed at shori suru

Torimachigaeru 取り間違える = to take something by mistake; from toru = to take + machigaeru = to mistake; cf. related terms listed at machigaeru

Torimaku 取りまく = to surround; *sand dunes surround the Tory's mall in Kuwait*; cf. related terms listed at kakomu

Torimodosu 取り戻す = to get back or take back; from toru = to take + modosu = to put back, to give back

Torinozoku 取り除く = to remove; from toru = to take + nozoku = to remove; cf. related terms listed at hazusu

Torio トリオ = trio

Toriokonau 執り行う = to hold a ceremony; *the Tories are in Oklahoma now, holding a ceremony*

Toriosaeru 取り押さえる = to capture, arrest; from toru = to catch + osaeru = to master or apprehend; cf. taiho suru = to arrest; cf. toraeru = to arrest, capture, understand; cf. toru = to catch; cf.

tsukamaeru = to capture, catch or seize

Torisaru 取り去る = to remove or eliminate; from toru = to take + saru = to leave; cf. related terms listed at hazusu

Torishimariyaku 取締役 = a company director, board member; from toru = to take + shimaru = to tighten + yaku = service, e.g., yaku ni tatsu = to be of service

Torisokonau 取り損なう = to fail to catch; from toru = to take + sokonau = to fail to do something

Toritsukeru 取り付ける = to install or furnish; from toru = to take + tsukeru = to attach; cf. sonaeru = to equip with, to prepare; cf. sonaetsukeru = to provide, equip, install

Toriyameru 取りやめる = to cancel; from toru = to take + yameru = to stop

Toriyoseru 取り寄せる = to order or send away for; from toru = to take + yoseru = send, gather or bring closer; cf. chuumon suru = to order or request

Toro トロ = fatty tuna (sushi); *I ate fatty tuna in Toronto*; cf. related terms listed at ryouri

Torokeru とろける = to melt, to be charmed (intransitive); *while riding on the toll road, Kennedy ruined his suit when some ice cream melted on it*; cf. tokeru = to melt or dissolve (intransitive)

Toru 取る = to get, take, pick up, to take off a hat or watch, etc.; *I will get some tomatoes from that room*; cf. related terms listed at hirou and at shutoku suru

Toru 捕る = to catch; *my toes were ruined when I used them to catch a scorpion*; cf. taiho suru = to arrest; cf. toraeru = to arrest, capture, understand; cf. toriosaeru = to capture or arrest; cf. tsukamaeru = to capture, catch or seize

Toru 採る = to hire, adopt, collect or pick up; *she picked up the tomatoes that were ruined and placed them in the trash*; cf. related terms listed at kaishuu suru and at yatou

Toru 撮る = to take (a photo); *I climbed onto Tolstoy's roof to take a photo*

Toshi 年 = year, elderly (an abbreviation of toshiyori); *Tolstoy's sheep was born that year*; cf. related terms listed at nen

Toshi 都市 = a city; *Tolstoy bought sheets in the city*; cf. related terms listed at shi

Toshiue 年上 = a senior, or an older person; from toshi = year + ue = above; cf. kourei = elderly; cf. other related terms listed at joushi

Toshiyori 年寄り = an elderly person; from toshi = year + yoru = to gather; cf. roujin = an elderly person

Toshiyoru 年寄る = to get old; from toshi = year + yoru = to gather

Toshokan 図書館 = a library; *Tolstoy showed his candle collection at the library*; cf. shosai = a library (home) or study; cf. zousho = a book collection or library

Totan とたん = just (now, at the moment, etc.); *Tony Blair's tank just arrived*

Totan ni とたんに = just as, as soon as; from totan = just + ni = at; cf. -tokoro = on the point of, just when

Totemo とても = very; *that totem pole in Oregon is very big*; cf. related terms listed at ooi ni

Totonoeru 整える = to put in order, prepare; the transitive form of totonou = to be ready or in order; cf. seiri suru = to arrange, put in order; cf. soroeru = to arrange, prepare, put in order, make uniform

Totonou 整う = to be ready or in order; *Tolstoy's toes and nose were ready for the cold*

Totsugeki 突撃 = assault, charge, attack; *I was toting Superman's guest keys when I came under attack*; cf. related terms listed at shuugeki

Totsugeki suru 突撃する = to attack; from totsugeki = assault, charge, attack; cf. related terms listed at osou

Totsugu 嫁ぐ = to get married (used for women); *Tolstoy's daughter asked him a tsuitcase (suitcase) and a goose before she got married*; cf. kekkon suru = to get married

Totsunyuu suru 突入する to enter or rush into; *after she entered the hospital, her two tots were born in nyuu yooku (New York)*; cf. related terms listed at hairu

Totsuzen no 突然の = abrupt or sudden; *the total time that Superman spent at the Zen center was less than a minute, and his departure was quite sudden*; cf. related terms listed at ikinari

Tottemo とっても = terribly, extremely, completely; this is a variant of totemo = very; cf. related terms listed at ooi ni

Tou 問う = to ask or inquire; *Tolstoy asked how many books he had sold*; cf. kiku = to hear or listen, to ask or enquire; cf. tazuneru = to ask, inquire or look for; cf. ukagau = to visit or ask

Tou 塔 = pagoda, tower; *some toads live in the tower*

Tou 島 = an island, usually used as a suffix, e.g., hantou = a peninsula; *animals lose their toes on that island*; cf. related terms listed at shima

Tou 頭 = head, counter for large animals; *Tony Blair has a big head*; cf. related terms listed at atama

Toubou 逃亡 = escape, flight; *he used a torpedo boat for his escape*; cf. dasshutsu = flight or escape; cf. tousou = escape, flight

Toubu 頭部 = head; *Tony Blair's boot flew off and hit me on the head*; cf. related terms listed at atama

Toubun 当分 = for the moment, for awhile; from touchi = this place + bun = fun = a minute; cf. related terms listed at toriaezu

Toubyou 闘病 = fighting against an illness; *Tony Blair suffered from B.O. (bacterial overgrowth) and had to fight against his illness*

Touchaku 到着 = arrival; *Tony Blair drank champagne and Kool-Aid while he waited for the queen's arrival*; cf. chaku = arrival, order of arrival (in a race); cf. otozure = a visit or arrival

Touchaku suru 到着する = to arrive; from touchaku = arrival; cf. related terms listed at tsuku

Touchi 当地 = this place, here; *we eat toast with cheese here*; cf. related terms listed at basho

Touchi 統治 = governing; *Tony Blair was the chief, and he concentrated on governing*; cf. seigyo = control, governing, checking

Touchou 登頂 = climbing to the summit; *the tortoise choked as it was climbing to the summit and let the rabbit go by*

Touchou suru 登頂する = to climb to the summit; from touchou = climbing to the summit; cf. related terms listed at noboru

Toudai 当代 = the present age; from touji = these days + dai = a certain age; cf. related terms listed at ima

Toudai 東大 = Tokyo University; an abbreviation of toukyou daigaku

Toudai 灯台 = lighthouse; from tou = lamp, e.g., dentou = electric light; + dai = platform

Toufu 豆腐 = tofu (bean curd)

Touge 峠 = a mountain pass or peak, a crucial point; *we climbed to the peak together*; cf. related terms listed at choujou

Tougei 陶芸 = ceramic art; from touki =

pottery + geijutsu = art; cf. related terms listed at geijutsu

Tougoku suru 投獄する = to imprison; *they imprisoned me for stealing toast and gold Kool-Aid*

Touhyou 投票 = voting, vote; *Tony Blair and the healer from Oregon awaited the voting*; cf. related terms listed at hyou

Touitsu 統一 = standardization, unification; *after the standardization of his diet, Tony Blair eats the same food every day*

Touji 当時 = those days, at that time, old days; *in those days, we often had to tow our Jeep*; cf. sai ni = in case of, at that time; cf. other related terms listed at mukashi

Toujiru 投じる = to throw into or invest; *after Tony Blair's Jeep was ruined, he threw himself into his work*; cf. related terms listed at nageru and at toushi suru

Toujou 搭乗 = boarding (a ship or plane); *Tony Blair and Joan of Arc planned on boarding the ship*; cf. jousha = taking a train or bus

Toujou 登場 = entry or appearance (on stage or screen); *Tony Blair and Joan made their appearances at different times*

Toujou jinbutsu 登場人物 = a character in a story or play; from toujou suru = to enter (a stage or story) + jinbutsu = a person

Toujou suru 搭乗する = to board (a ship or plane); from toujou = boarding

Toujou suru 登場する = to enter (a stage or story); from toujou = entry or appearance

Touka 桃花 = a peach blossom; *Tolstoy calculated the number of peach blossoms in his orchard*; cf. related terms listed at hana

Touka suru 投下する = to throw down or drop; *Tolstoy stood on the castle wall and dropped boiling tar on the attackers*; cf. otosu = to drop (transitive), to lose, to decrease; cf. other related terms listed at nageru

Toukei 統計 = statistics; *here are the statistics regarding the total number of cakes sold*

Touki 冬季 = winter season; *Tolstoy went to Kiev for the winter season*; cf. related terms listed at kisetsu

Touki 陶器 = chinaware, pottery; *Tolstoy's quiche is in that pottery*; cf. related terms listed at setomono

Toukou 投稿 = a post or written contribution (e.g., to a journal); *I submitted a post about tobacco corporations*; cf. related terms listed at sengen

Toukyoku 当局 = authorities; *the authorities closed the Toukyou Kool-Aid club*

Toukyouto 東京都 = the Tokyo metropolitan area; from toukyou = Tokyo + toshi = city

Toukyuu 等級 = grade, ranking; from tou = equivalent; *taking the toll road is equivalent to taking the train*; + kyuu = level or grade; cf. related terms listed at kyuu

Toumei 透明 = transparent, clean; *this tomato has transparent skin and is very clean*; cf. related terms listed at seijou

Tounan 盗難 = a burglary or robbery; *Tolstoy's nanny was the victim of a robbery*; cf. related terms listed at tsumi

Tounan'ajia (Tounanajia) 東南アジア = southeast Asian; from tou = east, e.g, toukyou = eastern capital; + nan = south + ajia = Asia

Tounyoubyou 糖尿病 = diabetes; from satou = sugar + nyou = urine (since diabetes causes sugar to spill into the urine) + byouki = sickness

Tounyuu suru 投入する = to throw into, invest, insert; *Tony Blair went to Nyuuyooku (New York) and threw himself*

into his *work*; cf. related terms listed at nageru and at toushi suru

Tourai suru 到来する = to arrive; *I will eat toast and rice after I arrive*; cf. related terms listed at tsuku

Touroku 登録 = registration, enrollment; *registration is held from too to roku (10 to 6)*; cf. nyuudan = enrollment

Touron 討論 = a debate or discussion; *in the debate, Tolstoy was often wrong*; cf. related terms listed at rikutsu

Tourui 盗塁 = a stolen base; from tou = to steal, e.g., goutou = a robber; + rui = a base; cf. related terms listed at rui

Tousaku 倒錯 = perversion; *his perversion caused him to eat too many tortillas and salty cookies*; cf. related terms listed at hentai

Tousen 当選 = being elected; *they toasted the senator when it was clear that she was being elected*

Tousha 当社 = this company; *this company sold tofu to the Shah*; cf. related terms listed at kaisha

Toushi 凍死 = freezing to death; *Tolstoy's sheep were freezing to death*; cf. related terms listed at eimin

Toushi 投資 = an investment; *Tony Blair's sheep are an investment*

Toushi suru 投資する = to invest; from toushi = an investment; cf. toujiru = to throw into or invest; cf. tounyuu suru = to throw into, to invest; to insert

Toushika 投資家 = an investor; from toushi = investment + ka = a person

Toushishintaku 投資信託 = an investment trust or mutual fund; from toushi = an investment + shintaku = a trust; cf. related terms listed at kikin

Tousho 当初 = at first, beginning; *at first, I went to the Toyota showroom*; cf. related terms listed at hajime ni

Tousou 逃走 = escape, flight; *the officer told the soldiers to make their escape*; cf. dasshutsu = flight or escape; cf. toubou = escape, flight

Toutei 到底 = (cannot) possibly, no matter how; *the toast on the table cannot possibly satisfy my appetite, no matter how much butter I spread on it*

Touten 当店 = this store; *they sell tobacco and tennis balls in this store*; cf. related terms listed at mise

Toutobu 貴ぶ = to value, respect; this can also be spelled 尊ぶ; *Tony Blair offered toasts of booze to people he respected*; cf. related terms listed at sonkei suru

Toutoi 尊い = sacred, important, valuable; this can also be spelled 貴い; *that tortoise toy is valuable*; cf. related terms listed at juuyou and kichou

Toutotsu 唐突 = sudden, abrupt; *there was a sudden decision to have Tony Blair tote his own suitcases*; cf. related terms listed at ikinari

Toutou とうとう = finally, at last; *Tony's tortoise finally arrived*; cf. related terms listed at yatto

Touwaku 当惑 = embarrassment, bewilderment; *when I accidentally drank Toner during the War on Kool-Aid, it caused me embarrassment*; cf. kyoushuku = gratitude or embarrassment

Towazu 問わず = regardless of; sometimes expressed as otowazu (honorific); from towanaide = towazuni = not inquiring, derived from tou = to ask or inquire

Touyou 東洋 = the Orient; *Toyotas come from the Orient*

Touyougaku 東洋学 = Eastern studies; from touyou = the Orient + gaku = study

Touzen 当然 = justly, natural; *if you only dip a toe into Zen, you will justly not achieve*

enlightenment; cf. related terms listed at tekitou

Touzoku 盗賊 = a robber or burglar; *the burglar stole some tofu and Zooey's Kool-Aid*; cf. related terms listed at hannin

Towazu 問わず = regardless of; *the toads in the washing machine at the zoo, regardless of, I did the laundry*

Tozan 登山 = mountain climbing; *Tolstoy went to Zanzibar for mountain climbing*

Tsuba 唾 = saliva; *when my tsuitcase (suitcase) arrived from Barcelona, it was stained with saliva*; cf. related terms listed at yodare

Tsubasa 翼 = wing; *when I took my tsuitcase (suitcase) to Barcelona's sandy beaches, I saw some birds with powerful wings*; cf. related terms listed at hane

Tsubo 坪 = a unit of area comprising 3.3 square meters, or 2 tatami mats; *when we attended the Tsuper (Super) Bowl, we were assigned a sitting area of 3.3 square meters*; cf. related terms listed at menseki

Tsubo 壺 = jar, pot, urn; *he took an urn to the Tsuper (super) Bowl*; cf. akibin = an empty bottle; cf. bin = a bottle, jar or decanter; cf. donburi = a porcelain bowl (for noodles, rice, etc.), or a meal served in such a bowl; cf. hachi = a bowl or flower pot; cf. isshoubin = a 1.8 liter bottle; cf. kabin = a vase; cf. kama = a pot in which rice is cooked; cf. kame = an earthenware jar; cf. kotsutsubo = a funerary urn; cf. nabe = a pot or pan; cf. sakatsubo = a sake jar; cf. uekibachi = a flower pot; cf. yakan = a kettle

Tsubu 粒 = grains, drops, counter for tiny particles; *the tsupervisor's (supervisor's) boots were covered with grains of rice*; cf. amatsubu = a raindrop; cf. itteki = one drop; cf. ootsubu = large drop, large grain; cf. ryuushi = a particle or grain; cf. shizuku = a drip or drop; cf. teki = a drop

Tsubureru つぶれる = to be smashed, become useless, go bankrupt; this can also be spelled 潰れる; *the tsuitcase (suitcase) where I keep my booze was pushed over by a red rooster, and the bottles were smashed*

Tsubusu つぶす = to smash, block or waste (time); this can also be spelled 潰す; *the agents smashed the tsuitcase (suitcase) full of booze in front of their supervisor*

Tsubuyaku つぶやく = to mumble or mutter; *the tsupervisor's (supervisor's) boot would strike the yakuza whenever he mumbled*

Tsuchi 土 = soil, earth; *my tsuit (suit) is cheap and shows soil stains*; cf. related terms listed at aka

Tsuchikau 培う = to nourish or cultivate; *this tsuchi (soil) is fertilized by cows, and that makes it easier for us to cultivate it*; cf. tagayasu = to plow or cultivate; cf. yashinau = to feed, nourish, support or cultivate

Tsugeru 告げる = to tell, inform or announce; *while drinking tsoup (soup) with the guests in his room, he informed them that he was raising his prices*; cf. related terms listed at shiraseru

Tsugi 次 = next, following; *next my tsuitcase (suitcase) was attacked by geese*; cf. ika = below, less than, the following, the rest; cf. ni tsuzuite = following, subsequently, after

Tsugi kara tsugi e to 次から次へと = one after another, in succession; from tsugi = next + kara = from + tsugi = next + e = to + to = with; cf. related terms listed at tsugitsugi ni

Tsugime 継ぎ目 = joint, seam; *the tsuitcase where I keep my guitar caused a mess when its seam split*; cf. related terms listed at kansetsu

Tsugitsugi ni 次々に = one after the other; from tsugi = next + -ni = a suffix that forms an adverb; cf. chikuji = one by one, sequentially, successively; cf. hitotsu

hitotsu = one by one, carefully; cf. renzoku shite = in succession; cf. tsugi kara tsugi e to = one after another, in succession; cf. zokushutsu = appearing one after the other

Tsugou 都合 = circumstances, convenience; *she had a tsuitcase (suitcase) of gold and every convenience so that she could deal with every circumstance*; cf. related terms listed at jitai

Tsugu 継ぐ = to succeed to, to inherit; *I had to tsue (sue) my goofy parents in order to be allowed to inherit money from my grandparents*; cf. hikitsugu = to succeed, to take over; cf. souzoku suru = to inherit; cf. uketsugu = to succeed to, to inherit; cf. yuzuriukeru = to inherit

Tsugunau 償う = to compensate; *I will compensate you for the tsuitcase (suitcase) that the goose is now nesting in*; cf. oginau = to supplement or compensate for

Tsui つい = in spite of oneself, against one's better judgment; *I give my child tsuits (sweets) in spite of myself*

Tsui ni ついに = finally, in the end; *my tsuite (sweet) niece showed up in the end*; cf. iyoiyo = more and more, increasingly, at last; cf. izure = which, soon, someday, in the end; cf. yatto = at last, barely; cf. youyaku = finally or barely

Tsui no 対の = a pair; *the tsuite (sweet) Norwegian only owned one pair of gloves*

Tsuide ni ついでに = incidentally, while doing something; *the tsuites (sweets) were on the deck and my niece ate some while walking by*; cf. related terms listed at nagara

Tsuihou 追放 = expulsion, banishment; *after my expulsion from my country, I lived in a tsuite (sweet) hotel*; cf. jokyo = removal; cf. kuchiku = expulsion; cf. shobun = expulsion

Tsuika 追加 = addition, supplement; *I have a tsuit (sweet) cat which I got as an addition to my grouchy one*; cf. tenka = an addition

Tsuika suru 追加する = to add or supplement; from tsuika = addition, supplement

Tsuikyuu suru 追求する = to pursue a goal, to chase; *he's pursuing a dream of a tsuite (sweet) cucumber farm*; cf. related terms listed at oikakaeru

Tsuiraku 墜落 = a plane crash or a fall; *at the site of the plane crash, they found a tsuite (sweet) raccoon*

Tsuiraku suru 墜落する = to fall or crash; from tsuiraku = a plane crash or a fall; cf. related terms listed at ochiru

Tsuite ついて – see ni tsuite

Tsuittaaa ツイッター = Twitter

Tsuiyasu 費やす = to spend time or money; *I spend time and money with tsuite (sweet) Yasuko*; cf. related terms listed at sugosu

Tsuka 塚 = a mound; *a tsuitcase (suitcase) that belonged to Karl Marx can be seen in a house near his burial mound*; cf. mogurazuka = a mound created by a mole

Tsuka no ma 束の間 = a moment; *since he had it in a tsuitcase (suitcase) in the car, the Norwegian mariner only needed a moment to locate his umbrella*; cf. related terms listed at shunkan

Tsukaana 塚穴 = a grave; from tsuka = a mound + ana = a hole

Tsukaeru 仕える = to serve; *he carries a tsuitcase (suitcase) of calendars for erudite people, and thus he serves the public*

Tsukai 使い = an errand or mission; from tsukau = to use

Tsukaikiru 使い切る = to use up, to exhaust, to wear out; from tsukau = to use + kiru = to cut or stop; cf. related terms listed at riyou suru

Tsukaikonasu 使いこなす = to handle (men), to master (a tool or a language); from tsukau = to use + konasu = to be able to use; cf. related terms listed at osaeru

Tsukaiwakeru 使い分ける = to use different things for different purposes; from tsukau = to use + wakeru = to divide

Tsukamaeru 捕まえる = to capture, catch or seize; *Tsuperman (Superman) calculated that the massive eruption was dangerous, and he decided to catch the lava*; cf. taiho suru = to arrest; cf. toraeru = to arrest, capture, understand; cf. toriosaeru = to capture or arrest; cf. toru = to catch; cf. other related terms listed at tsukamu

Tsukamaru 捕まる = to be caught; the intransitive form of tsukamaeru = to catch; cf. hamaru = to fall into or be caught, to fit in or into (intransitive); cf. mitsukaru = to be caught or found; cf. torawareru = to be caught

Tsukamu つかむ = to grasp or grip; *Tsuperman (Superman) calculated that the moon was falling, and he grasped it to push it back into orbit*; cf. nigirishimeru = to grasp tightly; cf. nigiru = to grasp or hold tight; cf. tsukamaeru = to capture, catch or seize

Tsukare 疲れ = fatigue; from tsukareru = to get tired; cf. hirou = fatigue

Tsukarekiru 疲れ切る = to be exhausted; from tsukareru = to get tired + kiru = to complete an action; cf. related terms listed at tsukareta

Tsukareru 疲れる = to get tired; *I left my tsuitcase (suitcase) in the car and chased the red rooster until I got tired*

Tsukareta 疲れた = tired; the past (or exclamatory) form of tsukareru = to get tired; cf. kutakuta = exhausted, mushy; cf. tsukarekiru = to be exhausted

Tsukaru 浸かる = to be soaked in, to be submerged; *I lent my tsuit (suit) to Karl Marx, and he ruined it by soaking it in water*

Tsukau 使う = to use; *I use this tsuitcase (suitcase) full of cauliflower to block the door*; cf. related terms listed at riyou suru

Tsukawasu 遣わす = to dispatch; *when my tsuitcase (suitcase) was taken by the wacky superintendent, I dispatched someone to find it*; cf. haken suru = to send (a person), to dispatch

Tsukejiru 漬け汁 = a sauce; from tsukeru = to soak + jiru = shiru = soup; cf. related terms listed at shiru

Tsukekuwaeru 付け加える = to add; from tsukeru = to attach + kuwaeru = to add or include; cf. kuwaeru = to add or include

Tsukemen つけ麺 = cold Chinese noodles with soup for dipping; *the tsutsukeesu (suitcases) the men had contained cold Chinese noodles*; cf. related terms listed at soba

Tsukeru 付ける = to attach, install, follow or pursue, make an entry, settle (accounts), grow leaves and many other meanings; *I attached my tsuitcase (suitcase) to the keg in my room*; cf. haru = to paste, stick or attach; cf. soeru = to attach to, to garnish a dish, to help or support; cf. tenpu suru = to attach or append; cf. other related terms listed at tadoru

Tsukeru 漬ける = to soak or marinade; *the tsuit (suit) that Ken ruined had been soaked in water*; cf. hitasu = to soak, dip, drench or dunk

Tsukeru 点ける = to turn on or light; *I turned on the light before hanging my tsuit (suit) in a Kenyan room*

Tsukeru 着ける = to wear (clothing or accessories); *I will wear the tsuit (suit) that Kennedy ruined*; cf. related terms at chakuyou suru

Tsukesaseru つけさせる = to cause to set (a price); the causative form of tsukeru = to set a price, among many other meanings

Tsuki 月 = moon, month; *tsuitcase (suitcase) keys are not needed on the moon*

Tsuki 突き = a thrust or stab or lunge; from

tsuku = to stab, strike or poke

Tsukiai 付き合い = association, relationship; from tsukiau = to associate with; cf. related terms listed at kanrensei

Tsukiatari 突き当り = dead end; *on the tsuki (moon), the Atari office is located at a dead end*

Tsukiau 付き合う = to associate with, to keep company; from tsuku = to adhere + au = to come together or match; cf. majiwaru = to keep company or mingle with, to have a sexual relationship with

Tsukidasu 突き出す = to push out, to thrust out; from tsuku = to stab or poke + dasu = to put out; cf. related terms listed at osu

Tsukihi 月日 = time, years; from tsuki = month + hi = day; cf. related terms listed at jikan

Tsukiji 築地 = reclaimed land, a district in Tokyo; *I left my tsuitcase (suitcase) keys in a Jeep on that reclaimed land*

Tsukiru 尽きる = to be used up; *the tsupervisor (supervisor) will keep the rooster until the stores of corn are used up*

Tsukisou 付き添う = to accompany, chaperone, take care of; from tsuku = to attach + soeru = to support; cf. douhan suru = to go together, to accompany; cf. other related terms listed at azukaru

Tsukitomeru 突き止める = to find out, locate, ascertain; *Tsuperman (Superman) gave the keys to Tolstoy's Mexican roommate, and I soon found out*; cf. related terms listed at kakunin suru and at mitsukeru

Tsukizuki 月々 = monthly; from tsuki = month + zuki = tsuki = month

Tsukkomu 突っ込む = to thrust into or jump into; from tsu = to protrude; *my tsuitcase (suitcase) protruded into the aisle of the train;* + komu = to crowd in; cf. related terms listed at tobu

Tsuku 付く = to adhere to, to stick, to be added, to come along with, to be connected, to be perceived, to be acquired and many other meanings; *my tsuitcase (suitcase) leaked Kool-Aid, and now it adheres to the floor*; cf. related terms listed at kuttsuku

Tsuku 就く = to start, set out, obtain a position; *when I set out to obtain a position, I brought along a tsuitcase (suitcase) of Kool-Aid harder*; cf. related terms listed at hajimaru

Tsuku 点く = to be ignited or to turn on; *my tsuit (suit) from Kuwait was ignited in the fire*

Tsuku 着く = to arrive or come in contact with; *she arrived with a tsuitcase (suitcase) of Kool-Aid and came in contact with some thirsty kids*; cf. otozureru = to visit or arrive; cf. touchaku suru = to arrive; cf. tourai suru = to arrive

Tsuku 突く = to stab, poke, strike, attack; *I used my tsuitcase (suitcase) full of Kool-Aid to strike the muggers*; cf. related terms listed at osou

Tsukue 机 = a desk; *the tsuitcase (suitcase) that we need for our quest is on the desk*

Tsukuri 作り = a structure or construction; this can also be spelled 造り ; from tsukuru = to create or produce; cf. related terms listed at kensetsu

Tsukuridasu 作り出す = to produce or create; from tsukuru = to make + dasu = to put out; cf. related terms listed at tsukuru

Tsukurizakaya 造り酒屋 = a sake brewery; from tsukuru = to make + zakaya = sakaya = liquor store; cf. shuzousho = a brewery, distillery

Tsukurou 繕う = to mend or repair; *before I could carry my tsuitcase (suitcase) on a Kuwaiti road, I had to repair its handle*; cf. related terms listed at shuuri suru

Tsukuru 作る = to create, make or produce; this can also be spelled 造る; *I carried a tsuitcase (suitcase) of Kool-Aid to my room and created some refreshing drinks*; cf. sanshutsu suru = to yield, produce or derive; cf. seisan suru = to produce; cf. tsukuridasu = to produce or create; cf. umu = to give birth, produce, lay (an egg)

Tsukusu 尽くす = to use up, to exert oneself, to devote, to serve (a person); *I exerted myself to get a tsuitcase (suitcase) full of Kool-Aid to Superman, but he soon used it up*; cf. related terms listed at zensho suru

Tsuma 妻 = a wife (one's own or another person's); *my wife is a tsuperior (superior) ma (mother)*; cf. related terms listed at kanai

Tsumamu つまむ = to pick up or eat with fingers, to pinch; *the tsupervisor (supervisor) brought some dried mackerel to the movie and picked it up with his fingers*; cf. hasamu = to hold or place between, to pinch; cf. other related terms listed at hirou

Tsumaranai つまらない = dull, uninspiring, unimportant, tedious, worthless; *the fact that I'm carrying my tsuitcase (suitcase) in the marathon at night is unimportant*; cf. fukujiteki = secondary

Tsumari つまり = that is to say, in other words; *people who live on the tsuki (moon) tend to marry; in other words, it can get lonely up there*; cf. sunawachi = or, that is, namely, in other words

Tsumaru 詰まる = to be packed, to be blocked; the intransitive form of tsumeru = to stuff

Tsumazuku つまずく = to trip or stumble; *the tsuma (wife) of the zookeeper was carrying cookies when she tripped*

Tsume 爪 = nail, claw; *I use my nails to open tsumetai (cold) cartons of milk*

Tsumekiri 爪切り = nail cutter; from tsume = nail + kiru = to cut

Tsumekomu 詰め込む = to cram or stuff (transitive); from tsumeru = to stuff + komu = to crowd in; cf. related terms listed at tsumeru

Tsumeru 詰める = to stuff, fill or pack into (transitive); *on the tsuki (moon), a merry rooster stuffs its mouth*; cf. kasaneru = to pile up, to stack up; cf. moru = to fill or pile up; cf. tsumekomu = to cram or stuff; cf. tsumu = to heap up

Tsumetai 冷たい = cold (object); *the ice in my tsuit (suit) melted in the Thai heat, and I sensed my leg getting cold*; cf. samui = cold (atmosphere)

Tsumi 罪 = a crime or sin; *his crime was to steal a tsuitcase (suitcase) full of meat*; cf. fusei = wrongdoing, unlawfulness, injustice; cf. hanzai = a crime; cf. sagi = a fraud or hoax; cf. settou = theft; cf. tounan = a burglary or robbery; cf. zaiaku = a crime; cf. zouwai = bribery

Tsumikomu 積み込む = to load (goods, etc.), to put on board; from tsumu = to heap up or load + komu = to crowd in; cf. noseru = to carry, load, transport

Tsumori つもり = intention, expectation – used after a plain speech verb and followed by desu or da in the present tense, deshita or datta in the past tense, and de imashita or de ita in the past progressive tense; *I have an intention to buy a tsuit (suit) for Maureen*

Tsumoru 積もる = to pile up (intransitive); *the tsuitcases (suitcases) in the moron's room are piling up*; cf. kasanaru = to be piled up, to happen at the same time, to accumulate

Tsumu 摘む = to pick tea, cotton, etc.; *I will pick flowers and put them in the tsuitcase (suitcase) that I'm taking to the moon*

Tsumu 積む = to heap up, accumulate, load (transitive); *people heap up tsuitcases*

(suitcases) on the <u>moon</u> because they rarely get a chance to return to earth; cf. tsumeru = to stuff, fill or pack into

Tsumugikata 紡ぎ方 = a way of spinning; from tsumugu = to spin + kata = a method

Tsumugu 紡ぐ = to spin (textiles); *she <u>spun</u> some cloth that was used to make <u>tsu</u>its (suits) for the <u>Moo</u>ney and his <u>goofy</u> friends*

Tsuna 綱 = a rope, cord, cable; *I survived the <u>tsunami</u> by holding onto a <u>rope</u>*; cf. nawa = rope

Tsunagaru つながる = to be tied together or connected to (intransitive); *the <u>tsunami</u> came up to the <u>garage roof</u>, but I was <u>connected to</u> a tree and survived*

Tsunagu つなぐ = to connect, link, fasten or tie; the transitive form of tsunagaru = to be tied together; cf. musubu = to tie; cf. shibaru = to tie or bind; cf. shimeru = to fasten (seatbelt), tie (necktie), strangle, tighten (transitive); cf. yuu = to tie up, braid, fasten (hair)

Tsunahiki 綱引き = tug of war; from tsuna = rope + hiku = to pull

Tsunami 津波 = a tidal wave

Tsune ni 常に = always, continually; *our lives will <u>tsoon</u> (soon) end, says my <u>niece</u>, <u>continually</u>*; cf. related terms listed at itsumo

Tsuno 角 = antler, horn; this can also be read as kado = an outside corner; *I keep a <u>tsu</u>itcase (suitcase) full of <u>notes</u> about <u>antlers</u>*

Tsunoru 募る = to advertise, recruit, intensify; *the <u>tsu</u>perior (superior) Norwegians in the <u>room</u> planned to <u>recruit</u> people for their cause*; cf. boshuu suru = to recruit

Tsurai 辛い = painful; *the <u>tsu</u>itcase (suitcase) is pressing <u>right</u> on my foot, and it's <u>painful</u>*; cf. kurushii = hard, painful

Tsuranaru 連なる = to stand in a row; *the <u>tsu</u>itcases (suitcases) on the <u>ranch</u> that the <u>nanny ruined</u> had been made to <u>stand in a row</u> in the shower*

Tsuranuku 貫く = to penetrate, to accomplish, to carry out; *after he <u>accomplished</u> his mission, <u>Tsu</u>perman (Superman) came to the <u>ranch</u> to buy <u>noodles</u> and <u>Kool-Aid</u>*; cf. related terms listed at hatasu and at shimiru

Tsurasa 辛さ = pain or bitterness; from tsurai = painful + sa = a suffix that makes a noun from an adjective; cf. related terms listed at itami

Tsureru 連れる = to take a person or pet, to lead; *this <u>tsu</u>itcase (suitcase) contains my <u>red rooster</u> which I'm <u>taking</u> to the veterinarian*

Tsureteiku 連れて行く = to take someone of lower status along; from tsureru = to take a person or pet + iku = to go

Tsuriageru 吊り上げる = to lift up or suspend; from tsuru = to suspend + ageru = to raise; cf. related terms listed at sageru

Tsurisageru 吊り下げる = to suspend from; from tsurusu = to hang up + sageru = to hang down; cf. related terms listed at sageru

Tsuri 釣り = fishing; from tsuru = to fish

Tsuru 吊る = to suspend or hang up; *my <u>tsu</u>itcase (suitcase) was <u>ruined</u> when I <u>hung</u> it <u>up</u> in the shower*; cf. related terms listed at sageru

Tsuru 釣る = to fish, to lure in; *his <u>tsu</u>itcase (suitcase) was <u>ruined</u> when he used it to store his catch while he <u>fished</u>*

Tsuru 鶴 = a crane; *there's a <u>crane</u> in the <u>tsu</u>itcase (suitcase) in my <u>room</u>*; cf. related terms listed at tori

Tsurugi 剣 = a sword; *that <u>tsu</u>itcase (suitcase) in the <u>room</u> contains my <u>gear</u>, including a <u>sword</u>*; cf. related terms listed at katana

Tsurumu つるむ = to go with a companion, to hang out with; *I left my tsuitcase (suitcase) in my room while I hung out with my friends*

Tsurusu 吊るす = to suspend or hang up; *my tsuitcase (suitcase) was ruined by a supervisor who hung it up in the shower*; cf. related terms listed at sageru

Tsurutsuru つるつる = smooth, slippery; *my tsuitcase (suitcase) will be ruined, I cried repeatedly, as it slid down the slippery cliff*; cf. related terms listed at namaraka

Tsutaeru 伝える = to inform, to hand down or transmit; *I must inform you that I have recovered the tsuitcase (suitcase) of the tanned erudite traveler*; cf. uketamawaru = to hear, to be told, to undertake, to take (a message or reservation), to comply; cf. other related terms listed at shiraseru

Tsutanai 拙い = clumsy, unskillful; *I cut a tsuit (suit) for Tarzan with a knife, but my work was unskillful*; cf. related terms listed at heta

Tsutau 伝う = to go along, to climb up or down; *carrying a tsuitcase (suitcase) full of towels, he went along to the laundromat*; cf. related terms listed at noboru

Tsutawaru 伝わる = to be handed down, transmitted or introduced; the intransitive form of tsutaeru = to hand down or transmit

Tsutome 勤め = job or responsibility; from tsutomeru = to be employed; cf. futan = responsibility, burden, charge; cf. sei = fault, responsibility; cf. sekinin = responsibility; cf. tantou = charge (duty)

Tsutomeru 努める = to make an effort; *people who live on the moon make an effort to tsuki (moon) tomeru (park) their moon buggies correctly*; cf. related terms listed at zensho suru

Tsutomeru 務める = to discharge one's duty; *people who live on the moon tsuki (moon) tomeru (park) their moon buggies and then discharge their duties*

Tsutomeru 勤める = to be employed; *people who are employed on the moon tsuki (moon) tomeru (park) their moon buggies outside their offices*

Tsutsu つつ (used after a verb stem) = while, even though, e.g., modoritsutsu = while returning; from tsuzuku = to continue; cf. related terms listed at nagara and at ni shiro

Tsutsu 筒 = a cylinder; *I hang big tsuits (suits) and small tsuits on this cylinder*

Tsutsumareru 包まれる = to be enveloped by; the passive tense of tsutsumu = to wrap up

Tsutsumi 堤 = an embankment or dike; *tsuitcases (suitcases) and tsuitcases of meat were lined up on the embankment*; cf. teibou = an embankment or dike

Tsutsumu 包む = to wrap up; *I wrapped up tsuits (suits) and tsuits before the move*

Tsutsushimu 慎む = to be discreet, to refrain from; *there were tsuits and tsuits and sheets scattered in the moonlight, but I was discreet and didn't tell anyone*; cf. hikaeru = to refrain from, to take notes, to be imminent (an event), to be in waiting; cf. miawaseru = to exchange glances, to postpone, to refrain from doing something

Tsuu 通 = a counter for letters, notes and documents; *I counted the number of documents in the tsuitcase (suitcase)*

Tsuugaku 通学 = commuting to school; *my tsuitcase (suitcase) holds a gallon of Kool-Aid when I'm commuting to school*; cf. tsuukin = commuting; cf. other related terms listed at nyuugaku

Tsuujiru 通じる = to lead to, reach by phone, communicate, flow, be knowledgeable; *the tsuitcase (suitcase) that the genius put in the room contains equipment that allows him to communicate with the outside world, and it may lead to a good outcome*; cf. itaru = to lead to, reach, result in; cf. nagareru = to flow

Tsuujite 通じて = through, throughout, by way of; from tsuujiru = to lead to or communicate; cf. related terms listed at nagara

Tsuujou 通常 = usual; *the tsuitcase (suitcase) that Joan of Arc carried was full of books, as usual*; cf. related terms listed at taitei

Tsuuka 通貨 = currency; *I bought this tsuitcase (suitcase) and this car with American currency*; cf. related terms listed at kinsen

Tsuuka 通過 = transit, passage; *my tsuitcase (suitcase) is in a car in transit*

Tsuukin 通勤 = commuting; *I carry a tsuitcase (suitcase) to the kindergarten where I work when I'm commuting*; cf. tsuugaku = commuting to school

Tsuukon 痛恨 = contrition, regretful, bitter; *she expressed contrition for throwing the tsuitcase (suitcase) at Conan*

Tsuukou 通行 = passage, traffic; *I wore a tsuit (suit) and a coat during the passage to Antarctica*; cf. related terms listed at ourai

Tsuukoudome 通行止め = road closed (seen on a sign); from tsuukou = passage + domeru = tomeru = to stop

Tsuun to ツーンと = pungently (smell); *I will put some bread into the toaster, and tsoon (soon) toast will be smelling pungently*

Tsuushin 通信 = communication; *the tsuitcase (suitcase) the Shinto priest is carrying contains communication equipment*; cf. renraku = contact or communication

Tsuushou 通称 = a nickname or alias, popular name; *Tsuuper (Super) Shorty is his nickname*; cf. related terms listed at namae

Tsuushoumei 通称名 = a nickname or alias;

from tsuushou = nickname + mei = name, e.g., yuumei = famous; cf. related terms listed at namae

Tsuuwa 通話 = telephone call, talking on the phone; from tsuujiru = to communicate + kaiwa = conversation

Tsuuyaku 通訳 = an interpreter or an interpretation; *the tsuitcase (suitcase) that the yakuza is carrying contains interpretations from our meeting*

Tsuuyou suru 通用する = to pass as, to pass muster; *with a tsuitcase (suitcase) full of yogurt, I will be able to pass as a salesman*

Tsuya 艶 = luster, glaze, polish; *the tsuitcase (suitcase) the Yankee carried had a shiny luster*; cf. koutaku = luster

Tsuyoi 強い = strong; *using my tsuitcase (suitcase) to carry yogurt is easy, since its handle is strong*; cf. ganjou = sturdy, strong; cf. joubu = healthy, hearty, strong; cf. kyouretsu na = intense, powerful; cf. kyouryoku na = powerful; cf. saikyou = the strongest; cf. takumashii = strong, dependable

Tsuyomeru 強める = to strengthen or emphasize; from tsuyoi = strong; cf. katameru = to harden, solidify, strengthen; cf. kyouchou suru = to emphasize; cf. kyouka suru = to strengthen

Tsuyu 梅雨 = rainy season (June and early July); compared to baiu, this is the more common pronunciation; *I took my tsuitcase (suitcase) to the Yukon during the rainy season*; cf. related terms listed at kisetsu

Tsuyu 露 = dew; *my tsuitcase (suitcase) of yucca was covered with dew*

Tsuzuite 続いて = continuing, next, furthermore (this is spelled tsuduite in electronic dictionaries); from tsuzuku = to be continued; cf. related terms listed at sara ni

Tsuzukeru 続ける = to continue, transitive (this is spelled tzudukeru in electronic dictionaries); *he continues the practice of leaving his tsuitcase (suitcase) at the zoo in Kenya which is ruining it*; cf. ganbaru = to persevere, do one's best; cf. nebarinuku = to stick it out or see through it to the end; cf. nebaru = to persist or be sticky

Tsuzuki 続き = a continuation (this is spelled tsuduki in electronic dictionaries); from tsuzuku = to be continued; cf. keizoku = a continuation

Tsuzuku 続く = to continue or to adjoin (this is spelled tsuduku in electronic dictionaries); the intransitive form of tsuzukeru = to continue

Tsuzumi 鼓 = a drum (spelled つづみ tsudumi in electronic dictionaries); *that drum solo is tsuitable (suitable) for Zooming*; cf. related terms listed at taiko

Tte って = something is reportedly true, speaking of, as for the one called, because, also used to indicate insistence or certainty; *reportedly she will play tennis*; cf. related terms listed at to iu koto wa

Tte iu koto da っていうことだ – see to iu koto desu

Tte iu koto wa っていうことは – see to iu koto wa

Tte iu no wa っていうのは – see to iu no wa

Ubaitoru 奪い取る = to snatch or plunder; from ubau = to rob + toru = to take; cf. related terms listed at nusumu

Ubau 奪う = to rob or fascinate; *the ubiquitous Austrian mobsters rob people and also fascinate them*; cf. kokoro wo ubau = to completely fascinate or attract; cf. other related terms listed at nusumu

Uchi 内 = inside, within, among, middle, center, while; *we keep Uruguayan cheese inside that cabinet, among other food items, while we are waiting for a refrigerator*; cf. related terms listed at chuubu and at naka

Uchi 家 = house, home; this is usually spelled うち; *we make uber cheese in my home*; cf. honba = home, habitat, center, authentic; cf. jitaku = one's home; cf. katei = home, household; cf. otaku = your honorable home or organization; cf. shataku = company-owned housing; cf. taku = a house or home; cf. other related terms listed at ie

Uchi ni うちに = while or among; from uchi = while (or among) + ni = at

Uchiageru 打ち上げる = to wash up (ashore), to dash (waves), to launch or shoot off, to finish or close (a performance); from utsu = to hit + ageru = to raise; cf. torikakaru = to begin or set out, to launch or start; cf. other related terms listed at owaraseru

Uchiawase 打ち合わせ = a preparatory meeting; from uchiawaseru = to make preliminary arrangements; cf. related terms listed at kaigi

Uchiawaseru 打ち合わせる = to make preliminary arrangements; from utsu = to strike + awaseru = to join together

Uchigawa 内側 = inside or interior; from uchi = inside, middle, center + gawa = side; cf. similar terms listed at hou

Uchikomu 打ち込む = to drive in (a nail, etc.), to hit (a ball, etc.); from utsu = to hit + komu = to crowd in; cf. related terms listed at utsu = to hit

Uchiwa うちわ = a nonfolding hand-held fan; *some uber cheese from Washington got onto my nonfolding hand-held fan*; cf. related terms listed at sensu

Uchiwa 内輪 = family or inner circle; from uchi = inside + wa = a round shape; *Washington's face had a round shape*; cf. related terms listed at kazoku

Uchuu 宇宙 = universe, cosmos, space; *in Uruguay we chew our meals inside to keep space aliens from stealing our food*; cf. related terms listed at sora

Uchuuhikoushi 宇宙飛行士 = astronaut; from uchuu = space + hikouki = airplane + shi = man

Uchuujin 宇宙人 = space alien; from uchuu = space + jin = person

Ude 腕 = arm; *the Uruguayan dentist has strong arms*; cf. ashi = foot or leg; cf. joushi = an arm or upper limb; cf. kashi = a leg; cf. kata'ude = one arm; cf. ryouashi = both feet; cf. shi = a limb (arm or leg), used as a word component

Udon うどん = Japanese noodles; *the Uruguayan donkey likes Japanese noodles*; cf. related terms listed at soba

Ue 上 = top, surface, upper part, above, over, up; *the ueitaa (waiter) is up there*

Ue 飢え = hunger, starvation; from ueru = to starve, to be thirsty or hungry; cf. gashi = starvation; cf. kuufuku = hunger

Uejini 飢え死に = death from starvation; from ueru = to starve + jinu = shinu = to die; cf. related terms listed at eimin

Ueki 植木 = a garden plant or tree, a potted plant; from ueru = to plant + ki = a tree; cf. related terms listed at ki and at shokubutsu

Uekibachi 植木鉢 = a flower pot; from ueki = a garden plant + bachi = hachi = a bowl; cf. related terms listed at tsubo

Ueru 植える = to plant, grow, raise (transitive); *that ueitaa (waiter) ruined my view when he planted that tree outside my window*; cf. maku = to sow, sprinkle, scatter

Ueru 飢える = to starve, to be thirsty or hungry; *I'm starving, thanks to Ueitoresu (waitress) Ruth's slow service*; cf. gashi suru = to die of starvation; cf. kawaku = to be thirsty; cf. other related terms listed at onaka ga suku

Ugokasu 動かす = to move (transitive), operate (machinery), influence; the transitive form of ugoku = to move; *the uber gopher casually moved dirt from its tunnel*; cf. idou suru = to move (an object); cf. iten suru = to move (a business, etc.); cf. nokeru = to move something; cf. soujuu suru = to operate or handle; cf. sousa suru = to operate (a machine); cf. un'ei suru = to manage or operate

Ugoku 動く = to move (intransitive); *the Uruguayan gopher keeps cool by moving underground*; cf. idou suru = to move (both transitive and intransitive); cf. unkou suru = to operate, move or revolve (intransitive)

Uirusu ウイルス = a virus

Uirususei shikkan ウイルス性疾患 = a viral disease; from uirusu = a virus + sei = nature or personality + shikkan = a disease; cf. related terms listed at byouki

Ujauja うじゃうじゃ = swarming, in clusters, tediously; *there were Uruguayan jars and Uruguayan jars in clusters inside the cupboard*

Uji 氏 = a clan; *that uber Jeep belongs to our clan*; cf. related terms listed at buzoku

Ukabu 浮かぶ = to float (intransitive), to have inspiration, to rest in peace; *at UC (University of California) they abuse men who are afraid of water by making them float in pools*

Ukagau 伺う = to visit or ask, to hear; *I rode in an Uber car and carried a gift of gauze bandages when I visited him*; cf. houmon suru = to visit; cf. otozureru = to visit or arrive; cf. tazuneru = to visit; cf. tazuneru = to ask, inquire or look for; cf. tou = to ask or inquire

Ukagau 窺う = to observe or watch; *I watched the Uruguayan carpenter build a gaudy shrine*; cf. related terms listed at miru

Ukaru 受かる = to pass (an exam); *if you pass the exam, you will receive uber cashews from Rudolph*

Ukeireru 受け入れる = to accept; from ukeru = to receive + ireru = to put in

Ukenagasu 受け流す = to ward off or elude; from ukeru = to receive + nagasu = to flush

Ukeru 受ける = to receive, to take (a class, etc.), to be affected or suffer from, to catch or get, to accept (a challenge); *I received an uber kettle from Rudolph*; cf. uketoru = to receive or interpret; cf. other related terms listed at morau and at wazurau

Uketamawaru 承る = to hear, to be told, to undertake, to take (a message or reservation), to comply; *an uber Kenyan ran a taxing marathon in Washington according to the rules, and I took him a message in which he was told that he had won*; cf. hikiukeru = to take charge of, to undertake; cf. tsutaeru = to inform, to hand down or transmit; cf. other related terms listed at kiku

Uketoru 受け取る = to receive or interpret; from ukeru = to receive + toru = to get, take, pick up

Uketsugu 受け継ぐ = to inherit or succeed to; from ukeru = to receive + tsugu = to inherit; cf. related terms listed at tsugu

Uketsuke 受付 = reception (desk); *when I was in the UK, I took my tsuutsukeesu (suitcase) to the reception desk*

Ukiyo 浮世 = floating world, transitory life; *in Uruguay, people live on quiche and yogurt in a floating world*

Ukkari うっかり = carelessly, inadvertently; *in the UK the bellhop carried my bags carelessly*; cf. karugaru = lightly, easily, carelessly; cf. nanige ni = inadvertently, without knowing

Uku 浮く = to float (intransitive); to have time or money left over; *in Uruguay the cool people float in pools when they have time left over*

Uma 馬 = a horse; *this horse belongs to an Uruguayan man*; cf. ba = a horse, used as a suffix; cf. mokuba = a wooden horse

Umai うまい = skillful, delicious (used by men), successful; if the meaning is "skillful," this can also be spelled 上手い (similar to a spelling for jouzu); if the meaning is "delicious," it can be spelled 美味い (identical to one spelling for oishii); *uber Mighty Mouse is skillful*; cf. oishii = delicious; cf. other related terms listed at jouzu

Umaku うまく = skillfully; the adverbial form of umai = skillful

Umami 旨味 = a 5th taste category recognized in Japan (apart from sweet, sour, salty, and bitter); *the uber Marine ate the meat and savored its 5th taste*; cf. related terms listed at aji

Umare nagara 生まれながら = by nature, naturally, by birth; from umareru = to be born + nagara = while or at the same time; cf. related terms listed at masa ni

Umarekawaru 生まれ変わる = to be born again, make a fresh start; from umareru = to be born + kawaru = to change, intransitive

Umareru 産まれる = to be born; this can also be spelled 生まれる; the intransitive form of umu = to give birth; cf. tanjou suru = to be born

Umaretehajimete 生まれて初めて = for the first time in one's life; from umareru = to be born + hajimeru = to begin

Umaru 埋まる = to be buried (in), to be filled (with); *the Uruguayan man was rumored to be buried in that forest filled with wild beasts*; cf. juuman suru = to be filled with

Ume 梅 = plum; *they have good plums in Uruguay and Mexico*; cf. related terms listed at kudamono

Umeboshi 梅干し = pickled Japanese plums; from ume = plum + bosu = hosu =

to dry

Umeru 埋める = to bury, to fill up (e.g., a hall, a seat or a vacant position), to plug gaps, to make amends, to cover; *the Uruguayan met ruin and had to bury his animals and fill up his swimming pool*; cf. uzumeru = to fill up, to bury (the face); cf. other related terms listed at houmuru

Umi 海 = the ocean; *the Uruguayan mediator took a trip to the ocean*; cf. chichuukai = the Mediterranean Sea; cf. kaiyou = ocean; cf. nihonkai = the Sea of Japan; cf. taiheiyou = the Pacific Ocean; cf. taiyou = ocean; cf. unabara = ocean

Umibe 海辺 = a beach; from umi = ocean + be = area; *there's a bench in this area*

Umigame ウミガメ = sea turtle; from umi = ocean + game = kame = turtle; cf. kame = turtle, tortoise

Umoreru 埋もれる = to be buried in; *the uber motorhome hit a red rooster, which was buried in the barnyard*; cf. umaru = to be buried in, to be filled with

Umou 羽毛 = down, feathers; *Uruguay has more feathers on its birds, compared to Paraguay*; cf. related terms listed at hane

Umu 産む = to give birth, produce, lay (an egg); this can also be spelled 生む; *she gave birth under an Uruguayan moon*; cf. related terms listed at tsukuru

Un 運 = luck, fortune; *the undertaker trusted in luck*; cf. related terms listed at kouun

Unabara 海原 = ocean; *the Unabomber played ball with some rascals near the ocean*; cf. related terms listed at umi

Unagasu 促す = to urge; *after he saw the unappreciated garden, Superman urged his friends to visit it*; cf. semaru = to come close, to urge

Unagi ウナギ = eel; *the unappreciated geese feasted on eels*

Unaru うなる = to groan or roar; *the Unabomber ruined the ambush when he groaned*; cf. related terms listed at naku

Unchin 運賃 = fare (transportation); *my Uncle Chin paid my fare*; cf. densha chin = train fare

Undou 運動 = exercise, sport, action, movement; *undoubtedly, the movement entailed in exercise is good for us*; cf. dousa = movement; cf. taisou = gymnastics, exercise

Undoukai 運動会 = an athletic meet, sports day; from undou = exercise + kaigi = a meeting

Undoushinkei 運動神経 = reflexes, motor nerves; from undou = exercise, movement; + shinkei = nerves, sensitivity

Un'ei (Unei) suru 運営する = to manage or operate; *the undertaker's aging father managed the business*; cf. soujuu suru = to operate or handle; cf. sousa suru = to operate (a machine); cf. ugokasu = to operate (a machine)

Unga 運河 = a canal; *undoubtedly Gandalf will help to build the canal*; cf. haisuikou = drainage, gutter, ditch; cf. hori = a canal, moat or ditch; cf. mizo = a ditch, groove or gap

Unkou 運行 = operation, revolution (planet), transportation; *Uncle Conan is in charge of the operation of our transportation system*

Unkou suru 運行する = to operate, move or revolve (intransitive); from unkou = operation, revolution, transportation; cf. related terms listed at ugoku

Unmei 運命 = fate or destiny; *the unlucky maid had to face her destiny*; cf. related terms listed at kouun

Unpan 運搬 = carriage, transport; *the clothing company arranged transport for the underpants*; cf. related terms listed at ourai

Unsou 運送 = shipping, shipment, transportation; *let's pack the unsold items for shipment*; cf. shukka = shipment, shipping

Unsougaisha 運送会社 = a shipping company; from unsou = shipping + gaisha = kaisha = a company; cf. similar terms listed at kaisha

Unten 運転 = operation of a car or machinery; *the unlucky tennis player was assigned the operation of a car during the big match*; cf. related terms listed at sousa

Unten suru 運転する = to drive a car or operate a machine; from unten = operation of a car or machinery; cf. related terms listed at sousa suru

Unto うんと = greatly, very much; *the previously untold stories affected me greatly*; cf. related terms listed at ooi ni

Unuboreru うぬぼれる = to be conceited; *after the unusual bore got a red rooster, he seemed more conceited than usual*

Unyoku 運良く = luckily; from un = luck + yoku = well, or nicely

Unzari suru うんざりする = to get disgusted, be fed up with; *when the Unabomber went to Zambia, he reacted to their machines by getting disgusted*; cf. related terms listed at akiru

Uppun 鬱憤 = anger, frustration (usually written うっぷん); *she felt anger about the Uruguayan punch that she was served*; cf. gekido = fury, outrage; cf. kankan = anger, clanging noise

Ura 裏 = back, rear, hidden aspect; *the uber ram lives in the back*; cf. related terms listed at ushiro

Uragiru 裏切る = to betray or deceive; from ura = back + giru = kiru = to cut; cf. azamuku = to deceive or trick; cf. damasu = to trick, cheat or deceive; cf. madowasu = to delude or seduce; cf. negaeru = to betray

Uramen 裏面 = the back side; from ura = rear + men = face; cf. related terms listed at hou and at men

Urami 恨み = a grudge, animosity; from uramu = to bear a grudge; cf. related terms listed at akui

Uramu 恨む = to bear a grudge; *he bears a grudge against the operators of the uranium mine on the moon*

Uranai 占い = fortune telling; *the fortune-telling lady said that I would inherit a uranium mine on the Nile*

Urayamashii 羨ましい = envious; *when we learned that the Uranium mine in the yama [mountain] was owned by Shiites, we were envious*; cf. related terms listed at netami

Urei 憂い = melancholy, sorrow, anxiety (this can also be spelled 愁い); *the Uruguayan rain enhances my sorrow*; cf. related terms listed at utsubyou

Ureru 売れる = to sell well; the potential form of uru = to sell

Ureru 熟れる = to ripen; *the uber red rooster likes to eat corn after it ripens*; cf. related terms listed at jukusu

Ureshii 嬉しい = happy, glad, pleased, pleasant; *when I checked the patient and saw how much urea (a major component of urine) she was making, I was pleased*; cf. related terms listed at shiawase na

Ureshiku omou 嬉しく思う = to feel happy; from ureshii = happy + omou = to feel

Ureyuki 売れ行き = sales, demand; from ureru = to be able to sell + yuku = iku = to go; cf. related terms listed at uriage

Uriage 売り上げ = sales; *if you try to sell urine to the aged, your sales will be poor*; cf. baibai = buying and selling; cf. baikyaku = selling, or a sale; cf. gyoushou = peddling; cf. hanbai = sales, marketing; cf. tokubai = a special sale; cf. ureyuki = sales, demand

Urikire 売切れ = sold out; from urikiru = to

sell out; from uru = to sell + kiru = to cut; cf. kanbai = sold out

Urinushi 売主 = seller or vendor; from uru = to sell + nushi = a master; cf. related terms listed at gyousha

Urotsuku うろつく = to loiter or hover; from urouro = loitering, restlessly + tsuku = adhere

Uro'uro (Urouro) うろうろ = loitering, restlessly; *the urologist waited at the urology clinic, loitering*

Uru 売る = to sell; *in Uruguay they sell wheat*; cf. akinau = to trade in or sell; cf. hatsubai suru = to sell; cf. orosu = to sell wholesale; yuzuru = to give way, hand over, sell, bequeath

Urumu 潤む = to moisten, to be blurred; *since tears moistened my eyes, the Uruguayan moon was blurred*; cf. related terms listed at shimeru

Uruoi 潤い = charm, profit, moisture; from uruou = to become moist, to profit; cf. miryou = fascination, charm; cf. other related terms listed at rieki

Uruou 潤う = to become moist, to profit; *our Uruguayan oat project profited us after the ground finally became moist*; cf. related terms listed at shimeru

Urusai うるさい = noisy, annoying; *the Uruguayan room that the scientist rented was noisy*; cf. souzoushii = noisy

Urushi 漆 = lacquer, lacquerware; *the Uruguayan sheep ate from lacquer bowls*; cf. slonghikki = lacquerware

Uruwashii 麗しい = beautiful, charming; *my Uruguayan washing machine was beautiful*; cf. related terms listed at utsukushii

Usabarashi 憂さ晴らし = a diversion or distraction; *the uber salaryman threw the barracuda at the sheep and took advantage of the distraction to escape*

Usagi うさぎ = a rabbit; *the Uber driver's coat was sagging in front because he was carrying a rabbit*

Useru 失せる = to disappear or vanish; *the computer user made it a rule to disappear from the chat room at 11 p.m.*; cf. synonyms listed at bossuru

Ushi 牛 = a cow; *the uber sheep fell in love with a cow*

Ushinau 失う = to lose something; *we have uber sheep now, and we would hate to lose any of them*; cf. related terms listed at okiwasureru

Ushiro 後ろ = back, rear; *my Uruguayan sheep roam at the rear of my house*; cf. ato = the rear, the rest; cf. kouhou = behind, in the rear; cf. ura = back, rear

Uso 嘘 = a lie; *when you say that you have uber solar panels, that's a lie*; cf. kyogi = a deception or lie; cf. nise = a falsehood or lie

Uso wo tsuku 嘘をつく = to tell a lie; from uso = lie + tsuku = to adhere; cf. itsuwaru = to lie, deceive or pretend

Usotsuki 嘘つき = a liar; from uso wo tsuku = to lie

Ussura 薄ら = slightly, faintly, dimly; *the usurer ate the ramen which was slightly spoiled*; cf. bonyari = dimly, faintly, absent-mindedly, carelessly, aimlessly; cf. wazuka ni = slightly, only

Usu 臼 = a mortar, i.e., a receptacle in which ingredients are crushed; *usually I use a mortar and pestle to crush my pills*

Usugiri 薄切り = thinly sliced; from usui = thin + giru = kiru = to cut

Usui 薄い = thin or light (color); *the usurer eats thin slices of light-colored bread*; cf. related terms listed at semai

Usumeru 薄める = to dilute; *the usurer gave the medicine to Rudolph after diluting it*

Usureru 薄れる = to fade or become dim; *the usurer's red rooster faded from sight*

Uta 歌 = a song; from utau = to sing; cf. chanson = a song; cf. fushi = knot (wood), joint (body), melody; cf. kashou = song, singing; cf. kayou = a song or ballad; cf. kayoukyoku = a popular song; cf. ko'uta = a ballad; cf. kyoku = a musical composition, a song; cf. min'you = a folk song; cf. naga'uta = a long epic song; cf. ongyoku = songs with samisen accompaniment; cf. ouenka = a cheering song; cf. senritsu = a melody; cf. shirabe = a tune, tone, writing style, investigation, inspection, examination; uta = a song with samisen

Uta 唄 = a song with samisen (a three-stringed lute), used as a word component; *I wrote a song about an Uruguayan tavern*

Utagai 疑い = doubt, question, suspicion; from utagau = to doubt or suspect; cf. gimon = a question or doubt; cf. giwaku = a suspicion or doubt; cf. mayoi = doubt, suspicion, hesitation; cf. shitsumon = a question or enquiry; cf. toi = a question; cf. yougi = a suspicion or charge

Utagau 疑う = to doubt or suspect; *in Utah, if you lose your gaudy jewelry, I doubt that you will get it back*

Utagawashii 疑わしい = doubtful; from utagau = to doubt or suspect; cf. related terms listed at ayashii

Utagoe 歌声 = a singing voice; from utau = to sing + goe = koe = voice; cf. related terms listed at koe

Utai 謡い = Noh chanting; *an Uruguayan tiger cannot learn Noh chanting*

Utau 歌う = to sing; *we sang in Utah and in Uruguay*

Utoi 疎い = ignorant, estranged from; *she was ignorant about certain uber toys*

Uto'uto (Utouto) うとうと = dozing; *riding in an Uber car on a toll road, I started dozing*

Utsu 打つ = to hit, beat, strike, to engage in (gambling, etc.), and many other meanings; *I utilized a souvenir to hit the burglar*; cf. ataru = to hit; cf. ateru = to touch or hit; cf. butsu = to hit (a person); cf. hataku = to beat, dust or knock; cf. iru = to hit or shoot (an arrow); cf. naguru = to beat up, punch or slap; cf. tataku = to beat or strike; cf. uchikomu = to drive in (a nail, etc.), to hit (a ball, etc.)

Utsu 撃つ = to fire a gun; *I was utilizing a supermarket when someone fired a gun*; cf. hanatsu = to fire, to release, emit

Utsu 討つ = to shoot at, attack, defeat, destroy; *I was utilizing a supermarket when someone attacked me*; cf. related terms listed at horobosu and osou

Utsubuse ni うつ伏せ = face down; *when I was utilizing the supermarket, I saw a boozed-up Segway rider and my niece lying face down on the floor*

Utsubyou 鬱病 = depression; from yuu'utsu = depression + byouki = sickness; cf. yuu'utsu = depression, melancholy; cf. urei = melancholy, sorrow, anxiety

Utsukushii 美しい = beautiful; *I utilize Superman's cushy dressing room to make myself beautiful*; cf. azayaka = colorful, bright, vivid, impressive, beautiful; cf. gouka = wonderful, gorgeous; cf. hade = showy, gaudy, colorful; cf. hanayaka = dazzling, gorgeous; cf. kirei = beautiful, pretty, clean; cf. taenaru = exquisite; cf. uruwashii = beautiful, charming;

Utsurisumu 移り住む = to change one's residence; from utsuru = to move + sumu = to reside; cf. related terms listed at hikkosu

Utsuru 移る = to move (one's lodging), to change or be infected with, to change target of interest; *utilizing Superman, Ruth moved to a new home*; cf. related terms listed at hikkosu

Utsushi 写し = a copy; from utsusu = to copy or take (a photo); cf. fukusei = a reproduction or copy

Utsushidasu 映し出す = to project onto a screen; from utsu = to project + dasu = to put out; cf. utsusu = to project (onto a screen), to reflect

Utsusu 写す = to copy or take (a photo); *when I needed someone to take a photo, I utilized my superior supervisor*

Utsusu 映す = to project (onto a screen), to reflect; *I utilize my superior supervisor to help me project movies onto a screen*; cf. hansha suru = to reflect; cf. utsushidasu = to project onto a screen

Utsusu 移す = to move or transmit something (transitive), to infect; *we utilized Superman to supervise the work when we moved a boulder*; cf. related terms listed at idou suru

Utsuwa 器 = container or receptacle, ability; *we utilize the supermarket's water to fill our containers*; cf. related terms listed at kan

Uttaeru 訴える = to sue, appeal or complain of; *that Uruguayan taxi driver is erudite, and he complains and sues when he is wronged*; cf. related terms listed at boyaku

Uwagi 上着 = jacket, outer clothes; *Uber warned that guitars left in cars should be covered with jackets to deter theft*; cf. kooto = a coat

Uwaki 浮気 = extramarital affair; *in Uruguay, it's considered wacky to have extramarital affairs*

Uwamawaru 上回る = to surpass or exceed; from uwa = above, e.g., uwagi = an outer garment; + mawaru = to turn; cf. related terms listed at oikosu

Uwasa うわさ = rumor, gossip; *I heard a rumor that they serve uber wasabi*; cf. similar terms listed at hanashi

Uwayaku 上役 = someone who is superior or senior; *the Uruguayan warrior's yak followed its superiors*; cf. related terms listed at joushi

Uyamau 敬う = to respect or venerate; *in Uruguay, the yama [mountain] owls respect and venerate their leader*; cf. related terms listed at sonkei suru

Uyoku 右翼 = right wing (politics); *the Uber driver drove yoku (well) and favored right-wing politics*; cf. sayoku = left wing (politics)

Uzuku うずく = to ache or throb; *when my heart aches, I often take an Uber to the zoo in Kuwait*; cf. itamu = to feel pain

Uzumaki 渦巻き = a whirlpool, spiral or coil; *when I went to an Uruguayan zoo wearing a Mackintosh (raincoat), I fell into a whirlpool*

Uzumeru うずめる = to fill up, to bury (the face); *the uber zoo sends me meeru (emails) that fill up my in-box*; cf. umeru = to bury, to fill up (e.g., a hall, a seat or a vacant position), to plug gaps, to make amends, to cover

Wa 和 = harmony, total; *the walrus lives in harmony with its ecosystem*; cf. related terms listed at chouwa

Wa 輪 = round shape (ring, circle etc.); *Washington's face had a round shape*; cf. related terms listed at maru

Wa 羽 = a counter for birds; *that bird ate my waffle*

Waarudo rekoozu ワールドレコード = world records

Waarudo tsuaa ワールドツアー = world tour

Wadai 話題 = topic, subject; *after the warlord died, he was the topic of many conversations*

Wafuku 和服 = Japanese clothing; from wa = harmony or Japanese style, e.g., washoku = Japanese food; + fuku = clothing; cf. related terms listed at fuku

Waga 我が = my, our, one's own; *the water*

and gas are my responsibilities

Wagagun 我が軍 = our army; from waga = mine or ours + guntai = army; cf. related terms listed at guntai

Wagakki 和楽器 = a traditional Japanese musical instrument; from wa = harmony or Japanese style, e.g., washoku = Japanese food; + gakki = musical instrument; cf. gakki = a musical instrument

Wagakuni 我が国 = one's country; from waga = my + kuni = country; cf. related terms listed at sokoku

Wagamama わがまま = selfish, spoiled; from waga = my + mama = as is, as you are; cf. jikochuushinteki = selfish

Wagasha 我社 = our company; from waga = my + kaisha = company; cf. related terms listed at kaisha

Wagashougai 我が生涯 = my lifetime; from waga = my + shougai = one's lifetime; cf. related terms listed at isshou

Wagaya 我が家 = my house; from waga = my + ya = house or store, e.g., honya = bookstore; cf. related terms listed at ie

Wagyuu 和牛 = Wagyu beef, Japanese beef; from wa = Japanese, e.g., washoku = Japanese food + gyuuniku = beef; cf. related terms listed at gyuuniku

Wakai 若い = young, immature; *that young person whacked me in the eye*; cf. related terms listed at osanai

Wakannai わかんない = I don't understand; an abbreviation of wakaranai

Wakare 分かれ = separation, parting; from wakareru = to separate or be divided, to part from; cf. bekkyo = separation of family members; cf. bunretsu = division, separation

Wakareru 分かれる = to branch, fork, separate or split; *the wandering cat and the red rooster split up and separated from each other*

Wakareru 別れる = to separate or be divided, to part from; the intransitive form of wakeru = to divide or share; cf. hanareru = to separate from or leave

Wakaru 分かる = to understand, know or recognize; *I understand that a war in California will ruin some cities*; cf. eru = to get, earn, understand, receive something undesirable (like a punishment); cf. ha'aku suru = to comprehend or understand; cf. kashikomaru = to understand humbly; cf. kikitoru = to hear or understand; cf. rikai suru = to understand; cf. ryoukai suru = to agree, consent or understand; cf. ryoushou suru = to understand or acknowledge; cf. sameru = to wake up or become sober, to understand; cf. shouchi suru = to understand; cf. toraeru = to arrest, capture or understand; cf. other related terms listed at shiru

Wakasu 沸かす = to boil, to heat (transitive); the transitive form of waku = to boil; cf. related terms listed at niru

Wake 分け = placement (in a class), a division; from wakeru = to divide or classify

Wake 訳 = reason, meaning, circumstance, case; *the reason Barbie stayed was to watch Ken work on the case*; cf. imi = meaning, sense, significance; cf. other related terms listed at riyuu

Wake de wa nai 訳ではない = wake ja nai = wake de wa arimasen = not necessarily; from wake = circumstance + de wa nai = it isn't; cf. related terms listed at kanarazu shimo

Wake desu 訳です (or wake da) = therefore or as a result; from wake = reason + desu = it is; cf. related terms listed at dakara

Wake ga nai 訳がない = not possible or unthinkable; from wake = circumstance + nai = not

Wake ja nai 訳じゃない – see wake de wa nai

Wake ni wa ikanai わけにはいかない (or wake ni wa ikenai, or wake ni wa ikimemasen) = impossible to do (although one wants to); from wake = circumstance + ni = to + ikanai = won't go; literally, then, this = to circumstance it will not (or cannot) go, or it doesn't accord with circumstances; cf. related terms listed at muri

Wakemae 分け前 = a share; *we will give a share of the water to Ken's maestro*; cf. bun = a share or quantity; cf. buntan = one's share or assignment

Wakeru 分ける = to divide, classify or share; *we will share the water in Ken's room*; cf. buntan suru = to share; cf. shikiru = to divide or partition

Waki 脇 = side or armpit; *I always carry my walkie talkie in my armpit*; cf. wakibara = the flank; cf. yokoppara = side of the body, or flank

Wakibara 脇腹 = the flank; from waki = side + bara = hara = the abdomen; cf. related terms listed at waki

Wakideru 湧き出る = to gush forth; from waku = to gush out + deru = to go out; cf. nagareru = to flow; cf. waku = to gush out, well up, appear

Wakimizu 湧き水 = spring water; from waku = to gush out + mizu = water; cf. related terms listed at mizu

Waku 枠 = a frame, framework, limit; *during the war against the Kool-Aid industry, we often fired at the enemy from inside gunport frames*; cf. wakugumi = a frame or framework; cf. other related terms listed at genkai

Waku 沸く = to grow hot, to boil (intransitive), to get excited; *during the war in Kuwait, water would boil, and then we would make coffee*; cf. related terms listed at nieru

Waku 湧く = to gush out, well up, appear; *watery Kool-Aid gushed out of the broken pitcher*; cf. related terms listed at arawareru and at wakideru

Wakugumi 枠組み = a frame or framework; from waku = frame + gumi = kumu = to assemble; cf. waku = a frame, framework, limit

Wakusei 惑星 = planet; *waffle mix and Kool-Aid packages are sold at all of the Safeway stores on the planet*

Wakuwaku ワクワク = trembling, nervous, excited; *when Washington drank Kool-Aid, he got excited*

Wameku 喚く = to yell or shriek; *he shrieked about his war memories from Kuwait*; cf. related terms listed at donaru

Wan 湾 = gulf, bay; *I wandered down to the bay*

Wangan 湾岸 = gulf coast; from wan = gulf or bay + gan = beach, e.g., kaigan = beach

Wangan sensou 湾岸戦争 = the Gulf War; from wangan = gulf coast + sensou = war

Wanpaku na 腕白な = naughty; *you were naughty when you only bought one pack of beer for the party*; cf. related terms listed at warui

Wanpiisu ワンピース = a dress or frock; from the English "one piece"

Waraidasu 笑い出す = to burst into laughter; from warau = to laugh + dasu = to put out; cf. related terms listed at warau

Warau 笑う = to smile or laugh; *a warrior named Raul Castro laughed at danger*; cf. hohoemu = to smile; cf. nikoniko suru = to smile; cf. waraidasu = to burst into laughter

Ware 我 = self; *Washington rested in this house, which belongs to my self*; cf. related terms listed at jibun

Wareme 割れ目 = a crack, fissure or chasm; *during the war, an emerald was lost in this fissure*; cf. hibi = crack, fissure

Warera 我ら = we; from ware = self + ra = suffix that makes the preceding pronoun plural; cf. similar terms listed at watashi

Wareru 割れる = to break, to be torn, to split or crack; the intransitive form of waru = to break; cf. related terms listed at yabureru

Wareware 我々 = we; from ware = self; cf. similar terms listed at watashi

Wari 割り = a proportion or rate; from waru = to divide or cut

Wari ni 割りに – see wari to

Wari to 割りと = relatively, comparatively; *the warrior's tone was relatively mild*; cf. hikakuteki = comparatively

Waribashi 割り箸 = splittable (disposable) chopsticks; from waru = to break glass or wood + bashi = hashi = chopsticks

Waribiki 割引 = a discount; *the wary beekeeper refused the discount offered by the peddler*; cf. hangaku = a 50% discount

Waru 割る = to break glass or wood, to divide (arithmetic) or cut; *when we played in the war ruins, we used to break glass or wood and divide the fragments*; cf. synonyms listed at kowasu

Waruguchi 悪口 – see warukuchi

Waruguse 悪癖 = a bad habit; from warui = bad + guse = kuse = a habit or characteristic; cf. related terms listed at shuukan

Warui 悪い = bad, wrong; *to throw water on King Louis was bad*; cf. aku = evil; cf. dame = bad or wrong; cf. fudoutoku = immoral; cf. gaiaku = evil, a bad influence; cf. saiaku = the worst; wanpaku = naughty

Warukuchi 悪口 = slander, abuse; from warui = bad + kuchi = mouth; cf. related terms listed at hihan

Washi ワシ = eagle; *the eagle is standing on the washing machine*; cf. related terms listed at tori

Washoku 和食 = Japanese-style food; from wa = harmony or Japanese style, e.g., wafuku = Japanese clothing; cf. related terms listed at tabemono

Wasureru 忘れる = to forget or leave behind; *when I washed Superman's red rooster, I forgot to use soap*; cf. okiwasureru = to mislay or leave behind

Wata 綿 = cotton; *the warlord targeted the cotton farm for extortion*; this can also be pronounced "men," with the same meaning; cf. related terms listed at momen

Watakushi 私 = I; *I am a Washington takushii (taxi) driver*; cf. related terms listed at watashi

Wataru 渡る = to cross (e.g., a bridge); to span, extend, continue or stretch (usually written わたる for these meanings); *Napoleon crossed a bridge at Waterloo*; cf. related terms listed at oudan suru

Watashi 私 = I; *I asked Wallace to create a tax shield*; cf. boku = I or me (used by men and boys); cf. ore = I, me (used by men and boys); cf. orera = we; cf. warera = we; cf. wareware = we; cf. watakushi = I; cf. watashidomo = we or I (humble)

Watashibune 渡し舟 = a ferry; from watasu = to carry across + bune = fune = ship; cf. related terms listed at fune

Watashidomo 私ども = we or I (humble); from watashi = I + domo ni = tomo ni = together; cf. related terms listed at watashi

Watashitachi 私達 = we or us; from watashi = I + tachi = a suffix denoting that the previous noun is plural

Watasu 渡す = to carry across, pass or hand over; *the warriors, Tarzan and Superman arranged for messages to be carried across, passed and handed over*; cf. related terms listed at hakobu

Waza 技 = skill, technique; *the warlord zapped me with a taser to show his skill*; cf.

gijutsu = skill, technique, technology; cf. kotsu = a knack; cf. nouryoku = skill, ability, competence; cf. tegiwa = skill, performance, tact

Wazawai 災い = calamity, disaster; *wacky Zambian warriors from the east caused the calamity*; cf. related terms listed at saigai

Wazawaza わざわざ = expressly, specially; *I brought my walrus zapper specially, since you're having a problem with them*

Wazuka ni わずかに = slightly, only; *unlike a bazooka, my wazuka fired wasps at the zoo's camel's knees and was only slightly effective*; cf. ussura = slightly, faintly, dimly

Wazurau 煩う = to worry about, to have trouble doing; *I'm worried about going to that wacky zoo with Raul Castro*; cf. related terms listed at shinpai suru

Wazurau 患う = to suffer from an illness; *the walrus at the zoo bit Raul Castro, and then he suffered from an illness*; cf. kakaru = to suffer from (among many other meanings); cf. ukeru = to receive, to take (a class, etc.), to be affected or suffer from, to catch or get

Wazurawashii 煩わしい = complicated, troublesome; *when the wacky zoo rabbits got into the washing machine, they were troublesome*; cf. related terms listed at fukuzatsu and at kimazui

Wo hajime をはじめ = including, as well as, not to mention; from wo = on or at + hajime = beginning; *wo hajime (at the beginning) of my book, I include the names of my parents as well as my friends*; cf. moura = comprising, including; cf. orosoka = neglect, negligence, not to mention, needless to say

Wo megutte をめぐって = in regard to, concerning (disputes); from meguru = to surround; cf. related terms listed at ni tsuite

Ya や = etcetera, an abbreviation of yara; cf. related terms listed at nado

Ya 夜 = night, used as a word component, e.g., konya = tonight; *the yak sleeps at night*

Ya 屋 = a shop, store or house, used as a suffix; *that store sells yachts*

Ya 矢 = an arrow; *I found an arrow in the yard*

Yabai やばい = dangerous, risky; *it's dangerous for a yak to ride a bike*; cf. related terms listed at kiken na

Yaban na 野蛮な = barbarous, uncivilized; *the yakuza banquet was uncivilized*; cf. related terms listed at mikai

Yabansei 野蛮性 = barbarism; from yaban = barbarous + sei = nature

Yabureru 敗れる = to lose or be defeated; *the Yankees drank booze and danced with red roosters, and they lost the battle*; cf. makeru = to lose

Yabureru 破れる = to be torn or broken; the intransitive form of yaburu = to break or tear; cf. kezureru = to be shaved or planed; cf. kireru = to break, to be cut, to wear out, to expire, to be used up, to cut well, to get angry, and many other meanings; cf. kudakeru = to be broken or smashed; cf. kowareru = to break; cf. oreru = to be broken or folded; cf. sakeru = to split or tear; cf. wareru = to break, to be torn, to split or crack

Yaburu 破る = to break, tear or violate; *my yak-skin boots were ruined when I broke their clasps*; cf. related terms listed at kowasu and at saku

Yacchimau やっちまう = yatte shimau = to do completely, implying making a mistake

Yachin 家賃 = rent; *here's the rent for the yacht of Mr. Chin*

Yado 宿 = an inn or lodging; *Yankees often doze at that inn*; cf. ryokan = a Japanese inn; cf. shukuhaku = lodging

Yadoru 宿る = to lodge or dwell; *the yaks*

and the <u>do</u>py <u>roos</u>ters <u>dw</u>ell outside; cf. related terms listed at ikiru

Yagate やがて = before long, soon; *the <u>ya</u>rd garbage is <u>terr</u>ible, and <u>before</u> <u>long</u> the neighbors will start complaining*; cf. related terms listed at mamonaku

Yagi ヤギ = goat; *the <u>goat</u> is in the <u>ya</u>rd with the <u>ge</u>ese*

Yahari やはり – see yappari

Yajirushi 矢印 = arrow (on a map or sign); *the <u>yacht</u> and the <u>Jeep</u> were <u>rushing</u> after <u>arrows</u> on signs*

Yajuu 野獣 = a wild animal; *<u>wild</u> <u>animals</u> consumed our <u>yams</u> and <u>juice</u>*; cf. related terms listed at doubutsu

Yakan やかん = a kettle; *my <u>yak</u> in <u>Canada</u> drinks from a <u>kettle</u>*; cf. related terms listed at tsubo

Yakan 夜間 = at night; from ya = night, e.g., konya = tonight; + kan = interval or space; cf related terms listed at tetsuya

Yakedo やけど = a burn (injury); *the <u>Yankee</u> <u>Kennedy</u> ate a <u>doughnut</u> fresh from the fryer which caused a <u>burn</u>*

Yakeru 焼ける = to be burned or roasted; the intransitive form of yaku = to bake or burn

Yaki imo 焼き芋 = roasted sweet potato; from yaku = to grill + imo = potato; cf. related terms listed at imo

Yakimono 焼き物 = earthenware, chinaware; from yaku = to bake + mono = thing; cf. related terms listed at setomono

Yakitori 焼き鳥 = chicken grilled on a skewer; from yaku = to grill + tori = bird; cf. related terms listed at ryouri

Yakkai na 厄介な = troublesome, awkward; *the <u>yacht</u>'s <u>kite</u> fell onto another boat, which was <u>troublesome</u>*; this can also be spelled やっかいな; cf. kimazui = awkward, embarrassing

Yakkyoku 薬局 = a pharmacy; *the <u>yakuza</u> came to the <u>Kyo</u>to <u>Kool</u>-Aid club thinking that it was a <u>pharmacy</u>*; cf. kussuriya = a pharmacy

Yakou 夜行 = night travel; from ya = night, e.g., konya = tonight; + kou = to go, e.g., ryokou = trip; cf. related terms listed at ryokou

Yaku 厄 = misfortune, disaster; *the <u>yak</u> met with <u>misfortune</u>*; cf. related terms listed at saigai

Yaku 役 = a role, service; *that <u>yakuza</u> plays the <u>role</u> of a tough guy*; cf. hitoyaku = a role, a contribution to a situation

Yaku 焼く = to bake, burn, roast, grill, toast; *that <u>yakuza</u> <u>bakes</u> <u>bread</u>*; cf. related terms listed at niru

Yaku 約 = about, approximately; *the <u>yakuza</u> was <u>about</u> 30 <u>years</u> old*; cf. daitai = approximately, about, general; cf. hodo = extent, degree, limits, moderation, approximate time, about so much; cf. karekore = roughly, almost, this and that; cf. -kurai (or -gurai) = about, approximately, almost, something like; oyoso = an estimate or outline, approximately

Yaku 訳 = a translation (this can also be read as wake = reason, circumstance); *the <u>yakuza</u> arranged for a <u>translation</u>*; cf. related terms listed at honyaku

Yaku 躍 = a leap, used as a suffix; *the <u>yakuza</u> took a <u>leap</u> out the window*

Yaku ni tatsu 役に立つ = to be useful or helpful; from yaku = service + tatsu = to stand

Yakudatsu 役立つ = to be useful or helpful; a variation of yaku ni tatsu = to be useful or helpful

Yakusha 役者 = an actor or actress; from yaku = role + sha = person; cf. yakuza = a member of the Japanese mafia; cf. related terms listed at haiyuu

Yakushin 躍進 = progress; *when the yakuza put new shingles on his house, people said that he was making progress*; cf. related terms listed at kaizen

Yakusoku 約束 = an appointment, promise or agreement; *I took my yak to an appointment for yak soaking*; cf. machiawase = an appointment; cf. yoyaku = a reservation or appointment; cf. other related terms listed at seiyaku

Yakuwari 役割 = a role, an assigning of duty; from yaku = a role or service + wari = a proportion or rate

Yakuza やくざ = a hoodlum or gangster; *the yakuza sailed his yacht from Kuwait to Zanzibar*

Yakyuu 野球 = baseball; *that baseball team mostly consists of yakking (talking) Cubans*

Yama 山 = a mountain; *the yak managed to climb the mountain*; cf. kouzan = high mountains; cf. meihou = a famous mountain; cf. oka = a hill; cf. saka = slope, hill; cf. renpou = a mountain range; cf. sangaku = mountains; cf. sanmyaku = a mountain range

Yamanobori 山登り = mountain climbing; from yama = mountain + noboru = to climb

Yamasuso 山裾 = the foot or base of a mountain; from yama = mountain + suso = the foot or base of a mountain; cf. fumoto = foot of a mountain, base

Yameru 止める = to stop an activity; *when the Yankee met Ruth, he stopped gambling*; cf. kuitomeru = to hold back or check; cf. taeru = to discontinue or cease; cf. tatsu = to cut off, discontinue; cf. tomeru = to stop or turn off (transitive); cf. yosu = to cease, desist

Yameru 辞める = to resign; *when the Yankee met Ruth, he resigned his position*; cf. related terms listed at jishoku suru

Yami 闇 = darkness; *the yaks meet in darkness*; cf. kurayami = darkness; cf. kuragari = darkness

Yamu 止む = to stop (intransitive); *I want you to stop buying so many yams*; cf. tomaru = to stop (intransitive)

Yamu wo enai やむを得ない = unavoidable, inevitable; from yamu = to stop + enai, the negative form of eru = to receive; cf. related terms listed at hitsuyou

Yamu wo ezu やむをえず = yamu wo ezuni = yamu wo enai de = unavoidably, inevitably; from yamu wo enai = unavoidable + de, which converts a negative verb to an adverb, e.g., tabenai = not to eat, tabenaide = not eating; cf. yoginaku = unavoidably, necessarily

Yanagi 柳 = willow; *the yak was nagging me under the willow tree*

Yane 屋根 = roof; *yaks in the Netherlands sleep under roofs*

Yanushi 家主 = landlord or landlady; *in the yard I saw new shingles that had been stacked by the landlady*; cf. related terms listed at okami and at shujin

Yappari やっぱり = as expected, after all, again; this can also be expressed as yahari; *the Yankees went to Paris after all, as expected*; cf. sasuga ni = indeed, as expected; cf. other related terms listed at kekkyoku

Yara やら = etcetera; *our yak ran away, etcetera*; cf. related terms listed at nado

Yarakasu やらかす = to perpetrate or to be guilty of; *if the yak or the ram kicked the candle over in Superman's tent, they may be guilty of causing the fire*

Yaridasu やり出す = to begin (transitive); from yaru = to do + dasu = to put out; cf. related terms listed at hajimeru

Yarikata やり方 = a way of doing something; from yaru = to do + kata = a method; cf. related terms listed at houhou

Yarimawashi やりまわし = making a turn; from yaru = to do + mawasu = to turn or spin

Yarinaosu やり直す = to redo; from yaru = to do + naosu = to repair

Yaritogeru やり遂げる = to accomplish; from yaru = to do + togeru = to accomplish; cf. related terms listed at hatasu

Yarou 野郎 = a guy or rascal; *the yak on the road was run over by a rascal*); cf. aitsu = that damn person; cf. related terms listed at yatsu

Yaru やる = to give to someone of equal or lower status or to a member of the speaker's in-group, to do, to get along; cf. related terms listed at ataeru and at suru

Yasai 野菜 = vegetables; *the Yankee scientist loves vegetables*; cf. daikon = a large white winter radish; cf. imo = potato; cf. kabocha = pumpkin, squash; cf. kinoko = mushroom; cf. nasu = eggplant; cf. negi = a green onion; cf. ninjin = a carrot; cf. renkon = lotus root; cf. tamanegi = an onion

Yasashii 易しい = easy, simple, plain; this is usually spelled やさしい; *the Yankee's sad sheep were easy to control*; cf. synonyms listed at kantan

Yasashii 優しい = kind, gentle, graceful; *the Yankee gave me satin sheets because he's kind and gentle*; cf. futokoro ga hiroi = is kind-hearted; cf. shinsetsu = kind, gentle

Yasashisa 優しさ = kindness, gentleness; from yasashii = kind, gentle, graceful + sa = a suffix that makes a noun from an adjective; cf. shinsetsu = kindness, gentleness

Yasei 野生 = wild (referring to plants or animals); *the yak felt safe back in the wild*; cf. honpou = unrestrained, free, wild

Yaseru やせる = to lose weight, to become thin, to become barren; *the Yankee will sell the rooster only if it loses weight*

Yashiki 屋敷 = estate, mansion, residence; *the yakuza (gangster) pressed the shift key when he wrote emails in his mansion, so that they would appear in capital letters*; cf. daiteitaku = a mansion; cf. teitaku = a mansion or residence

Yashinau 養う = to feed, nourish, support, cultivate; *I have to feed those Yankee sheep now*; cf. hagukumu = to nourish or nurture; cf. sodateru = to bring up or nurture; cf. tsuchikau = to nourish or cultivate; cf. other related terms listed at tagayasu

Yashu 野手 = fielder (baseball); from yakyuu = baseball + senshu = athlete

Yasuagari 安上り = cheap, economical; from yasui = inexpensive + agaru = to increase; cf. related terms listed at yasui

Yasui 安い = inexpensive; *the yak had a Swedish owner who fed it inexpensive hay*; cf. tegoro = handy, affordable; cf. yasuagari = cheap, economical;

Yasui 易い = easy (to do); *the yak's Swedish owner was easy to fool*

Yasumi 休み = a rest, break, days off, vacation; from yasumu = to rest; cf. daikyuu = compensatory time off; cf. ikoi = a rest; cf. kyuujitsu = a holiday or a day off; cf. kyuuka = holiday, day off; cf. kyuukei = a rest or break; cf. kyuuyou = rest, recuperation, recreation; cf. shukujitsu = a national holiday

Yasumu 休む = to rest or take a break; *the Yankee supervisor was in a mood to rest*

Yasuragi 安らぎ = peace of mind, tranquility; from yasuragu = to feel at peace; cf. heiwa = peace, tranquility

Yasuragu 安らぐ = to feel at peace; *after drinking yak soup at the ranch with Goofy, I felt at peace*; cf. anshin suru = to feel relief or peace of mind; cf. hotto suru = to feel relief, to relax

Yatai 屋台 = a cart (e.g., selling food), stall or stand; from ya = a shop + tai = dai = a stand; cf. related terms listed at mise

Yatoinushi 雇い主 = an employer; from yatou = to hire + nushi = a master

Yatou 雇う = to employ or hire; *when the Yankees grew tobacco, they had to hire many workers*; cf. kakaeru = to embrace or hold; to employ (a person); cf. saiyou suru = to adopt, accept or employ; cf. toru = to hire, adopt, take, collect or pick up

Yatsu 奴 = he, she, a guy, that person, a fellow (slang; usually spelled やつ); *that yacht club supervisor is a regular guy*; cf. related terms listed at aitsu

Yatsuhashi 八つ橋 = a sweet made from bean paste; from yatsu (or more correctly, yattsu) = eight + hashi = a bridge

Yatsura やつら = they; from yatsu = he + ra = a suffix that makes a preceding pronoun plural; cf. related terms listed at aitsu

Yatta! やった = hurray! *The Yankee tax collector said hurray when he finished work*

Yatte iku やっていく = to get along, manage; from yaru = to do + iku = to go

Yatte kuru やって来る = to turn up, come along; from yaru = to do + kuru = to come; cf. related terms listed at arawareru

Yatto やっと = at last, barely; *the yak's toes barely escaped the closing door, but they made it through at last*; cf. ayauku = barely, almost; cf. karoujite = barely; cf. toutou = finally, at last; cf. youyaku = finally or barely; cf. other related terms listed at tsui ni

Yatto no koto de やっとのことで = with great difficulty; from yatto = barely + koto = thing + de = of; literally, "of barely's thing"

Yawarageru 和らげる = to soften or mitigate; *the Yankee had a warrant to get the rooster, and he softened his voice to gain the bird's trust*

Yawaragu 和らぐ = to soften or calm down; the intransitive form of yawarageru = to soften or mitigate

Yawarakai 柔らかい = soft, tender; *since the yak warranted kind treatment, we used a soft touch to dress its tender wounds*

Yo 世 = world, era, age; *yogis are trying to save the world*; cf. related terms listed at jidai and sekai

Yo no naka 世の中 = the world, society, life; from yo = world; *yogis take care of the world*; + the possessive no + naka = inside; cf. seken = society, other people, the way of the world; cf. shakai = society; cf. other related terms listed at inochi and at sekai

Yoake 夜明け = dawn; *we finished the yogurt and a keg by dawn*; cf. akatsuki = daybreak, beginning, ending; cf. akegata = daybreak

Yobidasu 呼び出す = to summon; from yobu = to call out + dasu = to put out; cf. shoukan suru = to summon

Yobikakeru 呼び掛ける = to call out, to appeal; from yobu = to call + kakeru = to expend; cf. yobu = to call out, to summon, among other meanings

Yobina 呼び名 = a name or alias; from yobu = to call + na = name; cf. related terms listed at namae

Yobirin 呼び鈴 = a doorbell or buzzer; from yobu = to call + rin = small bell; *the small bell rings every day*; cf. related terms listed at suzu

Yobou 予防 = prevention; *I eat yogurt for my bones as a strategy for prevention of osteoporosis*; cf. boushi = prevention

Yobu 呼ぶ = to call out, to summon, among other meanings; *after the yogi drank booze, he called out to people on the street*; cf. yobikakeru = to call out or appeal

Yobun 余分 = surplus, extra; *yogurt and hamburger buns are among the surplus items, since we brought an extra supply*; cf. youbun = nutriment; cf. related terms listed at yoyuu

Yochi 余地 = room or space; *we have room for yogurt and cheese*; cf. related terms listed at kuukan

Yodare よだれ = saliva, drool; *Yoda turned red when I mentioned his drooling*; cf. daeki = saliva; cf. tsuba = saliva

Yodooshi 夜通し = throughout the night; from yoru = night + dooshi = tooshi = right through; from tooru = to pass through; cf related terms listed at tetsuya

Yogen 予言 = a prediction; *he made a prediction that the yogurt that Genghis would prefer was the peach-flavored one*; cf. related terms listed at yosoku

Yoginaku 余儀なく = unavoidably, necessarily; *if you serve the yogi nasty Kool-Aid, he will unavoidably retaliate*; cf. yamu wo ezu = yamu wo ezuni = yamu wo enai de = unavoidably, inevitably

Yogiru よぎる = to go by, to cross; *the yogi and his rooster went by my house*; cf. koeru = to cross over; cf. kosu = to exceed, pass, cross, move (residence); cf. oudan suru = to cross

Yogore 汚れ = dirt or a stain; from yogoreru = to get dirty; cf. shimi = a stain; cf. other related terms listed at aka

Yogoreru 汚れる = to get dirty or be stained; *if you give a dish of yogurt to a goat or a red rooster, it will get dirty*

Yogosu 汚す = to soil or stain (transitive); the transitive form of yogoreru = to get dirty

Yohou 予報 = a forecast; *the yogi was at home listening to the forecast*

Yoi 宵 = evening, the early hours of the night; *the yogi from India ate during the evening*; cf. related terms listed at ban

Yoi 良い = good; *if you eat yogurt in the evening it's good*; cf. related terms listed at ii

Yoin 余韻 = a reverberation, a lingering memory; *the yogi felt inaudible reverberations*

Yojinoboru よじ登る = to scramble up; from yojireru = to become twisted + noboru = to climb; cf. related terms listed at noboru

Yojireru よじれる = to become twisted; *the yogi's jeans were attacked by a red rooster and became twisted*

Yojouhan 四畳半 = 4 ½ tatami mats; from yo = four + jou = counter for tatami mats; *Joan of Arc sat on tatami mats*; + han = half; cf. related terms listed at tatami

Yokei 余計 = excessive, all the more, extra; *the yogi kicked his cage excessively*; cf. related terms listed at issou

Yoki 良き = goodness (a noun) or good (a na adjective, but usually the na is omitted); *the yogurt and quiche are good*; cf. yosa = goodness; cf. jintoku = benevolence, goodness

Yokin 預金 = bank deposit; *the yodeling king made a bank deposit*

Yokkyuu 欲求 = desire; *there is strong desire for yogurt in Cuba*; cf. related terms listed at shomou

Yoko 横 = side or width; *Yoko Ono watches her width*; cf. haba = width; cf. other related terms listed at fukin and at hou = direction or side

Yoko ni naru 横にする = to lie down; from yoko = side, sideways, horizontal + ni naru = to become; cf. fuseru = to lay an object upside down or face down, to lie down, to cast one's eyes down; cf. korogaru = to roll, fall over, lie down

Yokogiru 横切る = to cut across; from yoko

= side, sideways, horizontal + giru = kiru = to cut

Yokojiku 横軸 = a horizontal axis; from yoko = width + jiku = an axis; cf. related terms listed at jiku

Yokoppara 横っ腹 = side of the body, or flank; from yoko = side + para = hara = abdomen; cf. related terms listed at waki

Yoku 欲 = greed, desire; an abbreviation of yokubari = greed; cf. yokubari = greed; cf. other related terms at shomou

Yoku 良く = well, often, thoroughly; the adverbial form of yoi = good

Yoku 浴 = to bathe or bask in, used as a word component; *after I bathe, I eat yogurt and cookies*

Yoku 翌 = the next, the following, used as a word component; *the next thing to do is to make yogurt and cookies*

Yoku irasshaimashita 良くいらっしゃいました = welcome; from yoku = well + irassharu = to come honorably; cf. related terms listed at youkoso

Yokubari 欲張り = greed; *in Yosemite, Kuwait and Bali, the greed of tourists for stimulation is visible*; cf. yoku = greed, desire

Yokujitsu 翌日 = the next day; *the next day she ate yogurt and cookies with the jittery superstar*; cf. heijitsu = weekdays; cf. hi = sun, sunlight, day; cf. nichi = day, date; cf. senjitsu = yesterday, the other day; cf. sakujitsu = yesterday; cf. sokujitsu = the same day; cf. youbi = a day of the week

Yokujou 浴場 = a bath, bathtub, bathhouse, bathroom; *I eat yogurt and cookies with Joan at the bathhouse*; cf. related terms listed at furo and at senmenjo

Yokunen 翌年 = the next year; from yoku = next; *the next day she ate yogurt and cookies*; + nen = year

Yokusei 抑制 = control, restraint, suppression; *I need to exercise more control over my impulses to buy yogurt and cookies from Safeway*

Yokusei suru 抑制する = to control or curb; from yokusei = control or restraint; cf. related terms listed at shori suru

Yokushitsu 浴室 = a bathroom; from yoku = to bathe + shitsu = room; cf. related terms listed at senmenjo and at -shitsu

Yokushuu 翌週 = the next week; from yoku = next; *the next day she ate yogurt and cookies*; + shuu = week

Yokusou 浴槽 = a bathtub; *I eat yogurt and cookies in Somalia and then get into a bathtub*; cf. related terms listed at furo

Yome 嫁 = a bride, or one's daughter-in-law; *the bride's yogurt was melting*; cf. related terms listed at hanayome

Yome'iri (Yomeiri) 嫁入り = marriage; from yome = a bride + iri = entering, e.g., iriguchi = an entrance; cf. related terms listed at kekkon

Yomigaeru 甦る = to revive or rise from the dead; *the yogi will meet a gallant Eskimo who is rumored to have risen from the dead*; cf. okosu = to revive or raise up; cf. sosei suru = to revive

Yomu 読む = to read; *I read a review about a yodeling movie*; cf. haiken suru = to see or read humbly

Yonaka 夜中 = the middle of the night; from yoru = night + naka = middle; cf related terms listed at tetsuya

Yonezu 米酢 = rice vinegar; this can also be pronounced komezu; *the yogi had a network at the zoo that supplied rice vinegar*; cf. su = vinegar

Yopparau 酔っ払う = to get drunk; from you = to get drunk + parau = harau = to pay; cf. you = to get drunk

Yori より = more, also, than, out of, from,

since, compared to; *the yogi reads more than the monk*

Yori hoka よりほか = other than; from yori = more or than + hoka = other; cf. betsu to shite = other than, except for

Yori ooku より多く = more numerous; from yori = more + ooku = numerous

Yorikakaru 寄りかかる = to lean on; from yoru = to be inclined to, e.g., toshiyori = elderly person; + kakaru = to hang on; cf. noshikakaru = to lean on, to weigh on

Yorimo よりも = in comparison to, rather; from yori = compared to + mo = even

Yorisou 寄り添う = to cuddle together; from yoru = to drop in or go closer + soueru = to attach

Yorokobi 喜び = joy, delight; from yorokobu = to be happy or delighted; cf. related terms listed at shiawase

Yorokobu 喜ぶ = to be happy or delighted; this can sometimes be written 慶ぶ; *in the Yoropean (European) city of Cologne, the booze is good, and I'm delighted*; cf. etsu ni iru = to be gratified or happy

Yoron 世論 = public opinion; *you're wrong, since public opinion contradicts you*

Yoroshii よろしい = good; *Yoropean (European) sheets are good*; cf. related terms listed at ii

Yoroshiku よろしく = well, best wishes, treat me well; the adverbial form of yoroshii = good

Yoroshiku onegai shimasu よろしくお願いします = I beg you well, or please treat me well; from yoroshiku = treat me well + the humble "o" + negau = to ask + suru = to do

Yoroshiku tonokoto degozaimasu よろしくとのことでございます = (someone) sends you best wishes; from yoroshiku = best wishes + tonokoto = I'm told + degozaimasu = to exist humbly

Yoru 依る = to depend on, usually written よる; *whether the yogi keeps his room depends on his ability to pay the rent*

Yoru 夜 = night; *we eat yogurt under that roof at night*; cf. related terms listed at ban

Yoru 寄る = to gather, to approach, to drop in at; *please gather all of the pennies in your room before you drop in at my house*; cf. sekkin suru = to approach; cf. semaru = to come close, to urge; cf. tachiyoru = to drop in for a short visit

Yoru よる = to choose or select; *please choose some pennies from your room*; cf. related terms listed at erabu

Yoruosoku 夜遅く = late at night; from yoru = night + osoi = late

Yosa 良さ = goodness, merit, virtue; from yoi = good + sa, a suffix that creates a noun from an adjective; cf. bitoku = virtue; cf. jintoku = benevolence, goodness; cf. yoki = goodness, good; cf. zen = goodness, right, virtue

Yosan 予算 = a budget; *we have a budget for the yogi's sandals*

Yosen 予選 = a preliminary contest or heat; *when the yogi ran for senator, he had to compete in a preliminary contest*; cf. related terms listed at issen

Yoseru 寄せる = to send, gather or bring closer; *the yogurt seller rued the day when he gathered rodents, brought them closer to his home and sent them to his clients*; cf. related terms listed at atsumeru

Yoshiashi 善し悪し = good or bad, right or wrong; *the yodeling sheepherder asked some Shiites to explain why people are good or bad*

Yoshuu 予習 = preparation for a lesson; *the yogi surely does thorough preparation for his lessons*

Yosoku 予測 = a prediction or supposition; *the yogi got soaked in the downpour which followed his prediction of rain*; cf. kitai = anticipation; cf. yosou = expectation; cf. kasou = imagination, supposition, virtual; cf. katei = a supposition, hypothesis or conjecture; cf. yogen = a prediction;

Yosou 予想 = expectation; *the yoga class met the soldier's expectations*; cf. kitai = anticipation; cf. yosoku = prediction; cf. shokubou = expectation, hoping for

Yosou 装う = to serve or dish up; *the yogi asked the soldier to dish up the soup*

Yosu よす = to cease, desist; *the yogi's supervisor desisted from checking up on him*; cf. related terms listed at yameru

Yotei 予定 = a plan, arrangement or schedule; *our plan was to store the yogurt on a table*; cf. related terms listed at kikaku

You よう = appearing, seems to be, way to, method of, form or style, like or similar to; *the way that you make that yogurt seems to be good*; cf. related terms listed at -mitai

You よう = let's do, or I shall do; used as a suffix after the root of the plain speech form of an ru verb, e.g., tabeyou = let's eat; *let's eat yogurt*; cf. related terms listed at shou

You 洋 = west, used as a word component, e.g., youshoku = Western-style food; *they eat more yogurt in the west*

You 用 = a use, a job or errand; *the yogi found a use for his old newspapers*

You 酔う = to get drunk; *the yogi got drunk*; cf. yopparau = to get drunk

You ni ように = in order to, so that, as (someone) says; *the yogi's knee underwent surgery so that he would be able to walk again*

You ni naru ようになる = to reach the point that, to come to be that, to turn into; from you ni = in order to + naru = to become

You ni suru ようにする = to see to it that; from you ni = in order + suru = to do

You suru 擁する = to have or possess, to embrace; *I have some yogurt*; cf. related terms listed at motsu

You suru 要する = to need, demand, take or require; *we need a yogi in this town*

You suru ni 要するに = in a word, after all, in short; from you suru = to require + ni = for the purpose; literally this = for the purpose of requiring, or for the purpose of stating what is required

Youbi 曜日 = a day of the week; *I eat yogurt and beans every day of the week*; cf. related terms listed at yokujitsu

Youbou 容貌 = face, features, looks; *since the yogi was bored with his looks, he got a haircut*; cf. related terms listed at mitame

Youbun 養分 = nourishment; *the yogurt that Daniel Boone made was a nourishment for his family*; cf. related terms listed at eiyou

Youchi na 幼稚な = childish, puerile; *yodeling is a cheap activity for childish people*; cf. related terms listed at osanai

Youchien 幼稚園 = kindergarten; from youchi = childish + en = park, e.g., kouen = a park

Youfuku 洋服 = Western-style clothes; from you = west + fuku = clothing; cf. synonyms listed at fuku

Yougan 溶岩 = lava; *a yogi told Gandalf to watch out for lava*

Yougi 容疑 = a suspicion or charge; *the yogi faced a charge of embezzlement*; cf. related terms listed at utagai

Yougisha 容疑者 = a suspect; *the yogi used his sharp mind to identify the suspect*

Yougo 擁護 = protection; *the yogi's golf buddies arranged for protection from his creditors*; cf. related terms listed at hogo

Youhin 用品 = supplies, utensils; from you = a use + hin = goods or articles

Youi 容易 = easy, simple, plain; *for a Yosemite eagle, flying is easy*; cf. related terms listed at kantan

Youi 用意 = preparation, arrangements; *the yogi traveled east to make preparations for his class*; cf. junbi = preparation; cf. junbi bantan = every preparation, suggesting that one is completely ready; cf. shitajunbi = a preliminary preparation; cf. shitaku = preparations; cf. tehai = arrangements, preparations

Youin 要因 = a factor; *their yogurt is incredible, and that was a factor in my review*; cf. related terms listed at youso

Youji 幼児 = a young child; *the young child spilled yogurt on his jeans*; cf. related terms listed at kodomo

Youji 用事 = business, errand; *he went on an errand to buy yogurt for the genius*

Youjiki 幼児期 = early childhood, infancy; from youji = a young child + jiki = time or season; cf. younen jidai = childhood

Youjin 用心 = caution; *exercise caution when you wash the yogi's jeans*; cf. related terms listed at keikoku

Youkai 妖怪 = a ghost or phantom; *at Yosemite, the Kaiser met a ghost*; cf. related terms listed at yuurei

Youken 用件 = an important matter, a business matter; from you = a job or errand + ken = a matter; cf. related terms listed at ken

Youki 陽気 = merry, happy-go-lucky; *the yodeling king is merry*; cf. related terms listed at shiawase na

Youkoso ようこそ = welcome, nice to see you! *welcome! here is some yogurt from Colombia, which is low in sodium*; cf. oideyasu = welcome (used in shops); cf.

okoshiyasu = welcome (used in shops); cf. irasshai = welcome; cf. irasshaimase = welcome (used in shops); cf. yoku irasshaimashita = welcome

Youkou 要項 = outline, main point; *the main point is that we should keep the yogurt cold*; cf. gaiyou = an outline or summary

Youkyuu 要求 = a request or demand; *yogurt and cucumbers are among our requests*; cf. related terms listed at seikyuu

Youkyuu suru 要求する = to demand or request; from youkyuu = a request or demand; cf. related terms listed at tanomu

Youmou 羊毛 = wool; *the yogi moped around in a wool suit*; cf. related terms listed at ke

Younen jidai 幼年時代 = childhood; from youji = a young child + nen = years + jidai = era or times; cf. youjiki = early childhood, infancy

Yousai 要塞 = fortress, fortification; *the yogi found a scientist to help him build up his fortifications*

Yousangyou 養蚕業 = the sericulture (silkworm) industry; *the yogi ate sandwiches and gyoza as he prepared to enter the silkworm industry*; cf. related terms listed at kougyou

Yousei 妖精 = an elf or fairy; *a fairy guided the yodeling sailor*

Yousei no 陽性の = cheerful, positive; *the yodeling sailor is cheerful and positive*; cf. maemuki = facing forward, positive; cf. sekkyoku = positive, progressive; cf. other related terms listed at rakkanteki

Yousha 容赦 = pardon, forgiveness; *the yogi asked the Shah for forgiveness for his inability to speak Persian*; cf. related terms listed at kanben

Youshi 容姿 = appearance, looks; *the appearance of the yogi's sheep is bad*; cf. related terms listed at mitame

Youshi 用紙 = a blank printed form; from you = a use + shi = paper, e.g., shihei = paper money

Youshi 要旨 = the gist or main idea; *the gist of the conversation was that the yogi likes sheep*; cf. shushi = purpose, gist, tenor

Youshoku 洋食 = Western-style food; from you = west + shokuji = a meal; cf. related terms listed at tabemono

Youshoku 養殖 = fish (or pearl) farming, cultivation or raising; *the yodeler was shocked when we showed him our fish farming operation*

Youso 要素 = component, factor, element; *yogurt was eaten during Soviet times, but it was only one element in the diet*; cf. seibun = ingredient, component; cf. youin = factor

Yousu 様子 = condition, state, appearance; *the yogi's suit was in a bad condition, and its appearance shocked the audience*; cf. related terms listed at keisei and mitame

Youten 要点 = an emphasis or main point; from youshi = a main idea + ten = a point

Youtsuu 腰痛 = low back pain; *carrying too much yogurt in my tsuitcase (suitcase) caused my low back pain*; cf. related terms listed at itami

Youyaku ようやく = finally or barely; *the yogi and his yak were finally reunited*; cf. yoyaku = a reservation; cf. related terms listed at tsui ni and at yatto

Youyaku suru 要約する = to summarize; *to summarize, the yogi's yak is troublesome*; cf. related terms listed at matomeru

Yowabi 弱火 = a low fire; from yowai = weak + bi = hi = fire; cf. related terms listed at kaji

Yowai 弱い = weak; *your wife is getting weak*

Yowami 弱み = a weak point; from yowai = weak + mi = body; cf. related terms listed at nigate

Yowamushi 弱虫 = a coward or weakling; from yowai = weak + mushi = an insect or worm; cf. okubyou mono = a coward

Yoyaku 予約 = a reservation or appointment; *the yogi's yak had an appointment for a haircut*; cf. youyaku = finally or barely; cf. related terms listed at yakusoku

Yoyuu 余裕 = surplus; *we have a surplus of yogurt in the Yukon*; cf. amari = surplus; cf. kado = excess, immoderation; cf. kajou = excess, surplus; cf. saisan = profit, surplus; cf. yobun = surplus, extra

Yozakura kenbutsu 夜桜見物 = going out to look at cherry blossoms in the evening; from yoru = night + zakura = sakura = cherry + kenbutsu = sightseeing

Yozora 夜空 = night sky; from yoru = night + zora = sora = sky; cf. related terms listed at sora

Yu 湯 = hot water; *I soak in hot water in the Yukon*; cf. related terms listed at mizu

Yubi 指 = finger; *after I place this ring on your finger, you will be married*; cf. hitosashiyubi = an index finger

Yubisaki 指先 = fingertip; from yubi = finger + saki = end

Yubisasu 指差す = to point to (with finger); *the Yukon beef owner drank salty soup as he pointed to his cattle*; cf. related terms listed at sasu

Yubiwa 指輪 = a ring; from yubi = finger + wa = a round shape; *Washington's face had a round shape*

Yubune 湯船 = a bathtub; from yu = hot water + bune = fune = boat

Yuchaku 癒着 = adhesion, union, collusion; *the youths poured champagne and Kool-Aid into their wounds to promote adhesion*; cf. fuchaku = adhesion, cohesion; cf. yuugou = fusion, adhesion, blending

Yudan 油断 = negligence, inattentiveness; *the youthful dancer was charged with negligence*; cf. taiman = negligence

Yudaneru 委ねる = to entrust; *my youthful daughter never ruins the toys that I entrust to her*; cf. related terms listed at makaseru

Yude tamago ゆで卵 = a boiled egg; from yuderu = to boil + tamago = an egg

Yuden 油田 = an oil field; *the youthful dentist invested in oil fields*

Yuderu ゆでる = to boil; *the youthful debutante ruins eggs when she boils them*; cf. related terms listed at niru

Yuigon 遺言 = will, deathbed instructions; *some Yukon eagles that belonged to Gonzalez were bequeathed in the will*; cf. isho = a will; cf. yuigonsho = a written will

Yuigonsho 遺言書 = written will; from yuigon = will + sho = a document; cf. isho = a will; cf. yuigon = a will

Yui'itsu 唯一 (Yuiitsu) = only, sole, unique; *this Yukon eagle eats its food in a unique way, and it's the only one that eats that way*; cf. dokuji = original, unique; cf. dokutoku = unique, original, characteristic; cf. koseiteki = unique, individualistic; cf. myou = strange, odd, unique; cf. zanshin na = creative, original; cf. other related terms listed at dake

Yuisho 由緒 = history, pedigree, lineage, fame; *the Yukon Easter shows have a long history and have earned considerable fame*; cf. related terms listed at chimeido and at rekishi

Yuka 床 = a floor; *I keep my yucca on the floor*; cf. toko = a bed or floor

Yukai 愉快 = pleasant, cheerful; *the youthful Kaiser was pleasant and cheerful*; cf. related terms listed at kokoroyoi

Yukata 浴衣 = an informal summer kimono; *the youthful kata (honorable person) wore a summer kimono*; cf. related terms listed at fuku

Yuketsu 輸血 = a blood transfusion; from yu = to transport, e.g., yunyuu = to import + ketsu = blood

Yuki 行き = bound for, used as a suffix, e.g., toukyouyuki = bound for Tokyo; *the youthful king was bound for glory*

Yuki 雪 = snow; *this snow is yucky*; cf. gousetsu = a tremendous snowfall; cf. ooyuki = heavy snowfall

Yukidaruma 雪だるま = a snowman; from yuki = snow + daruma = a round doll modeled after Bodhidharma, a Buddhist monk who lived in the 5th century

Yukkuri (to) ゆっくり(と) = slowly, leisurely; *I eat my Yukon curry leisurely*; cf. related terms listed at shidai ni

Yukue 行方 = whereabouts, location; *the youth sold some Kool-Aid to the engineer, but he forgot its location and couldn't deliver it*; cf. shousoku = whereabouts

Yume 夢 = a dream; *the youthful mermaids enjoyed their dreams*; cf. akumu = a nightmare; cf. masayume = a dream come true

Yumi 弓 = bow (archery); *at the youth meeting, I saw many bows*

Yumiya 弓矢 = bow and arrow; from yumi = bow + ya = arrow

Yu'nyuu (Yunyuu) 輸入 = imported; *the yucca in Nyuuyooku (New York) is imported*; cf. hakurai no = imported

Yuragu 揺らぐ = to sway or shake; *the youth ran after the goose, whose wings began to shake*; cf. related terms listed at yureru

Yurai 由来 = origin, source, destiny; *European rice is the source of the illness*; cf. related terms listed at kigen

Yureru 揺れる = to sway, shake or rock (transitive); *the European restaurant was ruined when it shook during an earthquake*; cf. furueru = to tremble; cf. yuragu = to sway or shake (intransitive)

Yurui 緩い = lax, loose, slow; *you ruined the company because your efforts were too lax and slow*; cf. yuttari = comfortable, easy, loose; cf. other related terms listed at osoi

Yurukyara ゆるキャラ = a mascot character; from yurui = lax or loose (implying lighthearted) + character; cf. kigurumi = a cartoon-character costume

Yurumeru 緩める = to abate or loosen (transitive); *the youth ruled over the Mexican ruins until he loosened his grip*; cf. hanasu = to release or loosen

Yurumu 緩む = to abate or become loose; this is the intransitive form of yurumeru = to loosen

Yurushi 許し = forgiveness; from yurusu = to forgive; cf. related terms listed at kanben

Yurusu 許す = to forgive, accept, permit; *after the youths used a ruse on Superman, he forgave them*

Yushutsu 輸出 = export; *when the youth shoots across the border, his bullets become exports*

Yusou 輸送 = transportation; *in the Yukon, soldiers guard transportation facilities*

Yutaka na 豊かな = rich, abundant; *in Utah, a carpenter can find abundant work*; cf. houfu = abundant

Yuttari ゆったり = comfortable, easy, loose; *in that comfortable, loose atmosphere, the youth tarried too long and missed the train*; cf. yurui = lax, loose, slow; cf. other related terms listed at kantan

Yuu 結う = to tie up, braid, fasten (hair); *in the Yukon, people tie up their hair*; cf. related terms listed at tsunagu

Yuu suru 有する = to own or be endowed with; *I own land in the Yukon*; cf. hoyuu suru = to own; cf. motsu = to have or own; cf. megumareru = to be endowed with; cf. sonawaru = to be furnished, equipped or endowed with

Yuube 夕べ = evening, yesterday evening; *the youthful beggar comes in the evening*; cf. related terms listed at ban and at sakuya

Yuuben 雄弁 = eloquent; *the youthful Ben Franklin was eloquent*

Yuubin 郵便 = mail; *these European beans came in the mail*

Yuubinkyoku 郵便局 = the post office; from yuubin = mail + kyoku = bureau, office

Yuuboku 遊牧 = nomadism; *the youthful bony Kool-Aid salesman, who traveled a lot, compared his life to nomadism*

Yuuchou 悠長 = leisurely, slow, deliberate, easy-going; *in the Yukon, I did my chores in a leisurely way*; cf. related terms listed at osoi

Yuudachi 夕立 = evening rain shower; *the youth ate damp cheese during an evening rain shower*; cf. related terms listed at ame

Yuufuku 裕福 = wealth; *I know a youth in Fukuoka who acquired wealth*; cf. related terms listed at tomi

Yuuga 優雅 = elegant; *the youthful gambler wore elegant clothes*; cf. related terms listed at jouhin

Yuugai na 有害な = harmful; *that European guy has a harmful influence on my son*

Yuugata 夕方 = evening, dusk; from yuube = evening + kata = direction; cf. related terms listed at ban

Yuugohan 夕ご飯 = the evening meal; from yuu = evening + gohan = a meal; cf. similar terms listed at shokuji

Yuugou 融合 = fusion, adhesion, blending; *in the Yukon, our goal is a fusion of all cultures into one*; cf. setsugou = fusing or linking cf. other related terms listed at yuchaku

Yuuhan 夕飯 = the evening meal; from yuube = evening + gohan = a meal; cf.

similar terms listed at shokuji

Yuuhei suru 幽閉する = to confine; *the youth hated it when he was confined*

Yuuhi 夕陽 = evening sun, setting sun; from yuugata = evening + hi = sun; cf. synonyms listed at taiyou

Yuujin 友人 = a friend; *that youthful genius is my friend*; cf. related terms listed at tomodachi

Yuujin 有人 = manned, occupied, piloted; from yuu = to exist; *we exist in the Yukon*; + jin = person

Yuujou 友情 = friendship; from yuujin = friend + jou = emotion, e.g., aijou = love; cf. shinmitsusa = friendship, intimacy; cf. shinboku = friendship;

Yuukai 誘拐 = an abduction; *the youthful Kaiser was the target of an abduction*; cf. rachi = kidnapping, taking captive

Yuukan 夕刊 = evening newspaper; from yuube = evening + kankou suru = to publish; cf. related terms listed at shinbun

Yuukan na 勇敢な = brave; *brave people settled the Yukon in Canada*; cf. isamashii = courageous, invigorating

Yuukei (no) 有形(の) = material, physical; *the U.K. is part of the physical world*; cf. gutai = concrete, tangible, material

Yuuki 勇気 = courage; *when the Yukon was being settled, the key to survival was courage*; cf. dokyou = courage or audacity; cf. kimo = the liver, courage

Yuukou 有効 = valid, effective; *the youthful coach had a valid and effective plan*; cf. koukateki = effective

Yuukyuu 有給 = an abbreviation of yuukyuukyuuka = paid vacation; from yuu = to exist; *the Yukon exists*; + kyuuryou = salary + kyuuka = vacation

Yuukyuu no 悠久の = eternal; *after the unicorn was cured, it enjoyed eternal life*; cf. related terms listed at mugen

Yuumei 有名 = famous; *in the Yukon, mayonnaise is famous*; cf. chimei = famous; cf. chomei = famous; cf. nadakai = famous

Yuumeijin 有名人 = a celebrity; from yuumei = famous + jin = a person

Yuumoa ユーモア = humor, as in comedy

Yuumorasu ユーモラス = humorous

Yuunou 有能 = able, competent; *you know I'm competent*; cf. tekinin = competent

Yuurei 幽霊 = a ghost; *the youth raced against the ghost*; cf. rei = soul or ghost; cf. youkai = a ghost or phantom

Yuuri 有利 = advantageous, favorable; *universal reading skills are favorable for society*; cf. related terms listed at daijoubu

Yuuryoku 有力 = prominent, influential; from yuumei = famous + ryoku = power

Yuuryokusha 有力者 = an influential person; from yuuryoku = prominent, influential + sha = a person

Yuusei 郵政 = a postal system; *the Yukon saves money with its postal system*

Yuusen 優先 = preference, priority; *the youthful senator was given priority in the seating arrangements*

Yuusha 勇者 = a brave man or hero; this can also be pronounced yuuja; from yuuki = courage + sha = a person; cf. related terms listed at eiyuu

Yuushi suru 融資する = to finance or lend money; *the bank financed my Yukon sheep ranch*

Yuushoku 夕食 = the evening meal; from yuu = evening + shokuji = meal; cf. similar terms listed at shokuji

Yuushou 優勝 = a victory or championship; *I won a victory at the yucca show*; cf. related terms listed at shouri

Yuushuu 優秀 = outstanding, prominent, excellent; *the youth's shoes were outstanding and featured prominent laces*; cf. yuusuu = prominent; cf. other related terms listed at joutou

Yuusuu 有数 = prominent; *the youthful superintendent is a prominent member of the community*; cf. yuushuu = prominent

Yuu'utsu (Yuuutsu) 憂鬱 = depression, melancholy; *when the youth's uber tsuitcase (suitcase) was lost, he fell into a depression*; cf. related terms listed at utsubyou

Yuuwa 融和 = harmony; *the unicorns and the walruses live in harmony*; cf. related terms listed at chouwa

Yuuwaku 誘惑 = seduction, temptation; *the youths who fought the war against the Kool-Aid industry faced temptation during their leave hours*

Yuuyake 夕焼け = sunset; from yuugata = evening + yakeru = to be roasted or sunburnt; cf. nichibotsu = sunset

Yuuyo 猶予 = a postponement or reprieve; *the youthful yogi asked for a postponement or reprieve of his punishment*; cf. enki = postponement

Yuuyuu 悠々 = quiet, calm, leisurely; *the youthful unicorn moved in a quiet, calm and leisurely way*; cf. related terms listed at odayaka

Yuuzai 有罪 = guilty (of crime); *the youth from Zaire (former name of the Congo) was found guilty*; cf. muzai = innocent

Yuzuriukeru 譲り受ける = to inherit; from yuzuru = to bequeath + ukeru = to receive; cf. related terms listed at tsugu

Yuzuru 譲る = to give way, hand over, sell, bequeath; *the youthful zookeeper ruined the zoo when he gave way to pressure and handed over the crocodiles*; cf. related terms listed at uru

Za 座 = seat, position; *he held an important position in Zambia*; cf. related terms listed at seki

Zabuton 座布団 = a floor cushion; *Zach drank booze with Tony Blair while sitting on a floor cushion*

Zaiaku 罪悪 = crime, sin, vice; *in Zaire (former name of Congo), acupuncture was a crime*; cf. related terms listed at tsumi

Zaibatsu 財閥 = a financial combine or business conglomerate; *in Zaire (former name of the Congo), a guy in a bat suit formed a financial combine*; cf. related terms listed at kaisha

Zaidan 財団 = a foundation (institution); from zaisan = assets + dantai = a group of people

Zaijuu 在住 = residence; *due to the local zeitgeist (spirit of the age) and the orange juice, I am taking up residence in Florida*; cf. related terms listed at ie

Zaika 財貨 = stock, goods on hand; *we have Zairean cattle in stock*; cf. zaiko = stock or inventory

Zaiko 在庫 = stock or inventory; *we kept our inventory on the Zairean coast (Zaire = the former name of the Congo)*; cf. zaika = stock, goods on hand

Zaimoku 材木 = timber; *in Zaire (former name of the Congo), they would give more Kool-Aid to workers who harvested more timber*

Zairyou 材料 = material, ingredient; *in Zaire (former name of the Congo), Pope Leo found some of the ingredients for his recipes*; cf. genryou = raw materials; cf. sozai = a material or ingredient; cf. seibun = ingredient

Zaisan 財産 = assets, fortune, property; *in Zaire (former name of the Congo) I bought a sand mine with my fortune*; cf. related terms listed at tomi

Zaisei 財政 = public finance, financial affairs; from zaisan = assets + seiji = politics; cf. kinyuu = finance, money-lending

Zangyaku na 残虐な = cruel, inhuman; *in Zanzibar I met a geeky yakuza who was cruel*; cf. hidoi = inhuman, cruel, painful, violent, terrible

Zangyakusa 残虐さ = cruelty; from zangyaku = cruel + sa = a suffix that makes a noun from an adjective

Zangyou 残業 = overtime work; *in Zanzibar, gyoza makers often work overtime*; cf. related terms listed at shigoto

Zankoku na 残酷な = brutal, atrocious; *in Zanzibar, the corporation coolly ignored the brutal conduct of its employees*

Zannen 残念 = too bad, regrettable; *in Zambia my negative nephew's farm failed, which was too bad*; cf. ikan na = regrettable, unsatisfactory; cf. oshii = unfortunate or regrettable, almost but not quite, precious or valuable

Zanshin na 斬新な = creative, original; *the Zanzibarian shingles were an original design*; cf. related terms listed at yuiitsu

Zantei 暫定 = tentative, temporary; *in Zanzibar, the tailor found temporary work*; cf. rinji = temporary, extraordinary, emergency; cf. other related terms listed at toriaezu

Zaseki 座席 = a seat (transportation, theater); from za = to sit, e.g., zabuton = a floor cushion; + seki = a seat; cf. related terms listed at seki

Zasetsu 挫折 = a failure or setback; *when I went to Zambia to set up a super farm, I experienced some setbacks*; cf. related terms listed at shippai

Zasetsu suru 挫折する = to be frustrated, to collapse or fail; from zasetsu = a failure; cf. related terms listed at hazureru

Zashiki 座敷 = Japanese-style room with tatami flooring; *Zach found the missing shift key in the tatami room*; cf. related terms listed at -shitsu

Zasshi 雑誌 = a magazine; *Zachory Taylor liked sheep and subscribed to magazines about them*; cf. gekkanshi = a monthly magazine; cf. sasshi = a pamphlet; cf. shuukanshi = a weekly magazine

Zassou 雑草 = weeds; *the Zambian soldier cut down some weeds*

Zatsudan 雑談 = idle chat; *I showed Zach's tsuitcase (suitcase) to the dancer while we engaged in idle chat*

Zatsuon 雑音 = noise; *Zach's tsuitcase (suitcase) only makes noise when an unauthorized person touches it*; cf. souon = noise

Zatsuyou 雑用 = chores; *Zach's tsuitcase (suitcase) contained a yoke that he used for his chores with oxen*

Zatto ざっと = roughly, briefly, approximately; *Zach's toe was approximately three inches long, and he briefly examined it*

Zattou 雑踏 = a crowd, congestion; *a crowd of people examined Zach's swollen toe*; cf. related terms listed at dantai

Zawameku ざわめく = to be noisy, to rustle or murmur; *when Zach warred with the Mexican Kool-Aid gang, sometimes he was noisy and sometimes he murmured*

Zazen 座禅 = Zen meditation; from zaseki = a seat + zenshuu = Zen Buddhism

Zehi 是非 = by all means, definitely, really; *I really think that Zen can heal me*; cf. makoto ni = really, truly; cf. mattaku = really, entirely; cf. zehitomo = by all means; cf. zettai ni = absolutely, definitely, by all means

Zehitomo 是非とも = by all means; *I will go to the Zen temple for healing tomorrow, by all means*; cf. related terms listed at zehi

Zeikin 税金 = tax, duty; *the zany king collected taxes*; cf. genzei = a tax reduction; cf. juuzei = heavy taxes; cf. menzei = a tax exemption; cf. shuzei = a liquor tax

Zeitaku ぜいたく = luxury, extravagance; *my zany friend drinks only tap water and Kool-Aid although otherwise she lives in luxury*

Zekkei 絶景 = a superb view; *there is a superb view from that Zen cave*; cf. related terms listed at nagame

Zekkou suru 絶交する = to break off (a relationship); *the zesty coder broke off the relationship*

Zekkyou 絶叫 = a scream or shriek; *I heard a scream from a Zen temple in Kyouto*; cf. related terms listed at kakegoe

Zen 全 = all, whole, entire, used as a word component; an abbreviation of zenbu = all, everything

Zen 前 = former, before, in front of, used as a word component; *my former teacher became a Zen monk*; cf. related terms listed at saki ni

Zen 善 = goodness, right, virtue; *the Zen monk encouraged goodness, right and virtue*; cf. related terms listed at yosa

Zen 膳 = a counter for bowls of cooked rice; *the Zen monks used counters to remember the number of bowls of cooked rice that they ate*

Zenbou 全貌 = a full picture, the whole story; from zenbu = everything + youbou = looks

Zenbu 全部 = all, everything; *a Zen Buddhist told me that everything is an illusion*; cf. related terms listed at banji

Zenchou 全長 = overall length or span; from zenbu = everything + chou = long, e.g., chou kyori = long distance; cf. related terms listed at nagasa

Zenchou 前兆 = premonition, omen; *the Zen temple assigned me the chore of sweeping, and I had a premonition that my broom would break*; cf. engi = omen, sign of luck, origin, causation; cf. fukitsu = ill omen, unlucky, ominous; cf. kehai = indication, sign, presence; cf. kizashi = a sign or omen

Zendate 膳立て = setting the table; from zen = a counter for bowls of cooked rice + dateru = tateru = to set up

Zen'in (Zenin) 全員 = all members; from zenbu = everything + in = a group member

Zenin 是認 = approval; *the Zen monk said that the ninja met with his approval*; cf. kyoka = permission, approval; cf. shounin = approval, recognition, sanction

Zenkai 全開 = opening fully, full throttle; *the Zen monk kindly drove at full throttle when he took me to the hospital*

Zenkai 前回 = the previous time; from zen = before + kai = time

Zenkai suru 全快する = to recover completely (from illness); *practicing Zen and flying kites allowed me to recover completely*; cf. related terms listed at ryouyou suru

Zenkoku 全国 = countrywide, whole country; from zen = all, whole + koku = country

Zenmen 全面 = whole surface, entire; from zenbu = everything + men = surface; cf. related terms listed at men

Zenmenteki 全面的 = all-out, general, extensive, full-scale, over-all, complete; from zenmen = entire + teki = related to; cf. other related terms listed at habahiroi, at kanpeki na and at taitei

Zennen 前年 = the previous year; from zen = before, e.g., gozen = before noon; + nen = year; cf. related terms listed at kyonen

Zennin 善人 = a good person; *the Zen*

devotee was a _ninja_ and a _good_ _person_; cf. seijin = a saint

Zenryaku 前略 = a salutation in a letter indicating that the writer is dispensing with formalities; from zen = before, e.g., gozen = before noon; + ryaku = omission

Zenryoku 全力 = all one's power or energy; from zenbu = everything + ryoku = strength, e.g., nouryoku = ability; cf. isshou kenmei = with all one's might; cf. seiippai = the best of one's ability, with all one's might

Zensei 全盛 = culmination, heyday, peak; _that Zen sage is at the peak of his powers_

Zenseiki 前世紀 = the last century, ancient times; from zen = former + seiki = century

Zenshin 前進 = an advance, progress; _those who turned to Zen from Shinto made some progress_; cf. related terms listed at hattatsu

Zensho 善処 = making the best of, handling carefully; _at the Zen show, we were making the best of our resources and handling our customers carefully_

Zensho suru 善処する = to make an effort to solve a problem, to make the best of; from zensho = making the best of, handling carefully; cf. ganbaru = to persevere, to do one's best; cf. hagemu = to be diligent or make an effort; cf. tsukusu = to use up, to exert oneself, to devote, to serve (a person); cf. tsutomeru = to make an effort

Zenshou suru 全焼する = to burn completely; _the set for the Zen show burned completely_; cf. related terms listed at moeru

Zenshuu 禅宗 = Zen Buddhism; from Zen + shuukyou = religion; cf. related terms listed at shuukyou

Zensokuryoku 全速力 = full speed; from zen = all + soku = fast; _dry ground soaks up the rain fast_; + ryoku = force

Zensou 禅僧 = a Zen monk; from zenshuu = Zen Buddhism + sou = a monk; cf. related terms listed at juushoku

Zentai 全体 = whole; from zen = whole + tai = body, e.g., taijuu = body weight; cf. related terms listed at banji

Zentei 前提 = premise, prerequisite; _the Zen tape describes the prerequisites for meditation_

Zenzaisan 全財産 = everything one owns; from zenbu = everything + zaisan = property; cf. related terms listed at tomi

Zenzen 全然 = not at all in negative sentences, completely in positive sentences; _to sit in one Zen session followed by another Zen session is not at all what I want to do_; cf. chittomo = not at all; cf. ikkou ni = not at all (with negatives), completely; cf. issai = not at all (with negatives), everything (with positives); cf. kanzen ni = perfectly, entirely; cf. maru de = absolutely, entirely, completely; cf. nantomo = quite or extremely, in positive constructions; not at all, in negative constructions; cf. sukkari = thoroughly, completely; cf. suppori = completely, entirely; cf. zonbun (ni) = fully, to one's heart's content;

Zeppeki 絶壁 = a precipice; _a Zen monk visited Peking to see a precipice_; cf. related terms listed at dangai

Zessan suru 絶賛する = to praise highly; _they highly praised the Zen sandwiches that they were served at the temple_; cf. homeru = to praise, admire or speak well of; cf. shousan suru = to praise, admire, commend

Zetsubou 絶望 = despair; _the Zen monk took his tsuitcase (suitcase) to the bowling alley out of despair when he couldn't find another place to spend the night_

Zetsubouteki 絶望的 = hopeless; from zetsubou = despair + teki = related to

Zetsumetsu 絶滅 = extinction; _I was wearing_

my Zen tsuit (suit) when I met Superman, and he warned me about the possible extinction of the human race

Zettai ni 絶対に = absolutely, definitely, by any means; the zesty tiger that my niece saw definitely had stripes; cf. related terms listed at zehi

Zettaiteki 絶対的 = absolute; from zettai = absolutely + teki = related to

Zo ぞ = a particle used at the end of Japanese sentences to indicate emphasis; she put emphasis on the importance of the signs of the zodiac

Zoi 沿い = along, used as a word component; from zou = sou = to run along or follow a plan; cf. ni sotte = in accordance with, along

Zoku na 俗な = mundane, vulgar, common; Zooey's Kool-Aid is common and vulgar; cf. related terms listed at mittomonai

Zoku ni 俗に = commonly (slang); from zoku = common; cf. related terms listed at taitei

Zoku suru 属する = to belong to (e.g., to a group); I belong to Zooey's Kool-Aid club; cf. shozoku suru = to belong to

Zokuhen 続編 = a sequel or continuation; in the sequel, Zooey makes Kool-Aid for Henry

Zokusei 属性 = an attribute; Zooey's Kool-Aid is safe to drink and has other positive attributes; cf. related terms listed at tokuchou

Zokushutsu 続出 = appearing one after the other; zombies in Kuwait shoot supervisors, and these stories appear one after the other; cf. hitotsu hitotsu = one by one, carefully; cf. tsugitsugi ni = one after the other

Zonbun (ni) 存分(に) = fully, to one's heart's content; the zoning in the boondocks allows him to enlarge his house to his heart's content; cf. related terms listed at zenzen

Zonjiru 存じる = to know, think or feel humbly; in that zone they jeer at rumors started by those who humbly know very little; cf. related terms listed at omou and at shiru

Zou 像 = an image or statue, e.g., butsuzou = an image or statue of Buddha; I saw an image representing the signs of the Zodiac; cf. douzou = a bronze statue; cf eizou = images, pictures (screen); cf. ritsuzou = standing statue

Zou 象 = an elephant; elephants thrive in tropical zones

Zou 臓 = an organ of the body; zou (elephants) have big organs

Zouge 象牙 = ivory; from zou = elephant + ge = tusk; my guest wore a necklace of tusks

Zouka 増加 = increase, addition; there has been an increase in the number of zones where cars are allowed; cf. joushou = rising, ascending, climbing; cf. kyuuzou = sudden increase

Zouka suru 増加する = to increase; from zouka = increase, addition; cf. fueru = to increase

Zoukei 造詣 = knowledge, mastery; Zooey's cakes demonstrate a mastery of baking; cf. jukutatsu = mastery; cf. other related terms listed at chishiki

Zoukeifukai 造詣深い (this can also be pronounced zoukeibukai) = scholarship, learning; from zoukei = knowledge, mastery + fukai = deep; cf. related terms listed at chishiki

Zouki 臓器 = an internal organ; Zooey's quiche is good for our internal organs; cf. related terms listed at naizou

Zoukin 雑巾 = a dust cloth or cleaning cloth; Zooey's kindergarten was cleaned with dust cloths; cf. related terms listed at nuno

Zouri 草履 = Japanese sandals; *Zooey really likes her Japanese sandals*; cf. related terms listed at kutsu

Zousho 蔵書 = a book collection or library; *Zooey showed me her book collection*; cf. related terms listed at hon, at shuushuu and at toshokan

Zousui 雑炊 = rice gruel with fish, vegetables, etc.; *in the Canal Zone, a Swedish cook prepares rice gruel with fish*

Zoutei 贈呈 = a presentation (of a gift, etc.); *Zooey tasted the cookies that she was given during the presentation*

Zoutei suru 贈呈する = to donate or present a gift; from zoutei = a presentation; cf. related terms listed at ataeru

Zouwai 贈賄 = bribery; *Zooey wisely refused the offer of bribery*; cf. related terms listed at tsumi

Zouwai suru 贈賄する = to bribe; from zouwai = bribery

Zu 図 = a drawing or illustration; an abbreviation of zushi = illustration; cf. related terms listed at e

Zubon ズボン = pants or trousers; *I work for the zoo, and as a bonus they give us pants*; cf. nikkapokka = knickerbockers (men's baggy trousers)

Zugaikotsu 頭蓋骨 = a skull; *the zoo guide wore two coats over his skull to keep warm*; cf. related terms listed at hone

Zui 髄 = marrow or pith; *the zooming eagle eats the marrow from the bones of its prey*; cf. shinzui = essence or gist

Zuibun ずいぶん = very; this can sometimes be spelled 随分; *it was very frightening when the zooming eagle attacked Daniel Boone*; cf. related terms listed at ooi ni

Zujou 頭上 = overhead; from zu = head, e.g., zutsuu = headache; + jou = above, e.g., jouzu = skillful

Zukizuki ずきずき = throbbing pain; *the zookeeper dropped his zoo keys when he experienced a throbbing pain in his chest*; cf. related terms listed at itami

Zuni ずに = not doing, used as a suffix by replacing naide at the end of a negative progressive verb, e.g., tabenaide = tabezuni = not eating; *the zoo needs volunteers who are not working during the day*

Zunou 頭脳 = brains, head; *the zookeeper knows that she has brains*; cf. related terms listed at atama

Zushi 図示 = an illustration (showing in graphic form); *the zoo's sheep appear in this illustration*; cf. related terms listed at e

Zutsu ずつ = each or by (as in "one by one"); *I value each zoot suit and fold them one by one*; cf. related terms listed at hitotsu hitotsu

Zutsuu 頭痛 = a headache; *this zoot suit is giving me a headache*; cf. related terms listed at itami

Zutto ずっと = always, all the while, all the way, very much, far more; *the zookeeper told us that she wanted to help us very much and would be with us all the way*; cf. related terms listed at itsumo and also at ooi ni

Proper Nouns (names of people and places)

This list includes nearly all of the proper nouns found in the *Learn to Read in Japanese* books and their associated supplemental reading material. It also contains the names of the Japanese prefectures, the largest Japanese cities (more than 500,000 population) and the wards of Tokyo. Please **note** that many Japanese people's names, especially first names like Youko, are spelled in multiple different ways, and we are not able to provide all of the possible spellings for them. Japanese people often write first names like Youko using hiragana, to avoid confusion.

Adachi 足立 – a ward in Tokyo

Agawa 阿川 – surname

Aichi 愛知 – prefecture

Aihara 相原 – surname

Aiko 愛子 – female name

Akagi 赤木 – mountain, surname

Akihabara 秋葉原 – a district in Tokyo

Akiko 明子 – female name

Akita 秋田 – city, prefecture

Amami Ooshima 奄美大島 – island

Amanohashidate 天橋立 – a sandbar

Aoki 青木 – surname

Aomori 青森 – city, prefecture

Arakawa 荒川 – river, Tokyo ward

Arashiyama 嵐山 – a district in Kyoto

Ariakekai 有明海 – the Ariake Sea, near Kyuushuu

Asahi 朝日 – a newspaper

Asakusa 浅草 – a district in Taitou

Aso 阿蘇 – a volcano in Kyushu

Atsuko 厚子 – female name

Beikoku 米国 – the U.S., America

Bunkachou 文化庁 – the Agency for Cultural Affairs

Bunkyou 文京 – a ward in Tokyo

Chiba 千葉 – city, prefecture

Chichibu 秩父 – city

Chichuukai 地中海 – Mediterranean Sea

Chieko 千恵子 – female name

Chion'in (Chionin) 知恩院 – a temple in Kyoto

Chiyoda 千代田 – a ward in Tokyo

Chizuru 千鶴 – female name

Choukou 長江 – the Yangtze River in China

Chousen 朝鮮 – Korea

Chuubu 中部 – a region in the middle of Honshuu

Chuugoku 中国 – China, a region in western Honshuu

Chuunanbei 中南米 – Central and South America

Chuuou 中央 – a ward in Tokyo

Dougen 道元 – Zen monk in Kamakura era

Ebisu 恵比寿 – a district in Shibuya

Edo 江戸 – old name for Tokyo

Edogawa 江戸川 – a ward in Tokyo

Ehime 愛媛 – prefecture

Eikoku 英国, or igirisu イギリス – England

Fuji 富士 – mountain

Fujita 藤田 – surname

Fukui 福井 – city, prefecture

Fukuoka 福岡 – city, prefecture

Fukushima 福島 – city, prefecture, surname

Funabashi 船橋 – city

Gifu 岐阜 – city, prefecture

Ginza 銀座 – a district in Chuuou

Gomen Machi 後免町 – town

Gunma 群馬 – prefecture

Hachiouji 八王子 – city

Hakata 博多 – a ward in Fukuoka

Hakone 箱根 – town

Hamamatsu 浜松 – city

Hanada 花田 – surname

Hanako 花子 – female name

Haneda 羽田 – airport

Hanshin 阪神 – Oosaka and Koube

Haruki 春樹 – male name

Haruko 春子 – female name

Harumi 晴海 – a district in Chuuou

Hashimoto 橋本 – surname

Hatoyama 鳩山 – surname

Hayashi 林 – surname

Hayashida 林田 – surname

Hibiya 日比谷 – a park and subway line, Tokyo

Higashida 東田 – surname

Higashioosaka 東大阪 – city

Higashiyama 東山 – a district in Kyoto

Higuchi 樋口 – surname

Himeji 姫路 – city, castle

Hirayama 平山 – surname

Hiroshima 広島 – city, prefecture

Hirota 広田 – surname

Hokkaido 北海道 – prefecture, island

Honda 本田 – surname

Honkon 香港 – Hong Kong

Honshuu 本州 – the main island of Japan

Houjou 北条 – surname

Hyougo 兵庫 – prefecture

Ibaraki 茨城 – prefecture

Ichiko 壱子 – female name

Igirisu イギリス, or eikoku 英国 – England

Ikeda 池田 – surname

Imada 今田 – surname

Inoue 井上 – surname

Ise 伊勢 – city, shrine

Isesaki 伊勢崎 – city

Ishida 石田 – surname

Ishihara 石原 – surname

Ishikari 石狩 – city

Ishikawa 石川 – prefecture, surname

Itabashi 板橋 – a ward in Tokyo

Itou 伊藤 – surname

Iwate 岩手 – prefecture

Izu 伊豆 – a peninsula on Honshuu

Izumi 泉 – female name, surname

Junko 純子 – female name

Kagawa 香川 – prefecture

Kagoshima 鹿児島 – city, prefecture

Kamakura 鎌倉 – city

Kanagawa 神奈川 – prefecture

Kanako 加奈子 – female name

Kanazakura 金櫻 – a shrine in Koufu

Kankoku 韓国 – South Korea

Kansai 関西 – southwestern Japan, including Osaka

Kantou 関東 – a district that includes seven prefectures, including Tokyo

Kasai 葛西 – surname

Katou 加藤 – surname

Katsushika 葛飾 – a ward in Tokyo

Kawaguchi 河口 – city, lake

Kawasaki 川崎 – city

Keiichi 恵一 – male name

Keiko 恵子, or 慶子, or 啓子 – female name

Kenji 健司 – male name

Kibune 貴船 – town

Kihara 木原 – surname

Kimura 木村 – surname

Kinkakuji 金閣寺 – a temple in Kyoto

Kintarou 金太郎 – a fairy tale boy

Kishida 岸田 – surname

Kishiwada 岸和田 – city

Kita 北 – a ward in Tokyo

Kitadake 北岳 – mountain

Kitakyuushuu 北九州 – city

Kitamura 北村 – surname

Kiyohime 清姫 – a woman from a fairy tale

Kiyomizudera 清水寺 – a temple in Kyoto

Kobayashi 小林 – surname

Koizumi 小泉 – surname

Komoro 小諸 – city, castle

Koube 神戸 – city

Kouchi 高知 – city, prefecture

Koudaiji 高台寺 – a temple in Kyoto

Koufu 甲府 – city

Koushi 孔子 – Confucius

Koutou 江東 – a ward in Tokyo

Kouzanji 高山寺 – a temple in Kyoto

Kudou 工藤 – surname

Kumamoto 熊本 – city, prefecture

Kuroda 黒田 – surname

Kyouto 京都 – city, prefecture

Kyuushuu 九州 – island

Maeda 前田 – surname

Makoto 真 – male or female name

Maruyama 丸山 – city

Masako 正子 – female name

Masao 正男 – male name

Matsue 松江 – city

Matsumoto 松本 – surname

Matsushita 松下 – surname

Matsuyama 松山 – city, castle

Matsuzakaya 松坂屋 – department store

Meguro 目黒 – a ward in Tokyo

Michiko 道子 – female name

Mie 三重 – prefecture

Miikegun 三池郡 – the Miike district in Kyuushuu

Miki 三木 – female name

Minato 港 – a ward in Tokyo

Minoo 箕面 – city, waterfall, mountain

Mishima 三島 – surname

Mitsui 三井 – surname

Mitsukoshi 三越 – department store

Mitsunari 光成, or 三成 – male name

Miura 三浦 – surname

Miyagi 宮城 – prefecture

Miyazaki 宮崎 – city, prefecture, surname

Miyazu 宮津 – town

Miyuki 美雪 – female name

Mizuno 水野 – surname

Moe 萌 – female name

Mori 森 – surname

Morioka 盛岡 – city

Morita 森田 – surname

Murakami 村上 – surname

Nagano 長野 – city, prefecture

Nagasaki 長崎 – city, prefecture

Nagashima 長島 – town

Nagoya 名古屋 – city

Nakajima – see Nakashima

Nakamura 中村 – surname

Nakano 中野 – a ward in Tokyo

Nakashima 中島 – surname

Nakayama 中山 – surname

Nanbei 南米 – South America

Naoki 直樹 – male name

Naoko 直子 – female name

Naomi 直美 – female name

Nara 奈良 – city, prefecture

Narita 成田 – city

Natsumi 夏美 – female name

Nerima 練馬 – a ward in Tokyo

Nihon 日本 – Japan

Nihonbashi 日本橋 – district in Chuuou

Nihonkai 日本海 – Sea of Japan; cf. related terms listed at umi

Niigata 新潟 – city, prefecture

Nijoujou 二条城 – Nijou Castle

Nikkou 日光 – city

Nintoku Tenn'ou (Nintoku Tennou) 仁徳天皇 – the legendary emperor Nintoku

Nishimura 西村 – surname

Noda 野田 – surname

Nomura 野村 – surname

Nozawa 野沢 – town

O'inarisan (Oinarisan) お稲荷さん – the god of harvests and wealth

Oda 小田 – surname

Odaiba お台場 – an island in Tokyo Bay

Odawara 小田原 – city, castle

Ogasawara 小笠原 – island chain

Ogawa 小川 – surname

Okayama 岡山 – city, prefecture

Okinawa 沖縄 – prefecture

Ono 小野 – surname

Oohara 大原 – surname

Ooita 大分 – city, prefecture

Oosaka 大阪 – city, prefecture

Oota 大田 – a ward in Tokyo

Ootsu 大津 – city

Oubei 欧米 – Europe and the U.S., the West

Oushuu 欧州 – Europe

Ran 蘭 – male or female name

Ren 蓮 – male name

Roppongi 六本木 – a district in Minato

Sachiko 佐知子 – female name

Saga 佐賀 – city, prefecture

Sagamihara 相模原 – city

Saitama 埼玉 – city, prefecture

Saitou 斎藤 – surname

Sakabe 坂部 – surname

Sakai 堺 – city

Sakuragaoka 桜ヶ丘 – a district in Shibuya

Sakuragawa 桜川 – town

Sakurajima 桜島 – volcano

Sanai 佐内 – a building in Ginza

Sankei 産経 – a newspaper

Sanwa 三和 – a company

Sanyabori 山谷掘 – a park in Tokyo

Sapporo 札幌 – city

Satoshi 諭 – male name

Satou 佐藤 – surname

Sawamura 沢村 – surname

Sekida 世木田 – surname

Sendai 仙台 – city

Setagaya 世田谷 – a ward in Tokyo

Setsuko 節子 – female name

Shibutani 渋谷 – surname

Shibuya 渋谷 – a ward in Tokyo

Shiga 滋賀 – prefecture

Shikoku 四国 – island

Shimada 島田 – surname

Shimane 島根 – prefecture

Shimonoseki 下関 – city (the "no" is understood)

Shin'ichi (Shinichi) 真一 – male name

Shin'oosaka (Shinoosaka) 新大阪 – city

Shinagawa 品川 – a ward in Tokyo

Shingen 信玄 – a warrior who lived in the 1500's

Shinjuku 新宿 – a ward in Tokyo

Shirayukihime 白雪姫 – Snow White

Shisenshou 四川省 – Szechuan Province in China

Shizuoka 静岡 – city, prefecture

Suehiro 末広 – a restaurant in Ginza

Suginami 杉並 – a ward in Tokyo

Sumida 隅田 – a ward in Tokyo

Susumu 進 – male name

Suzuki 鈴木 – surname
Tadokoro 田所 – surname
Taiheiyou 太平洋 – Pacific Ocean; cf. related terms listed at umi
Taitou 台東 – a ward in Tokyo
Taiwan 台湾 – Taiwan
Takahashi 高橋 – surname
Takakura 高倉 – surname
Takamatsu 高松 – city
Takarazuka 宝塚 – city
Takayama 高山 – city
Takeda 竹田 – surname
Tamagawa 玉川 – hot spring
Tamura 田村 – surname
Tanabe 田辺 – surname
Tanaka 田中 – surname
Tarou 太郎 – male name
Teshima 手島 – surname
Tochigi 栃木 – city, prefecture
Tochousha 都庁舎 – the Tokyo Metropolitan Government building
Togawa 戸川 – surname
Tokushima 徳島 – city, prefecture
Toshima 豊島 – a ward in Tokyo
Tottori 鳥取 – city, prefecture

Toubu 東武 – a railroad company
Touhoku 東北 – a university in Sendai
Toukyou 東京 – city
Toyama 富山 – city, prefecture
Tsu 津 – city
Tsuchida 土田 – surname
Tsuda 津田 – surname
Tsukino 月野 – surname
Tsuutenkaku 通天閣 – a tower in Osaka
Uchida 内田 – surname
Ueda 上田 – surname
Umezawa 梅沢 – surname
Urashima 浦島 – surname
Urata 浦田 – surname
Ushiku 牛久 – town
Utsunomiya 宇都宮 – city (the "no" is understood)
Wada 和田 – surname
Wakayama 和歌山 – city, prefecture
Wakou 和光 – city
Waseda 早稲田 – a university in Shinjuku
Watanabe 渡辺 – surname
Yamada 山田 – surname
Yamagata 山形 – city, prefecture

Yamaguchi 山口 – city, prefecture, surname

Yamakawa 山川 – surname

Yamamoto 山本 – surname

Yamanashi 山梨 – city, prefecture

Yamashita 山下 – surname

Yamato 大和 – old name for Japan, former province

Yokohama 横浜 – city

Yomiuri 読売 – a newspaper

Yoshida 吉田 – surname

Yoshino 吉野 – an old province of Japan

Youko 洋子 or 陽子 – female name

Yoyogi 代々木 – a park in Shibuya

Yukiko 雪子 – female name

Yuu 優 – male name

Yuuma 悠真 – male name

Yuuta 悠太 – male name

Counting and Time Words

Counting Numbers (objects)

Hitotsu 一つ = 1 item

Futatsu 二つ = 2 items

Mittsu 三つ = 3 items

Yottsu 四つ = 4 items

Itsutsu 五つ = 5 items

Muttsu 六つ = 6 items

Nanatsu 七つ = 7 items

Yattsu 八つ = 8 items

Kokonotsu 九つ = 9 items

Too 十 = 10 items

Counting Numbers (people)

Hitori 一人 = 1 person

Futari 二人 = 2 people

Sannin 三人 = 3 people

Yonin 四人 = 4 people

Gonin 五人 = 5 people (and so on)

Days of the Month

Tsuitachi 一日 = 1st of the month

Futsuka 二日 = 2nd of the month

Mikka 三日 = 3rd of the month

Yokka 四日 = 4th of the month

Itsuka 五日 = 5th of the month

Muika 六日 = 6th of the month

Nanoka 七日 = 7th of the month

Youka 八日 = 8th of the month

Kokonoka 九日 = 9th of the month

Tooka 十日 = 10th of the month

Juuichinichi 十一日 = 11th of the month

Juuyokka 十四日 = 14th of the month

Hatsuka 二十日 = 20th of the month

Nijuuichinichi 二十一日 = 21st of the month

Nijuuyokka 二十四日 = 24th of the month

Sanjuunichi 三十日 = 30th of the month

Days of the Week

Nichiyoubi 日曜日 = Sunday

Getsuyoubi 月曜日 = Monday

Kayoubi 火曜日 = Tuesday

Suiyoubi 水曜日 = Wednesday

Mokuyoubi 木曜日 = Thursday

Kinyoubi 金曜日 = Friday

Doyoubi 土曜日 = Saturday

Mnemonic for the Days of the Week:

Suppose that you have a friend named Nietzche who gets you a coyote. You aren't sure what to feed it, but you think that sweet milk can do. The mnemonic is: <u>Nietzche</u> <u>gets</u> <u>yo</u>u a <u>coyote</u> *(Nichi Getsu Kayou)*. <u>Sweet</u> <u>milk</u> <u>can</u> <u>do</u> *(Sui Moku Kin Do)*.

Eras and Periods

Edo 江戸 – period (1603 – 1867)

Heisei 平成 – era (1989–2019)

Joumon 縄文 – period (14,000 – 300 BC)

Kamakura 鎌倉 – era (1192 – 1333)

Keiou 慶応 – era (1865-1868)

Meiji 明治 – era (1868 – 1912)

Shouwa 昭和 – era (1926-1989)

Yayoi 弥生 – era (300 BC - 300 AD)

Months of the Year

Ichigatsu 一月 = January

Nigatsu 二月 = February

Sangatsu 三月 = March

Shigatsu 四月 = April

Gogatsu 五月 = May

Rokugatsu 六月 = June

Shichigatsu 七月 (or nanagatsu) = July

Hachigatsu 八月 = August

Kugatsu 九月 = September

Juugatsu 十月 = October

Juuichigatsu 十一月 = November

Juunigatsu 十二月 = December

Number of Months

Ikkagetsu 1 カ月 = 1 month

Nikagetsu 2 カ月 = 2 months

Sankagetsu 3 カ月 = 3 months

Yonkagetsu 4 カ月 = 4 months

Gokagetsu 5 カ月 = 5 months

Rokkagetsu 6 カ月 = 6 months

Nanakagetsu 7 カ月 (or shikikagetsu) = 7 months

Hakkagetsu 8 カ月 (or hachikagetsu) = 8 months

Kyuukagetsu 9 カ月 = 9 months

Jukkagetsu 10 カ月 (or jikkagetsu) = 10 months

Juuyonkagetsu 14 カ月 = 14 months

Nijuukagetsu 20 カ月 (or nijikka getsu) = 20 months

Ordinary Numbers

Zero ゼロ = 0; this can also be expressed as 零 rei

Ichi 一 = 1

Ni 二 = 2

San 三 = 3

Yon 四 (or shi) = 4

Go 五 = 5

Roku 六 = 6

Nana 七 (or shichi) = 7

Hachi 八 = 8

Kyuu 九 (or ku) = 9

Juu 十 = 10

Juuichi 十一 = 11

Juukyuu 十九 (or juuku) = 19

Nijuu 二十 = 20

Shichijuu 七十 (or nanajuu) = 70

Hyaku 百 = 100

Nihyaku 二百 = 200

Sanbyaku 三百 = 300

Yonhyaku 四百 = 400

Gohyaku 五百 = 500

Roppyaku 六百 = 600

Nanahyaku 七百 = 700

Happyaku 八百 = 800

Kyuuhyaku 九百 = 900

Sen (issen) 一千 = 1,000

Nisen 二千 = 2,000

Sanzen 三千 = 3,000

Nanasen 七千 = 7,000

Hassen 八千 = 8,000

Kyuusen 九千 = 9,000

Man (ichiman) 一万 = 10,000

Niman 二万 = 20,000

Oku (ichioku) 一億 = 100,000,000 (one hundred million)

Chou (icchou) 一兆 = 1,000,000,000,000 (one trillion)

Time of Day

Ichiji 一時 = 1:00

Niji 二時 = 2:00

Sanji 三時 = 3:00

Yoji 四時 = 4:00

Goji 五時 = 5:00

Rokuji 六時 = 6:00

Shichiji 七時 (or nanaji) = 7:00

Hachiji 八時 = 8:00

Kuji 九時 = 9:00

Juuji 十時 = 10:00

Juuichiji 十一時 = 11:00

Juuniji 十二時 = 12:00

The Differences Between Wa and Ga
「は」と「が」の違い

1. Use は *wa* to indicate the **topic** of a sentence. For example, in the sentence あの人は先生です *ano hito wa sensei desu* ("as for that person over there, he is a teacher"), 人 *hito* is the *topic* of the sentence, not the subject. The subject is the silent pronoun "he" which is not expressed in Japanese but is understood. This silent pronoun can be seen when the sentence is translated: "as for that person over there, he is a teacher."

2. Use が *ga* to indicate the **subject** of a sentence. A subject is something that **exists** or that **does something**. For example, in the sentence 田中さんがあそこにいます *tanakasan ga asoko ni imasu* ("Tanaka exists over there"), Tanaka exists. In the sentence 秘書が辞めました *hisho ga yamemashita* ("the secretary resigned"), the secretary does something.

3. Many Japanese sentences contain a **topic followed by** は *wa* and then a **subject followed by** が *ga*. For example, 像は鼻が長いです *zou wa hana ga nagai desu* ("as for the elephant, it has a long trunk").

4. If you are **introducing** a **noun** (or pronoun) into conversation, **use** が *ga*. For example, the sentence 昨日田中さんが東京に来ました *kinou tanakasan ga toukyou ni kimashita* ("yesterday Tanaka came to Tokyo") introduces the subject Tanaka.

5. If a **noun has already been introduced** into conversation, **use** は *wa*. For example, 明日彼は大阪に帰ります *ashita kare wa oosaka ni kaerimasu* means "tomorrow he will return to Osaka," and it could be one of the next remarks you make about Tanaka.

6. To say that a noun is described by an **adjective,** using です *desu* or だ *da*, you may use either は *wa* or が *ga*:

a) Use が *ga* if you are referring to a **particular** noun, if you want to **single** a noun out **from a group**, or if you are **introducing** it as a subject. For example, 花がきれいです *hana ga kirei desu* ("the flower is pretty") suggests that we are talking about only one flower, or we are singling one out from a group, or we are introducing flowers into the conversation.

b) Use は *wa* if you are referring to something **general**, or to **more than one thing**. For example, 花はきれいです *hana wa kirei desu* could mean "flowers in general are pretty" or "the flower (or flowers) we've been discussing is (are) pretty." (Note that this sentence includes as a subject the silent pronoun "they" which becomes visible when translated into English: "as for flowers, they are pretty.")

7. Generally speaking, when using the "exist" verbs ある/あります *aru/arimasu* or いる/います *iru/imasu*, you should use が *ga*. For example, お金があります *okane ga arimasu* ("money exists") and 人がいます *hito ga imasu* ("a person exists").

However, if a clause ends in **"but,"** you may use は *wa* in clauses using あります **arimasu**. For example, お金はありますけど... *okane wa arimasu kedo...* ("there is money, but..."). The "but" in this clause may imply, for example, that you don't have time to spend the money. By using は *wa* in this sentence ending with "but," you suggest that there is a subject further along in the sentence (which may be left unstated).

8. After an **interrogative pronoun**, use が *ga*. For example, 誰が来ましたか *dare ga kimashita ka* ("who came?") or 何がいいですか *nani ga ii desu ka* ("what is good?").

You should also use が *ga* in **responding** to a question that contains such an interrogative pronoun. For example, you could respond to the two questions above by saying 恵子さんが来ました *keikosan ga kimashita* ("Keiko came") and この本がいいです *kono hon ga ii desu* ("this book is good").

9. If you are using この *kono*, その *sono*, あの *ano* or other **specific markers**, such as 今日の *kyou no* (today's), then you **don't need to use** が *ga* (unless you are responding to a question containing an interrogative pronoun) because your statement is already specific. For example, この部屋は狭いです *kono heya wa semai desu* ("this room is tight") is correct, even if you are introducing the room into the conversation. If you said この部屋が狭いです *kono heya ga semai desu,* you would be over-emphasizing the point that this room in particular is tight.

10. When you are describing one of the **five senses**, use が *ga*. For example, いい匂いが

する *ii nioi ga suru* ("it smells good"), and 甘い味がする *amai aji ga suru* ("it tastes sweet").

11. If you want to show a **contrast between two competing topics**, use は *wa*. For example, 昼は厚いです、夜は寒いです *hiru wa atsui desu, yoru wa samui desu* ("the days are hot, the nights are cold").

12. Use は *wa* **after** と *to* (used to show quotes) in **negative sentences**. For example, 高いとは思いません *takai to wa omoimasen* ("As for expensive, I don't think so").

13. In **subordinate clauses, use** が *ga*. For example, デビがフランスへ行くことを知っています *debi ga furansu e iku koto o shitte imasu* ("I am knowing that Debi will go to France").

14. **In some expressions,** が *ga* **is almost always used**. For example, ミルクが欲しいです *miruku ga hoshii desu* ("I desire milk"), スペイン語が分かります *supeingo ga wakarimasu* ("I understand Spanish"), 日本語ができます *nihongo ga dekimasu* ("I can do Japanese"), 時間がかかります *jikan ga kakarimasu* ("it takes time"), テニスが上手です *tenisu ga jouzu desu* ("he's good at tennis"), お腹が痛いです *onaka ga itai desu* ("the stomach hurts"), 砂糖がいります *satou ga irimasu* ("I need sugar"), and コーヒーが好きです *koohii ga suki desu* ("I like coffee").

15. When stating a **simple equivalence** using だ *da* or です *desu*, e.g., "it's a car" or "it's Tanaka," **don't** use は *wa* or が *ga*. Instead say things like 車だ *kuruma da* or 田中さんです *tanakasan desu*. However, you should use either は *wa* or が *ga* in more complex sentences employing です *desu*, depending on the circumstances. For example, 車がいいです *kuruma ga ii desu* ("the car is good," referring to a specific car), or 田中さんは先生です *tanakasan wa sensei desu* ("as for Tanaka, he is a teacher," implying that he has already been introduced into the conversation).

Books in the *Learn to Read in Japanese* Series

1. *Learn to Read in Japanese,* Volume I. Published in 2016, it teaches 608 target kanji and includes a kanji catalogue, plus 4,200 reading practice sentences.
2. *Learn to Read in Japanese,* Volume II. Published in 2018, it teaches 600 additional target kanji, with an expanded kanji catalogue. It includes 2,900 vocabulary terms and 1,660 sentences for reading practice. It also suggests extensive supplemental reading material.
3. *Learn to Read in Japanese,* Volume III. Published in 2020, it teaches 320 more target kanji, with an expanded kanji catalogue. It includes 2,100 vocabulary terms and 912 sentences for reading practice. It also suggests extensive supplemental reading material.
4. *Learn to Read in Japanese,* Volume IV. Published in 2022, it teaches 560 more target kanji. Due to space limitations, it does not include a kanji catalogue, which is published separately (see Item # 5, below). It includes 3,800 vocabulary terms and 1,623 sentences for reading practice.
5. *Core Kanji, a Catalogue of 2,088 Essential Kanji.* Published in 2022 and expanded in 2024, it includes memorable kanji descriptions, retrieval cues for kanji readings and comparisons among similar characters, as well as an index to 4,300 kanji pronunciations. It also contains tools that can be used for identifying kanji, a technique known as Kanji ID.
6. *Learn to Read in Japanese, a Glossary.* Published in 2020 and expanded in 2022, it lists more than 9,700 Japanese vocabulary terms, with definitions, mnemonics and comparisons among terms.
7. *Kanji Memorization Drills,* Version One. Published in 2025, it contains drills for learning to recognize and pronounce 608 kanji. A supplement to *Learn to Read in Japanese,* Volume I.
8. *Kanji Memorization Drills,* Version Two. Published in 2025, it contains drills for learning to recognize and pronounce 1,208 kanji. A supplement to *Learn to Read in Japanese,* Volume II.
9. *Kanji Memorization Drills,* Version Three. Published in 2025, it contains drills for learning to recognize and pronounce 1,528 kanji. A supplement to *Learn to Read in Japanese,* Volume III.
10. *Kanji Memorization Drills,* Version Four. Published in 2025, it contains drills for learning to recognize and pronounce 2,088 kanji. A supplement to *Learn to Read in Japanese,* Volume IV.

www.ingramcontent.com/pod-product-compliance
Lightning Source LLC
Chambersburg PA
CBHW060104170426
43198CB00010B/760